The Genealogy of Several Allied Families

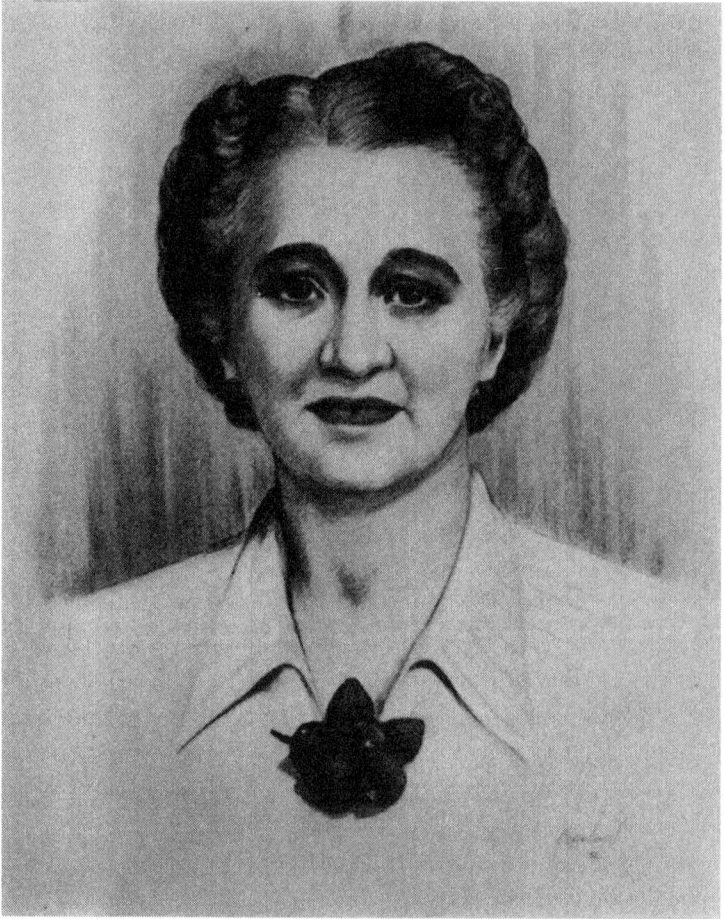

Laura Owen (Mrs. Clifford Uriah Johnson)

The Genealogy
of
Several Allied Families

FRAZER — OWEN — BESSELLIEU
CARTER — SHAW — WRIGHT — LANDFAIR
BRIGGS — NEILL — TIDWELL — JOHNSON
AND OTHERS

By

CHARLES OWEN JOHNSON

A FIREBIRD PRESS BOOK

PELICAN PUBLISHING COMPANY
Gretna 1998

Manufactured in the United States of America

Published by Pelican Publishing Company, Inc.
1000 Burmaster Street, Gretna, Louisiana 70053

To my mother
Laura Owen Johnson

NOTE

The asterisk (*) before the names in the "New England Ancestry of Henry Delos Briggs" indicates the person in each generation of the different families from whom Henry Delos Briggs directly descends.

TABLE OF CONTENTS

(John Almey — Thomas Almey — Christopher Almey — William Almey or Almy — Anna or Annis Almy — Phillis (Phillipa or Phillip) Greene — Caleb Carr — Caleb Carr — Merebah Carr — Sarah Greene — Henry Briggs — Michael Parker Briggs — Henry Delos Briggs)

(Arthur Aylsworth — Robert Aylsworth — Ephraim Aylsworth — M a r y Aylsworth — Phoebe Parker — Michael Parker Briggs — Henry Delos Briggs)

(Aldred Byccombe or Bickham — Charity Bickham — Giles Slocum — The Reverend Ebenezer Slocum — Johanna Slocum — Caleb Carr — Merebah Carr — Sarah G r e e n e — Henry Briggs — Michael Parker Briggs — Henry Delos Briggs)

(Clement Briggs— Thomas Briggs — Daniel Briggs — Captain Benjamin Briggs — Benjamin Briggs, Jr. — Lieutenant Michael Briggs — Henry Briggs — Michael Parker Briggs — Henry Delos Briggs)

(The Reverend Chad Brown — The Reverend John Brown — Mary Brown — Robert Aylsworth — Ephraim Aylsworth — Mary Aylsworth — Pheobe Parker — Michael Parker Briggs — Henry Delos Briggs)

(Thomas Butter — William Butter — Pierce Butter — Anne Butter — President John Coggeshall — Joshua Coggeshall — Humility Coggeshall — Henry Greene — Job Greene — Sarah Greene — Henry Briggs — Michael Parker Briggs — Henry Delos Briggs)

(Robert Carr — Caleb Carr — Caleb Carr — Caleb Carr — Merebah Carr — Sarah Greene — Henry Briggs — Michael Parker Briggs — Henry Delos Briggs)

LIST OF ILLUSTRATIONS

PREFACE

This genealogy is the result of well over fifteen years work. The limitations of space and finance have not permitted me to include all the material I've gathered. This limitation in mind, I've included only those families who have lived in Louisiana or Mississippi with two exceptions.

The Johnsons, Tidwells, Neills and Wrights settled in Mississippi in the early 1800's. The Carters, Landfairs and Shaws were in the Old Natchez District in the 1700's. The Owens moved from Mobile to New Orleans in the 1870's. The two exceptions to my inclusion of only those families who lived in Louisiana or Mississippi are the ancestral lines of Henry Delos Briggs on my father's side of the family and the Bessellieu, Cheche (Chichet or Souchet) and Frazer lines on mother's side. My great-grandfather, Henry Delos Briggs, came to Louisiana in 1857. His ancestors were early settlers of Massachusetts and Rhode Island, moving to New York just after the American Revolution. The Bessellieus and Cheches were among the earliest settlers of Charleston, South Carolina, though a branch of the Cheche descendants were later resident in East Greenwich and Newport, Rhode Island. The Frazers came to Charleston from Scotland just prior to the American Revolution. Some day, perhaps, it will be possible to publish another book to include the omitted lines.

As a lawyer, I'm most impressed with the "evidence" of any case and, for that reason, have given at some length and perhaps risk of being tedious, the proof of these lines. Family traditions often have a grain of truth beneath quite a lot of unintentional distortion and exaggeration. I've used traditions only as a starting point and by the use of public records — deeds, wills, administration papers, tax lists, census records, tombstone, church and other records — have tested their accuracy. Happily, in most instances they have proved to be surprisingly correct.

Ever so many people have given me help in compiling this book. Only a few can be named in the small space, but to all of them goes my deepest gratitude. My first interest in family history dates from stories of olden times told me by Claudia Pearce (Mrs. Charles W. Owen), who was my great-aunt by marriage, but known to me as "grandmother," as she reared my mother after the death of mother's mother. The genealogy of the Pearce and Tanner families has been very ably chronicled by Dr. George Mason Graham Stafford, grandson of Leroy Stafford, the youngest general on Lee's staff. My first technical instruction in the art of genealogical research was given me by Mrs. James R. Wooten, her daughter, Mrs. Elmer Slagle, and Mrs. David Garrett, all of Monroe, Louisiana.

On the Briggs lines no one has worked harder or done more than Elaine Briggs, wife of Dr. Kenneth Fleming of Canfield, Ohio. She, and my two great-aunts, Dea Briggs Williams and Mary Briggs Thompson of Oak Grove, Louisiana, aside from helping with the Briggs lines, have worked with me on the Wright and Landfair families. Mrs. Edith Briggs Peters and her father, Mr. Gardner Briggs, the author of two books on his branch of Briggs, have been of great assistance.

Mr. A. A. Wright of Eudora, Arkansas; Mr. Albert Sidney Wright and Mrs. Emmett Reed, of Warren County, Mississippi, have helped with the Wright family. Mr. and Mrs. John Lee Hyland and their daughter, Ceress Hyland Newell, were most gracious in working on Wright records with me. In all my research none has been more pleasant than one day I spent with them at their plantation home south of Vicksburg, which had formerly belonged to their kinsman, Mississippi's distinguished Chief Justice and Provisional Governor, William L. Sharkey.

Mr. Robert Lamar Landfair of Jackson, Mississippi, has been untiring in his efforts to unearth all possible records on the Landfair and Carter families.

First mention for work on the Shaw family rightly belongs to Miss Lena Carmena of Baton Rouge, Louisiana. Others who helped were the late Mr. J. W. McHugh of Zachary, Louisiana, his wife, Blanche Capdevielle McHugh, and Mr. Clarence Shaw, last of the Shaw name to live in Zachary, where they have lived since 1798.

Mamie P. Austin (Mrs. C. M. Rouzan) of Jackson, Louisiana, has been of great assistance on the Carters and principally the line of Hannah Carter (Mrs. Archibald Palmer). To Shirley B. Winston, Clerk of Court of West Feliciana Parish, do I owe thanks for my introduction to Mrs. Rouzan. Ella Norwood Pipes (Mrs. C. G. Dumas) of Dallas, Texas, has furnished much material on Palmers, Carters and Dicksons. Mrs. Dumas descends from the builders of the palatial Richland, antebellum home of the Honorable Charles E. Wilson, former United States Secretary of Defense, near Norwood, Louisiana. Winona Netterville (Mrs. Paul Henri Laroussini) of Baton Rouge worked with me principally on the Isaac Carter line. Judge Cecil Morgan of New York and Washington, in the midst of his busy life, was gracious in making available papers of his father, Mr. Howell Morgan, who did so much research on all of the Carter family. From Lillie Thompson (Mrs. James Sparks) of Monroe, Louisiana, I received help on the Parsons Carter line. With her charm

Mrs. Sparks reminds me of what I've read of her noted kinswoman, Varina Howell (Mrs. Jefferson Davis).

On the Johnsons, Neills, and Tidwells I have received help from Mrs. Margaret Newman of Lake Providence, Louisiana, former Dean of Women at Northeast State College, Mrs. E. T. Cashion of Lake Village, Arkansas, and the late Grace Peterson of St. Joseph, Louisiana.

On the Owen family special assistance was given me by my great-uncle, Colonel William Frazer Owen, and his wife, Mary Taylor Owen, both now deceased, but formerly of Mobile. Also by Mr. Paul Odendahl and Mr. John G. Owen of New Orleans, Dr. Harry Owen of Dallas, Celeste Vincent (Mrs. Ward Goodloe) of San Francisco, Mr. Ronald Vincent of Boston, Mary Lucylle Owen (Mrs. John N. Covanes, Jr.) of Fort Worth, Texas, and my mother.

Miss Eva Raymond Frazer Hughes of Clearwater, Florida, gave me much information on the Frazers. Ruth Davenport (Mrs. Charles Jackson Steward) of Orlando, Florida, sent material on the descendants of Rebecca Ripley by her first husband, Mr. William Eayres of Charleston, South Carolina.

Mr. Phillip Bessellieu of St. Petersburg, Florida, made photostats for me of the old Bessellieu Bible printed in England in 1738. An ancestor of his, Phillip Bessellieu, lived in Charleston during the American Revolution and an even earlier Phillip lived in the France of Louis XIV. Help was also given me by Mary Ann FitzSimons (Mrs. Donald McKay Allston) of Johns Island, South Carolina and by Louise Williams (Mrs. Alvin Cox) of Hardeeville, South Carolina.

My special thanks go to Miss Frances Flanders, Librarian of the Ouachita Parish Public Library in Monroe, who has taken such a great interest in local history and genealogy for many years and who has been so very kind to me when I have been in the library. I could not end this list of acknowledgements without mention of the great pleasure given me by many hours of delightful conversation on genealogy, local history and related topics with Mrs. Bridger Thornhill, Mrs. J. B. Dawkins, and Mrs. Robert Layton of Monroe and Mrs. Allen Turpin of Bastrop, Louisiana.

— Charles Owen Johnson

The Genealogy of Several
Allied Families

OWEN

JOHN GARLAND OWEN

Born: September 14, 1818, in Wilkes County, Georgia

Married: Susannah Rebecca Frazer on January 23, 1843, in Augusta, Georgia

Died: September 25, 1867, near Gardiner's Island, Alabama River

Children of John Garland and Susannah Rebecca (Frazer) Owen: Charles Wheadon Owen; Chauncey Hall Owen, born December 2, 1851, in Mobile, Alabama; Frank Stone Owen; Jo Hunter Owen, born December 12, 1845, in Mobile, Alabama, died March 29, 1846; John Garland Owen Junior; Catharine (Kate) Lee Owen; Martina Harper Owen; Robert Otis Owen; William Frazer Owen.

The Owen Bible from which much of the data on the children of John Garland Owen is taken was published in New York by Harper Brothers, 82 Cliff Street, in 1846. An inscription: "A sacred token from Alex Campbell to Susan R. Owen, January 1, 1847."

Some of the following material has been taken from the Frazer family Bible, now owned by Charles Owen Johnson and referred to hereafter as the "Frazer Bible." This Bible was printed and published by S. Walker, Washington Street, Boston. Stereotyped at the Boston Type and Stereotype Foundry. Late T. H. Carter Company.

1850 CENSUS, MOBILE COUNTY, ALABAMA, CITY OF MOBILE

1716, 1835

J. G. Owen born in 1819 in Georgia; Susan Owen born in 1825 in South Carolina; Martina H. Owen born in 1846 in Alabama; Jno Owen born in 1849 in Alabama; Wm M. Frazer born in 1800 in South Carolina.

1860 CENSUS, WARD NO. 6 MOBILE CITY, MOBILE COUNTY, ALABAMA

John G. Owen born in 1821 in Georgia; Susan R. Owen born in 1827 in South Carolina; Martina H. Owen born in 1847 in Alabama; John Owen born in 1849 in Alabama; Chancy H. Owen born in 1851 in Alabama; Catharine L. Owen born in 1853 in Alabama; William Owen born in 1856 in Alabama; Frank S. Owen born in 1859 in Alabama; Sarah A. Cox born in 1843 in South Carolina.

Obituary Notices from clippings in the Frazer Bible:

"Death of an Estimable Man

"A dispatch was received yesterday morning in town from Captain Johnson of the steamer Mist announcing the death of Capt. John Owen first clerk of the Mist, and an old steamboat man. He died on the boat at Selma and had been sick some time. He was one of the most popular men on the river and his loss will be universally regretted."

"Another Old Steamboatman Gone

"By dispatch from Capt Frank Johnson to Capt Cox President of the Trade Company we learn the melancholy intelligence of the death of Capt John G. Owen, one of the oldest, if not the best, of our river clerks. Capt Owen at the time of his death was clerk of the Mist, and died on board of that boat at Selma, yesterday morning at half past nine o'clock. For a period of nearly thirty years the deceased has been identified with steamboats and steamboating, sometimes captain, but generally clerk, standing among the latter confessedly at the top of the list, and no man ever possessed more universally the entire confidence of his employers throughout that long period than he did. He was, we should think, near fifty years of age, his health, for some time past, doubtless from a too close attention to business, having been precarious so much so, in fact, that he spent a portion of the summer at the springs, near Gadsden, and it was hoped with permanent relief. Capt Owen has been a resident of Mobile for over thirty years and leaves an interesting family to mourn their irreparable loss."

"Died at Selma Ala on (illegible) September 25th 1867 after (illegible) some months Capt John (illegible) 49 years.

In the death of this well (illegible) gentleman (illegible) concerned with the Alabama River the past thirty years the name of Captain Owen has become "familiar as a household word" along its banks, between this city and Montgomery, and but few, after so long and constant an intercourse with the travelling and business portions of our citizens have left behind them, as a valuable inheritance to their family, a fairer or more honored record than that of our deceased friend.

"To his many friends throughout Alabama and Georgia we know how painful this news will be, coming at a time when his life gave seeming promise of so much future usefulness, while to his suddenly bereaved wife and family in whom there existed so peculiarly a deep affection for their loving and indulgent father, we feel there is little can be said to temper their grief in this, their sad and painful season."

Susannah Rebecca second daughter of William M and Maria S Frazer was born on the 29th day of October 1823 in Charleston.

John G. Owen of Mobile Ala was married to Susannah Rebecca daughter of Wm M and Maria S. Frazer on the 24th January 1843 in Augusta Geo.

John G. Owen departed this life on the 25th day of September 1867 on board of Steamboat Mist at Gardner's Island Alabama River aged 49 years 11 days.

Susan R. Owen wife of Capt John G Owen and daughter of Wm M

and M. S. Frazer died in Mobile Ala on the 11th day of January 1870 aged 46 years.

Frazer Bible.

GEORGIA

WILKES COUNTY:

THIS INDENTURE made this the first day of January in the year of Our Lord One Thousand eight hundred and thirty-six between John G. Owen of the County of Wilkes and State aforesaid of the one part and Harris C. Jackson of the County and State aforesaid

WITNESSETH that the said John G. Owen for and in consideration of the sum of One Hundred Dollars to him in hand paid at and before the sealing and delivery of these presents the receipt whereof is hereby acknowledged hath granted bargained, sold and conveyed and doth by these presents grant, bargain sell and convey unto the said Harris C. Jackson his heirs and assigns:

All that tract or parcel of land situate lying and being in the County of Early and State aforesaid known and distinguished as Lot Number Three Hundred and Fifty two in Fifth District and drawn by the orphans of Garland Owen dec. of the County of Wilkes containing two hundred and fifty acres more or less.

TO HAVE AND TO HOLD said tract or parcel of land unto him the said Harris C. Jackson his heirs and assigns together with all and singular the rights, members and appurtenances thereof to the same in any manner belonging to his and their own proper use, benefit and behoof forever in fee simple. And the said John G. Owen for himself, his heirs and executors and administrators the said bargained premises unto the said Harris C. Jackson his heirs and assigns will warrant and forever defend the right and title thereof against himself and against the claims of all other persons whatever.

IN WITNESS WHEREOF the said John G. Owen hath hereunto set his hand and seal the day and year above written.

JOHN G. OWEN   (SEAL)

Signed, sealed and delivered in
presence of
Lewis S. Brown
John Jesseo, J.P.
Recorded Feby. 2nd, 1837.   JOHN W. PERRY CLK

GEORGIA, EARLY COUNTY

I, Bert Tarver, Clerk of the Superior Court of Early County, Georgia, do hereby certify that the above and foregoing is a true and correct copy of the original deed from John G. Owen to Harris C. Jackson, as the same appears of record in my office, in Deed Book "D", page 394.

Given under my hand and official seal of office, this the 18th day of April, 1958.

/s/ BERT TARVER   (SEAL)

CATHARINE (KATE) LEE OWEN

Born: January 3, 1854, in Mobile, Alabama

Married: Dr. Frederick Wespy on December 8, 1891, in New Orleans, Louisiana

Died: January 30, 1913, in New Orleans, Louisiana

MRS. KATE O. WESPY

The funeral of Mrs. Kate Owen Wespy took place from the Louisville and Nashville Railroad depot Sunday afternoon at 12:45 o'clock, the Reverend G. C. Tucker officiating. The interment was made in Magnolia Cemetery, many floral designs being placed upon the grave. The following acted as pallbearers: Messrs. E. J. Buck, H. M. Hood, J. C. Rich, George Duffie, George Stone and Benjamin Vincent.

MOBILE REGISTER, Monday, February 3, 1913.

Wife of Popular Newcomb College Professor Passes Away

Sorrow came to a large circle of devoted friends of Mrs. Kate Owen Wespy with the news announced yesterday of her death at her late residence, 1539 Exposition Boulevard. Mrs. Wespy was the wife of Professor Frederick Wespy who occupies the chair of German at Newcomb College. She had been in ill health for some time, and about two weeks ago her condition became critical. She died at midnight on Thursday. While her death was not unexpected there was no indication that she would pass away so quickly and Mr. Wespy, worn out for want of sleep, had been induced to take some rest. Dr. Mann of Tulane University was with Mrs. Wespy when she died and in response to a request to shift her pillow had done so, while with one hand he held her pulse. There was not a flutter of her pulse to mark her passing, death coming so swiftly, he said, that its beat ceased just as the request had passed her lips.

Mrs. Wespy was the daughter of the well-known antebellum steamboat owner of Alabama, Captain John Owen, who owned a line of boats that plied on the Tombigbee River. With the Civil War, Captain Owen's business was swept away like that of many others.

Mrs. Wespy, then Miss Owen, was married to her husband twenty-one years ago by Dr. A. Gordon Bakewell, Venerable Rector of Trinity Chapel, and Dr. Bakewell will conduct the funeral services this afternoon at four o'clock. Dr. George Cornelson, pastor of the First Presbyterian Church, who is Mr. Wespy's pastor, will assist. These services will be conducted at the residence of Mrs. Wespy's brother, Mr. C. W. Owen, 6039 Coliseum Street. Mr. Owen is assistant general freight agent of the Southern Pacific. Besides him, and her husband,

Mrs. Wespy is survived by her brother, Mr. Frank Owen, now in Waco, Texas; a sister, Mrs. F. F. Vincent; and a brother, Mr. W. F. Owen, President of the New Orleans, Mobile and Chicago Railroad, which is part of the Frisco Louisville and Nashville System.

It was first planned to hold the interment on Saturday in Mobile, Mrs. Wespy's home town where she was born and where her early life was spent. The impossibility, however, of getting in touch with many of her immediate relatives in distant cities caused a delay in the arrangements. Her remains were taken to her brother's residence yesterday morning and will remain there until 7 A.M. Sunday when they will be removed to the train which will carry them to Mobile. The interment will take place upon the arrival of the train in that city. It is owing to the very early hour that it will be necessary to leave this city on Sunday morning that the funeral will be held this afternoon.

New Orleans Daily Picayune, February 1, 1913.

CHARLES WHEADON OWEN

Born: August 11, 1864, in Mobile, Alabama

Married: Claudia Pearce on February 3, 1885, in Evergreen, Louisiana

Died: June 9, 1934, in Alexandria, Louisiana

C. W. Owen merchant Cheneyville, Louisville. It is difficult for anyone unfamiliar with merchandising to form a correct estimate of the magnitude of the trade in Cheneyville. Among those whose knowledge, courage and resolution have met with signal success may be mentioned Mr. C. W. Owen who is one of the prominent merchants of the town. Although he has been there but one year, he has already won a large patronage. He was born in Alabama, and there his youth and boyhood were spent. He was educated in New Orleans and became agent for the Union Pacific and Texas Pacific Railroads, being their agent at New Iberia for two years of that time. He married Miss Claudia Pierce (sic) daughter of Hon. S. S. Pierce (sic) of Avoyelles Parish, La., and to this union have been born two children: Claude P. and Chauncey H. Mr. Owen engaged in merchandising shortly after his marriage and this has occupied his attention ever since. He is the son of John and Susannah (Frasier) (sic) Owen, the father a native of Georgia but who resided in Mobile, Ala., the principal part of his life. He was a steamboat man and the owner of several steamers. The maternal grandfather was a French Huguenot.

Biographical and Historical Memoirs of Northwest Louisiana. Published by the Southern Publishing Company of Nashville and Chicago in 1890, page 584.

Hon. S. S. Pearce, planter, Evergreen, La. Mr. Pearce is one of the wealthiest and most successful planters in Avoyelles Parish and not only has the respect and confidence of all as a successful business man but is esteemed and held in the highet estimation socially. His parents, Stephen and Ann G. (Tanner) Pearce were natives of Georgi aand South Carolina respectively. The maternal grandfather was a native of South Carolina and the paternal grandfather was a native of Georgia. S. S. Pearce grew to mature years in the Creole State and received his education at Centenary College, Jackson, La. Although he was reared on his father's extensive plantation he was not compelled to farm labor owing to the numerous slaves his father always kept. At the age of eighteen years he commenced business for himself as a planter, his father and mother having died previous to this and this has been his chief calling in life. He has acquired nearly all his property through his own efforts and is a public spirited and enterprising citizen. He was elected to the Legislature from 1880 to 1882 and politically is one of the most influential men in this section. When twenty-one years of age he was married to Miss Mary E. Bennett who was but fifteen years of age, and they have seven living children: Sarah A. (wife of S. Tanner), Claudia (wife of C. W. Owen), Mansel K., Jennie, Stephen S., Addie G., and Heber L. Algernon B. died at the age of nineteen and was a promising young man. Mr. Pearce's success is unusual but is due largely to his excellent judgment and strict honesty and upright dealing and the proud position he now occupies as a representative citizen is a just tribute to his worth.

Biographical and Historical Memoirs of Northwest Louisiana Published by the Southern Publishing Company of Nashville and Chicago in 1890, pages 646-647.

For a genealogy of the family of Claudia Pearce Owen, see Dr. George Mason Graham Stafford's THREE PIONEER RAPIDES FAMILIES (PEARCE, TANNER AND ROBERTS) published by the Pelican Publishing Company. Also see Annie Elizabeth Miller's OUR FAMILY CIRCLE published in 1931 by the J. W. Burke Company of Macon, Georgia.

CHARLES W. OWEN, FREIGHT EXPERT, DEAD AT BUNKIE

Charles W. Owen, 69 years old, for many years an executive of the Southern Pacific Railway lines in New Orleans, died early Saturday at his home in Bunkie.

Mr. Owen had been associated with the Southern Pacific Railway lines for about 30 years before his retirement several years ago. His first position was that of local freight agent in Opelousas and then he was transferred to New Orleans as Assistant General Freight Agent in 1905. Subsequently he was made General Freight Agent. In 1920 Mr. Owen was sent to Houston, Texas, as Assistant General

Freight Traffic Manager. He remained in Houston until his retirement when he went to live on his plantation near Bunkie.

He was regarded as an expert in freight rate matters and handled many important rate adjustments for the line while he was in New Orleans and Houston.

Mr. Owen's only son Chancey H. Owen now holds a position which his father once held, that of Assistant General Freight Agent in New Orleans.

Mr. Owen was a native of Louisiana having been born in Rapides Parish (ERROR: he was born in Mobile, Alabama). Funeral services will be conducted this morning in Bunkie.

In addition to his son, he is survived by his widow, the former Miss Claudia Pearce, and a niece, Mrs. Clifford U. Johnson of Monroe, Louisiana.

TIMES-PICAYUNE, June 10, 1934

CHANCEY H. OWEN
LAST RITES TODAY

Funeral services for Chancey Hall Owen, 63, Assistant Freight Traffic Manager for Southern Pacific Lines in Houston, Texas, will be held Wednesday at 4 p.m. from the funeral home of P. J. McMahon and Sons, 4800 Canal. Interment will be in Hope Mausoleum.

Mr. Owen died at Southern Pacific Hospital in Houston on Monday.

After starting his railroad career with the Lake Charles and Northern Railroad in 1907, Mr. Owen joined the local freight office of the Southern Pacific Lines in 1908. He remained here until 1937, when he was transferred to Houston as Assistant Freight Traffic Manager. He was a native of New Iberia.

Mr. Owen is survived by his widow, Mallie Magee and a sister.

CHAUNCEY HALL OWEN

Married: Mallie Magee on June 14, 1911, in New Orleans, Louisiana
Died: June 5, 1950

FRANK STONE OWEN

Born: March 31, 1859, in Mobile, Alabama
Married: 1st: Laura Sue Schroeder in Palestine, Texas, on January 31, 1883, by the Reverend Edwin Wickens of St. Philip's Episcopal Church. Witnesses were Mrs. Schroeder, Mrs. Carr, and Mr. and Mrs. Deming. Laura Schroeder had been confirmed by the Right Reverend, the Bishop of Texas, Alexander Gregg, on October 9, 1881. Her brother, Henry William Schroeder, had been baptized in Rusk, Texas, and was con-

firmed by Bishop Gregg on November 21, 1880, in St. Philip's. Their father, John Henry Schroeder, Age 59, was buried on March 2, 1882, by the Reverend George Patterson. (Records St. Philip's Episcopal Church, Palestine Texas). Laura Sue Schroeder was born on August 21, 1861, in Nacogdoches, Texas, and died in Waco where she is buried in Oakwood Cemetery.

2nd: Ethel Mae Tyson

Children of Frank Stone and Laura Sue (Schroeder) Owen: Dr. Harry Owen of Dallas, Texas, born 1892; Laura Owen, married Dr. Clifford Johnson of Monroe, Louisiana, one son, Charles Owen Johnson; Robert Owen; Wallace Owen, died August 26, 1917.

Children of Frank Stone and Ethel Mae (Tyson) Owen: Katherine Elizabeth Owen; Ethel Louise Owen, born on February 1, 1907, died December 28, 1925; Helen Olive Owen; Juanita Christine Owen; Mary Lucylle Owen.

HELEN OLIVE OWEN

Born: March 10, 1914

Married: Andrew Alexander McWhorter of Port Arthur, Texas, on November 9, 1940

JUANITA CHRISTINE OWEN

Born: July 27, 1916

Married: L. B. McCay on January 21, 1939

Children of L. B. and Juanita Christine (Owen) McCay: Kathryn Ann McCay; Walter Bill McCay, born October 21, 1944.

KATHRYN ANN McCAY

Born: September 15, 1940

Married: Lloyd Carver III on February 14, 1959, in Hargill, Texas.

KATHERINE ELIZABETH OWEN

Born: October 9, 1909

Married: A. B. Wilkinson on August 6, 1941.

MARY LUCYLLE OWEN

Born: January 15, 1912

Married: John N. Covanes, Jr., on February 17, 1945

Children of John N. and Mary Lucylle (Owen) Covanes, Jr.: Helen Colleen Covanes, born December 2, 1949; John N. Covanes III, born November 10, 1946.

ROBERT O. OWEN

Born: January 21, 1885

Married: Margaret Gretta Swann on April, 1907

Died: December 11, 1941

Children of Robert O. and Margaret Gretta (Swann) Owen: W. F. Owen; Harry Stuart Owen, married Helen Patricia Evans; M/Sgt. Schroeder S. Owen.

SCHROEDER S. OWEN

Born: October 25, 1913

Married: Juanita Sanders on February 28, 1942.

W. F. OWEN

Born: October 10, 1914

Married: Bernice Inez Allison on February 28, 1940

Adopted Daughter of W. F. and Bernice Inez (Allison) Owen: Belinda Fern Owen, born February 3, 1956.

JOHN GARLAND OWEN, JUNIOR

Born: September 15, 1849

Married: Maggie Allen on May 18, 1880, in Houston, Texas

1880 Census, Subdivision No. 1, County of Harris, Texas

John G. Owen, born in 1850; Maggie Owen born in 1861.

MARTINA HARPER OWEN

Born: April 2, 1847, in Mobile, Alabama

Married: Frank S. Vincent on April 18, 1872, in Mobile, Alabama. Frank Strong Vincent was born on November 5, 1846, in Erie City, Pennsylvania.

Children of Frank Strong and Martina Harper (Owen) Vincent: Earl Starr Vincent, born October 29, 1883, in New Orleans, La.; Frank Massey Vincent, born February 2, 1873, in New Orleans, La.; George Owen Vincent, born September 29, 1875, in New Orleans, La.; John Garland Vincent, born January 1, 1886, in New Orleans, La.; Maude Vincent, born January 5, 1880 in New Orleans, La., died October 24, 1881.

1880 Census, City of New Orleans, Louisiana

Ward 1 or 2, 432, 168, 171

Frank Vincent born in 1847 in Pennsylvania; Martina Vincent born in 1848 in Alabama; Frank Vincent born in 1873 in Louisiana; Owen Vincent born in 1876 in Louisiana; Maud Vincent born in Dec 1869 in Louisiana; Wheedon Owen born in 1864 in Alabama.

Parents of Frank Vincent were born in Pennsylvania; those of Martina Vincent and Wheedon Owen: Father: Georgia; Mother: South Carolina.

George Calhoun Vincent. Born 1821. Died 1847. Wife deceased. Left two sons: George T. Vincent of San Francisco, California, and Frank Strong Vincent of New Orleans, Louisiana, who married Martina Owen of Mobile, Alabama. Has a son, Frank Massey Vincent in Marshall, Texas, G. Owen Vincent, New Orleans; and Earl Vincent, living in Little Rock, Arkansas. All three sons are married and have children.

OUR FAMILY OF VINCENTS. Boyd Vincent. Page 128. Published in Cincinnati by Stewart Kidd Company in 1924.

EARL STARR VINCENT

Born: October 19, 1883, in New Orleans, Louisiana
Married: Delphine McCown
Died: April 9, 1932

Children of Earl Starr and Delphine (McCown) Vincent: Eleanor Vincent; Lois Vincent.

Earl S. Vincent, 49, died suddenly at 11:40 o'clock, Friday morning in Lafayette, Louisiana.

Mr. Vincent was born October 19, 1882, in New Orleans, Louisiana. He was a citizen of Marshall for mnay years, leaving here about a year ago for Louisiana where he has since resided.

Mr. Vincent was a member of Trinity Episcopal Church of this city and a Mason, Shriner and Knights Templar.

He is survived by his wife, two daughters, Misses Lois and Eleanor Vincent of Marshall; two brothers, Frank M. Vincent of Dallas and G. Owen Vincent of New Orleans.

The body will be brought to Marshall Sunday morning for burial. Funeral services will be held at 9 o'clock from Rains and Herndon Funeral Home. Services will be conducted by Rev. Henry F. Selcer of Trinity Episcopal Church.

Burial will be in Greenwood Cemetery.

(The above is from a Marshall, Texas, newspaper clipping.)

LOIS VINCENT

Born: February 15, 1907, in Marshall, Texas
Married: William Jordan Burkart of Glendive, Montana, on June 26, 1934.

Children of William Jordan and Lois (Vincent) Burkart: Jordan Vincent Burkart, born December 7, 1935, an Ensign in the U.S. Navy; Michael Paul Burkart, born October 3, 1938, a student at Texas University.

1880 CENSUS, MARSHALL, TEXAS, WARD 3

Jerome G. McCowan born in 1840 in Alabama where his parents were born; Nancy J. McCowan, wife, born in 1849 in Alabama where her father was born, her mother was born in Georgia; Fannie McCowan, daughter born in 1875 in Alabama; Morgan McCowan, son, born in

1877 in Alabama; William Moore, brother-in-law, born in 1858 in Alabama.

The correct spelling of the name of the family listed as "McCowan" in the above census is McCown. Aside from the children listed above and the wife of Earl Starr Vincent, there was a son, James M. McCown of Mobile, Alabama.

ELEANOR VINCENT

Born: October 7, 1916, in Little Rock, Arkansas

Married: 1st: William Grant Richardson

2nd: Artis T. Alderman on August 11, 1958

Children of William Grant and Eleanor (Vincent) Richardson: James Vincent Richardson, born December 30, 1946.

FRANK MASSEY VINCENT

Born: February 2, 1873, in New Orleans, Louisiana

Married: Grace Finch on October 26, 1898

Died: April 19, 1955

Children of Frank Massey and Grace (Finch) Vincent: F. Ronald Vincent.

FRANK M. VINCENT FUNERAL ARRANGED

Funeral services will be held in Newton, Massachusetts, Thursday for Frank M. Vincent, 82, former Dallas resident for many years who died Tuesday night in the home of his son, F. Ronald Vincent, in Boston, Massachusetts. Burial will also be in Newton.

Vincent came to Dallas from Marshall where he worked for the Texas and Pacific Railway Lines. He lived here about 40 years before retiring and moving to Boston to live with his son in 1951. In Dallas he was associated with the Missouri-Kansas-Texas Railroad and the Dallas Power and Light Company. At the time of his retirement he worked as an accountant with the State Fair Park Association.

He was a Knight Templar and a member of the Episcopal Church.

Other survivors include a brother, Owen Vincent of New Orleans, Louisiana, and a grandson.

RONALD VINCENT

Born: December 20, 1899

Married: October 17, 1923.

Children of Ronald Vincent: Haywood Vincent.

HAYWOOD VINCENT

Born: August 14, 1924

Children of Haywood Vincent: Michael Vincent, born January 20, 1949; Ronald Vincent, born May 30, 1951.

GEORGE OWEN VINCENT

Born: September 29, 1875, in New Orleans, Louisiana

Married: 1st: Clara Gresham on October 11, 1899, in Baton Rouge, Louisiana. Married in St. James Rectory by Dean J. Wilmer Gresham, the Rector and brother of the bride.

2nd: Maude Castleman Werner in October, 1925

Died: November 12, 1949, in San Francisco, California

Children of George Owen and Clara (Gresham) Vincent: Celeste Gresham Vincent; Gresham Holt Vincent, born March 9, 1904, in New Orleans, married Louise McCoy in 1938 (?).

Mr. Vincent served for many years as Vice President of the Commercial Germania Trust and Savings Bank, the Commercial Trust and Savings Bank, the Canal Commercial Trust and Savings Bank and President of the New Orleans Bank and Trust Company and New Orleans Securities, Inc. He was a member of the Boston Club.

CELESTE GRESHAM VINCENT

Born: July 23, 1900, in New Orleans, Louisiana

Married: 1st: James L. Hiers of Beaufort, South Carolina, on September 27, 1922, in New Orleans, Louisiana

2nd: Ward Hazeton Goodloe in 1934

Children of James L. and Celeste Gresham (Vincent) Hiers: Celeste Gresham Hiers; James Lawrence Hiers.

The wedding of Miss Celeste Gresham Vincent, daughter of Mr. G. Owen Vincent to Mr. James Lawrence Hiers will claim especial interest in the social world today. It will be celebrated this evening at 7 o'clock at Christ Church Chapel on St. Charles Avenue.

...*THE TIMES PICAYUNE* September 27, 1922

A very lovely event of the fall was the wedding Wednesday of Miss Celeste Gresham Vincent, daughter of Mr. G. Owen Vincent to Mr. James Lawrence Hiers, son of Mr. and Mrs. Wade Hampton Hiers of Hampton, South Carolina. The wedding was celebrated at 7 o'clock at Christ Church Chapel and the ceremony was performed by the Reverend Robert S. Coupland, Rector of Trinity Episcopal Church. The greatest profusion of palms, smilax, and radiance roses decorated the chapel and tall Marie Antoinette baskets holding lovely clusters of radiance roses stood on either side of the altar. The bride who was given away by her father was radiant in a bridal gown of white satin fashioned on plain lines having on one side of the skirt a cascade of rose point lace and on the other side a platinum ornament. Her veil was held by a coronet of orange blossoms and she carried a large shower bouquet of lillies of the valley. The bridal party entered to the strains of the March from Lohengrin and Mendelssohn's March was played as the recessional. The bride had as her attendants, Mrs. William T. Coats as Matron of Honor and Misses Lillian Kahao and Ruben Carnal as bridesmaids. They wore especially lovely gowns of chiffon and Miss Kahao and Miss Carnal wore flesh colored chiffon and Mrs. Coats gown was of orchid color of chiffon. All carried shower bouquets of radiance roses. Mr. Hiers had as his attendants Mr. Loyless Hiers of Hampton, South Carolina as best man and Messrs. Carroll Bobb, William T. Coats, Walter Dunbar and Gresham Vincent, the latter a brother of the bride as groomsmen.

Miss Vincent has never been formally introduced but is one of the loveliest and most attractive members of the younger set in New Orleans. Mr. Hiers who was formerly of Hampton, South Carolina, has for the last few years been making his home here and is also well known both in the social and business world. There was no reception following the ceremony. Mr. and Mrs. Hiers have left on a bridal trip East and on their return will be at home in an apartment at 1311 Short Street.

THE TIMES PICAYUNE, Thursday, September 28, 1922.

Miss Clara Vincent's death recorded at City Board of Health April 1. 36 years. 1805 Carrollton.

THE TIMES PICAYUNE, April 2, 1913.

On Monday, March 31, 1913, at 5:30 o'clock p.m. Clara Celeste Gresham, wife of G. Owen Vincent died. Funeral will take place from her late residence, 1803 Carrollton Avenue this (Tuesday) afternoon April 1 at 4 o'clock. Interment in Metairie Cemetery.

THE TIMES PICAYUNE, April 1, 1913

Mr. and Mrs. G. Owen Vincent of Baton Rouge are at the St. Charles being in the city on a little wedding tour.

THE DAILY PICAYUNE, October 12, 1899.

W. H. GOODLOE, FORMER ST. LOUISAN, AMONG DEAD

Ward H. Goodloe one of the ten persons dead in the crash of an airliner near Edwall, Washington, was the son of Mr. and Mrs. Ward H. Goodloe of 330 West Lockwood Avenue, Webster Groves and a graduate of Webster Groves High School and a University of Missouri graduate.

His parents were notified last night by the President of Northwest Airlines.

Goodloe, 47, was discharged from the Navy on the West Coast and stayed there to become an executive in the American News Company, a magazine distributing agency operating over an eleven state area. He was one of the first naval officers to land on Guadalcanal in World War II.

He is also survived by his widow, Celeste in San Francisco and a brother, Allan M. Goodloe, an assistant United States Attorney for the Eastern District of Missouri. His father is President of a food brokerage firm bearing his name in the Merchant Exchange Building.

The older Goodloe was named District Manager of the Priorities Division of the Office of Production Management here at the start of World War II.

January 17, 1951, St. Louis GLOBE DEMOCRAT

REVEREND GRESHAM DIES, FORMER GRACE DEAN
City Church Leader Since 1909 Succumbs At 86

The Very Reverend James Wilmer Gresham who served for thirty years as Dean of Grace Cathedral and became one of the city's best known and most beloved Churchmen, died yesterday at St. Luke's Hospital after a three weeks illness. He was 86.

When Dean Gresham became dean in 1910 the Cathedral site atop Nob Hill was no more than a pile of rubble from the fire and earthquake.

He lived to see a great — though still unfinished — cathedral soaring out of the site.

Because he was so closely tied to that immense building project and to San Francisco, Dean Gresham once declined to become Episcopal Bishop of the Philippine Islands.

Doctor Gresham was born in Ocean Springs, Mississippi, into a family long prominent in Episcopal Church affairs in the Deep South.

He won his Bachelor of Divinity Degree at the University of the South in Sewanee, Tennessee, in 1895 and later was awarded an honorary doctorate. He was named as a deacon of the Church that same year and in 1896 was admitted to the priesthood.

He first served as curate of Trinity Church in New Orleans and in 1897 became Rector of St. James Church.

There followed Rectorships in Baton Rouge, Louisiana, and Charleston, South Carolina before he became in 1904 Rector of Trinity Episcopal Church in San Jose.

In 1909 he was called to Grace Cathedral as its Dean only to find no more than a clapboard chapel among the ruins.

He served for three decades working toward the completion of one of the city's greatest churches, tending his flock, a widely respected and immensely popular man.

It was in 1918 that he was unanimously elected Bishop of Philippines by the hierarchy of his Church.

After a week of thought and prayer, he respectfully declined the honor.

In 1939 he was retired from his post and at a special ceremony a special position as Dean Emeritus was established in his honor. It was this title he still proudly held at his death.

Dean Gresham was preceded in death by his wife, the former Emily Cooke who died in 1940. There were no children.

He is survived by only two immediate relatives, a niece, Mrs. Ward H. Goodloe of San Francisco and a nephew, Mr. Gresham H. Vincent of Greenville, Mississippi.

Funeral services under the direction of Halstead and Company will be held at 2 p.m. today in the Cathedral Chapel of Grace. Cremation will follow at Cypress Lawn Cemetery.

San Francisco *Examiner*, March 22, 1958

CELESTE GRESHAM HIERS

Born: March 9, 1927, in New Orleans, Louisiana

Married: George Franklin Prehmus in Schnectady, New York, on January 21, 1950

Children of George Franklin and Celeste Gresham (Hiers) Prehmus: Alan Prehmus born March 17, 1957; Cynthia Anne Prehmus born April 12, 1953, in Schnectady; Warren Dean Prehmus born August 11, 1955.

JAMES LAWRENCE HIERS II

Born: August 19, 1924, in New Orleans, Louisiana

Married: Marjorie Hillas Lithgow on January 10, 1953, in Morristown, New Jersey

Children of James Lawrence and Majorie Hillas (Lithgow) Hiers: James Lawrence Hiers III, born in Morristown, New Jersey, on June 10, 1955; Marjorie Lithgow Hiers born in Morristown, New Jersey, on April 29, 1958.

J. L. HIERS, JR., WEDS MARJORIE LITHGOW
Graduates of Yale and Smith Married in Morristown
Country Club Reception

Morristown, New Jersey. Miss Marjorie Hillas Lithgow, daughter of Mrs. Walter David Lithgow and the late Mr. Lithgow, was married here this afternoon to James Lawrence Hiers, Jr., of Stockton, son of Mrs. Ward Hazelton Goodloe of San Francisco and James Lawrence Hiers of St. Louis in the Presbyterian Church on the Green.

The Reverend Dr. Mutch performed the ceremony. There was a reception in the Morris County Country Club.

Given in marriage by her uncle, Robert M. Hillas of Greenwich, Connecticut, the bride had her sister, Miss Claire David Lithgow, as Maid of Honor. The other attendants were Mrs. Joseph Mangin of

Orange and Miss Barbara Ann Hillas of Madison, cousin of the bride. Carolyn Binney, cousin of the bride, was flower girl.

Mr. Hiers was his son's best man.

Mrs. Hiers was graduated from Kent Place School in Summit and Smith College. She is a granddaughter of the late Mr. and Mrs. Robert Hillas of Morristown and the late Mr. and Mrs. David G. Lithgow of New York.

Mr. Hiers is an alumnus of Yale. He is a grandson of the late Mr. and Mrs. Wade Hampton Hiers of Hampton, South Carolina, and the late Mr. and Mrs. G. Owen Vincent of New Orleans.

THE NEW YORK TIMES, January 11, 1953.

ROBERT OTIS OWEN

Born: July 31, 1861, in Mobile, Alabama

Married: Mary Ann Armstrong in New Orleans, Louisiana, on November 19, 1884

Died: March 7, 1912. Buried in Metairie Cemetery with his wife, Mary Ann Armstrong. She had been born in New Orleans on January 13, 1861, and died there on January 23, 1935.

Children of Robert Otis and Mary Ann (Armstrong) Owen: Alfred March Owen; Edith Frazer Owen; Edward Wallace Owen; Helen Frazer Owen born December 14, 1893, unmarried; James Blaine Owen; John Goronory Owen; Mary Olive Owen born on September 2, 1885, died in infancy; Robert Lee Owen born on May 31, 1895, died November 8, 1955, unmarried.

OWEN. On Thursday, March 7, 1912, at 2:20 o'clock a.m. Robert O. Owen, aged 50 years.

Funeral services at late residence 3606 Chestnut Street, this (Friday) morning at 11 o'clock.

Mobile and Meridian papers please copy.

New Orleans. March 8, 1912 Hall Mount Moriah Lodge No. 59, F. and A. M. The officers and members are hereby requested to assemble at the lodgerooms, Masonic Temple, this Friday, March 8, at 9:30 a.m. for the purpose of attending the funeral of Brother Robert O. Owen from his late residence, 3606 Chestnut Street. All Master Masons in good standing are fraternally invited to attend.

BY ORDER OF: M. M. BRADBURN, W.M.
ATTEST: JAMES I. RICHARD, SEC.

Daily Picayune, Friday, March 8, 1912

JAMES BLAINE OWEN CLAIMED BY DEATH

James Blaine Owen, 8226 Nelson Street, molasses company executive, died Wednesday at 2:45 p.m. at Baptist Hospital after a week's illness. He was 49 years old.

A native of New Orleans, Mr. Owen attended the public schools here and was a graduate of the Louisiana State University. He served in France during the World War as a First Lieutenant in the Army. For the past six years he had been traffic manager for the Commercial Molasses Corporation. He was a member of the traffic club of New Orleans.

Interment in Metairie Cemetery

ALFRED MARCH OWEN

Born: March 1, 1904, in New Orleans, Louisiana

Married: 1st: Emma Knight of New Orleans in Jackson, Mississippi, on March 1, 1928. Divorced.

2nd: Carrie Hurt in Baltimore, Maryland, on November 21, 1944

Children of Alfred March and Emma (Knight) Owen: Mary Ann Owen.

MARY ANN OWEN

Born: February 24, 1930

Married: Charles Vennum Grigsby on December 31, 1958

GRIGSBY-OWEN

The marriage of Miss Mary Ann Owen, daughter of Mrs. Emma Knight Owen to Mr. Charles Vennum Grigsby of New Orleans, son of Mrs. Charles Kent Priestman of Elmhurst, Long Island, New York, will be quietly celebrated Wednesday.

Greentrees Farm, the Hammond, Louisiana, home of the bride-to-be's cousin, Mrs. Edmond E. Talbot and Mr. Talbot will be the setting for the wedding, which will be attended only by the immediate families.

Miss Owen will have as her maid of honor her cousin, Miss Margaret Anne Knight of Baton Rouge, Louisiana, and as bridesmaid, Miss Olivia Gilliland.

Mr. Charles Stocker Fontelieu will be the best man.

The *TIMES-PICAYUNE*, Sunday, December 28, 1958

EDITH FRAZER OWEN

Born: March 11, 1888

Married: Paul Edward Odendahl on November 5, 1913, in New Orleans. Mr. Odendahl was born on March 17, 1886, the son of J. F. Odendahl, former President of the New Orleans Board of Trade, and partner in Glover and Odendahl.

Died: June 15, 1955

Children of Paul Edward and Edith Frazer (Owen) Odendahl: Paul Edward Odendahl, Junior.

J. F. ODENDAHAL, a member of the grain and flour firm of GLOVER AND ODENDAHAL is one of the advanced thinkers in business methods and leading men in the commercial circles of New Orleans, Louisiana. He was born in Rostack on the borders of the North Sea, in the Kingdom of Mecklinburg, Germany, in 1840 and came with his parents to America when but seven years of age. They located at Ft. Wayne, Indiana, and here he finished his education which had begun in Europe. At the age of nineteen, or in 1859, he entered the grain and milling business in St. Louis, Missouri, following that pursuit successfully until 1867 when he came South and located in New Orleans. Here he opened a grain and flour business with his present partner. The firm of GLOVER AND ODENDAHAL soon became known for their enterprise and reliability and remained unchanged until the present time, 1892. This firm is one of the largest and best known in the South, doing from $6,000,000 to $10,000,000 worth of business annually. They handle grain from the far Northwest and Pacific States and Texas to the southernmost parts of the Gulf of Mexico which latter places they supply with grain and flour. They sell flour to England and France, besides the large sales in various parts of the United States. This firm started with a small capital and now do a vast business. Wherever the name GLOVER AND ODENDAHAL is known, it is held in high esteem and respect and is a familiar one in all the large cities of the United States and many parts of the outside world. Mr. Odendahal married Miss Mary Schuricht of St. Louis, Missouri, and this union has been blessed with seven children: Fred H., a practicing physician of New Orleans, educated at St. Michael's College and graduated from the Rush Medical College, Chicago; Loula and Mary (twins); Adolph in business with his father; Emma, PAUL, and .... The entire family are members of the Lutheran Church. Mr. Odendahal is one of the leading members of the Board of Trade and has done much to build it up. He is a thorough American in all his ideas, a genial and accomplished gentleman and takes a prominent part in all social circles. He is essentially a progressive man of the New South. He is very liberal and charitable, giving freely of his means to those in distress and does much for the advancement of the city. BIOGRAPHICAL AND HISTORICAL MEMOIRS OF LOUISIANA, published by Goodspeed Company of Chicago, Volume 2, page 289.

PAUL EDWARD ODENDAHL, JUNIOR

Born: February 23, 1916

Married: Juanita Ann Todd on July 21, 1941. She was born on December 7, 1921

Children of Paul Edward and Juanita Ann (Todd) Odendahl: Jeanne Edith Odendahl born February 9, 1943; Robert Michael Odendahl born February 12, 1947.

EDWARD WALLACE OWEN

Born: August 15, 1886, in New Orleans, Louisiana

Married: Rita Desmarais on July 19, 1916, St. Stephen's Church, New Orleans

Died: March 20, 1940, in New Orleans, Louisiana

Children of Edward Wallace and Rita (Desmarais) Owen: Edward Wallace Owen, Jr.

EDWARD WALLACE OWEN, JUNIOR

Born: October 7, 1917, in New Orleans, Louisiana

Married: Lois Jeannette Bailey on December 27, 1943, in Atlanta, Georgia

Children of Edward Wallace and Lois Jeannette (Bailey) Owen: Frazer Nelson Owen born February 4, 1947, in Atlanta, Georgia.

JAMES BLAINE OWEN

Born: December 16, 1891, in New Orleans, Louisiana

Married: Katherine Nash Dearman on June 11, 1921, in Baton Rouge, Louisiana

Died: December 25, 1940, in New Orleans, Louisiana

Children of James Blaine and Katherine Nash (Dearman) Owen: Kathryn Lois Owen; Marcia June Owen.

KATHRYN LOIS OWEN

Born: September 14, 1929

Married: Robert Louis Giraud on June 26, 1954

Children of Robert Louis and Kathryn Lois (Owen) Giraud: Robert James Giraud born on April 1, 1958, in New Orleans, Louisiana; Suzette Lee Giraud born on March 27, 1955, in New Orleans, Louisiana.

MARCIA JUNE OWEN

Born: March 20, 1922

Married: Milton Hinrichs Lasker on April 2, 1941, in the Church of the Annunciation on South Claiborne Avenue in New Orleans.

Children of Milton Hinrichs and Marcia June (Owen) Lasker: Michael James Lasker born on November 2, 1944, in Boston, Massachusetts; Milton Owen Lasker born on January 7, 1943, in New Orleans, Louisiana.

JOHN GORONORY OWEN

Born: February 22, 1898

Married: Irene Alexander on September 1, 1923, in New Orleans, Louisiana. She was born on October 8, 1898

Children of John Goronory and Irene (Alexander) Owen: Irene Alexander Owen; John Goronory Owen, Junior.

JOHN GORONORY OWEN, JR.

Born: April 13, 1927

Married: Marilyn George on December 26, 1950

Children of John Goronory and Marilyn (George) Owen: James Blaine Owen born June 20, 1957; John Michael Owen born August 26, 1955.

IRENE ALEXANDER OWEN

Born: August 8, 1924

Married: Robert Emmet Byrne II on September 6, 1947

Children of Robert Emmet Byrne II and Irene Alexander Owen: Robert Emmet Byrne III born February 16, 1951; Renee Alexander Byrne born July 3, 1952; Susan Frazer Byrne born June 14, 1956.

COLONEL WILLIAM FRAZER OWEN

Born: March 31, 1856, in Mobile, Alabama

Married: 1st: Jennie O. Read on May 15, 1878, in Mobile, Alabama. She died Nov. 26, 1910

2nd: Mary Cornelia Taylor on September 15, 1921

Died: November 18, 1943. Buried Metairie Cemetery, New Orleans.

Colonel Owen served in the following capacities:

1906-1907 President of the New Orleans, Crowley and Western Railroad

July-Aug. Assistant to the President of the Mobile, Jackson and
1907 Kansas City Railroad

1907-1909 General Manager of the Mobile, Jackson and Kansas City Railroad

1910-1912 Vice President and General Manager of the New Orleans, Mobile and Chicago Railroad

1912-1913 President and General Manager of the New Orleans, Mobile and Chicago Railroad

1913-1916 Receiver of the New Orleans, Mobile and Chicago Railroad

1917-1918 President of the Gulf, Mobile and Northern Railroad

1918-1920 General Manager of the Gulf, Mobile and Northern Railroad and of the Meridian and Memphis Railroad under the United States Railroad Administration

See WHO'S WHO IN AMERICA 1916-1943

See WHO WAS WHO IN AMERICA Vol II 1943-1950. A. N. Marquis Company, Chicago, Illinois (1950)

1880 Census, Ward 4, Mobile, Alabama 5, 123, 164, 165
Harriet Read born in 1828 in New York; Emma C. Read born in 1854 in Alabama; William F. Owen born in 1852 in Alabama; Jennie O. Owen born in 1857 in Alabama; Jennie O. Owen born in 1879 in Alabama; Charles H. Read born in 1847 in Alabama.

The father of Harriet Read was born in France; her mother was born in Maine. The parents of Emma and Charles Read and Jennie Owen were born in New York. The parents of William F. Owen are incorrectly listed as born in Alabama.

The funeral of Mrs. Jennie Read Owen, wife of Vice President and General Manager W. F. Owen of the New Orleans, Mobile, and Chicago Railroad Company who died in Mobile Friday morning at 11 o'clock took place yesterday in New Orleans from Rayne Memorial Church, Reverend Dr. Rice, the pastor officiating.

On October 2, Mrs. Owen sustained a fall in her house. Her hip was fractured and it is believed other injuries resulted. She was removed to the Mobile Infirmary and about 10 days before her death was taken back home. The patient gradually grew worse despite efforts to save her life.

Mrs. Owen was a native of Mobile. She had resided here with her husband for several years, coming here again after he accepted service with the railroad in this city. Deceased leaves beside her husband one sister, Miss Emma Reed of New Orleans and other relatives in various parts of the United States. She was a member of the Rayne Memorial Church of New Orleans and served in church work while a resident of New Orleans.

MOBILE REGISTER, November 27, 1910

FUNERAL SET TODAY FOR COLONEL OWEN
RETIRED RAILWAY OFFICIAL IS STRICKEN ABOARD TRAIN TO NEW ORLEANS

Funeral services will be held in New Orleans Friday for Colonel William F. Owen, retired President of the old Gulf, Mobile and Northern Railroad and a native of Mobile.

Colonel Owen died unexpectedly in a New Orleans hospital about 12:30 a.m. Thursday after being stricken on a train while en route to New Orleans. He was apparently in good health when he left his residence, 1257 Selma Street for New Orleans.

Colonel Owen, 87 at the time of his death, served as President of the Gulf, Mobile and Northern until his retirement in 1920. He lived in New Orleans for 25 years, but had returned to Mobile to live about 1907.

He served in executive capacity for a number of railroads in this area during the half century he was in the railroad business. He began his career as a ticket agent for the New Orleans, Mobile and Texas Railroad in 1871 and headed the Gulf, Mobile and Northern from 1917 to 1920.

Colonel Owen is survived by the widowed, Mrs. Mary Taylor Owen of Mobile and several nieces and nephews in New Orleans and other relatives.

MOBILE REGISTER, Friday, November 19, 1943

Children of William Frazer and Jennie (Read) Owen: Thomas Bullock Owen, May 24, 1880, December 20, 1880; Emmie Cecile Owen, December 31, 1881, November 25, 1883; Jennie Read Owen, March 28, 1879, May 11, 1892; William Frazer Owen, Jr., March 17, 1886, October 18, 1899.

The above children are buried on Avenue G, 1 block from Metairie Avenue in Metairie Cemetery, New Orleans, with their parents:
Jennie O. Read wife of William F. Owen November 25, 1910
William Frazer Owen March 31, 1856   November 18, 1943

William Frazer Owen, Jr.
Memorial
Presented to City Park
By His Parents
1910

The above is the inscription on a drinking fountain in City Park in New Orleans.

William F. Owen married Jennie O. Read on May 15, 1878, in Mobile, Alabama. Thomas S. Bullock on the bond.

Frank S. Vincent and Martina H. Owen were married in Mobile on April 18, 1872 by J. A. Massey, Rector of Trinity Church, in the bride's house.

William M. Frazer married Mrs. Ann Hardy, a widow, on November 6, 1856, at the domicile of Mrs. Hardy in Mobile. They were married by J. H. Ingraham, Rector of St. John's Church.

Henry Hardy was married to Mrs. Ann Crosby on December 13, 1845, in Mobile. Wm. Hamilton, Pastor of the Government Street Church was the minister.

FRAZER

1. John Frazer came from Scotland when a boy and settled in South Carolina. He was a member of the artillery when killed at the Battle of Beaufort, 1779. His son, grandson, and great-grandson were hereditary members of the Ancient and Honorable Artillery Society of Charleston. John Frazer married Martha Milligan, a relative of Jacob Milligan, the South Carolina Revolutionary hero.

2. John Milligan Frazer (died 1826) and Rebecca Ripley, his wife.

3. Charles Peronneau Frazer (1805-1873) and Hannah Pratt Raymond, his second wife.

4. William Norton Hughes and Mary Geraldine Frazer, his wife.

   See Record of Eva Raymond Frazer Hughes, D.A.R. Number 22425, Volume 23, pages 146 and 147. See also Record of May Geraldine F. Hughes, D.A.R. Number 49692, Volume 50, pages 309 and 310.

Account of the Battle at Port Royal in which Lieu. Benj. Wilkins, of the Charlestown Artillery, Mr. John Fraser of same corps, John Williams, and John Craig volunteers, and four privates were killed. The above account is from the South Carolina and American General Gazette and is printed again in the South Carolina Historical and Genealogical Magazine, Volume 17, page 152.

"Last Saturday returned hither the detachment of Charlestown artillery and militia, which, with a part of Col. Skirving's regiment, beat the British light infantry on the 4th of last month on Port Royal Island. Our loss 8 killed and 25 wounded.
Charlestown artillery: Lieut. Benj Wilkins, private John Fraser killed.
Charlestown Light Infantry Volunteers, John Craig, private John Wiliams, killed.
Detachment Col. Skirving's regiment Sergeant Alexander Douglas killed
Capt Lushington's Camp of Charlestown Militia Privates Charles Smith, James Heathcott, Joseph Solomon killed.
(Wednesday, March 10, 1779.)
See Death Notices from the Gazette of the State of South Carolina, Published in the *South Carolina Historical and Genealogical Magazine*, Volume 50, page 204.
The following is taken from *The History of South Carolina in the Revolution 1775-1780* by Edward McCrady. Printed by the Macmillan Company, New York 1901. Pages 339-340.

"The Royal Army at Savannah having now been reenforced by the junction of the troops from St. Augustine, Prevost availing himself of his naval aid and of the interior navigation made lodgement on the island of Port Royal with two hundred men under Major Gardiner. On the 2d of February 1799 (The correct year is 1779. C.O.J.) General Moultrie with General Bull and about three hundred militia crossed the river and attacked and drove the British from the island. In this engagement General Moultrie had but nine regular soldiers, but he had with him a portion of the Charlestown battalian of artillery, which was no doubt the very best fighting material in the service. This was the elite corps Christopher Gadsden had organized and drilled. It had now been increased to a battalion of two companies under the command of Major Thomas Grimball, with Thomas Heyward, Jr., and Edward Rutledge, two of the signers of the Declaration of Independence, both still Members of Congress, as Captains.

On the 15th of January President Lowndes had issued orders to Major Grimball to detach fifty men from his battalion with two field pieces to join General Lincoln. A meeting of the officers was called, when it was resolved to turn out the battalion and read the orders to ascertain if volunteers sufficient would offer for the service, if not then to draw. The battalion turned out on the 16th and instead of fifty, eighty volunteered and were accepted under the command of Captains Edward Rutledge and Thomas Heyward, Jr. It was indeed to this corps that the success of the expedition was chiefly due. Heyward and Rutledge and Captain John Barnwell of the militia distinguished themselves in the action. Captain Heyward was wounded and Lieutenant Wilkins was killed. The British lost almost all their officers. The Americans had but eight men killed and twenty-two wounded. General Lee in his *Memoirs of the War in the Southern Department* observes that the occupation of Port Royal, on the part of Prevost, could not then be ascertained, nor has it since been developed.

List of killed or wounded at the action near Beaufort, February 9, 1799 (The correct year is 1779. C.O.J.) :

Killed: Lieutenant Benjamin Wilkins, John Fraser, John Craig, John Williams, Alexander Douglas, Charles Smith, James Heathcott, Joseph Solomon

Wounded: Honorable Captain Thomas Heyward, Captain Thomas McLaughlin, Lieutenant Brown, Lieutenant Sawyer, John Calvert, Francis Dearing, John Righton, John Lawrence, John Green, John Anthony, I. D. Miller, Anthony Watts, John Collins, Stephen Deveaux, William Rea, John Crosskeys, Michael Campbell, Ephraim Adams, Samuel Howard, John Graves, Thomas Feapue, John Oliphant, Ramsay's Revolution, Vol. II 391. Omitted in above lists, George Jervey and John Parsons, wounded.

The above is from *The History of South Carolina in the Revolution* by Edward McCrady. Printed by the Macmillan Company, New York. 1901. Pages 339-340.

Francis Bernard Heitman in his Historical Register of the *Officers of the Continental Army during the War of the Revolution April 1775-1783*, New Revised and Enlarged Edition, The Rare Book Shop Publishing Company, Inc., 1914, on page 236, mentions a John Frazer (S. C.), Lieutenant 4th South Carolina (Artillery) — 1777; killed at Beaufort 9th February 1779. In his preface to the book, Mr. Heitman notes, "The records given in this volume are not strictly official, for much of the data has not been obtained from official records, but in order to complete, as far as possible the service of each officer other sources of reliable information have been consulted and the data obtained therefrom included." It is indeed an odd circumstance that *two* persons named John Frazer of South Carolina should be killed at the Battle of Beaufort on the same day. Mr. Heitman lists John Frazer as a Lieutenant and places him in the 4th South Carolina (Artillery). No other record — those contemporaneous with the event — refer to him as an officer. They call him a "volunteer" or private. All other records associate John Fraser with the Charlestown Artillery. Many of the descendants of John Frazer were hereditary members of the Ancient and Honorable Artillery Society of Charleston.

JACOB MILLIGAN

Jacob Milligan of Bay Street was on the Poll List of the Charleston, South Carolina Municipal Elections in 1787.

South Carolina Historical and Genealogical Magazine Vol 56, page 47.

Died yesterday afternoon, in the bloom of life, after a long and tedious illness, Mrs. Margaret Milligan, wife of Mr. Jacob Milligan of this city. Friday, November 24, 1786.

Ibid, Vol 20, page 217.

Died. In England. Mary Milligan, wife of Mr. Jacob Milligan of this place. Gazette of Charleston Friday, December 20, 1793.

Ibid, Vol 22, page 24.

Married by the Rev. Parson Frost on Saturday last, George Manson, ship carpenter to the amiable relict of the deceased Captain Jacob Milligan, Harbor-Master of this port. Gazette of Charleston S.C. Monday, January 30, 1797.

Captain Jacob Milligan was a member of the Court Martial of Captain Joyner of the South Carolina.

South Carolina Historical and Genealogical Magazine Vol 10 page 114.

"Jacob Milligan, as a lieutenant of the *Prosper* in 1776, boarded the frigate *Actaeon*, as she lay burning and deserted by her crew, on the shoal where Fort Sumter now stands, and firing her guns at the British fleet, he brought off her flag ere she blew up."

Ibid, Vol 10, page 115.

"The sloop *Sally* commanded by Captain Benjamin Stone (one of the vessels fitted out by the merchants to scour the coast) returned into port with 5 men killed and 12 wounded — having engaged a large ship off Port Royal Bar — Captain Milligan lost the club of his hair and some skin by the enemy's shot —

Gazette of Charleston Wednesday, Dec 30, 1778

Ibid, Vol 50, page 129. See also McCrady SOUTH CAROLINA IN THE REVOLUTION published in 1901 by Macmillan Co. in New York page 160.

Jacob Milligan in 1790 Census of Charleston District of St. Philips and St. Michaels Parish had one male 16 and over, one male under 16 and 3 females.

Jacob Milligan filed Revolutionary claim in South Carolina.

ORIGINAL INDEX BOOK by Janie Revill page 241.

Captain Jacob Milligan S.C.N. 33 received a bounty grant as a Revolutionary Soldier (Continental). Recorded in 4th Volume of Bounty Grants in the Office of the Secretary of State.

South Carolina Historical and Genealogical Magazine Vol 7, page 222.

Captain Jacob Milligan testified at the Court of Inquiry on Lieutenant Fraser, 1780.

Ibid, Vol 5, pages 212-213.

1784

March 15th   The State of South Carolina
             To Jacob Milligan Dr-
             To One Year's Gratuity (allowed Commodore
             Gillon and his officers) as Captain in the
             Naval Department

Endorsed: The committee appointed on Captain Milligan's Petition report that they have examined the allegations contained in the said petition and are of the opinion that though Captain Milligan's claim is not within the letter it is within the spirit of the Acts of this State for making compensation to its servants. They are fully of opinion as well from the vouchers produced to them as from their personal knowledge of the active zeal and good conduct of the petitioner that he ought to be put on a footing with the officers of Commodore Gillon. They therefore recommend that the resolution of the legislature for granting a year's pay as a gratuity to Commodore Gillon's officers be extended to Captain Milligan.

South Carolina Historical and Genealogical Magazine

Vol 7, pages 99-100.

No 204 Issued the 7th April 1785 to Mr. Jacob Milligan for forty

Lib O   one pounds twelve shillings sterling for freight of rice and
corn for continental use in 1783. Account audited.

STUB ENTRIES TO INDENTS ISSUED IN PAYMENT OF
CLAIMS AGAINST SOUTH CAROLINA GROWING OUT OF THE
REVOLUTION. Books O to Q, page 40. A. S. Salley, Jr., 1915.

No 6   Issued the 23rd June 1784 to Captain Jacob Milligan for
Book H One Hundred and Fifty One pounds two shillings and six
         pence three farthings sterling for pay due him as Captain
of the Revenge Galley from 25th May 1782 to 15th March 1783. Account audited etc.

Idem Book G-H, page 64.

ANN CAROLINE MILLIGAN

Married, on Thursday last, Mr. Isaac Johnston to Miss Ann Caroline Milligan, daughter of Captain Jacob Milligan. Gazette of Charleston, Monday, May 27, 1793.

South Carolina Historical and Genealogical Magazine Vol 21, page 157.

Will of Ann Johnston in Vol 46 (1851-1856) page 109 *INDEX TO WILLS OF CHARLESTON COUNTY, SOUTH CAROLINA* Charleston Free Library (1950)

JOHN MILLIGAN

Jno Milligan testified at the Court of Inquiry on Lieutenant Fraser, 1780.

South Carolina Historical and Genealogical Magazine
Vol 5, pages 212-213.

John Milligan in 1790 Census of Charleston District, St. Philips and St. Michaels Parish with 1 male 16 and up and 3 females.

Will of John Milligan in Vol 28 (1800-1807) page 227
INDEX TO WILLS OF CHARLESTON COUNTY, SOUTH CAROLINA 1671-1868. Charleston Free Library (1950)

John Milligan filed Revolutionary Claim in South Carolina. Janie Revill *ORIGINAL INDEX BOOK*, page 241.

No 45 Book L
Issued the 20th September: 1784: to Mr. John Milligan for forty seven pounds ten shillings sterling for 9½ months service as Lieutenant on board the Revenge Galley commanded by Jacob Milligan from the 27th May 1782 to the 15th March 1783. Account audited etc.
STUB ENTRIES TO INDENTS FOR REVOLUTIONARY CLAIMS, BOOK L-N, page 10.

JOHN T. MILLIGAN

1860 CENSUS, 4TH WARD, CHARLESTON, SOUTH CAROLINA 392, 395
Jno T. Milligan born in 1816 in South Carolina; Mary Milligan born

in 1823 in South Carolina; William Milligan born in 1844 in South Carolina; John Milligan born in 1847 in South Carolina; Edward Milligan born in 1849 in South Carolina; Jacob Millgan born in 1851 in South Carolina.

John T. Milligan is listed as a "Master of Sail."

1870 CENSUS, WARD 8, CHARLESTON, SOUTH CAROLINA 1433, 1733

J. T. Milligan born in 1816 in South Carolina; Elizabeth Milligan born in 1843 in South Carolina; Jacob Milligan born in 1851 in South Carolina; Charles Milligan born in 1858 in South Carolina; George Milligan born in 1859 in South Carolina; Elizabeth Graham born in 1854 in South Carolina; Catharine Graham born in 1856 in South Carolina; Charles Gruber born in 1820 in South Carolina.

JOHN MILLIGAN FRAZER

Born: 1765-1774

Married: Rebecca Ripley on April 6, 1797, in Charleston, South Carolina

Died: 1826

Children of John Milligan and Rebecca (Ripley) Frazer: Charles Peronneau Frazer, George Ripley Frazer, James Lawrence Frazer, John Jacob Frazer, John Milligan Frazer, Martha Richards Frazer, Mary Ann Frazer, William Milligan Frazer.

John Milligan Frazer was a contractor and ship builder. In the City Directories of Charleston, he is listed as located on 10 Pinckney Street in 1801, on 26 Trott Street in 1802, 1803, 1806, and 1807. In 1822 Frazer and Sons was located on Daniel's Wharf in Charleston. In the 1829 Directory, Rebecca Fraser, widow, is listed as living on Laurens Street.

1800 CENSUS, CHARLESTON COUNTY, SOUTH CAROLINA Page 66

John M. Fraser

1 male born 1755-1774; 1 male born 1784-1790; 2 males born 1790-1800; 1 female born before 1755; 1 female born 1755-1774; 1 female born 1790-1800.

1810 CENSUS, CHARLESTON COUNTY, SOUTH CAROLINA Page 50

John M. Fraser

1 male born 1765-1784; 8 males born 1784-1794; 2 males born 1794-1800; 1 male born 1800-1810; 1 female born 1765-1784; 3 females born 1800-1810.

1820 CENSUS, CHARLESTON COUNTY, SOUTH CAROLINA Page 72

John M. Fraser

1 male born before 1775; 1 male born 1775-1794; 2 males born 1794-1804; 1 male born 1804-1810; 2 males born 1810-1820; 1 female born before 1775; 2 females born 1810-1820; 5 slaves.

The Manual of the Second Presbyterian Church of Charleston, South

Carolina, names John M. Frazer as a founder of the church in 1810. The Manual was published in 1894. See also the 1898 Yearbook of the City of Charleston, page 33.

A pamphlet, "A Sketch of the History and the Rules of the Charleston Ancient Artillery Society" published in 1901 by the Walker, Evans and Cogswell Company of Charleston, South Carolina, on page 18, contains an account of the part played in February, 1779, by the Charlestown Battalion of Artillery in the Battle of Beaufort. In 1808 the members of the Battalion organized a social and benevolent association, of which every member of the corps was a member under rules. As late as 1851 a few of the original members were surviving although it was chiefly composed of descendants of members of the old Battalion. (Idem page 22). John Milligan Frazer was admitted to membership on November 2, 1808. (Idem page 54) He was an officer (Stewart) that year. (Idem page 45). His Son, Charles Peronneau Frazer was admitted to membership on January 12, 1832. Charles Peronneau Frazer served as a Stewart from 1834 to 1840, as Secretary from 1854 to 1869 and as Secretary-Treasurer from 1870 until his death in 1873.

References to Charles Peronneau Frazer in "A Sketch of the History and the Rules of the Charleston Ancient Artillery Society" published in 1901 by the Walker, Evans and Cogswell Company of Charleston, South Carolina, may be found on pages 48, 49, 50 and 55. A son of Charles Peronneau Frazer named John Milligan Frazer was admitted to membership in the Society on May 13, 1851 (Idem page 56)

April 6, 1797. John Milligan Frazer of Charleston married Rebecca Eairr of the same place, widow. See St. Philip's Register (1754-1810) Smith and Huger, 1927, page 265.

March 12, 1788. William Eayres and Rebecca Ripley spinster were married per license. Ibid, page 242.

John M. Frazer bought a negro slave Jammy from John J. Pringle on 12 October 1809. See Bill of Sale Book 4-A, page 356 State Archives, Columbia, South Carolina.

John M. Fraser of Charleston held a lease from John Cochran and Louisa Durse for part of a lot on the south side of Tradd Street which he sublet or conveyed to Christopher Stanks, late of London. 1 February 1801. See Charleston Deed Book, D-7, page 381, Office of the Register of Mesne Conveyances.

John Milligan Frazer of Charleston bought a negro slave Isaac from William Chambers of Charleston for $400.00. See Bill of Sale Book 4-A, page 349, State Archives, Columbia, South Carolina.

Samuel Richards to his wife, Mary Richards, sole tradership deed. - April 1818. John M. Frazer Trustee with John J. Frazer a witness. Children: Thomas, Mary, and Martha Richards. Covers two plantations in Greenville District, a plantation in Anderson District, and other property. See Misc. Records 4-N, State Archives, Columbia South Carolina.

Samuel Richards married Mary Singleton, only daughter of Daniel Singleton. See Georgetown Gazette, Charleston Column. 12 December 1801.

John M Frazer and Samuel Richards as Trustee for five children of John M. Frazer. Mortgage to Thomas Bennett satisfied. Covered a lease of a lot in Winthrop Street No. 41, leased by Bartholomew Carrol as attorney for Edward Winslow for a period of twelve years from August 1, 1818 with all buildings. See Misc Mtg RRR, page 336, State Archives, Columbia, South Carolina.

John M. Frazier, a student at Mr. Nixon's Academy, won medals in English, Writing, and Arithmetic. See Charleston City Gazette and Daily Advr. May 6, 1791.

John M. Frazer borrowed money from William Cannon with the agreement that John M. Frazer make a trust deed to his sons, John J. Frazer and Wm. M. Frazer covering two lots, part of the property of the late Christopher Gadsden, plat reference, lots 115 and 116; also his public salt water bathing house. 9 May 1823. See Charleston Deed Books F-9, page 455 and L-9, page 316 or 386, Office of the Register of Mesne Conveyances.

John Milligan Frazer to his wife Rebecca Sole Dealer. 29 May 1820 John Jacob Frazer and William Milligan Frazer Trustees. Consideration $2,000. Two lots on Laurens Street running back to Vernon Street, leased land with a workshop facing on Laurens Street, slave Rachel, and a bathing establishment. See Misc Records 4-T page 414, State Archives, Columbia South Carolina.

John Milligan Frazer of Charleston gave Henry Bennett of Charleston a bond dated 29 January 1820. Just sum $600 and Penal Sum $1,200. See Misc Record UUUU, page 262, State Archives, Columbia, South Carolina.

John Milligan Frazer died intestate in 1826. His widow Rebecca and their children: John Jacob Frazer, William Milligan Frazer, Charles Peronneau Frazer, Mary Ann Frazer who married Wm. Crosby and had a son, Josiah Crosby, Martha Richards Frazer who married Geo. Osborne, James L. Frazer, and George R. Frazer. See Equity Bills Nos. 81 and 82 filed 16 July 1838. State Archives, Columbia, South Carolina.

John Milligan Frazer made a trust deed to Samuel Richards, printer, covering his home, slaves, etc. in favor of his children: John Milligan Frazer, John Jacob Frazer, William Milligan Frazer, Charles Peronneau Frazer, Mary Ann Frazer, and Martha Richards Frazer, First made 21 May 1812. Renewed 29 May 1823. See Misc Records 4-Y, page 276, and 4-E page 384, State Archives, Columbia, South Carolina.

REBECCA RIPLEY

Born: 1766

Married: 1st: William Eayres on March 12, 1788

2nd: John Milligan Frazer on April 6, 1797

Died: August 16, 1847

Children of William and Rebecca (Ripley) Eayres: Elizabeth Eayres.

William Airs in the 1790 Census of Charleston, South Carolina, Christ Church Parish, had one male over 16, one male under 16, one female and seven slaves.

William Eayres and Rebecca Ripley Spinster were married per license. See St. Philip's Register (1754-1810) Smith and Huger (1927) page 242

April 6, 1797, John Milligan Frazer of Charleston married Rebecca Eairr of the same place widow. See St. Philip's Register (1754-1810) Smith and Huger (1927) page 265

Rebecca Frazer was admitted to membership in the Second Presbyterian Church in Charleston in 1829, according to Church records.

Sacred to the memory of Rebecca Frazer, consort of John M. Frazer who departed this life August 16, 1847, in the 81st year of her life.

From a tombstone in the Frazer Plot in the Churchyard of the Second Presbyterian Church, Charleston, South Carolina.

Estate of George Ripley owned Indent from Book BB, page 590 S.C. Treasurer's Journal for 1780, page 280, Hist. Comm. Archives.

ELIZABETH MARY AYERS (EAYRES)

Born: 1793 in South Carolina

Married: Richard Cole of Charleston, formerly of Bristol, England

Died: After 1860

Children of Richard and Elizabeth Mary (Ayres) Cole: Mary Louisa Cole.

After the death of Richard Cole, Elizabeth Mary Ayres Cole and their daughter, Mary Louisa Cole, went to live in Hamburg, South Carolina, with James Frazer, half brother of Elizabeth Cole.

Information on the Coles and Stoys was sent me by Mrs. Charles Jackson Steward (Ruth Davenport) of 733 Conway Road, Orlando, Florida.

MARY LOUISA COLE

Born: May 2, 1817, in South Carolina (Charleston)

Married: John Walter Stoy on January 26, 1837, in Hamburg, South

Carolina. Mr. Stoy was born June 3, 1810, and died December 23, 1874, Augusta, Ga.

Died: October 25, 1898, Augusta, Georgia

Descendants of John Walter Stoy and Mary Louisa Cole:

Miranda Stoy.
Born 1838 (?)
Married: Garbert Wienges on April 30, 1857, Charleston, S. C.
Married: 2nd: Mr. Gordon

    Joseph Wienges
    Married: Eva Mims   Augusta, Georgia

        Mattie Wienges
        Married: William K. Hagler
            Evelyn Hagler

        J. Claud Wienges
        Married: Carrie Cotton
            Frances Caroline Wienges
            Married: William H. Kinney
            Martha Claud Wienges

        Howard J. Wienges
        Married: 1st: Evelyn Boon
            Barbara Mims Wienges
            Married: Roger Haskell Cross, Jr.

        Howard J. Wienges
        Married: 2nd: Nelle Menius

        Louis G. Wienges
        Paul C. Wienges
        Married: Marian Barber

    Ida Wienges
    Married: Leonard Verdery   Augusta, Georgia

        Louise Verdery

        Berteau Verdery
        Married: Gertrude Lewis
            Leonard F. Verdery

Floretta Stoy   Died in Mexico City
Born: 1840 in Augusta, Georgia
Married: James Chrietzberg   Died in Mexico City

    William Chrietzberg   Moved to New York

    Arthur Chrietzberg   Arthur Chrietzberg was su-
    Married: Senorita M. Guerrero   perintendent of a railroad in
                            Mexico. He, his wife, and four
        Floretta Chrietzberg   children were killed in a train
        Married: Enrique de Vaca   wreck.

Jose Luis de Vaca   Only survivor was Floretta de
Lupita de Vaca   Vaca, Atzcapotzalco, D.F.
Enrique de Vaca   Mexico.
James Chrietzberg
Arthur Chrietzberg
Emma Chrietzberg
Maria Chrietzberg

Emma Louisa Stoy
Born: 1842 in Charleston, South Carolina. Died in Augusta, Georgia.
Walter P. Stoy
Born: 1844 in Charleston, South Carolina. Died in Augusta, Georgia.
Married: Isabella Hayes

Walter J. Stoy
Married: Annie Jones   Atlanta, Georgia, 1879
Margaret Stoy
Married: R. F. Bateman

Isabel Augusta Stoy
Born: 1847 in Charleston, South Carolina
Died: 1921 Augusta, Georgia
William C. Stoy
Born: 1850 in Charleston, South Carolina
Died: 1912 Augusta, Georgia
Julian M. Stoy
Born: 1852 in Charleston, South Carolina
Married: Ida E. Cameron   Augusta, Georgia

Viola Stoy   Formerly lived in Savannah,
Married: William Tommins   Georgia. Now live in Colum-
    bia County, Georgia.

Alman Tommins
Married: Martha Wright Wilder
Evelyn Tommins

Harry E. Stoy
Married: Mae Belk
Julian M. Stoy, Jr.
Married: Ruth Lewis
Effie Stoy
Married: Forrest Glenn Croley
Jack Glenn Croley
Ada Evelyn Croley

Rosa A. Stoy
Born: 1854 in Charleston, South Carolina
Married: Joab L. Mauldin in 1879. Died: Anderson, South Carolina

— 33 —

Charles S. Mauldin Deceased
Married: Margaret Wright
   Virginia Caroline Mauldin

Frank S. Mauldin
Married: Beatrice Robertson
   Rosa Stoy Mauldin

J. Lawrence Mauldin Deceased

Jane Robertson Stoy
Born: February 12, 1856, in Charleston, South Carolina
Married: Joseph Benjamin Davenport on November 12, 1878. Mr.

Davenport was born on May 19, 1854 and died on January 22, 1943
Died: December 31, 1924 Augusta, Georgia

Joseph Benjamin Davenport, Jr. Died: 1945 North Augusta, S. C.
Born: October 5, 1879
Married: Ethel Lamkin on April 30, 1900

   Julian Benton Davenport
   Born: 1902
   Died: 1906

   Martha Benton Davenport
   Married: Harry Parker
   Walter Davenport
   Lamkin Davenport

Ruth Davenport
Born: February 6, 1881
Married: Charles Jackson Steward on December 14, 1911. Died: Dec.
24, 1951

   Davenport Steward, Decatur, Georgia
   Author and Journalist
   Born: February 24, 1913
   Married: Kathryn Henderson June 13, 1939
      Carole Henderson Steward
      Born: March 27, 1942
      Ruth Davenport Steward
      Born: May 7, 1944

Williams Dean Steward, M.D., F.A.C.P. Orlando, Florida
Born: November 25, 1914
Married: Martha Frances Boyd on June 30, 1939

   Frances Jouett Steward
   Born March 21, 1942
   Martha Dean Steward
   November 19, 1947

Boyd Gunter Steward
Born: August 22, 1952

Jack Barnett Steward
Born: June 6, 1917
Died: May 24, 1918

Charles Jackson Steward, Jr. Richmond Hill, New York
Born: March 29, 1920
Married: Nancy Harris on June 1, 1940

Harris M. Steward
Born: March 11, 1941

Mary Jacquelyn Steward
Jon Barnett Steward
Darrel Steward

Charles Jackson Steward, Jr.
Married: 2nd: Rose Mary Leo on February 9, 1952

Janet Rose Steward
Born: November 23, 1955

Michael Dean Steward
Born: October 4, 1957

Alice Davenport: Born Nov 11, 1883, Died in infancy

Warren C. Davenport: Born Nov 10, 1885. Resides North Augusta,
Georgia

Jouett Davenport: Born Mar 15, 1890, Augusta, Georgia

Warren Candler Davenport
Born: November 10, 1885
Married: Elena Virginia Jones September 10, 1907

Pearre Jones Davenport
Married: Mildred Smith
Pearre Jones Davenport
Anne Davenport
Jane Davenport

Harold Davenport
Married: Margaret Henson
Allan Davenport
Helen Davenport

Dorothy Jane Davenport
Married: 1st: Hanley Hiekes
Lealie Hiekes

Married:2nd: David Wirt
Kathy Wirt

Jonett Davenport
Born: March 15, 1890

Married: Annie Laurie Attaway on January 14, 1914

Resides: Augusta, Georgia

Jonett Davenport, Jr.

Eliza Williams Stoy

1880 CENSUS WARD 5 CHARLESTON, SOUTH CAROLINA PAGE 1
Supervisors District 2 Enumeration District 67 4, 3, 3
Martha A. Fraser born in 1835 in South Carolina; Fanny Gadsden born in 1806 in South Carolina was her mother. Both with their parents were born in South Carolina. Boarding with them was Robert H. Teasdale born in 1835 and also Rena Teasdale born in 1867, both born with their parents in South Carolina

1810 CENSUS, CHARLESTON COUNTY, SOUTH CAROLINA
Thos Cole: 1 male born 1765-1784; 1 male born 1800-1810; 1 female born 1784-1794

1820 CENSUS, CHARLESTON COUNTY, SOUTH CAROLINA
Mrs. E. Cole: 1 male born 1810-1820; 1 female born 1775-1794; 1 female born 1810-1820; 4 slaves

1830 CENSUS, CHARLESTON NECK, SOUTH CAROLINA
Eliza Cole: 1 male born 1810-1815; 1 female born 1790-1800; 1 female born 1815-1820; 2 slaves

1850 CENSUS, WARD 4, CHARLESTON, SOUTH CAROLINA 538, 555
Seth Prior born in 1813 in South Carolina; Rebecca Prior born in 1814 in South Carolina; Rebecca Weinges born in 1794 in Massachusetts; Garbet Weinges born in 1825 in South Carolina; Rebecca Prior born in 1835 in South Carolina; Elizabeth Prior born in 1836 in South Carolina; Cornelia Prior born in 1837 in South Carolina; Julia Prior born in 1844 in South Carolina; S. T. Prior born in 1847 in South Carolina

1860 CENSUS, WARD 6, CHARLESTON, SOUTH CAROLINA 508, 500
Gabot Weinges born in 1835 in South Carolina; Miranda Weinges born in 1840 in South Carolina; Joseph Weinges born in 1858 in South Carolina

1880 CENSUS, WARD 3, CHARLESTON, SOUTH CAROLINA PAGE 7
Supervisor's District 2, Enumeration District 58 42, 71
Mary Hanall (?) born in 1839 in South Carolina where her father was born. Her mother was born in Connecticut; Julia Hughes born in 1867 in South Carolina; Mary Hughes born in 1869 in South Carolina; Emilie Hughes born in 1872 in South Carolina; Ellen Hughes born in 1864 in South Carolina, all Hughes were children of Mary Hanall. Their father was born in South Carolina; William Hanal born in 1876 in South Carolina was the son of Mary Hanall. His father was born in South Carolina; Mrs. Frazer born in 1810 in

Connecticut where her parents were born was the mother of Mrs. Hanall

1830 CENSUS, CHARLESTON NECK, SOUTH CAROLINA

E. Bazeleau: 1 male born 1800-1810; 1 female born 1780-1790; 5 slaves

William N. Hughes, husband of Mary Geraldine Frazer, was admitted to membership in the Ancient and Honorable Artillery Society of Charleston, South Carolina, on December 14, 1868.

Victoria Alexine Frazer, daughter of Charles P. Frazer, died in infancy and is buried in the Frazer Plot in the Cemetery of the Second Presbyterian Church, Charleston.

John Milligan Frazer born ca 1829, the son of Charles P. Frazer had a son John Frazer and a daughter, Ethel Frazer. He lived at one time in Columbus, Georgia, and later in Mexico.

On August 17, 1780 Mary Henderson was buried. St. Philip's Register (1754-1810) Smith and Huger (1927) page 340

1860 CENSUS WARD NO. 5 CHARLESTON SOUTH CAROLINA, 124, 138

John W. Stoy born in 1811 in Georgia; Mary Stoy born in 1818 in South Carolina; Jas R. Christberg born in 1825 in South Carolina; Floretta Christberg born in 1840 in Georgia; Emma L Stoy born in 1842 in South Carolina; Walter Stoy born in 1844 in South Carolina; Isabel Stoy born in 1847 in South Carolina; William Stoy born in 1850 in South Carolina; Julian Stoy born in 1852 in South Carolina; Rosa Stoy born in 1854 in South Carolina; Jane Stoy born in 1856 in South Carolina; Eliza Stoy born in 1860 in South Carolina; Elizabeth M. Cole born in 1793 in South Carolina; Ann Loury born in Ireland; John W. Stoy was a merchant; Jas R Christberg, a broker, and Ann Loury, a servant.

1870 CENSUS WARD NO. 3, AUGUSTA, RICHMOND COUNTY, GEORGIA 146, 137

John W. Stoy born in 1812 in Georgia; Mary L. Stoy born in 1820 in South Carolina; Emma L. Stoy born in 1842 in South Carolina; Walter P. Stoy born in 1844 in South Carolina; Isabella A. Stoy born in 1847 in South Carolina; William C. Stoy born in 1849 in South Carolina; Julia M. Stoy born in 1851 in South Carolina; Rosa A. Stoy born in 1854 in South Carolina; Jane B. Stoy born in 1857 in South Carolina; Eliza W. Stoy born in 1859 in South Carolina

1880 CENSUS WARD NO. 3 AUGUSTA RICHMOND COUNTY GEORGIA MILLER STREET 102, 245, 351

Mary L. Stoy born in 1821 in Georgia (sic); Emma Stoy born in 1855 in South Carolnia; William Stoy born in 1847 in Georgia (sic); Isabella Stoy born in 1849 in Georgia (sic); Eliza Stoy born in 1862 in Georgia (sic); the parents of Mary L. Stoy were born in South Carolina.

CHARLES PERONNEAU FRAZER

Born: 1805 in Charleston, South Carolina

Married: 1st: Susan E. (?   )

2nd: Hannah Pratt Raymond on April 17, 1838

Died: 1873

Children of Charles Peronneau and Susan E. (?) Frazer: Edward Laurens Frazer; John Milligan Frazer.

Children of Charles Peronneau and Hannah Pratt (Raymond) Frazer: Mary Geraldine Frazer

1850 CENSUS CHARLESTON SOUTH CAROLINA PARISHES OF ST. PHILIP'S AND ST. MICHAEL'S 443, 447

Charles P. Frazer born in 1805 in South Carolina; Hannah P. Frazer born in 1808 in Connecticut; John M. Frazer born in 1829 in South Carolina; Edward L. Frazer born in 1832 in South Carolina; Mary G. Frazer born in 1838 in South Carolina; F. Kneuffer born in 1800 in Germany; Charles P. Frazer was listed as "Keeper of Baths" and F. Kneuffer as a "Homo. P Physician"; 6 slaves

Charles P. Frazer Trust Deed for benefit of his wife Hannah P. Frazer and his daughter Mary Geraldine Frazer. Casimer Patrick Trustee. 6 May 1843 covers 11 years lease on low water lot on Ashley River on which C. P. Frazer had a lease and bathing house. See Misc. Record 5-Z, page 511, State Archives, Columbia, South Carolina

1870 CENSUS WARD 2 CHARLESTON SOUTH CAROLINA 400, 592

Charles P. Frazier born in 1805 in South Carolina; Hannah Frazier born in 1810 in Connecticut; Mary Hughes born in 1838 in South Carolina; Eveline Hughes born in 1864 in South Carolina; Raymond Hughes born in 1863 in South Carolina; Martha J. Hughes born in 1867 in South Carolina; May J. Hughes born in 1869 in South Carolina; Maggie Taylor born in 1848 in Georgia; Mary Quinn born in 1820 in Ireland; Margaret Quinn born in 1858 in South Carolina; Charles P. Frazier was a "Collector of Rents." Maggie Taylor was a "nurse" and Mary Quinn a "cook."

Under advertisements in the back of the Augusta, Georgia Directory for 1841 is the following: "Victoria House, No. 139 King, corner of Princess Street, Charleston, South Carolina: The subscriber respectfully informs his friends and the travelling public generally that the above extensive and splendid establishment having undergone various improvements during the past season, he is prepared to accommodate them with permanent or transient board in the handsomest style; and in addition to his former arrangements he has fitted up a new and elegant dining room, capable of conveniently accommodating 100 persons.   Charles P. Frazer"

"Sacred to the Memory of Mrs. Susan E. Frazer consort of Charles P. Frazer who departed this life January 12, 1837 in the 33rd year of her life." From a tombstone in the Frazer plot in the Churchyard of the Second Presbyterian Church in Charleston, South Carolina.

Charles P. Frazer married Hannah Raymond on April 17, 1838 in Charleston, South Carolina. See Marriage Records of the Second Presbyterian Church in Charleston.

1840 CENSUS, WARD 4, CHARLESTON SOUTH CAROLINA
C. P. FRAZER, VICTORIA HOUSE
1 male born 1760-1770; 1 male born 1780-1790; 1 male born 1790-1800; 6 males born 1800-1810; 8 males born 1810-1820; 1 male born 1820-1825; 1 male born 1825-1830; 1 male born 1835-1840; 1 female born 1760-1770; 1 female born 1770-1780; 2 females born 1810-1820; 3 females born 1820-1825; 3 females born 1825-1830; 5 females born 1835-1840; 13 slaves. Nap Raymond born in 1761 was a Revolutionary Pensioner living with them.

1840 CENSUS, 3RD. WARD, 398 DISTRICT, AUGUSTA, RICHMOND COUNTY GEORGIA
Jno W. Stoy: 1 male born 1800-1810; 1 female born 1810-1820; 2 females born 1835-1840

1830 CENSUS, CHARLESTON COUNTY, SOUTH CAROLINA, WARD 3, PAGE 45
Rebecca Frazer: 1 male born 1770-1780; 1 male born 1790-1800; 2 males born 1800-1810; 1 male born 1810-1815; 1 male born 1815-1820; 1 male born 1825-1830; 1 female born 1800-1810; 2 females born 1810-1815; 2 females born 1815-1820; 6 slaves

1840 CENSUS, CHARLESTON COUNTY, SOUTH CAROLINA, CHRIST CHURCH PARISH
Mrs. R. Fraser: 1 male born 1830-1835; 1 male born 1835-1840; 1 female born 1800-1810; 7 slaves

EDWARD LAURENS FRAZER

"Sacred to the Memory of Edward Laurens Frazer who departed this life September 27, 1851, aged 18 years, 10 months and 10 days." From a tombstone in the Frazer plot in the Churchyard of the Second Presbyterian Church in Charleston, South Carolina.

GEORGE RIPLEY FRAZER

1850 CENSUS DIVISION NO. 73 RICHMOND COUNTY GEORGIA 118
George R. Frazer born in 1816 in South Carolina; Melvina C. Frazer born in 1820 in Georgia; Elizabeth Frazer born in 1846 in Georgia, child born in 1850 in Georgia; James Jackson born in 1838 in Georgia George Ripley, son of John M. and Rebecca Frazer, was born May 2, 1817 and was baptized June 20, 1817. See records of the Second Presbyterian Church in Charleston, South Carolina

1860 CENSUS, CITY OF BRUNSWICK, GLYNN COUNTY, GEORGIA 121, 212
George R. Frazer born in 1818 in South Carolina, Printer, married

within the year; Amanda A. Frazer born in 1825 in Georgia; Angelina McConn born in 1845 in Georgia; Jack McConn born in 1853 in Georgia; Virginia McConn born in 1848 in Georgia; Samuel A. Brockington (?) born in 1833 in Georgia

1870 CENSUS, BRUNSWICK, GLYNN COUNTY, GEORGIA, 158, 166
Geo. R. Frazer, Auctioneer, born in 1818 in South Carolina; Amanda Frazer born in 1832 in Georgia; Elizabeth Frazer born in 1865 in Georgia

1880 CENSUS, BRUNSWICK, GLYNN COUNTY, GEORGIA, 10
Amanda Frazer born in 1825 in Georgia, where her parents were born; Melvina Frazer, daughter, born in 1864 in Georgia

GEORGE R. FRAZER. Bvt 2nd Lieutenant, Captain Harris Independent Company, Georgia Infantry (Brunswick Rifles). Enlisted in Brunswick, Georgia.

JAMES L. FRAZER

1840 CENSUS 120TH DISTRICT RICHMOND COUNTY CITY OF AUGUSTA GEORGIA

J. L. Frazer born 1810-1820; James Lawrence Frazer born November 18, 1813 and baptized February 20, 1814. See Records of the Second Presbyterian Church, Charleston, South Carolina

Sacred to the memory of Elizabeth M. Frazer, consort of James L. Frazer, who died September 21, 1836, in the 19th year of her life. From a tombstone in the Frazer Plot in the Churchyard of the Second Presbyterian Church, Charleston, South Carolina

JOHN JACOB FRAZER

Born: Baptized April 30, 1798
Married: Sarah Townsend
Children of John Jacob and Sarah (Townsend) Frazer: John J. Frazer; Mary Frazer; William S. Frazer

1830 CENSUS CHARLESTON NECK SOUTH CAROLINA
John J. Frazer: 1 male born 1790-1800; 2 males born 1825-1830; 1 female born 1780-1790; 1 female born 1800-1810; 1 female born 1825-1830; 6 slaves

1840 CENSUS CHARLESTON NECK SOUTH CAROLINA
J. J. Fraser: 1 male born 1800-1810; 2 males born 1825-1830; 1 female born 1760-1770; 1 female born 1800-1810; 1 female born 1825-1830; 9 slaves

April 30, 1798. John Jacob son of John M and Rebecca Frazer was baptized. See St. Philip's Register (1754-1810) Smith and Huger (1927) page 17

John Jacob Frazer married Sarah Townsend daughter of Stephen Townsend Settlement 6 June 1821.

Died in Christ Church Parish on the 20th instant (June, 1799) Stephen Townsend Esq. one of the oldest inhabitants of that parish. Marriage and death Notices from the City Gazette. See South Carolina Historical and Genealogical Magazine Volume 25, page 157.

The following advertisement fixes an approximate date for the rebuilding of Christ Church which was burned by the British in 1783; Christ Church Parish April 21, 1787. Whereas the Vestry and Church Wardens of the Episcopal Church in the parish of Christ Church have resolved to rebuild the church and vestry house as speedily as possible, therefore public notice is hereby given to any person or persons that are inclined to undertake the rebuilding of the same. Stephen Townsend and Paul Pritchard, Church Wardens

The South Carolina Gazette and Morning Post May 8, 1787, See the South Carolina Historical and Genealogical Magazine, Volume 21, page 88

Died on Friday the 24th instant (August 1804) at her plantation in Christ Church Parish, Mrs. Sarah Townshend aged 52 years widow of the late Stephen Townshend: Her suavity of manners endeared her to a large circle of relatives and friends who sincerely deplore her loss. Marriage and Death Notices from the City Gazette. See South Carolina Historical and Genealogical Magazine Volume 28, page 49

Thomas Townsend son of Stephen and Sarah Townsend was born February 27, 1789; Stephen Townsend son of Stephen and Sarah Townsend was born October 2, 1786. Register of Christ Church Parish. See South Carolina Historical and Genealogical Magazine Volume 21, pages 148 and 149.

WILLIAM FRAZER

Married: Mary Gadsden

1850 CENSUS PARISH OF ST. PHILIP AND ST. MICHAEL CITY OF CHARLESTON, SOUTH CAROLINA 557, 565

Fisher Gadsden born in 1805 in South Carolina; Laura Gadsden born in 1807 in South Carolina; Christopher Gadsden born in 1829 in South Carolina; Mary Gadsden born in 1832 in South Carolina; Elizabeth Gadsden born in 1842 in South Carolina; Alston Gadsden born in 1844 in South Carolina; James Gadsden born in 1840 in South Carolina; Alexander Gadsden born in 1837 in South Carolina; William S. Frazier born in 1829 in South Carolina; John J. Frazier born in 1830 in South Carolina; Aramintha Air born in 1806 in South Carolina

Fisher Gadsden was the grandson of General Christopher Gadsden, Governor of the State of South Carolina, following the American Revolution, the son of Philip Gadsden and the brother of Christopher Edwards Gadsden, Fourth Bishop of the Episcopal Church in the Diocese of South Carolina and of Colonel James Gadsden, United

States Minister to Mexico. His wife was Laura Michau. See *History and Genealogy of Bellinger, DeVeaux and Allied Families*, pages 100-101.

1860 CENSUS WARD 5 CHARLESTON SOUTH CAROLINA 508, 571

William S. Fraser born in 1828 in South Carolina; Mary Fraser born in 1834 in South Carolina; Sarah Fraser born in 1808 in South Carolina; R. H. Teasdale born in 1834 in South Carolina

1850 Census Charleston County South Carolina Christ Church Parish 61, 81

Sarah Fraser born in 1785 in South Carolina; Rebecca Fraser born in 1808 in South Carolina; Martha Fraser born in 1825 in South Carolina; Galasha Fraser born in 1825 in South Carolina; Samuel Fraser born in 1834 in South Carolina; Jacob Fraser born in 1836 in South Carolina

1860 Census Charleston District South Carolina Christ Church Parish 27, 27

Rebecca Fraser born in 1810 in South Carolina; John S. Frasier born in 1834 in South Carolina Student of Medicine; Jacob Frasier born in 1837 in South Carolina

1870 Census Ward 5 Charleston South Carolina 165, 184

William Fraser born in 1834 in South Carolina; Augustus Luhn born in 1839 in South Carolina; Harriet Luhn born in 1841 in South Carolina; Lillie Luhn born in 1857 in South Carolina; Nannie Luhn born in 1854 in South Carolina; William Luhn born in 1870 in South Carolina

1880 Census Ward 6 Charleston South Carolina Page 11, Supervisor's District 2 Enumeration District 70 79, 126

William Frazer born in 1835 in South Carolina; James Gadsden born in 1845 in South Carolina; Birthplace of parents of William Frazer not given; of James Gadsden, South Carolina. Merchants.

1870 Census, Ward 5, Charleston South Carolina 166, 185

Mary Gadsden born in 1805 in South Carolina; Susan Gibbs born in 1810 in South Carolina; Sarah Fraser born in 1801 in South Carolina; Charles Smith born in 1828 in South Carolina; Sarah Smith born in 1838 in South Carolina; Marion Smith born in 1856 in South Carolina; Moultrie Smith born in 1858 in South Carolina

JOHN MILLIGAN FRAZER

Born: 1807
Died: December 9, 1826

MARTHA RICHARDS FRAZER

Married: George Osborne
Children of George and Martha Richards (Frazer) Osborne: Charles Frazer Osborne

According to Miss Eva Raymond Frazer Hughes the Osbornes had three sons, of whom Charles Frazer Osborne was the youngest.

A letter to Owen Johnson:

Miss Bettie Matthews
Williston, South Carolina

Sept. 26, 1949

Dear Mr. Johnson,

First I must explain why I am writing with a pencil. I am in my eightieth year and my vision is very bad so I use a special pencil so as to be able to read it.

Your letter was given to me and my sister because we are of the older set and are often consulted when folks are tracing residents of long ago.

A Mr. Charlie Osborne did live here many years ago and his mother who was a Charlestonian boarded in many homes in town. I knew them all, but not so intimately.

When his mother we called "Old Mrs. Osborne" died the neighbors in those days sat up at the home where the corpse was and I happened to be one of the visitors. She was proud of her ancestry and often related having danced with the Marquis de Lafayette when he made his second visit to this country and was in Charleston. I think this was in 1824. My sister says he had a brother, she thinks named George Osborne.

I will give you the following address "Mrs. Jack Fanning," 108 East Edisto, Columbia, South Carolina." Mrs. Fanning is his step-daughter, as he married a widow.

I hope you can get it straight, but will do anything I can to assist you.

Yours truly,
/s/ BETTIE MATTHEWS

CHARLES FRAZER OSBORNE

1880 CENSUS BARNWELL COUNTY SOUTH CAROLINA TOWN OF WILLISTON 153, 167

Chl F. Osborn born in 1851 in South Carolina. His father was born in Massachusetts and his mother was born in South Carolina; Angeline Osborn born in 1857 in South Carolina where her father and mother were born; Their daughter: Mary E. Osborn born in 1876 in South Carolina

MARY ANN FRAZER

Married: 1st: William Crosby
         2nd: Major Cartwell

Children of William and Mary Ann (Frazer) Crosby: Josiah Frazer Crosby

JUDGE JOSIAH F. CROSBY

1850 CENSUS WASHINGTON COUNTY, TEXAS 264, 264

J. F. Crosby born in 1828 in South Carolina; A. T. Crosby born in 1832 in Kentucky; Eliza Fral born in 1835 in Tennessee; J. F. Crosby was an attorney.

1860 CENSUS EL PASO COUNTY, TEXAS 124, 92

J. F. Crosby born in 1827 in South Carolina; Josafina Crosby born in 1840 in Pennsylvania; Willey Crosby born in 1858 in Texas; Joseph Crosby born in 1859 in Texas; Saml Endicott born in 1836 in Tennessee; J. F. Crosby was a Judge. Saml Endicott was his servant.

1870 CENSUS 3RD. WARD HOUSTON HARRIS COUNTY TEXAS 529, 539

Josiah F. Crosby born in 1828 in South Carolina; Josephine Crosby born in 1841 in Pennsylvania; William Crosby born in 1858 in Texas; Mary L. Crosby born in 1860 in Texas; Madeline Crosby born in 1862 in Texas; Indito Crosby born in 1864 in Texas; Josephine Crosby born in 1866 in Texas; Virginia Crosby born in 1868 in Texas; Josiah F. Crosby born in 1870 in Texas; Josiah F. Crosby was a lawyer.

1880 CENSUS HARRIS COUNTY TEXAS CITY OF HOUSTON PAGE NO. 22 SUPERVISOR'S DISTRICT NO. 4, ENUMERATION DISTRICT NO. (5) 76 159, 189

Jos. F. Crosby born in 1828 in South Carolina; Josephine B. Crosby born in 1841 in Pennsylvania; Wm. Crosby born in 1858 in Texas; Maria L. Crosby born in 1860 in Texas; Madelaine B. Crosby born in 1862 in Texas; Indita Crosby born in 1864 in Texas; Josephine B. Crosby born in 1867 in Texas; Virginia B. Crosby born in 1869 in Texas; Jos. F. Crosby, Jr. born in 1870 in Texas; Kate E. Crosby born in 1870 in Texas; Birthplace of parents of Jos. F. Crosby not given. His wife's parents were born in Pennsylvania.

The following extracts are taken from The War of the Rebellion, A Compilation of the Official Records of the Union and Confederate Armies, printed by the GPO in Wasihngton, D.C., 1882:

Memorandum of Lt Col Edwin A. Rigg

"Brigadier General Baylor arrived in San Antonio from Richmond some time in August bringing full authority to raise a force of 6,000 men and with instructions to retake and hold New Mexico at all hazards. The expedition is organizing in San Antonio now. C. H. Merritt of El Paso is quartermaster to the expedition. Judge Crosby, also of El Paso, is assitant adjutant general."

Supra, Series I, Volume 15, page 599

Letter from R. L. Robertson, U.S. Consul in Mazatlan, April 18, 1862, to General Wright, Commanding Army of the Pacific, San Francisco:

"* * * The grand aim and object of the leading men of Western Texas, Hart, of El Paso, Crosby and others is to annex to Texas Chichuahua and Sonora and I am of the opinion that they will on the receipt of

the news of the defeat in the South cause a diversion from New Mexico toward Sonora, providing they can get transportation, grain, etc. enough to reach the Gila * * *"
Supra, Series I, Volume 50, page 1013

Report of Brigadier General William Steele C.S.A. Operations in Indian Territory, 1863
"In conclusion, I would refer to the valuable assistance rendered me by my staff officers, Capt J. F. Crosby, as adjutant general * * * all these officers displayed zeal, energy, ability, and which I have found more rare, honesty."
Supra, Series I, Volume 22, page 36

Letter from S. Hart to General H. H. Sibley, El Paso, October 27, 1861
"A week since Judge Crosby called on me in reference to supplies for your brigade * * * You must especially heed Judge Crosby's and Mr. Richardson's instructions as to things here * * *"
Supra, Series I, Volume 50, Part I, page 683

Letter to Major Guy M. Bryan to Major General J. B. Magruder, Shreveport, Louisiana, September 2, 1863
"General: I am directed by Lieut. Gen. E. Kirby Smith to enclose to you a letter just received from Captain (J. F.) Crosby, assistant adjutant general of General Steele, in regard to affairs in the Indian Territory * * *"
Supra, Series I, Volume 26, page 200

Letter of J. F. Crosby to General H. H. Sibley, El Paso
October 27, 1861
"Sir: The mail has just arrived here from San Antonio and I am advised by Captain Walker, in command of Fort Bliss, that he will cause it to return forthwith. Colonel Baylor's dispatches will no doubt advise you of the condition of affairs here at this time. We are looking for Colonel Baylor with his entire force at any moment. The merchants and most of the families of this part of the country have pulled up stakes and gone to the Mexican side. Colonel Canby's force is said to be 2700 strong and that he will approach us in three columns, one via the river, one via El Jornada and another by Stanton—the latter intended to cut off Baylor's retreat. This seems to me rather a hazardous enterprise for a prudent man like Canby to embark in. You can imagine what an unsettled state the country hereabout is in. I for one shall stand my ground until the last moment, and will not cease to do all that can be done in the way of providing for your command, at least so long as I may have it in my power to remain. I have made arrangements with a responsible party to proceed at once and buy up a quantity of corn beans etc. in Mexico for

your use. None of these supplies as a matter of course will be brought on this side of the river until such time as they would be safe from the enemy. The party who will make these purchases is not known as a contractor for the Confederate States and will therefore run no risk in his purchases.

I regret not having received additional instructions per last mail. I shall engage all the arms and munitions possible to be had. I am sending an express to Sonora with a view, among other things of watching the California route. It may be that there is some intelligence between Canby and Sumner and that it is desirable to get Baylor out of the way to enable them to form a junction at Mesilla. This is however purely conjectural on my part. In great haste your obedient servant,

J. F. Crosby

Supra, Series I, Vol. 4, page 133

Letter from General H. H. Sibley to Colonel W. W. Loring from Hart's Mill, El Paso, Texas, June 12, 1861

"* * * Meanwhile, Colonel Magoffin, Judge Hart and Crosby are very much exercised and concerned on account of the public stores here in their unguarded condition * * *"

Supra, Series I, Vol. 4, page 55

Letter from Lt. Col Ed R. S. Canby to Major I. Lynde, Sante Fe, New Mexico, June 24, 1861

"Sir: Information has been received here that some movement is in contemplation from Fort Bliss against the interests of the Government in this Territory, at the head of which are Magoffin, Hart and Crosby * * *"

Supra, Series I, Vol. 4, page 57

Inclosure in letter from Col Ed R. S. Canby to the Adjutant General of the Army, Washington. Belen, New Mexico, January 25, 1862

"General Sibley and staff arrived in El Paso about a month ago; staff officers A. M. Jackson, Captain Dwyer and Judge Crosby, assistant quartermaster and receiver of property to be confiscated in New Mexico * * *"

Supra Series I, Vol. 4, page 89

Josiah F. Crosby was elected a delegate from Texas to the Democratic National Convention held in Charleston, South Carolina in 1860. See Wortham's *History of Texas* Volume 4, page 291. See also Southwestern Historical Quarterly, Volume 5, page 125

Josiah F. Crosby mentioned as District Attorney for the Third Judicial District. See Preston v. Walsh The Mercer Colony in Texas 1844-1883 Southwestern Historical Quarterly Volume 40, pages 127-128

From Records in the National Archives, Washington, D. C., is the information that Judge J. F. Crosby was on the Staff of General Sibley in 1861, the Staff of General Baylor in San Antonio in 1862, the Staff of General Steele in 1863 and the Staff of General E. K. Smith in 1864.

Josiah Frazier Crosby was born in Charleston, South Carolina, on January 3, 1829. After his father's death his mother moved to Washington County, Texas, where Crosby grew to manhood. When quite young, he was elected district attorney of the Third Judicial District but, because of poor health, he resigned in 1852 and moved to El Paso, where he was one of the six proprietors of the original townsite. He was elected to the legislature in 1854 and in 1857 was elected district judge of the territory west of the Pecos. At the outbreak of the Civil War he joined James Wiley Magoffin and Simeon Hart in enthusiastic support of the Confederacy. After the Union forces occupied the El Paso area, Crosby entered the Confederate Army serving with distinction as adjutant general on the staff of Brigadier General William Steele.

After the War Crosby settled in Houston, Texas, where he practiced law and engaged in various business activities. He promoted and, for a time, served as president of the Texas and New Orleans Railroad. In 1886 he returned to El Paso first to promote the "Corralitos" mining and railroad properties in Chihuahua, Mexico, and later to reside and practice law. He married Josephine Bremond in Austin, Texas, on August 30, 1856. He acquired considerable property in and around El Paso and was an active promoter of the White Oaks Railroad. He and his wife supported all and sponsored many of El Paso's charitable agencies.

In 1893 Judge Crosby established a law office in New York but most of his time was given to promoting sundry business enterprises. He soon returned to El Paso where he died January 5, 1904. He was buried in Concordia Cemetery.   J. L. Waller

BIOGRAPHICAL ENCYCLOPEDIA OF TEXAS (1880); TEXAS ALMANAC (1859); El Paso HERALD, January 5, 1904.

THE HANDBOOK OF TEXAS Volume 1 Austin 1952, pages 437-438 The Texas State Historical Association. Volume 2, page 562 mentions J. F. Crosby "who became prominent in local history" arrived during the 1850's.

From Owen White's OUT OF THE DESERT, The Historical Romance of El Paso, 1923, The McMath Company, Publishers, El Paso, Texas:

(Page 59) "And then one morning in the year 1859, in the midst of all of this period of lurid speculation as to El Paso's future we can draw for ourselves another picture. This time, however our picture is not imaginary; it is real, and it carries with it the final assurance that El Paso as an American town belonging to and settled by American people has at last arrived. In our picture we can see a young man, wearing a look of newly acquired responsibility and immense superiority walk into Ben Dowell's saloon and we can hear him announce in tones of undoubted authority, "It's a boy, Ben, set 'em up all around and pass the cigars."

"That young man was Judge J. F. Crosby and his announcement that his son, William Crosby, had just made his appearance in the world was also the announcement of the birth of El Paso's first native-born American."

(Page 65) First named in a list of El Paso's ante-bellum population is J. F. Crosby.

(Page 67) "The majority of El Paso's post-war citizens, however, were naturally Southern sympathizers. Among these were such men as Crosby etc. who had all served in the Confederate Army but who now came back to take up their tasks of making a living and building a city."

(Page 237) White Oaks Railroad was to connect El Paso with the coal fields at White Oaks, New Mexico.

(Page 334) "With the enthusiastic and optimistic eyes of youth he could see far into the future and so it was that (the later General) Anson A. Mills went to J. F. Crosby, the Gillette brothers and others interested in the place and suggested to them that they organize a town-site company and lay out a city. He finally prevailed upon them and was employed to plat the town and draw its first map. This map was signed February 28, 1859, and on its face we note that he has re-christened the settlement by officially calling it "The Town of El Paso"."

(Page 337) "In 1881 in partnership with Judge J. F. Crosby Major (General) Mills erected the Grand Central Hotel which was at the time of its completion, the largest hotel building in the State of Texas."

In the 1882-1883 TEXAS STATE GAZETTEER AND BUSINESS DIRECTORY, Standard Directory Company, Houston, Texas, Main Office: 20 N. Cherry Street, Nashville, Tennessee, is the following listing in Houston: "Josiah F. Crosby, Vice President and General Manager, The Texas and New Orleans Railroad." Also Josiah F. Crosby and Edward P. Hill, Attorneys.

In the 1884-1885 TEXAS STATE GAZETTEER AND BUSINESS DIRECTORY R. L. Polk and Company, 22 North Fourth Street, St. Louis are the following Houston listings:

Josiah F. Crosby, Vice President, Texas and New Orleans Railroad. Financial Agent, Houston, East and West Texas Railroad.

In the Beaumont listings are a picture and advertisement of the original Crosby House, John B. Goodhue, proprietor. Also an advertisement of the Crosby Opera House, seating 900.

The New Crosby Hotel, corner of Orleans and Crockett Streets, has been closely identified with the oil industry from boom days to stabilization. The nucleus of the present building was erected in 1903 on the site of the first structure built in 1880, and has since been remodeled. It is a five story building of Texas limestone faced with polished Vermont Metawell marble. Designed by Fred C. Stone and L. W. Pitts, it is in the modern style. For many years the Crosby House, as it was known, was the "pit," the "curb," and "exchange" of the oil industry and millions of dollars changed hands in its lobby and rooms. Its founder, Colonel John B. Goodhue, vice president of the East Texas Railroad, named the hotel for COLONEL J. F. CROSBY, president of the road.

See the Beaumont article in TEXAS Compiled by the Writers Program of the Works Progress Administration, 1949, page 201.

1860 Census, Travis County, Texas, Austin 782, 782

J. F. Crosby born in 1830 in South Carolina; J. Crosby born in 1840 in Pennsylvania; W. Crosby born in 1857 in Texas; M. L. Crosby born in 1860 in Texas; J. F. Crosby is listed as a lawyer.

The small town of Crosby in Harris County, Texas, not far from Houston, was named for Judge Crosby.

JOSIAH FRAZER CROSBY, lawyer, Houston, Texas, is a native of Charleston, South Carolina. He was born on the 3rd day of January, 1829. His grandfather Crosby, his father and mother were all natives of the same city. His grandfather Crosby was commander of a privateer during the War of 1812. His father, William Crosby, was a merchant, who, in early life, emigrated to Mobile, Alabama, where he pursued his mercantile occupation for some years, when he removed to Montgomery in the same state and resided there until his death in 1837. His mother whose maiden name was MARY ANN FRAZER, WAS THE DAUGHTER OF JOHN FRAZER, WHO WAS A SEA-FARING MAN AND THE OWNER OF LARGE MARITIME INTERESTS.

The subject of this memoir was the adopted child of his uncle, Josiah J. Crosby, a prominent lawyer of the early Texas bar, who took him to Texas in his ninth year, where he was reared and educated under the supervision of private instructors. In 1844 he began reading law with his uncle and the Honorable James Willie, ex-Attorney General of the State of Texas. In 1848 he was admitted to the bar in pursuance of a Special Act of the Legislature removing disabilities on account of age. Judge Willie of Galveston and Colonel Sexton of Marshall being admitted under the same Act and at the same time. In the year 1848 and before he was twenty years old, he entered upon the practice of law at Brenham, Washington County, in partnership with the Honorable James Willie, one of his preceptors. After practicing his profession for a few months, he was, upon the recommendation of Chief Justice Hemphill and Abner Lipscomb, Judges of the Supreme Court, appointed by Governor George T. Wood, District Attorney for that district, and in 1850 he was elected by the people to the same office. He resigned the office before 1852 and was succeeded by Judge A. H. Willie.

In 1852 he located at El Paso, in El Paso County and practiced his profession there until 1861. In 1854 he was elected to represent El Paso County in the State Legislature and in 1856 he was re-elected to the same office. In 1857 he was elected District Judge and served until the Civil War began. In 1861 he resigned his office and entered the Confederate Army and served in various official positions of honor throughout the war.

He was Acting Quartermaster General of the Army of New Mexico, under command of General Sibley. He was Adjutant General on the Staff of General Kirby-Smith. After the Battles of Mansfield and Pleasant Hill, he was ordered by General Kirby-Smith on a special mission to Europe for the purpose of procuring arms and munitions of war for the Confederate States. He was absent about nine months engaged in the object of his mission, returning to Texas in the early part of 1865. During the remaining months of the war he was in service under Governor Murrah of Texas.

In October of 1865, the war being ended, Mr. Crosby located in the City of Houston and resumed the practice of law, and has since resided there as an able lawyer and one of the most prominent and public spirited citizens. Since his location at Houston he has manifested but little active interest in politics, having devoted his time and attention principally to his profession and to his duties as Vice President and General Manager of the Texas and New Orleans Railroad. Mr. Crosby is President of the Street Railway Company of Houston, and devotes much of his time and conspicuous ability to the general interests of the city.

Mr. Crosby was married in 1850 to the daughter of Judge Thomas Johnson. She died in 1852. In 1856 he married again, to Miss Josephine Bremond, daughter of John Bremond, a merchant of Austin, Texas.

In politics, Mr. Crosby has always been remarkably firm and consistent in his adhesion to the Democratic Party and democratic principles. In religion he is an Episcopalian. His social qualities are faultless and devoid of all ostentatious display, yet firm and courteous toward all who come into his presence. Having through life applied himself to such employments as were suited to his large capabilities and labored only with a view to servicable, sincere and ennobling results, his achievements have not failed to yield him that assurance of security and contentment which proceeds from faithfulness of action and integrity of character.

The above was copied from the BIOGRAPHICAL ENCYCLO-PEDIA OF TEXAS, pages 38-39, published in 1880 by the Southern Publishing Company of New York, by Mr. J. L. Waller of 2905 Beanna Street, Austin, Texas.

REMAINS OF JUDGE CROSBY INTERRED
DECEASED WAS ONE OF TEXAS' BEST KNOWN MEN

The last sad rites were said over the remains of Judge Josiah F. Crosby at his late residence on Myrtle Avenue this morning at 10 o'clock.

Rev. G. H. Higgins, a retired Episcopal minister of this city, officiated at the funeral.

After the funeral at the residence, the remains were escorted to their last resting place in Concordia Cemetery.

The El Paso Bar Association attended in a body, as well as a large number of sorrowing friends.

The courts and county office also closed their morning in memory of the deceased and in order that all might attend the obsequies.

The pallbearers were from among his intimate friends during his long residence in this city and were Charles Richardson, Dr. W. N. Vilas, Dr. A. L. Justice, C. B. Eddy, R. C. Lightbody, and B. F. Hammett.

The remains were laid to rest in a temporary valut, which will serve as their resting place until a larger valut can be constructed for them.

The deceased was one of the most noted men in the state. He was admitted to the bar in 1848 by a special act of the legislature, removing his disabilities of minority. He at once entered into the practice of law at Brenham and when barely of age, was appointed district attorney for the district, to which place he was subsequently elected for another term by the people.

In 1852 the deceased came to El Paso and in 1854 and 1856 he was elected to the state legislature, when it meant traveling overland by stage to Austin through a country infested with Indians.

In 1857 he was elected Judge of El Paso in which position he served until the outbreak of the Civil War, when he entered the Confederate Army.

He served a great part of the time under General Sibley and was at one time Quartermaster General of the Department of New Mexico.

He was later Adjutant General on the Staff of General Kirby-Smith.

In 1864 he was sent by President Jefferson Davis to Europe to buy munitions of war for the Confederacy.

After the war he located in Houston and there served as President of the street railway company and General Manager of the Texas and New Orleans Railway, at present that part of the Southern Pacific System between Houston and New Orleans.

The deceased returned to El Paso from Houston and remained here the rest of his life, with an occasional visit to New York.

In 1856 he was married to Miss Josephine Bremond at Austin, while attending the legislature, her father being John Bremond, a merchant of Austin, at that time one of the leading merchants in the state. To them were born eight children: William Crosby of Guadalajara, Mexico; Mrs. G. Hardcastle of Houston; Mrs. H. R. Wood of El Paso; Miss Yndita Crosby of El Paso; Miss Josephine Crosby of El Paso; Mrs. E. Percy Moran of New York City; J. F. Crosby, Jr., now traveling in the South with a theatrical troupe; and Miss Catherine E. Crosby, who is in the Bermudas on a yatching trip.

> The above is copied from the El Paso HERALD,
> January 5, 1904

The business founded by Mr. John Bremond of Austin, father of Josephine Bremond, wife of Judge Josiah Frazer Crosby, is still in operation in 1960, 113 years after its founding, JOHN BREMOND COMPANY, WHOLESALE GROCERS, ESTABLISHED 1847, San Jacinto at Third Street, Austin, Texas.

WILLIAM MILLIGAN FRAZER

Born: July 2, 1800, in Charleston, South Carolina

Married: 1st: Maria Susannah Purdy on May 22, 1821, in Charleston, South Carolina

2nd: Mrs. Ann Hardy, widow, on November 6, 1856, in her residence in Mobile, Alabama. The minister was the Reverend J. H. Ingraham, Rector of St. John's Episcopal Church

Died: September 29, 1864, in Mobile, Alabama

Children of William Milligan and Maria Susannah (Purdy) Frazer: Ann Stevens Frazer; Emeline Maria Frazer; Francis Marion Frazer; James Robertson Frazer; Martha Jane Frazer, Mary Ann Frazer; Susannah Rebecca Frazer.

1840 CENSUS RICHMOND COUNTY 2ND WARD AUGUSTA, GEORGIA
William M. Frazer: 20 males born 1810-1820; 6 males born 1800-1810; 1 male born 1790-1800; 1 female born 1835-1840; 2 females born 1825-1830; 1 female born 1820-1825; 1 female born 1800-1810; 8 slaves

1850 Census Mobile County City of Mobile, Alabama 1716, 1835
J. G. Owen born in 1819 in Georgia; Susan Owen born in 1825 in South Carolina; Martina H. Owen born in 1846 in Alabama; Jno Owen born in 1849 in Alabama; Wm. M. Frazer born in 1800 in South Carolina

1860 Census Ward No. 6, City of Mobile, Mobile County Alabama
Wm M. Frazier born in 1800 in South Carolina; Ann Frazier born in 1818 in England; Charles Hardy born in 1843 in Alabama; Virginia Hardy born in 1849 in Alabama

1850 Census Mobile County City of Mobile Alabama 1974 2070
Henry Hardy born in 1812 in Maryland; Ann Hardy born in 1818 in England; Charles Hardy born in 1843 in Alabama; Virginia Hardy born in 1847 in Alabama

1870 Census Ward No. 8 City of Mobile Mobile County Alabama 363, 363
Chas Hardy born in 1845 in Alabama; Ann Frazier born in 1828 in England

William M. Frazer to George Osborne. Mortgage. July 1, 1828. See Misc Mtg 3-U, page 339, Hist Comm Columbia, S. C.

William M. Frazer made a trust deed of gift dated December 1, 1823, to his two daughters, Ann Stevens Frazer and Susanna Rebecca Frazer, with his two brothers, John J. Frazer and John M. Frazer, as trustees. See Misc. Records 4-Z, page 331, State Archives, Columbia, South Carolina.

William M. Frazer gave a mortgage to George Osborne on July 1, 1828. See Misc. Mtg., page 339, State Archives, Columbia, South Carolina.

Grocery store owned by William M. Frazer at No. 81 East Bay, Charleston, mentioned in Misc. 5-J, page 117, State Archives, Columbia, South Carolina.

Power of Attorney from John Cannon to William M. Fraser to collect all money due at Charleston. Dated December 8, 1824. See Misc. Records, 5-B, page 15, State Archives, Columbia, South Carolina.

"* * * in the presence of the fact that French had ceased to be spoken, or generally understood, especially by the children of the immigrants * * * a resolution was adopted in 1828, to reopen the church with the services wholly in English.

"The committee appointed to make the change consisted of the Hon. Elias Horry, Chairman, and Messrs. Joseph Manigault, William Mazyck, Senior, George W. Cross, Daniel Ravenel, Thomas S. Grimke, and William M. Frazer." See "A Historic Sketch of the Huguenot Church, Incorporated as the 'French Protestant Church', Charleston, S. C. Founded A.D. 1681-2 with a view of the Present Building, the

Fourth Successive Church Edifice upon the Same Site" Prepared by the Rev. C.S. Vedder, General Wilmot G. DeSaussure, and Mr. Daniel Ravenel. Printed in the Charleston, South Carolina Yearbook for 1885 on page 307.

"* * * This measure was adopted in 1828 when a committee was appointed to prepare, or cause to be prepared under their supervision a translation of the Book of Liturgies which had been used in the church and to adapt it to public service in our country with authority to employ persons to make, or aid in making, the translations. The committee were the Hon. Elias Horry, Chairman, and Messrs. Joseph Manigault, William Mazyck, Senr., George W. Cross, Daniel Ravenel, Thomas S. Grimke, and William M. Frazer. These gentlemen soon afterwards entered their work. Mr. Frazer attended only the first or preliminary meeting. He removed to Augusta, where he resided several years. He then removed to Mobile where he resided until his death in 1863. See Transactions of the Huguenot Society of South Carolina, No. 7, page 64. See also the *French Protestant Church in the City of Charleson, "The Huguenot Church": A Brief History of the Church and Two Addresses Delivered on the Two Hundred and Twenty Fifth Anniversary of the Founding of the Church April Fourteenth Nineteen Hundred and Twelve,* a pamphlet printed by Walker, Evans and Cogswell Company, Charleston, South Carolina.

William Milligan Frazer, son of John M. and Rebecca Frazer of Charleston, So Ca, was born in Charleston on the second day of July, 1800. William M. Frazer was married to Maria Susannah Daughter of Joseph and Johannah Purdy on the 22nd day of May, 1821 in Charleston. Died in Mobile, Ala., on the 29th of Sept., 1864, William M. Frazer (a native of Charleston, South Carolina) in the 65th year of his age. Frazer Family Bible.

The friends and acquaintances of the late William M. Frazer are respectfully invited to attend his funeral this Friday morning at 10 o'clock from his late residence, corner Government and Jefferson Streets. Carriages will be waiting at McDonald's Stables, opposite to the Public Square, till quarter to 10 o'clock.

MOBILE ADVERTISER AND REGISTER, Friday, September 30, 1864

September 30—Captain William M. Frazer, 64 years. Interment MOBILE ADVERTISER AND REGISTER, October 2, 1864

ANN STEVENS FRAZER

Born: April 6, 1822, in Charleston, South Carolina
Married: 1st: Madison Cox of Barnwell, South Carolina, on March 20, 1838
    2nd: Augustus B. Greene on April 19.... by the Rev. Mr. Cliett

Children of Madison and Ann Stevens (Frazer) Cox: Caroline Maria Cox born May 17, 1841, in South Carolina; Clement Cox born in 1847 in South Carolina; Elizabeth Augusta Cox born April 28, 1839, in Augusta, Georgia; Emma Cox born in 1843 in South Carolina; Sarah Ann Cox born in 1843 (?) in South Carolina; William Madison Cox born October 6, 1845, in South Carolina

Children of Augustus B. and Ann Stevens (Frazer) Greene: Ida Kate Greene born December 3, 1856

1840 Census, Barnwell District, South Carolina, 2nd Part

Madison Cox: 2 males born 1800-1810; 1 female born 1820-1825; 1 female born 1835-1840; 10 slaves

1850 Census, Barnwell District South Carolina 487, 487

Madison Cox born in 1810 in South Carolina; Ann Cox born in 1822 in South Carolina; Elizabeth Cox born in 1838 in South Carolina; Caroline Cox born in 1840 in South Carolina; Emma Cox born in 1843 in South Carolina; William Cox born in 1845 in South Carolina; Clement Cox born in 1847 in South Carolina; 11 slaves

EMELINE MARIA FRAZER

Born: April 10, 1830, in Charleston, South Carolina
Married: Henry Frazer, her first cousin

FRANCIS MARION FRAZER

Born: May 9, 1835, in Augusta, Georgia
Died: August 19, 1836, in Hamburg, South Carolina, and buried in the Schultz Hill Cemetery.

JAMES ROBERTSON FRAZER

Born: April 12, 1826, in Charleston, South Carolina
Died: July 25, 1826, in Charleston, South Carolina. Buried in the French Protestant (Huguenot) Churchyard.

MARTHA JANE FRAZER

Born: December 18, 1827, in Charleston, South Carolina
Married: William Wilson of Beach Island, South Carolina, on April 30, 1845, in Augusta, Georgia. See Frazer Bible.
Children of William and Martha Jane (Frazer) Wilson: Emma Wilson; Martha Wilson; Susan O. Wilson; William F. Wilson.

1850 CENSUS EDGEFIELD DISTRICT SOUTH CAROLINA 1932, 1935

William Wilson born in 1820 in South Carolina; Martha Wilson born in 1828 in Georgia; William Wilson born in 1847 in South Carolina; Martha Wilson born in 1848 in South Carolina

1860 CENSUS EDGEFIELD DISTRICT SOUTH CAROLINA BEACH ISLAND 771, 759

Wm Wilson born in 1817 in South Carolina; Martha Wilson born in

1827 in South Carolina; Wm F. Wilson born in 1848 in South Carolina; Susan O. Wilson born in 1851 in South Carolina; Wm Griffin born in 1836 in South Carolina

1870 CENSUS EDGEFIELD DISTRICT SOUTH CAROLINA HAMMOND TOWNSHIP; POST OFFICE: HAMBURG 128, 129

William Wilson born in 1817 in Georgia; Martha Wilson born in 1830 in Georgia; William Wilson Jr. born in 1847 in South Carolina; Emma Wilson born in 1864 in South Carolina

1880 CENSUS HAMMOND TOWNSHIP AIKEN COUNTY SOUTH CAROLINA 348, 348

William Wilson born in 1817 in South Carolina; Martha Wilson born in 1828 in South Carolina; Emma Wilson born in 1863 in South Carolina; the father of William Wilson was born in North Carolina; his mother and the parents of Martha Wilson were born in South Carolina.

MARY ANN FRAZER

Born: September 1, 1833, in Augusta, Georgia, where she died a few hours after birth and is buried.

SUSANNAH REBECCA FRAZER

Born: October 29, 1823, in Charleston, South Carolina

Married: John Garland Owen on January 24, 1843, in Augusta, Georgia

Died: January 11, 1870, in Mobile, Alabama

Children of John Garland and Susannah Rebecca (Frazer) Owen: Charles Wheadon Owen; Chauncey Hall Owen; Frank Stone Owen; Jo Hunter Owen; John Garland Owen, Junior; Catharine (Kate) Lee Owen; Martina Harper Owen; Robert Otis Owen; William Frazer Owen.

Died at her residence in this city, Mrs. Susan R. Owen, relict of the late Captain John G. Owen, a native of Charleston, South Carolina. Mobile DAILY REGISTER, January 16, 1870.

Interment. January 13. Mrs. John G. Owen, 46 years. Mobile DAILY REGISTER. January, 1870.

WILL OF SUSAN R. OWEN recorded in the courthouse, Mobile, Alabama, 3-704-400.

IN THE NAME OF GOD, AMEN. I, SUSAN R. OWEN, relict of the late JOHN G. OWEN, being weak in body, but of sound mind and memory, feeling a deep solicitude for the welfare of my children and desiring that they shall live together in harmony after my decease do will and desire that the following disposition shall be made of the property that I now hold and such as I shall die in possession of, viz.

FIRST. I appoint my daughter Miss Martina H. Owen to be my

executrix and do not desire that she shall be required to give any bond or security as such and I wish her to act as the guardian of my minor children that she may supervise their education and do what she can to fit them for the business of life and I enjoin upon them that they shall look up to and respect their oldest sister aforesaid and thereby make her task more easy and promote their own happiness and future well being.

SECOND. I have built two separate houses out of my own separate means fronting on the Shell Road about .... feet each including the lots that are enclosed around them, the improvements so placed thereon by me, constituting their principal value. These several lots and premises and improvements I give and devise as follows:

The most western one by the north side of the Shell Road opposite to the premises of Mrs. (name illegible) to my daughter MARTINA H. OWEN and the one adjoining and next east thereof to my daughter KATE LEE OWEN, for them to have and hold the same respectively in their own right forever and these houses, lots, and premises shall be all of my estate and that of my late husband that the said Martina H. and Kate L. Owen shall have and receive and I enjoin upon them to take care of my young children until they can provide for themselves.

THIRD. As to the house in which I live and the lot thereto attached, I wish to be retained without sale or division for the benefit of all my children except Martina H. and Kate L. aforesaid until the youngest of said children shall arrive at he age of 21 years. Said premises are at the northwest corner of Ann Street and the Shell Road.

FOURTH. While the last named premises shall remain unsold and undivided I desire the furniture to remain in the house for the benefit of all the family.

FIFTH. I give my watch and chain to my youngest child.

SIXTH. I wish that my children shall be reared in the faith and church in which they have been baptized. And now as a last request of a fond mother to her dear children I beseech them all and severally to avoid strife among themselves, to keep the little property they shall have together that they may live at one common house and try to assist each other in becoming useful, happy and respectable.

IN WITNESS of all which I have hereunto set my hand and seal this the 3rd day of May, 1869.

SUSAN R. OWEN (Seal)

In the presence of the testatrix and at her request we have hereunto set out hands as witnesses.

H. C. Chamberlain
T. W. Chamberlain

Tombs in the John G. Owen Plot in Magnolia Cemetery, Mobile, Alabama (Square 3, Lot 64) : Susan R. Owen and John G. Owen; Martina Owen Vincent, died November 20, 1920; Frederick Wespy, died July 13, 1928; Kate Owen Wespy, died January 30, 1913; Jo Hunter Owen, aged 3 months; Garland Vincent; Maude Vincent; Frank Strong Vincent, died July 6, 1922

Frederick Wespy was a Foundation Member of the Tulane University Chapter (Alpha of Louisiana) of Phi Beta Kappa, February 26, 1909. Charles Owen Johnson, his great-nephew, was elected to membership in 1946.

Births as recorded in a bible published by the American Bible Society, New York, 1864, and given to "Chat" H. Owen by his father, Jno. G. Owen, in May, 1865: Jno Owen 2d son of Jno G. and Susan R. Owen, 15 September, 1849; Chat Hall 2 Dec 1851 W. F. 31 Mar 1856 Frank Stone 31 Mar 1859 Robert Otis 29 July 1861

BESSELLIEU

MARK ANTHONY BESSELLIEU I

Mark Anthony Bessellieu I died in South Carolina before the 29th of September 1738. He was a French Huguenot. Family tradition says he came from Tours, France. His father is known in family tradition as Philip Anthony Bessellieu and was a minister in the French Protestant Church.

There are several references, following, to the "Bessellieu Bible." This old Bible was printed in London in 1738 by John Baskett, Printer to the King's Most Excellent Majesty and by the assigns of Thomas Newcomb and Henry Hills, deceased. The Bible is owned by Philip A. Bessellieu of St. Petersburg, Florida. Records from this Bible, the Frazer Bible, the Owen Bible, the Johnson Bibles and the Shaw Prayer Book were printed in BE IT KNOWN AND REMEMBERED, Bible Records, Volume I, Louisiana Genealogical and Historical Society, 1960.

"Among the names of French families in the early records of St. Thomas and St. Denis, and Orange Quarter were the Besselleus. The Parish of St. Thomas was created in 1706. Orange Quarter was part of St. Thomas Parish. In 1706 Orange Quarter was constituted a parish for the French under the name of "The Parish of St. Denis"* The first of the families came to Carolina between 1680 and 1690. See Arthur Henry Hirsch, *The Huguenots of Colonial South Carolina* (1928), page 23.

*St. Denis was the patron saint of the City of Paris, France.

According to Mrs. Richard W. Hutson in her "Notes on the Besselleu Family" published in the Transactions of the Huguenot Society of South Carolina, No. 51, page 33, the earliest reference to the name Besselleu in the Province of South Carolina is in the Miscellaneous Records, Probate Court, Charleston County, Volume 68, page 262, as follows:

"A true and perfect inventory of all the goods and effects belonging to the Estate of Mark Anthony Besseleu Dec'd taken and appraised (by us whose names are underwritten) this Twenty-ninth day of Sepr Anno Domini 1738" Then follows an itemized list of dry goods, hardware groceries a negroe wench etc. the total value of which is 350 pounds and 5 shillings. signed by John Laurens, Benj. Addison, Rice Price. Recorded Jan 9, 1739.

MARK ANTHONY BESSELLIEU II

Married: Martha Chichet (Cheche) on September 8, 1745, in Charleston, South Carolina

Died: Buried on April 7, 1765

Children of Mark Anthony and Martha (Chichet or Cheche) Bessellieu: Lewis Bessellieu; Mark Anthony Bessellieu III; Mary Bessellieu; Philip Anthony Bessellieu; Susanna Bessellieu.

The French and English Day School of Martha and Mark Anthony Bessellieu is mentioned in *Woman's Life and Work in the Southern Colonies* by Julia Cherry Spruill Published in 1938 by the University of North Carolina Press at Chapel Hill, North Carolina.

Mark Anthony Besselleu and Martha Chichet married on September 8, 1745. On April 7, 1765 Mark Anthony Besseleu was buried. See St. Phillip's Register (Smith and Huger, Salley) 1754-1810 Published in 1927, page 309.

Mark Anthony Besselleu was naturalized in South Carolina on August 14, 1747. See Publications of the Huguenot Society of London, England, Volume 24

Mark Anthony Besselleau was admitted as the 161st member of the South Carolina Society on December 6, 1748. See *Rules of the South Carolina Society Established in Charlestown in the said Province September* 1, 1737. *Originally Incorporated May* 1, 1751. Published by the Society on March 30, 1937, page 108.

An advertisement in the South Carolina Gazette on January 19, 1747:

"Whereas it is not well known that I keep a school in the Day, This is to give notice that I teach French, English, Writing and Arithmetic from the Hour of 9 to half an Hour after 11 in the Forenoon and from half an Hour after 1 to 4 in the afternoon at the House wherein Dr. Case lately lived in Broad Street.

"Whoever sends their children there may depend on their being carefully instructed by their most humble servant, Mark Anthony Besselleu. N. B. I continue to keep my French and English Evening School from the hours of 6 to 9 at said house where sundry goods are to be sold at reasonable prices.

On November 16, 1747 an advertisement in the South Carolina Gazette listed for sale cambricks, lawns, fans, necklaces, ribbons, callicoes, cotton gowns, knee buckles, salt petre, hats, caps, sealing wax, and sundry other things-reasonable-at their house near to Messrs. Smith and Palmer in Broad Street.

(signed) Martha and Mark Anthony Besseleu. This additional notice followed: "At the same house French and English Day School continues to be kept as usual, where sewing is also taught in the neatest manner by Martha Besseleu.

See Arthur Henry Hirsch, *The Huguenots of Colonial South Carolina* (1928), *page* 158.

LEWIS BESSELLIEU

Married: 1st: Susannah Wood on August 27, 1775. She died before
        May 22, 1786
      2nd: Elizabeth Young on August 19, 1790

Children of Lewis and Susannah (Wood) Bessellieu: John Bessellieu
Children of Lewis and Elizabeth (Young) Bessellieu: Benjamine Lewis Bessellieu; Mary Johanna Bessellieu

1790 CENSUS CHARLESTON DISTRICT ST. BARTHOLOMEW PARISH SOUTH CAROLINA

Lewis Besselue: 1 male of 16 years and over; 1 male under 16; 1 female

1790 CENSUS CHARLESTON DISTRICT ST. PHILIP'S AND ST. MICHAEL'S PARISH, SOUTH CAROLINA

1 male of 16 years and over; 1 female; 2 slaves

Louis Besselleu married Susannah Wood on August 27, 1775. See Annals and Parish Register St. Thomas and St. Denis Parish Robert F. Clute (1884) Printed in Charleston by Walker Evans and Cogswell, pages 26 and 44.

On 12 March 1716/17 a grant of 220 acres was made to one Robert Wood. In 1785 this tract was divided and owned half by John Rosemond and his wife, Rachel, and half by Lewis Besselieu. On 3 Nov 1786 John Rosemond and wife Rachel conveyed their half to Andre Michaux and on the same day Lewis Besselieu conveyed his one half to Andre Michaux. On the map of 1784 the tract is described as the property of the heirs of Robert Wood: "the probability is that the

Rosemonds and Besselieu were in some way the heirs of Robert Wood."

Andre Michaux was the celebrated botanist sent by the King of France to South Carolina. He lived in the old residence of Robert Wood. His journals are printed in the proceedings of the American Philosophical Society in 1888, Volume 26, No. 129. M. Michaux introduced the Camellia Japonica to South Carolina, as well as the Ginkgo and Candlebury tree. Nothing is now left of the old house of Robert Wood save broken bricks of the old chimney in a grove of oaks and magnolias. The property is called the French Garden. The railroad station called Ten Mile Hill or Ten Mile is situated on the tract half a mile east of the old residence and garden.

See the South Carolina Historical and Genealogical Magazine, Volume 29, pages 8 through 11.

Died in this city after a long illness Mrs. Susannah Besselleau, wife of Mr. Lewis Besselleau. Monday May 22, 1786. Ibid in Volume 51, page 27 and Volume 20 page 143.

Lewis Besseleu appointed guardian of Rachel Wood, infant. March 20, 1778. See Misc Records RR, page 466 Charleston

August 19, 1790. Lewis Bessileu and Elizabeth Young, spinster, were married per Lic by the Rev'd Thomas Frost. See St. Philip's Register (1754-1810) Smith and Huger, page 248

1810 CENSUS CHARLESTON DISTRICT SOUTH CAROLINA Page 57
Elizabeth Besseleau: 2 males born 1794-1800; 1 female born 1784-1794; 1 female born before 1765

Lewis Beselleu registers a deed of gift to Peter Smith. On 24 November 1792 of a "negroe wench" named Affee and one half a lot on Beaufain Street—in trust for the separate use, benefit and behoof of Elizabeth Besselleau his wife. See Book F-6 pages 447 and 449 of the Mesne Conveyance Office, Charleston, South Carolina.

Indenture dated 2 November 1786 concerns lease from Lewis Besselleu to Andrew Michaux of plantation in parish of St. James Goose Creek—111 acres. See Book Y-5 page 131 in the Mesne Conveyance Office, Charleston, South Carolina.

BENJAMINE LEWIS BESSELLIEU

Benjamine Lewis son of Lewis and Elizabeth Bessellieu was baptized on July 4, 1798. See Register of St. Philip's Parish (1754-1810) Smith and Salley (1927), page 17.

JOHN BESSELLIEU

Lewis Besselleau to John Besselleau "for the natural love and affection which he hath and beareth toward his beloved son John Besselleau" to whom he conveys one half of a lot on the north side of Beaufain Street—also a negro fellow named Simon and a negro wench named Chloe. 4 November 1792. Mesne Conveyance Record Office, Record Book F-6, pages 447 and 449, Charleston, South Carolina.

MARY JOHANNA BESSELLIEU

On October 12, 1801, Mary Johanna, daughter of Lewis and Elizabeth Bessillieu, was baptized. St. Philip's Register (1754-1810), Smith and Salley (1927), page 27.

MARY BESSELLIEU

On the 24th December 1768 John White and Mary Besselleu spinster were married per Lic by the Rev. Mr. Hart. August 27, 1769 Mary, wife of John White was buried. St. Philip's Register (1754-1810) Smith and Salley (1927) page 191.

PHILIP ANTHONY BESSELLIEU

Born: March 31, 1748

Married: Susannah Mason on April 10, 1771, in Charleston, South Carolina

Died: January 9, 1795

Children of Philip Anthony and Susannah (Mason) Bessellieu: Charles Bessellieu; Joanna Martha Bessellieu; Lewis Bessellieu; Mark Anthony Bessellieu IV, Martha Catharine Bessellieu; Mary E. Bessellieu; Philip Anthony Bessellieu; Philip John Bessellieu; Susannah Elizabeth Bessellieu.

1790 CENSUS SOUTH CAROLINA CHARLESTON DISTRICT ST. PHILLIPS AND ST. MICHAELS PARISH

Philip A. Bazeleau: 1 male over 16; 36 males under 16 (doubtless includes orphans) ; 5 females; 3 slaves

Philip A. Baziloe of 26 Bufan Street was on the Poll Lists of the Charleston, South Carolina Municipal Elections of 1787. See South Carolina Historical and Genealogical Magazine, Volume 56, page 48.

April 10, 1771 Philip Besseleu and Susannah Mason, spinster, were married per license. See St. Philip's Register (1754-1810), page 197.

Died on Friday morning last Mr. Philip Besselieu for several years master of the Orphan House school in this city; his wife and family have to lament the loss of an affection husband and father. Thursday January 13, 1795, issue of Charleston City Gazette. See South Carolina Historical and Genealogical Magazine, Volume 23, page 26.

The tombstone of Philip A. Besselleu "Tutor to the Orphants" in the French Protestant (Huguenot) Churchyard in Charleston, South Carolina, shows he died January 9, 1795, aged 47 years, 9 months and 10 days. The Bessellieu Family Bible lists his death on *February 25, 1795, aged 45 years, 11 months and 8 days*. As the *Gazette entry* shows, the tombstone entry is correct.

John Baptiste Chevanes releases to Phillip Anthony Besselieu all that plantation of one thousand acres in Camden District at the head of Taukaw Creek and Ox Swamp in consideration of the payment of 175 pounds. 4 Nov 1792. Charleston, South Carolina, Mesne Conveyance Office, Book z, page 404.

CHARLES BESSELLIEU

Born: May 14, 1776, Berresford's Bounty, St. Thomas, South Carolina

Married: 1st or 2nd: Mary Riley
        3rd: Annie Howell of Georgia

Died: 1844

Children of Charles and Annie (Howell) Bessellieu: Annie Cecilia Bessellieu; Charles Mason Bessellieu, married A. Wincey, died in New Orleans, Louisiana, listed as owning 5 slaves in 1860 in Beaufort District, South Carolina, member Co. B, 2nd S.C. Cavalry Hampton's Legion during the War Between the States. Jane Bessellieu, married the Reverend Dr. Hopkins, died in Texas; John Bessellieu; Julia Bessellieu, married the Reverend Dr. Perry, died Spartanburg South Carolina; Thomas Edward Bessellieu; Thurston Bessellieu, never married, died in Georgetown or Hardeeville, South Carolina, member Co. B, 2nd S.C. Cavalry, Hampton's Legion during the War Between the States; William Bessellieu

1820 CENSUS BEAUFORT DISTRICT, SOUTH CAROLINA ST. LUKE'S PARISH

Charles Besselleau: 1 male born 1775-1794; 1 male born 1804-1810; 1 male born 1810-1820; 1 female born 1775-1794; 1 female born 1804-1810; 2 females born 1810-1820; 29 slaves

1830 CENSUS BEAUFORT DISTRICT SOUTH CAROLINA ST. LUKE'S PARISH

Charles Besselleu: 1 male born 1770-1780; 1 male born 1800-1810; 1 male born 1825-1830; 1 female born 1800-1810; 2 females born 1810-1815; 1 female born 1820-1825; 1 female born 1825-830; 58 slaves.

1840 CENSUS BEAUFORT DISTRICT SOUTH CAROLINA ST. LUKE'S PARISH

Chas Bessellieu: 1 male born 1770-1780; 1 male born 1830-1835; 3 males born 1835-1840; 1 female born 1800-1810; 1 female born 1820-1825; 1 female born 1825-1830; 1 female born 1830-1835; 56 slaves.

1850 CENSUS BEAUFORT DISTRICT SOUTH CAROLINA ST. LUKE'S PARISH

Mrs. E. A. Besselleu born in 1806 in South Carolina; John Besselleu born in 1836 in South Carolina; Edward Besselleu born in 1838 in South Carolina; Mason Besselleu born in 1834 in South Carolina; Thurston Besselleu born in 1852 in South Carolina; Frazier Besselleu born in 1852 in South Carolina; 45 slaves.

Charles Besselleu was born Tuesday night 10 o'clock 14 May 1776
Berresford's Bounty St. Thomas.
Bessellieu Bible.

Charles son of Philip and Susannah Besselleu born May 14, 1776 and
bap July 21
Annals and Parish Register St. Thomas and St. Denis
Robert F. Clute (1884) Printed in Charleston by
Walker, Evans and Cogswell, page 50.

Mrs. Mary Besselleu wife of Charles Besselleu of Jacksonborough and
daughter of John Riley Senior died in the 18th year of her age.
See Georgetown Gazette Charleston Column for December 28, 1801.

Charles Besselleu granted 721 acres in Beaufort on November 6, 1809.
Land Grant on file, Office of the Secretary of State, Columbia, South
Carolina.

Charles Bessellieu married for the third time Annie Howell of Georgia. She died in Greenville, South Carolina.

Charles Bessellieu died in 1844 aged 68. He is buried in the Euhaw
Churchyard, Beaufort(now Jasper County) District South Carolina.
Bessellieu Bible.

Besselieu Plantation in Beaufort County South Carolina mentioned
on page 28 of the 42nd Volume of the South Carolina Historical and
Genealogical Magazine.

ANNIE CECILIA BESSELLIEU

Born: 1825-1826
Married: Benjamin Franklin Boyd
Children of Benjamin Franklin and Annie Cecilia (Bessellieu) Boyd:
Agnes L. Boyd; Benjamin H. Boyd; Charles Boyd; James Boyd; Mary
M. Boyd; Richard Boyd; William Thurston Boyd.

1850 CENSUS BEAUFORT DISTRICT SOUTH CAROLINA ST. LUKE'S PARISH
96, 96

B. F. Boyd born in 1816 in South Carolina; Cecilia Boyd born in 1826
in South Carolina; Benjamin H. Boyd born in 1846 in South Carolina;
James L. Boyd born in 1847 in South Carolina; Richard T. Boyd born
in 1849 in South Carolina.

1860 CENSUS BEAUFORT DISTRICT SOUTH CAROLINA ST. LUKE'S PARISH
197, 181

Benjamin F. Boyd born in 1812 in South Carolina; Cecilia A. Boyd
born in 1826 in South Carolina; Benjamin H. Boyd born in 1846 in
South Carolina; James Boyd born in 1848 in South Carolina; Richard
G. Boyd born in 1850 in South Carolina; Mary M. Boyd born in 1852
in South Carolina; Charles B. Boyd born in 1856 in South Carolina;
Agnes L. Boyd born in 1859 in South Carolina; Elihu W. Watson born
in 1835 in South Carolina; Richard Boyd born in ? in South Carolina;

H. Thurston Bessellieu born in 1843 in South Carolina; 44 slaves owned by Benjamin Boyd; 5 slaves owned by H. Thurston Bessellieu.

1880 CENSUS BEAUFORT COUNTY SOUTH CAROLINA YEMASEE TOWNSHIP VILLAGE OF HARDEEVILLE 8, 10

Benj F. Boyd born in 1815 in South Carolina; his wife, Cecilia Boyd born in 1825 in South Carolina.

Their children: Wm T. Boyd in 1865 in South Carolina; Chas A. Boyd born in 1856 in South Carolina and his wife, Florence E. Boyd born in 1857 in South Carolina — their children: Ben C. Boyd born in 1878 in S. C., A. M. Boyd born in 1880 in S. C. (girl) ; — Benjamin H. Boyd born in 1846 in South Carolina and his wife, Catte T. Boyd born in 1858 in S. C. The father of Benj F. Boyd was born in Virginia.

Annie Cecilia Bessellieu married Benjamin Boyd. She died at Hardeeville, S. C. See Bessellieu Bible.

AGNES LOUISE BOYD

Born: 1857
Married: Charles Addison Williams in 1879
Died: 1938

Children of Charles Addison and Agnes Louise (Boyd) Williams: Charles Addison Williams, Jr.; Amy Richard Williams, born 1882, died 1958, unmarried; Annie Cecile Williams, born 1883, died 1908, unmarried; Katie Williams; Louise Agnes Williams; Henry Reuben Williams; Mary Boyd Williams; Elizabeth Williams, born 1899, died 1904.

CHARLES ADDISON WILLIAMS, JR.

Born: 1880
Married: Frances Edith Greene.
Died: 1923

Children of Charles Addison and Frances Edith (Greene) Williams, Jr.: Charles Addison Williams III, born 1907, married Willie Mae Harrelson in 1951.

KATIE WILLIAMS

Born: 1885
Married: Clinton M. McTeer

Children of Clinton M. and Katie (Williams) McTeer: Clinton M. McTeer, Jr., born 1905, died in 1918; Charles Williams McTeer, born 1907, unmarried; Jack C. McTeer.

JACK C. McTEER

Born: 1909
Married: Elizabeth Hughes in 1932

Children of Jack C. and Elizabeth (Hughes) McTeer: Elizabeth, born 1936; Nancy, born 1938, married Frank Folsom in 1953.

LOUISE AGNES WILLIAMS

Born: 1888

Married: Alvin Zachary Cox in 1918

Children of Alvin Zachary and Louise Agnes (Williams) Cox: Alvin Zachary Cox, Jr.

ALVIN ZACHARY COX, JR.

Born: 1920

Married: Virginia Edwards

Children of Alvin Zachary and Virginia (Edwards) Cox, Jr.: Alvin Zachary Cox III, born 1946.

HENRY REUBEN WILLIAMS

Born: 1889

Married: Martha Wood Sipple in 1910 in Grahamville, South Carolina

Died: 1957

Children of Henry Reuben and Martha Wood (Sipple) Williams: Frances Sipple Williams.

FRANCES SIPPLE WILLIAMS

Born: 1911

Married: Daniel Hunter Wallace, Jr.

Children of Daniel Hunter and Frances Sipple (Williams) Wallace, Jr.: Martha Williams Wallace, born 1951.

MARY BOYD WILLIAMS

Born: 1893

Married: 1st: David Brown Roberts
2nd: Walter C. Peeples

Died: 1950

Children of David Brown and Mary Boyd (Williams) Roberts: Elizabeth Williams Roberts.

ELIZABETH WILLIAMS ROBERTS

Born: 1911

Married: Hamlin Beattie, Jr. in 1941

Children of Hamlin and Elizabeth Williams (Roberts) Beattie, Jr.: Hamlin Beattie III, born 1945; Elizabeth H. Beattie, born 1946.

BENJAMIN H. BOYD

Born: 1846

Married: Katherine Thompson Tison in 1876

Children of Benjamin H. and Katherine Thompson (Tison) Boyd: Martha Thelma Boyd, born 1878, died 1886; Pauline Louise Boyd, born 1884, lives in Hardeeville, South Carolina; Katherine Thompson Boyd; Mary Rebecca Boyd; Cecile Agnes Boyd, born 1895, died 1896.

KATHERINE THOMPSON BOYD

Born: 1887

Married: Ulric Jennings Beckham in 1909

Child of Ulric Jennings and Katherine Thompson (Boyd) Beckham: Katherine Boyd Beckham.

KATHERINE BOYD BECKHAM

Born: 1910

Married: 1st: Roy Jones in 1930
        2nd: Harold E. Blount in 1938

Children of Roy and Katherine Boyd (Beckham) Jones: Barbara Louise Jones

Children of Harold E. and Katherine Boyd (Beckham) Blount: Paula Katherine Blount, born 1940, married Billy Johnson in 1955; Harold Edward Blount, born in 1943; Oscar Ulric Blount, born in 1945; Rebecca Mary Blount, born in 1951.

BARBARA LOUISE JONES

Born: 1934

Married: Thomas Edward Pinckney in 1953

Children of Thomas Edward and Barbara Louise (Jones) Pinckney: Thomas Edward Pinckney, born in 1954; James Beckham Pinckney, born in 1956.

MARY REBECCA BOYD

Born: 1890

Married: Jesse C. Jennings in 1912

Died: 1958

Children of Jesse C. and Mary Rebecca (Boyd) Jennings: James Calvin Jennings; Sara Agnes Jennings.

JAMES CALVIN JENNINGS

Born: 1914

Married: Mary Alice Fowler in 1937

Children of James Calvin and Mary Alice (Fowler) Jennings: Jane Fowler Jennings, born in 1942.

SARA AGNES JENNINGS

Born: 1916

Married: James Leroy Massey in 1937.

WILLIAM THURSTON BOYD

Married: Mary Dalzell in 1902

Child of William Thurston and Mary (Dalzell) Boyd: William Thurston Boyd II.

WILLIAM THURSTON BOYD II

Born: February 29, 1908

Married: Madeline Davidson in October, 1930

Died: August 16, 1954

Children of William Thurston and Madeline (Davidson) Boyd II: William Thurston Boyd III, born October 12, 1938; Mary Janice Boyd, born January 12, 1941.

The Reverend W. T. D. Dalzell was born on the Island of St. Vincent on June 2, 1837. He died in Shreveport, Louisiana, on February 5, 1899. He was a graduate of Oxford University. He studied medicine before being ordained a priest in the Church of England in 1848. Mr. Dalzell settled in Philadelphia, but his sympathy during the War Between the States was with the South. He served as a Chaplain of a Texas Regiment during the war. After the war, he was Rector of Trinity Church in Houston.

Mr. Dalzell married Estelle Logan of New Orleans on November 1, 1866. He became Rector of St. Mark's in Shreveport where he remained with the exception of one year while he was at Grace Church in Memphis. Mr. Dalzell could have been a bishop, but refused to leave Shreveport. He was called a "maker of bishops." The new St. Mark's Church in Shreveport was a memorial to him. Dalzell Street in Shreveport is named for him.

Mr. Dalzell left three children: Dr. William Gregg Dalzell, Mrs. Andrew Jackson Ingersoll of Shreveport, and Mrs. William Thurston Boyd of Coushatta, Louisiana.

HISTORY OF SHREVEPORT AND SHREVEPORT BUILDERS by Lilla McLure and J. Ed Howe (1937).

JOHN HOWELL BESSELLIEU

Born: March 14, 1837

Married: Ann Earle Larisey on December 22, 1859, at White Point Plantation, Beaufort, South Carolina

Died: November 24, 1913

Children of John Howell and Ann Earle (Larisey) Bessellieu: Sara Bessellieu; Harry Bessellieu; Mary Bessellieu.

SARA BESSELLIEU

Born: October 6, 1873

Married: Henry L. Larisey on August 4, 1895

Died: January 4, 1946

Children of Henry L. and Sara (Bessellieu) Larisey: Vivienne Larisey; Karen Larisey, married G. C. Martschink of Charleston, South Carolina.

VIVIENNE LARISEY

Born: August 24, 1900

Married: Albert J. Kahrs on August 18, 1920, Charleston, South Carolina.

Children of Albert J. and Vivienne (Larisey) Kahrs: Anne Kahrs, married R. E. Johnson; Florence Kahrs, married James T. Risher, Jr.

1860 Census St. Luke's Parish Grahamville Beaufort District South Carolina

John H. Bessellieu born in 1837 in South Carolina; Anna E. Bessellieu born in 1843 in South Carolina; 1 slave.

John H. Bessellieu listed as a merchant

1870 Census St. Luke's Parish Beaufort County South Carolina Grahamville 764, 758

J. H. Besselieu born in 1834 in South Carolina; Anna Besselieu born in 1842 in South Carolina; Harry Besselieu born in 1862 in South Carolina; Mary Besselieu born in 1868 in South Carolina.

J. H. Besselieu listed as a dentist.

John H. Bessellieu was a member of Co. B, 2nd S. C. Cavalry Hampton's Legion during the War Between the States. Bessellieu Bible.

JULIA VIRGINIA BESSELLIEU

Married: The Reverend Duncan Perry

Children of the Reverend Duncan and Julia Virginia (Bessellieu) Perry: Mary Ann Perry; Lilly Perry; Rosa Perry, married Andrew Craneford, no children; Duncan Perry, married Jane Miller, no children; James Perry.

MARY ANN PERRY

Married: Samuel Gaillard FitzSimons

Children of Samuel Gaillard and Mary Ann (Perry) FitzSimons; Amy Perry FitzSimons; Theodore B. FitzSimons; Duncan Perry Fitz-Simons, died young; Thomas Porchet FitzSimons, died young; Samuel C. FitzSimons, died young; Mary Ann FitzSimons; Samuel Gaillard FitzSimons II.

AMY PERRY FITZ SIMONS

Married: James Pickens Walker.

Children of James Pickens and Amy Perry (FitzSimons) Walker: Amy Perry Walker, died as a baby; James Pickens Walker, Jr., married Ann Knight, no children; Emma Dee Walker; Mary Ann Walker.

EMMA DEE WALKER

Married: Robert Corbell

Died: May, 1959

Children of Robert and Emma Dee (Walker) Corbell: Robert Corbell, Jr.; James Corbell, died young; Dee Corbell.

MARY ANN WALKER

Married: Beverly McEwan

Children of Beverly and Mary Ann (Walker) McEwan: Christopher Gaillard McEwan; Nancy Fletcher McEwan; James Walker McEwan.

THEODORE B. FITZ SIMONS

Married: Clara Mather

Children of Theodore B. and Clara (Mather) FitzSimons: Theodore B. FitzSimons, Jr.; Clara Mather FitzSimons; Ann S. FitzSimons; William Huger FitzSimons.

MARY ANN FITZ SIMONS

Born: September 30, 1899

Married: Donald McKay Allston

Children of Donald McKay and Mary Ann (FitzSimons) Allston: Amy Perry Allston; Amarintha Theodora Allston; Donald McKay Allston II.

AMY PERRY ALLSTON

Born: August 22, 1921

Married: Henry Fishburne

Children of Henry and Amy Perry (Allston) Fishburne: Henry Fishburne, Jr.; Donald Allston Fishburne.

AMARINTHIA THEODORA ALLSTON

Born: November 21, 1923

Married: Robert McEwan

Children of Robert and Amarinthia Theodora (Allston) McEwan: Robert McEwan, Jr.; Amy Allston McEwan.

DONALD McKAY ALLSTON II

Born: February 21, 1925

Married: Margarita FitzSimons

Children of Donald McKay and Margarita (FitzSimons) Allston II: Donald McKay Allston III; Mary Ann Allston.

SAMUEL GAILLARD FITZ SIMONS II

Born: September 21, 1904

Married: Mary Hadden

Children of Samuel Gaillard and Mary (Haden) FitzSimons II: Samuel Gaillard FitzSimons III; Mary Ann FitzSimons; Grace Fitz-Simons.

LILLY PERRY

Married: William Coffin

Children of William and Lilly (Perry) Coffin: Perry Coffin, married, no children; Edward Coffin; Virginia Coffin; daughter who married Walton Wise Willette.

VIRGINIA COFFIN

Married: Percy Jones in Savannah, Georgia

Children of Percy and Virginia (Coffin) Jones: Virginia Jones; Ashley Jones.

(?) COFFIN

Married: Walton Wise Willette

Children: Margaret Willette; Walton Willette; William Willette.

THOMAS EDWARD BESSELLIEU

Born: December 30, 1838, on the Plantation on the Euhaw known as "Hebron"

Married: Harriet Euphemia Zealy of Grahamville, South Carolina, on June 21, 1859

Died: July, 1898, in Tybee, Georgia. Buried in Savannah, Georgia

Children of Thomas Edward and Harriet Euphemia (Zealy) Bessellieu: Alma Alice Bessellieu, born Savannah, Georgia, married Osborne R. Chancellor; Calbraith Butler Bessellieu, born 1880 in Savannah, Georgia, veteran Spanish American War and World War I, 1st Sergeant, 1st Tennessee Field Artillery 30 Division, fought at St. Miheil and Meuse Argonne, gassed October 23, 1918; Carrie Louise Bessellieu born in 1868 in Grahamville, South Carolina, married Jehu Wall, died in 1904 in Grahamville, where she is buried; Edward Cecil Bessellieu; Florence Irene Bessellieu, born Savannah, Georgia; Hattie Eloise Bessellieu, born in 1874 in Grahamville, South Carolina, married Wm. H. MacMillan, lived in Nashville, Tennessee in 1902, had two children: Dr. Wright MacMillan and Elsie MacMillan; James Zealy Bessellieu, born in 1863 in Grahamville, South Carolina, married Adele and Merrie Williams, died in Biloxi, Mississippi, October 1, 1918, and buried in Meridian, Mississippi; Julia Corrie Bessellieu, born in 1878, died Savannah, Georgia about 1882, buried in Grahamville, S. C.; William Mason Bessellieu, born 1872 in Savannah, Georgia, married Kate Sweat at Hardeeville, S. C.

1860 CENSUS BEAUFORT DISTRICT SOUTH CAROLINA ST. LUKE'S PARISH GRAHAMVILLE POST OFFICE 191, 175

T. Edward Bessellieu born in 1839 in South Carolina; Harriet E. Bessellieu born in 1842 in South Carolina; T. Edward Bessellieu was a "Surgeon Dentist." The Bessellieus lived with Wm. P. Zealy. 1 slave

1870 CENSUS BEAUFORT COUNTY SOUTH CAROLINA ST. LUKE'S PARISH GRAHAMVILLE 66, 69

T. E. Bessellieu born in 1839 in South Carolina; Harriet E. Bessellieu born in 1842 in South Carolina; James Z. Bessellieu born in 1864 in South Carolina; Edward C. Bessellieu born in 1866 in South Carolina; Carrie L. Bessellieu born in 1868 in South Carolina. T. E. Bessellieu was a Dentist.

1850 CENSUS BEAUFORT DISTRICT SOUTH CAROLINA ST. LUKE'S PARISH

Wm P. Zealy born in 1805 in South Carolina; Lydia A. Zealy born in 1810 in Georgia; Elizabeth Zealy born in 1833 in South Carolina; Theodore Zealy born in 1838 in South Carolina; James Zealy born in 1840 in South Carolina; Harriet Zealy born in 1842 in South Carolina; Oscar T. Zealy born in 1844 in South Carolina; Cornelia Zealy born in 1846 in South Carolina; Lydia Ann Zealy born in 1849 in South Carolina; Lydia Ann Arden born in 1833 in South Carolina.

1860 CENSUS BEAUFORT DISTRICT SOUTH CAROLINA ST. LUKE'S PARISH 191, 174

Wm P Zealy born in 1807 in South Carolina; Lydia A. Zealy born in (?) in Georgia; James E. Zealy born in 1840 in South Carolina; Oscar T. Zealy born in 1844 in South Carolina; Cornelia Zealy born in 1846 in South Carolina; Proctor Zealy born in 1852 in South Carolina; Alma A. Zealy born in 1854 in South Carolina; Wm. P. Zealy was a merchant and Postmaster. 19 slaves.

Thomas Edward Bessellieu was born on the plantation on the Euhaw known as "Hebron" on December 30, 1838. He married Harriet Euphemia Zealy of Grahamville, S. C., on June 21, 1859. That same year he graduated from the Baltimore College of Dental Surgery. He was a member of Co B, 2nd S.C. Cavalry, Hampton's Legion, during the War Between the States. He died at Tybee, Georgia, July, 1898, and is buried in Savannah, Georgia. Bessellieu Bible.

EDWARD CECIL BESSELLIEU

Born: February 11, 1866, Grahamville, South Carolina
Married: Emma Smith at Lincoln, New Mexico, January 7, 1888. She
    was born in Warrenburg, Missouri, September 1, 1871
Died: September 17, 1943

Children of Edward Cecil and Emma (Smith) Bessellieu: Clarence Cecil Bessellieu, born January 30, 1906, at Wilmington, North Carolina, married Mary Long of Wilmington, died September 18, 1942; Eleanor Bessellieu, born September 13, 1895, Savannah, Georgia, married George Payton Russell at Wilmington, North Carolina, on December 21, 1916, their children: Thomas, Edward, and George Payton Russell Jr. (born June 21, 1927), resided Chathan, Mendham, and Westfield, New Jersey, in 1936; Emily Bessellieu, born October 4,

1897 Savannah, Georgia, married Norman Eldridge Hudson July 1919 Wilmington, North Carolina, their children: Norman Eldridge Jr. born October 19, 1921 in Wilmington and Jerry Hudson born in 1935; Harriet Myrtle Bessellieu, born September 24, 1888 at Roswell, New Mexico, married Wm. A. Garrison of Orange Springs Florida at Ocala Florida; Parralee Bessellieu born March 1, 1903 in Wilmington North Carolina, married Lt. James Byron McCumber of Roanoke Virginia, on November 28, 1922, he was a graduate of Blackstone Military Academy, later served as Captain Headquarters Company North Carolina National Guard at Wilmington, their son, Bobby McCumber, was born in 1935 in Wilmington; Philip Arthur (Billy) Bessellieu, born November 22, 1915, in Wilmington, North Carolina, married Jane La Boiteaux of Washington, D. C. at St. Petersburg, Florida on March 15, 1941; Thomas Edward Besselieu, born July 16, 1890, Savannah, Georgia.

THOMAS EDWARD BESSELLIEU II

Born: July 16, 1890, Savannah, Georgia
Married: Mary Burnett Owen on March 8, 1923

Children of Thomas Edward and Mary Burnett (Owen) Bessellieu II: Eleanor Burnett Bessellieu; Thomas Edward Bessellieu III, born August 4, 1927, Jacksonville, Florida; Anthony Owen Bessellieu, born February 2, 1930, Jacksonville, Florida.

ELEANOR BURNETT BESSELLIEU

Born: October 28, 1923
Married: Doctor William P. Horton on September 6, 1947, Wilmington, North Carolina.

WILLIAM F. BESSELLIEU

Married: Mattie Henningway

1860 CENSUS CITY OF MONTICELLO COUNTY OF DREW ARKANSAS 529, 529

W. F. Bessellieu born in 1833 in South Carolina; Martha A. Bessellieu born in 1843 in Mississippi; Ja Lande born in 1835 in France; J. L. Haynes born in 1832 in Tennesee; Wm Akin born in 1832 in South Carolina; W. F. Bessellieu was a doctor and J. L. Haynes was Deputy Sheriff.

1870 CENSUS MARION TOWNSHIP DREW COUNTY ARKANSAS 124, 124

William Beslue born in 1834 in South Carolina; Martha Beslue born in 1844 in Mississippi; Elizabeth Beslue born in 1860 in Arkansas; Margret Beslue born in 1862 in Arkansas; Wilson Beslue born in 1864 in Arkansas; William Beslue born in 1866 in Arkansas; Annah Beslue born in 1869 in Arkansas; Fanny and Joseph Black servants are listed. William Beslue is listed as a teacher.

William Bessellieu born in 1834 in South Carolina; Mattie Bessellieu born in 1843 in Mississippi; Maggie Bessellieu born in 1863 in Arkansas; Wilson Bessellieu born in 1865 in Arkansas; Willie S. Bessellieu born in 1867 in Arkansas; Annie Bessellieu born in 1870 in Arkansas; Mamie Bessellieu born in 1872 in Arkansas; Wytie (?) Bessellieu born in 1876 in Arkansas. The father of Mattie Besselleiu was born in South Carolina, while her mother was born in Mississippi.

William F. Bessellieu had ten children of whom only seven were living in 1890. He practiced medicine in Monticello many years since 1860. He filled the offices of county assessor for several years. His son, Wilson F. Bessellieu in 1888 bought a one-half interest in the Arkansas City Journal, which had the largest circulation of any county paper in the state. The paper did county work for Desha and Chicot Counties.

See Biographical and Historical Memoirs of South Arkansas Published by the Goodspeed Publishing Company 1890 pages 932, 1006 and 1007.

JOHANNAH MARTHA BESSELLIEU

Born: February 25, 1784, Wentworth Street, Charleston, South Carolina

Married: Captain Joseph Purdy of New York on June 5, 1800, in Charleston, South Carolina

Died: June 16, 1804, in Charleston, South Carolina

Children of Captain Joseph and Johannah Martha (Bessellieu) Purdy: Maria Susannah Purdy.

1800 CENSUS CHARLESTON DISTRICT (Page 70)

Joseph Purdy: 1 male born 1774-1784; 1 female born 1774-1784.
Joanna Martha Besselleu born Wednesday morning half past 10 o'clock 25 Feb 1784 Wentworth Street Charleston.
Bessellieu Bible.

On June 5, 1800, Joseph Purdy of Charleston Mariner and Johanna Besselleau of the same place were married per Lic. See St. Philip's Register (1754-1810) Smith and Huger (1927) page 271.

Joseph Purdie and Johanna Besselleu were married in Charleston, S. C., on June 6, 1800. See William Montgomery Clemens North and South Carolina Marriage Records (1927), pages 29, 224.

Married on Thursday evening last, by Reverend Mr. Frost, Mr. Joseph Purdie to Miss Johannah Bessellew, both of this city. June 9, 1800, Monday issue Charleston City Gazette. See South Carolina Historical and Genealogical Magazine, Volume 26, pages 134 and 135. Died on Saturday morning last in the 21st year of her age, Mrs. Johannes M.

Purdie, third daughter of Mr. Philip A. Besseleu, late of this city deceased. She bore the pains of a long illness with much fortitude and submitted to the will of her Creator patiently in the end. Wednesday June 20, 1804 issue of Charleston City Gazette. Ibid, page 225 of Volume 27.

Capt Joseph Purdy of New York was married to Johannah Besselleu of Charleston So Ca on the 5th day of June 1800.

Johannah Purdy died on the 16th June 1804 in Charleston at 2 o'clock A.M.

Frazer Family Bible.

MARIA SUSANNAH PURDY

Born: December 22, 1801, in Charleston, South Carolina

Married: William M. Frazer on May 22, 1821, in Charleston, South Carolina

Died: September 28, 1850

Maria Susannah Frazer, wife of William M. Frazer, departed this life at the residence of William Wilson, her son-in-law, in Barnwell District, South Carolina, on Saturday morning the 28th day of September at 9 o'clock and was buried in his family burying ground near his residence in Beach Island Barnwell District South Carolina by his special request.

Frazer Bible.

LEWIS BESSELLIEU

Lewis Besselleu was born Friday morning at Quarter after 3 o'clock 26 March 1779 St. Thomas.

Bessellieu Bible.

Lewis son of Philip and Susannah Besselleu born Mar 26, 1779 and bap Apl 6.

See Annals and Parish Register of St. Thomas and St. Denis Parish Robert F. Clute (1884) Printed in Charleston by Walker, Evans and Cogswell, page 50.

CAPTAIN MARK ANTHONY BESSELLIEU

1800 CENSUS CHARLESTON DISTRICT SOUTH CAROLINA Page 50

Mary Anth Besseliue: 1 male born 1774-1784; 1 female born 1774-1784.

Mark Anthony Besselleu was born the Saturday morning 22nd October 1774 at Quarter after One St. Thomas.

Bessellieu Bible.

Mark Anthony, son of Philip and Susannah Besselleu, born October 22, 1774, and bap Nov 13

See Annals and Parish Register of St. Thomas and St. Denis Parish

Robert F. Clute (1884) Printed in Charleston by Walker Evans and Cogswell, page 50.

Married on Thursday evening last, by the Rev. Mr. Frost Captain Mark A. Besselleu to Miss Maria Williams, both of this city. See the South Carolina Historical and Genealogical Magazine, Volume 26, page 169. Copied from the Charleston City Gazette.

September 11, 1800. Mark Anthony Besselleu of Charleston, Mariner, and Maria Williams, of the same place were married per Lic. See St. Philip's Register (1754-1810) Smith and Huger, page 271.

May 25, 1802. John Cowan of Charleston and Maria Basilleau of the same place, widow, were married per Lic. Ibid, page 274.

MARTHA CATHARINE BESSELLIEU

Martha Catharine Besselleu was born Monday night half past 11 o'clock 30th January 1786 Beaufain Street Charleston.
Bessellieu Bible

Married on Sunday evening last, in Jacksonborough, by the Rev. Thomas D. Bladen, Mr. Joseph Dilgar to Miss Martha Catharine Besseleu.

See Wednesday, April 25, 1804 issue of Charleston City Gazette printed in South Carolina Historical and Genealogical Magazine, Volume 27, page 221.

MARY E. BESSELLIEU

1830 CENSUS CHARLESTON SOUTH CAROLINA WARD NO. 4 (Page 98)
Mary E. Maull: 2 males born 1800-1810; 1 male born 1810-1815; 1 male born 1815-1820; 1 female born 1780-1790; 3 females born 1810-1815; 2 slaves.

Mary E. Besselleu born Tuesday night at half past 8 o'clock 29 January 1782 St. Thomas. Bessellieu Bible.

Married on Saturday evening last by the Rev. Mr. Frost, Mr. David Maull of Jacksonborough to Miss Mary E. Besselleu of this city. November 4, 1799 issue Charleston City Gazette. See South Carolina Historical and Genealogical Magazine Volume 26, page 48.

November 2, 1799. David Maul of Charleston and Mary Besselew of the same place were married per Lic.
See St. Philip's Register (1754-1810) Smith and Huger (1927) page 270.

David Mason Maull born 15 May 1811 Seven o'clock in the morning. Charles W. Maull departed this life on 22 February aged 22 years. David Maul father of James departed this life February 1816 (?) in the 40 (?) year of his age.

Mary E. Maull mother of James departed this life July 1 in the 68 year of her age.
Bessellieu Bible.

PHILIP ANTHONY BESSELLIEU

Philip Anthony Besselleu was born on Friday morning at 6 o'clock the 27th of February, 1778, in St. Thomas. Bessellieu Bible.

Philip Anthony, son of Philip and Susannah Bessellieu born February 27, 1778. Bap March 17

Philip A. Bessellieu son of Philip A. Besselleu was buried March 19, 1778.

See Annals and Parish Register of St. Thomas and St. Denis Parish Robert F. Clute (1884) Printed in Charleston by Walker, Evans and Cogswell, pages 50 and 96.

PHILIP JOHN BESSELLIEU

1820 CENSUS BEAUFORT DISTRICT SOUTH CAROLINA ST. LUKE'S PARISH
Philip J. Besseleau: 1 male born 1775-1794; 1 slave.

1830 CENSUS BEAUFORT DISTRICT SOUTH CAROLINA ST. LUKE'S PARISH
Phillip J. Bessellieu: 1 male born 1780-1790; 6 slaves.

1840 CENSUS BEAUFORT DISTRICT SOUTH CAROLINA ST. LUKE'S PARISH
P. Bessillieu: 1 male born 1790-1800; 8 slaves.

1850 CENSUS BEAUFORT DISTRICT SOUTH CAROLINA ST. LUKE'S PARISH
264, 164

Philip J. Bessellieu born in 1787 in South Carolina; 5 slaves.

Philip J. Bessellieu was a tavern keeper.

Philip John Bessellieu was born February 14, 1788, in Charleston, South Carolina. Bessellieu Bible.

February 28, 1788, Philip John, son of Philip Anthony and Susanna Besileau was baptized. See St. Philip's Register (1754-1810) Smith and Huger, 1927, page 107.

"A summer retreat was a necessary of life with the people of Coosa-whatchie. To live in the village two summers was an impossibility for all white men with one exception, just enough to prove the rule. The exception was Mr. Bessellieu who kept a shop and furnished gentlemen of the bar with board and lodging. He was able to dwell with bilious fever and country fever, as Indian conjurers, handle poisonous serpents without harm. His mother must have annoited him when an infant with some medical charm. He was a wizard so far and yet he seemed in all besides a plain and simple-hearted man. To all but him a summer in Coosawatchie was death."

From the Autobiography of William John Grayson published in the South Carolina Historical and Genealogical Magazine, Volume 51, page 109.

SUSANNAH ELIZABETH BESSELLIEU

Susannah Besselleu was born at the house of J. Henderson the 12th May 1773 Wednesday in Charleston. Bessellieu Bible.

January 25, 1793 Susannah Elizabeth daughter of Philip and Susannah Besseleau was baptized.

St. Philip's Register (1754-1810) Smith and Huger (1927) page 123.

Married on Thursday evening last. Mr. Abraham Joy to Miss Susannah Besseleau. Monday February 6, 1792 issue Charleston City Gazette. South Carolina Historical and Genealogical Magazine Volume 21, page 122.

December 30, 1797. Mary Elizabeth daughter of Abraham and Elizabeth Joye was baptized.

1800 Census Charleston South Carolina page 68

Abraham Joy: 2 males born 1784-1790; 2 males born 1774-1784; 1 male born 1755-1774; 1 female born 1790-1800; 1 female born 1755-1774; 3 slaves.

Probate Court, Charleston, S. C., Volume 28, page 340. Will of Abraham Joy of the City of Charleston. Mentions wife, Susannah, after her death all property to go to son Abraham Philip and daughter, Mary Susannah. October 6, 1802. Witnesses: John M. Frazer, James Dean, John Wagoner. Proved before Charles Lining, Esq. O.C.T.D. October 22, 1802. Susannah qualified as Executrix. Recorded Will Book (1800-1807), page 310, Book D.

SUSANNAH BESSELLIEU

1810 CENSUS CHARLESTON DISTRICT SOUTH CAROLINA Page 57

Sus Gisendanner: 1 male born 1794-1800; 1 female born before 1765; 1 female born 1765-1784.

1820 CENSUS CHARLESTON DISTRICT SOUTH CAROLINA

Susannah Gisendenner: 1 male born 1810-1820; 1 female born before 1775; 3 females born 1775-1794; 2 females born 1794-1804; 2 females born 1804-1810; 2 females born 1810-1820.

Susannah Gissendanner died January 1829 aged 77 years and 8 months.

Also

Susannah Gissendenner departed this life on the (illegible) 1829, aged 78 years.

Bessellieu Bible.

On December 31, 1795, John Gissendanner and Susannah Bessileau spinster were married per Lic by the Rev'd Thomas Frost. See St. Philip's Register (1754-1810)

Smith and Huger (1927) page 259. June 8, 1799 Mr. John Gissendanner was buried in the French Church yard.

Charles Besselleu and Susannah Gissendanner to (or from) Andrew Swindershine Bill of Sale, a slave, 13 Jan 1798. See Misc LLL, page 173, State Archives, Columbia, S. C.

Mrs. Hutson in "Notes on the Bessellieu Family" published in Transactions No. 51 of the Huguenot Society of South Carolina names Susannah as the daughter of Philip Anthony and Susannah (Mason) Bessellieu. She was rather the sister of Philip, who did have a daughter Susannah Elizabeth who married Abraham Joy in 1792.

BESSELLIEUS WHO SERVED IN THE CONFEDERATE ARMY DURING THE WAR BETWEEN THE STATES AS FOUND IN THE NATIONAL ARCHIVES, WASHINGTON, D. C.

JOHN H. BESSELLIEU. Private. Company B, 2 South Carolina Cavalry. Enlisted 1861 in Grahamville, South Carolina. Transferred to the Navy on December 30, 1863.

JOHN H. BESSELLIEU. Private. Company C, Cavalry Battalion, Hampton Legion, South Carolina. Captain T. E. Sireven's Company. Born 1837, Grahamville, South Carolina. Blue eyes. Light hair. Light complexion. Five feet, eleven inches. Enlisted Beaufort District, South Carolina.

The Honorable G. W. Randolph
Secretary of War
My Dear Sir:

While in the city the other day I heard it rumored about that we had a squadron of vessels in the English channel and having some experience in seafaring life, I thought of applying to you for a situation aboard one of the Confederate vessels as Lieutenant or Midshipman. As to my character and standing I will refer you to Brigadier General Wade Hampton and to the Hon. L. M. Ayer, Congressman from my congressional district. In hopes of hearing from you as soon as possible, I have the honor to be your most obediently and respectfully,

JOHN H. BESSELLIEU

H. THURSTON BESSELLIEU. Private. Company C, Cavalry Battalion, Hampton Legion, South Carolina. Born 1843. Enlisted Grahamville, Beaufort District, South Carolina

T. E. BESSELLIEU. Captain Stuart's Company (Beaufort Voluntary Artillery) South Carolina Artillery. Enlisted Yorktown 1862.

H. T. BESSELLIEU. Company B, 2 South Carolina Cavalry. Corporal. Sergeant. Born in 1843 in Beaufort District, South Carolina. Grey eyes. Dark hair. Light complexion. Five feet, eight inches. His horse was killed in action at Brandy Station, Virginia, August 1, 1863. He was wounded and captured near Culpeper.

The Surgeon General
Richmond, Virginia

Through:

Surgeon F. D. Cunningham,
Medical Director,
District of Arkansas

Sir:

I beg leave respectfully to withdraw my application for a transfer and hereby tender my resignation as Surgeon in the Provisional Army of the Confederate States to take effect on the first day of June proximo. Ill health as shown in the accompanying certificates, much impaired recently, is my only reason for pursuing this course and while I yield reluctantly I still entertain the hope that should the contest in which we are engaged be unfortunately protracted, I may again be restored to the service of my country. With sentiments of esteem, your obedient servant,

W. F. BESSELLIEU

C. MASON BESSELLIEU. Private. Company B, 2 South Carolina Cavalry. Enlisted June 19, 1861, Grahamville, South Carolina. Transferred to 1 South Carolina Infantry

CHARLES M. BESSELLIEU. Private. Company A, Infantry Regiment, Hampton Legion, South Carolina. Born in 1840 in Beaufort District, South Carolina. Grey eyes. Black hair. Light complexion. Five feet, eight inches. Enlisted Columbia, South Carolina.

C. MASON BESSELLIEU. Private. Company C, Cavalry Battalion, Hampton Legion, South Carolina. Enlisted Beaufort District, South Carolina, 1861. Grahamville.

T. EDWARD BESSELLIEU. Sergeant. Company C, Cavalry Battalion, Hampton Legion, South Carolina. Born 1839. Enlisted Grahamville, Beaufort District, South Carolina.

T. EDWARD BESSELLIEU. Sergeant. Company B, 2 South Carolina Cavalry. Transferred to Beaufort Volunteer Artillery on August 27, 1863. Enlisted Grahamville 1861.

CHECHE (CHICHET OR SOUCHET)

JOANNAH CHECHE

Born: December 24, 1723

Married: Charles Reily on July 10, 1763, in Charleston, South Carolina

Died: ca February 20, 1784.

Children of Charles and Joannah (Cheche) Reily: Charles Reily Probate Court, Charleston, South Carolina, Volume 20, page 339. The Will of Joanna Reyley of Charles Town, S.C. Province of S.C. Mentions Mary Magdalen Flagg, daughter of George Flagg. To sell three slaves after paying debts, etc., one-third to Mary Flagg and two-thirds to nephews, Philip and Lewis Bessellew for the purpose of educating their children. Second best feather bed to Susannah, daughter of Philip Bessellew and the rest of the estate to Mary Magdalen Flagg, daughter of George Flagg. August 21, 1783. Codicil. Sister, Martha Bessellew to receive an equal share of that part of my interest which I have bequeathed unto the children of Philip and Lewis Bessellew, also ten guineas of the same to George Flagg, Jr. to purchase mourning. January 19, 1784. Proved before Charles Lining, Esq. O.C.T.D. February 20, 1784. Recorded in Will Book A (1783-1786), page 280.

Philip A. Besselleu gave George Flagg a receipt dated 26 Feb 1785 for a legacy left his children by Joanna Reily. See Miscellaneous Records LLL, page 65, State Archives, Columbia, South Carolina.

From the Bessellieu Bible:

Joanna Cheche was born Dec. 24, 1723.

Charles Reily and Joanna Reily were married July 10, 1763 in Charles Town.

Charles Reily was born in August 1765.

Charles Reily died September 14, 1782 in the 67th year of his age.

MARTHA CHECHE (CHICHET)

Married: Mark Anthony Bessellieu II on September 8, 1745

Died: After August 13, 1765

Children of Mark Anthony and Martha (Cheche or Chichet) Bessellieu II: Lewis Bessellieu; Mark Anthony Bessellieu III; Mary Bessellieu; Philip Anthony Bessellieu; Susanna Bessellieu.

Martha Besselleu of Charleston, widow, one of the daughters of Jeanne Chicher (Chicker?), late of Charleston, Deceased, relinquished her one-third of her mother's estate to James Henderson, son-in-law of Jeanne Chicher, as he had taken care of Jeanne for the past several years. The estate consisted chiefly of two negro slaves named George and Jack, the children of a negro slave named Hannah, which slaves had been given the deceased by Martha Marthant, widow. Dated August 13, 1765, and recorded June 5, 1769. Volume 91-A, pages 114-115, Miscellaneous Records, Probate Court, Charleston County, South Carolina.

MARY CHECHE

Born: 1727

Married: James Henderson. (Mrs. Waveland S. FitzSimons of Charleston found information typed on a sheet of paper and inserted into a copy of FLAGG FAMILY RECORDS (1907) written by Norman Gershom Flagg and C. S. Flagg which indicates that James Henderson was the son of John and Rachel Henderson of Scotland)

Died: August 17, 1780

Children of James and Mary (Cheche) Henderson: Mary Magdalene Henderson.

Graves in the Churchyard of the French Protestant (Huguenot) Church, Charleston, South Carolina:

James Henderson died 19 April 1773, aged 61.

Mary Henderson, wife of James Henderson, died 17 August 1780, aged 53.

See Transactions of the South Carolina Huguenot Society No. 57, page 41.

Probate Court, Charleston, South Carolina, Book 15, page 485

Will of James Henderson of Charles Town, S.C. mentions wife, Mary and son-in-law, George Flagg of Charles Town, Painter. April 3, 1773. Executor, George Flagg. Witnesses: Wm. Darby, E. Brenau, Wm. Print. Proved by virtue of a Dedimus from Hon. Wm. Bull, Esq. Lt. Gov. to Wm. Nisbet, Esq. 30 April 1773.

Two Henderson births found in the Bessellieu Bible: "On February 23, 1748/9 was born Jean Henderson, son of Samuel and Jane Henderson" and "Joanna Henderson was born August 14, 1751

MARY MAGDALENE HENDERSON

Born: 1752

Married: George Flagg in 1770

Died: Friday, June 30, 1775

Children of George and Mary Magdalene (Henderson) Flagg: George Flagg, Jr.; Mary Magdalene Flagg.

Volume 83 of the D.A.R. Lineage Book, page 280, shows George Flagg was born in 1741 in Boston, Masachusetts, and died in 1824 in Charleston, South Carolina. He was a member of the Sons of Liberty of Charleston and the last survivor of that body. In 1780 George

Flagg was sent by the British to St. Augustine, Florida, where he was confined as a prisoner of war for nearly a year.

Richard Walsh in his CHARLESTON'S SONS OF LIBERTY, 1763-1789, (1959), University of South Carolina Press, notes on page 12 that George Flagg and Benjamin Hawes taught drawing to the youth of Charleston for many years, on page 18 that George Flagg and Benjamin Hawes bought a 15 ton vessel in 1763 and entered the coastal and West Indian trade, on page 30 that George Flagg, the artist, was a leader of the American Revolutionists as a member of the Fellowship Society, on page 31 that George Flagg opposed the Stamp Act and the Declaratory Act, on page 65 that George Flagg was a member of the Provincial Congress in 1776, and on page 117 that George Flagg was elected to the City Council of Charleston in 1783.

In D. E. Huger Smith and A. S. Salley, Jr., *Register of St. Philip's Parish, Charleston, 1754-1810,* (1927), page 194, is the entry that on the 14th July, 1770, George Flagg and Mary Magdalene Anderson, Spinster, were married per License. The Index to the book shows Henderson, Mary Magdalene, married George Flagg, 194, (Anderson).

GEORGE FLAGG, JR.

Born: June, 1772

Married: Mary Dickerson (1774-1809) in 1795. She was of Santee, South Carolina

Died: June 11, 1812

Children of George and Mary (Dickerson) Flagg, Junior: Caroline Flagg, married a Mr. Trescott; Anna Matilda Flagg; Georgiana Belle Flagg; Eugenia Flagg.

ANNA MATILDA FLAGG

Born: 1801

Married: Charles Harris West in 1825. Mr. West was born in 1796 and died in 1876.

Died: 1876

Children of Charles Harris and Anna Matilda (Flagg) West: Charles Harris West, Junior; Eugene Webster West.

CHARLES HARRIS WEST, JUNIOR

Born: 1831

Married: Serena E. Cobia (1833-1873) in 1851

Died: 1880

Children of Charles Harris and Serena E. (Cobia) West, Junior: Rosa West.

ROSA WEST

Born: 1865

Married: G. L. Bailey in 1886

Children of G. L. and Rosa (West) Bailey: Serena Cobia Bailey.

EUGENE WEBSTER WEST

Married: Rosa Magdalene Cobia

Children of Eugene Webster and Rosa Magdalene (Cobia) West: Anna Emily West.

GEORGIANA BELLE FLAGG

Born: May 28, 1803

Married: Doctor St. John Phillips (1797-1879).

Died: March 8, 1868

Children of Dr. St. John and Georgiana Belle (Flagg) Phillips: Eliza Mary Phillips; Eugenia Gordon Phillips; Julia Caroline Phillips; Anna Richardson Phillips.

JULIA CAROLINE PHILLIPS

Married: Henry W. Kinloch

Children of Henry W. and Julia Caroline (Phillips) Kinloch: St. John Phillips Kinloch; Henry Otis Kinloch; Francis M. Kinloch.

MARY MAGDALEN FLAGG

Born: June 14, 1773, in Charleston, South Carolina

Married: Ray Greene on July 23, 1794, in St. Philip's Episcopal Church, Charleston, South Carolina

Died: July 21, 1817, in East Greenwich, Rhode Island

The Honorable Ray Greene, husband of Mary Magdalen Flagg, was the Attorney-General of Rhode Island at the time of their marriage. He later served as United States Senator from Rhode Island and was appointed to the Federal Judiciary by President John Adams. Mr. Greene's father, William Greene, served as Governor of Rhode Island. His mother, Catharine Ray, was the aunt of Katharine Littlefield, who married the Greene's cousin, Major General Nathaniel Greene, at the William Greene home. Mr. Greene's brother, Samuel, married Mary, daughter of Colonel Joseph Nightingale of Providence. His sister, Phoebe Greene, married Samuel Ward, son of Governor Ward of Rhode Island and his sister Celia Greene married Colonel William Greene, their cousin. Mr. Greene's grandfather, William Greene, Senior, served as Governor of Rhode Island. His wife was his second cousin, Catharine Greene. Mr. Greene's great-grandparents were Captain Samuel and Mary (Gorton) Greene. His great-great-grandfather was Major John Greene, Deputy Governor of Rhode Island, whose father, Surgeon John Greene founded the family in this country. This marriage interests me since it involves the marriage of a member of my mother's father from Charleston, South Carolina, to a member of my father's family, in Rhode Island, 128 years before my parents' marriage at Owendale Plantation in Louisiana.

Children of Senator Ray and Mary Magdalen (Flagg) Greene: George Flagg Greene, born September 20, 1795, died at St. Mary's, Georgia, December 16, 1821, unmarried; Lieutenant Governor William Greene; Catharine Ray Greene; Mary Elizabeth Greene, born February 21, 1804, died young; Isabella Mary Greene.

LIEUTENANT GOVERNOR WILLIAM GREENE

Born: January 1, 1797
Married: 1st: Abigail (Abby) Brackett Lyman, daughter of Erastus Lyman, Esq. of Northampton, Massachusetts, on April 30, 1821. She died July 18, 1862.
2nd: Mrs. Caroline Manchester, widow and daughter of Lemuel Burge, on November 17, 1867, in the Episcopal Church in East Greenwich, Rhode Island.

Children of Lieutenant Governor William and Abigail (Lyman) Greene: Anna Jean Lyman Greene, born April 30, 1827, died July 31, 1831; Catharine Ray Greene.

CATHARINE RAY GREENE

Born: November 20, 1824
Married: Dr. Frederick Christian Roelker on February 1, 1853, in Cincinnati, Ohio

Children of Dr. Frederick Christian and Catharine Ray (Greene) Roelker: William Greene Roelker, born June 12, 1854, married Eleanor Jenckes; Amie L. Roelker, born 1856; Fritz Greene Roelker, born June 14, 1857; Henry Roelker, born July 17, 1858; Catharine Elizabeth Roelker, born January 27, 1860; Emil Hastings Roelker, born November 29, 1861, died June 10, 1864.

CATHARINE RAY GREENE

Born: July 18, 1799
Married: Dr. James Varnum Turner, son of Dr. Peter Turner, on August 27, 1815. Dr. Peter Turner was a Surgeon in the American Revolution. His home built about 1774 in East Greenwich, Rhode Island, is described in the Rhode Island Guide published in 1937 by the Federal Writers Project of the Works Progress Administration. He was a member of the Society of the Cincinnati.
Died: January 16, 1875, in Newport, Rhode Island.

Dr. James Varnum Turner moved to Newport in 1837 and practiced medicine with his brother, Dr. William Turner, Dr. Oliver C. Turner, and his son, Dr. Henry E. Turner.

Children of Dr. James Varnum and Catharine Ray (Greene) Turner: Dr. Henry E. Turner; Mary Flagg Turner, born March 26, 1818, in

East Greenwich; Elizabeth Child Turner, born March 5, 1820, in East Greenwich, lived unmarried in Newport in 1897; Isabella Greene Turner; George Flagg Turner; Peter James Turner; Charles W. Turner; Richard Ray Turner, born November 27, 1831, died 1859, unmarried; William Greene Turner, born October 21, 1833, in Newport, he was a Captain in the Second Rhode Island Volunteers in the War Between the States, he was a sculptor, living in Florence, Italy, he designed the statue of Commodore Perry on the Mall, Washington Square, in Newport; Francis Lincoln Turner, born on December 27, 1835, in Newport, studied medicine in the Albany Medical College, married Catharine Munro, daughter of George C. and Elizabeth S. (Melville) Munro, in Newport on March 29, 1864, died without issue; Catharine Ray Turner, born on April 18, 1837, in Newport, unmarried.

ISABELLA GREENE TURNER

Born: May 25, 1822, Warwick, Rhode Island
Married: Francis Lawton, the son of the Honorable Edward and Mary (Engs) Lawton of Newport.
Children of Francis and Isabella Greene (Turner) Lawton: Catharine Greene Lawton, born July 8, 1845, married Alfred Roelker, merchant of New York; Francis Lawton, born June 28, 1848, lawyer in New York; Mary Engs Lawton, born May 14, 1850, married David Fales, lawyer in Chicago; Henry B. Lawton, born February 24, 1852.

GEORGE FLAGG TURNER

Born: March 26, 1824
Married: Caroline Amelia Stevens, daughter of Joseph E. and Sarah D. Stevens of Newport, on September 4, 1861
Died: October 6, 1864, as a Second Lieutenant, 5th Rhode Island Volunteers, at Newbern, North Carolina.
Children of George Flagg and Caroline Amelia (Stevens) Turner: Lillias Eliza Turner, born April 14, 1863, and died August 4, 1863.

DOCTOR HENRY E. TURNER

Born: June 15, 1816, Warwick, Rhode Island
Married: Ann Eliza Stevens, daughter of Joseph E. and Sarah D. Stevens of Newport, on July 18, 1844
Died: 1897 in Newport
Dr. Henry E. Turner was a graduate of the University of Pennsylvania in 1836. He served as a member of the Rhode Island General Assembly in 1847-8 and as President of the State Board of Health in 1880. Dr. Turner served as Vice President of the Rhode Island Society of the Cincinnati, membership in which is based on descent from an officer of the American Revolution and passes only to the eldest son. Dr. Turner served as President of the Redwood Library

in Newport. This library was founded in 1747 by Abraham Redwood who married a Coggeshall and is buried in the Coggeshall Cemetery located on the corner of Victoria and Coggeshall Streets in Newport. It is still housed in the original building and is the oldest library still so housed, in this country. Dr. Turner also served as President of the Newport Historical Society.

Children of Doctor Henry E. and Ann Eliza (Stevens) Turner: Sarah Catharine Turner, born May 6, 1845, died Feb. 20, 1865; Anna Stevens Turner, born September 30, 1846; Joseph Lincoln Turner, born October 1, 1848, died Sept. 6, 1873; Henry Edward Turner, Jr., born August 17, 1851; James Varnum Turner, born Feb. 22, 1853, died March 4, 1853; Thomas P. Turner, born February 11, 1856.

PETER JAMES TURNER

Born: April 20, 1826.

Married: 1st: Marianna B. Baylies, daughter of Dr. Hersey Baylies of Astoria, New York, on August 11, 1851, she died on June 27, 1854.

2nd: Eliza Wells Baylies, sister of Marianna B. Baylies.

Children of Peter James and Marianna B. (Baylies) Turner: William Bradford Turner, born August 4, 1852.

CHARLES W. TURNER

Born: June 12, 1828, Portsmouth, Rhode Island.

Married: Anna Mary Coffin on June 1, 1861

Children of Charles W. and Anna Mary (Coffin) Turner: Elizabeth Turner, born February 9, 1863; James Varnum Turner, born June 9, 1864; Isabella Greene Turner, born November 30, 1866; Mary Luce Turner, born October 10, 1868; Catharine Ray Turner; Ruth Carter Turner; Francis Turner.

ISABELLA MARY GREENE

Born: February 22, 1805

Married: Joseph Sherbourne Jenckes on May 16, 1833

Died: August 1, 1863 in Terre Haute, Indiana.

Mr. Jenckes prepared for college at the Greenwich and Exeter Academies. In 1824 he graduated from Brown University, of which his grandfather, Joseph, had been a trustee. Mr. Jenckes served as a Judge in Indiana.

Children of Joseph Sherbourne and Isabella Mary (Greene) Jenckes: Joseph S. Jenckes, Jr., born April 4, 1834, married Mary E. Laight, daughter of Daniel B. and Mary (Bull) Laight of Louisville, Kentucky, on May 6, 1860, no children; William Greene Jenckes; George Flagg Jenckes, born November 22, 1843, lumber dealer; Ray Greene Jenckes.

WILLIAM GREENE JENCKES

Born: January 7, 1836

Married: Mrs. Mary Linder (nee Kimball) on July 6, 1874.

William Greene Jenckes received an M.A. from the University of Wisconsin and an LL.B. from Cincinnati Law School.

Children of William Greene and Mary (Kimball) Jenckes: Belle Jenckes, born May 3, 1875, in London, England, died May 7, 1887, Indianapolis, Indiana; Mary Jenckes, born July 4 and died July 20, 1876, Davenport, Iowa; Joseph S. Jenckes, born 1877; George Flagg Jenckes, born 1878; Ray Greene Jenckes, born 1881.

RAY GREENE JENCKES

Born: July 4, 1847.

Married: 1st: (?) Miller.

        2nd: Grace Floyd on August 14, 1874.

Daughter of Ray Greene and Grace (Floyd) Jenckes: Grace Louise Jenckes, born June 9, 1878

In Volume VI, April, 1947, No. 2 issue of "Rhode Island History" published by the Rhode Island Historical Society, there is an interesting letter to James Varnum Turner from Miss Elizabeth Turner of Newport dated September 11, 1869. The letter is printed on pages 74 to 82. Miss Turner notes that all the children of Governor William Greene and Catharine Ray were "remarkably handsome" except Mrs. Ward. Among the notable weddings held at Governor Greene's home were those of Major General Nathaniel Greene, a cousin of the Greenes, to the niece of Catharine Ray Greene and the wedding of Dr. Benjamin Franklin's niece to Dr. Elihu Greene, a cousin.

Miss Turner notes that Ray Greene, "your great-grandfather married Mary Magdallin Flagg, daughter of George Flagg of Charleston, South Carolina. His wife was Mary M. Henderson, granddaughter of Philip and Martha Souchet, Huguenots who took refuge in this country at the time of the Revocation of the Edict of Nantes which protected them."

In speaking of the visits of Dr. Benjamin Franklin to the Governor Greenes, Miss Turner writes, "He loved to sit at the window of the old west parlor overlooking the beautiful valley. Last summer I had the pleasure of seeing Mrs. H(arriet) B(eecher) Stowe (authoress of *Uncle Tom's Cabin*) seated there. She and her sister were calling at Uncle's."

Miss Turner writes of the children of Ray Greene and Mary Magdallin Flagg, "Grandpapa Greene had four children: George Flagg, William, Catharine Ray, and Isabella Mary who was the mother of the Jenckes family. Their mother said their dispositions were like the ingredients of a bowl of punch. Uncle George was the milk, Uncle

William the spirit, Mother the sugar, and Auntie, the lemon. How ever that might have been, we loved Auntie dearly and I never saw that she was very sharp. Uncle George was a very pious young man and well prepared for the sudden death which awaited him. He was drowned in the St. Mary's River. Your Uncle Henry brought his remains home many years after and they are buried in the old burying ground on the hill. Uncle William became a lawyer in Cincinnati, married Miss Lyman of Northampton and had two little girls, but in 1831 he brought his family East for the summer and in passing through Providence, the carriage door was not properly fastened and the youngest, Anne Jean, was thrown out and died in a few hours. I was a little girl then but shall never forget the shock and Aunt Abby's inconsolable grief. She was only thirty, but her hair became perfectly white almost immediately. The elder child, Catharine Ray, grew up, married Dr. Frederick Roelker and died last year with her youngest child, Emil, of scarlet fever. She left five children: Willie, Annie, Fritz, Harry and Kate Roelker. Aunt Abby had died the year before. Also Aunt Isabella Jenckes. Uncle came two years since to make the old farm his permanent home. My mother was well described as sugar, for except for your cousin, Sadie, I never saw anyone who approached her in gentleness, sweetness and quiet dignity. Not deficient in pride either, or in spirit — In school, the teacher, Aunt Mumford, wished her to ask her Father to send her a bushel of meal. She spoke up indignantly, though a very little girl, "My Papa don't sell meal. My Papa's a gentleman' — Grandpapa Greene had indeed no fancy for farming having been educated in a very different way. (He was taken to the Academy in Philadelphia by Benjamin Franklin.) Being quite a boy during the Revolution, he was invited on board the French Fleet while in Narragansett Bay to become familiar with the language and lived for some time on board with the officers. He afterwards graduated at Yale College and became a lawyer under the instruction of Uncle Varnum from whom your name descends (James Mitchell Varnum, First Colonel of the Kentish Guards, later Brigadier General in the Continental Army and Judge for the Northwest Territory. General Varnum's home, built in 1773, still stands in East Greenwich, Rhode Island. Guests in the old home included George Washington, the Marquis de Lafayette, and Tom Paine). He (Ray Greene) was Attorney General of Rhode Island from 1794 to 1798 when he was elected Senator to Congress, being then in his 34th year. In 1801 he was appointed by President Adams and Senate, District Judge of the Rhode Island District, but when Jefferson came in, he sent him a Commission either intentionally or accidentally which had some fatal irregularity in it. The mortification and disappointment were too much for him after having resigned his seat in Congress in the certainty of the new appointment and his mind gave way and never recovered its healthy tone, though he lived many years. I remember him even in his childishness as a magnificent old man with courtly manners and address. He, too, loved to sit at that beautiful west window, and I remember his soft white curls playing in the breeze as he sat there. We always found him a sympathizing friend ready to take our part when scolded. I remember that on one occasion Mary said, 'Oh, Grandpa, it's only because you like us.' His wife, Mary Flagg, was educated at Bethlehem and played delightfully on the piano; also excelled in painting, embroidery and the modern languages and various accomplishments of the day. None of us remember her at all, but Mother loved to dwell upon her charms, so we feel quite acquainted with her."

Mr. Carl Van Doren in his BENJAMIN FRANKLIN (Viking Press, New York, 1938) writes of the friendship of Catharine Ray Greene and Benjamin Franklin in these terms, "Though Franklin and Catharine Greene met so seldom their devoted friendship never grew less and they exchanged from time to time for more than thirty years letters which are as delightful as any in the language. Long lapses made no difference to them nor the long distances between them. Her sister's husband, Samuel Ward, was three times Governor of the Province and after independence her own husband was for eight years Governor of the State. But she seldom mentioned public affairs any more than Franklin did. They wrote about their families and casually about themselves — the two selves that had met and loved each other and needed nothing else to keep their affection perfectly alive. One of his letters, she said, "gave me great pleasure, as it gave me fresh proof of your own dear self.' She called him in that formal age "my dearly beloved friend," sent him "as much love as you wish" and signed herself "your friend that loves you dearly." After many years she told him, "I impute great part of the happiness of my life to the pleasing lessons you gave me in that journey." Franklin, at eighty-three, wrote her, "Among the felicities of my life I reckon your friendship, which I shall remember with pleasure as long as that life lasts."

In her delightful book, THIS WAS MY NEWPORT, (1944), University Press, Cambridge, Massachusetts, Maud Howe Elliot, daughter of Julia Ward Howe, gives an interesting description of the Turners and Greenes. Julia Ward Howe was the author of the "Battle Hymn of the Republic." Her brother, Samuel Ward, banker and author, married Emily Astor, daughter of William B. Astor. Their first cousin, Ward McAllister, drew up New York Society's famed List of the 400. Their grandfather was Colonel Samuel Ward who married Phebe Greene, the daughter of Governor William Greene and Catharine Ray, and the sister of United States Senator Ray

Greene who married Mary Magdalen Flagg of Charleston. These Wards descend from Surgeon John Green not only through Phebe (Greene) Ward, but also through her husband, Colonel Samuel Ward. His mother, Anna (Ray) Ward was the daughter of Deborah (Greene) Ray, the granddaughter of Job Greene, the great-granddaughter of Deputy Governor John Greene and the great-great granddaughter of Surgeon John Greene.

On pages 75 and 76 of her book, Maud Howe Elliot writes, "Dr. Henry Turner, Mother's cousin, lived at the corner of Touro and School Streets. His house adjoined the office and here I spent many happy hours—for the Turners welcomed my mother when she came to town for the day and needed a place to park the children. Cousin Kate Turner gave music lessons to generations of Newporters. I found Dr. Turner a rather frightening personage, with his prim old-fashioned dress and formal manners. He wore a high white neckcloth, carried a cane with a yellowish ivory knob — and I faintly remember him in evening dress with a frilled shirt and dark blue broadcloth coat with brass buttons. Dr. Peter Turner had been Perry's Surgeon at the Battle of Lake Erie and had lived in this same gambrel-roofed house. The Turners owned many beautiful pieces of furniture, family heirlooms — a unique dining room table remembered best of all and a Malbone miniature of General Nathaniel Greene in a scarlet coat. Dr. Turner was interested in genealogy. He and mother talked endlessly about the family history. This I considered to be a sign of second childhood. How could anybody be interested in knowing what Greene married what Ward; where the Tillinghast strain came in and the ramifications of the Simon Ray family of Block Island? Here I am today, browsing about old letters, trying to dig up these same old stories. The Wards and Greenes were closely related and as Mother kept open house to kinsfolk of every degree, they were frequent visitors. We made many trips to East Greenwich on the mainland, where we were entertained at the house of Lieutenant Governor William Greene."

Dr. D. H. Greene in his HISTORY OF EAST GREENWICH, RHODE ISLAND, (1877) J. A. and R. A. Reed of Providence, Printers, gives this glimpse of Mary Magdalen (Flagg) Greene on page 56, "Music was then a rare accomplishment, though two pianos were owned in this village previous to the year 1800 — one belonging to Mrs. Ray Greene, mother of the present (Lieutenant) Governor William Greene and the other to Mrs. Anne Greene, widow of Nathaniel, son of General Greene."

Dr. Greene notes on page 202 that Senator Ray Greene in 1802 drew the Charter for Kent Academy and that Dr. Peter Turner and Elihu Greene were among the incorporators.

On pages 161-163, Dr. Greene describes Dr. Peter Turner, the son of William Turner of Newark, New Jersey and the grandson of Captain William Turner of Newport, as short, rather stout, very erect and active in his movements, sociable and fond of conversation. "The first syringa, the first white lilac and the first crown imperial ever seen in East Greenwich were in Dr. Turner's famous garden. Their love of flowers was characteristic of every member of Dr. Turner's family and has descended and remained with them to this day." Dr. Turner was buried with Masonic Honors in East Greenwich, but his remains were removed to Newport in the family burying ground of his descendants.

JOHNSON

JASON URIAH HENRY JOHNSON

Born: January 17, 1834, in Madison County, Mississippi

Married: Lourana Smith Neal Tidwell on November 1, 1854, in Hinds County, Mississippi

Died: December 19, 1898, in Chicot County, Arkansas

Children of Jason Uriah Henry and Lourana Smith Neal (Tidwell) Johnson:

> Hattie Ruth Johnson
> Jason Uriah Johnson
> Loucinda Elizabeth Johnson
> Louisa Ann Johnson Born November 25, 1856. Died 1858
> Lourana Eldora Johnson
> Margaret Johnson
>
> Robert F. Johnson Born November 25, 1872 Died August 29, 1883
>
> Thomas B. Johnson Born May 23, 1880 Died April 22, 1882

Jason U. Johnson married *Lurena* S. Tidwell on November 1, 1854. J. J. Bennett was the bondsman. See Book 3, pages 425 and 426, Hinds County, Mississippi, at Raymond. The license was issued October 31, 1854.

1850 CENSUS, MADISON COUNTY, MISSISSIPPI 414, 424

Mary Bennett born in 1799 in South Carolina

John J. Bennett born in 1828 in Mississippi

Susan Bennett born in 1832 in Alabama

William Bennett born in 1830 in Mississippi

Alexander Bennett born in 1833 in Mississippi

Julia Bennett born in 1838 in Mississippi

Jason Johnson born in 1836

1860 CENSUS, BAYOU MASON TOWNSHIP, CHICOT COUNTY, ARKANSAS
191, 191

Jacon U. Johnson born in 1835 in Mississippi
Lamania Johnson born in 1839 in Mississippi
Margaret A. Johnson born in 1859 in Arkansas

1870 CENSUS, BAYOU MACON TOWNSHIP, CHICOT COUNTY, ARKANSAS
12, 15

J. U. Johnson born in 1835 in Mississippi (male)
L. R. Johnson born in 1838 in Mississippi (female)
M. A. Johnson born in 1860 in Arkansas (female)
L. E. Johnson born in 1861 in Arkansas (female)
J. U. Johnson born in 1866 in Arkansas (male)
L. R. Johnson born in 1868 in Arkansas (female)
T. Hernden born in 1856 in Arkansas (male)

1880 CENSUS, BAYOU MASON TOWNSHIP, CHICOT COUNTY, ARKANSAS
184, 186

Jason Johnson born in 1835 in Mississippi
Lourania Johnson born in 1839 in Mississippi
Jason Johnson born in 1869 in Arkansas
Loucinda Johnson born in 1863 in Arkansas
Lula Johnson born in 1870 in Arkansas
Robert Johnson born in 1872 in Arkansas
Ruth Johnson born in 1877 in Arkansas
Baby Son born 1880 in Arkansas
The mother of Jason Johnson Senior was born in Mississippi

FROM THE CIRCUIT CLERK'S OFFICE, CHICOT COUNTY, ARKANSAS:

Deed Book K, page 33: 16 June 1860: Crop mortgage from J. U. Johnson to Scranton Sweet, both of Chicot County, Arkansas.

Deed Book T, page 553. 20 September 1876. Deed of land from Jason U. Johnson, Lourana S. N. Johnson, his wife, and G. G. Tidwell, to A. J. Marshall, all of Chicot County.

Deed Book Pl, page 99. 7 December 1894. Deed respecting property of the Methodist Church at Eula, Arkansas. J. U. Johnson, a trustee

Deed Book S1, page 234. 23 March 1899. J. U. Johnson, Jr., represents the Estate of J. U. Johnson, Sr., Deceased.

Deed Book S1, page 599. 27 June, 1899. Mrs. Lourana S. N. Johnson, Widow, of Chicot County, Arkansas, grants the plantation where she lived to Jason U. Johnson of Oak Grove, Louisiana, reserving possession during her lifetime. On her death Jason U. Johnson was to pay money to Andrew Jason Jackson, Rufus Jackson, Mrs. Maggie A. Ralph, Mrs. Bettie Stephenson, and Mrs. Ruth J. Murphy.

Deed Book S1, page 635. 1 November 1899. Andrew Jason Jackson, Rufus Jackson, Mrs. L. S. N. Johnson have all died. Mrs. Bettie

Stephenson, Mrs. Maggie Ralph, and Jason U. Johnson are three of the four surviving children of Jason U. Johnson, Senior, and Mrs. Lourana S. N. Johnson.

Deed Book U1, page 450. 29 January 1901. Mortgage from J. U. Johnson, Jr. and Susie Johnson, his wife to J. B. Jones of Memphis, Tennessee, and Pritchett McCormack and Company of Memphis.

Deed Book B2, page 56. 12 March 1904. Note of A. G. Anderson to J. U. Johnson.

In his *HISTORY OF EUDORA, ARKANSAS*, Mr. E. T. Cashion, Vice President of the Bank of Lake Village, Arkansas, mentions:

1. Jason U. Johnson and Hardy Stephenson as Confederate soldiers.
2. The first residence in Eudora (no longer standing) was the W. H. Stephenson home, built about 1858 by Mr. Scranton Sweet.

HATTIE RUTH JOHNSON

Born: July 27, 1876, in Carmel, Arkansas

Married: 1st: John Cantie Murphy, Senior, who was born in Alabama on July 15, 1851, and died on February 28, 1900, on November 1, 1892.

2nd: Jessie Hardy Cooper I on October 9, 1901, in Vicksburg, Mississippi. Mr. Cooper was born on December 22, 1862, and died November 9, 1914.

Died: December 12, 1909

Children of John Cantie and Hattie Ruth (Johnson) Murphy, Senior:

John Cantie Murphy, Junior. Born on September 18, 1899, in Lake Providence, Louisiana. Died on March 19, 1900

Lula Eldora Murphy. Born in January, 1896 in Lake Providence, Louisiana. Died on August 14, 1897.

Margaret Ruth Murphy. Born on January 20, 1894, on the Walnut Grove Plantation in West Carroll Parish, Louisiana.

Children of Jessie Hardy and Hattie Ruth (Johnson) Cooper I:
Charles Wheeler Cooper, Senior and Jessie Hardy Cooper II

MARGARET RUTH MURPHY

Born: January 20, 1894, on Walnut Grove Plantation in West Carroll Parish, Louisiana

Married: Earnest Newman on September 10, 1919, in Lake Providence, Louisiana. Mr. Newman was born on November 7, 1888 on the Willow Point Plantation in East Carroll Parish, Louisiana. He died on September 9, 1938.

CHARLES WHEELER COOPER, SENIOR

Born: February 28, 1909, in Lake Providence, Louisiana

Married: Faustine Couch on July 10, 1914, in Kerens, Texas

Children of Charles Wheeler and Faustine (Couch) Cooper, Senior:
Charles Wheeler Cooper, Junior. Born April 28, 1940, in Atlanta,
Georgia
Joel Hardy Cooper. Born on March 9, 1945, in Atlanta, Georgia.

JESSIE HARDY COOPER II
Born: August 17, 1902, in Lake Providence, Louisiana
Married: 1st: Robbie Mae Dameron on December 15, 1921, in Jackson, Mississippi
2nd: Eula Matile Neill on April 8, 1928, in Winnfield, Louisiana
3rd: Martha Bell on August 17, 1948, in Baton Rouge, Louisiana
Children of Jessie Hardy and Eula Matile (Neill) Cooper II: Jessie
Hardy Cooper III

JESSIE HARDY COOPER III
Born: February 19, 1933, in South Bend, Indiana
Married: Sara Armstrong on August 18, 1956 in Delhi, Louisiana
Children of Jesse Hardy and Sara (Armstrong) Cooper III: Cynthia
Dianne Cooper. Born August 8, 1957.

JASON URIAH JOHNSON
Born: July 4, 1866, Chicot County, Arkansas
Married: Sue Briggs on March 15, 1893, in Oak Grove, Louisiana
Died: December 27, 1906
Children of Jason Uriah and Sue (Briggs) Johnson: Clifford Uriah
Johnson, Clyde Briggs Johnson, Jason Henry Johnson

CLIFFORD URIAH JOHNSON
Born: November 10, 1897, in Oak Grove, Louisiana
Married: Laura Owen at Owendale Plantation, Bunkie, Louisiana, on
December 21, 1922
Child of Clifford Uriah and Laura (Owen) Johnson: Charles Owen
Johnson
Dr. Clifford U. Johnson, President of the Ouachita Parish Medical
Society and on the medical staff of both the St. Francis and Riverside
Sanitariums, has been prominently identified with the medical profession in Monroe for more than fifteen years, and is generally regarded as a man highly schooled in the science of medicine and surgery. He is a graduate of the Tulane University of Medicine, Class
of 1920, following which he was an interne in the Charity Hospital
at New Orleans, for one and one-half years. While in his junior year
at Tulane he entered the Naval Unit at the College which is attached

to the Algiers Naval Station at New Orleans, and was discharged in 1921. He continued to draw inactive pay from the Naval Reserve for two and one-half years. Upon locating in Monroe he became house physician at St. Frances Sanitarium and held that position for one year. He began the private practice of his profession in Monroe January 1, 1923.

Dr. Johnson was born at Oak Grove, Louisiana, November 10, 1897. His father, Jason U. Johnson, was a farmer and operator of sawmills, cotton gins and various other interests. He was a native of Arkansas. His grandfather was J. U. H. Johnson, a native of Copiah County (Incorrect: Madison County), Mississippi, born January 17, 1834. He died at Eula, Arkansas, December 19, 1898. He was also a farmer and was justice of the peace of Chicot County, Arkansas, for 15 years. He also served as tax Collector in his county for a short while. He was a lifelong Democrat and an active member of the Methodist Church; a Mason, Knight of Pythias and Woodman of the World. His wife, the grandmother of this subject, was Lourana Smith Neal Tidwell, who was born at Meridian, Missisisppi, November 7, 1854 (Incorrect: She was born in Mississippi on December 12, 1838, Madison County).

Dr. Johnson's mother was Susie S. Briggs, daughter of Henry D. Briggs and Sarah Elizabeth Wright Briggs of Oak Grove, Louisiana. She was born March 31, 1878, at Oak Grove, and died December 6, 1926. She was married to Jason U. Johnson at Oak Grove on March 16, 1893, and they were the parents of four sons, one of whom died in infancy. They were Jason H. Johnson with the Monroe Wholesale Hardware Company, Clyde B. Johnson, an attorney of Eudora, Arkansas, and this subject.

In 1899 Dr. Johnson's father moved from Oak Grove to Eudora, Arkansas, where Dr. Johnson attended school up to the third grade. Thereafter the family moved to Monroe and he attended the Ouachita Parish School and graduated from the high school in 1915. He then entered Tulane University to study medicine, completing the course in 1920.

Fraternally he is a member of Chi Zeta Chi and Alpha Omega Alpha, which, locally, was formerly known as the Stars and Bars honorary fraternity. He is a 32nd degree York Rite and Royal Arch Mason, a Knight Templar, member of the American Legion and the Methodist Church.

Dr. Johnson was married December 21, 1922, to Laura Owen who was reared by her uncle, C. W. Owen, an Official of the Southern Pacific Railroad. She is a native of Waco, Texas. They have one son, Owen Johnson, aged 11 years.

The above biography is taken from Volume 2, page 822, of *EASTERN*

LOUISIANA, A HISTORY OF THE WATERSHED OF THE OUACHITA RIVER AND THE FLORIDA PARISHES, edited by Frederick W. Williamson and George T. Goodman.

An out-of-town wedding which will interest many here was that of Miss Laura Owen, daughter of Mr. and Mrs. Charles W. Owen of Bunkie, Louisiana, to Dr. Clifford U. Johnson of Monroe, Louisiana, which was celebrated in Bunkie Thursday, December 21 [1922] at 5:30 o'clock at the home of the bride's parents. The reception rooms of the home were prettily decorated with bride's roses and maiden hair ferns. At one end of the living room was an improvised altar where the ceremony was performed by the Reverend George of Bunkie. The bride was given away by her father and was especially lovely in an afternoon gown of blue satin Canton crepe, with hat to match and carried a shower bouquet of bride's roses. Mendlesohn's wedding march was played by Mrs. Otis Tanner just before the bridal party entered Mrs. Charles Bordelon sang "At Dawning." The only attendant was Mr. Chancey Hall Owen, brother of the bride, who acted as best man to the bridegroom. A reception followed the ceremony. After a short bridal trip Dr. and Mrs. Johnson will be at home to friends in Monroe, Louisiana. Among the out-of-town guests were Mrs. Susie S. Johnson and Mr. Clyde B. Johnson of Monroe, Louisiana, mother and brother of the groom; Mr. and Mrs. Chancey Hall Owen, and Mr. Benjamin S. Atkinson of Texarkana, Texas. (From an unidentified newspaper clipping).

CLYDE BRIGGS JOHNSON

Bohn: April 16, 1901, in Eudora, Arkansas

Married: Neva Johnson of Monroe, Louisiana

Children of Clyde Briggs and Neva (Johnson) Johnson: Clyde Briggs Johnson, Jr.; Marian Kay Johnson; Patricia Sue Johnson — Born August 18, 1930; Neva Ann Johnson — Born August 22, 1926

PATRICIA SUE JOHNSON

Born: August 18, 1930

Married: Walker Leroy Felts on August 19, 1948

Children of Walker Leroy and Patricia Sue (Johnson) Felts: Clyde Steven Felts — Born September 4, 1951; Robert Walker Felts — Born February 14, 1950.

JASON HENRY JOHNSON

Born: November 27, 1895, in Oak Grove, Louisiana

Married: Sarah Margaret Richardson

Children of Jason Henry and Sarah Margaret (Richardson) Johnson: Jason Johnson — Born September 5, 1926; Nancy Briggs Johnson —

Born July 12, 1931; Sarah Sue Johnson — Born December 22, 1927; Thomas Henry Johnson — Born May 13, 1936.

JASON RUFFIN JOHNSON

Born: September 5, 1926

Married: Dorothy Tucker on September 5, 1952

Children of Jason Ruffin and Dorothy (Tucker) Johnson: Barbara Susan Johnson. Born June 26, 1955

SARA SUE JOHNSON

Born: December 22, 1927

Married: John K. Dupuy on October 6, 1950

Children of John K. and Sara Sue (Johnson) Dupuy: Carolyn Ann Dupuy — Born May 1, 1953; Margaret Camille Dupuy — Born November 6, 1954; John Michael Dupuy — Born April 29, 1956.

LOUCINDA ELIZABETH JOHNSON

Born: June 26, 1862

Married: William Hardy Stephenson on January 28, 1883. Mr. Stephenson died on September 7, 1922

Died: August 6, 1930

Children of William Hardy and Loucinda Elizabeth (Johnson) Stephenson:

Gerald Renard Stephenson

Lula Elizabeth Stephenson. Born December 19, 1888. Died on June 9, 1890

Mamie Grace Stephenson

Morton Basil Stephenson

Robert Stephenson

Roderick Eustace Stephenson

William Harold Stephenson

Willye Myrtle Stephenson

1870 Census, Bayou Macon Township Chicot County Arkansas Grand Lake 152, 176

H. F. Stephenson born in 1820 in Georgia (male)
E. Stephenson born in 1846 in Mississippi (female)
S. Stephenson born in 1849 in Alabama (male)
G. Stephenson born in 1852 in Alabama (male)
B. Stephenson born in 1854 in Alabama (male)
W. Stephenson born in 1859 in Arkansas (male)
M. Stephenson born in 1867 in Arkansas (female)
U. Stephenson born in 1870 in Arkansas (male)

1880 Census, Bayou Macon Township Chicot County Arkansas 246, 250

Hardie Stevenson born in 1821 in Georgia
Elizabeth Stephenson born in 1848 in Mississippi
William Stevenson born in 1860 in Arkansas
Laura Stevenson born in 1864 in Arkansas
John Stevenson born in 1870 in Arkansas
Mollie Stevenson born in 1874 in Arkansas
(male) Stevenson born in 1872 in Arkansas
(female) Stevenson born in 1876 in Arkansas
Fannie Stevenson born in 1879 in Arkansas
Parents of Hardie Stevenson were born in South Carolina. Father of William and Laura born in Georgia; mother in Alabama.

GERALD RENARD STEPHENSON

Born: December 5, 1904

Married: Inez Karber on January 6, 1924. Divorced.

Children of Gerald Renard and Inez (Karber) Stephenson: Frances Louise Stephenson

FRANCES LOUISE STEPHENSON

Born: November 13, 1927

Married: Robert Duncan Brown on March 12, 1949

Children of Robert Duncan and Frances Louise (Stephenson) Brown: Robert Duncan Brown, Jr. — Born on February 3, 1951; Francis David Brown — Born June 14, 1953

MAMIE GRACE STEPHENSON

Born: June 29, 1886

Married: Ward William Stevens on June 22, 1909
   Mr. Stevens died on January 6, 1916

Died: March 10, 1956

Children of Ward William and Mamie Grace (Stephenson) Stevens: Bowman Stevens, Ward William Stevens, Myrtle Louise Stevens.

MYRTLE LOUISE STEVENS

Born: January 5, 1912

Married: 1st: Hugh Bowen of Grenada, Mississippi, on August 21, 1926. Divorced.

    2nd: Carl Shipp, Jr., of Wisner, Louisiana, on August 19, 1937

Children of Hugh and Myrtle Louise (Stevens) Bowen: Dr. William Ward Bowen; Myrtle Ann Bowen — Died on birth on June 3, 1931; Jewell Ray Bowen

DOCTOR WILLIAM WARD BOWEN

Born: November 11, 1927

Married: Betsy Ann Green of Monroe, Louisiana, on June 12, 1951

Children of Doctor William Ward and Betsy Ann (Green) Bowen: Charlotte Ann Bowen — Born March 3, 1952; Cynthia Louise Bowen —Born September 29, 1953; William Ward Bowen, Jr. — Born December 17, 1954; Elizabeth Emily Bowen — Born June 3, 1958.

JEWELL RAY BOWEN

Born: January 9, 1934

Married: Priscilla Joan Spooner of Boston, Massachusetts

Children of Jewell Ray and Priscilla Joan (Spooner) Bowen: Jewell Ray Bowen, Jr. Born November 2, 1956

SAMUEL BOWMAN STEVENS

Born: December 26, 1915

Married: Nancy Frazier Booth on July 17, 1937, in All Souls Memorial Episcopal Church in Washington, D.C.

Children of Samuel Bowman and Nancy Frazier (Booth) Stevens: Donna Stevens — Born July 20, 1940; Louise Stevens — Born January 12, 1944; Joyce Ann Stevens — Born September 13, 1950

WARD WILLIAM STEVENS

Married: 1st: Alice Kiser on March 31, 1937. Divorced.
2nd: Juanita Armes on September 20, 1946.

Children of Ward William and Alice (Kiser) Stevens: Ward William Stevens III. Born January 15, 1938. Graduate in Engineering from Rennsalear Polytechnic in Troy, New York. Sandra Louise Stevens. Born March 5, 1941

Children of Ward William and Juanita (Armes) Stevens: Mona Lynn Stevens — Born November 6, 1947; Janis Carrol Stevens — Born January 9, 1951; Shelley Melissa Stevens — Born October 2, 1953.

MORTON BASIL STEPHENSON

Born: December 1, 1899

Married: Eunie Williams on September 8, 1937

ROBERT STEPHENSON

Married: 1st: Jimmie Worthington on June 21, 1907. She died January 10, 1915.
2nd: Pearle Oslin Seale on March 10, 1917

Children of Robert and Jimmie (Worthington) Stephenson: Gladys Stephenson.

GLADYS STEPHENSON

Born: July 23, 1910

Married: Dale Allsbury on December 25, 1938

Children of Dale and Gladys (Stephenson) Allsbury: Robert Dale Allsbury. Born April 16, 1944

RODERICK EUSTACE STEPHENSON

Born: January 14, 1894

Married: Annie Allen in 1916

WILLIAM HAROLD STEPHENSON

Born: October 30, 1896

Married: Frankie Gray Lumpkin on December 21, 1915

Chlidren of William Harold and Frankie Gray (Lumpkin) Stephenson: William Harold Stephenson II, Minnie Elizabeth Stephenson, Frances Jean Stephenson, Walter Lumpkin Stephenson, Gloria Ann Stephenson, Edwin Faust Stephenson.

WILLIAM HAROLD STEPHENSON II

Born: December 4, 1916

Married: 1st: Lucille Marie Goff in 1939

2nd: Carolyn P. Manning in 1942

Children of William Harold and Lucille Marie (Goff) Stephenson: Lucille Marie Stephenson and Alice Joel Stephenson.

Children of William Harold and Carolyn P. (Manning) Stephenson: William Harold Stephenson III — Born March 9, 1943; Sandra Susan Stephenson. Deceased.

LUCILLE MARIE STEPHENSON

Born: December 29, 1939

Married: 1st: Hobart Barret Filer

2nd: Claude Rice in 1959

Children of Hobart Barret and Lucille Marie (Stephenson) Filer: Harold Barrett Filer — Born November 28, 1958.

ALICE JOEL STEPHENSON

Born: November 29, 1941

Married: Frank Hanley O'Donnell on November 10, 1959

Children of Frank Hanley and Alice Joel (Stephenson) O'Donnell: Twins: Barbara Joel O'Donnell. Born May, 1960, and Theresa Alice O'Donnell. Born May, 1960. Deceased.

MINNIE ELIZABETH STEPHENSON

Born: October 9, 1918

Married: 1st: Joseph John Carmody, Sr., in 1944. Died 1950.

2nd: Talmadge (Bill) Leroy Crabtree in 1954

Children of Joseph John and Minnie Elizabeth (Stephenson) Carmody, Sr., Joseph John Carmody, Jr. Born March 6, 1946

Children of Talmadge (Bill) Leroy and Minnie Elizabeth (Stephenson) Crabtree: Jeannie Crabtree — Born May 17, 1955; Tab Crabtree — Born February 10, 1957; Bob Crabtree — Born June 17, 1959.

FRANCES JEAN STEPHENSON

Born: August 14, 1921

Married: James Woodall Durham on August 26, 1939

Children of James Woodall and Frances Jean (Stephenson) Durham:
Jimmie Frances Durham. Born August 26, 1941
William Walter Durham. Born January 10, 1943
Donald Harold Durham. Born August 13, 1952

JIMMIE FRANCES DURHAM

Born: August 26, 1941

Married: Maxwell Pace

Children of Maxwell and Jimmie Frances (Durham) Pace:
Maxwell Pace, Jr. Born September 17, 1959

WALTER LUMPKIN STEPHENSON

Born: May 13, 1924

Married: 1st: Lillie Mae Williams in August, 1942
        2nd: Mary Frances Blalock on November 25, 1948

Children of Walter Lumpkin and Lillie Mae (Williams) Stephenson:
Walter Frank Stephenson. Born May 17, 1946. Died May 21, 1946

Children of Walter Lumpkin and Mary Frances (Blalock) Stephenson: Glenn Alan Stephenson—Born August 12, 1952; Mary Catharine Stephenson—Born June 4, 1954; Judy Ann Stephenson—Born April 17, 1957.

GLORIA ANN STEPHENSON

Born: August 25, 1926

Married: John Leonard Earney on June 1, 1946

Children of John Leonard and Gloria Ann (Stephenson) Earney:
John Stephenson Earney. Born February 16, 1947
David Edwin Earney. Born December 28, 1948
Janice Ann Earney. Born August 21, 1952
Marilyn Gloria Earney. Born December 19, 1953
Floyd Sheldon Earney. Born May 26, 1955
Frank Leonard Earney. Born March 7, 1959

EDWIN FAUST STEPHENSON

Born: March 18, 1930

Married: Geraldine Broodway on May 10, 1952

Children of Edwin Faust and Geraldine (Broodway) Stephenson:

Edwin Faust Stephenson, Jr. Born December 7, 1952
Ronald Lee Stephenson. Born July 18, 1955
Kaley Don Stephenson. Born November 26, 1957

WILLYE MYRTLE STEPHENSON

Born: April 23, 1891

Married: Elbert Thomas Cashion on December 23, 1913

Children of Elbert Thomas and Willye Myrtle (Stephenson) Cashion:
Clotilda Corinne Cashion, Dorothy Lee Cashion, Elbert Thomas
Cashion, Jr., Marlys Ann Cashion.

CLOTILDA CORINNE CASHION

Born: November 30, 1914

Married: Charles Morris on May 7, 1936

Children of Charles and Clothilda Corinne (Cashion) Morris:
Charlotte Corinne Morris. Born June 6, 1942
Dorothy Diane Morris. Born Sepetmber 1, 1939

DOROTHY LEE CASHION

Born: March 22, 1917

Married: Louis East on September 24, 1942

Children of Louis and Dorothy Lee (Cashion) East:
Robert Cashion East. Born June 23, 1947
Thomas Collier East. Born November 20, 1945

ELBERT THOMAS CASHION, JUNIOR

Born: March 19, 1923

Married: Fanchon Hampton

Children of Elbert Thomas and Fanchon (Hampton) Cashion, Jr.
Karen Cashion. Born April 27, 1954
Michael Stuart Cashion. Born May 20, 1947
Paul Thomas Cashion. Born April 10, 1951

MARLYS ANN CASHION

Born: February 14, 1929

Married: Charles Linwood Turnage on July 1, 1944

Children of Charles Linwood and Marlys Ann (Cashion) Turnage:
Betty Carol Turnage. Born April 5, 1945
Charles Clifton Turnage. Born August 19, 1955

LOURANA JOHNSON

Born: May 28, 1869

Married: Andrew Jackson who was born August 19, 1863, and died
     February 3, 1942 on August 19, 1884

Died: September 8, 1895

Children of Andrew and Lourana (Johnson) Jackson: Andrew Jason Jackson. Born April 18, 1886. Died July 27, 1899

Rufus Jackson. Born February 8, 1890. Died July 28, 1899. All the Jackson family are buried in the Oak Grove, Louisiana, cemetery.

1880 CENSUS, WARD 4, WEST CARROLL PARISH, LOUISIANA 34, 34

A. Jackson born in 1829 in Alabama
Mary A. Jackson born in 1850 in Mississippi
Andrew Jackson Jr. born in 1864 in Louisiana
Julia Jackson born in 1866 in Louisiana
Henry Jackson born in 1868 in Louisiana
Sallie Jackson born in 1870 in Louisiana
Lillia Jackson born in 1876 in Louisiana

MARGARET ANN JOHNSON

Born: October 15, 1859, in Arkansas
Married: Ben M. Ralph on March 8, 1876
Died: June 10, 1937

1880 CENSUS, BAYOU MACON TOWNSHIP, CHICOT COUNTY, ARKANSAS 80, 82

Benjamin Ralph born in 1854 in Arkansas
Maggie Ralph born in 1860 in Arkansas
The parents of Benjamin were listed as born in Tennessee
and the parents of Maggie Ralph were born in Mississippi.
See record of Jason Uriah Henry Johnson.

1850 CENSUS, PLANTERS TOWNSHIP, CHICOT COUNTY, ARKANSAS 30, 30

James H. Ralph born in 1815 in Tennessee
Sarah Ralph born in 1817 in North Carolina
Duncan G. Ralph born in 1843 in Arkansas
Robert H. Ralph born in 1849 in Arkansas

1860 CENSUS, MASONA TOWNSHIP, CHICOT COUNTY, ARKANSAS 73, 73

James H. Ralph born in 1820 in Tennessee
Sarah Ralph born in 1823 in North Carolina
Robert H. Ralph born in 1849 in Arkansas
James A. Ralph born in 1851 in Arkansas.
Benjamin M. Ralph born in 1854 in Arkansas
John W. Ralph born in 1857 in Arkansas
Charles S. Ralph born in 1860 in Arkansas

1870 CENSUS, MASONS TOWNSHIP, CHICOT COUNTY, ARKANSAS 24, 24

James H. Ralph born in 1820 in Tennessee
Sarah Ralph born in 1823 in North Carolina
James A. Ralph born in 1851 in Arkansas

Benjamin Ralph born in 1854 in Arkansas
John W. Ralph born in 1858 in Arkansas
Charles Ralph born in 1860 in Arkansas
Richard Ralph born in 1864 in Arkansas

1880 BAYOU MACON TOWNSHIP, CHICOT COUNTY, ARKANSAS 8, 9

Sarah Ralph born in 1825 in North Carolina. Her parents were born in North Carolina.

Margaret Ann Johnson born October 15, 1859 married Ben M. Ralph on March 8, 1876. See Johnson Bible owned by Mrs. Margaret Newman of Lake Providence, Louisiana.

TIDWELL

FRANCIS TIDWELL

Born: ca 1780

Married: Rebecca (?)

Died: 1840 in Madison County, Mississippi

Children of Francis and Rebecca (?) Tidwell:

Charlotte Tidwell, David F. Tidwell, Edna Ann Tidwell, Gibeon Gibson Tidwell, Richard Tidwell, Tennessee Tidwell

No will or other paper listing all of the children of Francis Tidwell has been found. The above listing of his children is likely incomplete and the proof for it (given hereafter) is necessarily indirect.

Mrs. Ettie (Tidwell) McCall in her *McCALL, TIDWELL AND ALLIED FAMILIES* (1931), Atlanta, Georgia, notes that three Tidwell brothers, John, Richard, and Robert came to Westmoreland County, Virginia, in the late 1600's. They were devout members of the Church of England and strong adherents of the King. John Tidwell is described as "a man of large wealth and influence in Virginia." (*Virginia Magazine of History and Biography*, Volume 10, pages 96 and 97).

By 1790 those with the surname Tidwell had moved to other states. There is yet, however, a town named Tidwell in Westmoreland County and Tidwell descendants still reside in the Old Dominion. They are descendants of Colonel Reuben Lindsay of Albermarle County and his wife, Hannah Tidwell, through their daughters, Elizabeth Lindsay, wife of Major General William Fitzhugh Gordon and Maria Lindsay, wife of Captain Meriweather Lewis Walker.

I have searched census records from 1790 through 1860 in all all the Southern States, as well as the Confederate Military Records.

The Tidwells lived throughout all the South and are all likely descendants of the three original Tidwell brothers.

1820 CENSUS, JEFFERSON COUNTY, MISSISSIPPI
Francis Tidwell
1 male born 1775-1794
2 males born 1804-1810
4 males born 1810-1820
1 female born 1775-1794
4 slaves

1830 CENSUS, JEFFERSON COUNTY, MISSISSIPPI
Francis Tidwell
1 male born 1780-1790
2 males born 1800-1810
1 male born 1810-1815
1 male born 1815-1820
2 males born 1820-1825
1 male born 1825-1830
1 female born 1780-1790
1 female born 1820-1825
22 slaves

1840 CENSUS, MADISON COUNTY, MISSISSIPPI
Francis Tidwell
1 male born 1770-1780
1 male born 1810-1820
1 male born 1820-1825
1 female born 1780-1790
1 female born 1825-1830

In 1802, the mark and brand of Francis Tidwell was described in Book B, page 229, Adams County, Mississippi.

In 1805, John Bullin and wife sold property to Francis Tidwell. See Book D, page 253, Adams County, Mississippi.

Francis Tidwell and wife, Rebecca, deeded land to Nathaniel Harrison on May 14, 1827. See Deed Book B, page 98, Jefferson County, Mississippi.

PETITION TO CONGRESS BY CITIZENS OF THE TERRITORY

August 25, 1802

To the Honorable the Senate and House of Representatives of the United States in Congress Assembled:

We the Undersigned, Citizens of the Mississippi Territory, pray your honorable Body that the Land Office to be opened for this country may be held within the Bounds of the same, and that the actual Settlers on the vacant lands of the United States may have a preemption right secured to them —

We further pray for the following alterations in the Ordinance of 1787 (To Wit) that the right of Suffrage may be extended to every male person of full age, being a Citizen of the United States, and who has had his residence within the Territory for the last six months preceding the election.

That all officers of the Territorial Government shall be appointed by the Governor of the Territory, by and with the advice and consent of the Council.

That the Office of Territorial Judge be abolished: and that the appointment of all our Judicial Officers shall be made by the Governor by and with the advice and consent of the Council: and that they shall be removable only by impeachment.

That the members of the Legislative Council shall henceforth be chosen at the same time, in the same manner and for the same term as the Members of the House of Representatives of the Territory.

These proposed alterations in the Ordinance would remove some needless and inconvenient encroachments on our rights as American Citizens — they are suited to our local situation, far distant from our parent Government, and would obviate many serious evils under which we now labor. We on our part therefore pray for these alterations and we trust to the justice and goodness of the Government of the United States, for a compliance on their part.

Francis Tidwell a signer of the above Petition. See pages 159-160 and 168 of Clarence Edwin Carter's *Territorial Papers of the United States*, Volume 5, Territory of Mississippi 1798-1817. U.S. GPO Washington 1937.

FRANCIS TIDWELL joined upwards of 200 of the "most respectable characters" of the Mississippi Territory in signing a testimonial to the character of Colonel John Steele, who was appointed Secretary for the Government of the Mississippi Territory in 1798. Colonel Steele was Acting Governor of the Mississippi Territory following the Departure of Governor Winthrop Sargent for Boston, Massachusetts, on April 3, 1801, and until the arrival of his successor, Governor William Charles Cole Claiborne, on November 23, 1801. According to an affiant, Stephen Bullock, "None who stand high in this country, I believe, have refused their signatures except Colonel Cato West, Colonel Green and the Governor, the last two of whom, admitted the truth of every thing stated in the paper, but apprehended that the object of it (in case Colonel Steele shall not be reappointed) was to injure Mr. Jefferson (the then President of the United States) and, therefore, wished to decline giving it their signature." The Testimonial was used in connection with the Petition of Colonel Steele for his salary as Secretary and Acting Governor of the Mississippi Territory.

See Clarence Edwin Carter's *Territorial Papers of the United States*, Territory of Mississippi 1798-1817, Volume 5, pages 241 et seq., 249. Printed in Washington in 1937 by the GPO.

1841. Francis Tidwell deceased. His son-in-law, Thomas J. Smith, an attorney, took out letters of administration to test the validity of land sales to a Mr. Hill. Richard Tidwell joined in those sales. Cause No. 654, Madison County, Mississippi Minute Book A, page 715. March 12, 1844.

Thos. J. Smith of Madison County, Admr Est of Francis Tidwell dec'd vs. H. R. Hill, James Dick, and William J. McLean, 1845. Drawer 94, Case No. 3425 Madison County, Mississippi. *MISSISSIPPI COURT RECORDS 1799-1859 FILES OF HIGH COURT OF ERRORS AND APPEALS* by Mary Louise Flowers Hendrix, 408 Dunbar Street, Jackson, Mississippi.

TAX ROLLS:

ADAMS COUNTY, MISSISSIPPI

1805 Francis Tidwell, living in or near the Town of Washington (near Natchez), 2 polls, 5 slaves
1807 Francis Tidwell, Land on St. Catherine's Creek, 1 poll
1808 through 1810 Francis Tidwell, 1 poll

JEFFERSON COUNTY, MISSISSIPPI

1811 Francis Tidwell 1 poll
1815 Francis Tidwell 1 poll
1817 Francis Tidwell Land on "D" Creek; 1 poll
1818 Francis Tidwell Land on Cole's Creek; 1 poll
1819 through 1825 Francis Tidwell, 1 poll
1825 through 1828 Francis Tidwell, 9 slaves. No poll.
1829 through 1831 Francis Tidwell 11 slaves. No poll.

CLAIBORNE COUNTY, MISSISSIPPI

1828 Francis Tidwell Land on James Creek. Same in 1829 and 1830. No poll in any year.

MADISON COUNTY, MISSISSIPPI

1833 Francis Tidwell 8 slaves. No poll.
1834 Francis Tidwell 27 slaves. No poll.
1835 Francis Tidwell 34 slaves. No poll.
1836 Francis Tidwell 41 slaves. 1 poll.
      Francis Tidwell and Company. 10 slaves.
1837 Francis Tidwell 57 slaves. 1 poll.
1838 F. and R. Tidwell. 57 slaves. 1 poll.

These Tax Rolls are on microfilm in the Department of Archives and

History in Jackson, Mississippi. Where "No poll" is assessed, it means the person is either overage or a resident of another county.

Deed Book B, page 98, Chancery Clerk's Office, Fayette, Jefferson County, Mississippi. 14 May 1827.

FRANCIS TIDWELL AND REBECCA, HIS WIFE, OF JEFFERSON COUNTY, MISSISSIPPI. To Nathaniel Harrison of same. Consideration $1,600. Parcel of land in Jefferson County, part of fractional Section 26 T 10, R 1 E, beginning at a sassafras tree on the N.W. corner of the tract, running from thence N 81 degrees east, following the old Section line, 42 chains, 73 links to a poplar tree, standing on the bank of TIDWELL CREEK, thence down with the meandering of said creek to a gum tree, thence S 54 degrees 30 minutes west, 19 chains, 97 links to a post oak, thence S 50 degrees West, 25 chains, 50 links to a post on the western boundary of said Section 26, thence following the west boundary of said Section, N 9 degrees west, 47 chain to a sassafras the place of beginning, 144.3 acres /s/ FRANCIS X TIDWELL, REBECCA X TIDWELL. Test: Jno. A. Watkins.

1816 CENSUS, JEFFERSON COUNTY, MISSISSIPPI FROM DEPARTMENT OF ARCHIVES AND HISTORY, JACKSON, MISSISSIPPI

FRANCIS TIDWELL

1 male born before 1795
3 males born after 1795
1 female born before 1795
2 females born after 1795

Deed Book B, page 472

23 November 1832

Samuel McCalby and Rebecca, his wife, and R. A. Cain of Madison County, Mississippi (Nancy, the wife, of Cain)

To:

FRANCIS TIDWELL, of same

Consideration: $2,500. Land in Madison County, Mississippi. W½ of NW¼, Sec. 9, T8, R3E, SW¼ Sec. 9, T8, R3E; SE¼, Sec. 8, T8, R3E; N½ of E½ of SW¼, Sec. 8, T8, R3E; N½ of W½ of SW¼, Sec. 8, T8, R3E; N½ of E½ of NE¼, Sec. 17, T8, R3E. 520 acres. /s/ Rebecca McCalby, R. A. Cain, Nancy Cain. Ack. by all including Samuel on Feb. 3, 1833

Deed Book C, page 212

12 June 1835   A Bond.

FRANCIS TIDWELL OF MADISON COUNTY, MISSISSIPPI to Owen Royse, John A. Hackett, and RICHARD TIDWELL

Amount of bond is stated in body of document $72,000, but the individual notes total only $36,000; 1 note for $10,000 due Jan. 1, 1836; 1 note for $13,000 due Jan. 1, 1837; 1 note for $13,000 due Jan. 1,

1838 in favor of Hays, Walker and Johnson, dated Madisonville (the old County Seat of Madison County) June 12, 1835, negotiable at Planter's Bank of Mississippi at NATCHEZ. Document signed Francis X Tidwell. Ack. by signer 27 July 1835. Also on p 214 an Agreement signed by Owen Royse, J. A. Hackett and Richard Tidwell (This was in connection with a land deal mentioned next below)

Deed Book C, page 211
Madison County, Miss.
12 June, 1835
Andrew C. Hays, Harvey M. Walker and John B. Johnson
To:
FRANCIS TIDWELL

Consideration: $36,000. 1,231.85 acres of land, certain slaves, live stock, etc. (All the land was in Township 8, Range 3 East). /s/ Hays, Walker, and Johnson per H. M. Walker. Test: E. R. Anderson, Jos. Riddle, Jr., John C. Turner. Ack. by Jos Riddle Jr. 27 Feb. 1835

Deed Book G, page 523
27 February, 1840   Bill of Sale
FRANCIS TIDWELL AND RICHARD TIDWELL OF MADISON COUNTY, MISSISSIPPI
TO
Jesse Cage

Consideration: $17,246.12. For certain slaves. /s/ Francis "T", his mark, TIDWELL, RICHARD TIDWELL. Test: John F. Cook. Ack. by John F. Cook, 2 March, 1840

CHARLOTTE TIDWELL

Married: 1st: John C. Neill on July 20, 1818, in Jefferson County, Mississippi. See Marriage Book "A", page 97.

2nd: Lawrence W. Ludlow on February 1, 1839, in Madison County, Mississippi

Children of John Caraway and Charlotte (Tidwell) Neill:
Charles Culbertson Neill, Tennessee Neill, Aaron L. Neill, Richard T. Neill, David F. Neill, Gibeon G. Neill.

DAVID TIDWELL

David Tidwell married Malinda M. Moore on July 13, 1833, in Madison County, Mississippi. Book E, page 155. Bondsman, William Moore, father of the bride.

Deed Book B, page 292, Chancery Clerk's Office, Madison County, Mississippi
10 June, 1834
DAVID TIDWELL and MALINDA MARTHA TIDWELL, his wife of Madison County, Miss.

TO

William M. Haden of same

79.20 acres in Madison County, E½ of Nw½, Sec. 18, T8, R3E.

/s/ DAVID F. TIDWELL, MALINDA TIDWELL

Ack by signers same date

This land had been secured from the United States, Jan. 14, 1833

Deed Book K, page 304, Chancery Clerk's Office, Madison County, Mississippi

23 Sept 1844   DEED OF GIFT

William Moore of Madison County

TO

MALINDA M. TIDWELL of Madison County.

Consideration: Natural love and affection which he bears his daughter, the said Malinda M. Tidwell: 9 slaves

/s/ W. Moore.

Test: Allen Moore, T. S. NEIL

Ack by THOS. S. NEIL, 10 October 1846

Deed Book M, page 261, Chancery Clerk's Office, Madison County, Mississippi

17 Sept. 1851

James Joyce of Rankin County, Miss.

TO

D. F. TIDWELL of *Hinds* County, Miss.

80 acres in Madison County, E½ of NW¼, Sec. 3, T10 R4E

/s/ James Joyce, Miranda B. Joyce.

Test: Arch Anderson, Nath'l or Watkins Wilkinson

Ack by Arch Anderson in Rankin County 18 Sept 1851 also by Miranda B. Joyce.

Deed Book O, page 83, Chancery Clerk's Office, Madison Co., Miss.

14 Jan 1853 DAVID F. TIDWELL and MALINDA M. TIDWELL, his wife of *Rankin County*, Miss. to S.W. Latham of Madison Co.

80 acres in Madison Co. E½ of NW¼ Sec 3 T10 R4E. /s/ DAVID F. TIDWELL, MALINDA M. TIDWELL. Ack. 19 Jan 1853

Tax Rolls, Madison Co.

1834 David Tidwell 1 poll

1836 David Tidwell 1 poll

EDNA ANN TIDWELL

Born: 1814 in Mississippi

Married: 1st: Fauntley Estes on July 23, 1829 in Jefferson County, Mississippi

         2nd: Thomas Johnson

Children of Fauntley and Edna Ann (Tidwell) Estes:

Emma R. Estes, Fauntley F. Estes, Margaret O. Estes, Sarah F. Estes.
Children of Thomas and Edna Ann (Tidwell) Johnson:
Viola Johnson

1830 CENSUS WARREN COUNTY MISSISSIPPI
Fauntley Estes
2 males born 1800-1810
1 female born 1810-1815
3 slaves

1850 CENSUS MADISON COUNTY MISSISSIPPI 2, 2
Edna Estes born in 1814 in Mississippi
Sarah F. Estes born in 1835 in Mississippi
Margaret O. Estes born in 1838 in Mississippi
Fantly F. Estes born in 1842 in Louisiana
Emma R. Estes born in 1844 in Mississippi
3 slaves

Edney Ann Tidwell married Fauntley Estes on July 23, 1829, in Jefferson County, Mississippi, according to courthouse records.

1860 CENSUS, MADISON COUNTY, MISSISSIPPI 387, 385
Thomas Johnson born in 1812 in Virginia, Planter
Edna A. Johnson born in 1813 in Mississippi
Emma R. Estes born in 1845 in Mississippi
Viola Johnson born in 1852 in Mississippi

GIBEON GIBSON TIDWELL, SENIOR

Married: Elizabeth Caroline Neill (Neal) in Claiborne County, Mississippi, on December 29, 1826
Died: September 19, 1838
Children of Gibeon Gibson and Elizabeth Caroline (Neill or Neal) Tidwell:
Clarissa A. Tidwell. Born May 25, 1829. Died July 20, 1862
Dorothy E. Tidwell. Born October 17, 1831. Married a Mr. Leggitt. Died October 6, 1852
Gibeon Gibson Tidwell, Jr. Born December 31, 1833.
John Caraway Tidwell. Born April 27, 1836. Died June 14, 1837
Louisa A. Tidwell. Born October 31, 1827. Died February 12, 1837.
Lourana Smith Neal Tidwell. Born December 12, 1838.

The dates given above were from an old record sent by Mrs. E. T. Cashion of Lake Village, Arkansas. The record also shows E. C. Tidwell (Elizabeth Caroline) died on July 14, 1862 and S. G. Herndon died on January 1, 1867.

Gibeon G. Tidwell granted a 99 year lease of all of NE¼ Section 24 Range 10 N-1 E by the Trustee of Schools. Francis Tidwell and Richard Tidwell joined in the execution of a bond for payment of the consideration which was secured by a mortgage. Deed Book "B", pages 577 and 597, Jefferson County, Mississippi.

Gibeon G. Tidwell and Elizabeth Tidwell, his wife, quitclaimed the above land to Benjamin F. Jones. October 13, 1832. Deed Book "B", page 620, Jefferson County, Mississippi.

In the January Term, 1835, Gibeon G. Tidwell was appointed Administrator of the Estate of John C. Neal. In 1838 he executed several deeds. On the death of Gibeon G. Tidwell (he was killed by his brother-in-law, Lawrence Ludlow) Richard Tidwell was appointed Administrator of the Estate of Gibeon G. Tidwell. Later Len C. Harris was appointed Administrator de bonis non of the Gibeon G. Tidwell Estate.

File 489, File 660

TAX ROLLS, DEPARTMENT OF ARCHIVES AND HISTORY, JACKSON, MISS. Madison County, Mississippi

1835 Gipson Tidwell, 1 poll, 23 slaves
1836 G. G. Tidwell, 1 poll, 16 slaves
1837 G. G. Tidwell, 1 poll, 23 slaves
1838 G. G. Tidwell, 1 poll, 20 slaves

DEED BOOK C, PAGE 437, CHANCERY CLERK'S OFFICE, MADISON COUNTY, MISSISSIPPI

3 March, 1836

GIBEON G. TIDWELL, Admr. of Estate of John C. Neel, late of Madison County, Miss.

To

George Robinson of same

168 acres in Madison County. NE¼ of Sec. 2, T7, R2E.

/s/ GIBEON G. TIDWELL, Admr of Estate of J. C. Neel

Ack by signer, 14 March, 1836.

DEED BOOK I, PAGE 386, CHANCERY CLERK'S OFFICE, MADISON COUNTY, MISSISSIPPI

28 April, 1846

Thomas Fletcher, U. S. Marshal of Southern District of Mississippi. (Writ of fieri facias, issued at suit of Andrew Conner against GIBEON G. TIDWELL, FRANCIS TIDWELL, RICHARD TIDWELL, and WILLIAM RAINEY

TO

James A. McAlester of Davidson County, Tennessee

1,580 acres in Madison County. W½ Sec. 9; E½ Sec. 8; N¼ of SE¼, Sec. 8 E½ of NE¼ and E½ of SE¼, Sec. 7, SE¼, Sec. 6; E½ Sec. 17; SE¼ Sec. 23, all of T8 R3E.

/s/ Thos Fletcher, Marshal

Ack by signer 11 May, 1846

DEED BOOK G, PAGE 722, CHANCERY CLERK'S OFFICE, MADISON COUNTY, MISSISSIPPI

10 April, 1840   Quit Claim, Release of Dower

ELISABETH C. TIDWELL of Madison County, Miss.
TO William A. Matthews of same.

Release and quit claim all her rights, title of dower to a certain tract of land, belonging to Her husband, now deceased, GIBEON G. TIDWELL, etc. NE¼ Sec. 25, SE¼ and W½ of NE¼ Sec. 24, T8 R2E and W½ of SW¼, Sec. 18 and W½ of NW¼, Sec. 19, T8 R3E
541 acres
/s/ ELIZABETH TIDWELL.
Ack by signer. 18 April 1840

CLARISA A. TIDWELL

Born: May 25, 1829
Married: Obadiah Herndon   May 18, 1847
Died: July 20, 1862

Children of Obadiah and Clarisa (Tidwell) Herndon:
Alzo (?) F. Herndon (male), Cornelia A. Herndon, Lovit Oliver Herndon, Somerfield G. Herndon, Thomas W. Herndon

1860 CENSUS, WARD NO. 5, CARROLL PARISH, LOUISIANA 685, 658

Clarisa A. Herndon born in 1830 in Mississippi
Cornelia A. Herndon born in 1848 in Mississippi
Somerfield G. Herndon born in 1850 in Mississippi
Alzo F. Herndon born in 1853 in Mississippi
Thos W. Herndon born in 1856 in Arkansas
Lovit Oliver Herndon born in 1859 in Louisiana
Elizabeth C. Tidwell born in 1810 in Mississippi
Clarisa A. Herndon is listed as a widow and Elizabeth C. Tidwell as a widow and mother.

Deed J-330 (1858) Sale by Obadiah C. Herndon and his wife, Mrs. Clarissa Ann Tidwell to Mrs. Elizabeth C. Tidwell, widow of Gibeon G. Tidwell. East Carroll Parish, Louisiana.

Deed M-558 (1867) Sale by O. C. Herndon to John T. Ludeling. East Carroll Parish, Louisiana.

1850 CENSUS, CLAIBORNE COUNTY, MISSISSIPPI 366, 364

Obadiah Herndon born in 1816 in Alabama
Clarrisa Herndon born in 1829 in Mississippi
Cornelia Herndon born in 1848 in Mississippi
Summerfield Herndon born in 1850 in Mississippi

1880 CENSUS, WARD 4, WEST CARROLL PARISH, LOUISIANA 12, 12

Thos. Herndon born in 1857 in Arkansas. His father was born in Alabama and his mother was born in Mississippi.

Obadiah Herndon and Clarissa A. Tidwell, May 18, 1847, H. M. Hart, Bondsman. Book F, page 235, Marriage Licenses Madison County, Mississippi. Also page 35 of Robert Chester and Marie Luter Upton MARRIAGE RECORDS OF MADISON COUNTY, MISSISSIPPI. On page 31 O. C. H. Herndon is listed as Bondsman, Washington L. Bell and Mrs. Martha Kirkpatrick, November 18, 1845

CORNELIA A. HERNDON

Born: 1848 in Mississippi

Married: 1st: Andrew J. Marshall

         2nd: George Peterson

Children of Andrew J. Marshall and Cornelia Herndon: Allison Marshall, Margaret Marshall, Marion A. Marshall, Robert Marshall, Thomas Marshall, William Marshall.

Children of George and Cornelia (Herndon) Peterson:
George Peterson — Lived in Oklahoma; Grace Peterson — Lived in St. Joseph, Louisiana.

1870 CENSUS, BAYOU MASON TOWNSHIP, CHICOT COUNTY, ARKANSAS
A. J. Marshall born in 1842 in Georgia (male)
C. A. Marshall born in 1848 in Mississippi (female)
M. A. Marshall born in 1868 in Arkansas (male)
R. Marshall born in 1870 in Arkansas (male)
L. O. Hernden born in 1860 in Louisiana (male)
G. Peterson born in 1842 in Denmark (male)

1880 CENSUS, BAYOU MACON TOWNSHIP, CHICOT COUNTY, ARKANSAS
201, 215
Andrew Marshall born in 1843 in Georgia
Cornelia Marshall born in 1848 in Mississippi
Their Children:
Marion Marshall born in 1868 in Arkansas
Robert Marshall born in 1870 in Arkansas
Willie Marshall born in 1872 in Arkansas
Thomas Marshall born in 1874 in Arkansas
Allison Marshall born in 1876 in Arkansas
Margaret Marshall born in 1879 in Arkansas
The parents of Andrew Marshall were born in South Carolina.
The father of Cornelia Marshall was born in Alabama; her mother, in Mississippi

GIBEON GIBSON TIDWELL, JUNIOR

Born: December 31, 1833

Married: Mary E. McKee, aged 16 years, on 29 November 1855, Chicot County, Arkansas. Book B, page 120, Marriage Licenses.

Children of Gibeon Gibson and Mary E. Tidwell: Dortha Tidwell and John W. Tidwell

Gideon G. Tidwell Pvt Co A 31st La Inf. En Monroe, Louisiana, April 12, 1862. Roll Feb 1 to Mar 1, 1863, Present. Federal Rolls of Prisoners of War, Captured and Paroled at Vicksburg, Mississippi, July 4, 1863. Roll of Prisoners of War CSA Paroled at Monroe, Louisiana, June 12, 1865. Res Carroll Parish, Louisiana.

Gideon G. Tidwell. Pvt Co F 27th La Inf Rolls of Prisoners of War CSA Paroled at Monroe, La., June 12, 1865. Res. Winn Parish, Louisiana.

Booth's *RECORDS OF LOUISIANA CONFEDERATE SOLDIERS*, Volume 3, page 832.

DEED BOOK N, PAGE 360, MADISON COUNTY, MISSISSIPPI.

1 January 1855. Gibeon Tidwell (Junior) of Madison County as one of the heirs of Gibeon G. Tidwell, sold to Willie Lyons, all right title and interest to a tract of land in Madison County: NE¼ Sec. 25, Township 8, Range 2 East; E½ of SE¼, Sec. 24; W½ of NE¼; W½ of SE¼, sec. 24, T8, R2E, 380 acres.

1860 CENSUS WARD NO. 5, CARROLL PARISH, LOUISIANA 684, 657
Gibbe Tidwell born in 1835 in Tennessee
Mary E. Tidwell born in 1841 in Tennessee
Dortha E. (?) Tidwell born in 1858 in Arkansas
Jno. W. Tidwell born in 1860 in Louisiana

1870 CENSUS BAYOU MACON TOWNSHIP CHICOT COUNTY ARKANSAS 146, 166
G. G. Tidwell born in 1836 in Mississippi (male)
M. E. Tidwell born in 1844 in Tennessee (female)
E. D. Tidwell born in 1858 in Arkansas (female)
J. W. Tidwell born in 1860 in Louisiana (male)
A. Hernden born in 1852 in Mississippi (male)
M. Wilson born in 1852 in Arkansas (male)

Deed Book U, page 132, Chicot County, Arkansas. 1 September 1877. Deed of land from B. H. Jackson and Elizabeth Jackson, his wife, to G. G. Tidwell, all of Chicot County, Arkansas. Acknowledged before Jason U. Johnson, J.P.

Deed Book U, page 134, Chicot County, Arkansas. 19 September 1877. G. G. Tidwell sold land to Henry F. Holt.

JOHN W. TIDWELL

Born: 1860 in Louisiana

1880 CENSUS, BAYOU MACON TOWNSHIP, CHICOT COUNTY, ARKANSAS 304, 308

John Tidwell born in 1860 in Louisiana. His father was born in Mississippi and his mother was born in Tennessee.

Deed Book B1, page 587, Chicot County, Arkansas. 26 February 1883. Crop mortgage from J. W. Tidwell of Chicot County, Arkansas to Cohn and Weis. Also mortgages in 1886, 1887, 1888 and 1889.

LOURANA SMITH NEAL TIDWELL

Born: December 12, 1838

Married: Jason Uriah Henry Johnson on November 1, 1854, in Hinds County, Mississippi

Died: October 6, 1899

Children of Jason Uriah Henry and Lourana Smith Neal (Tidwell) Johnson: Hattie Ruth Johnson, Jason Uriah Johnson, Loucinda Elizabeth Johnson, Louisa Ann Johnson, Lourana Johnson, Margaret Ann Johnson, Robert F. Johnson, Thomas B. Johnson

Jason U. Johnson married Lurena S. Tidwell on November 1, 1854. J. J. Bennett was the bondsman. See Book 3, pages 425 and 426, Hinds County, Mississippi, at Raymond. The license was issued on October 31, 1854.

RICHARD TIDWELL

Born: 1807 in Mississippi

1840 CENSUS MADISON COUNTY MISSISSIPPI

Richard Tidwell born 1800-1810

119 slaves

1860 CENSUS POLICE DISTRICT NO. 4 JEFFERSON COUNTY MISSISSIPPI
187, 182

Richard Tidwell born in 1807 in Mississippi

Deed Book I, page 386, 19 November, 1842, Madison County, Mississippi. Richard Tidwell released grazing rights to the west half of 16th section, Township 8, Range 3 East. It had been leased for 99 years.

TAX ROLLS, MADISON COUNTY, MISSISSIPPI

1834 Rich'd Tidwell 1 poll

1835 Richard Tidwell 1 poll

1838 F. and R. Tidwell. 1 poll. 57 slaves.

Deed Book "A-2", page 134, Chancery Clerk's Office, Fayette, Jefferson County, Mississippi. May 23, 1818. The Brand and Marks of RICHARD TIDWELL: Brand 33, Marks: Left Ear: Swallow Fork; Right Ear: Crop and Underbitt.

From the Department of Archives and History, Jackson, Mississippi Drawer No. 94, Case No. 3425, from Madison County, Miss. Cases before the Superior Court

Thos. J. Smith, Admr of Francis Tidwell, deceased, 1842, vs James Dick, McLain and Hill

Transfer of considerable acreage of land in Madison County, Miss. The trade supposed to have taken place 25 April 1840.

FRANCIS TIDWELL, FATHER, NOW DECEASED.

RICHARD TIDWELL, SON.

FRANCIS TIDWELL DIED IN FALL OF 1840.

Newspaper File No. 767. Canton HERALD, Canton, Miss. Nov. 28, 1838, page 4, Col. 4. THE ESTATE OF GIBEON G. TIDWELL, deceased. Letters of Administration granted to undersigned Sept Term of Court 1838. /s/ R. TIDWELL, ADM'R.

Issue of Dec 26, 1838, page 4, col. 2. ESTATE OF GIBEON G. TIDWELL, deceased. By Order of the Court, November Term, 1838; Sale of Property at late residence on Tuesday, 1st day of January, 1839; 27 negroes; stock, household goods, feed, etc. /s/ RICH'D TIDWELL. From Department of Archives, Jackson, Miss.

Deed Book K, page 706, Chancery Clerk's Office, Fayette, Jefferson County, Miss. 14 Sept, 1860. Mortgage R. TEDWELL

To: John McCusker. Tidwell is indebted to McCusker $200, a note and pledges a slave, John, aged 47, as security. /s/ R. TEDWELL and ack. in Jefferson County, Miss, 14 Sept, 1860.

TENNESSEE TIDWELL

Born: 1827 in Mississippi

Married: Thomas J. Smith on December 30, 1841, Madison County, Mississippi

Children of Thomas J. and Tennessee (Tidwell) Smith: Charles Smith, Francis Smith, H. L. Smith (male), Thomas B. Smith.

1850 CENSUS, MADISON COUNTY, MISSISSIPPI 3, 3

Thomas J. Smith born 1813 in North Carolina; Tennessee Smith born 1827 in Mississippi; Charley Smith born 1848 in Miss.; Francis Smith born 1839 in Miss.; 4 slaves. Also employed 18 other slaves.

1860 CENSUS, MADISON COUNTY, MISSISSIPPI 399, 397

Thomas J. Smith born 1813 in North Carolina; H. L. Smith born in 1852 in Mississippi (male); Thomas B. Smith born 1859 in Mississippi; Margaret O. Estes born 1839 in Mississippi.
Jno. W. Combs born in 1824 in North Carolina, Overseer. Thomas J. Smith was a planter and saw mill owner.

1870 CENSUS, MADISON COUNTY, MISSISSIPPI, DISTRICT 3, 22, 22

Thomas Smith born 1814 in North Carolina; Margaret Smith born 1839 in Miss.; Lawson Smith born 1853 in Miss.; Lee Smith born 1863 in Miss.; Mary Smith born 1866 in Miss.; Albert Tidwell born 1845 in Miss., Preacher; Edna Temple born 1856 in Miss.

1880 CENSUS, MADISON COUNTY, MISSISSIPPI, TOWNSHIP 8, E ONE-HALF OF BEAT NO. 3, 63, 72

Thomas J. Smith born 1812 in North Carolina where his parents were born; Margaret Smith, wife, born 1839 in Mississippi where her parents were born; Lawson Smith, son, born 1853 in Mississippi; Lee Smith, son, born 1863 in Miss.; Emma Smith, daughter, born 1866 in Miss.

NEAL

AARON NEILL, SENIOR

TAX ROLLS:

Jefferson County, Mississippi

1803 through 1807 Aaron Neill

1808, 1810 Aaron Neill Land on Cole's Creek; 1 poll

1811 Aaron Neill 1 poll; 4 slaves; Land on Bayou Pierre

1812 and 1813 Aaron Neill 2 polls and 1 poll respectively; 3 slaves; Land on Cole's Creek

1815 and 1816 Aaron Neill 1 poll; 5 slaves

1817 Aaron Neill 1 poll; 5 slaves

Claiborne County, Mississippi

1819 through 1821 Aaron Neill 1 poll; 6 slaves

1825 Aaron Neill Estate Land South Fork of Bayou Pierre; 3 slaves

1828 and 1829 Aaron Neill Estate Land on South Fork of Bayou Pierre

Census Records from the Department of Archives and History, Jackson, Mississippi

Jefferson County, Mississippi, 1805, Aaron Neill 1 male born before 1784; 4 males born after 1784; 1 female born before 1784

Jefferson County, Mississippi, 1808, Aaron Neill, 1 male born before 1787, 5 males born after 1787, 1 female born before 1787

Jefferson County, Mississippi, 1810, Aaron Neill, 1 male born before 1789, 5 males born after 1789, 1 female born before 1789, 1 female born after 1789

CENSUS RECORDS FROM THE DEPARTMENT OF ARCHIVES AND HISTORY, JACKSON, MISSISSIPPI:

1816 Census, Jefferson County, Mississippi

Aaron Neal

1 male born before 1795

6 males born after 1795

1 female born before 1795
2 females born after 1795

1820 Census, Claiborne County, Mississippi

Aaron Neel

1 male born before 1775
1 male born 1794-1804
1 male born 1802-1804
2 males born 1804-1810
2 females born 1804-1810
5 slaves

Deed Book "A-2", page 131 Chancery Clerk's Office, Fayette, Jefferson County, Mississippi. November 14, 1808. The Brand and Marks of AARON NEIL; Brand: A N; Marks: Left Ear: Crop; Right Ear: Underbitt.

From *AMERICAN STATE PAPERS* 1789-1815. Page 898. Register C. November 1806. Entered November 15, 1806. No. 11. Recorded September 4, 1806. Vol. .., Page .... Granted to AARON NEEL, ORIGINAL SETTLER, 300 acres on Bayou Pierre.

Land Entry Book, Claiborne County, Mississippi, Page 13. Fractional Section 7 — Township 10 — Range 2 East. 296.65 acres for AARON NEIL. October 26, 1815. Duplicate issued October 20, 1820.

McBee's NATCHEZ COURT RECORDS 1767-1805, Page 524. No. 780: Unrecorded land claim. Claimant AARON NEIL; 20 March 1804. Wit: James Milligan, 25 Sept 1804. Certif D-11, issued 4 Sept 1806. AARON NEIL claims the preemption of 300 acres in Jefferson County (now Claiborne) on waters of Tabor's Creek of Bayou Pierre, by cultivation and habitation by said Neil.

Probate File N-1, Claiborne County Mississippi. ESTATE OF AARON NEILL. Bond $6,000. JOHN C. NEIL and CHARLES NEIL, Administrators. /s/ JOHN C. NEIL, CHARLES NEIL, FRANCIS X TIDWELL, William Cessna. Test: P. A. Van Dorn, Clerk. Letters of Administration to JOHN C. NEIL and CHARLES NEIL on the 8th of October, 1821.

Estate appraised at $3,382.25, 21 November 1821 by Joshua Saxon, Samuel Saxon, and Bunberry Scott.

Pursuant to an order of the County and Probate Court of Claiborne County appointing Commissioners to make a Division of the Estate of Aron Neel Deceased equally between the Heirs of sd. Decd. We H. T. Irish, George Tannehill and R. L. Caldwell have this day met and proceeded as follows (to wit)

Division of Negroes

One negro man Peter appraised to $650 drawn by Elizabeth Neel
One negro boy Elijah appraised to $500 drawn by C. C. Neel
One negro boy named Burreel appd to $600 drawn by Lovett Neel

*Susannah Rebecca Frazer
(Mrs. John Garland Owen)*

Below — Captain John Garland Owen

Above — John G. Owen, II   *Below — Robert O. Owen*

One negro boy Sam appraised to $500 drawn by Lurenna Neel
One money Lott of $650 drawn by R. Neel
Money lott of $650 drawn by Thos. S. Neel

Division of Money

Notes on Thomas S. Neel for	$269.54
One on John S. Chambless	$500
H. T. Irish	$ 22.07
J. C. Neel	$455.56
John H. Shanks	$146.13
Francis Tidwell	$100
	1493.30
Negro property	2250
Money paid heirs	1505.23
	$5248.53

Six heirs — each heir's share $874.75

STATE OF MISSISSIPPI   Personally appeared before the undersigned one of the Justices of the CLAIBORNE COUNTY Peace for the County afd H. T. Irish, George Tannehill and R. L. Caldwell who maketh oath that they have honestly, impartially and faithfully made a distribution of the PERSONAL ESTATE of Aaron Neel decd equally between the heirs to the best of our skill and judgment agreeably to the above statement 26 March 1827.

Geo Tannehill   R. L. Caldwell J.P.   H. T. Irish
    State of Mississippi
    County of Claiborne

    I, J. Mack Jones, Clerk of the Chancery Court in and for the County and State hereby certify that the foregoing instrument is a true and correct copy of the original as it appears filed in the records in this office in the papers in the Estate of Aaron Neill.

    Witness my hand and official seal this 7th day of July, 1960

           J. Mack Jones, Clerk
           By L. Hamilton   D.C.
    To the Register of the Orphans
    Court of Claiborne County

           Let Letters of
Administration issue to JOHN C. NEILL on the Estate of Aaron Neill on his entering into Bond with Charles Neill and Francis Tidwell as Securities in the penalty of four thousand dollars.
23 Sept 1821
Same affidavit by the Clerk as above, as to True and Correct Copy.

In the 1800 Census of Kentucky as compiled by G. Glenn Clift, Assistant Secretary of the Kentucky Historical Society, and published in 1954 in Frankfort are AARON NEEL of Muhlenberg County and AARON NEEL of Warren County.

AARON L. NEILL (NEAL)

TAX ROLLS:

Claiborne County, Mississippi

1825 Aaron L. Neele Land on South Fork of Bayou Pierre; No poll
1829 Aaron L. Neale Land on South Fork of Bayou Pierre
1830 Aaron L. Neel Land on South Fork of Bayou Pierre; 1 poll;
   3 slaves

Madison County, Mississippi

1833 A. L. Neil, 1 poll, 5 slaves
1834 A. L. Neil, 1 poll, 7 slaves
1835 A. L. Neil, 1 poll, 7 slaves
1836 A. L. Neil, 1 poll, 9 slaves
1837 A. L. Neil, 1 poll, 8 slaves
1838 A. L. Neil, 1 poll, 8 slaves
1839 A. L. Neil Land on Pearl River, 9 slaves, 1 poll
1840 A. L. Neil Land on Pearl River, 1 poll, 9 slaves

Aaron L. Neil to Eliza Penelope Caldwell; marriage license dated 20 December 1827. Consent by R. L. Caldwell, father of the bride. Marriage Licenses, Claiborne County, Miss., Book 2, page 332.

1820 Census, Claiborne County, Mississippi, Robert L. Caldwell, 1 male born 1775-1794; 1 male born 1804-1810; 2 males born 1810-1820; 1 female born 1775-1794; 1 female born 1804-1810; 2 females born 1810-1820; 6 slaves

1830 Census, Claiborne County, Mississippi, Robert L. Caldwell, 1 male born 1770-1780; 1 male born 1800-1810; 1 female born 1780-1790; 2 females born 1815-1820; 1 female born 1820-1825; 1 female born 1825-1830; 15 slaves

1830 CENSUS, CLAIBORNE COUNTY, MISSISSIPPI
Aaron L. Neill
1 male born 1800-1810
1 female born 1800-1810
1 female born 1825-1830
6 slaves

1840 CENSUS, MADISON COUNTY, MISSISSIPPI
A. L. Neal
1 male born 1800-1810
1 male born 1830-1835
2 males born 1835-1840
1 female born 1810-1820
1 female born 1825-1830
1 female born 1830-1835
1 female born 1835-1840
13 slaves

1850 CENSUS, MADISON COUNTY, MISSISSIPPI
Aaron L. Neal born in 1807 in Mississippi
Eliza F. Neal born in 1810 in Kentucky
Aaron L. Neal born in 1833 in Mississippi
Mary A. Neal born in 1835 in Mississippi
George W. Neal born in 1837 in Mississippi
Emma C. Neal born in 1847 in Mississippi
Aaron L. Neal Jr. born in 1825 in Mississippi
24 slaves

1860 CENSUS, MADISON COUNTY, MISSISSIPPI 469, 467
A. L. Neal born in 1806 in Mississippi, Planter
Elizabeth P. Neal born in 1809 in Kentucky
Wm. Langford born in 1838 in Georgia, Overseer
33 slaves

1870 CENSUS, MADISON COUNTY, MISSISSIPPI
POLICE DISTRICT NO. 3, 95, 95
Aaron L. Neal born in 1807 in Mississippi
Susan Ford born in 1831 in Mississippi
Lucy Ford born in 1859 in Mississippi

Deed Book C, page 357. 1 February 1836. A. L. Neel and E (lizabeth) Penelope, his wife of Madison County, Mississippi, sell 400 acres of land there to James W. B. Hutchins for $10,887.50. Witnessed by Moses Goff. (This land was secured by a grant from the United States).

SUSAN E. NEILL

Born: ca 1830-1831

Married: James C. Ford. John R. Lambuth on bond, December 1, 1846. Page 33, Robert Chester and Marie Luther Upton, MARRIAGE RECORDS, MADISON COUNTY, MISSISSIPPI

1850 CENSUS, MADISON COUNTY, MISSISSIPPI 728, 742
James C. Ford born in 1825 in Alabama
Susan E. Ford born in 1830 in Mississippi
Lavinia E. Ford born in 1849 in Mississippi

1860 CENSUS, MADISON COUNTY, MISSISSIPPI 389, 389
J. C. Ford born in 1825 in Alabama
Susan E. Ford born in 1830 in Mississippi
Eldora Ford born in 1849 in Mississippi
Lovett R. Ford born in 1851 in Mississippi
Lucy V. Ford born in 1858 in Mississippi

CHARLES C. NEILL (NEAL)

Tax Rolls:

Claiborne County, Mississippi

1823 Charles Neill Land on South Fork of Bayou Pierre: 1 poll; 2 slaves

1827 Charles C. Neale

1828 Charles Neale; 1 poll; 1 slave

1829 Charles Neale; 1 poll; 1 slave

1830 Charles C. Neel Land on South Fork of Bayou Pierre; 1 poll; 2 slaves

1831 Charles C. Neill Land on South Fork of Bayou Pierre; 1 poll; 2 slaves

Madison County, Mississippi

1836 C. C. Neel 1 poll, 4 slaves

1839 C. C. Neil Land on Pearl River, 1 poll; 5 slaves

Charles C. Neel to Emeline Terry, license 19th December, 1829, W. B. Goff, Bondsman. Book 3, page 92, Marriage Licenses, Claiborne County, Mississippi.

Deed Book D, page 231, Madison County, Mississippi, 25 Jan, 1837, Charles C. Neal and Emeline M. Neal, his wife, of Madison County, sold land to William Harris of Adams County, Miss. Land in Madison County: E½ of SE¼ and S½ of E½ of NE¼, Sec 13, T8, R2E, 116 acres; W½ of SE¼, Sec 13, T8, R2E, 77 acres; S½ of W½ of NE¼, Sec 13, T8, R2E, 38 acres, a total of 232 acres on Bear Creek. Deed Book P, page 460, Madison County, Mississippi, Deed of Gift, 24 December 1860, Charles C. Neal of Madison County to Melinda Ann A. Goff of same. Consideration: $1. One negro girl, Peggy, aged 16 years; one negro girl, Eliza, aged 7 years, slaves for life, with reversion in event she has no heirs of her body. Test: C. L. Gilmer, J. H. Jeffries.

1830 Census Claiborne County Mississippi

Charles Neil

1 male born 1800-1810
1 female born 1800-1810
1 female born 1825-1830
6 slaves

1840 Census Madison County Mississippi

Chas. C. Neal

1 male born 1790-1800
1 male born 1835-1840
1 female born 1800-1810
1 female born 1830-1835
5 slaves

1850 CENSUS MADISON COUNTY MISSISSIPPI

Charles C. Neal born in 1800 in Kentucky
Emeline Neal born in 1810 in Kentucky
Malinda Neal born in 1830 in Mississippi
Charles Neal born in 1837 in Mississippi
Eugene Neal born in 1840 in Mississippi
Mary Neal born in 1843 in Mississippi
Margaret Neal born in 1847 in Mississippi
Martha Neal born in 1849 in Mississippi
8 slaves

1860 Census, Madison County, Mississippi 806, 804

Charles C. Neel born in 1800 in Kentucky, Planter
Emeline M. Neel born in 1810 in Kentucky
Margaret Neel born in 1847 in Mississippi
Martha E. Neel born in 1850 in Mississippi
Sallie R. Neel born in 1851 in Mississippi
Jno. K. Goff born in 1830 in Mississippi

1870 Census, Madison County, Mississippi, Police District 1, 897, 896

Charles C. Neel born in 1800 in Kentucky
Emeline M. Neel born in 1809 in Kentucky
Margaret Neel born in 1848 in Mississippi
Martha Neel born in 1850 in Mississippi
Sarah Neel born in 1852 in Mississippi
Neals buried in Sharon, Madison County, Mississippi.
Copied by Lamar Landfair of Jackson, Mississippi:
Maggie Neel, Wife of J. W. Unger died April 23, 1897.
Martha L. Neel, December 21, 1849—March 6, 1934.
Charles C. Neel, May 2, 1800—February 4, 1885
Emeline M., wife of Charles C. Neel, March 26, 1810—February 10, 1885
Miss Sallie R. V. Neel 1851—July 24, 1883 or 1888
Elizabeth, wife of C. L. Neel died April 4, 1862, aged 52 years, 10 months and 24 days.
Charles C. son of C. C. and E. M. Neel died June 8, 1859, aged 15 years.
Martha Jane daughter of T. S. and R. M. Neel born March 26, 1826 and died May 2, 1843.

ELIZABETH CAROLINE NEILL (NEAL)

Born: 1810-1811 in Mississippi
Married: Gibeon Gibson Tidwell on December 29, 1826, in Claiborne County, Mississippi, John C. Neill on the bond. Book 2, page 283.
Died: July 14, 1862, Carroll Parish, Louisiana
Children of Gibeon Gibson and Elizabeth Caroline (Neill or Neal)

— 125 —

Tidwell: Dorothy E. Tidwell, Gibeon Gibson Tidwell, Jr., Lourana Smith Neal Tidwell, John Caraway Tidwell, Louisa A. Tidwell, Clarissa A. Tidwell.

1850 CENSUS, MADISON COUNTY, MISSISSIPPI 740, 754
Elizabeth Tidwell born in 1811 in Mississippi
Dorothy Tidwell born in 1831 in Mississippi
Gibeon Tidwell born in 1834 in Mississippi
Loriana Tidwell born in 1838 in Mississippi
1 slave

1860 CENSUS, WARD NO. 5, CARROLL PARISH, LOUISIANA, CALEDONIA
Clarisa A. Herndon born in 1830 in Mississippi
Cornelia A. Herndon born in 1848 in Mississippi
Somerfield G. Herndon born in 1850 in Mississippi
Alzo (?) Herndon born in 1853 in Mississippi
Thomas W. Herndon born in 1856 in Arkansas
Lovit Oliver Herndon born in 1859 in Louisiana
Elizabeth C. Tidwell born in 1810 in Mississippi
Clarisa A. Herndon is listed as a widow and Elizabeth C. Tidwell as widow and mother.
1 slave
Gibeon G. Tidwell was the administrator of the estate of his mother, Elizabeth Caroline Tidwell, who died in 1862.
See Succession of Elizabeth Caroline Tidwell, Drawer No. 64, East Carroll Parish, Louisiana.

LOURANA NEILL

William B. Goff to Lourana Neel, 4th October, 1827.
John C. Neel, Bondsman, Book 2, page 322, Marriage Licenses, Claiborne County, Mississippi

1830 Census, Claiborne County, Mississippi

William B. Goff

1 male born 1800-1810
1 male born 1825-1830
1 female born 1800-1810

1840 Census, Claiborne County, Mississippi

Wm. B. Goff

1 male born 1800-1810
1 male born 1825-1830
1 male born 1830-1835
1 female born 1810-1820
1 female born 1820-1825
1 female born 1835-1840
2 slaves

ROBERT NEILL (NEAL)

TAX ROLLS

Claiborne County, Mississippi

1827 Robert Neale. Land on Carr's Creek. 1 poll; 1 slave

1828 Robert Neal Land on South Fork of Bayou Pierre; 1 poll; 2 slaves

1829 Robert Neale Land on South Fork of Bayou Pierre; 1 poll

1830 Robert Neel. South Fork of Bayou Pierre; 1 poll

1831 Robert Neal Land on South Fork of Bayou Pierre; 1 poll

Madison County, Mississippi:

1834 Robert Neil, 1 poll; 1 slave

1835 Robert Neil, 1 poll; 1 slave

Robert Neil to Ann Raines, 2 Feb. 1826, Charles C. Neel, Bondsman. Book 2, page 238, Marriage Licenses, Claiborne County, Mississippi. Robert Neil to Polly Thedford, 19 Aug. 1830. Thomas S. Neel, Bondsman. Book 3, page 136, Marriage Licenses, Claiborne County, Mississippi.

Robert Neel and Mary, his wife, sell land in Claiborne County, Mississippi, to John Langhorn of Claiborne County. 10 May 1834. Deed Book 0, page 316, Chancery Clerk's Office, Claiborne County. The Neels were living in Madison County.

1830 Census, Madison County, Mississippi, Robert Neil, 1 male born 1800-1810, 1 female born 1800-1810

THOMAS NEILL (NEAL)

TAX ROLLS

Claiborne County, Mississippi

1825 Thomas Neele. Land on South Fork of Bayou Pierre; 1 poll

1827 Thomas S. Neale. Land on Carr's Creek; 1 poll

1828 Thomas Neale. Land on South Fork of Bayou Pierre; 1 poll; 1 slave

1829 Thomas Neale. Land on South Fork of Bayou Pierre; 1 poll; 1 slave

1830 Thomas S. Neel. Land on South Forth of Bayou Pierre; 1 poll; 3 slaves

1831 Thomas Neill. Land on South Fork of Bayou Pierre; 1 poll; 1 slave

Madison County, Mississippi

1833 Thos. Neil. 1 poll, 2 slaves

1834 Thos. L. Neil, 1 poll, 3 slaves

1835 Thomas Neil. 1 poll, 8 slaves

1836 Thomas S. Neil. 1 poll, 6 slaves

Thomas S. Neel to Rebecca Roblin, 30 November 1826. Robert Neel, Bondsman. Edward Roblin, father of the bride, gave his consent.

Book 2, page 277, Marriage Licenses, Claiborne County, Mississippi.
1820 Census, Jefferson County, Mississippi, Edward Roblin, 1 male born 1775-1794; 4 males born 1810-1820; 1 female born 1775-1794; 1 female born 1804-1810; 1 female born 1810-1820

1830 Census, Jefferson County, Mississippi, Edward Roblin, 1 male born 1770-1780; 1 male born 1810-1815; 1 male born 1815-1820; 1 male born 1820-1825; 1 male born 1825-1830; 1 female born 1790-1800; 1 female born 1810-1815; 1 female born 1815-1820; 1 female born 1825-1830

Page 459 M. J. Berry's MARRIAGE AND CEMETERY RECORDS, HINDS COUNTY, MISSISSIPPI, 1951. Bethesda (Presbyterian Cemetery eight miles southeast from Utica). Rebecca M., wife of Thos. S. Neel, born November 25, 1809, died January 29, 1880. J. W. Neel, 1830-1918.

1830 CENSUS CLAIBORNE COUNTY MISSISSIPPI
Thomas L. Neil

1 male born 1800-1810
1 female born 1800-1810
1 female born 1825-1830
7 slaves

1840 CENSUS MADISON COUNTY MISSISSIPPI
Thomas Neil

1 male born 1800-1810
1 male born 1830-1835
1 female born 1800-1810
1 female born 1825-1830
12 slaves

1850 Census, Hinds County, Mississippi 562, 562
Thomas S. Neil born in 1802 in Mississippi
Rebecca M. Neil born in 1809 in Mississippi
James W. Neil born in 1830 in Mississippi
Charles G. Robbins born in 1826 in Mississippi
20 slaves

1860 Census, Hinds County, Mississippi
Post Office: Auburn
1494, 1517
T. S. Neil born in 1803 in Mississippi (male)
R. Neil born in 1808 in Mississippi (female)
J. W. Neil born in 1834 in Mississippi (male)
30 slaves

1870 Census, Township No. 14, Hinds County, Mississippi
Utica 141, 157

Wesley J. Neel born in 1830 in Mississippi

Rebecker M. Neel born in 1809 in Mississippi
Alice Roblin born in 1858 in Mississippi
Callie (?) Roblin born in 1860 in Mississippi

Deed Book C, page 87. 25 July 1834. Tho's. S. Neel and Rebecca, his wife, of Madison County, Mississippi, sell land in Madison County to Jno. S. Gooch. Deed signed by T. S. and Rebecca Neel and acknowledged by them on January 17, 1835.

Deed Book 6, page 61, Chancery Clerk's Office, Brandon, Rankin County, Mississippi, 1 February 1839. From: THOMAS S. NEAL AND REBECCA M. NEAL OF RANKIN COUNTY, MISSISSIPPI to: James L. Callahm. Consideration: $2,295 for a tract of land in Rankin County, Mississippi, the W½ of SE¼, Sec 32, T8, R4E, etc. 79.95 acres; also the NE¼ Sec 32, T8, R4E, also the SE¼ of Sec 32, T8, R4E, also the NE¼ of NW¼, Sec 32, T8, R4E, also the NW¼ of NW¼ of Sec 33, T8, R4F, etc. /s/ T. S. NEAL AND R. M. NEAL. Acknowledged by signers 2 Feb 1839 and Recorded 12 January 1841.

Deed Book 27, page 483, Chancery Clerk's Office, Raymond, Hinds County, Mississippi. 22 July 1859. From: William E. Mallett and Eliza M. Mallett, his wife, of Hinds Co., Miss. TO: THOMAS S. NEAL OF SAME. Consideration: $2,650 for land in Hinds County, Miss., the E½ of NE¼ and SE¼ of Sec 22 and the SW¼ of Sec 23, all in T4, R4E, 400 acres. /s/ William E. Mallett and Eliza M. Mallett. Acknowledged by signers on 22 July 1859.

Deed Book 31, page 730, Chancery Clerk's Office, Raymond, Hinds County, Mississippi. 22 Jan 1869. From: Gerard B. Downey, Commissioner in Chancery, of the one part and REBECCA M. NEIL, OF THE OTHER PART, ALL OF HINDS COUNTY, MISSISSIPPI. Witnesseth: Chancery Court of Hinds County, Second District, by Decree, the 14th of December, 1868, in a certain Claim, wherein THOMAS S. NEIL ADMINISTRATOR, was Complainant and W. F. Williams, et al, were defendants, appointed said Downey Commissioner, etc. with authority to sell etc. the E½ of NE¼, Sec 22 and the SE¼ of Sec 22 and the N½ of E½ of SW¼, Sec 22 and 35 acres in W½ of NE¼ of Sec 22 and the SW¼, of Sec 23, all in T4, R4W, 475 acres. REBECCA M. NEIL highest bidder, $475. /s/ G. B. Downey, Comm, Ack. 23 Jan 1869.

Probate File 3031. THE ESTATE OF THOMAS S. NEIL. Petition of James W. Neil of Hinds County, Miss., presents that *his father, Thomas S. Neil* of same county, departed this life on the 26th day of May, 1862, intestate, leaving your petitioner as his only child and heir and *his mother, Rebecca M. Neil* as his only distributees and prays for administration on the Estate. /s/ J. W. Neil. 1 Oct 1866. Appointed October Term of Court, 1866.

JOHN C. NEILL (NEAL)

Born: 1794-1800

Married: Charlotte Tidwell on July 20, 1818, in Jefferson County, Mississippi. Book A, page 97.

Died: 1834-1835 in Madison County, Mississippi

Children of John C. and Charlotte (Tidwell) Neill (Neal):

Aaron L. Neill (Neal), Charles Culbertson Neill (Neal), David F. Neill (Neal), Gibeon G. Neill (Neal), Richard T. Neill (Neal), Tennessee Neill (Neal).

Tax Roll of Jefferson County for 1818 shows John Neill, 1 poll.

Tax Roll of Claiborne County for 1827 shows Caroway Neale: 240 acres 3/2 land on Carr's Fork; 1 poll; 4 slaves

Birth and Death Record for Jefferson County for 1822 shows John C. Neal reported 1 white birth and 1 white death in the year.

Land Entry Book of Claiborne County, page 47 shows Section 6 Township 19, Range 4 East. 160.92 acres for John C. Neil.

1830 Census, Jefferson County, Mississippi, Carroway Neel: 1 male born 1790-1800; 1 male born 1815-1820; 2 males born 1820-1825; 2 males born 1825-1830; 1 female born 1790-1800; 1 female born 1815-1820; 6 slaves

1820 Census, Jefferson County, Mississippi, John C. Neil 1 male born 1794-1804, 1 male born 1810-1820; 1 female born 1794-1804; 1 female born 1810-1820

Minute Book A, pages 547 and 551 Madison County, Miss. JOHN C. NEAL ESTATE. Probate File No. 489, January Term of Court, 1835. GIBEON G. TIDWELL, ADMINISTRATOR. Names G. G. NEAL, A. L. NEAL, R. T. NEAL, C. C. NEAL AND TENNESSEE BROWN AS CHILDREN AND WIDOW CHARLOTTE NEAL AS HEIRS. Charlotte Neal, his widow has since married J. W. (or L. W.) Ludlow (Book F, page 30, Feb 23, 1837). All of age in past two years including A. L. Neal and R. T. Neal, December 19, 1846. Departed this life sometime in 1834 or 1835. ELIZABETH TIDWELL, WIDOW OF G. G. TIDWELL (SENIOR), AN HEIR(?) OF JOHN C. NEIL AND HER CHILDREN ELIZABETH TIDWELL, LOUISIANA (?) TIDWELL, GIBEON G. TIDWELL (JUNIOR), DOROTHY TIDWELL, CLARISSA A. TIDWELL, MINOR HEIRS OF GIBEON G. TIDWELL (SENIOR), DECEASED.

Deed Book K, page 377, Madison County, Mississppi
24 October 1846
SAMUEL J. BROWN AND TENNESSEE, HIS WIFE: C. C. NEIL AND SARAH, HIS WIFE: A. L. NEIL: R. T. NEIL AND ELIZA HIS WIFE: HEIRS AT LAW OF J. C. NEIL, DECEASED, OF

COUNTY OF RANKIN, STATE OF MISSISSIPPI TO: William A. Moore of Madison County, Miss.

Consideration: $280. Land in Madison County; sold our right, title E½ of SW¼ and W½ or SE¼, Sec 18, T8, R3E. /s/ S. J. BROWN, T. BROWN, C. C. NEIL, A. L. NEIL, R. T. NEIL Ack by S. Brown and Tennessee Brown his wife, 24 Oct 1846. Sarah and Eliza Neil signed in another deed, recorded DBk, K, p 607, 30 Oct 1847. (This tract was sold to Heirs of John C. Neil DBk. E, p 379, 16 Nov 1835, 319,80 acres, by Moses Goff.)

From: Chancery Clerk's Office, Brandon County, Miss.:
Deed Book 7, page 261, 20 May 1843. From Asa Myers of Scott County, Miss. To: GIBEN G. NEEL and AARON NEEL OF RANKIN COUNTY, MISS. Consideration: One negro girl, Leah and $100 for land in Rankin County, Miss. the W½ of SE¼ of Sec 36, T6, R5E. /s/ Asa Myers. Frances X Myers. Ack. by signers 20 May 1843.

Deed Book 9, page 348. 2 March 1847. From Moses B. Rankin and Christian H. Rankin, his wife of Rankin County, Miss. To: GIDION G. NEEL. Consideration: $65 for tract of land in Rankin County, Miss., the S½ of E½ of NE¼ of Sec. 11, T5, R5E, 40.24 acres. /s/ Moses B. Rankin and Christian H. Rankin. Ack. by signers 3 Mar 1847

Deed Book 9, page 331 2 March 1847. From Moses B. Rankin and Christian H. Rankin, his wife of Rankin County, Miss. To: AARON NEEL OF RANKIN COUNTY, MISS. Consideration: $360 for 120 acres.

Deed Book 9, page 93. 7 Feb 1846. From: A. L. NEEL, G. G. NEEL AND MASSENA NEEL OF RANKIN COUNTY, MISS. To: Kinzie Winstead of Scott County, Miss. Consideration: $400 for tract of land in Rankin County, Miss., the W½ of SE¼, Sec. 36, T6, R5E. /s/ A. L. NEEL, G. G. NEEL, MASSENA NEEL, WIFE OF G. G. NEEL. Ack. by signers on 7 Feb 1846

Deed Book 10, page 430. 7 August 1850. From: AARON L. NEIL OF RANKIN COUNTY, MISS. to SAMUEL J. BROWN OF SAME. Consideration: $230 for tract of land in Rankin County, Miss., the W½ of SE¼ and N½ of E½ of SE¼, Sec 11, T5, R5E, 120 acres. /s/ AARON L. NEIL. Test: E. M. Myers. Ack. by signer 7 Aug 1850.

C. C. NEILL (NEAL)

Born: 1817-1818 in Missisippi

Married: Sarah

Died: After 1880

1850 Census, Polk County, Texas
46, 46
C. C. Neil born in 1817 in Mississippi

Sarah Neil born in 1820 in Missisippi
Louisa Neil born in 1843 in Mississippi
Tennessee Neil born in 1846 in Mississippi
Mary Neil born in 1849 in Mississippi
1870 Census, Tyler County, Texas
233, 233

Culberson C. Neil born in 1818 in Mississippi
Sarah Neil born in 1827 in Alabama
Louisa Neil born in 1844 in Mississippi
George Neil born in 1859 in Texas
Tennessee Neil born in 1846 in Mississippi
Lucinda Neil born in 1859 in Texas
1880 Census, Tyler County, Texas, Precinct 3
164, 169

C. C. Neil born in 1818 in Mississippi, where his father was born. His mother was born in Louisiana.
Sarah Neil was born in 1827 in Alabama
Louisa Neil born in 1844 in Mississippi
George Neil born in 1860 in Texas
Deed Book I, page 24, Chancery Clerk's Office, Madison County, Mississippi
18 October, 1841
Sam Hamblen, Sheriff of Madison County, Miss.
TO:
Culbertson S.; Tennessee, Aaron, Richard; and David Neel of Madison County, Miss., Heirs of John C. Neel
160 acres in Madison County E½ of SW¼ and W½ of SE¼, Sec. 18, T 11, R3E. Sig. Samuel Hamblin, Sheriff. Ack. by signer, 18 Oct 1841.

DAVID F. NEILL (NEAL)

Born: Ca 1833 in Mississippi

Deed Book N, page 218   Power of Attorney   Chancery Clerk's Office
24 May, 1854   Madison County,
David F. Neel of Polk County, Texas   Mississippi
TO
Wm M. Ludlow of Tyler County, Texas

I appoint Ludlow my true and lawful Attorney, etc. to sue, demand, etc., my share or interest, as one of the HEIRS AT LAW of my deceased father, late of Madison County, Mississippi, the name of my late father is Carnwea Neel etc. to bargain, sell, etc.

/s/ DAVID F. NEEL. Ack. by signer, 24 May, 1854.

Deed Book N, page 233, Chancery Clerk's Office, Madison County, Mississippi
6 July, 1854

David F. Neel of Polk County, Texas
TO
Erasmus Williams of Madison County, Mississippi
An undivided one fifth part, as one of the Heirs of the Estate of John
C. Neel, late of said County, deceased, land in Madison County, Miss.,
160 acres, E½ of SW¼ and W½ of SE¼, Sec. 18, T8, R2E. /s/ D. F.
NEIL by his Atty, Wm M. Ludlow, Ack. by Ludlow as Atty, 6 July
1854.

1850 Census, Polk County, Texas 44, 44
L. W. Ludlow born in 1815 in Mississippi
Charlotte Ludlow born in 1812 in Mississippi (date obviously incorrect)
Sarah Ludlow born in 1836 in Mississippi
Lanier Ludlow born in 1844 in Mississippi
David F. Neil born in 1833 in Mississippi
48, 48
C. M. Ludlow born in 1800 in Tennessee
Mahala Ludlow born in 1836 in Mississippi
Mary Ludlow born in 1840 in Mississippi
John Ludlow born in 1843 in Mississippi

1860 Census, Tyler County, Texas, 417, 426
C. M. Ludlow born in 1801 in Tennessee (male)
J. B. Schofield born in 1827 in Alabama (male)
M. Schofield born in 1838 in Mississippi (female)
S. Schofield born in 1854 in Texas (male)
D. Schofield born in 1859 in Texas (male)

RICHARD T. NEILL (NEAL)

1860 Census, Rapides Parish, Louisiana 142, 145
Richard Neal born in 1827 in Mississippi
Eliza Neal born in 1828 in Georgia
Emily Bass born in 1840 in Louisiana
Martha Ann Neal born in 1846 in Mississippi
John C. Neal born in 1848 in Mississippi
Aaron L. Neal born in 1850 in Texas
Henry C. Neal born in 1852 in Texas
Mary Jane Neal born in 1854 in Texas
Laura V. Neal born in 1856 in Texas
Marriage Licenses, Book 2, page 295, Rankin County, Mississippi.
Richard T. Neel and Eliza Perry, License 17 October 1845:
Ceremony 21 October 1845. Aaron L. Neel, Bondsman.

CONFEDERATE WAR RECORDS, NATIONAL ARCHIVES, WASHINGTON
JOHN C. NEILL. Private. Old Company J, 10 Mississippi Infantry.
Captain George R. Fearn's Company, 10 Regiment Mississippi Volunteers. Enlisted Canton, Mississippi 1861

JOHN C. NEILL. Private. Company E, 27 Mississippi Infantry. Enlisted Carthage 1862.

TENNESSEE NEAL (NEILL)

Born: 1820 in Mississippi

Married: James Brown, Jr.

Children of James and Tennessee (Neal or Neill) Brown, Jr.:
Alice Brown, Ann Brown, Charlotte Brown, George Brown, James Brown, Laura Brown.

1850 CENSUS, RANKIN COUNTY, MISSISSIPPI 629, 629

James Brown, Jr. born in 1813 in Louisiana
Tennessee Brown born in 1820 in Mississippi
Laura Brown born in 1836 in Mississippi
Charlotte Brown born in 1838 in Mississippi
Ann Brown born in 1840 in Mississippi
James Brown born in 1842 in Mississippi
George Brown born in 1845 in Mississippi
Alice Brown born in 1849 in Mississippi
3 slaves

1840 CENSUS, RANKIN COUNTY, MISSISSIPPI

S. J. Brown

1 male born 1810-1820
1 female born 1820-1825
3 females born 1835-1840
3 slaves

1840 CENSUS, RANKIN COUNTY, MISSISSIPPI

James Brown

1 male born 1780-1790
1 male born 1820-1825
1 male born 1825-1830
1 female born 1780-1790
1 female born 1820-1825
29 slaves

1850 CENSUS, RANKIN COUNTY, MISSISSIPPI 619, 619

James Brown born in 1785 in South Carolina
Nancy Brown born in 1787 in South Carolina
29 slaves

BRIGGS

HENRY DELOS BRIGGS

Born: January 6, 1835, in Otsego County, New York

Married: Sarah Elizabeth Wright on January 19, 1871, in East Carroll Parish, Louisiana

Died: December 20, 1900, in Oak Grove, Louisiana

Children of Henry Delos and Sarah Elizabeth (Wright) Briggs: Delia Elizabeth Briggs, Dorrell D. Briggs, Eri Briggs, Henry Delos Briggs, John Cheatham Briggs, Mary Briggs, Ollie Briggs, Orrin Briggs, Sue Saphronia Briggs.

1850 Census, Otsego County, New York Town of New Lisbon 1161, 1282

Amariah Smith born in 1806 in New York

Kesia Smith born in 1828 in England

Delos Briggs born in 1835 in New York

Amariah Smith born in 1850 in New York

Jane Briggs born in 1837 in New York

1860 CENSUS, TOWN OF FLOYD, WARD 6 CARROLL PARISH LOUISIANA 868, 838

Henry D. Briggs born in 1834 in New York

1870 CENSUS, TOWN OF FLOYD CARROLL PARISH LOUISIANA 4, 4

Henry D. Briggs born in 1836 in New York

1880 CENSUS, WARD NO. 3 WEST CARROLL PARISH LOUISIANA 115, 121

H. D. Briggs born in 1835 in New York

S. E. Briggs born in 1851 in Louisiana

J. C. Briggs born in 1872 in Louisiana

Dorrel D. Briggs born in 1874 in Louisiana

Orrin Briggs born in 1876 in Louisiana

Susie S. Briggs born in 1878 in Louisiana

Thos Wright born in 1869 in Louisiana

The parents of Henry D. Briggs were born in New York. The father of S. E. Briggs and Thos. Wright (brother of S. E. Briggs) was born in Mississippi and their mother was born in Louisiana.

H. D. Briggs Pvt Co H 3rd Inftry. Enlisted May 17, 1861, New Orleans, La. Present on all rolls May 1861 to December, 1862. Detailed on recruiting service January and February, 1863. Captured and paroled at Vicksburg, Mississippi, July 4, 1863. Reported in camp for exchange at Nachitoches, Louisiana, before April 1st, 1864. Paroled at Shreveport, Louisiana, June 22, 1865. Residence: Carroll Parish, Louisiana. Andrew B. Booth LOUISIANA CONFEDERATE SOLDIERS, Volume 2, page 116.

DORRELL D. BRIGGS

Born: January 4, 1873

ERI BRIGGS

Born: September 1882

HENRY DELOS BRIGGS

Born: February 8, 1885
Married: Boyce Sadler in Monroe, Louisiana
Died: June 22, 1922

JOHN CHEATHAM BRIGGS

Born: November 13, 1871
Died: August 26, 1926

ORRIN BRIGGS

Born: December 20, 1875
Married: Emma Fowler on October 31, 1923

DELIA ELIZABETH BRIGGS

Born: September 21, 1889
Married: Jerry T. Williams on November 10, 1909

Children of Jerry T. and Delia Elizabeth (Briggs) Williams:
Jerry Moore Williams. Born September 16, 1910.
Died: May 29, 1912
Laura Mae Williams. Born December 30, 1916
Mary Lucille Williams. Born September 23, 1912
Died September 12, 1915
Sarah Elizabeth Williams. Born July 17, 1929
Sue Irene Williams. Born January 17, 1915
Thomas Arthur Williams. Born May 10, 1919

LAURA MAE WILLIAMS

Born: December 30, 1916
Married: Godfrey Meloncey Soniat du Fossat on June 14, 1947.
Mr. Soniat's ancestor, Chevalier Guy Soniat du Fossat, was born in the Chateau du Fossat in 1726 and came to Louisiana in 1751. He wrote a history of Louisiana.

Children of Godfrey Meloncey and Laura Mae (Williams) Soniat du Fossat:
Marie Elaine Soniat du Fossat. Born February 3, 1949
Paul Meloncey Soniat du Fossat. Born October 7, 1953
Thomas Meloncey Soniat du Fossat. Born December 16, 1951
William Michael Soniat du Fossat. Born April 5, 1956
Yvonne Elizabeth Soniat du Fossat. Born March 19, 1948

SARAH ELIZABETH WILLIAMS

Born: July 17, 1929
Married: Charles Edward Cox on May 4, 1952
Children of Charles Edward and Sarah Elizabeth (Williams) Cox:
James Steven Cox. Born January 29, 1958.

At Left — General Albert Gallatin Carter of Linwood Plantation

Right—Sarah Elizabeth Wright (Mrs. Henry Delos Briggs)

Dorrell Wright

Mary Ann Landfair
(Mrs. Dorrell Wright)

Below — Jason Uriah Henry Johnson

Below — John Anthony McHugh

SUE IRENE WILLIAMS

Born: January 17, 1915

Married: Roy Howard on June 30, 1960

THOMAS ARTHUR WILLIAMS

Born: May 10, 1919

Married: 1st: Helenjane Ruth Martin on May 9, 1949. Divorced.
2nd: Linda Jane Rankin on December 27, 1957, in Hayward, California

Children of Thomas Arthur and Helenjane Ruth (Martin) Williams:
Jerry Thomas Williams. Born January 12, 1950
Suzanne Michele Williams. Bohn February 7, 1951

MARY BRIGGS

Born: June 30, 1880

Married: Jarman Stewart Thompson on November 5, 1902

Children of Jarman Stewart and Mary (Briggs) Thompson:
Elizabeth Briggs Thompson, Emma Elise Thompson

ELIZABETH BRIGGS THOMPSON

Born: June 20, 1906

Married: November 25, 1926, to Buren Perritt

Children of Buren and Elizabeth Briggs (Thompson) Perritt:
Margaret Ann Perritt, Mary Elizabeth Perritt

MARY ELIZABETH PERRITT

Born: April 27, 1928

Married: Benjamin Earle Cooke, Jr., on June 3, 1949

Children of Benjamin Earle Cooke, Jr. and Mary Elizabeth Perritt:
Jan Elizabeth Cooke. Born March 25, 1955
Cathy Anne Cooke. Born February 26, 1960

MARGARET ANN PERRITT

Born: September 28, 1936

Married: Clifton Benson Love, Jr., on December 21, 1957, in Minden, Louisiana

ELISE THOMPSON

Born: November 28, 1904

Married: John Leonard Wall on November 24, 1927

Children of John Leonard and Elise (Thompson) Wall:
Barbara Jean Wall

BARBARA JEAN WALL

Born: February 13, 1929

Married: William Andrew Jackson on June 1, 1950
Children of William Andrew and Barbara Jean (Wall) Jackson:
Charles Robert Jackson. Born January 18, 1959
Cheryl Lynn Jackson. Born September 27, 1954
John David Jackson. Born December 2, 1952.

OLLIE BRIGGS

Born: February 22, 1887
Married: Edna Harper
Died: October 8, 1937

Children of Ollie and Edna (Harper) Briggs: Charlotte Dale Briggs, Edna Carolyn Briggs, Elaine Briggs, Frances Elizabeth Briggs, Henry Delos Briggs, John C. Briggs, Martha Dea Briggs.

"The untimely passing of Ollie Briggs, planter and banker of Oak Grove, Louisiana, robbed that community of a man who had been one of its most useful citizens for more than a quarter of a century. His town, his parish, and his friends were a passion with him, and he never tried of giving his support to wholesome progress. No history of northeast Louisiana, written by the most learned historian would be quite complete without setting down in type for the guidance of future generations, the life and activities of Ollie Briggs of Oak Grove. May his accomplishments be a shining light to guide the footsteps of his children to the success they so justly deserve for having been born of such a father.

"Mr. Briggs was a member of a pioneer family in West Carroll Parish. He was born at Oak Grove, February 22, 1887, and died October 8, 1937. His father, Henry Delos Briggs, was a native of New York State, born in Otsego County, January 6, 1835. He settled in Louisiana before the Civil War and became a large planter, owning and operating the first cotton gin in West Carroll Parish. He died December 20, 1900.

"Mr. Briggs' mother was born Sarah Elizabeth Wright. She was a native of East Carroll Parish, born May 11, 1851, and died at Oak Grove January 12, 1917. They were married at Floyd, Louisiana, January 19, 1871 and were the parents of eight children, as follows: Mrs. Mary B. Thompson, Mrs. J. T. Williams, and Orrin Briggs, a planter and ginner, all of Oak Grove, Louisiana, Dorrell Briggs in the real estate business in Sonora, California; the deceased are Ollie Briggs, subject of this sketch, John C. Briggs, planter, banker and gin operator; Mrs. Sue B. Johnson, who gave the land for the courthouse, and Henry D. Briggs, attorney of Monroe, Louisiana.

"Ollie Briggs attended school at Briggs' Community School House, and then came to Oak Grove and completed his high school course.

Thereafter he attended the Paragould Business College at Paragould, Arkansas.

"His first business connection was with the Bank of Oak Grove as assistant cashier, beginning in 1907, at the time of its organization. He remained with this institution until 1930 when he resigned to take over the management of the vast Briggs Estate, which consists of hundreds of acres of land, town property and three cotton gins. He also maintained an insurance office and during the World War he served as a member of the Board of Food Administration. He also served as a member of the Fifth District Levee Board, an honorary appointment. In short, he had a part in every activity making for community progress in all lines. For four years he served as a member of the Board of Aldermen of Oak Grove; he likewise served as a member of the parish and cotton commissions; was a notary public for thirty years; charter member of the Lions Club, and a member of the Masonic Lodge, Royal Arch, Delhi Chapter, member of the Woodmen of the World Lodge, and also of the Knights of Pythias. He served as a representative of the Tallulah Production Credit Association.

"Mr. Briggs was married to Edna S. Harper of Winn Parish, Louisiana, September 6, 1890, and she still resides in the family home at Oak Grove. They were parents of seven children as follows: Elaine Briggs Fleming, born July 23, 1912, a graduate of Louisiana State University in 1932, married to Dr. Kenneth Fleming of Youngstown, Ohio; Frances Elizabeth, born March 12, 1914, graduated from Louisiana State University and now in charge of her father's business interests; John C. born November 5, 1916; Henry Delos born May 10, 1924; Edna Carolyn born May 1, 1928; Martha Dea born May 13, 1930; and Charlotte Dale born October 12, 1931, all residing in the family home in Oak Grove.

"Mr. Briggs succumbed to a complication of heart aliments after an illness of several months. Funeral services were held at the family home and drew a great throng of his friends from all parts of the parish, attesting to the high esteem in which he was held as a citizen and civic leader."

Biography of Ollie Briggs as taken from Page 1248, Volume 3, *Eastern Louisiana, A History of the Watershed of the Ouachita River and the Florida Parishes* Edited by Frederick William Williamson and George T. Goodman

CHARLOTTE DALE BRIGGS

Born: October 22, 1931

Married: William Eugene Scott, Jr., of Lake Providence, Louisiana, on June 18, 1949

Children of William Eugene and Charlotte Dale (Briggs) Scott, Jr.:
William Eugene Scott III. Born on August 10, 1955

EDNA CAROLYN BRIGGS

Born: May 1, 1928

Married: Lawrence Bell Brashier, Jr., on October 21, 1950. Mr. Brashier was born in Orange, Texas, on August 5, 1927

Children of Lawrence Bell and Edna Carolyn (Briggs) Brashier, Jr.:
Lawrence Bell Brashier III. Born in Shreveport, Louisiana, on September 26, 1951

John David Brashier. Born on September 3, 1952, in Shreveport, Louisiana.

Catharine Dale Brashier. Born on September 28, 1956, in Shreveport, Louisiana.

ELAINE BRIGGS

Born: July 23, 1912

Married: Dr. Kenneth Fleming of Youngstown, Ohio, on June 24, 1937

Children of Dr. Kenneth and Elaine (Briggs) Fleming:
Henry Briggs Fleming—Born November 14, 1942.

FRANCES ELIZABETH BRIGGS

Born: March 12, 1914

Married: Arnold Floyd Kuykendall on December 27, 1947

MARTHA DEA BRIGGS

Born: May 13, 1930

Married: Franklin Lee Baxter on April 12, 1952

Children of Franklin Lee and Martha Dea (Briggs) Baxter: John Everett Baxter—Born January 14, 1953; Mark Briggs Baxter—Born June 30, 1954; Robert Edwards Baxter—Born September 8, 1955.

SUE SAPHRONIA BRIGGS

Born: March 31, 1878, in Oak Grove, Louisiana

Married: Jason Uriah Johnson on March 15, 1893, in Oak Grove, Louisiana

Died: December 6, 1926, in Monroe, Louisiana

Children of Jason Uriah and Sue (Briggs) Johnson: Clifford Uriah Johnson, Clyde Briggs Johnson, Jason Henry Johnson.

THE NEW ENGLAND ANCESTRY
OF
HENRY DELOS BRIGGS

ALMY

JOHN ALMEY OF DUNTON - BASSETT, COUNTY LEICESTER, ENGLAND

Living in Dunton-Bassett about the middle of the 16th century. Dunton-Basett is nine miles south of Leicester and four miles north of Lutterworth, the parish of which John Wycliffe was rector 1374 to 1384.

Married (?) Reignolds

Children of John and (? Reignolds) Almey:

Thomas Almey

See *English Ancestry of William Almy* N.E.H.G.R. Vol 71 p 319
References to the New England Historical and Genealogical Register are abbreviated N.E.H.G.R.

THOMAS ALMEY OF DUNTON - BASSETT, COUNTY LEICESTER, ENGLAND

Born: Probably about 1530

Married Joan Wale, the daughter of Thomas Wale of Dunton-Bassett. She was buried there October 31, 1604.

Children of Thomas and Joan (Wale) Almey:

*Christopher Almey

William Almey of Bitteswell, Co. Leicester (a small parish one mile north of Lutterworth), yeoman

Born about 1556. His will of 18 March 1628/9 mentions sons, William and Andrew. Requests to be buried in the Church "at my seat's end."

Thomas Almey of Badby County Northampton. Living in 1618 when apparently he entered the Almey pedigree in the Visitation of Northamptonshire (Printed in Metcalfe's Visitation of Northamptonshire, London, 1887, page 61) Married 1st Agnes (Andrew) Cowper, daughter of Nicholas Andrew, brother of Thomas Andrew. She was widow of John Cowper. Married 2nd Alice Marsh, daughter of Lawrence Marsh of Northampton

John Almey of Lutterworth Co. Leicester. Died before 23 September 1636 when administration of his estate was granted to his widow

Anna Almey. Married 1st at Leire co. Leicester (a parish four miles northwest of Lutterworth) on 20 June 1592 Frances Smyth of Leire. Married 2nd Anna (?)

See *English Ancestry of William Almy* N.E.H.G.H. Vol 71 p 319

CHRISTOPHER ALMEY, GENTLEMAN, OF SOUTH KILWORTH, COUNTY LEICESTER, ENGLAND

Married: 1st: (?) Clarke of Lutterworth, Co. Leicester

　　　　2nd: By license of 1606 Anne or Annie Greene, widow, of Hurley, co. Warwick, who was buried at South Kilworth 5 March 1622/3.

Buried: 4 October 1624 at South Kilworth

Children of Christopher and (? Clarke)

Joan Almey. Living 2 October 1624. Married by license of 1618 (in which she is called "Katharine") to John Paule of Ashby Parva, co. Leicester, yeoman. See Vol. 38, page 8 Index Library of the British Record Society Limited London 1910 Leicestershire Marriage Licenses 1570-1729, page 318.

Mary Almey. Living unmarried 2 October 1624.

*William Almey.

Will of Christopher Allmey of South Kilworth Co. Leicester, Gentleman, 2 October 1624. Printed in N.E.G.H.R. Vol 71, page 314. Also printed in Putnam's Genealogical Quarterly Magazine Vol 4, page 249 (Jan 1904). Mentions dau Marie Allmey, son-in-law John Paule and children: Willm, Christopher, and Richard, Joane Paule, wife of John Paule of little Ashby co. Leicester, Yeoman, only son, William Allmey. Requests to be buried in Church or Churchyard of South Killworthe.

From the Records of the Court of Requests (In Public Record Office London and Printed in N.E. G.H.R. Vol 71 p 318) In 1625 Edward Clement, clerk, sued William Almey yeoman son and Executor of Christopher Almey deceased about the parsonage of Lutterworth and a bond connected therewith. William Almey of Bitteswell co. Leicester yeoman aged 68 deposed that the late Christopher Almey was reputed to be an honest man. Court of Requests James I Bundle 397 1606 Christopher Allmey of South Killworth and Anne Greene widow of Hurley co. Warwick. See Vol 38 p 8 Index Library of the British Record Society London 1910 Leicestershire Marriage Licenses 1570-1729.

See *English Ancestry of William Almy* N.E.H.G.R. Vol 71 p 320

WILLIAM ALMY (ALMEY), GENTLEMAN, OF SOUTH KILWORTH, COUNTY LEICESTER, ENGLAND AND OF SAUGUS

(LYNN) MASSACHUSETTS, SANDWICH, IN THE PLYMOUTH COLONY, AND PORTSMOUTH, RHODE ISLAND

Born: Probably at Dunton-Bassett or South Kilworth, Co. Leicester, England about 1600 (Pope's *Pioneers of Massachusetts* says he deposed 20 (4) 1654, aged about 53 years.)

Married: At Lutterworth, co. Leicester, England, by license of 1626, Audrey Barlowe of Lutterworth, who was born about 1602 and was living 28 February 1676/7.

Died: Probably at Portsmouth, Rhode Island, between 28 February 1676/7 when he made his will and 23 April 1677 when his will was proved.

Children of William and Audrey (Barlowe) Almy:

*Anna or Annis Almy

Catharine Almy. Married Bartholomew West who was the son of Matthew West and who died before 1703.

Christopher Almy Born about 1631. Brought by parents to New England, aged 3. Married July 9, 1661 to Elizabeth Cornell daughter of Thomas and Rebecca Cornell. Died 30 January 1712/3. Deputy from Portsmouth, Rhode Island. Assistant to the Royal Governor, Sir Edmund Andros, 1690. Captain, 1692. Elected Governor of Rhode Island, 1693, but refused to serve.

John Almy.

Colonel Job Almy Born 1601 Died 1684. Married Mary Unthank, daughter of Christopher and Susanna Unthank, who married 2nd Thomas Townsend and who died after 1724. Colonel Almy served as a Deputy from Warwick, Rhode Island to the Colonial Assembly, 1670-1672 and as Indian Commissioner, 1673.

William Almy
Executor of his father's will, which he proved 29 October 1624.

Defendant in suit in Court of Requests in 1625 which had been begun against his father.

In Massachusetts Bay Colony 1631

Returned to England

With wife, Audrey and children Anna (Annis) and Christopher came to New England in the *Abigail* in 1635

Lived at Saugus (Lynn) Massachusetts a year or two

A founder of Sandwich in Plymouth Colony

Received land grant in Portsmouth Rhode Island 14 November 1664
Freeman at Portsmouth 1655, Juryman, Commissioner, Served in Rhode Island General Assembly 1656, 1657, 1663

ANNA OR ANNIS ALMY OF SOUTH KILWORTH, COUNTY LEICESTER, ENGLAND, OF SAUGUS (LYNN) MASSACHU-

SETTS, SANDWICH IN THE PLYMOUTH COLONY, AND PORTSMOUTH, RHODE ISLAND

Baptized: South Kilworth, co. Leicester, England

Married: Major John Greene, Deputy Governor of Rhode Island ca 1648

Died: May 6, 1709

See *English Ancestry of William Almy* N.E.H.G.R. Vol 71 p 321-2

See *The Genealogical Dictionary of Rhode Island* by John Osborne Austin, p. 236

See *Historic Families of America* Published by Charles Kingsbury Miller in Chicago in 1897 pp 14-15

AYLSWORTH

ARTHUR AYLSWORTH

Came to America from either England or Wales before July 29, 1679, when he and 41 others signed a Petition to the King of England.

Married: Mary Brown of Providence, Rhode Island, the daughter of the Reverend James Brown and the granddaughter of the Reverend Chad Brown and of the Reverend Obadiah Holmes, through her mother, Mary Holmes

Died: Between November 7, 1725, and September 13, 1726.

The family lived in Quidnesset, North Kingstown, Rhode Island.

Children of Arthur and Mary (Brown) Aylworth:

Arthur Aylsworth. Born 1685. Married Mary Franklin. Moved to West Greenwich (then a part of East Greenwich) Rhode Island, before June 29, 1723. He died in July 1761.

Catharine Aylsworth. Married (?) Greene.

Chad Aylsworth. Named for the Reverend Chad Brown, his great-grandfather. Born 1696. Married 1st in Newport, Rhode Island, to Elizabeth Major, daughter of David Major of the Island of Guernsey, on November 15, 1725. Elizabeth and her sister, Mary Major, came to Newport in 1717 and united with Trinity Church. David Major's estate—principally London property—was turned into the Bank of England. Elizabeth (Major) Aylsworth died at Foster, Rhode Island. Married 2nd Mary Wood, who was living when his will was made on April 23, 1757. The will was proved on May 22, 1773.

Elizabeth Aylsworth. Married (?) Dolliver, perhaps the son of Joseph Dolliver, Senior, who died in East Greenwich in 1731. Before

1726 she married 2nd Peleg Card. She probably died before his will was made on September 17, 1764.

John Aylsworth. Married Dorcas Jones, the daughter of Josiah and Elizabeth Jones of East Greenwich, where they lived as early as December 22, 1718. John Aylsworth died in North Kingstown where his will was proved May 15, 1771.

Martha Aylsworth. Married John Davis before December 1, 1727, and lived ,in East Greenwich where he died before February 25 1737-8.

Mary Aylsworth. Married John Greene, son of Benjamin and Humility (Coggeshall) Greene and grandson of John and Joan Greene of North Kingstown. See Ray Greene Huling's article in Narragansett Historical Register, Vol II, No 3, pp 167-8.

Philip Aylsworth. Born 1692. Married Rachel Greene, daughter of Daniel and Rebecca (Barrow) Greene and granddaughter of John and Joan Greene of North Kingstown.

*Robert Aylsworth

Thomas Aylsworth

Arthur Aylsworth was a Ratemaker in 1699, a Viewer of Fences and Supervisor of Highways, June 5, 1699. He deeded land to Henry Tibbets on September 21, 1697.

The will of Arthur Aylworth mentions:

Sons: Philip, Chad, Robert, Arthur, and John, and

Daughters: Mary Green, Elizabeth Dolliver, Katherine and Martha Aylsworth

See N.E.H.G.R. Vol 35, p 91

ROBERT AYLSWORTH

Married: Ann Davis on May 20, 1708. Lived ten years near the Quidnesset homestead and then lived in that part of North Kingstown called Exeter

Died: Before February 25, 1760.

Children of Robert and Ann (Davis) Aylsworth:

Amey Aylsworth. Married Joshua Rathburn.

Anna Aylsworth. Married (?) Austin.

*Ephraim Aylsworth

Mary Aylsworth. Married on September 28, 1739, to Nathaniel Pettis, perhaps the son of William and Mary Pettey

Robert Aylsworth. Married Susanna Reynolds, perhaps a daughter of Joseph Reynolds whose will was executed in 1722.

Sarah Aylsworth. Married Jabez Tucker.

Will of Anna (Davis) Aylsworth dated May 4, 1760 and proved November 10, 1761. Executor was son Ephraim. Mentioned in the will: son Robert, son-in-law, Jabez Tucker, grandson, Robert Petty daughter Amey Rathbun daughter Anna Austin.

Ann (Davis) Aylsworth administered the Estate of her husband, Robert Aylsworth. Ephraim Aylsworth, Joshua Rathbun, Robert Petty, and Robert Aylsworth receipted for legacies. Jabez Tucker receipted for Hannah Tucker granddaughter of Robert Aylsworth.
Aylsworth Descendants pages 41, 48-49

EPHRAIM AYLSWORTH

Married: Alice Pettey, the daughter of William and Mary Pettey. She was born June 4, 1718. The Petteys lived in Charlestown, Rhode Island.

Died: Before August 11, 1767, when the inventory of his personal property was presented to the Exeter Town Council and his son, William, was appointed Administrator.

August 11, 1767 Robert Aylsworth gave Ephraim and Alice (Pettey) Aylsworth 50 acres of land.

The Ephraim Aylsworth family lived three-fourths of a mile from Lewis City on Black River. Several children died there and it was thought the place was unhealthy. Alice Aylsworth was taken to Connecticut where she lived with a Douglas family.

Children of Ephraim and Alice (Pettey) Aylsworth:

Alice Aylsworth. Married Moses Clark on November 18, 1773. He was born on December 29, 1751, the son of Thomas and Bridget (Barber) Clark, who had been married on December 17, 1732 and lived in Richmond, Rhode Island.

Anna Aylsworth. Born August 3, 1746
Ephraim Aylsworth. Born December 2, 1750
Lucina Aylsworth
*Mary Aylsworth
Nathan Aylsworth
Peleg Aylsworth
Solomon Aylsworth

William Aylsworth. Born October 3, 1744. Died before September 13, 1768, probably single. In his will made on June 21, 1768, he names all his brothers and sisters.

MARY AYLSWORTH

Born: February 13, 1748

Married: Elisha Parker of Coventry, Rhode Island, on January 15, 1767

Died: September 24, 1828,

H. E. Aylsworth *Arthur Aylsworth and His Descendants in America*

(1887) Narragansett Historical Publishing Company, Providence, Rhode Island

Sylvester Aylsworth *A Register of the Aylsworth Family* (1840) Bennett, Backus and Hawley, Franklin Square, Utica, New York

BICKHAM

ALDRED BYCCOMBE (BICKHAM) OF OLD CLEEVE, COUNTY SOMERSET, ENGLAND

Married: Hellen or Ellen (?)

Died: Will proved 2 Feb 1610/1611

Children of Aldred and Hellen or Ellen Byccombe (Bickham):

Aldred Bickham

Ann Bickham. Married (?) Lanham

Charity Bickham. Married Philip Slocum

Joane Bickham. Married John Studdier

Mary Bickham

William Bickham

Will of Charity Slocombe, widow, of the Parish of Old Cleeve, County Somerset, England, dated 21 Nov 1642 and proved 26 Jan 1642/3:

Mentions brother: Aldred Bickham

Sister: Joane Studdier

Kinswomen: Isoll Oatford and Mary Wills

Son: Giles Slocombe who is made executor.

The first mention of Giles Slocum in New England is on 4 September 1648 when he received land in Portsmouth. Mr. G. Andrews Moriarty Jr. in N.E.H.G.R. Vol 70 pp 283-284 says there can be little doubt that Giles Slocombe of Old Cleeve and Giles Slocum of Portsmouth, Rhode Island, are identical. Giles was probably a near relative of Anthony Slocum of Taunton.

Dr. Charles Elihu Slocum in SLOCUMS OF AMERICA says Giles is the son of Anthony, who moved from Taunton, Massachusetts, to Albermarle County in Carolina. His will dated 26 Nov 1688 and proved 7 Jan 1689/90 does not mention Giles or the children of Giles. It is probable therefore they were not father and son.

Will of Aldred Byccombe of Old Cleeve, County Somerset, England, clothier dated 21 July 1610 and proved 2 Feb 1610/11 by his relict Helen Byccombe, mentions—

Daughters: Charitie, Mary, Joane

Brother: William

Son: William

Brother-in-Law: Thomas Cridland

Son: Aldred

Isott Lanham daughter of daughter Ann Lanham, deceased

Somersetshire Wills Series 2 p 67.

Will of Ellen Bickham of Old Cleeve, County Somerset, England, widow dated 24 June 1642 and proved 20 June 1646, mentions—

Sister: Anne Ashe

Daughters: Charity Slocombe, Joan (wife of John Studdier)

Cousins: Nicholas and Roger Colles

Uncle John Colles's widow

Son Aldred's daughter: Ellen

Son: William

Somersetshire Wills series 2 p 68.

Will of William Bickham of Old Cleeve, County Somerset, England, Bachelor dated 2 Mar 1626 and proved 12 June 1627, mentions—

Aldred Bickham Jr.

Brother: Aldred

Brother-in-Law: John Studdier

Mother: Ellen Bickham

Somersetshire Wills Series 2 p 67

Will of Aldred Bickham of Old Cleeve County Somerset, England, Clothier dated 7 Feb 1651 and proved 24 May 1652, mentions—

Son: Richard to whom was given "a silver salt guilded with gold and six silver spoons, according to his grandfather's will to remain forever to the eldest son of his line and blood."

Wife: Thomasine

Daughter: Ellen Escott wife of Richard Escott

Son: Aldred

Son: William

Son: Hugh

Daughters: Johan, Mary and Anne Bickham and Isott Bickham

Granddaughters: Mary and Joan Escott

Brother-in-Law: Hugh Slocombe

Somersetshire Wills Series 3 p 87.

See N.E.H.G.R. Vol 70 pp 283-284

CHARITY BICKHAM OF OLD CLEEVE, COUNTY SOMERSET, ENGLAND

Married: Philip Slocum of Old Cleeve, County Somerset England, on November 20, 1621.

Died: Before 26 Jan 1642/3.

BRIGGS

CLEMENT BRIGGS, FELMONGER OF BERMONDSEY STREET SOUTHWARK DISTRICT, LONDON, ENGLAND

Born: ca 1600 in England

Married: 1st: Joanne Allen in 1630 or 1631

2nd: Elizabeth (?) about 1638. She died about 1691

Died: 1648

Children of Clement and Joanne (Allen) Briggs:

Jonathan Briggs. Born June 14, 1635, in Weymouth, Massachusetts. Married Experience (?) who with their son Jonathan was granted administration of his estate (Page 112 Vol 1 Bristol County, Mass., Probate Records) on November 18, 1690. See Book 2, pages 242 and 243 for division of estate. Jonathan Brigg lived at Taunton in 1662, 1668, 1672. Purchaser of North Purchase (now known as Easton) in 1668.

*Thomas Briggs

Children of Clement and Elizabeth (?) Briggs:

Clement Briggs. Born about November 1, 1642 or 1643, in Weymouth, Massachusetts. Married Hannah Packard, daughter of Samuel Packard of Bridgewater, Mass. Died November 7, 1669. Hannah (Packard) Briggs married 2nd Thomas Randall and she died on April 20, 1727. Administration papers are in Boston.

David Briggs. Born August 23, 1640, in Weymouth, Mass. Married on October 26, 1676 to Mary Barber of Southampton, Long Island, New York. Died between November 13, 1683, and November 11, 1685. In a History of Southampton it is stated that in 1674 David Briggs received land from Robert Fordham.

Elizabeth Briggs. Married June 25, 1689, to Elkanah Babbitt, son of Edward I. Babbit and Sarah Farne.

John Briggs. Received land at Plymouth in his father's will. Little is known positively of him. Some claim he is the same as John Briggs of Newport in 1638 and Portsmouth in 1642, though such is not probable.

Remember Briggs. Married Mary (?) of Weymouth, Mass. Died May 1696

Clement Briggs landed at Plymouth, Massachusetts, on November 19, 1621. He came in the *Fortune*. See N.E.H.G.R. Vol. 1, p 124.

In London, England, District called Southwark, Clement Briggs was a felmonger or tanner and dealer in hides. See Plymouth Colony Records Vol XII: 34, 35.

On August 29, 1638, Clement Briggs sold land in Plymouth to Robert Heeks (Hicks) and also made a deposition which shows that in 1616 he lived with Mr. Samuell Lathame in Barmundsey (Bermondsey) Street, Southwark District, London, England. N.E.H.G.H. Vol. 2, p 244

Clement Briggs and his wife both left books in their wills.
Plymouth Colony Records Vol XII:5 Clemente Brigges alloted one acre of land in 1623 and on May 22, 1627, he received a heifer brought on the ship *Jacob*. Plymouth Colony Records XII:9.

On March 5, 1639-40 Clement Briggs was named as one of 58 "purchasers" and an "old comer" of Plymouth. Plymouth Colony Records Vol II:177

Between 1627 and 1630 Clement Briggs moved to Dorchester and married in 1630 or 1631 Joan Allen. See The Records of the Governor and Company of the Massachusetts Bay in New England Vol 1.83.
Governor Bradford in a letter of 1631 to John Winthrop mentions the move of Clement Briggs to Dorchester. From Dorchester Clement Briggs moved to Weymouth, Mass., where his oldest son, Thomas, was born in 1633. Clement Briggs was fined for allowing an Indian in his house. Rec Gov Mass 1.132

Clement Briggs sold four acres of land to John Browne in what is now Kingston, Mass. Plymouth Colony Records 12:22

Mr. Savage, a descendant of Clement Briggs, in his Genealogical *Dictionary* mentions that Joan Allen (wife of Clement Briggs) was forbidden to "come into the company of Arthur Warren." Rec Gov Mass 1.219, 1.123

Clement Briggs was found "Not Guilty" of an extortion charge. Rec Gov Mass 1:247

Land of Clement Briggs mentioned Rec Gov Mass 1.123 (1639) and 1.163 (1640).

The Will of Clement Briggs is dated December 23, 1648, and proved 24 October 1650. It is in the Suffolk County Registry of Probate and has been printed in the New England Historical and Genealogical Register Vol 7 p 233

See Holmes Directory etc. p 31. Also N.E.H.G.R. Vol 18, p 368 N.E.G.H.R. Vol 9, p 171 for mention of Thomas son of Clement Briggs borne 14 (4) 1633. See N.E.H.G.R. Vol 9, p 347 mentions Estate of Clement Briggs.

Daniel Axtell bought one-half of the Briggs Grant in Bridgewater (later Abington) which was given to the children of Clement Briggs "old comer" by the Plymouth Colony in 1664 N.E.H.G.R. Vol 30, p 239

Will of Elizabeth Briggs second wife of Clement Briggs is in Vol 8 p 49 of the Probate Court of Suffolk County, Boston, Massachusetts. Samuel Packard in W. 1655-1664. Selectman. Removed to Bridgewater. His daughter Hannah married Clement Briggs Jr. who died 1669. Packard and his daughter settled the Briggs Estate. She married 2nd Thomas Randall of Easton. N.E.H.G.R. Vol 46 p 187

Robert Tucker of W. 1647-51 Overseer of Clement Briggs' will in W. 1648-9. N.E.H.G.R. Vol 46 p 188

Weymouth Mass Records

Tho:son of Clement Briggs borne 14 (4) 1633
Jonathan son of Clement Briggs borne 14 (4) 1635
David Briggs son of Clement Brigs borne 23 (6) 1640
Clemant sonne of Clement Bregs borne 1 (11) 1642
See N.E.H.G.R. Vol 8 p 348, Vol 9, p 171

Will of Clement Brigs of Waymouth 24 (8) 1650 mentions sons Thomas, Jonathan, Clement, David, John, and Remond (?) N.E.H.G.R. Vol 7 pp 233-4

See The Colonial Ancestry of the Family of John Greene Briggs and Isabell Gibbs De Groff by Harry Tallmadge Briggs of Poughkeepsie, New York, and John Greene Briggs of West Babylon, Long Island, New York (1940) pages 276-294

THOMAS BRIGGS, SENIOR

Born: June 14, 1633, at Weymouth, Massachusetts
Married: Ann (?   )
Died: Before April 1, 1696

Children of Thomas and Ann (?   ) Briggs:
*Daniel Briggs

Samuel Briggs   Married July 27, 1692 to Mary Hall daughter of Samuel Hall and Elizabeth White, daughter of Nicholas White. Samuel Briggs is mentioned in Chaffin's *History of Easton, Massachusetts*, as a son of Thomas Briggs

Mary (Hall) Briggs married 2nd on March 17, 1706-7 to Benjamin Caswell. Samuel Briggs died after January 1706.

Susannah Briggs married John Cobb

Thomas Briggs Jr. Probably born in Taunton, Massachusetts. Moved to Rhode Island where he was ferryman at Kingston. Married Martha (?   ). Freeman of East Greenwich, Rhode Island in 1703. He and Martha deeded land there on March 17, 1709 to son-in-law Samuel Gardiner. The will of Thomas Briggs Jr. was executed on January 4, 1724, and proved on December 25, 1736.

Thomas Briggs Senior was among the first settlers of Taunton, Massachusetts. He was joint owner with Richard Briggs of land in Norton and Mansfield, Massachusetts.

150 acres of land granted to Thomas Briggs, son of Clement Briggs deceased. June 7, 1659. See New Plymouth Records 3:164.

On March 16, 1696, Thomas Briggs Senior deeded land to his son Samuel Briggs.

The Inventory of Thomas Briggs Senior was dated April 1, 1696. His youngest son Samuel administered the estate. Land given sons, Thomas Daniel and Samuel. Left also daughter, Susannah, wife of John Cobb.

See H. T. Briggs, *Briggs*, pages 208-210.

DANIEL BRIGGS

Born: 1665

Married: Lydia (?   )

Died: 1730

Children of Daniel and Lydia (?   ) Briggs.

*Captain Benjamin Briggs

Deliverance Briggs. Married Seth Jones of East Greenwich, Rhode Island, son of Jeremiah and Mary Jones on October 28, 1732.

Hannah Briggs (Twin of Martha Briggs) Married Joseph Gardiner.

Martha Briggs (Twin of Hannah Briggs) Married Samuel Spencer, son of Michael Spencer of East Greenwich, Rhode Island on May 28, 1719.

Mercy Briggs Married William Card of East Greenwich, Rhode Island on June 13, 1733.

Daniel Briggs was born on the farm deeded to Thomas Briggs Senior on June 7, 1659 "on the way to Deadum".

On October 7, 1702, Daniel Briggs of Patience Island bought 90 acres in East Greenwich, Rhode Island from Joseph Wait.

Daniel and Lydia Briggs sold six acres of land in East Greenwich to Thomas Matteson on June 13, 1710.

Daniel Briggs received property from the Estate of his father, Thomas Briggs, Senior.

The will of Daniel Briggs was dated September 9, 1727, and was proved March 28, 1730. The will made son Benjamin Executor and named daughter Martha Spencer, wife of Samuel Spencer, daughter Hannah, wife of Joseph Gardiner and daughters, Deliverance and Mercy Briggs.

See H. T. Briggs, *Briggs*, pages 126 and 127

CAPTAIN BENJAMIN BRIGGS

Born: May 5, 1695

Married: Susannah Spencer on March 17, 1719-1720, in East Greenwich, Rhode Island

Died: November 25, 1759, in East Greenwich, Rhode Island

Children of Captain Benjamin and Susannah (Spencer) Briggs:

*Benjamin Briggs, Junior.

Deliverance Briggs. (Given in H. T. Briggs, *Briggs* but not in the list of Arnold in V.R.R.I. Vol I Kent Co. East Greenwich p 101)

Daniel Briggs. Born August 13, 1731. Married September 4 or 8, 1754, to Welthian Sweet, daughter of Captain Benjamin Sweet and Susannah Spencer, daughter of Robert Spencer and cousin of Susannah Spencer Briggs.

Elizabeth Briggs. Born July 8, 1721. Died June 15, 173.. Married Robert Sweet, son of Benjamin Sweet and Susannah Spencer.

Job Briggs. Born November 16, 1740. Died 1804. Married Susan Potter, daughter of Thomas Hazard Potter and Patience Wilkinson.

Job Briggs went to Potter, Yates County, New York, and later removed to Michigan. Mrs. Patience (Wilkinson) Potter lived with her son-in-law, Job Briggs after the death of her husband.

John Briggs. Born August 5, 1737. Married Susanna

Orpah Briggs. Born March 18, 1725-6. Married Benjamin Sweet, son of Captain Benjamin and Susannah (Spencer) Sweet, on April 23, 1746.

Samuel Briggs. Born August 31, 1733.

Thomas Briggs. Born July 1, 1720. Died August 10, 1720

Thomas Briggs. Born October 13, 1728. Married Abigail or Almy .... He lived in East Greenwich, Rhode Island, but the first deed of a land purchase in Dutchess County, New York, is by Thomas Briggs of Tiverton, Mariner, September 6, 1751.

James Newell Arnold, *Vital Records of Rhode Island* (abbreviated V.R.R.I.)

East Greenwich, Births and Deaths
(PP. 146-7)

Elizabeth Spencer of Michael and Elizabeth	born Sept	22,	1694
Samuel	Mar	2,	1696
Susannah	Mar	13,	1698
John	Jan	5,	1700
Abner	Jan	8,	1702-3
Isabel	June	6,	1705
Johanna	Jan	1,	1708-9
Johanna	died Mar	11,	1708-9
Mary	Jan	31,	1709-0
Ruth	Apr	24,	1711

| Orpha | Oct 31, 1713 |
| Michael | Apr 27, 1718 |

(P. 102)

Capt Benjamin Briggs died aged 64 y 6 m 20 ds Nov 25, 1759.

Warwick, Births and Deaths

Deborah Greene of Capt John and Ann	born Aug 10, 1649
John	June 6, 1651
William	Mar 5, 1652-3
Peter	Feb 4, 1654
Peter	died Aug 12, 1723
Job	Aug 24, 1656
Phillis	Oct 7, 1658
Richard	Feb 8, 1660
Anne	Mar 19, 1662-3
Catharine	Aug 15, 1665
Audrey	Dec 27, 1667
Samuel	Jan 30, 1670

Capt John Greene died aged 89 Nov 27, 1708

Ann wife of Capt John Greene died aged 82 May 6, 1709

The will of Robert Spencer mentions receipt from Benjamin Sweet.
John Osborne Austin, *Genealogical Dictionary of Rhode Island* page
187.

East Greenwich, Births and Deaths

(P. 158)

Robert Sweet of Benjamin and Susannah	born June 28, 1718
Ruth	May 8, 1720
Benjamin	Feb 6, 1721-2
Henry	Nov 10, 1723
Frances	Mar 8, 1725-6
Theodosha	Oct 30, 1727
Susanna	July 25, 1729
Amey	Apr 22, 1731
Welthian	Feb 3, 1732-3
Hannah	Nov 19, 1734
Theophilus	Dec 16, 1736
David	Dec 2, 1738

(P. 101)

Thomas Briggs of Benjamin and Susannah	born July 1, 1720
	died Aug 10, 1720
Elizabeth	July 8, 1721
Benjamin	Sept 25, 1723
Orpah	Mar 18, 1725-6
Thomas	Oct 13, 1728

Daniel	Aug	13, 1731
Samuel	Aug	31, 1733
John	Aug	5, 1737
Job	Nov	16, 1740

(P. 146)

John Spencer of John and Susannah	born	Apr	20, 1666
Mycael		May	28, 1668
Benjamin		June	22, 1670
William		July	1, 1672
Robert		Nov	6, 1674
Abner		Dec	4, 1676
Abner	died	May	11, 1759
Thomas		July	22, 1679
Thomas	died	Apr	25, 1752
Susannah		Dec	1, 1681
Peleg		Dec	4, 1683

Thomas Spencer listed above was the first English child born in East Greenwich.

Kent County, Volume 1
East Greenwich Marriages

(P. 11)

Benjamin Briggs and Susannah Spencer by John Spencer, Justice, March 17, 1719-0.

Benjamin Briggs Jr. of Capt Benjamin of E. Greenwich and Theodosia Sweet of Capt Henry of W. Greenwich married by Henry Tibbitts, Justice, June 7, 1747.

(P. 66)

Michael Spencer and Elizabeth (?) married by John Heath, Justice, Nov 16, 1682.

Susannah Spencer and Benjamin Briggs Mar 17, 1719-20.

(P. 75)

Theodosia Sweet and Benjamin Briggs Jr. June 7, 1747
East Greenwich, Births and Deaths

(P. 157)

Henry Sweet of Henry and Mary	born	Mar	11, 1682
John		Mar	24, 1684
Joseph		Mar	7, 1687
Benjamin		Mar	29, 1690
Mary		Feb	10, 1692
Johannah		Feb	13, 1695
William		Aug	1, 1698
Eals (daughter)		July	10, 1700

Ruth	July 10, 1700
Elizabeth	Feb 25, 1704
Susanna	May 17, 1706
Griffin	Sept 17, 1709
Hannah	Feb 8, 1711-2

BENJAMIN BRIGGS, JUNIOR

Born: September 25, 1723, in East Greenwich, Rhode Island

Married: Theodosia Sweet on June 7, 1747, in East Greenwich, Rhode Island

Children of Benjamin and Theodosia (Sweet) Briggs, Junior:

Elizabeth Briggs. Born December 6, 1748. Died January 13, 1749
Jeremiah Briggs. Born September 28, 1753
Joseph Briggs. Born December 5, 1749
Lydia Briggs. Born February 13, 1755. Died July 14, 1755
*Micael Briggs. Born September 16, 1751
Ruth Briggs. Born September 3, 1747

See H. T. Briggs, *Briggs*, page 94

See V.R.R.I. Vol I Kent Co East Greenwich Births and Deaths, page 102.

CAPTAIN JOSEPH BRIGGS

Born: December 5, 1749, in East Greenwich, Rhode Island

Married: Patience Gardner on May 19, 1779, in Bennington, Vermont

Died: March 29, 1832, in Pittsfield, Otsego County, New York
Children of Captain Joseph and Patience (Gardner) Briggs:
Silas Briggs
The following records are from the *History of Otsego County, New York* by Duane H. Hard Published by Everts and Fariss 714-716 Filbert Street, Philadelphia in 1878

(Page 287) Joseph Briggs from the Green Mountain State was among the first of many settlers. Mr. Briggs was a Captain in the War of the Revolution. Silas Briggs, a son was nine when he came with his father. Frank H. Briggs, the son of Silas Briggs, occupies the old homestead which has remained in the family nearly a century.

(Page 290) First School Tax in District No. 2 in 1814 in Pittsfield: Joseph Briggs, Joseph Briggs Jr., Silas Briggs

(Page 286) Pittsfield was formed from Burlington

(Page 289) Those competent as Pittsfield jurors in 1814: Silas Briggs, Joseph Briggs

(Page 289) Those competent as jurors on July 3, 1798: Joseph Briggs

(Page 289)   Joseph Briggs chosen constable and collector
Joseph Briggs named postmaster
Joseph Briggs one of the petitioners for a road
July 15, 1799
Joseph Briggs is Commissioner of Highways

Declaration of Mrs. Patience Briggs, wife of the late Captain Joseph Briggs, made to obtain a pension under the Law of the United States passed July 4, 1836. The original declaration is in the National Archives in Washington, D. C., Record Group No. 15A W16512

Mrs. Briggs swore that she married Captain Joseph Briggs on May 19, 1779, at Bennington County, Vermont, Samuel Robinson, a Justice of the Peace officiating.

That they lived in Pownall, Vermont.

That Captain Joseph Briggs died at Pittsfield, Otsego County, New York, on March 29, 1832

That her husband and his brother, Michael Briggs were in the Revolutionary War.

That her husband served as a Lieutenant under Captain Goff in the Vermont Militia.

That Captain Goff deserted and in 1778 her husband received a commission as Captain signed by Thomas Chittenden, the Governor of Vermont, and dated April 23, 1778.

That Joseph Briggs had the following service:

As Lieutenant, for six months in 1775, 1776, and 1777

As Captain for six months in 1778, 1779, 1780, and 1781.

That Joseph Briggs served under General Ethan Allen, Colonel Seth Warner, Major Bronson, Colonel Herrick of Springfield, Colonel Samuel Robinson

That Joseph Briggs was at the taking of Ticonderoga, in the Battle of Bennington, and in various other battles.

That her maiden name was Patience Gardner.

That she was born in East Greenwich, Rhode Island

That her parents moved to Vermont when she was very young

That Joseph Briggs was born in East Greenwich too

That Joseph Briggs was born on December 5, 1749 and that she was born on December 31, 1757

That Joseph Briggs was attached to the 2nd Regiment of the Vermont Militia

That there is a record of their marriage and the date of birth of her husband and of herself in their family Bible

That she and her husband lived in Pownall Vermont until February 1794 when they moved to Pittsfield

That the following persons were acquainted with her husband: General Augustus C. Welch, Charles Medbury, Esquire, Major Silas A. Conkey, Edward C. Williams, Esquire, General Henry De Forest, Hon. Nathan Taylor, Hon. James C. Walworth.

1810 CENSUS OTSEGO COUNTY NEW YORK TOWN OF PITTSFIELD

J. Briggs
1 male born before 1755
1 male born 1784-1794
1 male born 1800-1810
1 female born before 1755
1 female born 1755-1784
1 female born 1794-1800

1830 CENSUS OTSEGO COUNTY NEW YORK TOWN OF PITTSFIELD

Joseph Briggs
1 male born 1740-1750
1 male born 1820-1825
1 female born 1750-1760

1840 CENSUS OTSEGO COUNTY NEW YORK TOWN OF NEW LISBON

Patience Briggs
1 female born 1750-1760
1 female born 1800-1810

SILAS BRIGGS

Born: 1783 in Vermont
Married: Ruby (?   )
Died: After 1860
Children of Silas and Ruby (?   ) Briggs:
Almira Briggs. Deceased in 1893
Caleb Briggs. Lived in West Burlington, Otsego County, New York, in 1893
Francis Briggs, Senior
Horace Briggs. Lived in Boston in 1893
Joseph Briggs. Lived in Massachusetts in 1893.
The following is from the *Biographical Review of Otsego County, New York* published in 1893 by the Biographical Review Publishing Company of Boston. Page 827.

Frank Briggs was born in Pittsfield in 1870. He was the son of Frank Briggs of Pittsfield, who died in 1892, aged 67. He was the grandson of Silas Briggs, a native of Otsego County, who died upwards of 60 years old. Silas Briggs had the following children: Almira, deceased, Joseph who lives in Massachusetts, Caleb of West Burlington, Horace who lives in Boston, Mass., and Frank Briggs Sr.

who married Elizabeth Brown. Their children were: Rosa, deceased, Lilly, wife of Lott Davis of New Berlin, and Frank, who married in March, 1892 to Irene Pudney, daughter of Andrew Pudney of Otsego County

1830 CENSUS OTSEGO COUNTY NEW YORK TOWN OF PITTSFIELD
Silas Briggs
1 male born 1780-1790
1 male born 1810-1815
1 male born 1815-1820
2 males born 1820-1825
1 male born 1825-1830
1 female born 1780-1790
1 female born 1800-1810
1 female born 1810-1815
1 female born 1815-1820

1840 CENSUS OTSEGO COUNTY NEW YORK TOWN OF PITTSFIELD
Silas Briggs
1 male born 1780-1790
1 male born 1810-1820
2 males born 1820-1825
1 male born 1825-1830
1 female born 1780-1790

1850 CENSUS OTSEGO COUNTY NEW YORK TOWN OF PITTSFIELD
Silas Briggs born in 1783 in Vermont
Ruby Briggs born in 1787 in Rhode Island
Francis H. Briggs born in 1825 in New York
Silas Briggs born in 1837 in New York

1860 CENSUS OTSEGO COUNTY NEW YORK TOWN OF PITTSFIELD
Francis H. Briggs born in 1825 in New York
Elizabeth Briggs born in 1842 in New York
Silas Briggs born in 1783 in Vermont
Phebe Briggs born in 1787 in Rhode Island

1870 CENSUS OTSEGO COUNTY NEW YORK TOWN OF PITTSFIELD
Francis Briggs born in 1825 in New York
Elizabeth Briggs born in 1844 in New York
Rosa Briggs born in 1861 in New York
Lilla Briggs born in 1863 in New York
Francis Briggs born in 1870 in New York (male)

CALEB BRIGGS
Born: 1820-1821 in New York
Married: Hulda (?   )
Children of Caleb and Hulda (?   ) Briggs: Albert **Briggs,**

Alice Briggs, Charles E. Briggs, Helen Briggs, Mary Briggs, Masilla
(?) Briggs, Ruth Briggs.

1850 CENSUS OTSEGO COUNTY NEW YORK TOWN OF MORRIS
22, 24

Caleb Briggs born in 1821 in New York
Hulda Briggs born in 1825 in New York
Ruth Briggs born in 1847 in New York
Mary Briggs born in 1849 in New York

1860 CENSUS OTSEGO COUNTY NEW YORK TOWN OF BURLINGTON

Caleb H. Briggs born in 1820 in New York
Hulda Briggs born in 1824 in New York
Ruth Briggs born in 1847 in New York
Mary Briggs born in 1848 in New York
Masilla Briggs born in 1851 in New York
Hellen Briggs born in 1853 in New York
Charles E. Briggs born in 1855 in New York
Allis Briggs born in 1858 in New York
Albert Briggs born in 1859 in New York
Ruth Briggs born in 1844 in New York

FRANCIS BRIGGS, SENIOR

Born: 1825 in New York
Married: Elizabeth Brown
Children of Francis and Elizabeth (Brown) Briggs:

Francis Briggs, Junior, who married in March 1892 to Irene Pudney,
daughter of Andrew Pudney of Otsego County.

Lilly Briggs who married Lott Davis of New Berlin, New York
Rosa Briggs. Deceased in 1893.

LIEUTENANT MICHAEL BRIGGS

Born: September 16, 1751, in East Greenwich, Rhode Island
Married: Sarah Greene on December 28, 1775, in the then Town of
    Jerico (later Hancock), Berkshire County, Massachusetts
Died: February 10, 1828, in Burlington, New York

Children of Lieutenant Michael and Sarah (Greene) Briggs:

Eunice Briggs. Married George Gardner.

Gardner Briggs. Born in Otsego County, New York, on January 29,
1796. Married on July 4, 1821 to Selinda Sheldon. Died September
25, 1855.

Griffin Briggs. Born in Otsego County, New York, on March 29,
1782. Married 1st Rachel Sweet on March 11, 1802. Married 2nd
Susannah Parsons on April 21, 1814. Died on September 2, 1829.
Griffin Briggs was a soldier of the War of 1812.

*Henry Briggs. Born 1780. Married Phebe Parker.

Michael Briggs, Junior. Born 1775.

Ruth Briggs.

Thomas Briggs. Born 1803. Married Melinda Merchant, according to O. G. Briggs, *Descendants of the Sons of Michael and Sarah (Green) Briggs*. However, in *Marriages taken from the Otsego Herald and Western Advertiser and Freeman's Journal, Otsego County Newspapers from 1795-1840* Volume 1 compiled by Gertrude Audrey Barber, page 39 is the following: May 4, 1828, Burlington, New York, Thomas Briggs to Eleanor Merchant.

See *Descendants of the Sons of Michael and Sarah (Green) Briggs of Otsego County, New York State* Compiled by Orlo Gardner Briggs, Milwaukee, Wisconsin. Published by his wife, Lucy Adelaide Briggs. Printed by the Sugar River Printing Company T. L. Reese, Manager, Albany, Wisconsin. Copy of the book in the Library of Congress was presented by Mrs. Edith Briggs Peters, 1408 Randall Street, Beloit, Wisconsin. A Copy was placed in the State Historical Library, Madison, Wisconsin. See Pages 10, 11, 35.

1790 CENSUS ALBANY COUNTY NEW YORK HALFMOON TOWN

Michael Briggs
1 male born before 1774
2 males born after 1774
4 females

1800 CENSUS OTSEGO COUNTY NEW YORK TOWN OF BURLINGTON

Michael Briggs
1 male born before 1755
1 male born 1774-1784
1 male born 1784-1790
1 male born 1790-1800
1 female born 1755-1774
1 female born 1774-1784
1 female born 1784-1790
1 female born 1790-1800

1810 CENSUS OTSEGO COUNTY NEW YORK TOWN OF BURLINGTON

M. Briggs
1 male born before 1755
1 male born 1794-1800
1 male born 1800-1810
1 female born before 1755
1 female born 1755-1784

1820 CENSUS OTSEGO COUNTY NEW YORK TOWN OF BURLINGTON

Michael Briggs
1 male born before 1775
2 males born 1794-1804

1 male born 1802-1804
1 female born before 1775
1 female born 1775-1794

AFFIDAVIT OF PATIENCE BRIGGS OF THE TOWN OF PITTS-FIELD, COUNTY OF OTSEGO, STATE OF NEW YORK

Patience Briggs swore that:

She was 79 years old

She is the widow of Captain Joseph Briggs deceased who resided in the Town of Pownall in the State of Vermont and served in the Army in the Revolution.

She was well acquainted with Michael Briggs and his wife Sarah Briggs

During the war they lived in Pownall, but afterwards moved to Burlington, Otsego County, New York, where Sarah still resides.

Deponent made a declaration of the services of Joseph Briggs, her husband, to obtain a pension under the Act of July 4, 1836.

Michael Briggs was in the Army with her husband in 1775 until he came home sick in the fall of that year.

Michael Briggs was an Orderly Sergeant, Ensign and Lieutenant and served as such under her husband in his company nearly all the time her husband was in the service.

Her husband and Michael Briggs were brothers.

At Ticonderago, Michael Briggs had a ball shot through the stock and cut off the ramrod of his gun within about a hand breadth of his hand and she has seen the gun.

In the Revolution Joseph and Michael Briggs generally went away into the service together.

Michael Briggs served in the war more than three years, in the years 1775, 1776, 1777, 1778, 1779, 1780, 1781, and 1782.

The Saturday before Joseph Briggs died he told her that he had been in the Revolutionary Army 4 years and upwards.

Joseph and Michael Briggs were in the taking of Ticonderoga and Crown Point, in the Battle of Bennington and Saratoga and they served under General Arnold, Allen, Gates, and Stark and Colonels Warner, Herrick, and Warren and Major Branson

Sworn and Signed before the Judge of Otsego County in 1837.

"These may certify the Honorable General Assembly of Vermont that we the subscribers have been well acquainted with Eld. Benjamin Gardners conduct concerning the present war, as we live in the neighborhood with him, and he and his family is in our company. He was agreed to defend his country by always going at the first notice of any alarm or whenever men is sent for, by encouraging men to list, by contributing men, arms money clothes provision and any necessary that was wanting so that he (word illegible) his family has been behind in their duty by money or . . . .

Signed in Pownall Oct 13 . . . . . . by Joseph Briggs Capt, Lt. Mikel Briggs, Ensign John Doaller, and Hugh Thompson.

George R. Thompson, Deputy Secretary of State of Vermont certified the above as a true copy in his office at Montpelier on March 12, 1855.

THOMAS CHITTENDEN ESQ CAPTAIN GENERAL, GOVERNOR AND COMMANDER IN CHIEF IN AND OVER THE STATE OF VERMONT

TO MICHEAL BRIGGS GENTLEMAN

You being elected Ensign of the Company of Militia in Pownall Reposing especial trust and confidence in your patriotism, valour, conduct and fidelity: I do by these presents In the Name of the Freemen of this State Authorize and Impower you to take the charge of sd company as their Ensign. You are therefore carefully and dilligently to discharge the duty of Ensign of a company by doing and performing all manner of things thereunto belonging and I do strictly charge and require all officers and soldiers under your command to be obedient to your orders as Ensign and you are carefully and dilligently to observe and obey such orders and Directions from time to time as you shall receive from me or the Governor of this State for the time being or other of your Superior Officers according to the rules and Discipline of War and the Laws of this State for which this Commission shall be your Sufficient Warrant. Given under my hand in Council Arlington April 23d 1778

BY HIS EXCELLENCY'S
COMMAND   THOS CHITTENDEN
M. LYON, D. SECY

AFFIDAVIT OF SILAS GARDNER OF CUYAHOGA COUNTY, THE STATE OF OHIO, MIDDLEBURGH TOWNSHIP

Silas Gardner swore that:

He was well acquainted with Michael Briggs of Burlington, Otsego County, New York and lived near to him in Burlington about twenty-five years.

He left Burlington in 1819.

Michael Briggs has been dead more than twenty years.

He heard Michael Briggs say he held a Lieutenant's Commission in the Revolutionary War.

Deponent is 72 years old. He has often heard Michael Briggs tell how long he was in service. He thinks it was more than six months, but thinks it was less than a year.

Subscribed and Sworn on October 3, 1853 before Morris Hepburn, Justice of the Peace.

AFFIDAVIT OF CLARK GARDNER OF BURLINGTON OTSEGO COUNTY NEW YORK

Clark Gardner swore that:

He was well acquainted with Michael Briggs who was a Revolutionary Soldier

He lived near Michael Briggs from 1794 until his death in February 1828.

He heard him say he enlisted under Captain Stewart and went to Manchester and was with Col. Warner, Putnam and Arnold at Skenesborough and that he saw Putnam and Arnold or Allen clash their swords together repecting a barrell of rum at which time Col. Warner interfered and settled the difficulty. He went to Ticonderoga and was there an officer of the guard. The day after the skirmish or battle he was relieved from the guard and went onto the battle ground and picked up a large powder horn with the name of Stephen (surname illegible) and number of Regiment and date of the year cut upon it and also a verse cut in it. The said horn remained in his possession until his death and deponent has often seen it. Michael Briggs was with Schuyler when he retreated from Ticonderoga and was in the Battle of Bennington and had his gun barrell dented or smashed by a ball from the enemy which he threw down and took in exchange a gun from a fellow soldier then dead. Deponent heard Michael Briggs say he was an Ensign and saw him show how they exercised the colours in Service. Deponent heard Michael Briggs say he was often out when an alarm that the enemy was approaching was sounded, for a few hours and days at times.

Sworn and Signed before William M. Fairchild (?) J.P. Oneida County, New York, on 18 February 1854.

AFFIDAVIT OF MRS. LOVINA BURLINE AND MRS. LIVONA KEECH, THE FORMER OF THE TOWN OF AUGUSTA, ONEIDA COUNTY, NEW YORK, AND THE LATTER OF THE TOWN OF STOCKBRIDGE, MADISON COUNTY, NEW YORK

They swore that:

They were well acquainted with Mrs. Sarah Briggs late of the Town of Augusta and knew her for thirty years before her death which occurred in Augusta on February 12, 1849, as deponent Lovina recollects. Deponents were present at her death. Sarah Briggs was the widow of Michael Briggs who died in the Town of Burlington, Otsego County, New York

Each deponent lived near Michael Briggs when he died and believe he was in the Army in the American Revolution.

AFFIDAVIT OF CLARK GARDNER OF THE TOWN OF BURLINGTON COUNTY OF OTSEGO, THE STATE OF NEW YORK

Clark Gardner swore that:

He was well acquainted with Michael Briggs late of the Town of Burlington, County of Otsego, State of New York

He knew him from 1794 to the time of his death in Burlington on the 11th day of February, 1828 and that he attended his funeral.

Michael Briggs left the following children surviving:
Ruth Briggs, Griffin Briggs, Henry Briggs, Eunice Gardner, the wife of George Gardner, Thomas Briggs, and Gardner Briggs

All the children were now dead (28 June 1854) except:
Eunice Gardner, Thomas Briggs, and Gardner Briggs

Gardner Briggs made application for pension money on account of the Revolutionary services of Michael Briggs.

Sworn before Hiram Kinne, Surrogate, on 28 June 1854

AFFIDAVIT OF G. HERRINGTON OF THE TOWN OF BURLINGTON, COUNTY OF OTSEGO STATE OF NEW YORK

G. Herrington swore that:

He was well acquainted with Michael Briggs late of the Town of Burlington, County of Otsego for 38 years.

That Michael Briggs died on the 11th day of February 1828 and he attended his funeral.

That Eunice Gardner, Thomas Briggs, and Gardner Briggs are his only children still surviving.

He heard the above affidavit of Clark Gardner and knows of his own knowledge that all the facts stated therein are true.

In the State of New York, County of Oneida, before W. G. Cummings, J.P., appeared Gardner Briggs, a resident of Augusta, in the County of Oneida, in New York, who being duly sworn states that he is the son of Michael Briggs and Sarah Briggs, deceased, late of the County of Otsego, and State of New York who was a Revolutionary Officer and that he is interested as a claimant in the pension for which application has heretofore been made by Sarah Briggs and constitutes F. E. Hasler of Washington, D. C. his attorney to establish the claim.

Signed on December 1, 1852 with David Stilson a witness. Alexander Rae, Clerk of Oneida County, certified that W. G. Cummings was a J.P. on December 4, 1852.

For Military Service of Michael Briggs, Elisha Parker, and Job Greene, see D.A.R. Record of Elaine Briggs Fleming National Number 328946 and also D.A.R. Record of Mary Briggs Thompson National Number 353873.

Affidavits of Military Service of Michael and Joseph Briggs may be found in the National Archives, Record Group No. 15 A.

Revolutionary Descent of Mrs. Ruth J. H. Parker Kyner, born in West Burlington, New York, and the wife of James H. Kyner is found in Daughters of the American Revolution Lineage Book, Volume 91, page 173

1. David G. Parker (1822-1881) Married 1852 to
   Susannah Bolton (1817-1885)

2. Alexander Parker (1768-1845). Married 1793 to
   Joannah Gardner (1777-1860)

3. Elisha Parker (1746-1813). Married Maria Ellsworth
   (1747-1828)

Elisha Parker served as an ensign and lieutenant 1776-1778 in Captain Josiah Gibb's Company, Colonel William Richmond's Regiment. He was born in Rhode Island and died in Burlington, New York.

Civil War Record of Michael P. Briggs from the Adjutant General, Albany, New York:

"Machael P. Briggs, residence, New Berlin, Chenango County, New York, enlisted May 3, 1861, at Utica as a private, Co. F, 26th N.Y. Vol Inf, but was discharged May 19, 1861, not having been mustered into the service of the United States".

Job Greene was a private in Captain Elijah Dewey's Company at the Battle of Bennington, August 16, 1777. Tuttle's ROLLS OF VERMONT.

GARDNER BRIGGS

Born: January 29, 1796, in Otsego County, New York

Married: On July 4, 1821, to Selinda Sheldon who was born on April 30, 1803, and who died on October 13, 1875.

Died: September 25, 1855

Children of Gardner and Selinda (Sheldon) Briggs:

Aaron Briggs. Born in New York on March 13, 1826. Died February 9, 1845

Alonzo Briggs. Born in Oneida County, New York, on January 23, 1838. Married on December 22, 1866, to Amelia E. Hepson of Jefferson County, Wisconsin.

Erastus Briggs. Born in New York on November 16, 1829, and died on September 22, 1840.

Erastus Thomas Briggs and Ervin Briggs.

Eunice Briggs. Born in Otsego County, New York, on December 25,

1827. Married her first cousin, John Parmley Briggs, the son of Griffin Briggs.

Daniel Wesley Briggs

DANIEL WESLEY BRIGGS

Born on January 23, 1838, in Oneida County, New York

Married: Almira L. Scofield of Rock County, Wisconsin

Died: March 6, 1917

Children of Daniel Wesley and Almira (Scofield) Briggs:

John Scofield Briggs. Born on October 3, 1871, in Rock County, Wisconsin.

Pearl May Briggs. Born on February 12, 1880, in Carpenter, Iowa.

ERASTUS THOMAS BRIGGS

Born on March 10, 1841, in Oneida County, New York

Married: 1st Elmira H. Pelton of Janesville, Wisconsin, on November 17, 1867

2nd Elsie Walker of Johnstown, Wisconsin

Died: November 11, 1926

Children of Erastus Thomas and Elmira (Pelton) Briggs:

Arthur Gardner Briggs. Born on May 21, 1870, in Jefferson County, Wisconsin.

Ervin Henry Briggs. Born on September 26, 1868, in Jefferson County, Wisconsin.

Frank Alonzo Briggs. Born on March 30, 1872, in Adams County, Wisconsin.

George Wesley Briggs. Born on April 12, 1878, in Dane County, Wisconsin.

Child of Erastus Thomas and Elsie (Walker) Briggs:

Ray Chester Briggs. Born in Arcadia, Texas, on December 20, 1910. Lives in Dallas, Texas.

ERVIN BRIGGS

Born on June 9, 1833, in Oneida County, New York

Married: Ann Torrey, who was born on October 14, 1836, and who died on April 23, 1912

Died: August 6, 1864, in Andersonville Prison, Georgia.

He was a member of the 1st Wisconsin Cavalry.

Children of Ervin and Ann (Torrey) Briggs:

Cora Lucretia Briggs. Born on November 28, 1859, in Jefferson County, Wisconsin. Married Marshall C. Crawford of Juneau County, Wisconsin, and lived in Mauston, Wisconsin.

Henry Gardner Briggs. Born on December 7, 1854, in Oneida County, New York. Married Josephine S. Delap on December 24, 1882. He died on December 4, 1930. His wife lived in Mauston, Wisconsin.

Ina Ervin Briggs born on April 12, 1864, in Jefferson County, Wisconsin. Married Rupert Rhodes of Juneau County, Wisconsin, on April 2, 1885. Died on February 27, 1886.

Mary Caroline Briggs. Born on November 1, 1857, in Jefferson County, Wisconsin. Married Rodney Severance on February 18, 1885. She lived in Mauston, Wisconsin.

Mary Josephine Briggs. Born on September 1, 1856, in Jefferson County, Wisconsin. Died on October 22, 1856.

GRIFFIN BRIGGS

Born: March 29, 1782, in Otsego County, New York

Married: 1st Rachel Sweet on March 11, 1802. She was born in 1786 and died on January 14, 1813

2nd Susannah Parsons on April 21, 1814. She was born on October 20, 1798, and died August 21, 1865.

Died: September 2, 1829

Children of Griffin and Rachel (Sweet) Briggs:

Lyman Briggs. Born in New York on September 1, 1803.
Died March 5, 1892

Children of Griffin and Susannah (Parsons) Briggs:

Daniel Briggs

Gardner P. Briggs. Born in New York on December 31, 1820.
Died on March 20, 1821.

Chloe Briggs. Born in New York on May 10, 1822.
Died July 14, 1822.

Henry Briggs. Born in New York on December 23, 1816.
Died March 14, 1832.

John Parmley Briggs

Griffin Briggs, Jr. Born in New York on April 19, 1829.
Died December 31, 1847.

Mary Ann Briggs. Born in New York on September 20, 1815.
Died March 21, 1880.

Spencer Briggs

William Briggs

1830 CENSUS OTSEGO COUNTY, NEW YORK TOWN OF NEW LISBON

Susanna Briggs
2 males born 1815-1820
2 males born 1820-1825
2 males born 1825-1830

1 female born 1760-1770
1 female born 1790-1800
1 female born 1820-1825

1840 CENSUS OTSEGO COUNTY NEW YORK TOWN OF BURLINGTON
Susan Briggs
1 female born 1760-1770
1 female born 1790-1800
1 female born 1810-1820

1850 CENSUS OTSEGO COUNTY NEW YORK TOWN OF BURLINGTON
HOUSE NO. 663, FAMILY NO. 734

Susanna Briggs born in 1799 in New York
Mary A. Briggs born in 1815 in New York

HOUSE NO. 676, FAMILY NO. 734
John Briggs born in 1828 in New York
Eunice Briggs born in 1828 in New York
Aaron Briggs born in 1849 in New York

1860 CENSUS JEFFERSON COUNTY WISCONSIN KOSKONING POST OFFICE
FORT ATKINSON
1494, 1490
Wesley Briggs born in 1838 in New York
Alonzo Briggs born in 1835 in New York
Erastus Briggs born in 1841 in New York
Salinda Briggs born in 1803 in New York

1495, 1491
John Briggs born in 1828 in New York
Eunice Briggs born in 1828 in New York
Aaron Briggs born in 1849 in New York
Henry Briggs born in 1852 in New York
Alice Briggs born in 1856 in Wisconsin
Albert Briggs born in 1858 in Wisconsin
Ada Briggs born in 1859 in Wisconsin

1225, 1220
Ervin Briggs born in 1834 in New York
Ann T. Briggs born in 1837 in New York
Henry G. Briggs born in 1855 in New York
Mary C. Briggs born in 1858 in Wisconsin
Cora L. Briggs born in 1859 in Wisconsin

DANIEL BRIGGS

Born: March 18, 1817, in New York

Married: On January 1, 1846, to his cousin, Harriet Parsons, who
was born on September 23, 1827, and died on May 15, 1912

Died: June 26, 1903

Children of Daniel and Harriet (Parsons) Briggs:

Ann Eliza Briggs   Born in New York on September 6, 1850
Married on September 24, 1870 to Evan Olesono who had been born in Norway. She died on March 13, 1912.

Charles Edward Briggs   Born in Wisconsin on March 14, 1855
Married on January 20, 1878, to Kate Belle Clement

Ida Jane Briggs   Born in Wisconsin on August 2, 1861. She married 1st on November 28, 1875 to Lewis Helm and she married 2nd to Merton Henry Cummings.

Lelah Briggs. Born in Wisconsin on April 14, 1865. Married 1st Henry P. Travis. Married 2nd on December 14, 1886 to Hiram Howard. Married 3rd on April 17, 1887 to Charles H. Card.

Lyman Henry Briggs. Born in New York on January 20, 1853.
Married Eva Bancroft of Rock County, Wisconsin, lived in Janesville.

Nancy A. Briggs. Born in New York on December 18, 1848.
Married on December 18, 1866, to Daniel B. Lovejoy of Rock County, Wisconsin. Died on November 3, 1897.

1850 CENSUS OTSEGO COUNTY NEW YORK TOWN OF PITTSFIELD
William Briggs (brother of Daniel) born in 1823 in New York
Amy J. Briggs born in 1826 in New York

JOHN PARMLEY BRIGGS

Born: April 3, 1827, in New York

Married: 1st Eunice Briggs, his first cousin, the daughter of Gardner Briggs, on August 29, 1847. She was born on December 25, 1827, and died on September 9, 1865

2nd Marilla Bates of Michigan in 1865

3rd Mary E. Smith on December 2, 1879

Died: May 16, 1900

Children of John Parmley and Eunice (Briggs) Briggs:

Aaron Griffin Briggs. Born Oneida County, New York, on December 21, 1848. Married on July 4, 1870, to Lydia A. Scofield of Rock County, Wisconsin. Married 2nd Lena Green of Rusk County, Wisconsin. Died on December 17, 1926.

Ada Estella Briggs. Born on November 16, 1859, in Jefferson County, Wisconsin. Married on March 10, 1877 to Philo Sterling, Jr., of Juneau County, Wisconsin.

Albert Parmley Briggs. Born on May 12, 1858, in Jefferson County, Wisconsin. Married Fredericka Moote on January 1, 1880.

Alice Florilla Briggs. Born on May 3, 1856 in Jefferson County, Wisconsin. Died on September 18, 1874.

Henry Ervin Briggs. Born in Otsego County, New York, on July 26, 1851. Married on July 19, 1880 to Sarah Jane Rodwell of Sauk County, Wisconsin. Died on February 27, 1888.

Orlo Gardner Briggs. Born on July 27, 1861, in Jefferson County, Wisconsin. Married Lucy Adelaide Chase of Wilton, Wisconsin, on April 15, 1886.

SPENCER BRIGGS

Born: May 10, 1825, in New York
Married: Sarah Ann Parker on December 13, 1848
Died: February 3, 1885

Children of Spencer and Sarah Ann (Parker) Briggs:

Annie Briggs. Born in Otsego County, New York, on January 26, 1856. Married Peter Card on April 3, 1877. She died on June 26, 1921.

Elvira D. Briggs. Born in Otsego County, New York, on April 3, 1853. Died on May 15, 1871.

Ida M. Briggs. Born in Otsego County, New York, on January 7, 1858. Died on July 25, 1865.

1850 CENSUS OTSEGO COUNTY NEW YORK TOWN OF PITTSFIELD
Spencer Briggs born in 1825 in New York
Sarah Briggs born in 1829 in New York

1870 CENSUS OTSEGO COUNTY NEW YORK TOWN OF NEW LISBON
Spencer Briggs born in 1825 in New York
Sarah Briggs born in 1831 in New York
Elvira Briggs born in 1853 in New York
Ann Briggs born in 1856 in New York

WILLIAM BRIGGS

Born in New York on May 21, 1823

Married: Amy Bruce on January 10, 1847. Amy Bruce was born on December 26, 1825.

Died: September 17, 1900
Child of William and Amy (Bruce) Briggs:

Eva Briggs. Born in Otsego County, New York, on November 15, 1860. Married to David H. Webster on December 19, 1877.

1850 CENSUS OTSEGO COUNTY NEW YORK TOWN OF PITTSFIELD 58, 58
William Briggs born in 1823 in New York
Amy J. Briggs born in 1826 in New York

1870 CENSUS OTSEGO COUNTY NEW YORK TOWN OF PITTSFIELD
William Briggs born in 1823 in New York
Anna Briggs born in 1826 in New York
Eva Jane Briggs born in 1851 in New York

HENRY BRIGGS

Born: ca 1780
Married: Phoebe Parker
Died: Before January 26, 1846
Children of Henry and Phoebe (Parker) Briggs:
Michael Parker Briggs.

1810 Census Otsego County New York Town of Burlington
H. Briggs
1 male born 1784-1794
1 male born 1800-1810
1 female born 1784-1794
1 female born 1800-1810

1820 Census Otsego County New York Town of Burlington
Henry Briggs
1 male born 1775-1794
1 male born 1804-1810
1 female born 1775-1794
1 female born 1804-1810
1 female born 1810-1820

1830 Census Otsego County New York Town of Burlington
Henry Briggs
1 male born 1780-1790
1 male born 1800-1810
1 male born 1810-1815
1 female born 1760-1770
1 female born 1770-1780
1 female born 1780-1790
1 female born 1800-1810
2 females born 1825-1830

1840 Census Otsego County New York Town of Burlington
Henry Briggs
1 male born 1780-1790
1 male born 1830-1835
1 female born 1750-1760
1 female born 1770-1780
1 female born 1780-1790

AFFIDAVIT OF CORA E. CARPENTER OF MORRIS, OTSEGO
COUNTY, NEW YORK: ON FILE WITH THE DAUGHTERS OF
THE AMERICAN REVOLUTION PAPERS OF ELAINE BRIGGS
FLEMING OF OAK GROVE, LOUISIANA, AND YOUNGSTOWN,
OHIO
STATE OF NEW YORK

COUNTY OF OTSEGO
TOWN OF MORRIS

Cora E. Carpenter, being duly sworn, deposes and says:

1. That she resides in the Town of Morris, County of Otsego, and State of New York.
2. That she is the wife of Stanley Carpenter.
3. That she is the daughter of Eri Parker and Phila Chase, his wife.
4. That she is familiar with the family genealogy.
5. That Abraham Parker was the grandfather of this deponent.
6. That Alexander Parker was the great-grandfather of this deponent.
7. That Elisha Parker was the great-great grandfather of this deponent.
8. That this deponent has been told many times by members of her family that Phebe Parker was the sister of the above-mentioned Alexander Parker and
9. That she was the wife of Henry Briggs.
10. That the above-mentioned Alexander Parker was born in 1767 and that he died in 1845.
11. That she knows that Michael Parker Briggs, who died at the residence of this deponent's father was the son of Henry Briggs and the above-mentioned Phebe Parker Briggs.
12. That Henry Delos Briggs was the son of Michael Parker Briggs.
13. That she remembers and knew Henry Delos Briggs.
14. That this deponent was not acquainted with the wife of Michael Parker Briggs, but that she has been informed and believes that the wife of Michael Parker Briggs was Sophronia Matteson.
15. That Michael Parker Briggs was a Civil War veteran; that he came back from the Civil War and died at the home of this deponent's father, as is above recited.

CORA E. CARPENTER

Notary Seal and Signature

Conveyances and Deeds, Cooperstown, New York:

Volume 78, page 202

1829 — Between Susannah Briggs of Burlington Twp, Otsego County, New York, widow of Griffin Briggs, late of Burlington, deceased, and also as guardian of Mary Ann Briggs, Henry Briggs, Daniel Briggs, William Briggs, Spencer Briggs, Parmley Briggs, and Griffin Briggs, infant children and heirs at law of said Griffin Briggs, deceased, parties of the first part and Henry Briggs of the township, county, and state aforesaid of the second part — land situated Twp.

Burlington, Lot 15 Bowne Patent bounded on north by Lot 14 formerly owned by Jeremiah Briggs; east, by Lot 16 formerly owned by Oliver Gardner; south by land formerly owned by Alexander Parker and on west by land formerly belonging to Samuel Sweet containing in the whole lot one hundred acres more or less.

Henry Briggs, party of the second part having indemnified said infant children against the payment of a mortgage, etc.

/signed/ SUSANNAH BRIGGS

Sworn to before George Clyde, Commissioner
February 20, 1846

Conveyances and Deeds, Cooperstown, New York

Volume 57, page 279

Indenture   19 March 1828   Between Sarah Briggs, Thomas Briggs, Ruth Briggs, George Gardner and Eunice Gardner, his wife, Gardner Briggs and Selinda, his wife, Griffin Briggs, and Susannah, his wife of the first part and Henry Briggs of the second part of Burlington Twp. of Otsego County, State of New York. Parties of the first part for consideration of the sum of $100 have sold, quit-claimed etc. unto said party of the second part a piece of land in Burlington: that part of Lot 15 Bowne Patent, the whole lot being the same that Michael Briggs, late of Burlington, etc.

Parties of the first part have hereunto set their hands and seals the day and year first above written.

SARAH BRIGGS, SELINDA BRIGGS, GARDNER BRIGGS, GEORGE BRIGGS, RUTH BRIGGS, SUSANNAH BRIGGS, GRIFFIN BRIGGS.

Signed and delivered in presence of George C. Clyde
19 March A.D. 1828.

George Gardner and Eunice Briggs, his wife, known as grantors.
Recorded November 5, 1836.

January 28, 1846 — Phebe Briggs widow of Henry Briggs, late of Burlington of the first part and Willet Chase of the Twp. of New Lisbon, of the second part. Party of the first part in consideration of $75 paid to her by Halsey Spencer of Edmeston quitclaims etc all her claim of the following lot of land in Typ. Burlington south half of Lot 15 in Bowne Patent, also a house lot owned by Lyman Briggs which is bounded on north by other half of said lot 15, on east by lands of Nicholas Gardner, on south by Twp. line Burlington, on west by lands of Samuel Sweet and containing 50 acres more or less with all hereditaments etc. thereunto belonging.

PHEBE BRIGGS

Witness
David B. St. John, Justice
28 Jan A.D. 1846

MICHAEL PARKER BRIGGS

Born: 1808-1810 in New York

Married: Saphronia Matteson ca 1832

Died: March 21, 1864

Children of Michael Parker and Saphronia (Matteson) Briggs:

Andrew J. Briggs, Emily Elvira Briggs, Henry Delos Briggs, James Polk Briggs, Julia Briggs, Lewis Cass Briggs, Mary Frances Briggs, Phoebe Jane Briggs, Rachel Briggs, Sarah Briggs.

1840 CENSUS OTSEGO COUNTY NEW YORK TOWN OF BURLINGTON

M. P. Briggs

1 male born 1800-1810

1 male born 1830-1835

1 female born 1810-1820

2 females born 1835-1840

1850 CENSUS OTSEGO COUNTY NEW YORK TOWN OF NEW LISBON

Michel P. Briggs born in 1810 in New York

Suffrona Briggs born in 1817 in New York

Sally A. Briggs born in 1839 in New York

Emma Briggs born in 1841 in New York

James Briggs born in 1843 in New York

Rachel L. Briggs born in 1845 in New York

Lewis Briggs born in 1846 in New York

Job Briggs born in 1849 in New York

Phebe Briggs born in 1787 in Vermont

Conveyances and Deeds, Cooperstown, New York

Volume VV, page 227

Henry Briggs of the Twp. of Burlington in the County of Otsego of the first part and Michael P. Briggs of the same place of the second part for the sum of $400 paid by the party of the second part, 50 acres of land, Town Lot Number 15 in Bowne Patent bounded on the north by Lot Number 14 now in the possession of George Gardner and on the east by land of Oliver Gardner, and on the south by line of Twp of New Lisbon and on the west by land of Samuel Sweet.

Witness   Signed

J. C. Walworth 15 Jan 1832   HENRY BRIGGS

Recorded 16 Jan 1832

Volume 104, page 408

Phebe Briggs of the Twp of Pittsfield, Otsego County and Michael Briggs of the same Twp, land in Twp of New Lisbon February 15, 1854

Liber 112 of Conveyances, page 184

Michael P. Briggs and his wife, Sophronia, deeded land on May 14, 1857, to Henry D. Briggs

Michael Briggs died intestate March 21, 1864. Letters of administration were issued on June 22, 1864, to James Briggs. In the papers connected with the Estate is one in which James Briggs states, "Respectfully showeth that your petitioner is the oldest son now living except a brother in the Rebel Army of Michael Briggs late of the Town of New Lisbon in the County of Otsego, deceased leaving no widow."

1870 CENSUS OTSEGO COUNTY NEW YORK TOWN OF NEW LISBON

Lewis C. Briggs born in 1847 in New York
Mary J. Briggs born in 1848 in New York
Julia M. Briggs born in 1869 in New York

1870 CENSUS OTSEGO COUNTY NEW YORK TOWN OF BUTTERNUTS
397, 393

Andrew J. Briggs born in 1848 in New York
Antoinette Briggs born in 1846 in New York
Their marriage was in May, 1870.

1860 CENSUS OTSEGO COUNTY NEW YORK TOWN OF PITTSFIELD

Michael Briggs born in 1808 in New York
Emma Briggs born in 1842 in New York
Rachel Briggs born in 1845 in New York
Lewis Briggs born in 1846 in New York
Andrew Briggs born in 1848 in New York
Frances Briggs born in 1853 in New York

1870 CENSUS OTSEGO COUNTY NEW YORK TOWN OF BURLINGTON

Caleb Briggs born in 1820 in New York
Hulda Briggs born in 1824 in New York
Charles Briggs born in 1855 in New York
Albert Briggs born in 1857 in New York
Alice Briggs born in 1859 in New York

1850 CENSUS MADISON COUNTY NEW YORK LENNOX 502, 502

Gardner Briggs born in 1796 in New York
Celinda Briggs born in 1803 in New York
Alonzo Briggs born in 1835 in New York
Daniel W. Briggs born in 1838 in New York
Erastus Briggs born in 1841 in New York

1830 CENSUS OTSEGO COUNTY NEW YORK TOWN OF BURLINGTON
Thomas Briggs
1 male born 1800-1810
1 female born 1810-1815
1 female born 1825-1830

EMILY ELVIRA BRIGGS

Born: July 28, 1841, in Burlington, Otsego County, New York

Married: Hiram Orlando Woodard on September 23, 1863

Died: May 10, 1906

Children of Hiram Orlando and Emily Elvira (Briggs) Woodward:
Bennie Butler Woodard. Born April 3, 1877. Married on June 27, 1906, to Louise Gassler. They had a daughter, Catherine Emily Woodard (called Mildred) who was born in Johnson City and Married Kenneth Miller.

Charles Henry Woodard. Born August 27, 1868

Frank Etson Woodard. Born September 28, 1870. Married in Binghamton on June 10, 1896, to Emma Julia Ochse. They had a daughter, Hazel Emilie Woodard born on October 5, 1897 in Norwich, who married George Smith

Fred Marvin Woodard. Born June 30, 1866. Married Julia Miranda Follett on April 25, 1888. They had the following children: Bertha Victoria Woodward, born April 8, 1901, who married Chester G. Lookwood on June 3, 1925, in Norwich, New York. Ivan Dewitt Woodard who was born July 1, 1888 and married on September 3, 1926, to Josephine Adams at Syracuse, New York. Mary Emilie Woodard. Born August 7, 1894. Married Lewis M. Crandall on June 23, 1920, in Norwich, New York. Ruth Olive Woodard. Born February 1, 1903. Married June 21, 1922 at Norwich to Everett B. Adams.

Lewis M. Crandall and Mary Emilie Woodard had the following children: Lewis Woodard Crandall born August 7, 1921 and Bettie Jane Crandall born October 2, 1923.

Ivan Dewitt Woodard and Josephine Adams had a son, Ivan Robert Woodard born February 21, 1928.

Harry Lee Woodard. Born August 8, 1879. Died December 10, 1893

Wallace Edwin Woodard. Born January 8, 1873. Married on June 27, 1906 to Katie McCarta. They had the following children: Catharine Emily Woodard born January 30, 1905 who married Millard Clayton. Dorothy Ethel Woodard who was born December 21, 1903 in Norwich and married Joseph Laden in Norwich.

JAMES POLK BRIGGS

Born: May 12, 1843

Married: Hellen A. (?   ) who was born on September 22, 1844, and died on December 22, 1927

Died: August 18, 1912 in Norwich, New York

Children of James Polk and Hellen A. (?   ) Briggs:

Howard W. Briggs. Born February 5, 1874.

Jason H. Briggs. Born December 3, 1884. Died September 3, 1919

Mildred Briggs. Born January 3, 1880

JULIA BRIGGS

Married: Mr. Hunter

Julia (Briggs) Hunter was a doctor practicing at Carbondale, Pennsylvania, when she was killed by a train. Her husband was a minister and her two sons, Virgil and Junius Hunter are professors in a college in California.

LEWIS CASS BRIGGS

Born: April 21, 1846

Married: Mary Josephine Ballard on July 4, 1868. She was born on
August 9, 1847 and died February 12, 1928

Died: December 17, 1925. Lewis Cass and Mary Josephine (Ballard)
Briggs are buried in the Hartwick Cemetery.

Children of Lewis Cass and Mary Josephine (Ballard) Briggs:

Claude Evelyn Briggs. Born October 9, 1875. Died September 13, 1914, unmarried. Buried in Hartwick Cemetery.

Earl Delos Briggs. Born December 12, 1892. Unmarried.

Elizabeth Pearl Briggs. Born January 18, 1890. Married on October 10, 1931, to Lavern Fuller.

Elbertie Idella Briggs. Born December 13, 1879. Married on January 25, 1898 to Andy L. Hall.

Their daughter, Nellie Josephine Hall was born on November 8, 1898.

She married on September 17, 1917 to Clark Kraus.

They had two children: Walter A. Kraus born January 18, 1919 and Zada E. Kraus born November 24, 1920

Elsie Ballard Briggs. Born July 10, 1886. Married Andrew J. Telfer born January 31, 1882.

Their daughter Ervina May Telfer was born June 13, 1904.

She married on June 25, 1927 to Byron Sabine.

Their daughter, Marie Belle Telfer, married John Chamberlain on May 17, 1930. Marie Belle Telfer was born on December 12, 1906.

They had two sons: John Telfer Chamberlain born on May 1, 1932 and Lee Brian Chamberlain born August 6, 1936.

Ina Blanche Briggs. Born April 30, 1888. Married on September 25, 1914, to Caryl L. Smith.

Their son, Caryl L. Smith, Jr., was born April 13, 1918.

Their daughter, Elnora Smith was born on September 29, 1925.

She died in Middlefield, Conn., on April 27, 1927.

Their daughter Josephine E. Smith was born on March 6, 1917.

Their daughter Laone R. Smith was born on November 25, 1919.

Their son Marvin E. Smith was born on June 8, 1921.

Their daughter Mary Hazel Smith was born on December 8, 1932.

Their son Stuart P. Smith was born on September 9, 1915.

James Cass Briggs. Born September 20, 1884. Married Mary E. Loughney.

Their daughter, Frances Elizabeth Briggs was born February 19, 1922.

Their daughter Margaret Mary Briggs was born May 7, 1918.

Their son Marvin E. Briggs was born March 7, 1913.

Their daughter Mary Helen Briggs was born August 13, 1916.

Jennie Belle Briggs. Born August 18, 1870. Married on February 26, 1896 to James Balcom who was born on September 30, 1871 and who died on November 17, 1921 and is buried in the Hartwick Cemetery.

Their son Claude L. Balcom was born on February 27, 1903.

He married Emma Bliss on February 5, 1927.

Their son Edward Balcom was born on June 2, 1929.

Their daughter Irene Beverly Balcom was born September 30, 1934.

Their daughter Virginia Belle Balcom was born on July 5, 1927.

Their daughter Eleanor Balcom was born on May 1, 1939.

Their son Hugh Balcom was born on December 5, 1906 and died on July 17, 1924.

Josephine Luella Briggs was born on September 13, 1877. She married on February 12, 1896 to Lewis Knoch who was born on September 13, 1867 and who died on December 2, 1930 and is buried in the Hartwick Cemetery.

Julia May Briggs. Born February 24, 1869. Married on April 19, 1894 to George T. Luce who was born on January 29, 1857 and who died on April 16, 1919 and is buried in the Hartwick Cemetery.

Their daughter Cornelia M. Luce was born on March 16, 1895.

She married Walter Bagg on August 5, 1922.

Their son Torry Briggs Luce was born on October 29, 1896. He married Mildred Martin on January 14, 1917.

Their son Torry James Luce was born on December 29, 1923.

Their daughter Sally Barbara Luce was born May 9, 1925.

Leon Russell Briggs was born on February 16, 1874. Unmarried.

Lewis Theodore Briggs was born on February 18, 1872. Unmarried.

Mary Dorothy Briggs. Born on February 15, 1882. Married on December 12, 1900 to Amasa Balcom who was born on April 16, 1873 and who died on March 22, 1895. Mary Dorothy Briggs died on February 8, 1921, and is buried with her husband in the Hartwick Cemetery.

Their son Clifford A. Balcom was born on August 2, 1901.

Their daughter Edna M. Balcom was born on October 22, 1906.
She married Theodore Hoffman on June 2, 1931.

Their son, Harold Balcom, born July 9, 1903. Married Gladys Tubbs.

Their son Harold Donald Balcom was born on May 4, 1932.

Their daughter Mary Balcom was born on August 31, 1929.

1870 CENSUS OTSEGO COUNTY NEW YORK TOWN OF NEW LISBON
108, 118

Lewis C. Briggs born in 1847 in New York

Mary J. Briggs born in 1848 in New York

Julia M. Briggs born in 1869 in New York

Lewis C. Briggs enlisted in Co H, 152d New York Volunteers 1862.
He was in the Battles of the Wilderness, Spottsylvania, Court House,
Hatcher's Run, Burgess Farm, and Reams Station. He was mustered
out with the regiment July 13, 1865.

Page 222 *History of Otsego County New York* Duane H. Hurd
Published by Everts and Fariss 714-16 Filbert Street, Philadelphia
(1878)

From Vol 100 N.E.G.H.R. p 172

Otsego County, New York Chase or Woodley Hill Cemetery

Spencer Briggs died Apr 24, 1882 56 y 11 m 14 d

Sarah A Briggs wife died Feb 3, 1885 55 y 1 m 21 d

Willis L. Briggs son died Nov 30, 1851 3 m 12 d

Ida M Briggs daughter died July 20, 1865 7 y 6 d

Elvira Briggs daughter died May 15, 1871 18 y 1 m 12 d

Thurs Apr 21, 1814 Griffin Briggs married Susannah Persons by the
Reverend Jonathon Sweet.

Vol 61 N.Y.G.H.R. p 40

PHOEBE JANE BRIGGS

Married: Mr. Parcelle

Children of (?   ) and Phoebe Jane (Briggs) Parcelle:

Charles F. Parcelle. Born 1858. Died 1932. Married Julia Emerson
who died in May 1931. They had a daughter, Grace Parcelle.

Ella May Parcelle. Born 1855. Married Gilbert Edgette, who was
born in 1854. They had a daughter, Elsie Mae Edgette.

Mary S. Parcelle. Born 1860. Married George Anderson. They had
a daughter, Mabel G. Anderson.

RACHEL BRIGGS

Married: F. M. Hadlock who was born on March 23, 1866 in Norwich and who died in July 1928

Died: July 29, 1898

Children of F. M. and Rachel (Briggs) Hadlock:

George Lee Hadlock. Born on March 23, 1866. Married on October 27, 1887 to Nora Barr.

Their daughter Berry Hadlock was born on April 28, 1894. She married Clarence Figary in November, 1917.

Their daughter Irene Hadlock was born on September 20, 1899.

Raphael A. Hadlock. Born on September 9, 1871. He married on March 28, 1894 to Flora Howard.

Their son Glen (?) Hadlock was born in November 1900. He married Sarah White.

Their daughter Rachel Hadlock was born on June 8, 1896 and died on January 8, 1905.

Stella Hadlock. Born May 3, 1869. Married Anthony Markiewicz. Died on June 26, 1915.

Their daughter Bessie M. Markiewicz was born on December 18, 1899. She married William Ubbens on June 15, 1920.

Their son Edwin G. Ubbens was born on December 23, 1924.

Their son Robert F. Ubbens was born on July 15, 1922.

Their daughter Francis A. Markiewicz was born on February 29, 1904. She married Elmer Hodge in 1931.

Their son Francis Earl Hodge was born on June 1, 1932.

BROWN

THE REVEREND CHAD BROWN OF HIGH WYCOMBE, COUNTY BUCKS, ENGLAND, AND OF PROVIDENCE, RHODE ISLAND

Came with his wife, Elizabeth, and son John, aged 8, in the ship, *Martin* to Boston in July, 1638.

Chaddus Browne and Eliz Sharparowe married at High Wycombe, co. Bucks, England, 11 September 1626. N.E.H.G.R. Vol 80, p 74, Vol. 65, p 84. Phillimore's Buckinghamshire Parish Registers, Marriages, Vol 6 p 11.

The final "e" was dropped by all descendants of Chad Browne except the Glocester, Rhode Island, branch.

Chad Browne died in or before 1663. He was called "deceased" in 1663 in a deed from William Field. His wife died about 1672.

Hague says in his *Historical Discourse* of Chad Browne:

> Contemporary with Roger Williams, he possessed a cooler temperament and was happily adapted to sustain the interests of religion just where that great man failed. We know only enough of his character to excite the wish to know more; but from that little it is clear that he was highly esteemed as a man of sound judgment and of a Christian spirit. Often referred to as the arbitrator of existing differences, in a state of society where individual influence was needed as a substitute for well digested laws, he won that commendation which the Savior pronounced when he said, "Blessed are the peace-makers, for they shall be called the children of God."

> The home of Chad Browne was at the corner of present day Market Square and College Street in Providence. Brown University occupies part of the lot. He was buried on his lot (on a spot now occupied by the Court House), but was removed in 1792 to the North Burial Ground where his gravestone, then erected, may be seen with the following inscription: "In memory of Chad Brown Elder of the Baptist Church in this town. He was one of the original Proprietors of the Providence Purchase. Having been exiled from Massachusetts for conscience sake. He had five sons: John, James, Jeremiah, Chad and Daniel Who have left a numerous posterity. He died about A.D. 1665. This Monument was erected by the Town of Providence."

> Chad Browne was a witness of the nuncupative will of Sylvester Baldwin of Aston Clinton, co. Bucks, England, who died on the *Martin* and whose will was proved on 13 July 1638 before Deputy Governor Dudley of Massachusetts.

1638　Chad Browne signed in Providence the Compact denying religious interference in civil affairs.

1642　Ordained pastor of the First Baptist Church of Providence, the Mother Church of that Faith in America. Either Roger

Williams or Chad Browne was the first pastor. See Henry King's *Historical Catalogue of the First Baptist Church in Providence.*

1640 Chad Browne served on a committee to adjust the disputed boundary between Providence and Pawtuxet.

1640 Chad Browne served on a committee to report the first written form of government of Providence Colony.

"Chadde Browne the son of Arthure Browne of Melcheborne in the Countie of Bedford yoman hathe put himself ap'rentice" in 1570. Waters of *Genealogical Gleanings in England* says this Chadde Browne *may* be the father of the Rhode Island Chad Browne. N.E. G.H.R. Vol 47 pp 266-7.

Chad Browne left a will (as shown by references in deeds), but its contents are unknown. In 1672 there was a general readjustment of the estate.

Children of the Reverend Chad and Elizabeth (Sharparowe) Brown:

Daniel Brown

James Brown. Removed to Newport.

Jeremiah Brown. Removed to Newport.

*John Brown

Judah or Chad Brown. Died May 10, 1663 unmarried

THE CHAD BROWNE MEMORIAL by Abby Isabel (Brown) Bulkley (1888) Brooklyn *Daily Eagle*, Brooklyn, New York, pages 7-9.

JOHN BROWN

Born: 1630

Married: Mary Holmes

Died: About 1706

Children of John and Mary (Holmes) Brown:

Deborah Brown

James Brown. Born 1666. Married on December 17, 1691, to Mary Harris, daughter of Andrew and Mary (Tew) Harris and granddaughter of William and Susannah Harris and Richard and Mary (Clarke) Tew. Mary Harris was born on December 17, 1671 and died on August 18, 1736. James Brown was Pastor of the First Baptist Church. From 1705 to 1725 he was a member of the Town Council of Providence and from 1714 to 1718 he was the Town Treasurer of Providence. James Brown died on October 28, 1732. Obadiah and James Brown, sons of James Brown, and Nicholas, Joseph, John and Moses Brown, grandsons of James Brown, by his son James Brown, laid the foundations of the Brown fortune, one of the oldest and largest in the United States, by their investment in shipping, manufacturing and merchandising. The family were benefactors of Rhode Island

College, which was renamed Brown University in the family's honor and which is located on the grounds of the old residence of the Reverend Chad Brown.

Ensign John Brown. Born March 18, 1662. Married on June 9, 1696, to Isabel Matthewson, daughter of James and Hannah (Field) Matthewson and granddaughter of John Field. She died after 1719. They lived in Johnston, Rhode Island. Ensign John Brown died on September 19, 1719.

Martha Brown. Married Joseph Jenckes who was born in 1656. He was the grandson of the first Joseph Jenckes of Buckinghamshire, England, who emigrated with the Winthrop Company in 1630 and settled in Lynn, Massachusetts, where he erected the first brass and iron foundry on the continent. His eldest son, Joseph Jenckes, established himself in the same business in Pawtucket, Rhode Island, where Martha Brown's husband, Joseph Jenckes, was born. Joseph Jenckes held the following positions: Deputy, Speaker of the House of Deputies, Major for the Main, Deputy Governor 1715-1727, Agent to settle the boundary dispute between Rhode Island, Massachusetts, and Connecticut, Governor, 1727-1732.

*Mary Brown

Obadiah Brown. Over 16 in 1688. Married Mary (   ). Died on August 24, 1716.

Sarah Brown. Married on November 14, 1678, to John Pray son of Richard and Mary Pray. He died on October 9, 1730.

Sarah (Brown) Pray died after 1733.

John Brown
Juryman
1654 Commissioner on Union of Towns
1659 Surveyor of Highways
Baptist Elder
Moderator
Member of the Providence, Rhode Island, Town Council
Deputy
Governor's Assistant, 1665-1666
Chad Brown Memorial pp 10-15
S.C.W. p 70

MARY BROWN

Daughter of John and Mary (Holmes) Brown
Granddaughter of the Reverend Chad Brown and the
Reverend Obadiah Holmes
Married: Arthur Aylsworth
Died: Before 1726
See N.E.H.G.R. Vol 80 pp 73-86

See CHAD BROWNE MEMORIAL pp 14-15
See John Osborne Austin's GENEALOGICAL DICTIONARY OF
RHODE ISLAND pp 258-261

BUTTER

THOMAS BUTTER OF DEDHAM, COUNTY ESSEX, ENGLAND, CLOTHIER

Testator of 1555

Born Ca 1500

Died: Between 20 August and 15 October, 1555

Married: 1st

2nd Marion (?) Living 20 August 1555

A juror at a manor court at Dedham on Monday after St. Martin the Bishop 21 Henry VIII (1529) and on Monday in the feast of St. Edmund, King and Martyr, 23 Henry VIII (1531)

Acquired 3 roods of meadow in Chaldewall, east of the River Stour. On 16 July 29 Henry VIII (1537) at the Manor Court of Over and Nether Hall, Dedham, he is called a native.

He was a prosperous clothier at Dedham and possessed a good estate in copy lands.

Henry Sherman, ancestor of the Shermans of Watertown, Massachusetts, was one of his executors and probably a relative or connection by marriage.

Children, probably by his first wife:

Agnes Butter. Born ca 1529. Living 20 Aug 1555. Married before then to a Mr. Rolfe.

Alice Butter. Born ca 1527. Living 3 and 4 Philip and Mary (1556-7) Married before 20 Aug 1555 Christopher Percyvall living 3 and 4 Philip and Mary (1556-7). Child John Percyvall living and under 20 on 20 Aug 1555. Probably others.

Alice Butter "Younger daughter". Born ca 1530. Living unmarried 20 Aug 1555.

Daughter. Born ca 1523. Died before 20 August 1555. Married a Mr. Wulman living 20 Aug 1555, when they had two children over 20 living.

John Butter. Born ca 1525. Living 12 Oct 21 Elizabeth (1579)

Child: John Butter. Living and of age 21 Oct 1579. Probably other children. See will of Thomas Butter 1555.

Margaret Butter. Born ca 1532. Living unmarried 20 Aug 1555.

Sibell Butter. Born ca 1531. Living unmarried 20 Aug 1555.

*William Butter. Born ca 1521

Children of Thomas Butter probably by his second wife: Ann Butter, Grace Butter, Faith Butter, Mary Butter. Child unborn on 20 Aug 1555 when Thomas Butter made his will.

See Vol 76, pp 292-293 N.E.H.G.R.

Will of Thomas Butter of Dedham, co Essex, Clothier dated 20 Aug 2 and 3 Philip and Mary (1555)

Request to be buried in the Dedham Parish Church where he had been accustomed to sit if he should die in the Parish of Dedham.

Mentions:

Wife: Marion

Son John: half a dozen silver spoons

Son William: Signet of gold. To his wife a silver goblet.

Alice Precyvall daughter

Alice Butter youngest daughter. Two silver spoons and a silver salt with the cover which was her grandmother's.

Daughter Sibell: Two silver spoons

Daughter Margaret: Two silver spoons

Daughters: Faith, Mary, Grace and Ann

Harry Sherman's wife: A silver pot.

Nuncupative Will of Marion Butter, Dedham, Co. Essex, widow declared 6 Oct 1606. Mentions Elizabeth and Mary Skinner, daughter Bosseti's children, son Thomas Welles.

Vol 76 pp 278-9, 281, N.E.H.G.R.

WILLIAM BUTTER OF DEDHAM, COUNTY ESSEX, ENGLAND, CLOTHIER

Testator of 1593

Born: Ca 1521

Buried: Dedham 8 November 1594

Married: 1st: Ann Gurdon who was buried at Dedham 22 Aug 1563
2nd: Marion (?   ) before 1567. She was the widow of a Mr. Willes. Probably she was also the wife of a Mr. Skinner. She had a son, Thomas Willes, living 6 Oct 1606 when she made him executor of her nuncupative will. She had a daughter who married a Mr. Bosetti and was apparently dead in 1606.

Juror at Manor Court on 7 Oct 2 and 3 Philip and Mary (1555) and subsequent Manor Courts.

Elected Constable at court held 9 Nov 1559.

He was, like his father, a wealthy and prosperous clothier, and acquired a considerable estate in copylands. The Will of William Littlebury of Dedham, co. Essex, dated 20 July 1571 makes William Butter of Dedham Clothier and Peirs Butter his son along with Shermans, Sparhawks, and Upchurs trustees for certain purposes. See Vol 50 p 133 N.E.H.G.R. and Waters GENEALOGICAL GLEANINGS IN ENGLAND, Vol 2, p 1124.

Children of William and Ann (Gurdon) Butter:

Alice Butter. Bapt Dedham 8 Nov 1562. Living 16 Apr 1645 when mentioned in the will of her niece, Ann (Butter) Coggeshall. Married before 30 May 1593 to (John?) Morfew.

Edward Butter. Born ca 1560. Buried Dedham 11 Dec 1568.

*Pierce Butter. Born ca 1550

Richard Butter. Born ca 1555. Living Aug 1599 when mentioned in the will of his brother, Pierce Butter.

Thomas Butter. Born ca 1553. Living 3 Oct 1597 but apparently dead in Aug 1599 when brother Pierce Butter made his will. Married between 27 Aug and 30 Sept 1585 to Elizabeth Crushe, daughter and coheiress of Robert Crushe, late of Roxwell, co. Essex, England, deceased. Thomas Butter was a defendant in a suit in Chancery brought by Pierce Butter May 1595.

Frances Butter bapt Dedham 24 Feb 1566/7. Probably died before 30 May 1593 was the daughter of William Butter by his second wife. See Volume 76, pp 293-4 N.E.H.G.R. Also Vol 95 p 72 N.E.H.G.R. Vol 76 pp 279-80 N.E.H.G.R. shows William's will naming Pierce Butter as a son.

PIERCE BUTTER OF DEDHAM AND COLCHESTER, COUNTY ESSEX, ENGLAND, CLOTHIER

Born: ca 1550

Married: 1st: at Dedham on 21 February 1574/5 Edith Skynner who was buried at Dedham 22 April 1576

2nd: Possibly the daughter of Hugh May of Dedham

3rd: Thomasine (?   ) Tomson, widow of John Tomson, probably ca 19 Nov 34 Eliz (1591) and certainly before 4 Aug 34 Eliz (1592).

By John Tomson she had the following children: John, William, Ann, Elizabeth, Thomazin, Sara, all living in August 1599 when mention in the will of Pierce Butter and also named in a Chancery Suit of 24 July 1601.

Died: Between 27 August and 3 October 1599 at Colchester, co. Essex, England

Pierce Butter was on the Court Manor Roll on 30 March, 15 Eliz (1573) and was often a juror in the Manor Court, his last appearance being on 6 June 41 Eliz (1599).

In the last years of his life, Pierce Butter lived in Colchester in the parish of St. James. His will disposes of a large estate, including considerable plate, and shows he was a clothier of the most prosperous type.

Children of Pierce Butter by his second wife:

*Anne Butter

James Butter. Born ca 1587. Living 26 January 1624/5 when mentioned in the will of his brother, John Butter. His father devised to him lands and houses in Much Okeley (Great Oakley), co. Essex

John Butter. Of Thorington, co. Essex, yeoman. Testator of 1624/5. Baptized Dedham 11 May 1585. Married Margaret (?   ) living in May 1626 when as Executrix she proved her husband's will.

Daniel Butter. Of Dedham, clothier. Testator of 1608/9. Baptized at Dedham 20 Nov 1582. Died between 14 March 1608/9 and 10 Nov 1609.

Pierce Butter. Bapt Dedham 17 Oct 1581. Living 26 Jan 1624/5

Children of Pierce Butter by his third wife:

Mary Butter. Born ca 1592 . Died apparently before 26 Jan 1624/5 when her children were mentioned in her brother, John Butter's will. Married a Mr. Stokes.

Will of Pierce Butter of Colchester, co. Essex, England, Clothier.
Dated August 41 Elizabeth (1599) mentions—
Sons: William, Peirce, Daniel, James, John Butter
Daughters: Ann and Mary Butter
Cousin Harry Sherman
Brother Richard Butter
Children of brother Thomas Butter, particularly Samuel Butter.
Sister Sara Northie, widow
Sister Morphewe
Tomson children
See N.E.H.G.R. Vol 73, pp 280-1

Will of Daniel Butter of Dedham co Essex, England, Clothier
Dated 14 Mar 1608/9 mentions brother William
See N.E.H.G.R. Vol 76, p 281

Will of John Butter of Thorington, co .Essex, yeoman.
26 Jan 1624/5.
To be buried in the Church of Thorington.
Mentions:

Wife Margaret Butter

Brothers Pearce and James Butter

Kinsmen: George Lincoln of Sutton, co. Suffolk, Samuel Backley of Dedham, John Cogshall and Edward Rand.

Sister Ann Cogshall

John Cogshall son of Ann Cogshall

Ann and Katherine, daughters of Ann Cogshall

Children of sister Stokes: Thomasen and Mary

Judith Butter, wife of brother William Butter

William and John Butter, his uncle's sons

Aunt Morphewe

Children of brother-in-law John Rand: Ann, Edward, John, Nicholas, Robert George, Samuel, Benjamin, Susan, Mary, and Sarah Rand

Children of brother-in-law Samuel Backley: Samuel, John and Elizabeth Backley.

See Vol 73, p 20 N.E.H.G.R.

ANNE BUTTER OF HALSTEAD AND CASTLE HEDINGHAM, COUNTY ESSEX, ENGLAND

Born: ca 1583

Married: ca 1600 John Coggeshall "the Younger" of Halstead, County Essex, Gentleman.

Died: Will dated April 16, 1645 and proved November 10, 1648

The Will of Anne Coggeshall of Castle Hedingham, co. Essex, England, Widow, Dated April 16, 1645, Proved November 10, 1648, may be found in Waters, *Genealogical Gleanings in England*, Vol 1, p 472. Also N.E.G.H.R. Vol. 47, pp 402-3.

The Will mentions:

Son John Coggeshall now dwelling in New England

Uncle of Son John named John Butter

Grandchild: Henry Raymond (The Visitation of Essex 1634

Publications of the Harleian Society, Vol 13, p 475 shows Anne Coggeshall married Richard Raymond, son of Henry and Joan (Perry) Raymond of Much Dunmow, co. Essex, England)

Granddaughter: Anne Raymond, daughter of Richard

Grandchildren (of Son John Coggeshall) : John, Anne, Mary, Joshua, and James Coggeshall

Grandchildren (of Daughter Anne Raymond) : John, Richard, and Elizabeth Raymond

CARR

ROBERT CARR

Born: In the British Isles on October 4, 1614

Married: (?   )

Died: Between April 30 and October 4, 1681 in Newport, Rhode Island

Children of Robert Carr:

*Caleb Carr

Elizabeth Carr. Born 1651 in Newport. Married 1st about 1670 to James Brown son of the Reverend Chad and Elizabeth (Sharparowe) Brown. He died in 1683. She married 2nd Samuel Gardiner, son of George and Herodias Gardiner.

Esek Carr. Born Newport. Married Susanna (?   ) in 1684. Died Little Compton, Rhode Island in 1744. He was a cooper.

Margaret Carr. Born Newport. Married on November 27, 1670, to Richard Hartshorne, the son of Hugh Hartshorne. Richard Hartshorne was born in Leicestershire, England, on October 24, 1641, and died probably in Middletown, New Jersey, on May 3, 1722. When George Fox Founder of the Society of Friends or Quakers visited America, he stayed with Richard and Margaret (Carr) Hartshorne and speaks of them in his Journal. Richard Hartshorne served as Speaker of the New Jersey Assembly from 1687 to 1708.

Mary Carr. Born Newport. Married 1st John Hicks. Married 2nd Ralph Earle, born 1660 and died 1757, the son of William and Mary (Walker) Earle.

Robert Carr. Born Newport. Married Elizabeth Lawton daughter of George and Elizabeth (Hazard) Lawton. Robert Carr was a merchant of Newport, where he died. His will was dated July 8, 1703 and proved February 5, 1704. Elizabeth died 1724.

Robert Carr came to Boston in 1635. On February 21, 1638, he resided in Portsmouth, Rhode Island. On March 16, 1641, he was a freeman of Newport, Rhode Island. Executors of his will were William Clarke, son-in-law, to the Reverend Roger Williams and his brother, Caleb Carr, later Governor of Rhode Island.

CALEB CARR

Born: Newport, Rhode Island

Married: Phillis Greene

Died: 1690 in Jamestown, Rhode Island

Children of Caleb and Phillis (Greene) Carr:

*Caleb Carr

Job Carr Born 1685. He died January 23, 1753. He married Mehitable Sherman who was born in Kingstown on March 4, 1688, and died November 3, 1751.

Mary Carr Born Jamestown, Rhode Island. Married to Benjamin Peckham. He was born June 9, 1684, and died in 1761. They lived in South Kingstown, Rhode Island. They were members of the Society of Friends. The daughter of their son, Benjamin Peckham, (Alice Peckham Rathbone) became a Quaker leader.

Phillis Carr Born December 8, 1688 in Jamestown, Rhode Island. Died probably in Newport Rhode Island. Married Edward Boss, son of Edward and Susannah Boss. Edward Boss, born January 20, 1685, and died December 25, 1752, was a merchant in Newport.

Their children: Mary, Truelove, Abigail, Edward, Hannah, Susannah, Joseph, Phillis, and Benjamin, who married Katharine Wightman on September 22, 1750.

Robert Carr born January 2, 1678. Died young.

Robert Carr Born June 7, 1683 in Jamestown, Rhode Island. Died Swansea, Massachusetts October 12, 1722. Married in Swansea on October 21, 1708 to Hannah Hale, born in Warren Rhode Island (or Swansea, Mass.) on May 8, 1690 and died in Warren. See N.E.G.H.R. Vol 70, page 25. Their Children: Mary, Robert, Hannah and Caleb.

William Carr. Born October 16, 1681, in Jamestown, R.I. Died before 1711. Married on February 8, 1708-9 to Abigail Barker, daughter of James and Sarah (Jefferay) Barker and granddaughter of James Barker, Deputy Governor of Rhode Island. They had son, Robert.

Caleb Carr was one of the first settlers of the Island of Conanicut (or Jamestown) in Narragansett Bay. His father, Robert was one of the original purchasers of the island from the Indians. By his will, Robert Carr, left his land there to his son Caleb. The will of Caleb Carr dated January 27, the 1st of William K of Gt. B. was proved in Newport 30 March 1690. The will mentions his brother-in-law, Peter Greene, son of John Greene, Deputy Governor of Rhode Island and his cousin Nicholas Carr, son of Caleb Carr, Governor of Rhode Island.

CALEB CARR

Born: March 26, 1679, in Jamestown, Rhode Island
Married: 1st: Joanna Slocum on April 30, 1701. 2nd: Mary (?)
Caleb and Joanna (Slocum) Carr were Quakers. In 1731 Caleb moved to West Greenwich Rhode Island and settled on Carr's Pond.
Children of Caleb and Joanna (Slocum) Carr:
*Caleb Carr Born Jamestown on November 6, 1702

Joseph Carr. Born Jamestown about 1704. Married in West Greenwich on June 21, 1741 to Percilla (Priscilla) (?)

Mary Carr. Born about 1707

Patience Carr. Born Jamestown about 1705. Married on July 9, 1723 to John Westgate (Westgeate)

William Carr. Born in Jamestown on December 26, 1708. Married on April 19, 1733, in East Greenwich, Rhode Island, to Elizabeth Cory, daughter of William Cory.

Children of Caleb and Mary (?) Carr:

Benejah Carr. Born Jamestown about 1713. Married Louisa (?)

Captain Charles Carr. Born Jamestown about 1715. Married in East Greenwich, Rhode Island, on December 18, 1735, to Hannah Hopkins, daughter of Joseph Hopkins. Census of 1744 shows Captain Carr in East Greenwich. For 30 years he was a deacon of the Baptist Church of East Greenwich. He served as a Representative from East Greenwich to the Rhode Island General Assembly and was Sheriff of Kent County. It was while he was Sheriff that thirteen pirates paid for their misdeeds with their lives at the yard arm of ships in the Bay of East Greenwich. *Carr Book* by A. A. Carr pp 21-2, 38-41.

CALEB CARR

Born: Jamestown, Rhode Island on November 6, 1702

Married: Sarah Richmond who was born on November 8, 1711 and died November, 1798

Died: 1769 in West Greenwich, Rhode Island

Children of Caleb and Sarah (Richmond) Carr:

Caleb Carr Born June 19, 1744. Married 1772 to Abigail Very. Died 1793 in Stephentown, New York. He had been born in West Greenwich, Rhode Island. Caleb was the oldest of five Carr brothers who moved from West Greenwich to Stephentown, Rensselaer County, New York. *Landmarks of Rensselaer County* says that, "Nathaniel Rose, Edward Carr and Caleb Carr came early to the southern part of the town." D.A.R. records show Caleb Carr was a corporal in the Massachusetts Militia in the Revolutionary War.

Comfort Carr Born on August 7, 1741, in West Greenwich, Rhode Island. Married May 25, 1760 to Benjamin Greene.

Edward Carr. Born on July 4, 1753 in West Greenwich, Rhode Island. Married 1st Eleanor Spencer on December 15, 1776. She was the daughter of William and Mary Spencer and was born in East Greenwich, Rhode Island, on June 22, 1754. She died in Stephentown, New York, on March 20, 1798. He married 2nd Mary Brown Green (widow) on September 27, 1798. She was born on May 7, 1752 and died in Stephentown on January 19, 1806. He married 3rd Sarah

Potter (widow) on May 26, 1806. She was born May 24, 1750 and died on December 25, 1831. He married 4th Margaret Lamfier (widow) on August 12, 1832. She was born on June 14, 1766, and died on August 19, 1836. Married 5th Bridget Williams (widow) on December 14, 1836. She was born on May 25, 1780 and died in 1884. Deacon Edward Carr was one of the founders of the Stephentown Baptist Church about 1795.

Eleazer Carr. Born West Greenwich, Rhode Island on April 22, 1746. Married Eleanor Stafford who died on October 26, 1813. A deed from Stephen Van Rensselaer to Eleazer Carr is dated July 17, 1787, and covers land in Stephentown. A 1794 deed refers to Eleazer Carr as of Hancock, Mass. He died on July 19, 1816.

Joshua Carr. Born December 28, 1748. Married 1st Sarah Stafford. Married 2nd Elizabeth Colegrove.

Mary Carr. Born February 18, 1731. Married Thomas Rogers

*Merebah Carr

Patience Carr. Born August 7, 1729

Rebecca Carr. Born West Greenwich, Rhode Island, on May 29, 1732. Married Job Harrington on March 18, 1749

Richmond Carr. Born West Greenwich, Rhode Island on April 4, 1751. Married Mary Richmond who died in Pavillion, New York, in 1839. He died in Stephentown, New York.

Robert Carr. Born West Greenwich, Rhode Island, on December 22, 1735. Married Rebecca Brayton, the daughter of Thomas Brayton of Coventry, Rhode Island, on December 4, 1754.

Susannah Carr. Born West Greenwich, Rhode Island on February 3, 1734. Married Nicholas Whitford on November 18, 1752.

Thurston Carr. Born West Greenwich, Rhode Island, on July 2, 1756. Married 1st Audrey Spencer, twin sister of Eleanor Spencer, who married Edward Carr. Audrey Spencer was born June 22, 1754 and died before 1798. Married 2nd Anna Doty. Thurston Carr died in 1812 in Stephentown New York.

Caleb Carr and Sarah Richmond Carr spent most of their lives near Carr's Pond, West Greenwich, Rhode Island.

In the 1790 Census some of the above Carrs are listed as "Kerr." That is not the way their descendants or any of the Rhode Island family spelled the name. A. A. Carr in the *Carr Book* put it down "to the fancy of the census enumerator."

MEREBAH CARR

Born: July 3, 1739, in West Greenwich, Rhode Island
Married: Job Greene on February 3, 1757, in West Greenwich
Died: July 12, 1785

Job and Merebah (Carr) Greene moved to the northern part of Vermont.

Arthur Adkins Carr of Ticonderoga, New York *The Carr Book* (1947). Tuttle Publishing Company, Rutland, Vermont. Edson I, Carr *Carr Family Records* Published in 1894 by Herald Printing House of Rockton, Illinois. John Osborne Austin's *Genealogical Dictinary of Rhode Island* p 39

COGGESHALL

JOHN COGGESHALL OF DEPWALL IN HUNDON 1461, FOXWELL IN CHILTON 1477, MORTIMER'S IN HUNDON 1481

Testator of 1488

Died 1488

Married: Alice (?   )

Children of John Coggeshall: John Coggeshall, Katherine Coggeshall, Richard Coggeshall of Ketyton, Master William Coggeshall of Mortimer's in Hundon and son William

Will of John Coggeshall of Hundon, Senior. Dated 14 Feb 1487/8. Proved 24 May 1488

Directed that he be buried in Hundon Churchyard. Mentions lands in Wood Street, Hundon

Wife Alice Coggeshall

Master William Coggeshall Vol 99 p 322 N.E.H.G.R.

Son John Coggeshall

Son Richard Coggeshall

Daughter Katherine Coggeshall

Vol 100 pp 14-24 N.E.H.G.R.

JOHN COGGESHALL OF GOSFIELD, COUNTY ESSEX, ENGLAND

Of Gosfield

Occ in Hundon

1487, 1492

Testator of 1501

Married: *Perhaps* the sister of Robert Parker

Children of John Coggeshall:

John Coggeshall

Richard Coggeshall

Roger Coggeshall. Of Fornham St. Martin, co. Suffolk, Gentleman. Died 26 April 1541. Will proved 2 July 1541. Married Elizabeth Smyth, widow of Edmund Boldero. John Coggeshall, son of Roger and Elizabeth, was born in 1527 and died in 1599. He married first Anne Rowe, daughter of John Rowe and second, Elizabeth Bacon, daughter of George Bacon of Hesset.

See the Inquisition Post Mortem of Roger Cogkesale of Fornham St. Martin, co. Suffolk, England, Gentleman taken at Ipswich 6 April 34 Henry VIII (1543) Son John Coggeshall and nephew Henry Coggeshall mentioned.

A Chancery Case of Roger Coggeshall sets out that William Coggeshall deceased was seised of the Manor of Hagdon Hall, co. Suffolk, England; that William Coggeshall was dead; that his son, William Coggeshall, was dead; and that the property should go to the said Roger Coggeshall as son and heir of John Coggeshall, brother of the elder William Coggeshall.

The Will of Roger Coggeshall of Fornham St. Martin, co. Suffolk, England, was dated 23 April 1541 and was proved 2 July 1541. It mentions his brother William Cocksall of Waltham and his sons, Henry, John, Nicholas, and Roger Coggeshall and his daughters, Besse and Dorothy Coggeshall, his uncle, Richard Coksall and his wife, Elizabeth and son, John.

The Visitation Pedigree of the Coggeshalls of Fornham St. Martin, co. Suffolk, begins with Roger Coggeshall. See account of Coggeshalls in Muskett's *Suffolk Manorial Families*.

*William Coggeshall of Gosfield 1524 and of Waltham 1541 and 1543.

The will of John Coggeshall of Gosfield is dated 13 Sept 1501 and was proved 31 Jan 1502. It mentions sons: Roger, John, William and Richard.

N.E.H.G.R. Vol 100 pp 14-24.

WILLIAM COGGESHALL OF GOSFIELD AND WALTHAM, COUNTY ESSEX, ENGLAND, CLOTHIER

Of Gosfield, 1524

Of Waltham, 1541, 1543

Children of William Goggeshall:

Dorothy Coggeshall. Under 21 on 26 April 1541

Elizabeth Coggeshall. Under 21 on 26 April 1541

Henry Coggeshall. Servant of Roger Coggeshall, his uncle, in 1541.

*John Coggeshall of Munchensies

Nicholas Coggeshall. Under 21 on 26 April 1541

Roger Coggeshall. Under 21 on 26 April 1541

"John Cokesall son of William Cokesall of Waltham Essex clothier" is mentioned as free of London on November 17, 1542 in Charles Welsh *Register of Freeman of London* 1532-52, p. 10

The Reverend William Holman (1669-1730) is the historian of Halstead, co. Essex, England. In *Holman's Halstead* the Reverend T. G. Gibbons, Vicar of the Parish, in writing of Munchensies, says of John Coggeshall, first in Halstead in 1553, "He was of London merchant" Page 55.

See N.E.H.G.R. Vol 99 pp 315-322.

JOHN COGGESHALL, GENTLEMAN, OF MUNCHENSIES, HALSTEAD, COUNTY ESSEX, ENGLAND

Free of London 1543.

Purchased Munchensies before 1553

Died January 1 and was buried at Halstead 3 January, 1600/1.

Married 1st Elizabeth (?   )

Children of John and Elizabeth (?   ) Coggeshall:

John Coggeshall "the Elder." Born ca 1560. Living 27 December 1600 when named in his father's will.

Richard Coggeshall. Born cs 1557. Living 27 December 1600 when mentioned in his father's will.

Married 2nd Katharine (?Wangford) about 1564. Katharine survived her husband and was one of the two executors who proved his will at Braintree, co. Essex, 8 Jan 1600/1 and Katharine was living on 22 March 1608/9 when she and her son John were taxed 5s. on goods valued at £3.

Children of John and Katherine (?Wangford) Coggeshall:

Elizabeth Coggeshall. Married the Reverend John Watson, Vicar of Halstead. Died 23 February 1604/5.

*John Coggeshall "the Younger"

Katherine Coggeshall (probably by second wife, but possibly by first wife). Baptized 26 December 1564. Married at Halstead 2 March 1583/4 Thomas Harrington. Children living unmarried when named in will of grandfather, John Coggeshall: Katherine Thomas Anne Susan (See Visitation of Essex)

John Coggeshall held Munchensies in Halstead near Coggeshall Bridge. He made great additions to the house. At one time he was a London merchant. At Halstead he built an almshouse with the following inscription: "John Coggeshall did Bild this Hous in Ao MD63---." See The Coggeshalls in America by Charles Pierce Coggeshall and Thelwell Russell Coggeshall Published in 1930 by C. E. Goodspeed and Company of Boston, Massachusetts, pages 3 and 4.

John Coggeshall (Coggeshall, Coxall, Cockshall) on Lay Subsidies for Co. Essex at Halstead in 1566/7, 1572, 1599, 1600. N.E.H.G. R. Vol 73, page 21

John Coggeshall, Gentleman, of Munchensies, Halstead, co. Essex, England, built an almshouse at Halstead with the following inscription: "John Coggeshall did Bild this Hous in Ao MD63." Beneath are his arms: Argent, a cross between four escallops sable and below them the motto: "Truth by this selfe." These are the arms of the knightly family of Coggeshall of Coggeshall. See N.E.H.G.R. Vol 73 p 28.

Elizabeth Coggeshall, the daughter of John Coggeshall, married the Reverend John Watson, Vicar of Halstead. She is buried at Halstead. A small brass mural to her memory is now fixed to the south wall of the south aisle of the Church. Incised on the brass is the figure of a woman attired in Elizabeth costume with ruff and high crowned hat kneeling at a fald stoll on which is an open book. Before her are kneeling figures of her two sons and behind her are three kneeling daughters. Beneath is the inscription: "Here lieth Elizabeth the wife of John Watson the daughter of John Coggeshall gent. who was buried February the 23rd Ao Dni 1604." See N.E.H.G.R. Vol 73 p 29

Will of John Coggeshall the Elder of Halstead co Essex, Gentleman, 27 December 1600.

Expresses desire to be buried in the chancel of the parish church of Halstead. His executors are instructed to put a marble stone upon his grave with some superscription in brass or else some inscription of brass upon the church wall near his grave with his "Whole arms and schochern in the same to be graven."

The will mentions:

Daughter: Elizabeth Watson and son-in-law, John Watson

Son: John Coggeshall the Younger

Wife: Katherine

Son: John Coggeshall the Elder by my late wife Elizabeth Alice Wangford, daughter of brother-in-law, John Wangford

Children of Daughter Katherine: Katherine, Thomas, Anne, and Susan

Proved Braintree co. Essex, England, 8 Jan 1600/1.

Commissary Court of London for Essex and Herts Somerset House, 1601, no. 31.

John Coggeshall was one of the Trustees under the Will of William Martin, clothier, who left money for the erection of a grammar school in Halstead.

In 1580 John Coggeshall signed a petition to remove the Dutch

clothiers from Halstead. State Papers Dom Eliz Vol CXLVI no. 63
See N.E.H.G.R. Vol 99 p 317

Coggeshall entries in Parish Registers of Halstead Co. Essex 1564-
1640 printed in N.E.H.G.R. Vol 73, page 21 (Some printed in East
Anglian New Series Vol 5, page 79.

JOHN COGGESHALL "THE YOUNGER" OF HALSTEAD, COUNTY ESSEX, ENGLAND

Baptized on July 29, 1576

Married: Anne, daughter of Pierce Butter, clothier of Dedham and
Colchester

Buried: August 4, 1615

Children of John Coggeshall "the Younger" and Anne (Butter) Coggeshall:

Anne Coggeshall. Born April 2, 1604. Married Richard Raymond.
See The Visitation of Essex.

Catharine Coggeshall. Baptized April 18, 1607. Buried s.p. May
14, 1640.

*John Coggeshall, President of the Colony of Rhode Island and the
Providence Plantations

The Coggeshalls In America pp 4 and 5. On p 5 it is said that Anne
Coggeshall was *baptized,* not *born* on April 2, 1604.

JOHN COGGESHALL, FIRST PRESIDENT OF THE COLONY OF RHODE ISLAND AND OF THE PROVIDENCE PLANTATIONS

Baptized: April 2, 1601, Halstead, co. Essex, England

Married: Mary (?   ) in England. She was born there probably about 1604 and died in Newport, Rhode Island, on November
8, 1684

Emigrated: To Boston, Massachusetts, in the ship *Lynn* in 1632 with
Roger Williams

Admitted freeman at Roxbury, Massachusetts, on November 6,
1632

United with the First Church, Boston, Massachusetts, April 20,
1634, where he was elected a deacon

Lived on Washington Street, opposite Water Street, next to the
home of Anne Hutchinson

"Wherever his name occurs, it invariably has the prefix 'Mr.'
signifying in those times dignity and quality and indicating some-
thing more than the simple form of polite address of the present
day."

1634-1637 Deputy from Boston to the Massachusetts
General Assembly

1640-1644 Governor's Assistant, Rhode Island, to which he moved
in 1637, settling at Providence. A founder of Newport,
Rhode Island.

1647 Moderator

1647 Elected the First President of the Colony of Rhode Island
and of the Providence Plantations

Died: November 17, 1647. Buried in the Coggeshall Cemetery,
located on the corner of Coggeshall and Victoria Avenues, Newport, Rhode Island.

In Austin's *Genealogical Dictionary of Rhode Island*, p 49 and *The
Rhode Island Historical Magazine*, Vol 5 p 174 the year of John
Coggeshall's birth is given as 1591. This date was obtained by accepting as correct the age at death as given on his gravestone, but
the gravestone was set up several years after his death. According
the Friends' record recognition of greater accuracy, his age at death
was 48 years. See Arnold's *Vital Records of Rhode Island*, Vol 7,
p. 95.

See Chapin's *Documentary History of Rhode Island*, pp 182-184, for
a letter John Coggeshall wrote in 1647.

See Holmes' *Directory* etc. p 42

Children of John and Mary (?   ) Coggeshall:

Ann Coggeshall Born co. Essex England about 1622. Died Newport
Rhode Island March 6 1688/9 Married November 15, 1643, to
Peter Easton, son of Governor Nicholas and Ann (Clayton)
Easton and brother of Governor John Easton. Peter Easton was
born in 1622 and died February 12, 1693/4.

Bediah Coggeshall Baptized First Church, Boston, July 30, 1637.
Probably died young. Listed in *Coggeshalls in America* as a son,
but Savage in his *Dictionary* Vol 1 p 421 says "Bedaiah" may
have been a daughter.

Hananiel Cogeshall (daughter) Baptized in First Church, Boston,
May 3, 1635. Probably died young

James Coggeshall Born probably in England about 1628. Mentioned
in his grandmother's will as living April 16, 1645. Savage in his
Dictionary Vol 1 pp 293 and 421 says James Coggeshall (Coxsall)
married Mary daughter of Governor Henry Bull

John Coggeshall Born co. Essex England about 1620. Died Newport
Rhode Island October 1, 1708. Buried in the Coggeshall Cemetery
in Newport. Married 1st Elizabeth Baulstone (or Baulston)
daughter of William and Elizabeth Baulstone of Portsmouth on
June 17, 1647. She was born at Portsmouth August 1639 and died

there October 1, 1700. John Coggeshall divorced her on May 25, 1655 and she married Thomas Gould.

John Coggeshall married 2nd Patience Throckmorton daughter of John and Alice (Staut) Throckmorton of Providence in December 1665. She was born about 1640 and died at Newport in 1677 and was buried in the Coggeshall Cemetery.

John Coggeshall married 3rd at Yarmouth in Plymouth Colony (or Boston?) to Mary Hedge daughter of Captain William Hedge Senior and widow of Samuel Sturgis. She was born in Yarmouth in 1648 and died in Newport August 22, 1731, where she is buried in the Coggeshall Cemetery. John Coggeshall served as Governor's Assistant 1663 et seq General Treasurer 1664 et seq. Deputy 1665 et seq General Recorder 1676 et seq, Major of the Island 1683-1685, Petitioner to the New Charter granted by King Charles II in 1663, Delegate to the First Council held by the Royal Governor, Edmund Andros, Deputy Governor, 1686-1690

*Joshua Coggeshall

Mary Goggeshall Born co. Essex England. Mentioned in her grandmother's will as living on April 16, 1645.

Wayte or Wait Coggeshall (daughter) Baptized First Church, Boston, September 11, 1636. Died July 9, 1718. Married December 18, 1651 Daniel Gould, a minister of the Society of Friends. He was born about 1625, the son of Jeremiah and Priscilla (Grover) Gould and died March 26, 1716.

See *The Coggeshalls in America* by Charles Pierce Coggeshall and Thelwell Russell Coggeshalll Published in 1930 by C. E. Goodspeed and Company of Boston, Massachusetts, pages 6 to 13.

John Coxsall, June 1632, to New England. N.E.H.G.R. Vol 14 p 300

John Coggshall and Mary his wife are mentioned as church members by the Reverend John Eliot of Roxbury, Massachusetts. N.E.H.G.R. Vol 35 p 23

JOSHUA COGGESHALL OF COUNTY ESSEX, ENGLAND, AND PORTSMOUTH, RHODE ISLAND

Born: ca 1623 in County Essex, England

Married: 1st: Joan West on December 22, 1652, at the Newport, Rhode Island home of his brother-in-law, Peter Easton, son of Governor Nicholas Easton and brother of Governor John Easton.

2nd: Rebecca Russell, a Quakeress from Hawkshead, Lancashire, England. She later moved to Lewes, Delaware, and Married Thomas Harford. N.E.H.G.R. vol 18, p 241

Children of Joshua and Joan (West) Coggeshall:

Caleb Coggeshall. Born Portsmouth on December 17, 1672

Daniel Coggeshall. Born April 1665 in Portsmouth (On p 28 of the *Coggeshalls In America*, it is said that he was born in Middletown, Rhode Island. Middletown was formerly part of Newport and is near Portsmouth. See pp 24-5 of the book.) Married Jamestown, Rhode Island on October 23, 1689 to Mary Morey, daughter of Joseph and Mary (Wilbour) Morey of Jamestown. She was born there October 7, 1672, and died in Portsmouth after 1724. In 1698 Daniel Coggeshall served as a member of the Town Council of Jamestown.

In May 1704 he was appointed Head Warden of Jamestown. In 1704 and 1706 he was a Deputy from Jamestown. In 1711 and 1715 he was Deputy to the General Assembly from Portsmouth. He was buried at the Portsmouth Friends Burying Ground.

*Humility Coggeshall

John Coggeshall. Born on December, 1659 in Portsmouth. Married Mary Stanton, daughter of John and Mary (Harndell) Stanton in Portsmouth. She was born in Newport on June 4, 1668, and died in Portsmouth on May 11, 1747. He died in Portsmouth on May 1, 1727.

John and Mary Coggeshall are buried on their farm, located between the farm of his brother Joshua on the south and the farm of his brother Daniel on the north. Their gravestones are still standing.

Joshua Coggeshall. Born Portsmouth in May, 1656. Married first Mrs. Sarah (George) Griffin, widow of Benjamin Griffin and daughter of Richard and Elizabeth George on May 13, 1681, in Newport. She died in Middletown, R.I., on March 20, 1697. Married second Sarah (?) on August 26, 1697, in Newport. She died after 1716.

Joshua Coggeshall. Born Portsmouth in May, 1656. Married first, was at Newport (now Middletown) near Portsmouth. He was admitted a freeman of Portsmouth on June 4, 1677.

Josias Coggeshall. Born Portsmouth in November, 1652. Married in Portsmouth Mary Sturgis, daughter of Widow Mary Sturgis, third wife of Major John Coggeshall. She was born in Boston and died in Newport.

Mary Coggeshall. Born in Portsmouth in February, 1655.

Children of Joshua and Rebecca (Russell) Coggeshall:

Isaac Coggeshall. Born Portsmouth about 1677. Married Sarah Harford, daughter of Thomas Harford of Lewes, Delaware, who was the stepfather as well as the father-in-law of Isaac Coggeshall. Died in Lewes before October 15, 1710.

Preserved Coggeshall, Gentleman. Born and died in Lewes, Delaware. Married Rebecca Harford, daughter of Thomas Harford of Lewes. Preserved Coggeshall died intestate. Letters of Administration were granted 1 April 1727. In 1706 he was an attorney. He was a Recorder under William Penn 1718 to 1721. He was Registrar of Wills. He was a subscriber to the building fund of St. Peter's Church in the Town of Lewes. Thomas Harford's will dated August 25, 1709 and proved on December 4, 1716, names his wife, Rebecca Russell, widow of Joshua Coggeshall and mother of Isaac and Preserved Coggeshall.

Pictures of the homes of Daniel, John and Joshua Coggeshall, Jr., may be found in *The Coggeshalls in America* by Charles Pierce Coggeshall and Thellwell Russell Coggeshall, published in 1930 by C. E. Goodspeed and Company of Boston, pages 14-16.

Joshua Coggeshall:

Came to America with his father in the ship *Lyon* on September 16, 1632. Served as Governor's Assistant 1669, 1672-6; Deputy 1664 et. seq. Buried on his own grounds in Portsmouth, Rhode Island.

HUMILITY COGGESHALL

Born: January, 1670, in Portsmouth, Rhode Island

Married: Benjamin Greene in Portsmouth

Died: After 1719

See John Osborne Austin's *Genealogical Dictionary Of Rhode Island* Published by Joel Munsell's Sons, Albany, New York (1887) page 49 From Chancery Proceedings in the Public Record Office, London, England, is a complaint of John Coggeshall the Younger, son and heir of John Coggeshall the Elder, late of Halstead, County Essex, Gentleman, being in minority under the age of twenty-one years, by Anne Coggeshall, widow, his mother and guardian assigned. Dated 26 June 1620. See Vol 73, pp 22-23 N.E.H.G.R.

COLEMAN

RICHARD COLEMAN

Will of Richard Coleman
Proved 3 Feb. 1457/8
Wife Agnes
To each son and daughter
Son Stephen

Will of Agnes Coleman of Waldingfield Parva
Dated 10 Dec. 1476
Proved 18 May 1477
Daughter Joan
Husband Richard
Son Richard
Son John
N.E.G.H.R. Vol 48, pp 513-5, Vol 94, pp 236-7

JOHN COLEMAN OF LYNES HALL, SUFFOLK

Will of John Colman, the Elder
Of Little Waldingfield
Will dated 19 December, 1505
Proved 5 March 1505/6
Will mentions:
Wife Katherine
Sons: Edward and William
Daughters: Agnes and Alice
Brother: Richard
Nephews: Robert and Richard, sons of brother Richard
Son-in-law: John Gurdon
Will of William Colman of Thorington, Essex, Gentleman
29 July 1586
Proved: 18 Nov 1586
Mentions:
Wife Anne
Brother-in-law Richard Symnell
Daughters: Jane, Elizabeth, Martha, Joane
Brother: Edward
Sister-in-law Jane Simnell
Cousin John Colman (under 21)
Brother-in-law Thomas Symnell
Sister-in-law Martha Saffold

Sister Taylecote and her daughter Jane Lambert
Sister Rachel, my wife's sister
Brother-in-law Lawrence Symnell
N.E.G.H.R. Vol 48, pp 513-5, Vol 94, pp 236-7

ANN COLEMAN

Married: John Gurdon of Assington Hall, County Suffolk, before 19
Dec 1505

DODGE

TRISTRAM DODGE

Sailed April 1661 from Taunton, Massachusetts, with 15 original
settlers for Block Island, Rhode Island. Robert Dodge *Tristram
Dodge and Descendants* (1886)

Rev. S. T. Livermore *History Of Block Island* (1876) pp 17 and 327
says Tristram Dodge was with first party of settlers on Block Island.
Simon Ray Sr. of Block Island (New Shoreham) grandfather of
Anna Ray who married Governor Samuel Ward and Catharine who
married Governor William Greene said February 28, 1718-19, "* * *
and Tristram Dodge Sr., a fisherman came from Newfoundland and
ye freeholders willing for to settle him on s'd island gave unto him
and his heirs forever three acres of land which land ordered by freeholders for to be measured unto him said Dodge situated and being
on ye South East of ye Harbor that now is joining the land of John
Rathbon."

Harris *Block Island Epitaphs* p 10 says the grave of Tristram Dodge
is not marked.

Descendants of David Britain Dodge, son of John Dodge and grand-
son of the first Tristram, have records that the sons of Tristram
Dodge followed him in 1667 and that they came from the north of
England near the river Tweed.

May 4, 1664 Freeman

1676 Sergeant

1720 Dead, Intestate

Children of Tristram Dodge:

Ann Dodge. Given as daughter of Tristram Dodge, Sr., in Austin's
Genealogical Dictionary Of Rhode Island. In view of the Rathbone
record given below this would seem in error. New Shoreham records
say Ann Dodge married November 11, 1686, John Rathbone Jr., who

died in 1723, the son of John Rathbone who died in 1702 and Margaret Rathbone. The Rathbone Genealogy by John C. Cooley says Ann Dodge was his second wife and adds her father settled Block Island in 1662 and died in 1723 but fails to mention his name.

Israel Dodge. July 1670 Freeman. October 1, 1720. Sells Block Island land formerly belonging to his father, Tristram, to his brothers, John, Tristram, and William Dodge of Block Island. 1694 On farm in North Parish (Montville) New London, Connecticut. 1707 Bought land in Montville of Samuel Rogers. 1719 He and his wife, Hannah, gave their son, John, land. 1725. Gave land to sons, William and Samuel.

John Dodge. July 1670 Freeman. Married Mary (?   ) on February 4, 1696. Bought land from brother Israel of New London on Block Island October 1, 1720. Sold land there February 1, 1724-5.

*Margaret Dodge. Theron Royal Woodward in DESCENDANTS OF TRISTRAM DODGE pp 5-8 says he has no record of her except that given by John C. Cooley of Oswego, New York in his Rathbone Genealogy (1898). Cooley says John Rathbone, the son of John Rathbone and the grandson of Richard Rathbone was born ca 1634 and married Margaret Dodge the daughter of Trustrum Dodge. Their children as listed: Thomas Rathbone born 1657 married Mary Dickens; John Rathbone born 1658, married Ann Dodge; Sarah Rathbone, born 1659, married Samuel George; William Rathbone, born 1661, married Sarah (?   ); Joseph Rathbone born 1670, married Mary Mosher; Samuel Rathbone, born 1672, married Patience Coggeshall.

Tristram Dodge. Freeman Block Island July 1670. Married on January 7, 1680 to Dorcas Dickens, daughter of Nathaniel Dickens. Will dated July 26, 1733 and proved on June 7, 1735.

William Dodge. Married Sarah George, the daughter of Peter and Mary George.

MARGARET DODGE

Married: John Rathbone II

GREENE

The Greenes of Rhode Island with Historical Records of English Ancestry 1534-1902 Compiled from manuscripts of Major General George Sears Greene by Louise Brownell Clarke. Printed by Knickerbocker Press of New York in 1903 finds indirect evidence of the descent of the Warwick Greenes from the Northampton Greenes in the following circumstance:

Major John Greene, Deputy Governor of Rhode Island, wrote a letter to the Honorable Sir Robert Southwell, Knight, one of the Secretarys of State to their Majesties Privy Council, Whitehall, London, on 21 December 1692. The letter was received by Sir Robert 4 July 1693.

It was to introduce Christopher Almy, brother-in-law of the Deputy Governor and who was himself elected Governor of Rhode Island in 1693, but refused to serve. The letter of Deputy Governor Greene was sealed with red Wax impressed with arms, three bucks trippant.

These arms were sent by him to an official in England. It was illegal to use arms to which one did not have a right by grant or inheritance. These arms were recorded in Herald's College as borne by Robert Greene of Gillingham, Dorsetshire, England. These arms were those borne by the Greenes of Boughton and Greene's Norton, Northhamptonshire.

In Vol 103, p 186 Mr. G. Andrews Moriarty (a genealogist writing in the New England Historical and Genealogical Magazine) finds this indirect evidence unconvincing. In the same article Mr. Moriarty finds unproven the assertion made in the *Greene* book that Richard Greene, Gentleman, who succeeded to Bowridge Hill in 1608 was married to Mary Hooker, daughter of John Hooker (alias Vowell) who was Chamberlain of the City of Exeter, England, 12 Sept 1534 and who represented Exeter in Parliament. This John Hooker (alias Vowell) was said in the *Greene* book to be the uncle of the celebrated divine, Richard Hooker, Rector of Bascombe, County Wilts and Prebendary of Salisbury. Mary, his daughter, was said to be the grand niece of the Lord Archbishop Grindal of Canterbury. See History of Exeter, England, Astor Library, New York City.

ROBERT GREENE OF BOWRIDGE HILL, PARISH OF GILLINGHAM, COUNTY DORSET, ENGLAND

Taxed on subsidy rolls 1543, 1547, 1558

Children of Robert Greene:

Alice Greene. Married a Mr. Small. Received a legacy from her brother, Peter Greene, as also did her daughter, Elizabeth Small.

Ann Greene. Married Roger Capps of Gillingham. Ann and her son, Richard Capps, received a legacy from Peter Greene.

John Greene of Gillingham. Received a legacy from his brother, Peter Greene.

Peter Greene, Gentleman. Died May 31, 1583. By will left bequests to his wife, Joan, and to his brothers and sisters.

*Richard Greene, Gentleman.

The following material from various wills can be found in The Greenes of Rhode Island with Historical Records of English Ancestry, 1534-1902, compiled from the Manuscripts of Major-General George

Sears Greene by Louise Brownell Clarke Printed in 1903 by the Knickerbocker Press of New York:

Will of Peter Greene of Bowridge Hill, the son of Robert Greene, Proved in the Prerogative Court of Canterbury at London on June 1, 1583 Mentions—

Brother John Greene

Sister: Alice Small and her daughter, Elizabeth Small
Johane Greene my wieff
Ann Capps wife of Roger Capps (my sister)
Richard Greene sonne of my brother, Richard Greene

(See Pages 737-738)

RICHARD GREENE, GENTLEMAN, OF BOWRIDGE HILL, PARISH OF GILLINGHAM, COUNTY DORSET, ENGLAND

Taxed on Subsidy Rolls, 1587
Will dated May 10, 1606. Proved May 3, 1608.
Children of Richard Greene:
Katharine Greene. Married a Mr. Turnor
*Richard Greene

Will of Richard Greene. Proved May 3, 1608, by son, Richard.
Mentions:
Grandson Peter Greene
Brother Peter Greene
Grandson Robert, son of my son, Richard
Grandson John, son of my son, Richard   Pages 738-740
Joane Greene, wife of Peter
Daughter, Katharine Turnor
Mary, wife of son Richard

Will of Robert Greene of Cucklington, brother of Surgeon John
    Greene
Proved January 7, 1650
"To my brother, John Greene in New England all my   Page 741
Latin books if he come for them."
Son Robert

Will of Richard Greene, brother of Surgeon John Greene
Proved at London June 23, 1617 by his father
Mentions:
Brothers Peter, Robert, John
Sisters Rebecca Downton, Mary Rachel, and Ann Greene
Wife Agnes
Will of Rachel Perne, sister of Surgeon John Greene
Dated March 31, 1656. Proved November 13, 1656
Widow of Richard Perne

Sons Richard and John   Page 741
Son-in-law Edward Rawson
Bowridge Hill now in possession of Richard Greene

RICHARD GREENE, GENTLEMAN, OF BOWRIDGE HILL, PARISH OF GILLINGHAM, COUNTY DORSET, ENGLAND

Succeeded to Bowridge Hill Estate in 1608. Executor of his father's will.

Married: Mary Hooker

Children of Richard and Mary (Hooker) Greene:

Ann Greene. Baptized at Gillingham August 31, 1595

Married Giles Stagg of Little Newton

*Surgeon John Greene

Mary Greene. Mentioned in brother, Richard Greene's will.

Peter Greene, Gentleman. Son and Heir to Bowridge Hill.

Mentioned in his grandfather's will. Married Joan (?   )
Issue recorded in Gillingham Parish Register.

Rachel Greene. Married Richard Perne of Gillingham.

Mentioned in brother Richard Greene's will. Edward Rawson married Rachel Perne, their daughter. Richard Perne named Edward Rawson an overseer and Rachel, Executrix of his will.

Richard Perne died on April 11 or 12, 1636. In Lib III, pp 413-5 of Suffolk Deeds is a document wherein Edward Rawson is to receive £300 as a marriage portion from Richard Perne and was to add £600 to be used to buy land to be settled on his wife, Rachel. Rachel Perne died leaving a will dated March 31, 1656, proved November 13th following. She was possessed of a living in the Parish of Gillingham, Dorsetshire called Easthaimes, by lease granted under the hand of William Lord Stowerton or Stourton during the Reign of King Charles I. She left in her will "Legacy of £40 to daughter, Rachel Rawson in New England." The Rawsons came to America in 1637-8, soon after their marriage. Edward Rawson was Secretary of the Massachusetts Bay Colony. See Ancestry of Edward Rawson by Ellery Bicknell Crane, Worcester, Mass. (1887) pp 13, 22-23.

Rebecca Greene. Married (?   ) Downton

Richard Greene. Of Salisbury. In his will dated April 28, 1614 (mem. "Vicesimo nono Septmb 1616") he styles himself "of the Close of the Canons of the Cathedral Churche of Sarum (Salisbury) County of Wilts, Gent." He died s.p. 1617 leaving property to his father, his wife Agnes, and to his brothers and sisters. He left his Latin books to his brothers, Robert and John. His will was proved in London by his father and brother, John, June 23, 1617.

Robert Greene of Cucklington, County Somerset, England, Gentleman. Died 1650. His will dated October 21, 1649, was proved January 7, 1650-1. He gave his Latin books to his "brother John Greene in New England." All other property was given to his son, Robert Greene.

Thomas Greene. Baptized May 18, 1599, and buried August 15, 1599.

SURGEON JOHN GREENE OF BOWRIDGE HILL, PARISH OF GILLINGHAM, COUNTY DORSET, ENGLAND, AND OF PROVIDENCE AND WARWICK, RHODE ISLAND

Born: ca 1590, Bowridge Hill, Parish of Gillingham, County Dorset, England

Married: 1st: Joanne Tattershall in St. Thomas Church, Salisbury, county Wilts, England, on November 4, 1619.
She died soon after their arrival in Rhode Island.

2nd: Alice Daniels, widow

3rd: Phillipa (name always written "Phillip") (?   ) in London, England, ca 1644. She died March 11, 1687. In 1668 she had deeded all her houses and lands to her stepson, Major John Greene, Deputy Governor of Rhode Island.

Died: January, 1659

Children of Surgeon John and Joanne (Tattershall) Greene:

James Greene. Baptized in St. Thomas Church, Salisbury, co. Wilts, England, on June 21, 1626. Married 1st Deliverance Potter, daughter of Robert and Isabel Potter. She was born 1637 and died 1664. Married 2nd Elizabeth Anthony, daughter of John and Susanna Anthony of Portsmouth, Rhode Island. She died in 1698. James Greene was a freeman of Warwick in 1647. He served in the following offices: Town Clerk, 1661, Member General Assembly, Commissioner, Deputy and Assistant. He died on April 27, 1698. His great-grandson was Major General Nathaniel Greene of Revolutionary War fame.

*Major John Greene, Deputy Governor of Rhode Island

Joan (Jone) Greene. Baptized in St. Thomas Church, Salisbury co. Wilts, England, on October 3, 1630. Married John Hade or Haden.

Mary Greene. Baptized in St. Thomas Church, Salisbury, co. Wilts, England, on May 19, 1633. Married ca 1654 to James Sweet, son of John and Mary Sweet. James Sweet was a freeman in 1655, Commissioner from Warwick 1653-8-9 and a juryman in 1656. James Greene died in 1695.

Peter Greene. Born Salisbury, England. Baptized at St. Thomas Church Mar 10, 1621-2. Died Feb 1659. Married Mary Gorton, daughter of Samuel and Elizabeth Gorton. Samuel Gorton was born in 1592 at Gorton, near Manchester, England. He served in Rhode Island as Magistrate, Corporator, Foreign Commissioner, Assemblyman, Judge, Senator, and in 1651 as President or Governor. After the death of Peter Greene, Mary Gorton married John Sanford who held the following offices in Rhode Island: General Treasurer 1655-61; Commissioner 1656-63; General Recorder 1656-76; Attorney-General 1663-71 Deputy 1664-86; Assistant 1664-80; Member of Sir Edmund Andros' Council 1686.

Thomas Greene. Born and Baptized at Salisbury, County Wilts, England, June 4, 1628. Married June 30, 1659, to Elizabeth, the daughter of Rufus and Margaret Barton of Old Warwick. Commissioner 1662; Deputy 1667-84; Assistant 1678-85. Died June 5, 1717.

Richard Greene. Baptized at Salisbury England, March 25, 1624.
Will of Surgeon John Greene
Proved Jan 7, 1659
Executor Wife Phillip
Sons: John, Peter, James, Thomas
Daughter: Mary Sweet
Grandchild: Ann Hade

Will of Deputy Governor John Greene
Proved Dec 20, 1708
Executors: Sons: Peter, Job, Richard, Samuel
Daughters: Deborah Torrey, Ann Greene, Catharine Holden, Audry Spencer, Phillip Dickenson, Granddaughter Mary Dyer.
John Osborne Austin GENEALOGICAL DICTIONARY OF RHODE ISLAND page 88-9
1647 Member First Town Council of Warwick
1648 Commissioner (Representative of Warwick in General Assembly)
1649 Magistrate, Assistant, Member Town Council
1650, 5, 6, 7 Commissioner
Much of the large estate of Surgeon John Greene, after the passage of 300 years, is still in the possession of his descendants.

MAJOR JOHN GREENE, OF SALISBURY, COUNTY WILTS, ENGLAND, AND OF PROVIDENCE, RHODE ISLAND, DEPUTY GOVERNOR OF RHODE ISLAND

Baptized: St. Thomas Church, Salisbury, co. Wilts, England, on August 15, 1620
Married: ca 1648 Anna (Ann or Annis) Almy
Died: November 27, 1708, in Warwick, Rhode Island
Children of Major John and Anna (Almy) Greene:

Anne Greene. Born March 13, 1662-3. Married Thomas Greene of Potowomut on May 27, 1686. Died 1713.

Audrey Greene. Born December 27, 1667. Married ca 1692 to John Spencer of East Greenwich, the son of John and Susannah Spencer.

John Spencer served as Deputy many years between 1699 and 1729 and as Speaker of the House of Deputies from 1712 to 1729. He was born on April 20, 1666, and died in 1743. Andrey (Greene) Spencer died on April 17, 1733. Their son, John Spencer, born June 10, 1693, married on September 13, 1716, to Mary Fry and after her death he married on February 26, 1740, to her sister, Elizabeth Fry. Mary and Elizabeth Fry were daughters of Thomas Fry, Deputy Governor of Rhode Island from 1727 to 1729 and his wife, Welthyan (Greene) Fry.

Catharine Greene. Born August 8, 1665. Married 1688 at Warwick, Rhode Island to Lieutenant Charles Holden, the son of Captain Randall and Frances (Dungan) Holden of Old Warwick. Lieutenant Charles Holden was born on March 22, 1666, and died on July 21, 1717. He served as a Deputy from Warwick from 1710 to 1716. Captain Randall Holden came from Salisbury, co. Wilts, England. He signed the first compact at Portsmouth, Rhode Island in 1638. In 1642-43 he was one of the original proprietors of Warwick. He accompanied Governor Samuel Gorton and Surgeon John Greene, father of Deputy Governor John Greene, on a trip to England to redress wrongs of the Colony. Through his mother, Lieutenant Charles Holden was the great-grandson of Lewis Latham (born 1570 and died ca 1670), Falconer to His Majesty, King Charles I of England.

Deborah Greene. Born in Warwick on August 10, 1648. Married ca 1699 to William Torrey, who was born in England in 1638 (?), the son of Captain William Torrey of Weymouth, Massachusetts. Captain Torrey was the great-great grandson of William Torrey of Combe St. Nicholas, co. Somerset, England. The Reverend Samuel Torrey, the brother of William, married Mary Rawson, the daughter of Edward Rawson, Secretary of the Massachusetts Bay Colony, who had married Rachel Perne, first cousin of Deputy Governor John Greene. William Torrey died on January 11, 1718. His will is in Boston (Suffolk County Records, Vol XX, page 206. Deborah (Greene) Torrey died in Weymouth, Massachusetts, on February 8, 1729, where she is buried with her husband.

Major Job Greene. Born in Warwick on August 24, 1656. He married Phebe Sayles, the daughter of John and Mary (Williams) Sayles and granddaughter of Roger Williams, on January 22, 1684. She was born in 1658 and died in 1744. Major Greene served as a Deputy thirteen terms ,as Assistant for nine years and as Speaker of the House of Deputies. He was Major for the Main in 1715. He died on July 6, 1745. John Sayles served as Assistant 1653-5-7-9, as Commissioner 1655-9, Town Clerk 1655-7, Warden 1658, Town Treasurer 1659-60, Deputy 1669-71, 74, 76, 77, 78, and as a Member of the Town Council 1670-1.

John Greene. Born in Warwick on June 6, 1651. Died before February 1, 1686.

Captain Peter Greene. Born in Warwick on February 4, 1654. Married on December 16, 1680, to Elizabeth Arnold, daughter of Stephen and Sarah (Smith) Arnold of Pawtuxet, Rhode Island. She was born on November 2, 1659, and died on June 5, 1728. Stephen Arnold was the son of William and Christian (Peck) Arnold and the grandson of Richard Arnold, who came to New England in 1635 from the Cheselbourne, co. Dorset, England, first to Providence and then to Pawtuxet.

Stephen Arnold served as a Deputy from Warwick 1664 to 1690 and as an Assistant from 1672 to 1698. Captain Greene served as a Deputy from Warwick for ten years. His will was dated May 14, 1718 and was proved on September 2, 1723. He died on August 12, 1723.

*Phillis (Phillipa or Phillip) Greene

Richard Greene. Born in Warwick on February 8, 1660. Married on February 16, 1692, to Eleanor Sayles, the daughter of John and Mary (Williams) Sayles and the granddaughter of Roger Williams. She died on March 11, 1714. Richard Greene served as a Deputy from 1699 to 1704 and as an Assistant from 1704 to 1711. His will was dated May 20 and was proved July 2, 1711.

Captain Samuel Greene. Born January 30, 1670-71. He married on January 24, 1694-5 to Mary Gorton, daughter of Captain Benjamin and Sarah (Carder) Gorton and granddaughter of Governor Samuel Gorton. She was born on October 31, 1673 and died in January 1731-2. Captain Greene served as a Deputy and as a Justice of the Peace.

He was the father of Governor William Greene, the grandfather of Governor William Greene, Jr., the great-grandfather of United States Senator Ray Greene, and the great-great grandfather of Lt.-Governor William Greene, of Major-General George Sears Greene, and of Brigadier General Alphonso Greene.

William Greene. Borne in 1652 and died in 1678 in Newport. He married Mary Sayles on December 17, 1674. She was the daughter of John and Mary (Williams) Sayles and the granddaughter of Roger Williams.

See THE GREENES OF RHODE ISLAND by L. B. Clarke Published in New York in 1903 Pages 59-75

JOHN GREENE

Town Clerk

Surveyor

One of 24 named in the Permanent Charter granted in 1663 by King Charles II to the Colony of Rhode Island. One of ten assistants named in that Charter.

On instructions from the King named a member of Sir Edmund Andros Council in 1688 with John Coggeshall.

Major for the Main 1683 to 1686, 1690 to 1691, 1696

Representative to the General Court 1652 to 1663

Deputy 1664, 1674, 1677, 1680

Assistant 1660 to 1690

Warden for Warwick 1658

General Recorder (Secretary of State) 1652, 1653, 1654

General Solicitor 1665

Attorney General 1657, 1658, 1659, 1660

Deputy Governor 1690 to 1700

His gravestone still stands on his old farm, Greene's Hold, which he purchased from the Indians October 1, 1642, and which was owned by his family until it was sold to John Brown of Providence on October 6, 1782. The gravestone reads: "Here lyeth the body of John Greene Esq and late deptie Governr he departed this life in ye 89 year of his age November ye 27 1708." The gravestone of his wife, Anna Almy reads: "Here lyeth the body of Ann ye wife of Major John Greene She deceased in ye 82nd year of her age May ye 6th 1709."

THE GREENES OF RHODE ISLAND WITH HISTORICAL REC-
ORDS OF ENGLISH ANCESTRY, 1534-1902 Compiled from manuscripts of Major-General George Sears Greene by Louise Brownell Clarke Printed by the Knickerbocker Press of New York in 1903 Pages 70-83

PHILLIS GREENE

Born: October 7, 1658, in Warwick, Rhode Island. Daughter of John Greene, Deputy Governor of Rhode Island and his wife, Ann Almy.

Married: Caleb Carr, son of Robert Carr and nephew of Caleb Carr, Governor of Rhode Island. Robert Carr was one of the original purchasers of the Island of Conanicut in Narragansett Bay. He left all his land at Conanicut (alias Jamestown) to Caleb, his eldest son and Caleb and Phillis lived there until the death of Caleb Carr.

The will of Caleb Carr proved in Newport March 30, 1690, mentions his brother-in-law, Peter Greene.

After the death of Caleb Carr, Phillis (Greene) Carr married Charles Dickinson, son of John Dickinson and Elizabeth Howland, daughter of John Howland of the Mayflower.

See *THE GREENES OF RHODE ISLAND* by L. B. Clarke Published in New York in 1903 Pages 59-75

See *THE GREENES OF RHODE ISLAND WITH HISTORICAL RECORDS OF ENGLISH ANCESTRY,* 1534-1902 Compiled from manuscripts of Major-General George Sears Greene by Louise Brownell Clarke. Printed by the Knickerbocker Press of New York in 1903 Pages 70-83

See *THE CARR BOOK* Published by Arthur A. Carr in Ticonderoga, New York, in 1947 Page 11

GREENE

JOHN GREENE

John Greene lived in 1639 with Richard Smith, Sr., in North Kingstown Rhode Island.

No relation is known between John Greene then of North Kingstown and John Greene of Warwick and John Greene of Newport.

John Greene in 1663 with Richard Smith Sr. declared himself in favor of being under jurisdiction of Connecticut rather than Rhode Island. May 20, 1671. John Greene takes Oath of Allegiace to Rhode Island. January 1, 1672. John Greene and five others buy of the Indians a tract of land in Narragansett. In 1672 and 1674 he is a witness to deeds.

July 21, 1679. John Greene makes affidavit in support of the title of Richard Smith, Jr., to lands in the vicinity of Wickford.

July 29, 1679. John Greene and 41 others of Narragansett sign a Petition to the King praying him to end boundary dispute between Connecticut and Rhode Island.

March 24, 1682. John Greene deeds land to sons Daniel and James Greene. Land bounded partly by land of son John. His wife in 1682 was named Joan.

July 16, 1686. John Greene signs an Address to the King.

May 13, 1692. John Greene witnesses a deed. Probably died within next four years as his name does not appear in a list of Kingstown freemen of 1696.

H. T. Briggs, *Briggs* pp 223-225 says John Greene married Joan Beggarly ca 1642. He names also children in addition to those named in DESCENDANTS OF JOSEPH GREENE OF WESTERLY, RHODE ISLAND, AND OTHER BRANCHES OF THE GREENES OF QUIDNESSET OR KINGSTOWN, RHODE ISLAND, by Frank L. Greene, Published in 1894 by Joel Munsell's Sons, Albany, New York, hereinafter referred to as Greene, *Joseph Greene.* Frank Greene says "probably" Benjamin Greene is the son of John Greene, but the evidence is "not conclusive."

Children of John and Joan (Beggarly) Greene:

*Benjamin Greene

Daniel Greene. Married at Newport July 16, 1689 (perhaps a second marriage) to Rebecca Barrows. Lived in North Kingstown where he died in 1730. Had seven children.

Edward Greene. Married Mary Tibbits, the daughter of Henry and Sarah (Stanton) Tibbits. Lived in North Kingstown. They had sons, as is hown by the will of their grandfather Tibbits, but their names have not been preserved.

James Greene. Born 1655. Died 1728. Married 1st Elizabeth (?) and married 2nd Ann (?   ). Lived in North Kingstown and had sons, John and James of whom nothing more is known.

John Greene, Jr. Born June 6, 1651. Died October 6, 1729. Married Abigail (?   ). Lived in East Greenwich, Rhode Island and in that part of Warwick set off as Coventry. Had eleven children.

See John Osborn Austin *GENEALOGICAL DICTIONARY OF RHODE ISLAND* pp 86-87.

BENJAMIN GREENE

Born: Probably in Quidnesset (North Kingstown) Rhode Island, ca 1665.

Married: ca 1687 to Humility Coggeshall

Died: Will dated January 7, 1719, and proved in East Greenwich, Rhode Island, on March 5, 1719. In the will he mentions his wife Humility and 12 children (three under 18).

Children of Benjamin and Humility ((Coggesshall) Greene:

Ann Greene. Born ca 1694. Married David Tennant, the son of Alexander Tennant of Kingstown. Lived in Kingstown.

Benjamin Greene. Born ca 1692. Married March 19, 1714, to Eleanor Randall of Westerly, where he settled.

Caleb Greene. Born after 1700. Admitted freeman of North Kingstown 1727 and died the same year. Probably not married. Willed property to his brother, Joshua Greene.

Catherine Greene. Born ca 1700. Probably married on December 23, 1721, to her cousin, Daniel Greene, Jr. Lived in North Kingstown. Died before 1738.

Deborah Greene. Born after 1700. Married in East Greenwich on September 18, 1729, to William Reynolds, the son of James Reynolds. Lived in West Greenwich, where the births of her children is recorded.

Dinah Greene. Born after 1700.

*Henry Greene

John Greene. Born ca. 1688, probably in Quidnesset. Married Mary Aylsworth, the daughter of Arthur and Mary (Brown) Aylsworth, the granddaughter of the Reverend John and Mary (Holmes) Brown and the great-grandghter of the Reverend Chad and Elizabeth (Sharparowe) Brown and of the Reverend Obadiah and Katherine (Hyde) Holmes. On October 13, 1726 John Greene gave a receipt for his wife's share of her father's estate. In 1732 John Greene is styled "lieut. John." On January 9, 1733-4 John Greene of East Greenwich purchases 149 acres in West Greenwich. In 1743 he sells farms belonging to his father and his brother Caleb, both deceased.

Married 2nd in West Greenwich to Priscilla Bowen (or Barney) who survived him. He died in West Greenwich March 29, 1752. Will made March 26 and proved April 25, 1752.

HENRY GREENE

Born: About 1696

Married: Margaret Rathbone on May 15, 1724, in East Greenwich, Rhode Island

Died: February 21, 1752, in West Greenwich Rhode Island

Children of Henry and Margaret (Rathbone) Greene:

Amey Greene. Born September 10, 1727

Anne Greene. Born November 4, 1736. Married perhaps in West Greenwich, Rhode Island, on January 26, 1758, to George Tibbitts

Benjamin Green. Born July 17, 1729. Married Mehitable Tripp of Exeter, daughter of Job Tripp. Lived in West Greenwich and Exeter. Mr. Douglas N. Greene of Syracuse, New York, is preparing a sketch of Benjamin's descendants.

Christian Greene. Born January 22, 1740. Married probably in Exeter on March 6, 1760, to Job Greene, son of her cousin Phillip (John, Benjamin, John) and lived in West Greenwich.

Humility Greene. Born February 12, 1725. Married her second cousin, Silas Greene (John, John, John) and had five children in West Greenwich.

Jeremiah Greene. Born April 11, 1743. Perhaps it was he who married in Exeter on July 20, 1765, to Deborah Cammell.

*Job Greene

Mary Greene. Born May 18, 1726. Died young.

Mary Greene. Born May 29, 1731.

Nathan Greene. Born May 29, 1731.

JOB GREENE

Born: March 2, 1735, in East Greenwich, Rhode Island

Died: January 25, 1792, in Vermont

Married: In West Greenwich, Rhode Island, by Isaac Sheldon, J. P., on February 3, 1757, to Meribah Carr

Children of Job and Meribah (Carr) Greene:

Amy Greene born September 7, 1782

Eunice Greene born October 17, 1757

Gardner Greene born July 19, 1779

The Reverend Henry Greene. Born July 17, 1761, probably in West Greenwich, Rhode Island. Died in Parishville, St. Lawrence County, New York, on January 20, 1849. Married 1st Abigail Moon, daughter of Asa and Deborah Moon on January 24, 1782. Abigail Moon was born September 30, 1764, and died in Vermont on April 17, 1824. Married 2nd on September 29, 1824, to Mrs. Betsey Munson, widow of Ephraim Munson of New Haven, Vermont. When a young man he united with the Baptist Church in Jericho, Vermont, under the pastorate of Elder Clark Rogers. He commended preaching in Clarendon, Rutland County, Vermont, in 1785, and was ordained to the Baptist ministry in Wallingford on October 4, 1787, where he preached twenty years. In 1808 he moved to Cornwall, Vermont, then to Shoreham, and closed a long and successful pastorate at Parishville, New York, having baptized over a thousand converts. He was Chaplain of the Vermont Legislature and also a chaplain of a regiment in Addison County.

Job Greene born November 7, 1765

Margaret Greene born probably in West Greenwich on August 5, 1763, and died July 13, 1845. Married about 1782 to Abel Potter, Jr., son of Abel and Hannah Potter. Abel Potter, Jr., was born in Vermont (Probably in Halifax) on March 13, 1760, and died March 13, 1846

Meriba Greene born June 11, 1772

Mility (Humility?) Greene born May 19, 1774 and died January 1, 1852

Nathan Greene. Born November 7, 1767. Some of his descendants are said to be living in St. Albans, Vermont.

Polly Greene born February 20, 1779

*Sarah Green born January 1, 1759

Susannah Greene born January 13, 1770

The birth of only Eunice Greene is recorded in West Greenwich, Rhode Island, though it is almost certain that several others were born there.

He doubtless removed early to Vermont, perhaps in Halifax or vicinity at first and farther north later.

SARAH GREENE

Born: January 1, 1759

Married: Lieutenant Michael Briggs on December 28, 1775, in the then Town of Jerico (now Hancock), Massachusetts

Died: February 12, 1849, in Augusta, New York

John Austin's *Genealogical Dictionary of Rhode Island* p 87 V.R.R.I. Kent Co. East Greenwich pp 119-120

AFFIDAVIT OF MRS. SARAH BRIGGS

She swore that:

She was 77 years old, the widow of Michael Briggs, an officer of the Revolutionary Army

on December 28, 1775 she married Michael Briggs in the then Town of Jerico, Massachusetts, the Reverend Clark Rogers officiating.

Michael Briggs died on the 10th day of February, 1828, in the Town of Burlington, Otsego County.

Deponent now resides in Burlington and has not married again since the death of her husband, Michael Briggs.

During the American Revolution Michael and Sarah Briggs lived in Pownel, Vermont, where she first became acquainted with Michael Briggs. She went home to her father's house in Massachusetts to be married.

In the spring of the year before they were married, the first of April according to her best recollection, Michael Briggs joined the Army as an Orderly Sergeant in Capt. Stewart's Company under General Arnold and Ethan Allen.

In his lifetime she often heard him tell of being at the taking of Ticonderoga and Crown Point.

He remained in the Service the whole of that summer until he was discharged and returned home sick in the fall of the year as will appear by his discharge hereunto annexed.

In the winter after their marriage she removed to Pownel to live with her husband. He joined a Company of minutemen commanded by Capt Wright.

After their marriage her husband served with the Army not less than one third part of the time till the close of the war. The greatest part of his service was rendered in Captain Joseph Briggs' Company. Captain Briggs was his brother. They served at Hubbardton and various posts on the northern frontier.

Michael Briggs was in the Battle of Bennington and at the taking of Burgoyne. After receiving the annexed Commission he served as an Ensign in Capt Briggs Company until he was promoted to the office of Lieutenant. His Commission as a Lieutenant is lost or destroyed and she does not know the date of it. After receiving his Commission he served at least one third part in each year to the end of the war.

Michael Briggs served more than two and one half years, but the specific terms of service she cannot state. He served with Generals Stark and Gates and Colonels Warner, Herrick and Warren.

Sworn and subscribed before Judge James C. Walworth of Otsego County, New York, on May 24, 1837

AFFIDAVIT OF HENRY GREENE OF THE TOWN OF PARISH-VILLE, THE COUNTY OF ST. LAWRENCE, THE STATE OF NEW YORK

Henry Greene swore that:

He was well acquainted with Michael Briggs deceased.

Michael Briggs was a soldier in the Revolution.

Michael Briggs was in the Battle of Bennington, 1777.

His sister Sarah was the widow of Michael Briggs.

He saw them married some one or two years previous to the Battle of Bennington.

He cannot certify the length of time Michael Briggs served, but always understood it was six months.

Sworn and subscribed before Eliphelet Leonard J. P. on 11 August 1848

AFFIDAVIT OF EUNICE DEAL OF POWNAL, COUNTY OF BENNINGTON, STATE OF VERMONT

Eunice Deal swore that:

She was 79 years old the 17th day of October last past.

That Sarah Briggs, the widow of Michael Briggs, who resides in the Town of Burlington, in the County of Otsego and State of New York, is her sister.

That on the 28th day of December, 1775, in the Town of Jerico, now the Town of Hancock in the County of Berkshire and State of Massachusetts, the said Sarah was married to Michael Briggs by a minister named Clark Rogers

Her name before her marriage was Sarah Greene and when she married she was not sixteen years old.

Michael and Sarah lived in the Town of Pownal, County of Bennington, State of Vermont, during the Revolution and for many years afterwards, later moving to New York.

Michael Briggs was a Lieutenant and was in the Battle of Burlington and at the taking of Burgoyne

Michael Briggs was in the service of his country the greatest part of the period of the Revolution, according to her best recollection.

The marriage of Michael Briggs and Sarah Greene was at the house of deponent's father and she was present.

Sworn and Signed in Pownal, Vermont, on the 27th day of February, 1837

GRIFFIN

ROBERT GRIFFIN

Came to America before 1655.
Settled at Newport, Rhode Island.
1656   Commissioner.

Children of Robert Griffin:
Benjamin Griffin. One of the patentees of 5,000 acres of land in East Greenwich, Rhode Island.

Mary Griffin. Married Thomas Fry of Newport. Their son, Thomas Fry, Deputy Governor of Rhode Island, deeded on July 14, 1710, land to "cousin John Spencer" for a burial place.

Susannah Griffin. Married Dr. John Spencer of East Greenwich.

See H.T. Briggs, *Briggs* p 296.

See Austin's *Genealogical Dictionary of Rhode Island* p 89

SUSANNAH GRIFFIN

Married: Dr. John Spencer of East Greenwich, Rhode Island
Died: After 1684

GURDON

GURDON

ADAM DE GURDON
Had a rent in Tystede from King John
Died: 1214
His son:
SIR ADAM DE GURDON, KT.
Held lands in Tystede and Selborne
Died: 1231 leaving by Ameria, his wife, two sons
His son:
SIR ADAM DE GURDON, KT.
Bailiff of Alton temp King Henry III
Outlawed for treason and rebellion as one of the Montfort faction
After the Battle of Evesham he retired with a band of followers into the New Forest
Afterwards King Edward I pardoned him and appointed him Keeper

of the Forest of Wolmer and employed him in high military commands

Married: By special Papal License to Constantia de Venuz and resided at the Temple, Selborne, Hants (now occupied by the Earl of Selborne). The estate which still bears the name of Gurdon Manor was left to his daughter Joanna, wife of Richard Achard. The arms of Sir Adam are still borne by the family.

His nephew: ROBERT GURDON Moved to London. Sheriff 1314 Died 1343

His son: JOHN GURDON Merchant in London Died: 1385

His son: THOMAS GURDON Clyne, Kent Died: 1439

His son: JOHN GURDON Clyne, Kent

Succeeded in 1465 by his son, John Gurdon of Dedham

JOHN GURDON

Of Dedham, County Essex, England.

His name appears in the court rolls as early as 8 Nov 1407

Married: Joan

Died after 1451-2

Children of John and Joan Gurdon:

*John Gurdon

John Gurdon Probably "the middler" of Dedham. Called "Senior" 1492-8. Died ca 1498. Married Olive

William Gurdon. Probably of Dedham.

Vol. 95, pp 69-72 N.E.H.G.R.

JOHN GURDON

Called John the elder in 1480, when there were living John Gurdon "the middler" and John Gurdon, Jr., the testator of 1504.

Died an old man between 13 August 1487, the date of his will and 14 Jan 1487/8, the date the will was proved.

Married: 1st Margaret (?   ) who died after 1472.

2nd Matilda (?   ) who died 13 August 1487.

Children of John Gurdon:

*John Gurdon

Jone Gurdon. Died before 13 August 1487

Alice Gurdon. Died before 13 August 1487

Isobel Gurdon. Married Thomas Martin of Wrabnees.

Robert Gurdon, Clothier. Born ca 1455. Died 1503.

Robert and three children are named in the will of his father, John Gurdon.

William Gurdon. d.s.p. 1502. Court Roll dated at Dedham on Wednesday in Whitweek 17 Henry VII (1502) states: "William Gurdon, Jr., died since the last court."

Will of John Gurdon dated 13 August 1487. See Vol 94, pp 232-3 N.E.G.H.R.

Masses to be said for his parents John and Joane Gurdon his wife, Margaret, Alice and Joane, his daughters.

Mentions:

Wife Matilda

Son: John

Daughters of his son Robert: Agnes and Margaret

Son of his son Robert: Robert

Daughter of his son John: Joane

Sons of his son John: John the elder and John the younger.

Thomas Martyn Junr son of Tho Martyn Senr of Wrabnase and Isabella, his wife, the daughter of testator.

William Gurdon, his brother.

JOHN GURDON OF DEDHAM, COUNTY ESSEX, ENGLAND, CLOTHIER

Will of John Gurdon of Dedham in ye Diocess of London

Dated 3 April 1504

Proved 21 May 1504

First bequeaths his soul to Almighty God, Our Blessed Lady St. Mary ye Virgin and to all ye holy company in Heaven.

Requests that his body be buried in ye Church or Churchyard of Our Lady at Dedham.

Mentions:

Joane his wife

John his son

Christian his daughter

Vol 94, p 234 N.E.G.H.R., Vol 95, pp 70-1

Children of John and Joan Gurdon:

Christina Gurdon. Born ca 1480. Married Robert Craddock of Dedham Joan Gurdon. Under 16 in 1487

John Gurdon the Elder. Under 16 in 1487. d.s.p. He is called John Gurdon the elder, son of John Gurdon the younger, i.e., the elder John of John Gurdon Jr.'s two sons John.

John Gurdon the Younger. Under 20 years of age on 3 April 1504.

JOHN GURDON, OF DEDHAM, LITTLE WALDINGFIELD, AND GREAT WALDINGFIELD, OF THE MANOR OF ASSINGTON, COUNTY SUFFOLK, ENGLAND

Born: About 1485

Married: 1st: before December 19, 1505, to Anne Coleman, daughter of John Coleman of Little Waldingfield.

2nd: before 1537/8 Alice (?   )

Died: 1556

Children

Alice Gurdon Married 1st: (?   ) Bunne; Married 2nd: Robert Thorpe of Brent Ely

*Anne Gurdon who married William Butter of Dedham

Anne Gurdon Married Roger Wincoll of Little Waldingfield

Jane Gurdon. Married 1st: (?   ) Cole. Married 2nd: William Cardinal of North Bromley, co. Essex

John Gurdon. d.s.p. in 1555/6

Katharine Gurdon. Married Richard Lawrence of Spexhall, co. Suffolk, Testator of 1560. She died before 1561.

Mary Gurdon. Married Anthony Rows of Badinghouse who in his will dated 22 November 1559 calls Robert Gurdon his brother-in-law.

Robert Gurdon. Married Rose (Sexton) Appleton, daughter of Robert Sexton and widow of William Appleton.

Their son, John Gurdon of Assington, co. Suffolk, married Amy Brampton, daughter of William Brampton of Letton, Co. Norfolk.

Their grandson, Brampton Gurdon of Assington married Muriel Sedley, daughter of Martin Sedley of Morley, co. Norfolk Their great-granddaughter, Muriel Gurdon married in June 1633 Richard Saltonstall, Esquire, eldest son of Sir Richard Saltonstall of Essex who began the settlement of Watertown, Massachusetts, in 1630. Richard Saltonstall born in 1610 came with his father, Sir Richard, to New England in 1630, but returned to England in 1631. In 1635 with his wife Muriel and young daughter he left England and settled at Ipswich Massachusetts.

John Gurdon and his son, Robert Gurdon, purchased Assington Hall from Sir Miles Corbett. See the listing of a direct descendant of John Gurdon, Sir Betram Francis Gurdon, K.G., M.C. of Letton and Cranworth, Norfolk, the Third Baron Cranworth, in Burkes *Peerage, Baronetage and Knightage* 1956

Will of Richard Saltonstall citizen and merchant taylor of the City of London, dated 25 August 1665 and proved 16 October 1667 mentions:

Cousin Philip Gurdon, Doctor in Phisicke

Cousin Anne Gurdon, the daughter of my uncle John Gurdon, Esquire, and Amy Gurdon, his sister

N.E.G.H.R. Vol 48 pp 511-2

Will of Elizabeth Barrett, widow, late the wife of Edward Barrett, Esquire, dated 27 May 36 Elizabeth and proved 18 October 1594 mentions:

Elizabeth Gurdon, daughter of son-in-law Brampton Gurdon, Esq.

Amy Gurdon and Judith Gurdon, two other of his daughters, Sir Robert Litton, Knight, my father

Will of Robert Gurdon of Assington in the diocese of Norwich within the County of Suffolk, esquire, dated 3 April 1578 and proved 12 May 1579 mentions:

wife Rose

son John

Daughter Elizabeth Waldgrave

Children of Elizabeth Waldgrave: Thomas, John, Elizabeth, Brampton Gurdon, son of son John

sister Wincoll

Daughter Appleton and her son Isaac Appleton

Will of William Littlebury of Dedham Essex dated 20 July 1571 and proved 26 January 1575 mentions:

Wife Bridget

Cousin Edward Littlebury of Gray's Inn son of Humfrey Littlebury of Hagwordingham in Lincolnshire

Thomas Appleton of Little Waldingfield Suffolk, Gentleman, my late wife's brother

Edward Waldgrave of Lawford, Essex

Robert Gurdon of Asson, Suffolk, Esq and John Gurdon his son

William Butter of Dedham Clothier and Piers Butter his son

ANNE GURDON

Buried at Dedham, County Essex, England, 22 Aug 1563

Married: William Butter of Dedham, Clothier. He was born ca 1521 and buried at Dedham 8 Nov 1594

HARNDEL

JOHN HARNDEL

Died: February 6, 1687, in Newport, Rhode Island

1673 Juryman

1685 Will drawn. Proved 1687. Mentions daughter Mary wife of John Stanton, daughters of Mary and Hannah (of Stantons) and daughter, Rebecca, wife of Hugh Mosher

Children of John Harndel:

Mary Harndel. Born 1646. Died young.

Mary Harndel. Born 1647. Married John Stanton son of Robert and Avis Stanton. She died 1678. Rebecca Harndel. Married Hugh Mosher who was born 1633 and died 1713. They were the parents of Nicholas, John, Joseph, Mary, James, Daniel, and Rebecca Mosher.

John Osborne Austin's *Genealogical Dictionary of Rhode Island* page 93.

REBECCA HARNDEL

Married: The Reverend Hugh Mosher

HOLMES

ROBERT HULME OF REDDISH, PARISH OF MANCHESTER, ENGLAND

Robert Hulme is buried in Stockport. January 14, 1604-5. His wife is buried in the Collegiate Church (now Cathedral) in Manchester.

September 7, 1610

The will of Robert Hulme was dated August 11, 1602 and proved at Chester January 28, 1604-5. He bequeathed his lands to his eldest son, Robert, and to his widow, Alice.

Children of Robert and Alice (?   ) Hulme:

Jane Hulme. Named in father's will, when she was unmarried.

John Hulme. Named in father's will. An Executor.

*Robert Hulme

Daughter whose child, George Hoyd is named in her father's will.

N.E.G.H.R. Vol 64 pp 237-9

The American Family of Obadiah Holmes by Colonel J.T. Holmes, Columbus, Ohio, (1915) p 11

ROBERT HULME

Baptized: August 18, 1578

Married: Katherine Johnson in Stockport near Manchester on October 8, 1605. She was buried at Stockport on September 8, 1630.

Buried: On November 12, 1640, at Stockport, England

Children of Robert and Katherine (Johnson) Hulme:

Joan Hulme. Baptized at Didsbury on February 2, 1610-1611

John Hulme. Baptized at Stockport on May 3, 1607. Matriculated at Brasenose College, Oxford University 18 November 1625 aged 17. Not named in father's will, so probably dead before 1640. Listed at Oxford "son of Robert Hulme of Reddish pleb."

Joseph Hulme. Buried in Stockport 13 June 1623.

Joseph Hulme. Named in his father's will in 1640. Under 21, His father left him all his books.

Nathaniel Hulme. Baptized Didsbury 12 July 1618. Buried at Stockport 10 September 1631.

*The Reverend Obadiah Hulme (Holmes)

Robert Hulme. Baptized at Stockport on March 25, 1621. Inherited his father's holdings at Reddish. He owned a tan yard and pits at Meadowcroft in Middleton and had a place of business at Manchester. He was ruling elder of the church at Gorton during the Commonwealth, approved 11 December 1649. Member of First Classis 1651-1660. Several times delegate to the Provincial Assembly at Preston. Buried at Gorton on November 17, 1697. His will was proved at Chester on October 11, 1698. In his will he is described as "of Reddish, yeoman". He was married at the Collegiate Church, Manchester, England, on 6 November 1641, to Ann Thorpe, who was buried in Gorton on 16 November 1672. They had two sons: John and Obadiah Hulme.

Samuel Hulme. Buried at Stockport on November 2, 1613

Samuel Hulme. Matriculated Brasenose College, Oxford University, 15 February 1632-3, aged 16. B.A. 17 May 1636. Mentioned in his father's will.

See N.E.H.G.R. Vol 64 pp 237-9.

THE REVEREND OBADIAH HOLMES OF COUNTY LANCASTER, ENGLAND, OF SALEM AND REHOBOTH, MASSACHUSETTS, AND OF NEWPORT, RHODE ISLAND

Baptized: Didsbury, England on March 18, 1609-1610

Married: Katherine Hyde on November 20, 1630, at the Collegiate Church (now Cathedral), Manchester, England.

Died: 1682

Children of the Reverend Obadiah and Katherine (Hyde) Holmes:
Hopestill Holmes. Married (?   ) Taylor.
John Holmes. Buried in Stockport, England, on June 27, 1633.
John Holmes. Born 1649. Married on December 1, 1671, to Frances

Holden, the daughter of Randall and Frances (Dungan) Holden. Frances Holden was born in 1649 and died in 1679. After her death, John Holmes married Mary, the widow of William Green and the daughter of John and Mary (Williams) Sayles and the granddaughter of Roger Williams, on October 12, 1680. Mary Green had been born in 1652 and died in 1713. John Holmes served as Deputy from Newport 1682, 1704-5 and as General Treasurer of the Colony of Rhode Island 1690-1703, 1708-9. He died on October 2, 1712.

Jonathon Holmes. Born near Manchester, England, 1633-4. He married Sarah Borden, the daughter of Richard and Joan (?   ) Borden in 1664-5. He was a founder of Middletown, Monmouth County, East Jersey. In New Jersey he served as a Deputy in the General Assembly, 1668, 1680, as a Justice, 1672, and as a Captain of the Middletown Company, 1673. He moved back to Newport, Rhode Island, in 1683-4, where he served as Deputy 1690-1, 1696, 1698-1702, 1706-1707, and as Speaker of the House of Deputies 1696-8, 1700-1. He died in October, 1713.

LYDIA HOLMES. Probably born in Rehoboth, Massachusetts. Married in 1663 to Captain John Bowne, the eldest son of William and Ann Bowne. Captain Bowne came with his father to Gravesend, Long Island, where he was alloted a plantation on September 20, 1647. He purchased land there from Sir Henry Moody. He was a Representative to the Hempstead Convention in 1665. He removed to Middletown, New Jersey where he was a patentee under the Monmouth Patent issued by the Duke of York on April 8, 1665. He was a resident there as early as 1667. He took the Oath of Allegiance in 1668. He was a member of the Provincial Assembly in 1680 and Speaker of the Provincial Assembly of New Jersey in 1682. He was a Justice of Monmouth County in 1683. He died in 1684. Their daughter, SARAH BOWNE, married Judge Richard Salter, who in 1695 was elected a member of the House of Deputies and in 1704 was a member of the Second Asembly of Representatives. HANNAH SALTER, granddaughter of Lydia Holmes, married Mordecai Lincoln. Her brother, Richard Salter, was Chief Justice of the Supreme Court of New Jersey. JOHN LINCOLN, great-grandson of Lydia Holmes, moved from Pennsylvania where his parents had lived to Virginia. ABRAHAM LINCOLN, great-great grandson of Lydia Holmes, served as a Captain of the Virginia Militia during the American Revolution. He moved to Kentucky where he owned a total of some 3,200 acres of land. THOMAS LINCOLN, great-great-great grandson of Lydia Holmes, was born in Rockingham County, Virginia, later lived in Kentucky, Indiana, and Illinois ABRAHAM LINCOLN, great-great-great-great grandson of Lydia Holmes, served as the 16th President of the United States. See ANCESTRY OF ABRAHAM LINCOLN by J. Henry

Lea and J.R. Hutchinson (1909), Houghton and Mifflin, Boston and New York.

*Mary Holmes

Martha Holmes. Baptized in Salem, Massachusetts, on May 3, 1640. Died 1682.

Judge Obadiah Holmes. Baptized in Salem, Massachusetts, on June 9, 1644. Married Hannah Cole. Moved to Staten Island, New York, where he served as Clerk of Court and Judge under Governor Leisler. He moved to Cohansey, New Jersey, where he died before June 10, 1723, and where he is buried. For twelve years he had served as Judge of the Salem County Court.

Samuel Holmes. Baptized in Salem, Massachusetts, on March 20, 1642. Married Alice Stillwell, daughter of Nicholas and Ann (Van Dyke) Stillwell. Moved to Gravesend, Long Island. Died 1679.

The original will of the Reverend Obadiah Holmes is printed in Vol 67, pp 21-23 N.E.H.G.R. It mentions daughters: Mary Brown, Martha Odlin, Liddiah Browne, and Hopestill Taylor, sons: John, Obediah, Samuel and Jonathon Holme, and wife Katherine Holme. Dated April 9, 1681, Newport, Rhode Island.

In a letter to all his children, the Reverend Holmes in 1675 mentions sons: Joseph, John, Obediah, Samuel, and Johnathon, daughters: Hope, Martha, Mary, Lidiah

N.E.H.G.R. Vol 67, p23, Vol 64, pp 237-9 shows Reverend Holmes was the son of Robert Hulme of Reddish in the Parish of Manchester, Lancashire, England, and was baptized 18 March 1609/10.

In letters the Reverend Holmes says:

"The twentieth day of the tenth month in the year 1675 I Obediah Hullme now come to the evening of the day being sixty nine years old or thereabouts***"

In writing of his parents:

"Three sons they brought up aright to the University at Oxford"
He writes of "my brother Robert Hullme"
"For Robert Hullme at his house in Redish near Gorton Chapel in the Parish of Manchester. In Lancashire".

The Newport Historical Society has lately come into possession of an autographed volume, written in 1675 by Obadiah Holmes who was minister of the First Baptist Church, but who went to Massachusetts to preach. Having no license, he was arrested by the Puritan Magistrate, confined in jail, and finally sentenced to be publicly whipped at the tail of a cart. N.E.H.G.R. Vol 22 p 351, Vol 39 p 42.

Obadiah Holmes came to Salem, Massachusetts, in 1639 where he had a land grant. He manufactured glass there. In 1646 he moved to Rehoboth, Massachusetts In 1650 he left the Congregational Church and founded the Baptist Church. He moved to Newport, Rhode Island where he bought a 400 acre farm. In 1651 he went with John Crandall and John Clarke to Lynn, Massachusetts. Mr. Clarke preached on the Sunday there. The Three were fined, but Obadiah Holmes would not pay the fine and suffered instead a public whipping. He bore the scars (which he was wont to call the marks of the Lord Jesus) for years afterwards. In 1652 he was pastor of the First Baptist Church in Newport and continued so until his death in 1682. He was buried on his farm with his wife.

The Reverend Obadiah Holmes was a Commissioner 1656-8 and frequently a Member of the General Assembly. His will dated 9 April 1681 is in the possession of Henry Bull, Esq., of Newport.

In the reading room of the Long Island Historical Society in Brookyln is a pendulum clock with this incription:

"This clock was presented by John H. Baker, Esq., of Brooklyn in May 1869 to the Long Island Historical Society. The clock has been running for over 200 years. It was brought to this country from London in 1639 by the Reverend Obadiah Holmes at whose death it passed to his oldest son (living) Jonathon, then to Jonathon's son, Joseph, who left it to his son, John Holmes, who was the great-grandfather of the donor."

Chad Brown Memorial by Abby Isabel (Brown) Buckley pp 150-2 John Osborne Austin's *Genealogical Dictionary of Rhode Island* pp 103-4 Published by Joel Munsell's Sons, Albany, New York (1887) Obadiah Holmes was mentioned in the letter of Governor John Endecott to John Leverett, Colonial Agent in England.

N.E.H.G.R. Vol 1, p 220

MARY HOLMES

Married: The Reverend John Brown, son of the Reverend Chad Brown of Providence, Rhode Island

Died: 1690

Genealogical Dictionary of Rhode Island by John Osborne Austin, Published by Joel Munsell's Sons Albany, New York, (pages 103, 258)

JEOFFREYS

CAPTAIN ROBERT JEOFFREYS

Born 1605

Of Charlestown, Massachusetts, and Newport, Rhode Island 1635. Came from London in ship *Elizabeth and Ann*. His age was given as 30 and the age of his wife, Mary, as 27, that of his son Thomas as 7, daughter Elizabeth 6 daughter Mary 3, maid servant Susannah Brown 21 and Hannah Day 20.

1636. His wife united with the Church

1638 Inhabitant of Newport

1639 He and 3 others are chosen to proportion land.

1640-1-2 Treasurer for Portsmouth and Newport

1643-4 Treasurer for Newport

1642 Captain

A physician

Children of Captain Robert and Mary (?) Jeoffreys:

*Elizabeth Jeoffreys. Born 1629

Jethro Jeoffreys. Born 1638. Died April 6, 1739

Mary Jeoffreys. Born 1632.

Thomas Jeoffreys. Born 1628

See John Osborn Austin's *Genealogical Dictionary of Rhode Island* page 330.

See N.E.H.G.R. Vol 14 p 314

See Holmes *Directory of Ancestral Heads of New England Families*, 1620-1700 (referred to as "Holmes Directory") page 132.

ELIZABETH JEOFFREYS

Born: 1629

Married: John Sweet II

Died: 1684

MOSHER

STEPHEN MOSHER OF MANCHESTER, ENGLAND

Child of Stephen Mosher:

Ensign Hugh Mosher

Brothers of Stephen Mosher:

John Mosher. The son of John, Hugh Mosher, went from Manchester to London where he became a member of the East India Company. He went to Calcutta, India, where his investments in real estate were valued at several millions of pound sterling. On his return to England he was honored with knighthood, being created a baron. He left no children.*

Thomas Mosher. The son of Thomas, Hugh Mosher, sailed from London in the *James* and reached Boston in 1632. He removed to Maine where he bought Great Island and Little Island in Casco Bay. He moved to Falmouth where he died in 1666, leaving two sons, James and John Mosher.

George Mosher

William Mosher. Appointed road overseer on September 2, 1616. Will recorded in Register of Probate Court, Manchester, England, in 1621. In 1614 William Mosher is described as a "silk Weaver". In 1619, he is described as a "gentleman". He left Mary and John Mosher.

*Hugh Mosher, son of John Mosher, went to India as secretary to Governor Charnock. His estate was valued at £32,000,000 on his death.

Tradition located the Mosher Family in Alsace, northeast France, in 1580, near Strassburg. The located in England (to escape religious persecution) in Manchester, Chester, and London.

See William C. Mosher, *Mosher Family* published in Alhambra, California, in 1898, pages 10-14, hereinafter referred to as *"Mosher Family"*.

ENSIGN HUGH MOSHER

Married: Lydia Maxon

Died: 1694 in Newport, Rhode Island

Children of Ensign Hugh and Lydia (Maxon) Mosher: Daniel Mosher, *The Reverend Hugh Mosher—Born 1633, James Mosher, John Mosher, Joseph Mosher, Nicholas Mosher.

1669 Hugh Mosher appointed Ensign of a military company. Fought in King Philip's War.

1674 Hugh Mosher ordained Pastor of the Baptist Church in Dartmouth, Massachusetts

1676 Hugh Mosher received a fifth part of the township of Westerly, Rhode Island on August 4.

See *Mosher Family*, pages 12-14

Hugh Mosher came to Boston, Mass., in 1632, settled at Salem, Mass. Removed to Newport, Rhode Island in 1661 and afterwards to Westerly, Rhode Island. See Holmes Directory etc. page 168

THE REVEREND HUGH MOSHER

Born: 1633 in Providence, Rhode Island

Married: Rebecca Harndell, daughter of John and Sarah Harndell

Died: 1713

Children of the Reverend Hugh and Rebecca (Harndell) Mosher:

Daniel Mosher. Born 1678. Married Elizabeth Edwards 1704. Died 1751

James Mosher. Born 1675. Married 1st Catharine Tosh July 6, 1704. Married 2nd Mary Duval May 22, 1714. Lived New London, Connecticut.

John Mosher Born 1668. Married Experience Kirby on May 5, 1692. Died August, 1739

Joseph Mosher. Born 1670. Married Lydia Taber who was born in 1673 and died in 1743. Died 1754

*Mary Mosher

Nicholas Mosher. Born 1666

Rebecca Mosher. Born 1677

See *Mosher Family* pages 14-17

MARY MOSHER

Born: 1672 or 1679

Married: Joseph Rathbone on May 19, 1691

Died: 1748

Mosher Family pages 15-16

The Reverend Hugh Mosher:

1660 The Reverend Mosher and five others of Newport buy land in Westerly, Rhode Island

1661 A share of land apportioned to the Reverend Mosher, who didn't live there long, however, if at all.

1663 The Reverend Mosher gave testimony in which he said he was about 30

1668 The Reverend Mosher bought a Portsmouth, Rhode Island, farm of Thomas Lawton

1676 The Reverend Mosher was a Member of the Court Martial of Indians held at Newport

1684   The Reverend Mosher was pastor of the Baptist Church at Dartmouth

1709   October 12 The Will of the Reverend Mosher was drawn. It was proved December 7, 1713. Son James was an executor. Friend and Kinsman Jeremiah Clarke and Captain John Stanton of Newport were overseers. Grandson Hugh of son Nicholas, sons, John, Joseph and Daniel named.

John Osborne Austin's *Genealogical Dictionary of Rhode Island* page 135. Published by Joel Munsell's Sons, Albany, New York, 1887.

MOTT

JOHN MOTT

Died: Living November 13, 1654

Child of John Mott:

Adam Mott

Adam Mott of Portsmouth, Rhode Island, had an aged father, John Mott, who was at Portsmouth as early as 1639. On 13 November 1654 the Town of Portsmouth voted "to pay John Mott's passage to Barbados and back again if he cannot be received."

John Ruffe of Barbados, planter and James Bycott (Upcot) of the same, barber, sell 4 March 1656/7 to Capt. William Mott, of the same place, gentleman, part of a messuage where said Mott now liveth.

See N.E.H.G.R. Vol 68 p 179

ADAM MOTT OF CAMBRIDGE, ENGLAND, ROXBURY, MASSACHUSETTS, AND PORTSMOUTH, RHODE ISLAND

Born: 1596

Married: 1st: (?   )

           2nd: Sarah (?   ). Born 1604.

Died: Between April 2 and August 31, 1661

Children of Adam Mott and his first wife:

Adam Mott. Born 1622. On October 1647, he married Mary Lott, the daughter of Sarah Mott, by a former husband.

*Elizabeth Mott

John Mott. Born 1620

Jonathon Mott. Born 1625

Children of Adam and Sarah (?   ) Mott:

Eleazer Mott. Born in Rhode Island

Gershom Mott. Born in Rhode Island

Jacob Mott. Born in Massachusetts.

In July 1634, Adam Mott came from Cambridge, England, with his second wife, Sarah, four children by his fromer wife, and Mary Lott, the daughter of Sarah by a former husband, in the ship *Defence*.

May 25, 1636. Freeman in Massachusetts. Land grant in Hingham. Members of the First Church in Roxbury.

Moved to Portsmouth, Rhode Island, where he received a land grant in 1638.

Will dated April 2, 1661, and proved August 31, 1661.

See Genealogy of Charles Myrick Thurston by his son C.M. Thurston Published by John F. Trow and Co., 50 Greene St., N.Y. pp 10-11

See N.E.H.G.R. Vol 14, p 319, Vol 2, p 251, Vol 35, p 245, Vol 68 p 179

ELIZABETH MOTT

Born: 1628/9 in England

Married: Edward Thurston in June 1647

Died: September 2, 1694

Before leaving England, Adam Mott brought testimony from the Justices of Peace and minister in Cambridge of his conformity to the Orders and Disciplines of the Church of England. He had taken the Oath of Allegiance and Supremacy. John Osborne Austin's GENEALOGICAL DICTIONARY OF RHODE ISLAND page 344 Published by Joel Munsell's Sons, Albany, New York 1887

PARKER

THOMAS PARKER

Born: May 20, 1725

Married: Jane Bennett on January 5 or 11, 1743-4

Children of Thomas and Jane (Bennett) Parker:
Eilzabeth Parker. Born January 1, 1749
*Captain Elisha Parker
Jane Parker. Born February 9, 1756
Samuel Parker. Born May 14, 1748
Sarah Parker. Born March 29, 1752
Thomas Parker Born September 6, 1744
Thomas Parker. Born February 18, 1754

See Vital Records of Rhode Island Vol 1 Kent County Coventry Births and Deaths, pp 83-4

Thomas Parker, son of George Parker, deceased of Warwick married Jane Bennett on January 5 or 11, 1743-4.

V.R.R.I. Vol 1 Kent Co. Coventry p 41

CAPTAIN ELISHA PARKER

Born: August 6, 1746, in Coventry, Rhode Island

Married: Mary Aylsworth on January 15, 1767

Died: March 19, 1813, in Burlington, New York

Children of Captain Elisha and Mary (Aylsworth) Parker:
Alexander Parker
John Parker
*Phoebe Parker
Samuel Parker
Others

From the West Burlington, Otsego County, New York, Cemetery:
Elisha Parker (Rev. Soldier) died March 22, 1813, aged 67
Mary Parker, his wife, died September 24, 1828, aged 81
John Parker, their son, died April 8, 1820, aged 46

Children of Abraham and Patience Parker: Grandchildren of Alexander:
John Parker died 1826 Mar 30 aged 5 mos 15 ds
Sally Parker died 1827 aged 4 mos
Charles Parker died 1822 aged 1 d
Norman Parker died 1822 Feb 4 aged 1 d
Samuel Parker died Mar 17, 1823 aged 75
Margaret Parker his wife died Mar 17 1813 aged 66

Abraham Parker died Feb 4, 1868, aged 72 yrs 8 mos 14 ds
Patience Parker his wife died July 15, 1861 aged 65 yrs 11 mos 29 ds
Joanna Parker their daughter died May 10, 1850 aged 17 yrs 1 m 6 ds
Alexander Parker (Rev Soldier) died Feb 27, 1845 aged 78
Sarah Parker his wife died June 4, 1792 aged 19 yrs
Joannah Parker his wife died June 28, 1860 aged 82 yrs 10 mos
Polly Parker their daughter died April 24, 1830 aged 3 yrs
Copied from Vol 104, p 47 N.E.H.G.R.

James Newell Arnold *VITAL RECORDS OF RHODE ISLAND, KENT COUNTY, VOL. 1*

Marriages Coventry:

Thomas Parker of George dec of Warwick and Jane Bennett married by Randall Rice Justice Jan 5 or 11, 1743-4 (P 41)

Jane Bennett and Thomas Parker Jan 5 or 11, 1743-4 (P 6)

Elisha Parker of Coventry and Mary Aylesworth of West Greenwich married by Phillip Greene Jan 15, 1767 (P 41)

Mary Aylesworth and Elisha Parker Jan 15, 1767 (P 4)

Marriages West Greenwich:

Elisha Parker of Coventry and Mary Aylesworth of West Greenwich married by Phillip Greene Justice Jan 15, 1767 (P 41)

Mary Aylesworth and Elisha Parker Jan 15, 1767 (P 4)

Coventry Births and Deaths

Thomas Parker of George dec of Warwick May 20, 1725 (P 83)

Alexander Parker of Elisha and Mary born Jan 8, 1768

From Chase or Woodley Hill Cemetery, Otsego County, New York

Thomas Ervine son of Alexander and Ellen Parker died October 28, 1818 aged 1 y 2 mos 3 ds
Printed Vol 100 p 172 N.E.H.G.R.

ALEXANDER PARKER

Born: January 8, 1768, in Coventry, Rhode Island

Married: 1st: Sarah Gardner, daughter of Abram Gardner of Pownal, Vermont, on January 1, 1791. Sarah died on May 27, 1792

2nd: Joanna Gardner, sister of Sarah Gardner, in February 1793

Died: February 27, 1845, in West Burlington, Otsego County, New York

Child of Alexander and Sarah (Gardner) Parker:

David Parker. Born October 29, 1791. Died March 7, 1793

Children of Alexander and Joanna (Gardner) Parker:

Abraham Parker. Born May 27, 1796

Alexander Parker. Born April 13, 1814
Betsey Parker. Born March 2, 1808
David G. Parker. Born November 28, 1822
Elisha Parker. Born August 15, 1802
Ira Parker. Born April 25, 1805
Mehitable Parker. Born January 1, 1811
Polly Parker. Born August 15, 1798
Sarah Parker. Born November 9, 1817

The above dates of birth were sent me by Mrs. Otis M. Parker of Edmeston, New York. She copied them from the Parker Bible, which gives the date of death of Sarah Gardner as June 2, 1792. The dates of birth of Sarah Gardner: July 27, 1773 and of Joanna Gardner: August 28, 1777.

1810 CENSUS OTSEGO COUNTY NEW YORK TOWN OF BURLINGTON
A. Parker

1 male born from 1755-1784; 1 male born 1794-1800; 1 male born 1800-1810; 1 female born 1755-1784; 1 female born 1794-1800; 1 female born 1800-1810

1820 CENSUS OTSEGO COUNTY NEW YORK TOWN OF BURLINGTON
Alexander Parker

1 male born before 1775; 1 male born 1794-1804; 1 male born 1802-1804; 1 male born 1804-1810; 1 male born 1810-1820; 1 female born before 1775; 1 female born 1775-1794; 1 female born 1794-1804; 1 female born 1804-1810; 2 females born 1810-1820.

1830 CENSUS OTSEGO COUNTY NEW YORK TOWN OF BURLINGTON
Alexander Parker

1 male born 1760-1770; 1 male born 1800-1810; 1 male born 1810-1815; 1 male born 1820-1825; 2 females born 1770-1780; 1 female born 1810-1815; 1 female born 1815-1820

1840 CENSUS OTSEGO COUNTY NEW YORK TOWN OF BURLINGTON
Alexander Parker

1 male born 1760-1770; 1 male born 1820-1825; 1 male born 1835-1840; 1 female born 1770-1780; 2 females born 1810-1820

ABRAHAM PARKER

Born: Mary 27, 1796, in New York
Married: Patience (?   )
Died: After 1850

Children of Abraham and Patience (?   ) Parker: Abigail Parker, Eri Parker, Jenette Parker, Harriet Parker.

1830 CENSUS OTSEGO COUNTY NEW YORK TOWN OF EDMESTON
Abraham Parker

1 male born 1790-1800; 1 male born 1815-1820; 1 male born 1820-1825; 1 male born 1825-1830; 1 female born 1815-1820

1840 CENSUS OTSEGO COUNTY NEW YORK TOWN OF EDMESTON
Abraham Parker

1 male born 1790-1800; 1 male born 1820-1825; 1 male born 1825-1830; 1 female born 1790-1800; 1 female born 1825-1830; 1 female born 1830-1835; 2 females born 1835-1840

1850 CENSUS OTSEGO COUNTY NEW YORK TOWN OF EDMESTON 609, 676
Abraham Parker was born in 1796 in New York
Patience Parker was born in 1796 in New York
Eri Parker was born in 1828 in New York
Abigail Parker was born in 1830 in New York
Jenette Parker was born in 1836 in New York
Harriet Parker was born in 1837 in New York

ALEXANDER PARKER

Born: April 13, 1814, in New York

Married: Eliza (?)

Died: After 1860

Children of Alexander Parker and Eliza (?) Parker: Adelbert Parker, Charles Parker, Evelyn Parker, Fanny Parker, John Parker, Lewis Parker, Miranda Parker, Louisa Parker, Stuckely Parker, Mary Parker, Willis D. Parker,

1840 CENSUS OTSEGO COUNTY NEW YORK TOWN OF NEW LISBON
Alexander Parker

1 male born 1810-1820
1 male born 1820-1825
1 male born 1835-1840
1 female born 1810-1820
1 female born 1835-1840

1850 CENSUS OTSEGO COUNTY NEW YORK TOWN OF NEW LISBON 1265, 1387
Alexander Parker was born in 1814 in New York
Eliza Parker was born in 1815 in New York
Willis D. Parker was born in 1836 in New York
Stuckely D. Parker was born in 1838 in New York
Miranda Parker was born in 1839 in New York
Charles Parker was born in 1841 in New York
Eveline Parker was born in 1843 in New York
Lewis Parker was born in 1846 in New York
Mary Parker was born in 1847 in New York

1860 CENSUS OTSEGO COUNTY NEW YORK TOWN OF BURLINGTON
Alexander Parker was born in 1814 in New York

Eliza Parker was born in 1815 in New York
Charles Parker was born in 1841 in New York
Evelyn Parker was born in 1843 in New York
Lewis Parker was born in 1846 in New York
Mary Parker was born in 1849 in New York
John Parker was born in 1851 in New York
Adelbert Parker was born in 1852 in New York
Louisa Parker was born in 1854 in New York
Fanny Parker was born in 1855 in New York

DAVID G. PARKER

Born: November 28 (or 29), 1822, in West Burlington, New York

Married: Susannah Bolton, the daughter of Lemuel and Ruth Bolton of Pownal, Vermont, on May 27, 1852

Died: May 25, 1881

Children of David G. and Susannah (Bolton) Parker: Dexter A. Parker of Edmeston, Ella M. Parker (Born September 16, 1853. Died June 15, 1859), Isaac B. Parker, Otis M. Parker, Ruth J. H. Parker,

1850 CENSUS OTSEGO COUNTY NEW YORK 619-687 TOWN OF BURLINGTON
David Parker born in 1823 in New York
Joanna Parker born in 1776 in Vermont
Sarah Parker born in 1818 in New York
James Noble born in 1839 in New York

1870 CENSUS OTSEGO COUNTY NEW YORK TOWN OF BURLINGTON
David Parker born in 1821 in New York
Susannah Parker born in 1817 in New York
Isaac Parker born in 1856 in New York
Dexter Parker born in 1858 in New York
Otis Parker born in 1859 in New York
Hettie Parker born in 1862 in New York

ABSTRACT OF WILLS OF OTSEGO COUNTY, NEW YORK From 1845 to 1850, Volume 5, Copied and Compiled by Gertrude Audrey Barber

(P 8)

P. 365 Will of Alexander Parker of Burlington

Dated March 20, 1844

Probated: December 29, 1845

Mentions:

Wife: Joanna
Sons: Ira
      Abraham
      Elisha

Alexander
David

Daughters: Mehitable
Sarah
Grandson: Willis D. Parker
Executor: James C. Walworth of Burlington
Witnesses: Pitman Cook
Truman Moss

HISTORY OF OTSEGO COUNTY NEW YORK by Duane H. Hard Published
by Everts and Fariss 714-16 Filbert Street, Philadelphia

Alexander Parker was of English origin
His grandfather was from England
Alexander Parker was a native of Rhode Island, born January 8, 1768
His father was Elisha Parker, born August 6, 1746, in Rhode Island
His mother was Maria Ellsworth born near Plymouth, Massachusetts
His parents had 11 children, all born in New England
Captain Elisha was in the Revolution

After 1800 Elisha Parker settled on a farm in Burlington owned by
his grandson, David G. Parker

Maria Parker died September 24, 1828
Elisha Parker died March 19, 1813
Alexander Parker married Joanna Gardner, daughter of Abram

Gardner of Pownell, Vermont in February, 1793. She was born
there on August 28, 1777. Their children: Abram, Elisha, Ira,

Betsey, Mehitable, Alexander, Jr., Sarah, David, G. four are dead
Alexander Parker's first wife was Sarah Gardner, sister of Joanna
Gardner. They were married about January 1, 1791. They had one
boy: David born October 29, 1791 and died March 7, 1793. Mrs. Sarah
Parker died May 27, 1792. Alexander Parker died February 27, 1845.
Mrs. Joanna Parker died June 22, 1860. David G. Parker born in
West Burlington on November 29, 1822. He married Susannah Bolton
on May 27, 1852. She was the daughter of Lemuel and Ruth Bolton
from Pownell, Vermont. Susannah Bolton was born on July 14, 1817.
Their children: Ella Born September 16 1853 Died June 15, 1859,
Isaac B., Dexter A., Otis M., Ruth J. M. Parker.

ELISHA PARKER

Born: August 15, 1802 on the Parker farm in Burlington
Married: Drusilla Hubbard in 1827. She died October 27, 1878
Died: February 1878

Children of Elisha and Drusilla (Hubbard) Parker: Elijah E. Parker
(born in 1841 in New Lisbon, New York), Leroy L. Parker, Mary L.
Parker, Sarah A. Parker. Maria J. Parker

1840 CENSUS OTSEGO COUNTY NEW YORK TOWN OF NEW LISBON
Elisha Parker
1 male born 1800-1810
1 male born 1820-1825
1 male born 1830-1835
1 female born 1800-1810
1 female born 1825-1830
2 females born 1830-1835

1860 CENSUS OTSEGO COUNTY NEW YORK TOWN OF BURLINGTON
Elisha Parker born in 1802 in New York
Drasilla Parker born in 1808 in New York
Elijah Parker born in 1840 in New York
Marium Parker born in 1844 in New York

1870 CENSUS OTSEGO COUNTY NEW YORK TOWN OF NEW LISBON
Elisha Parker born in 1802 in New York
Drusilla Parker born in 1809 in New York
Elijah Parker born in 1841 in New York
Marian Parker born in 1844 in New York
Leroy Parker born in 1862 in New York
Eugene Parker born in 1863 in New York
William Parker born in 1865 in New York
Minnie Parker born in 1868 in New York
Alva Parker born in May 1870 in New York

The following is from the *Biographical Review Otsego County New York* Published by the Biographical Review Publishing Company of Boston in 1893:

Isaac B. Parker:

Descendant of one of the earliest pioneers

His great-grandfather Elisha Parker of English parentage, his father having come to Rhode Island about 150 years ago.

Elisha Parker was born August 6, 1746. He married Maria Ellsworth, a native of Plymouth, Mass. They had 11 children. Alexander Parker, Isaac's grandfather, was the oldest. All of the children were born in New England.

Elisha Parker was a Captain in the Revolution. In 1800 he came to Otsego County. He died in March 19, 1813. His wife died on September 24, 1828.

Alexander Parker was born in Rhode Island on January 8, 1768. As a small boy he served in the American Revolution as a servant to General George Washington. He married in January 1791 to Sarah Gardner of Pownal, Vermont. She was the daughter of Abram Gardner. She died on May 27, 1792. In February, 1793, Alexander Parker married Joanna Gardner, sister of Sarah. Their Children:

Abram, Polly, Elisha, Ira, Betsey, living in Edmeston at 85, Mehitable, living at 83, Alexander Jr., living in Cleveland, Ohio at 80, Sarah, David G., father of Isaac. Alexander Parker died in West Burlington on February 27, 1845. Joanna Parker died on June 22, 1860

David G. Parker was born in West Burlington on November 29, 1822. On May 27, 1852 he married Susannah Bolton, daughter of Lemuel and Ruth Bolton formerly of Pownal, Vermont. Their children: Ella M., Isaac B., Dexter A. of Edmeston, Otis M., Ruth J. David Parker died on May 25, 1881.

(See Page 784)

Elijah E. Parker:

Born in New Lisbon in 1841. His father was Elisha Parker who was born on the Parker farm in Burlington in 1803. His grandfather, Alexander Parker, was born on January 8, 1768. He was the son of Maria Ellsworth a native of Plymouth, Mass. and Elisha Parker born on August 6, 1746 in Rhode Island. They had 11 children all born in New England. After 1800 he bought the farm in Burlington where his great-grandson, Isaac Parker now lives.

Elisha Parker died on March 19, 1813. His father was an Englishman. Maria Ellsworth died on September 24, 1828.

Elijah E. Parker descends through Elisha, David Parker's son.
Elisha Parker married Drusilla Hubbard in 1827. Their children were: Mary L., Sarah A., Maria J., Leroy L., Elijah E.
Elisha Parker died in February 1878 and Drusilla died on October 27, 1878.

IRA PARKER

Born: April 25, 1805 in New York
Married: Almeda (?)
Died: After 1850

Children of Ira and Almeda (?) Parker: Fidelia Parker, Lewis Parker, Mary Parker, Rosattha (?) Parker, Samuel Parker.

1850 CENSUS OTSEGO COUNTY NEW YORK TOWN OF EXETER
Ira Parker was born in 1805 in New York
Almeda Parker was born in 1807 in New York
Fidelia Parker was born in 1827 in New York
Samuel Parker was born in 1836 in New York
Lewis Parker was born in 1839 in New York
Mary Parker was born in 1841 in New York
Rosattha (?) Parker was born in 1843 in New York

MEHITABLE PARKER

Born: January 1, 1811

Married: Pittman Cook

Pitman Cook came in 1800 to Otsego County, New York, and married the daughter of Alexander Parker who came to West Burlington in 1790, then 22.

Hurd HISTORY OF OTSEGO COUNTY NEW YORK page 99

Captain Joseph Briggs, another veteran of the War, came early from Vermont, He and his son Silas were prominent citizens. Pittsfield. Burlington. In 1790 came Alexander Parker. Other respected families of the olden times whose names have been perpetuated are those of Col. David Gardner and Capt Elisha Parker, a soldier of the Revolution.

Edward F. Bacon, OTSEGO COUNTY Published 1902 by the Oneonta Herald, Oneonta, New York

1850 Census, Burlington, Otsego County, New York 622, 690

Pitman Cook born in 1793 in Massachusetts

Mehitable Cook born in 1810 in New York

Halsey (?   ) Cook born in 1823 in New York (male)

Maria Cook born in 1829 in New York

1860 Census, Burlington, Otsego County, New York 171, 171

Pitman Cook born in 1792 in Massachusetts

Mehitable Cook born in 1812 in Massachusetts

Elisha Parker who resides near Garratsville has been a resident of New Lisbon since 1802.

Page 220 HISTORY OF OTSEGO COUNTY, NEW YORK Duane H. Hurd Published by Everts and Fariss 714-16 Filbert Street, Philadelphia (1878)

PHOEBE PARKER

Born: October 1, 1787

Married: Henry Briggs

Died: After 1860

RATHBONE

RICHARD RATHBONE

Born: ca 1574

Married: Marion Whipple, sister of Captain John Whipple who mentioned her in his will made at Ipswich, Essex County, Massachusetts, on December 19, 1616, and probated on January 28, 1618.

Children of Richard and Marion (Whipple) Rathbone:

*John Rathbone

Joseph Rathbone. Born 1600

Thomas Rathbone

The Reverend William Rathbone. Born 1598. Preached in Vermont in 1630. Spoken of in a work published in 1637 and reprinted in "Historical Collections of Massachusetts"

None of their children left issue except the youngest, John.

John C. Cooley, *Rathbone Genealogy* (1898) Press of the Courier Job Print, Syracuse, New York.

Douglas Merritt *Richard Rathbone* (Rhinebeck, New York)

JOHN RATHBONE I

Bron: About 1610

Married: About 1633 (?   )

Child of John Rathbone I:

John Rathbone II. Born ca 1634. Married Margaret Dodge

See Cooley *Rathbone* p 13

JOHN RATHBONE II

Born: ca 1634

Married: Margaret Dodge

Died: Before October 6, 1702

Children of John Margaret (Dodge) Rathbone II:

John Rathbone. Bron ca 1658 in Roxbury, Mass. Twice married. The name of his first wife whom he married on June 20, 1680 is not known. He married Ann Dodge on November 11, 1686 (one account says 1686). John Rathbone was admitted freeman on May 1, 1696. He was appointed a Deputy for New Shoreham to the General Court. In 1676 he was a Surveyor of Highways. From 1681-1684 he was a Deputy.

In Austin's genealogical Dictionary p 66 Ann is given as a daughter of Tristram Dodge. In view of the record of John C. Cooley in the *Rathbone Genealogy* that the father of the John Rathbone who married Ann Dodge married Margaret Dodge, the daughter of Tristram Dodge, Austin seems in error. New Shoreham records say Ann Dodge married on November 11, 1686, to John Rathbone Jr. who died in 1723, the son of John who died in 1702 and add that her father settled Block Island in 1662 and died in 1723 but do not give his name. See *The Dodge Genealogy* by Theron Royal Dodge, Chicago, Illinois, 1904, p 6

*Joseph Rathbone

Samuel Rathbone. Born August 3, 1672, on Block Island. Married Patience Throckmorton Coggeshall, the daughter of Major John and Patience (Throckmorton) Coggeshall on November 3, 1692. She was born in Newport on August 13, 1669 and died on August 3, 1747. Samuel Rathbone was admitted freeman on January 2, 1693. He was a Constable in 1708 and an Ensign in 1695. In 1705 he owned land in Common Neck. He was admitted freeman in North Kingstown, R. I. He died on January 25, 1757, on Block Island.

Sarah Rathbone. Born June 10, 1659. Married 1st Samuel George on December 20, 1678. He died on April 12, 1692. She married 2nd on September 1, 1710, John Ball, the son of Peter and Mary Ball.

Thomas Rathbone. Born on Block Island in 1657. Married on April 21, 1685, to Mary, the daughter of Nathaniel and Joan Dickens. Freeman May 5, 1696. Deputy 1700, 1703, 1704, 1705, 1711, 1730, 1731. Freeman of New Shoreham in 1711. Representative in the General Assembly of Rhode Island in 1709, 1711, 1731. In 1702 he was appointed a Committee to audit the General Treasurer's accounts. He died on December 20, 1733. From Smith's History of Dutchess County, New York published in 1882 by Mason and Company of Syracuse, p 362, Thomas Rathbone (Rathbun) of New Shoreham gave land in Pecapshe (Poughkeepsie) in 1730 to certain relatives.

William Rathbone. Born in Mass. Married Sarah (?   ) on December 18, 1688. Appointed Constable. Admitted freeman on May 5, 1696. On October 10, 1698, Juryman. Deputy 1682, 1704. In 1718 sold brother Samuel land on Block Island. On July 31, 1710, bought land in Lynne, Connecticut.

His will was dated December 18, 1680.

John Rathbone II:

1660 Lived at Roxbury, Massachusetts

August 17, 1660. John Rathbone II met at the house of Dr. John Alcock in Roxbury, Mass., to confer about the purchase of Block Island. One of the 16 purchasers of Block Island.

1661 Sailed with other settlers from Taunton

1676 Surveyor of Highways

1682-1684 Representative of Block Island to the Rhode Island General Assembly

December 28, 1683 Deeds property to his daughter Sarah, the wife of Samuel George

July 16, 1686 Signed Petition to the King of England

October 6, 1702 Will proved. Wife named executrix. Sons named: John, William, Joseph, and Samuel.

See Cooley, *Rathbone* pp 14-16, 73, 707-708, 762-763.

See Douglas Merritt (Rhinebeck, New York) *Richard Rathbone*. See pp. 184-186 of Vol 67 N.E.H.G.R. for entries from the Bible (printed 1725) of "Samuel Rathbun, son of the immigrant John Rathbun who came without doubt from Lancashire, England, and probably settled at Dorchester, Massachusetts, whence he moved to Block Island with the first settlers in 1661."

JOSEPH RATHBONE

Born: About 1670 Block Island, Kings Co., Town of Exeter, Rhode Island

Married: Mary Mosher on May 19, 1691

Died: 1749

Children of Joseph and Mary (Mosher) Rathbone:

Benjamin Rathbone. Born February 6, 1710

Elizabeth Rathbone. Born March 14, 1692.

Grace Rathbone. Born July 16, 1695, in Colchester, Connecticut. Married Joseph Gates on May 9, 1714

Hannah Rathbone. Born March 21, 1706. Married (?) Eldred

Job Rathbone. Born April 1, 1712. Married Mary Harris in 1737.

Joseph Rathbone. Born October 4, 1707 in Exeter, R. I. Married Abigail Wilbur daughter of William Wilbur. She was born August 21, 1703. Joseph Rathbone was admitted a freeman in 1734.

*Margaret Rathbone

Mary Rathbone. Born March 6, 1697. Married John Garner of North Kingston, R. I. Died 1724.

Mercy Rathbone. Born February 4, 1703. Married John Bleven on November 8, 1727. He died on August 25, 1728

Rebekah Rathbone. Born March 14, 1694. Married Josiah Harris on May 9, 1714

Joseph Rathbone

Admitted freeman in 1696 with brothers Thomas, William and John.
His father and mother deeded him 70 acres and a house.
He had 25 acres on Common Neck.
His father and mother deeded him December 28, 1688, 39 acres and 6 acres at Harbor Neck and 10 acres beyond there. Deeds signed John and Margaret Rathbone.
April 30, 1734. Made freeman of North Kingstown.

The will of Joseph Rathbone dated December 26, 1748, mentions:
Son Joseph's son, Joseph
Heirs of son, Job
Heirs of deceased daughter, Grace Gates
Deceased daughter Rebecca Harris
Granddaughter Abigail Gates
Daughter of Jannah Eldred
Daughters Elizabeth Rathbone, Mary Gorton, Margaret Greene and
Mercy Rathbone.

MARGARET RATHBONE

Born: November 29, 1700, in East Greenwich, Rhode Island

Married: Henry Greene in East Greenwich, Rhode Island, on May 15, 1724.

Died: February 28, 1742

See Cooley *Rathbone* pp 755-760

See Douglas Merrit *Richard Rathbone*

See John Osborne Austin's *Genealogical Dictionary of Rhode Island*, page 159 Publish by Joel Munsell's Sons, Albany, New York (1887)

SLOCUM

PHILIP SLOCUM OF OLD CLEEVE, COUNTY SOMERSET, ENGLAND

Married: Charity Bickham on November 20, 1621, in Old Cleeve County Somerset, England

Children of Philip and Charity (Bickham) Slocum:
Giles Slocum

GILES SLOCOMBE

Born: Somersetshire (?   ), England

Married: Joan (?   ) who died at Porthmouth, Rhode Island, 31st 6 mo 1679

Died: 1682

Children of Giles and Joan (?   ) Slocombe:

*The Reverend Ebenezer Slocum born in Portsmouth 25th day of first month (March), 1650 (Quaker dating system)

Eliezer Slocum Born Portsmouth 25th day of Tenth Month, 1664. A resident of Dartmouth Township, New Plymouth in 1684 or before. Married Elephel Fitzgerald. Will of Eliezer Slocum proved 30 July 1727 is in the Probate Office at Taunton, Bristol County, Massachusetts.

The Honorable Giles Slocum. Born 25th day of First Month (March), 1647, in Portsmouth. Married Anne Lawton, daughter of Thomas Lawton of Portsmouth on March 26, 1669. He removed to Dartsmouth Township, New Plymouth in 1669 or before and became a resident of Portsmouth before 30 April 1678 when he was admitted a freeman. From 1685 to 1690 he was Deputy (or Colonial Representative) from Portsmouth in 1687. Town Councilman in 1690. Assistant (or Colonial Senator) 1696, 1698, 1700, 1703, 1705, 1708, 1712.

Johanna Slocum. Born Portsmouth 16th day of Third Month, 1642. Married Jacob Mott, son of Adam Mott and his wife, Sarah Mott. Jacob Mott was a distinguished Minister of the Society of Friends. The Reverend Edward Peterson in his history of Rhode Island (New York 1853) writes that the Mott family "have ever been highly respectable".

Captain John Slocum. Born Portsmouth 26th day of Third Month 1645. Removed to east New Jersey in May 1668, where he took the Oath as a freeholder. Married before 1674 to Meribah Parker (?). Will dated 6 April 1698 and proved 2 February 1702 is in the State House, Trenton, New Jersey.

Mary Slocum. Born Portsmouth 3rd day of Fifth Month 1660. Married Eighth Month 30th 1679 to Abraham Tucker, the son of Henry and Martha Tucker. Mary Slocum died Seventh Month 25th 1689. Abraham Tucker who was born Tenth Month 13th 1653 died in 1725. He married 2nd Hannah Mott.

Nathaniel Slocum. Born Portsmouth 25th day of Tenth Month 1652. Moved to Shrewsbury, East New Jersey, before 1679. Died August 1702 in Shrewsbury. In his will dated 28 July 1702 and proved 19 March 1703 and located in the State House, Trenton, New Jersey, his wife is called "Hannah".

The Reverend Peleg Slocum. Born Portsmouth 17th day of Sixth Month 1654. Married Mary Holder of Providence probably in 1680. Mary Holder was the great-granddaughter of the Reverend Edward (Francis?) Marbury of Lincolnshire, England, Rector of St. Martin Vintry, London and his wife,Bridget Dryden, great-aunt of the celebrated English poet.

Samuel Slocum. Born probably about 1657. Married and lived in Newport, Rhode Island.

Giles Slocombe settled at Portsmouth, Rhode Island, in 1638.

The following are from Township Records of Portsmouth, Rhode Island, Deeds of Perth Amboy and Trenton, New Jersey, *Rhode Island Colonial Records,* Records of Colony of New Portsmouth:

1650 Deed from John Cranston of Portsmouth to Giles Slocum
1651 Giles Slocum to Thomas Gunnings
1655 Giles Slocum made a freeman of Portsmouth

1657 Giles Slocum receives land from John Cranston
1657 Giles Slocum receives land from John Randall of Portsmouth
1657 Giles Slocum received land from Town of Portsmouth
1667 Giles Slocum receives land from Robert Carr of Newport in Navisink, New Jersey
1668 Giles Slocum receives land from William Brenton
1669 Giles Slocum receives land in Dartsmouth New Plymouth from the Brewsters
1670 Giles Slocum receives New Jersey land from John Wood
1679 Giles Slocum receives land in Shrewsbury, New Jersey, from Thomas Lawton
1672 Giles Slocum receives land in Shrewsbury, New Jersey, from Thomas Lawton
1672 Giles Slocum gave Portsmouth land to son, Giles
1676 Giles Solcum gave land in Shrewsburg and Navisink, New Jersery, to son, John
1676 Giles Slocum gave daughter, Johanna Mott land in Shrewsbury, New Jersey

Joan Slocum, wife of Giles, died at Portsmouth 31st 6 mo 1679. He died in 1682

Will of Giles Slocum
Proved Mar 12, 1683
Executor: Daughter Joanna Mott
Sons: Samuel, John, Giles, Ebenezer, Nathaniel, Peleg, Eliezer
Daughters: Mary Tucker, Johannah Mott

Will of Mary T. Slocum
Dated Nov 5, 1729
Codicil Nov 7, 1732
Executor: Son-in-law Samuel Dyer

Sons: Samuel, Giles, Joseph
Daughters: Abigail Thomas
Grandchildren:
Patience Carr daughter of Caleb
Caleb, Joseph and William Carr
David Greene
Ebenezer, Mary and Ruth Slocum
Thomas Rogers
Susanna Greene
Mercy and Elizabeth Thomas
William, Rebecca, Benjamin, Hannah, Sarah, Ebenezer, and Amey Burling
Susanna Thurston daughter of brother Jonathon

John Osborne Austin *Genealogocial Dictionary of Rhode Island* pp 181-3

THE REVEREND EBENEZER SLOCUM

Born: 25th day of First Month (March), 1650, in Portsmouth, Rhode Island

Married: Mary Thurston

Died: 1715

Children of the Reverend Ebenezer and Mary (Thurston) Slocum:
Abigail Slocum. (Twin of Joseph). Born February 21, 1697. Married George Thomas.

Deliverance Slocum. Born August 15, 1691. Married Thomas Rogers
Desire Slocum. Born March 12, 1688. Married Samuel Dyer on January 19, 1709-10.

Ebenezer Slocum. Born March 12, 1688. Married Naomi Barton daughter of Benjamin Barton of Warwick. Ebenezer died in Jamestown in October 1715. His widow married Edward Carr on July 13, 1721.

Elizabeth Slocum. Born January 1, 1677-8. Married Peter Greene, son of James Greene. Their intention of marriage was declared in Friends Meeting, Portsmouth, R. I., on October 17, 1695.

Giles Slocum. Born the 19th day of the 12th Month 1695 in Jamestown. Married Mary (?). Admitted freeman in Warwick in 1723, where he died on March 26, 1750. His widow died on January 2, 1763. He was a slaveholder.

*Johanna Slocum

Joseph Slocum (Twin of Abigail). Born 21st day, 2nd Mo 1697. Married Mary (?). Admitted freeman in East Greenwich in 1732.

Mary Slocum. Born June 21, 1679. Married David Greene on January 3, 1698-9

Mercy Slocum. Born 14th day 7th month 1693.
Died Jan 10, 1714.

Rebecca Slocum. Born November 13, 1682. Married William Burling (Burlingham or Burlingame?)

The Honorable Samuel Slocum. Born March 2, 1684 on Canonicut Island, Jamestown Township, Rhode Island.

Deputy to the Rhode Island General Assembly for Jamestown 1718.

Removed to North Kingstown before 1729.

Admitted a freeman there in 1734. His estate was administered there Apr 4, 1741.

The Reverend Ebenezer Slocum settled in Canonicut Island, Jamestown, where his father gave him land in 1678.

Deputy for Jamestown to the Rhode Island General Assembly in 1679. Held the office ,sometimes as Speaker, until his death in 1715.

Counsellman, Head Warden, Moderator of Town Meetings

An early proprietor of East Greenwich. A Quaker Minister.

See sketch concerning the Reverend Ebenezer Slocum from *Piety Promoted* compiled by John Field and quoted in SLOCUMS IN AMERICA.

N.E.G.H.R. Vol 34, p 393

From Transcript of Parish Registers of Old Cleeve, County Somerset, England, Preserved in Diocesan Registry at Wells, co. Somerset.

1621 Philip Slocum married Charity Beckham on November 20

1623 Giles Slocum son of Philip baptized 28 September.

Somerset Protestation Roll 27 Feb 1642 Old Cleeve

Giles Slocum

In custody Librarian, House of Lords.

N.E.H.G.R. Vol 78 pp 395-6

Will of Reverend Ebenezer Slocum

Dated Dec 10, 1714

Proved Apr 20, 1715

Executors Ebenezer (son) and widow Mary

Cousin Jacob Mott of Portsmouth was an overseer

Sons Samuel, Giles, Joseph, daughters Mercy, Abigail, Desire, wife of Samuel Dyer, Rebecca wife of William Burling, Elizabeth wife of Peter Greene

John Osborne Austin *Genealological Dictionary of Rhode Island* pages 181-3

JOANNA SLOCUM

Born: 1680 in Jamestown, Rhode Island

Married: Caleb Carr, Grandson of Major John Greene, Deputy Governor of Rhode Island and Grandnephew of Caleb Carr, Governor of Rhode Island. April 30, 1701 in Jamestown

Died: December 30, 1708.

Genealogical Dictionary of Rhode Island. John Osborne Austin. Joel Munsell's Sons, Albany, New York, 1887. Pages 181 and 201

SPENCER

JOHN SPENCER

Married: Christian Baker

Children of John and Christian (Baker) Spencer:

*John Spencer, Senior, Gentleman of St. George's Parish, Edworth, Bedfordshire, England. Dead 9 June 1558.

Robert Spencer, Gentleman of St. Albans, County of Hertford, England. Married Frances Foster, the daughter of John Foster of Bramfield.

William Spencer, Gentleman of Southmylles, Bedfordshire England. Married Isabella Osborn, the daughter of Edward Osborn of Northampton.

See William Henry Spencer, THE SPENCER FAMILY RECORD, pages 13-14

See SPENCERS OF BEDFORDSHIRE by the Reverend John Holding M.A., Vicar of Stotfold, co. Bedford, England.

See Heralds Visitations of Bedfordshire.

This John Spencer who married Christian Baker is the son of Robert Spencer of Southmylles, County Bedford, England, and the grandson of John Spencer, Gentleman of Southmylles, County Bedford, England. 14 Edward IV.

JOHN SPENCER OF EDWORTH, COUNTY BEDFORD, ENGLAND

Born: ca 1500

Married: Anne (Merrill?) who was buried at Edworth, co. Bedford, England 16 June 1560.

Buried: 9 June 1558 at Edworth, co. Bedford, England. He was called "senior" at his burial.

Children of John and Anne (Merrill?) Spencer:

Gerard Spencer. Born ca 1543. Married at Edworth 30 July 1568 to Ellen Whyston. Will dated 8 July 1576 and proved 20 May 1577 calls him "of Biggleswade, yeoman". The will names his son Richard (under 21), his daughter, Agnes, his daughter, Johan (under age), his wife, Elen, his god-daughter, Johan Spencer, his brother's daughter. His brother Michael Spencer is named an executor.

John Spencer. Buried at Edworth, co. Bedford, England, 21 April 1560 as the son of Ann Spencer, widow.

*Michael Spencer. Born ca 1530-1535.

Mr. Donald Jacobus, *The American Genealogist*, Vol XXVII No. 2 pp

79-81 says the Spencer Genealogy has not been established back of this John Spencer.

The Reverend John Holding M.A., Vicar of Stotfold, co. Bedford, England, in his *Spencers of Bedfordshire* names this John Spencer as a third son of John and Christian (Baker) Spencer, whose other two sons are named in the Heralds Visitations of Bedfordshire.

See Henry F. Waters *Genealogical Gleanings in England* for the will of Richard Spencer of London who left property to the four New England Spencer brothers.

See F. G. Emmison Bedfordshire Parish Register Series.

The will of Ann Spencer dated 13 June 1560 and proved 21 April 1651 calls her "widow" in Edworth, Beds. The will mentions son Gerard, son Michael, son John, Elizabeth Lymer, Alice Austin, brother Edward's children, Nicholas and John Merrill.

MICHAEL SPENCER OF EDWORTH AND STOTFOLD, COUNTY BEDFORD, ENGLAND

Born: ca 1530-1535

Married: 1st: at Edworth on 20 January 1555/6 to Agnes Limer (W.H.S. Spencer Family Record p 14 calls her Annis Liner or Miner). She was buried at Edworth on 23 Feb 1561/2

2nd: about 1563 to Elizabeth (?   ) who was buried at Stotfold 18 Nov 1599 as wife of Michael Spencer indicating he was alive. The Spencer family moved frmo Edworth to Stotfold between 1571 and 1576.

Children of Michael and Agnes (or Annis Limer, Liner, Miner) Spencer:

Anne Spencer. Baptized 24 July 1560

John Spencer. Baptized Edworth, co. Bedford, England, on 20 April 1577. He had two sons: Daniel Spencer, grocer of London, who married Sarah Audley of Hutchin and Francis Spencer who died in London in 1636. In his will found in Waters *Genealogical Gleanings in England* he describes himself as a brewer of the parish of St. Giles without Cripplegate. He appointed as the overseer of his will his uncle, Richard Spencer, haberdasher of London and his brother Daniel.

Michael Spencer. Baptized at Edworth, co. Bedford, England 20 April 1557. Buried 15 April 1560.

Children of Michael Spencer, *probably* by Elizabeth. *Certainly* Gerard and Richard Spencer were by Elizabeth:

Alice Spencer. Baptized 30 August 1566.

Catharine Spencer. Married (?   ) Bland.

Gerard Spencer. Baptized 20 May 1576. First of the children baptized at Stotfold. Recorded as "Gerat", but his name is spelled "Gerard" at the baptism of his own children.

Joan Spencer. Baptized at Edworth 21 August 1564.

Richard Spencer, Gentleman. Baptized 9 July 1580. Died in London in May or June 1646. His will was dated 17 March 1645. A codicil was dated 29 May 1646. The will was proved 8 June 1646. The will is printed in Waters *Genealogical Gleanings in England,* pp 514-515

The will mentions:

THOMAS SPENCER, son of brother, Thomas Spencer. Copyhold lands in St. Michael's Parish near St. Alban's co. Hertford. DANIEL SPENCER of London, grocer, son of brother, John Spencer, deceased. Eight messuages in parish of St. Mary Lothbury in London. This Daniel Spencer was at death of Cony Hatch co. Middlesex. He left a will dated July 1665 and proved 6 November 1668. See Waters *Genealogical Gleanings in England* p 913. He died a wealthy man leaving land in Lothbury near Greene's Court, London, in Hitchin, Hippoletts and Preston, co. Hertford, including the Red Lion Inn in Hitchin, in Gravesend and Rochester, Kent, and Tilbery, Essex.

SARAH AND HANNAH BLAND, daughters of sister, Katherine Bland, deceased. ELIZABETH TOMLYNS, widow, daughter of brother Jarrard Spencer deceased, a messuage in Grace Church Street. DANIEL SPENCER Lands in Kent and Essex, he to make payments to Anthony and Jarrard Spencer, sons of brother, Thomas Spencer, deceased and to the two children of Margaret Spencer, deceased.

£50 each to brothers JARRARD SPENCER, THOMAS SPENCER, MICHAEL SPENCER and £50 to children of brother William Spencer. On 8 January 1648/9 Gerrard Spencer appointed Thomas Broughton of Watertown, Massachusetts, and Samuel King of London, England, attorneys to collect his legacy under the last will of Richard Spencer, late of London, linen draper and at the same date Michael Spencer of Linne did likewise. (Aspinwall Notarial Records (1903) 182, 190)

On 19 January 1648/9 Michael Spencer signed in Boston a bill of exchange for part of legacy of "my Unckle Richard Spencer" and directed to "my loving cousin Mr. Danyell Spencer Grocer in Friday Streete in London". The bill was protested 5 April 1650 (Quarterly Courts of Essex County 4:385 quoted in Waters *Genealogical Gleanings in England* p 515

Thomas Spencer. Baptized Edworth co. Bedford 12 March 1571 Buried Stotfold co Bedford 13 June 1631 as "Thomas Spencer, gent.".

See Donald Lines Jacobus *The Four Spencer Brothers,* The American Genealogist Vol XVII, o. 2, pp 81-85.

W.H.S. *Spencer Family Record* p 18 has Michael Spencer baptized

May 27, 1558, John Spencer baptized August 20, 1564, and another Michael Spencer baptized August 30, 1566

GERARD SPENCER OF STOTFOLD, COUNTY BEDFORD, ENGLAND

Baptized: 20 May 1576 in Stotfold, co. Bedford, England St. Mary's Parish.

Married: Alice Whitbread or Whitbred (of a family of some prominence) at Upper Gravenhurst, co. Bedford, England, on 10 November 1600.

Died: Before 1646.

It is quite possible that Gerard Spencer and his family moved from Stotfold to London where Gerard's brother, Richard Spencer, had become a prosperous haberdasher, before the four brothers went to New England.

Children of Gerard and Alice (Whitbread or Whitbred) Spencer:

Elizabeth Spencer. Baptized 31 October 1602. Married (?) Tomlins.

Ensign Gerard Spencer. Baptized Stotfold, co. Bedford, England, 25 April 1614. Married 1st Hannah (?). Married 2nd Rebecca (Porter) Clark baptized at Felsted, co. Essex, England 16 September 1630 and died 9 January 1682/3 (recorded at Saybrook), the daughter of John and Ann (White) Porter of Windsor and widow of John Clark of Saybrook. Gerard Spencer settled in Lynn, Massachusetts, later came to Hartford, then to Haddam, Connecticut.

Henry Spencer. Baptized 11 August 1605. Buried 20 October 1607.

John Spencer. Baptized 22 January 1603/4. Died young or without issue before 1646 since he was not named nor his issue in the will of his uncle, Richard Spencer.

*Michael Spencer.

Richard Spencer. Baptized 11 December 1608. Buried May 6, 1614.

Sergt Thomas Spencer. Baptized Stotfold, co. Bedford, England 29 March 1607. Married 1st Ann Derefeld born abt 1610. Married 2nd at Hartford 11 September 1645 to Sarah Bearding who died before 1674, the daughter of Nathaniel Bearding. See N.E.H.G.R. July 1951. Sergt Thomas Spencer died in Harford, Connecticut, 11 September 1687. His will names as an overseer his "cousin" Samuel Spencer, actually his nephew, the son of William Spencer. Samuel Spencer was born ca 1638 and died ca 1716.

William Spencer. Baptized Stotfold, co. Bedford, England, on 11 October 1601. Married 1st Agnes (probably, Tucker) William Spencer died in 1640 in Hartford, Connecticut. His will 4 May 1640 mentions cousin Matthew Allyn and brother, John Pratt. The reason for concluding Agnes was a Tucker are stated in the New York Genealogical and

Biographical Record 71:220. Investigations are in progress to prove she was the daughter of Richard and Agnes (Wyatt) Tucker which would relate her to Matthew Allyn's Wyatt wife and she may have been a sister of John Pratt's wife, thus explaining the terms in William Spencer's will.

See Jacobus *The Four Spencer Brothers*, The American Genealogist Vol XXVII, No. 2, pp 84-85, Vol 27, No 3 pp 162-165

See William Henry Spencer's *Spencer Family Record* p 18

MICHAEL SPENCER OF STOTFOLD, COUNTY BEDFORD, ENGLAND, AND LYNN, MASSACHUSETTS

Born: Baptized on May 5, 1611, in Stotfold, co. Bedford, England

Married: Isabel (?   ) who died in Salem, Mass., on October 9, 1674. She married 2nd Thomas Robbins of Salem who was born about 1618 and who was living in 1681. Robbins married 2nd on March 11, 1674/5 to Mary Gould, widow of Richard Bishop

Died: 1653 in Lynn, Massachusetts

Children of Michael and Isabel (?   ) Spencer:

*Doctor John Spencer. See discussion below.

Michael Spencer. Born ca 1648. Married ca 1672 to Rebecca Sweetman living 1723, the daughter of Thomas Sweetman. He had children: Rebecca born Nov 4, 1673, Susannah born Apr 6, 1680. Susannah married John Olin in East Greenwich, Rhode Island, on Oct 4, 1708.

Michael born Apr 16, 1682, Thomas born February 3, 1688, Ammi Ruhamah born July 11, 1690

Susannah Spencer born ca 1643. Deposed Oct 12, 1728 aged about 85. Married at Salem, Mass., on Aug 4, 1664, to Daniel Bacon (of Daniel Bacon, of Michael Bacon). Daniel Bacon was born ca 1641. Susannah Spencer likely lived at Salem with her mother and stepfather.

William Spencer. Born 1652? Died 1712/3. May *not* be son of Michael and Isabel Spencer. William Spencer was of record in Saybrook in 1686.

Austin in his *Genealogical Dictionary of Rhode Island,* page 186, suggests Doctor John Spencer of East Greenwich, Rhode Island, *may* have been the son of this Michael Spencer of Stotfold, England, and Lynn, Massachusetts and *may* have been identical with the John Spencer mentioned in the will of his uncle John Spencer of Newbury, Massachusetts. This John Spencer of Newbury came over on the *Mary and John* in 1634 He represented Newbury in the General Court of Masachusetts in 1635, was made a captain in 1635, but returned to England in 1638. His will was executed on August 1, 1637 and was proved on March 29, 1649. The nephew John Spencer died unmarried in Jamaica before December 1656, when administration on his estate was granted to his half sister, Anne Filliol, his mother, Penelope, brother Thomas, and sister Rachel having renounced. This nephew John was the son of Thomas Spencer, Gentleman, born ca 1593 and buried at Kingston-upon-Thames, Co. Surrey on June 29, 1648. He had married at St. Peters, Paul's Wharf, on September 25, 1623, to Penelope (Jernegan) Fillioll, widow of Western Fillioll. See Probate Records of Essex County 1:107-8, Waters *Genealogical Gleanings in England* pp 467-8, 553 *Genealogical Dictionary of Maine and New Hampshire* pp 650-1 Doctor John Spencer of East Greenwich died in 1684. He is *definitely* not the John Spencer who died in Jamaica unmarried and who was the nephew of John Spencer of Newbury, Mass., whose will is in Vol 46 p 45 N.E.H.G.R.

See Jacobus *The Four Spencer Brothers* in Vol 27, No 2 pp 86-7 of the American Genealogist

Administration on the Estate of Michael Spencer was granted on November 29, 1653, to Gerard Spencer of Lynn, who is called the brother of Michael Spencer when he brought in the inventory.

Doctor John Spencer of East Greenwich, Rhode Island, had a son Michael Spencer. This plus the fact that a *proved* son of Michael Spencer of Stotfold, England, and Lynn, Mass., settled in East Greenwich Rhode Island after Doctor John Spencer had settled there earlier establishes a *presumption* that Doctor John Spencer is also the son of Michael Spencer of Stotfold, Eng., and Lynn, Mass., There is *direct evidence*: The will of Michael Spencer, son of Michael Spencer of Stotfold, Eng., and Lynn, Mass., named as oveseers in 1723 in East Greenwich, Rhode Island, kinsman Major Thomas Fry and Thomas Spencer, the son of Doctor John Spencer. Major Thomas Fry was later Deputy Governor of Rhode Island. Michael Spencer proved son of Michael Spencer of Stotfold, Eng., and Lynn, Mass., had witnessed a deed on March 11, 1688/9 which Major Thomas Fry had from his father, Thomas Fry Senior. On July 14, 1710, Thomas Fry deeded to his *cousin* John Spencer for love 13½ rods for a burial place. It appears both Spencer families of East Greenwich were related to Thomas Fry.

See Jacobus *Four Spencer Brothers* etc. Vol 27, No 3 pp 163-4, 168 of the American Genealogist

William Henry Spencer in the *Spencer Family Record* published in New York in 1907, p 19 says Michael Spencer had *two* children and that "It is not known that any descendants of this emigrant brother are living.

George W. Steele in *Thomas Steele of Boston* published in 1905 in Los Angeles pp 51-2 says Austin is wrong and John Spencer of East Greenwich is not the son of Michael of Lynn and the nephew of John Spencer who had a Salem will proved in 1648.

R. C. Spencer of Milwaukee in a small book thought John Spencer of East Greenwich was the son of Sir Robert Spencer.

JOHN SPENCER

Born: ca 1638

Married: Susannah Griffin

Died: 1684

Children of John and Susannah (Griffin) Spencer:

Abner Spencer. Born December 4, 1676. Married Susannah Wells. Died May 11, 1759

Benjamin Spencer. Born June 22, 1670. Married 1st Martha (?). Married 2nd Patience Hawkins. Married 3rd Susannah. Died 1723.

John Spencer. Born April 20, 1666. Married Audrey Greene, daughter of Major John Greene, Deputy Governor of Rhode Island.

*Mycal Spencer.

*Robert Spencer.

Susannah Spencer. Born December 1, 1681. Married Richard Briggs, son of John and Frances Briggs, on September 23, 1700.

Thomas Spencer. Born July 22, 1679. The first English child born in East Greenwich, Rhode Island. Married 1st Elizabeth, the daughter of Giles and Elizabeth (Hall) Pearce. Married 2nd Elizabeth (?). Married 3rd Sarah, widow of Benjamin Howland.

Peleg Spencer. Born December 4, 1683. Married Elizabeth Coggeshall, daughter of Joshua Coggeshall and granddaughter of John Coggeshall, the First President of the Colony of Rhode Island and of the Providence Plantations. Peleg Spencer died March 9, 1763

William Spencer. Born July, 1672. Died 1748. Married Elizabeth (?). Married 2nd Elizabeth Burlingame Arnold.

See T.H. Briggs, *Briggs* pp 210-212

See Jacobus *The Four Spencer Brothers,* The American Genealogist Vol 27 No 3 p 168

John Spencer:

1668   Freeman of Newport
1671   Juryman
1677   John Spencer and others receive 5000 acre land grant in East Greenwich, Rhode Island
1677
to   Town Clerk, East Greenwich, Rhode Island
1683
1678   Conservator of Peace
1680   Deputy
1684   Died intestate. Town Council made his will. Widow Susannah Executrix. Sons: John, Michael, Benjamin, William, Robert, and Peleg Spencer mentioned with daughter Susanna

John Osborne Austin's *Genealogical Dictionary of Rhode Island* pages
186-8

JOHN SPENCER. Married Audrey Greene, daughter of Major John
Green, Deputy Governor of Rhode Island.
1699-1700-4-5-9-14-24-6-9 Deputy
1704   Justice of the Peace
1712-1729   Speaker of the House of Deputies
1743   Will proved.

MICHAEL SPENCER Born May 28, 1668. Died October 10, 1748
1700   Contributed toward building of Meeting House for Quakers
       at Mashapaug
1706-7-15   Deputy

September 28, 1748. Will proved November 26, 1748.
Son John Spencer named Executor. To wife Elizabeth use of all
household articles, all bonds, liberty of dwelling house, negro man Pero
and keep of a cow and firewood. To my son Samuel a gun, canoe, and
property he already has by deed. To son-in-law Joseph Bailey and my
daughter Elizabeth Bailey certain land during their lives and then to
go to Robert Bailey. To son Abner Spencer certain land for life and
then to go to grandson Michael Spencer. To daughters SUSANNAH
BRIGGS, Mary Johnson and Ruth Winslow £90 each. To four daughters all household goods, bonds, money sheep and negro man Pero at
decease of wife. To son John Spencer all homestead, farming tools, etc.

BENJAMIN SPENCER. Born June 22, 1670. Died 1723
Contributed toward building Meeting House for Quakers at
Mashapaug
1709-18   Deputy

WILLIAM SPENCER. Born July 1, 1672. Died 1748
1696   Freeman
1703   Contributed toward building Meeting House for Quakers at
       Mashapaug
1709   He and others buy 1824 acres of land in Narragansett near
       Devil's Foot
1714-24-6-7-9   Deputy
1734-5   Justice of Inferior Court of Common Pleas for Kings County

PELEG SPENCER Maried Elizabeth Coggeshall, daughter of Joshua
and granddaughter of John Coggeshall, First President of the Colony
of Rhode Island and of the Providence Plantations.
1709-11-16-28   Deputy

THOMAS SPENCER. Born July 22, 1679. Died April 25, 1752.
Physician.
First English child born in East Greenwich, Rhode Island.
1703   Freeman

1704-7-10-14-15-19-21-29-30-31-33-35-36-37-38-
31-48-49-50-51   Deputy

1720-21-27   Clerk of Assembly

1734-5   Justice for the Inferior Court of Common Pleas for the County of Providence.

1738   Speaker of the House of Deputies

1741   Appointed to Committee to represent and manage the affairs of the Colony before the Commissioners to hear and determine boundaries between Rhode Island and Massachusetts

1741   He and two others are appointed by the Assembly to set off part of Warwick into a township to be called Coventry

Austin in his *Genealogical Dictionary* notes a portion of the offices may have been held a contemporary Thomas Spencer, the son of Michael Spencer.

ROBERT SPENCER. Married 1st Theodosia Whalley.

1696   Freeman

1721   Deputy

1723   Inhabitant of North Kingstown

1736.   Administration on the estate of his son, Robert.

1749, July 26.   Administrator George Reynolds who married his daughter, Joanna Spencer brought in an account. Receipts from John and Michael Spencer, Philip Green and *Benjamin Sweet* for £84, from Joseph Boss for £85 2s from Thomas Place, Jr., for £234

See John Osborn Austin's *Genealogical Dictionary of Rhode Island* Joel Munsell's Sons Albany New York 1887 pp 186-187

MICHAEL SPENCER

Born: May 28, 1668

Married: Elizabeth (?   ) on November 16, 1682

Died: October 10, 1748

Children of Michael and Elizabeth (?   ) Spencer:

Abner Spencer. Born January 8, 1702-3

Elizabeth Spencer. Born September 22, 1694. Married Joseph Bailey on July 28, 1726

Isabel Spencer. Born June 7, 1705

Joanna Spencer. Born January 1, 1708. Died March 11, 1708-9

John Spencer. Born January 5, 1700. Married May 7, 1730 to Lydia Gardiner, daughter of Nicholas Gardiner.

Mary Spencer. Born January 31, 1710

Michael Spencer. Born April 27, 1718

Orpha Spencer. Born October 31, 1713. Died March 6, 1726 unmarried

Ruth Spencer. Born April 24, 1711. Married Job Winslow

Samuel Spencer. Born March 2, 1696. Married May 28, 1719, to Martha Briggs, daughter of Daniel and Lydia Briggs.

*Susannah Spencer. Married Captain Benjamin Briggs, son of Daniel and Lydia Briggs.

SUSANNAH SPENCER

Born: March 13, 1698, in East Greenwich, Rhode Island
Married: Captain Benjamin Briggs on March 17, 1719-1720 in East
    Greenwich

CAPTAIN ROBERT SPENCER

Born: November 6, 1674, in Newport, Rhode Island
Married: 1st: Theodosia Whaley on July 15, 1697
         2nd: Susanna, widow of Joseph Reynolds
         3rd: Martha, widow of Joseph Hopkins and sister of Theodosia Whaley

Died: 1748

Children of Captain Robert and Theodosia (Whaley) Spencer:

Anna Spencer. Born June 7, 1699. Married Thomas Place

Caleb Spencer. Born July 20, 1713

James Spencer. Born February 6, 1716

Johannah Spencer. Born March 12, 1712 (T.H. Briggs, *Briggs* has birth on September 29, 1711. Marriage to George Reynolds, son of Joseph and Susanna Reynolds).

Martha Spencer. Born September 8, 1700. Married on March 22, 1722 to Jeremiah Boss, son of Edward Boss and Susannah Wilkinson

Michael Spencer. Born December 27, 1709

Nathaniel Spencer. Born September 4, 1715

Robert Spencer. Born March 1-5, 1704

Ruth Spencer. Born May 20, 1702. Married her cousin, John Spencer, son of William Spencer and grandson of Dr. John Spencer.

Samuel Spencer. Born February 3, 1717-8

*Susannah Spencer

Theodosia Spencer. Born November 8, 1703 (T.H. Briggs, *Briggs* has birth as December 8, 1705 and marriage to Philip Greene on September 14, 1732).

Theophilus Spencer. Born September 16, 1707

See V.R.R.I. Vol 1 Kent Co East Greenwich Births and Deaths p 147
See Austin p 187
See T.H. Briggs *Briggs* pp 129-130

SUSANNAH SPENCER

Born: March 4, 1697-8 in East Greenwich, Rhode Island
Married: Benjamin Sweet

Susannah Spencer of Robert and Theodetia born Mar 4, 1697-8

Ann	June 7, 1699
Martha	Sept 8, 1700
Ruth	May 20, 1702
Theodosia	Nov 8, 1703
Robert	Mar 1, 1704
Theophilus	Sept 16, 1707
Michael	Dec 27, 1709
Johannah	Mar 12, 1712
Caleb	July 20, 1713
Nathaniel	Sept 4, 1715
James	Feb 6, 1716
Samuel	Feb 3, 1717-8

Arnold's *Vital Records of Rhode Island*, Volume 1, Kent County, East Greenwich Births and Deaths, page 147

SWEET

JOHN SWEET I OF DEDHAM AND SALEM, MASSACHUSETTS, AND PROVIDENCE, RHODE ISLAND

Came to America ca 1630 from England or Wales.

Married: Mary (?   ) who died in 1681

Died: 1638

Chapin says, "John Sweet's lot in Providence is that on which the State House now stands".

Name of "Sweet's Cove" given an inlet near the residence of John Sweet at Salem, Massachusetts.

In 1637 John Sweet went with Roger Williams to Providence, Rhode Island.

The widow of John Sweet returned to Salem and married Ezekiel Holliman and changed the name of Meribah Sweet to Renewed Sweet. The widow's will was proved July 31, 1681.

Children of John and Mary (?   ) Sweet:

James Sweet. Born 1622. Married Mary Greene, daughter of John and Joan (Tattersall) Greene. Died 1695

*John Sweet II

Meribah (later Renewed) Sweet. Married John Gereardy.

See T.H. Briggs, *Briggs* pp 296-298

See Austin pp 194-195

JOHN SWEET II

Born: 1620

Married: ca 1651 (?   )

Died: 1677

Children of John and Elizabeth (?   ) Sweet:

Benjamin Sweet; Daniel Sweet, born 1657; Daughter, name unknown; *Henry Sweet; James Sweet; Jeremiah Sweet; John Sweet, born ca 1653/4; Richard Sweet, married Rachel; William Sweet, married Thankful.

John Sweet II:

1655   Freeman

1660   Commissioner

1663   April 17, Sold Francis Darby of Warwick dwelling house lot bought of Henry Townsend

1671   May 20, Took Oath of Allegiance

1675   Grist Mill at Potowomut burned by Indians

1677   Now in Newport, he sells meadow in Warwick to Randall Holden

1677   Will made at Newport names wife Elizabeth, and children: John, Daniel, James, Henry, Richard, Benjamin, William, Jeremiah, and a daughter.

See Austin pp 194-5

HENRY SWEET

Born: ca 1661 in Warwick, Rhode Island

Married: (?   )

Children of Henry Sweet:

*Benjamin Sweet

Eals Sweet (Daughter, Twin of Ruth Sweet) Born July 10, 1700

Elizabeth Sweet. Born February 25, 1704. Married Peter Wells on December 11, 1733

Griffin Sweet. Born September 15, 1709. Married Presilla Sweet, daughter of William Sweet, on October 24, 1736

Hannah Sweet. Born February 8, 1711/2

Henry Sweet. Born March 11, 1682

Johannah Sweet. Born February 13, 1695. Married on February 18, 1718 to Robert Vaughn

Joseph Sweet. Born March 7, 1687. Married Rachel Edmunds on May 26, 1709

John Sweet. Born March 24, 1684

Mary Sweet. Born February 10, 1692. Married on October 18, 1739, to Hezekiah Matterson

Ruth Sweet (Twin of Eals Sweet) Born July 10, 1700. Married on December 15, 1720, to Henry Matterson

William Sweet. Born August 1, 1698. Married to Elizabeth Peirce, daughter of Jeremiah Peirce on February 1, 1727/8.

Susanna Sweet. Born May 17, 1706

See Austin p 194

See V.R.R.I. Vol 1 Kent Co. East Greenwich, Births and Deaths p 157

See T.H. Briggs, *Briggs* pp 128-9

CAPTAIN BENJAMIN SWEET

Born: March 29, 1690, in Warwick, Rhode Island

Married: Susannah Spencer

Children of Captain Benjamin and Susannah (Spencer) Sweet:

Amey Sweet. Born April 22, 1731

Benjamin Sweet. Born February 6, 1721-2. Married April 23, 1746 to Orpah Briggs, daughter of Captain Benjamin and Susannah (Spencer) Briggs

David Sweet. Born December 2, 1738

Hannah Sweet. Born November 19, 1734. Married on February 25, 1749 to James Matteson

Henry Sweet. Born November 10, 1723

Francis Sweet. Born March 8, 1725-6

Robert Sweet. Born June 28, 1718

Ruth Sweet. Born May 8, 1720. Married June 6, 1740 to George Sweet.

Susannah Sweet. Born July 25, 1729. Married June 15, 1749 to Nathan Bennett

*Theodosha Sweet. Married on June 7, 1747 to Benjamin Briggs, Junior, son of Captain Benjamin and Susannah (Spencer) Briggs.

Theophilus Sweet. Born December 16, 1736

Welthian Sweet. Born February 3, 1732-3. Married September 4 or 8, 1754 to Daniel Briggs, son of Captain Benjamin and Susannah (Spencer) Briggs.

THEODOSIA SWEET

Born: October 30, 1727, East Greenwich, Rhode Island

Married: Benjamin Briggs, Jr., on June 7, 1747, in East Greenwich.

THURSTON

EDWARD THURSTON

Born: 1617

Married: Elizabeth Mott in June 1647

Died: March 1, 1707, aged 90

Children of Edward and Elizabeth (Mott) Thurston:

Content Thurston. Born June 1667

Daniel Thurston. Born April 1661. Of Newport. Married Mary Easton. Will made July 18, 1712

Edward Thurston. Born April 1, 1652. Freeman on May 6, 1679. Died December 7, 1690, aged 38.

Elizabeth Thurston. Born February 1650

Ellen Thurston. Born March 1655. Married 1674 to George Havens

John Thurston. Born December 1664. Freeman May 6, 1690. Died on October 22, 1690

Jonathon Thurston Born January 4, 1659. Of Little Compton. Married Sarah (?). Died 1740 aged 81.

*Mary Thurston

Rebecca Thurston. Born April 1662. Married 1st Peter Easton. Married 2nd Weston Clarke.

Samuel Thurston. Born August 24, 1669. Of Newport. Married Abigail Clarke, daughter of Latham and Hannah (Wilbor) Clarke and granddaughter of Jeremiah and Frances (Latham) Clarke. Hannah Wilbor was the daughter of Samuel and Hannah (Porter) Wilbor and granddaughter of Samuel and Ann (Bradford) Wilbor. Hannah Porter was the daughter of John Porter. Ann Bradford was the daughter of Thomas Bradford. Frances Latham was the daughter of Lewis Latham, Freeman May 5, 1696. Will dated May 13, 1740; proved November 2, 1747.

Quaker

1655 Freeman

1663 Commissioner

1667-71 through 74, 80 through 86 Deputy

1675, 1686, 1690, 1691 Assistant

1686 With other Quakers Edward Thurston signed an Address to the King in regard to the Writ of Quo Warranto. They desired to be excused from bearing arms, being a peaceable people and willing to pay all just rates and duties for carrying on the Commonwealth's affairs.

1690 Deputy Governor Greene, Edward Thurston and five other

Assistants write King William and Queen Mary congratulating them on their Accession to the Crown and informing them that since the deposition of Sir Edmond Andros, the former government under the Charter had been reassumed.

In his will Edward Thurston names grandson Edward (of son Edward) four surviving sons: Jonathon, Daniel, Samuel and Thomas; granddaughter Elizabeth (of son Jonathon), sons-in-law Weston Clarke and the Reverend Ebenezer Slocum and two granddaughters Slocum.

MARY THURSTON

Born: February, 1657

Married: The Reverend Ebenezer Slocum, who later served as Speaker of the Rhode Island General Assembly

Died: November 16, 1732

Descendants of Edward Thurston in Rhode Island by Chrales Myrick Thurston. 1858. New York

Genealogical Dictionary of Rhode Island. John Osborne Austin. Joel Munsell's Sons, Albany, New York. 1887. page 201.

WEST

MATTHEW WEST

1636 Of Lynn, Massachusetts
1637 Freeman
1646 Of Newport, Rhode Island
1655 Freeman

Children of Matthew West

Barthlomew West. Died 1703. Of Portsmouth, Rhode Island and Monmouth, New Jersey. Married Catharine Almy, daughter of William Almy of South Kilworth, co. Leicester, England, and of Saugus (Lynn), Massachusetts, Sandwich in the Plymouth Colony, and Portsmouth, Rhode Island, Gentleman.

Francis West.

*Joan West.

John West.

Nathaniel West. Died 1659 of Newport.

Robert West. Died 1697. Of Providence and Portsmouth, Rhode Island and of Monmouth, New Jersey.

See John Osborn Austin's *Genealogical Dictionary of Rhode Island*, pages 218-219.

See *The Coggeshalls in America* by Charles Pierce Coggeshall and Thelwell Russell Coggeshall Published in 1930 by C.E. Goodspeed and Company of Boston, pp 14-16.

JOAN WEST

Born: 1631

Married: Joshua Coggeshall, son of John Coggeshall, First President of the Colony of Rhode Island and the Providence Plantations, on December 22, 1652, at the Newport home of Peter Easton, brother-in-law of Joshua Coggeshall and son of Governor Nicholas Easton.

Died: April 24, 1676

Genealogical Dictionary of Rhode Island by John Osborne Austin, pages 49, 218-219. Published by Joel Munsell's Sons Albany, New York 1887.

WHALLEY

THEOPHILUS (ROBERT) WHALLEY

Born: 1616

Married: Elizabeth Mills in Virginia. She was born in 1645 and died in 1715

Died: 1720

Theophilus Whalley is believed to be the son of Richard Whalley of Kirkton Hall, Nottinghamshire, England and a member of Parliament in the last year of Queen Elizabeth's reign. His brother, Colonel Edward Whalley, married Frances Cromwell, a cousin of Oliver Cromwell, Lord Protector of England. After his marriage in Virginia, he returned to England where his Regiment took part in the execution of King Charles I. See H.T. Briggs, *Briggs* pp 213-214.

Theophilus Whalley is said to have been of wealthy parents and to have had a collegiate education; in support of which he is quoted as saying, "till he was eighteen years of age, he knew not what it was to want a servant to attend him with a silver ewer and napkin whenever he wanted to wash his hands". Theophilus Whalley went to Virginia where he served in a military capacity. He returned to England where he was an officer in the Parilamentary Army.

1649 Regiment of Theophilus Whalley takes part in the Execution of King Charles I.

1660 Theophilus Whalley married in Virginia where part of his children were born.

1680 Theophilus Whalley moved to Kings Town Rhode Island from Virginia because of religious differences. Theophilus Whalley lived by fishing, weaving and teaching. He was conversant with Hebrew, Greek, and Latin. His services as a penman were brought into requisition in deeds and papers. The visits of distinguished men from Boston and other places perhaps account for the persistently held tradition that he was one of the regicide judges and had signed the death warrant of King Charles.

1710 120 acres in East Greenwich conveyed to Theophilus Whalley.

1711 Theophilus Whalley and his wife, Elizabeth, deed land in East Greenwich to their son, Samuel.

In the latter part of his life, Theophilus Whalley moved to the house of his son-in-law, Joseph Hopkins in West Greenwich. Theophilus Whalley was buried with honors (military) on Hopkins Hill.

Children of Theophilus (Robert) and Elizabeth (Mills) Whalley:

Ann Whalley

Elizabeth Whalley. Married Charles Hazleton, the son of Charles Hazleton. She died in 1752.

Joan Whalley

Lydia Whalley. Married John Sweet.

Martha Whalley. Born 1680. Died 1773. Married 1st Joseph Hopkins who was the son of Thomas and Sarah Hopkins and who died May 15, 1735. She married 2nd Robert Spencer, the son of Dr. John and Susanna (Griffin) Spencer.

Samuel Whalley. Married a daughter of Samuel Hopkins.

*Theodosia Whally. Married July 15, 1697 to Robert Spencer, son of Dr. John and Susanna (Griffin) Spencer.

See John Osborn Austin's *Genealogical Dictionary of Rhode Island* page 221.

THEODOSIA WHALLEY

Married: Robert Spencer on July 15, 1697

Genealogical Dictionary of Rhode Island. John Osborne Austin. Joel Munsell's Sons Albany, New York. 1887. Page 221

Whalley Family. The Reverend Samuel Whalley. Ithaca, New York. Andrus and Church 1901

LANDFAIR

THOMAS LANDFAIR

Married: Ann (Anna) Carter, daughter of Nehemiah and Rachel Carter

Died: Before April 4, 1816

Children of Thomas and Ann (Carter) Landfair:

William Landfair. Born 1795-1802.

Robert Landfair. Born after 1802 and before 1816.

David (Davis) Landfair. Born 1795-1802.

Eunice (Unis) Landfair. Born 1795-1802.

Jesse Landfair. Born after 1802 and before 1816.

Wellington Landfair. Born after 1802 and before 1816.

The name Landfair is spelled many different ways in the old records: Lanphire, Landfare, Landfar, Landfeir, Landfier, Lamphear, Lanphier, Landphier, Lamphear, Lanphire, etc.

West Feliciana Parish, Louisiana. SUCCESSION OF THOMAS LAMPHEAR. File No. 62. Deliberation of the FAMILY MEETING of the minor heirs of THOMAS LAMPHIRE, DECEASED, held April 3, 1816.

Court of Probate, 3 April 1816.

Upon application of friends of minor heirs of THOMAS LAND-PHIER, late of this parish, deceased, It is ordered that a meeting of family and friends do take place at my office this day at 12 o'clock for the purpose of recommending a Tutor and Undertutor to JESSE, ROBERT AND WELLINGTON LAMPHIER, minors as aforesaid and for that purpose the following persons are summoned to be and appear at the time and place above mentioned: viz. MRS. HANNAH PALMER, PARSONS CARTER, A D A M PALMER, COLONEL WILLIAM KIRKLAND, DAVID DORTCH AND MALACHI BURNS. /s/ John H. Johnson, Parish Judge.

STATE OF LOUISIANA   To the Honorable John H| Johnson, Judge of PARISH OF FELICIANA   the parish aforesaid and of the Court of Probate in and for the same, the Petition of WILLIAM AND DAVIS LANPHIRE, minor adults and SONS OF THOMAS LAN-PHIRE and U N I S LANPHIRE, DAUGHTER OF THE SAME THOMAS, late of the parish aforesaid, dec'd, represents, That the said minors in consequence of the death of their father and mother are left without proper guardians and recommend ADAM PALMER as their Curator ad bona and JOHN AUSTIN, Esq., as their Curator ad litis and pray that the court may take the necessary measures for having them appointed and qualified as such.

Parish of Feliciana.

<pre>
Witness: his
John H. Mills   WILLIAM   X   LANPHIRE
                                          mark
                                          his
                                DAVIS   X   LANPHIRE
                                        mark
                                          her
                                UNIS   X   LANPHIRE
                                       mark
</pre>

STATE OF LOUISIANA   Court of Probate, Present,
PARISH OF FELICIANA   John H. Johnson, Parish Judge.

At a meeting of the Curator ad bona, Curator ad litis, tutor, under-tutor and FAMILY OF THE MINOR HEIRS OF THOMAS AND ANN LANPHIRE, late of the parish aforesaid, dec'd, held at the office of the Judge aforesaid Parish on the 4th day of April A.D. 1816 present MRS. HANNAH PALMER, ARCHIBALD PALMER, PARSONS CARTER, ADAM PALMER, JOHN AUSTIN, Esq., HENRY BENNET and SAMUEL ADAMS, who being duly sworn on the Holy Evangelists of Almighty God to declare the Truth, the Whole Truth, and nothing but the Truth, declare that it is their opinion that it will be to the interest of the said minors to have a sale made of their personal property as the same will be perishable and have to go to waste.

SWORN AND SUBSCRIBED TO
BEFORE ME THE DATE ABOVE
John H. Johnson
Parish Judge

<pre>
ADAM PALMER, Curator ad bona   her
and Tutor   HANNAH   X   PALMER
JOHN AUSTIN, Curator ad litis   mark
and Undertutor   ARCHIBALD PALMER
                                PARSONS CARTER
                                HENRY BENNETT
                                         his
                                SAMUEL   X   ADAMS
                                         mark
</pre>

STATE OF LOUISIANA   Know all men by these presents that we PARISH OF FELICIANA   ADAM PALMER and ARCHIBALD PALMER Senr both of the parish aforesaid are held and firmly bound unto JESSE LANPHIER ROBERT LANPHIRE AND WELLING-TON LANPHIER, minors under tutorship, their heirs, executors, Curators and Guardians that may hereafter be appointed in the sum of One Thousand and Three Hundred Dollars lawful money of the United States . . . . which payment well and truly to be made, we bind ourselves, our heirs, executors and administrators firmly by these presents, signed with our proper hands this Fourth day of April 1816

Whereas the above bounden ADAM PALMER had been appointed by the Judge of the Parish of Feliciana Tutor to the aforesaid minors

Now the condition of the foregoing obligation is such that if the above bounden ADAM PALMER shall truly and faithfully discharge the duties enjoined on him by Law as Tutor aforesaid and well and truly deliver the Estate of the said JESSE, ROBERT AND WELLINGTON LANPHIRE, minors aforesaid to themselves, their Curators or to their assigns, then this obligation to be void, otherwise to remain in full force and virtue.

Witnesses present

his	ADAM PALMER (Seal)
Samuel X Adams	ARCHIBALD PALMER (Seal)
mark	

John H. Mills

We the undersigned in FAMILY MEETING consider the above Bond and Surety sufficient and accordingly accept the same. Parish of Feliciana. April 4, 1816.

Witnesses:
Abraham Lobdell
John H. Mills

his
SAMUEL X ADAMS
mark

her
HANNAH X PALMER
mark

PARSONS CARTER

ARCHIBALD PALMER
HENRY BENNETT
JOHN AUSTIN, Undertutor

JOHN H. JOHNSON
Parish Judge

STATE OF LOUISIANA   Know all men by these presents that we PARISH OF FELICIANA ADAM PALMER and ARCHIBALD PALMER SENR of the State and Parish aforesaid are held and firmly bound unto WILLIAM LANPHIRE, DAVIS LANPHIRE, AND UNIS LANPHIRE, their heirs, executors, curators and guardians that may hereafter be appointed in the sum of One Thousand, Three Hundred Dollars, lawful money of the United States to which payment well and truly to be made we bind ourselves, our executors and administrators firmly by these presents, signed with our proper hands this Fourth day of April, A.D. 1816.

Whereas the above bounden ADAM PALMER has been appointed by the Judge of the Parish of Feliciana, Curator ad Bona of the aforesaid WILLIAM, DAVIS, AND UNIS LANPHIRE, minors above the age of fourteen years. Now the condition of the foregoing obligation is such that if the above bounden ADAM PALMER shall truly and faithfully discharge the duties enjoined on him by Law as Curator aforesaid, and well and truly deliver the Estate of the said WILLIAM, DAVIS AND UNIS LANPHIRE to themselves or to their assigns on their attaining the age of majority, then the above obligation to be void, else to remain in full force.

Witnesses present:

<table>
<tr><td>Samuel</td><td>his
X
mark</td><td>Adams</td><td>ADAM PALMER (Seal)
ARCHIBALD PALMER (Seal)</td></tr>
</table>

Witnesses present:

Samuel   his   X   Adams   mark

John H. Mills

ADAM PALMER (Seal)
ARCHIBALD PALMER (Seal)

We the undersigned in FAMILY MEETING consider the above Bond and Security sufficient and accordingly accept the same.

Witnesses:

Abraham Lobdell
John H. Mills

her
HANNAH   X   PALMER
mark
ARCHIBALD PALMER
HENRY BENNETT

PARSONS CARTER
his
SAMUEL   X   ADAMS
mark
JOHN AUSTIN, Curator Ad Litis
John H. Johnson
Parish Judge

Among many receipts in the Estate are the following to show the different spelling of the name:

Rec'd of Thomas Landfar by the hands of Mr. Parsons Carter the sum of four dollars eighty six and (sic) cents being in full for his state and parish tax for the year 1815.

April 3rd 1816

Ewell Dalton
Collector

Rec'd of Adam Palmer nine dollars and six cents in full of the state parish tax on the Estate of Thomas Landfare for the year Eighteen Hundred and Sixteen.

April 22d 1817

W. M. Clellan

Thomas Landfair

1816   To Thomas Brannan Dr.

Pair shoes $1.00
Gallon Whiskey 1.00
                 ———
                 $2.00

Received the above in full
Thompsons Creek
April 25th 1817   (Name illegible)

STATE OF LOUISIANA   In conformity to an order of John H. PARISH OF FELICIANA   Johnson, Probate Judge of the ...... a Meeting of the family of the minor children of Thomas Lamphear dec'd, to wit: William, Unis, David, Jesse, Robert and Wellington took place at my office as Ex Officio Notary .... present: Mrs. Hannah Palmer, Pearce Nowland, Archibald Palmer, John Wheeler and Alvah Palmer who being duly sworn on the Holy Evangelist of Almighty God to declare the truth the whole truth and nothing but the truth ...

give as their opinion that it would be to the advantage of .... to have ascertain tract of land .... Four hundred arpans lying on Black Creek sold .....

Witnesses: Jany 17, 1818
JOHN J. (?   )
JOSEPH CHISHOLM

HANNAH her X PALMER
mark
PEARCE NOLAND
ARCHIBALD PALMER
JOHN his X WHEELER
mark
ALVAH PALMER

I approve of the above.

JOHN AUSTIN, Under Tutor

JOHN H. JOHNSON   Parish Judge

I certify the above to be a true photostatic copy of the original Proces Verbal of Family Meeting filed in Succession of Thomas Lamphear in this office.

SHIRLEY B. WINSTON
Dy Clerk
West Feliciana, La.
(SEAL)

David Holsten sells to George Frederick Favre represented by Hypolite Twottier 500 arpents of land in Feliciana bounded by land of Charles Adams, Jonathon Cunningham, John Noland, THOMAS LAMPHIER, and James Rowell.

Spanish West Florida Records, Volume XI, page 74.

Census of the Inhabitants of the District of Natchez under the Dominion of Spain, 1792:

District of Second and Sandy Creek.   NEHEMIAH CARTER AND TOMAS LANDPHIER.

Mississippi Historical Society. Dunbar Rowland. Centenary Series. Volume I. Jackson, Mississippi. 1916. Page 421.

Also published in Dunbar Rowland's MISSISSIPPI, THE HEART OF THE SOUTH, Volume I.

Mr. Lamar Landfair of Jackson, Mississippi, sent this information on the 1792 Cencus, after having read it on film in the state archives:

District of Second and Sandy Creek:
Jese Carter: 4 males; 7 females; 11 negroes
Nehemiah Carter: 6 males; 3 females; 3 negroes
Tomas Landphier: 2 males; 2 females
District of Homochito:
Archwaldo Palmer: 3 males; 4 females
District of Santa Catalina:
Cornelio Shaw: 2 males; 2 females

The following are from THE NATCHEZ COURT RECORDS, 1767-1805, by May Wilson McBee, published by Edwards Brothers, Ann Arbor, Michigan, 1953:

(Page 301) *Francis Lansphier* versus Jeremiah Routh, who had a contract with your petitioner to build a bateau of certain dimensions for $80, payable in merchandise, on condition of delivery of said bateau to your petitioner by the 15th of December 1782 and on the penalty to pay your petitioner $2 per day until delivered; asks for the damage occasioned by his negligence as your petitioner has been forced to delay *his* voyage; also a note for $48. /s/ F. LANSPHIER. 23 Jany 1783.

(Page 274) Book F, Natchez Court Records, page 272. William Mulhollan versus THOMAS LANDPHIER. Mulhollan represents that THOMAS LANDPHIER did one day this week maim, wound and cripple one of the petitioner's oxen so that the oxen has become useless and his dependence for making his crop was the use of said oxen for the support of his family and the payment of his rent. 14 June 1794. /s/ Wm. Mulhollan. Colonel Hutchins is authorized to call before him THOMAS LANDPHIER and examine into the nature of the complaint of the petitioner and on finding said LANDPHIER guilty of the charge laid against him without sufficient cause or reason he will have him brought to this fort. I hereby commit THOMAS LAND-PHIER to the fort there to remain until a discharge has been sent him by Mulhollan. Declaration of David Mitchell that with Samuel Phipps on Friday last he went to view THOMAS LANDPHIER'S cornfield fence on the complaint of William Mulhollan against him for wounding and maiming his ox and he heard LANDPHIER say he was only sorry he had not killed him. Declaration of John Kinnard that he saw at THOMAS LANPHIER'S the wounded ox which had been struck in the back with a hatchet, it seems and LANPHIER said he would rather kill the ox than lose his corn. LANPHIER being confined to the fort was brought before His Excellency, the deposition being read to him, he was reprimanded and ordered to pay the damage for the ox and remain confined for his punishment for his threats. /s/ John Girault. 20 June 1794. Appeared Ebenezer Rees and said he would be responsible for the conduct of THOMAS LANPHIER that he may be released. /s/ Ebenezer Rees.

(Page 88) Thomas Lampheer owes money to the Estate of Eliphalet Richards. Natchez. 11 October 1791.

(Page 114) Thos. Lanphur a witness to the Will of Ezekiel Forman. 7 May 1795. Executors of the will: Ebenezer Rees, Sir William Dunbar, Banajah Osman. Colonel Osman, the last named executor, owned Windy Hill Manor, where he was visited by his close friend, the former Vice President of the United States, Aaron Burr.

(Page 554) Claimant: Thomas McCrora, 29 Mar 1804. Wit: Landon Davis, 29 Mar 1804. Wit: John Bullen, 24 Nov 1804. Certificate B-211 issued Feb 19, 1807. Miss. Ter. Thomas McCrora, the legal representative of THOMAS LANPHIER claims a donation of 640 acres. THE SAID THOMAS LANPHIER DID, ON THE DAY THE SPANISH TROOPS EVACUATED THE SAID TERRITORY, ACTUALLY INHABIT AND CULTIVATE THE SAID TRACT, HE BEING THEN THE HEAD OF A FAMILY AND CLAIMING NO LAND BY BRITISH OR SPANISH SURVEY IN SAID TERRITORY. /s/ Thomas McCrory// Paper: I, THOMAS LANPHIER BARGAIN AND SELL AN IMPROVEMENT WITH FOUR ACRES OF CORN TO MORDECAI RICHARDS OF THE HOMOCHITO FOR $25 TO BE PAID IN COTTON DELIVERED AT NATCHEZ, THIS IMPRIVEMENT BEING VACANT LAND ABOVE HUGH DAVIS ON THE HOMOCHITTO, 11 Oct 1798. Wit: James Smith, Charles Adams. /s/THOMAS LANPHIER. In fine handwriting on the side, "On 8 Nov 1804, personally and voluntarily appeared before the subscriber, alcalde of the second division of New Feliciana, in Province of West Florida, and in the presence of two assisting witnesses, THOMAS LANPHIER, the within grantee (?), and being duly sworn, DEPOSES THAT THE WITHIN SIGNATURE IS HIS OWN PROPER HANDWRITING and acknowledges this to be his voluntary act. /s/ William Gildart, John Mears, Isaac Johnson.// The reverse of the paper: "Mordacai Richards obligates myself to make over to John Bullen THOMAS LANPHIER'S RIGHT TO AN IMPROVEMENT ON THE HOMOCHITTO ABOVE HUGH DAVIS, 29 Nov 1798. See American State Papers, Public Lands, Washington, Gales and Seaton, 1860, page 893, Volume 1.

(Page153) Thomas Lanphier's note for $100 in the Inventory of the Estate of Jesse Dewitt. 21 July 1794.

WILLIAM LANDFAIR

Born: 1795-1802

Married: 1st: Catharine Shaw. Died in October, 1833, in East Baton Rouge, Parish.

2nd: Polly Lisenbee on December 11, 1834, in East Feliciana Parish, Louisiana.

3rd: Mrs. Elmira Ellis on August 28, 1850, in Carroll Parish Louisiana

Died: December, 1853, in Carroll Parish, Louisiana

Children of William and Catharine (Shaw) Landfair: Mary Ann Landfair and Rachel Landfair.

Children of William and Polly (Lisenbee) Landfair: Frances Landfair, Robert H. Landfair, Susan Landfair.

Children of William and Elmira (?) Landfair: William Margaret Landfair. (Daughter)

1830 Census, East Baton Rouge Parish Louisiana
William Landfair 1 male born 1770-1780, 2 males born 1800-1810,
1 female born 1790-1800, 1 female born 1825-1830, 1 slave

1840CENSUS EAST BATON ROUGE PARISH, LOUISIANA
William Landfair
1 male born 1800-1810
1 male born 1835-1840
1 female born 1810-1820
1 female born 1820-1825
2 females born 1825-1830
1 female born 1830-1835
1 female born 1835-1840
6 slaves

1850 CENSUS CARROLL PARISH, LOUISIANA
William Landfair born in 1810 in Louisiana
Susan Landfair born in 1837 in Louisiana
Frances Landfair born in 1843 in Louisiana
Robert H. Landfair born in 1848 in Louisiana
    4 Slaves

Henry Lisenbee settled in November 1809 land in Louisiana east of the
Mississippi River and the Island of New Orleans and west of the Pearl
River (Parish of Feliciana). See American State Papers, Public
Lands, etc., Volume 3, page 68.

William Lanfair married Mrs. Elmira Ellis on August 28, 1850. See
Marriage Book A (1832-1858) East Carroll Parish, Louisiana.

William Lanfair died in Carroll Parish, Louisiana, in December, 1853.
He and Elmira Lanfair had a daughter, William Margaret Landfair.
Elmira Lanfair married a Mr. Keegan after the death of William
Lanfair. See Succession of William Lanfair, Drawer No. 37, East
Carroll Parish, Louisiana.

1850 CENSUS CARROLL PARISH, LOUISIANA 204, 204
Elmira Ellis born in 1816 in Tennessee
Marietta Ellis born in 1847 in Louisiana

1860 CENSUS, CARROLL PARISH, LOUISIANA 850, 851
John Keegan born in 1827 in Ireland
Elmira Keegan born in 1815 in Tennessee
William M Landfair born in 1852 in Louisiana

William Lanfair, Vendor. Power of Attorney to Isaac Kemp. September 11, 1837. Book F, page 272, East Feliciana Parish, Louisiana.

William Lanfair sells 581 acres to Alexander French on May 10, 1838.
Book G, pages 84-85, East Feliciana Parish, Louisiana

William Lanfair mortgages two slaves to Robert W. Newport on November 7, 1838. Book G, page 212, East Feliciana Parish, Louisiana

Marriage Book A, page 404, Carroll Parish, Louisiana. John Keagan married Mrs. Elmira Landfair on September 30, 1855, in the house of Mrs. Nancy Cole. Recorded August 28, 1857

Book E, Pages 348 and 349, East Feliciana Parish, Louisiana
Estate of Rhoda Young, wife of Henry Lisenbee.
Mentions:
Polly Lisenbee, wife of William Landfair
Susan Lisenbee, wife of T.B. Brown

Also the children of Rhody and Thomas Young: Holly (Robert Brashier is her tutor) ; Martha Ann, Synthia Ann

Book G, Page 211, East Feliciana Parish, Louisiana
John C. White, John Morgan and William Lanfair, Wm. Tucker and David Lizenby to decide matters touching the minor children of Susan Lizenby dec'd wife of T.B. Brown. 1838.

Wm Lanfair sold John C. Walker 270 arpents in East Baton Rouge Parish bounded on the west by Lilly, on the east by Savage, on the north and south by lands formerly owned by William McFarland, being land William Lanfair bought of Jacob and Lewis Crumbholts on 30 December 1828. Book JQ-page 73, East Baton Rouge Parish, Louisiana. April 18, 1838.

William Lanfair to John Ayres. Book ND, page 161.

December 23, 1831. East Baton Rouge Parish.

William Lanfair to John Ayres. Book MI, page 430, East Baton Rouge Parish, Louisiana

William Lanfair. Tutor Oath. Book SC, page 26. East Baton Rouge Parish. November 25, 1837.

Rachel Lanfair and Mary A. Lanfair by their tutor to John C. Walker. Book JQ, page 73. East Baton Rouge Parish. April 18, 1838.

William Lanfair married Mary Lisenbee on December 11, 1834. Book X, page 150. East Feliciana Parish, Louisiana.

Landfair Deeds, East Carroll Parish, Louisiana

1851. J.J.B. and Emily Johnson to Robert Landfair. G-22.

1852. When William C. Lanfair paid Dorrell Wright a certain sum of money, Dorrell Wright will deliver to him property purchased at a sheriff's sale on October 2, 1832 in the Suit of RACHEL LANFAIR AND HUSBAND, W.W. KENT VS. WM. LANFAIR ET AL No. 599 6th Judicial District Court with the understanding that on his death the property would be divided between Mary Ann Wright, the wife of Dorrell Wright, Susan Lanfair, Franky Lanfair, and Margaret Lanfair, the children of William Lanfair. G-211.

1855.   H. and T. Montgomery to Robert C. Lanfair. H-227.

1856.   S.A.L. and G.H. Bonner to Robert C. Lanfair. I-64.

1856.   J.J.B. and Emily S. Johnson to Robert C. Lanfair. I-221.

1857.   Donation from Sylvanus C. Floyd to Robert C. Lanfair. I-340.
J.H. and Margaret Bonner to R.C. Landfair. J-459

1860. Subrogation from William T. Oliver to Robert C. Lanfair. L-134.
1877. George R. and Emma Hurley to Susan E. Landfair. P-512
1875. E.L. Kent to Mrs. S.E. Lanfair. P-189.
1875. Peter J. Guier to Mrs. S.E. Lanfair. P-190
1871. John W. Keller to Emma Landfair. O-66
1869. Angus Smith to Susan E. Landfair. N-315.

IN THE SUCCESSION OF CATHARINE SHAW, DECEASED

RACHEL LANFAIR Husband   NO. 597
Wm. W. Kent   Probate
VS.
WILLIAM LANFAIR ET AL

Sixth Judicial District Court Parish of East Baton Rouge State of Louisiana.

Petition of William Lanfair of the Parish of East Feliciana represents: That his wife Catharine Shaw died in the month of October 1833 and that her succession was duly opened in the Parish of East Baton Rouge where your petitioner then resided, that there were issue of his marriage with the said Catharine, two children now minors: Mary Ann and Rachel to whom your petitioner is desirous of being confirmed as their natural tutor. Petitioner suggests the propriety of appointing William Shaw Jr. of the Parish of East Baton Rouge, the maternal uncle of said minors, their Under Tutor. (Signed) David D. Avery, Attorney for Petitioner.

On November 18, 1837, the Court then confirmed William Lanfair Natural Tutor to his minor children: Mary Ann and Rachel Landfair and appointed as Under Tutor, William Shaw, Jr.

Petition of the Natural Tutor for Family Meeting

William Lanfair of the Parish of East Feliciana represents that he has been confirmed as Natural Tutor of his minor children, Mary Ann and Rachel Lanfair who are issue of his marriage with Catharine Shaw late of the Parish of East Baton Rouge and that the succession of Catharine Shaw has been opened. Petitioner wants to exchange a tract of land held in community (275 arpents located at about 18 miles north of the Town of Baton Rouge) for two slaves, Maria aged 22 and her child aged 18 months, the property of Parsons P. Carter. Petitioner prays that a Family Meeting composed of Mr. John McHugh, Philip McHugh and Jeremiah McHugh, relations and Mr. William Thomas and Benjamin Bryan friends of said minors be assembled and that William Shaw Jr. the maternal uncle and Under Tutor of the said minors be cited to attend. (Signed) David D. Avery Atty for Petitioner. IT IS ORDERED that a family meeting composed of Mr. John McHugh, Phillip McHugh and Jeremiah McHugh relations and Mr. William Thomas and Benj Bryan friends of the said minors assemble in Baton Rouge on Saturday 25th Inst. 1837 to deliberate the prayer of William Lanfair their Natural Tutor and that William Shaw their Under Tutor be notified to attend. Nov 21, 1837

Land and Slaves valued by B. Bryan and Jno. A. McHugh and Wm Lanfair authorized to effect exchange.

Petition of Rachel Lanfair wife of William W. Kent of the Parish of Carroll

Represents mother Catharine Shaw died in 1833 in the Parish of East Baton Rouge and that her Succession has been opened. That her Sister Mary Ann has married Dorrell Right of the Parish of Carroll. That her father William Lanfair was confirmed Natural Tutor and exchanged 275 acres of land in East Baton Rouge known as Buhlers Plain for two slaves. That her mother and father had community property: horses, cattle, hogs, household and kitchen furniture and a negro woman Lydia. That her mother had separate property: horse, stock, furniture, cash, which her father used for his private purposes. That her father has sold or used personal property belonging to the community. That the slaves, Lydia, Maria, and Green are worth hire. That Maria and Lydia have had children. That her father has rendered no account of his tutorship. That her father and tutor William Lanfair, her sister, Mary Ann Lanfair and her husband, Dorrell Right be cited to answer this petition. (Signed) A.M. Dunn Atty for Petitioner.
SUMMONS To William Lanfair residing in the Parish of Carroll Tutor to Rachel Lanfair, now wife of William W. Kent served on William Lanfair on October 1, 1850, in the Town of Providence, by Wm. L. Knox, Sheriff.

SUMMONS To Mrs. Mary Ann Lanfair, wife of Dorrell Right and the said Dorrell Right residing in the Parish of Carroll, served on October 8, 1850, on Mrs. Mary Ann Lanfair at her residence about 15 miles from Providence.

SALE OF LAND, WILLIAM LANFAIR TO JOHN C. WALKER
William Lanfair in behalf of his minor children Mary Ann and Rachel sells 270 arpents of land in East Baton Rouge Parish bounded on the west by Lilley; on the east by Savage; on the north and south by lands formerly owned by William McFarland being the same land that he the said William Lanfair purchased of Jacob and Lewis Crumholts representing their mother by Power of Attorney on 13 December 1828 Sale to John C. Walker on 9 April 1838.

ACCOUNT TO WILLIAM KENT AND WIFE FROM WILLIAM LANFAIR For Board of Mrs. Kent in 1846. For provisions, cattle, furnishings, costs of maintaining slaves: Green, Leanna, and Maria, should they be decreed to belong to heirs of Catharine Shaw.

East Baton Rouge, July 12, 1851

Dear Sir:

You will confer a favor if at your earliest convenience you will inform me the exact amount of the judgment recently rendered in favor of Rachel Kent v. W. Lanfair, also the amt. of Clerk's fees and Sheriffs and also, please ask Major Dunn the amt. of his claim and inform me of the whole sum to be paid. This will give you perhaps a little trouble, and it will be duly appreciated.

I am responsible for the whole sum, and as I am not able to advance the money, I had written to Mr. Kent several days ago to be prepared with funds to pay by the middle of July, which of course he has done and I presume nothing is needed but for him to know how much to send. Please let me know as soon as you can and I will write to him immediately for the money and instanter upon the receipt of it, I will send it down. I can't come unless I get well, I have been confined to my bed since the 10 inst with violent fever, and am writing to you as I lye in bed.

Yours
Respectfully
JNO. A. McHUGH

ACCOUNT TO DORRELL WRIGHT AND WIFE MARY ANN

Expenses of raising slaves: Green, Leanna, and Maria should they be decreed to belong to Estate of Catharine Shaw.

SUCESSION OF CATHARINE SHAW	597 Probate
RACHEL LANFAIR AND HUSBAND	Sixth Jud Dist Ct Par
VS.	of East Baton
WM. LANFAIR ET AL	Rouge

Testimony for Plaintiff

Letters of Tutorship granted defendant

Mortuary Proceedings in Succession of Catharine Shaw, mother of Plaintiff

Proces Verbal of Family Meeting mentioned in Petition
Deed: William Lanfair to John C. Walker
Testimony of William Shaw:

He is acquainted with William Lanfair. Plaintiff and her sister Mary Ann are the only children of the marriage of William Lanfair and Catharine Shaw. Catharine Shaw died about 1833. He knew the negro woman Lydia which belonged to the community of said Lanfair and wife and he knows the slaves Maria and Green which were obtained in the land exchange since the death of Catharine Shaw. After the death of Catharine Shaw witness had the living and care of plaintiff until the fall of 1845. She married in the Spring of 1846. Witness then valued the services of the slaves and other community property.

DECREE IN THE MATTER OF THE SUCCESSION OF CATHARINE SHAW

The action was brought by the daughter against her father and tutor to render an account, to settle the community and to make a partition of property. The parties were cited. A default judgment was rendered. An account was filed by defendant Lanfair. The cause was assigned for trial. Judgment for plaintiff. It was decreed that plaintiff was part owner of the negro slaves Lydia, Maria and Green and whatever increase there was of slaves. That the slaves be partitioned between defendant plaintiff and her sister, Mary Ann Lanfair wife of Dorrell Right: one half to defendant and one half to plaintiff and Mary Ann, her sister.

Defendant has received revenues of the slaves from the death of Catharine Shaw. He has personal property belonging to the community and separate property of the deceased. July 28, 1851. J.J. Burk Judge Sixth Jud. District WRIT OF FI FA issued to the Sheriff of the Parish of Carroll In the Matter of the Succession of Catharine Shaw Rachel Lanfair and husband Wm. W. Kent vs. William Lanfair No. 597 Probate Sixth Judicial District Court Parish of East Baton Rouge, Louisiana

Writ returned "No property" by Wm L. Knox Sheriff of Carroll Parish.

ALIAS FI FA issued. Judge William B. Robertson, August 12, 1852. William Lanfair pointed out for seizure the improvement, houses and clearing and fences where he lived. The sheriff also seized Leanna a slave girl 14 years old and Green a slave boy 15 years old. D.C. Jenkins Dep. Sheriff.

On 24 August 1852, the above property was advertised in the "Carroll Watchman" and a copy was posted on the courthouse door. Sale was made to Dorrell Wright

Edna Bishop Brock, Clerk of the Sixth Judicial District Court and Ex-Officio Notary Public in and for the Parish of Carroll and State of Louisiana, furnished me on January 6, 1958, a true and correct copy of the above preceedings "Rachel Lanfair, husband Wm. W. Kent vs. William Lanfair et al", docket number 596 on the docket of the Sixth Judicial District Court in and for the Parish of East Baton Rouge. Also of "E. Lanfair vs. Dorrell Wright" Docket No. 2408 in the Tenth District Court in and for the Parish of Carrol, State of Louisiana

A true and correct copy of the first proceedings "Rachel Lanfair etc" had been furnished the court in East Carroll by Chas. Nephler, Deputy Clerk of the Court in East Baton Rouge Parish, a century before (January 18, 1856). The Rachel Lanfair papers were filed in the "E. Lanfair vs. Dorrell Wright" suit.

STATE OF LOUISIANA
PARISH OF EAST FELICIANA

BE IT REMEMBERED that I, Fielden L. Gordon, an acting Justice of the Peace in and for the State and Parish aforesaid and one authorized to solemnize marriages therein did by virtue of a License issued by the Honorable Thomas W. Scott, Parish Judge in and for the State and Parish aforesaid authorizing the solemnizing the rites of matrimony between Mr. WILLIAM LANFAIR and Miss MARY LISENBY BOTH OF THE STATE AND PARISH AFORESAID they acknowledging the same to be of their own free will and accord, done in said State and Parish on the Eleventh day of December Eighteen Hundred and Thirty Four....in the presence of the attesting witnesses: WILLIAM D. CARTER, Phillip Simms, and Evin Edwards—all of full age. In testimony whereof the parties and witnesses sign hereunto with me the Justice aforesaid the day and date aforesaid.

Witnesses:

W. D. Carter   Wm. Landfair
P.A. Sims   Mary Lisenbe
E. Eddings (?   )

        Fielden L. Gordon
        Justice of the Peace.

A TRUE AND CORRECT COPY
This 29 day of Dec 1959 /s/ Robbye Armitage, Dy Clerk of Court

MARY ANN LANDFAIR

Born: 1827-1830

Married: Dorrell Wright, Junior, on February 24, 1848, in Carroll
    Parish, Louisiana

Died: 1870-1880

Children of Dorrell and Mary Ann (Landfair) Wright, Junior:
Anna Wright; Mattie Wright; Sarah Elizabeth Wright; Susan Wright; Thomas Wright.

RACHEL LANDFAIR

Rachel Landfair married William W. Kent on April 9, 1845. Marriage Book "A" (1832-1858) page 88, East Carroll Parish, Louisiana.

1850 Wm W Kent and wife, Rachel Kent, both of full age sell land to James P. Thompson on December 13, 1850 Conveyance Book F page 351, Carroll Parish, La.

John W. Hays sells land to Mrs. Rachel Kent widow of William W. Kent deceased on May 12, 1858. Conveyance Book H page 453 and J, page 261, Carroll Parish, La.

March 16, 1859. Uriah Kent father of William W. Kent and father-in-law of Rachel Kent both deceased. Succession Book I page 424. Rachel

Kent was administratrix of her husband on July 5, 1858. Succession
Book I page 230, Carroll Parish, La.

1850 Census Carroll Parish Louisiana 193, 193
Uriah Kent Born in 1800 in Georgia
Evira Kent born in 1802 in Georgia
Ephraim R. Kent born in 1828 in Mississippi
Joseph S. Kent born in 1832 in Mississippi
Calista W. Kent born in 1838 in Mississippi
Lucretia A. Kent born in 1840 in Mississippi

1860 Census Carroll Parish Louisiana 875, 846
Uriah Kent born in 1800 in Georgia
Maria Kent (wife) born in 1820 in Alabama
Richard P. Mabry born in 1846 in Alabama
Mary J. Mabry born in 1848 in Aalabama
David A Mabry born in 1853 in Louisiana

931, 901
Ephraim R. Kent born in 1828 in Mississippi
Sarah Kent born in 1828 in Louisiana
Ephraim L. Kent born in 1856 in Louisiana
Mary C. Kent born in 1856 in Louisiana
Ephraim L. and Mary C. Kent are listed as orphans.

Rachel Kent died on November 16, 1858. Succession Book I, pages
424, 429, Carroll Parish, La.

Tutorship of W.W. and Rachel Kent Children: Ephraim L., John W.
and Mary C. Kent. Book J, page 39, 41, Carroll Parish, La.

1860 Census, Carroll Parish, Louisiana, Ward 6, Floyd 812, 786
Elijah Gray born in 1826 in South Carolina
Lucretia A. Gray born in 1840 in Mississippi
John W. Kent born in 1852 in Louisiana

940, 908
Joseph S. Kent born in 1834 in Mississippi
Francis A. Kent born in 1839 in Mississippi
John W. Kent born in 1855 in Louisiana
Sarah E. Kent born in 1859 in Louisiana

Ward 5, Oak Grove
447, 439
Isaac N. Kent born in 1824 in Georgia
Salena A. Kent born in 1852 in Louisiana

FRANCES DREW LANDFAIR

Born: December 12, 1838, in Louisiana, the daughter of William C.
and Mary (Lisenbee) Landfair.

Married: James Franklin White, the son of James White and Sarah
Slocum. He was born on February 13, 1836, in Alabama, and died
on November 19, 1899 in Pine Bluff, Arkansas

Died: September 16, 1891, in Drew County, Arkansas

/Children of James Franklin and Frances Drew (Landfair) White:

Fannie Louise White. Born June 19, 1884, in Drew County. Married Tom Hale. Died January 6, 1919

Eugene Thomas White. Born May 10, 1872, in Star City, Lincoln County, Arkansas

James Henry White. Born April 14, 1875, in Drew County. Married Addie Ellis on January 4, 1894. Died July 6, 1942

Luella White. Born April 4, 1879, in Drew County Died August 11, 1898.

Mattie White. Born December 15, 1882, in Drew County. Married William J. Wilson on May 10, 1900. Still Living in 1958.

Susan White. Born ca 1862 in Drew County

William White. Born ca 1864 in Drew County

Frances Landfair, the daughter of William Landfair, had Robert C. Landfair as her tutor. On his resignation, her brother-in-law, James C. Palmer, was appointed her tutor. Tutorship Proceedings of Frances Lanfair, Drawer 37, East Carroll Parish, Louisiana.

EUGENE THOMAS WHITE

Born: May 10, 1872, in Star City, Lincoln County Arkansas

Married: Patsy Clementine Ozment on August 13, 1891. She was born the daughter of James G. and Rachel Caroline Ozment on January 10, 1870, in Drew County. She died in March, 1916

Died. October 30, 1910

Children of Eugene Thomas and Patsy Clementine (Ozment) White:

Daughter. Born ca 1893

Edgar Housten White. Born January 9, 1895 in Moody, Drew County, Arkansas. Married Bessie Burt on November 24, 1917

Emma White. Born April 26, 1898, in Moody, Married Jack Spurlock on October 7, 1917. Died March 2, 1935

Eva Jean White. Born April 7, 1910, in Moody. Married Lawton Heard on June 15, 1929.

Claude White. Born ca 1900 in Moody. Died ca 1909

James E. White. Born February 14, 1908, in Moody. Married (1) Ruthie May Andrews on October 1, 1927 (2) Ora Myrtle White on March 21, 1937

Jesse Monroe White

Maggie White. Born March 15, 1902 in Moody. Married (1) Olin Dougherty on May 17, 1917 and (2) John Cash on March 1, 1922

Otis Lee White. Born in Moody on June 7, 1906. Married Effie Belle Hayes on April 7, 1928

Walter Dewey White. Born October 4, 1905 in Moody. Married Hattie Cummings on July 26, 1925. Died February 17, 1937

JESSE MONROE WHITE

Born: August 23, 1896, in Moody, Drew County, Arkansas.

Married: Lola Mae Hayes, the daughter of John Vol Hayes and Dora Catharine Breedlove on December 24, 1921. Lola Mae Hayes was born in Florence, Drew County, Arkansas, on February 27, 1905

Died: January 12, 1934

Children of Jesse Monroe and Lola Mae (Hayes) White:

Betty Jean White. Born January 11, 1931, in Florence. Married Vance Houge, Junior

Frances White. Born January 17, 1927, in Florence. Married Rastue L. Martar.

James Monroe White. Born March 1, 1924 in Winchester. Married Helen Louise Idleman on April 6, 1956

Lamar Hayes White. Born November 14, 1922 in Winchester. Married Vivian Lucille Johnson on February on February 6, 1945.

Virginia Ruth White. Born July 11, 1929, in Florence. Died June 17, 1935.

LAMAR HAYES WHITE

Born: November 14, 1922, in Winchester, Drew County, Arkansas

Married: Vivian Lucille Johnson on February 6, 1945. She was born October 13, 1925, in Cresent, Salt Lake County, Utah, the daughter of James Harold and Sophia Charlotte (Larsen) Johnson.

Children of Lamar Hayes and Vivian Lucille (Johnson) White:

Linda Kay White. Born July 6, 1953, in Price, Carbon County, Utah.

SUSAN LANDFAIR

Born: 1837-1838 in Louisiana

Married: James Palmer on December 23, 1856, in the house of R.C. Landfair. Marriage Book A, page 405, Carroll Parish, La.

Children of James and Susan (Landfair) Palmer:
Eugenia Palmer

ROBERT LANDFAIR

Born: 1808-1810 in Louisiana

Married: 1st: Eliza Bonner
2nd: Susan E. McCandless on June 27, 1852

Died: May 14, 1878. Succession Drawer L, West Carroll Parish, Louisiana

Children of Robert and Eliza (Bonner) Landfair: Emma A. Landfair,

Hiram Landfair, James L. Landfair, Robert J. Landfair, Thomas M. Landfair, William H. Landfair.

Children of Robert and Susan E. (McCandless) Landfair: Ida Landfair, Samuel Landfair, Thomas Landfair, Walter Landfair.

1850 CENSUS, CARROLL PARISH, LOUISIANA
Robert Landfair born in 1808 in Louisiana, Planter
Eliza Landfair born in 1826 in Georgia
William H. Landfair born in 1831 in Mississippi, Student
James L. Landfair born in 1834 in Mississippi
Robert Landfair born in 1836 in Mississippi
Thomas M. Landfair born in 1838 in Louisiana
Hyram Landfair born in 1844 in Texas
Emma A. Landfair born in 1848 in Louisiana
Hamilton Ingram born in 1840 in Mississippi
Benjamin Ingram born in 1841 in Mississippi
9 slaves

1860 CENSUS, DREW COUNTY, ARKANSAS
Robert C. Landfair born in 1810 in Louisiana
Susan Landfair born in 1835 in Alabama
Robert J. Landfair born in 1838 in Mississippi
Loucresa E. Landfair born in 1844 in Mississippi
Hiram Landfair born in 1845 in Texas
Emma Landfair born in 1848 in Louisiana
Ida Landfair born in 1853 in Louisiana
Samuel Landfair born in 1858 in Louisiana
James Palmer born in 1831 in Louisiana
Susan A. Palmer born in 1838 in Louisiana
Eugenia Palmer born in 1859 in Louisiana
11 Slaves

1870 CENSUS, CARROLL PARISH, LOUISIANA
Robert C. Landfair born in 1810 in Louisiana
Susan Landfair born in 1837 in Alabama
Ida Landfair born in 1853 in Louisiana
Thomas Landfair born in 1863 in Arkansas
Walter Landfair born in 1868 in Louisiana

R.C. Landfair married Susan E. McCandless on June 27, 1852. See Marriage Book A (1832-1858), page 245, East Carroll Parish, Louisiana.

Robert Landfare (Landfair) was on the tax rolls of Madison County, Mississippi, for 1830, 1833 (2 slaves), 1834 (3 slaves), 1835 (3 slaves) 1836 (10 slaves), 1837.

Eliza Bonner, consort of Robert Lanfair. Born June 6, 1816. Died January 14, 1852. Buried in the Old Forrest Cemetery, Forrest Louisiana. Her father was Josiah Bonner, born May 4, 1787, and died on December 9, 1851.

LOUISIANA TOMBSTONE INSCRIPTIONS OF EAST AND WEST CARROLL PARISHES, Copied and Published by the Louisiana Society, Daughters of the American Revolution, Volume 6, pages 135 and 112

Nicholas D. Ingram married Lavinia Emeline Bonner, sister of Eliza Bonner Landfair, on December 23, 1839, in Madison County, Mississippi. Book F, page 84.

1850 Census, Carroll Parish, Louisiana 349, 349
James L. Bonner born in 1812 in Georgia

1850 Census, Carroll Parish, Louisiana 115, 115
Josiah Bonner born in 1790 in Georgia
Elizabeth M. Bonner born in 1816 in Mississippi
Sample Bonner born in 1849 in Louisiana
William H. Scanton (?) born in 1842 in Ind.
John M. Scanton (?) born in 1843 in Ind.
2 slaves

1860 Census, Carroll Parish, Louisiana, Ward 5, Oak Grove 764, 734
Gabreal H. Bonner born in 1811 in Georgia
Margaret E. Bonner born in 1812 in South Carolina
Wilbur F. Bonner born in 1842 in Mississippi
James J. Bonner born in 1848 in Mississippi
Mary E. Bonner born in 1850 in Mississippi
7 Slaves

1860 Census, Carroll Parish, Louisiana, Lake Providence 244, 234
Nicholas D. Ingram born in 1812 in Kentucky Planter
Hamilton B. Ingram born in 1841 in Mississippi Student
Benjamin S. Ingram born in 1843 in Mississippi Student
James Loflin born in 1850 in Louisiana Orphan
Alexander H. Embrey born in 1833 in Virginia Overseer
James Loflin Owned $1,000 property.

Nicholas D. Ingram awned $32,000 Real Estate and $43,000 Personal Estate.
41 Slaves

Nancy Williams Hubert, mother of Eliza Ann Bonner (Mrs. Robert C. Landfair), was a first cousin of the Honorable Hiram G. Runnels elected Governor of Mississippi in 1833 and of his brother, Hardin Dudley Runnels, whose son, Hardin Richard Runnels, served as Speaker, Texas House of Representatives, in 1853 and 1855, and was elected Governor of Texas over General Sam Houston in 1855. Governor Runnels of Mississippi and Hardin Dudley Runnels were the sons of Colonel Harmon Runnels who served in the Mississippi Constitutional Convention of 1817 and his wife, Hester Hubert, born in 1762 in North Carolina, the sister of Gabriel Hubert and the aunt of his daughter, Nancy Williams Hubert. Gabriel and Hester Hubert were two of the children of Benjamin B. Hubert, a French Huguenot who married Mrs. Mary Williams, widow of Paul Williams of Frederick County, Virginia in 1748. From Virginia the Huberts moved to Caswell County, North Carolina, and in 1785 or 1786 they moved to Warren County (then part of Wilkes County), Georgia. The will of Benjamin B. Hubert was signed July 26, 1793, and was the first recorded in Warren County, Georgia.

GENEALOGY OF THE FAMILY OF BENJAMIN B. HUBERT, A HUGUENOT, by Miss Sarah Donelson Hubert of Barnett, Warren County, Georgia, published in 1897 by the Franklin Printing and Publishing Company of Atlanta, Georgia. This booklet was loaned to the author by Mr. Robert Lamar Landfair of Jackson, Mississippi.

Mr. Robert Lamar Landfair sent this list of the children of Thomas Bonner and Margaret Jones: Jourdan Bonner who married Polly Adams on October 3, 1811; Zadock Bonner who married Lucy Ridgeway; Thomas Bonner; Whitmal Bonner; William Bonner born in 1774; Willis Bonner; Josiah Bonner born May 5, 1787 and married Nancy Williams Hubert and died on December 9, 1851; Deborah Bonner who married Richard Vanderford; and Elizabeth Bonner.

Mr. Robert Lamar Landfair sent this information on Josiah Bonner and Nancy Williams Hubert. Josiah Bonner was born on May 5, 1787 in Green County, Georgia, and died on December 9, 1851 in Carroll Parish, Louisiana. He married Nancy Williams Hubert on February 2, 1810, in Clarke County, Georgia.

Nancy Williams Hubert was born on October 20, 1791, in Georgia and died in Madison County, Mississippi, in 1834 or 1835.

Josiah Bonner and Nancy Williams Hubert were the parents of the following children: Gabriel Hubert Bonner born December 20, 1810, in Clarke County, Georgia, married Margaret E. Brown on May 28, 1831, and died on November 4, 1861; James Lucien Bonner born August 29, 1812 in Clarke County, Georgia, married Sarah Ann L. Reid on October 30, 1851, and died in West Carroll Parish, Louisiana, on September 13, 1853; Eliza Ann Bonner born on June 6, 1816, in Clarke County, Georgia, married Robert C. Landfair in 1830-1831, and died on January 14, 1852, in West Carroll Parish, Louisiana; Thomas Jones Bonner born June 8, 1818, in Clarke County, Georgia and died on April 30, 1843; Hiram Runnels Bonner born on October 22, 1820 in Lawrence County, Mississippi and died November 13, 1853, in West Carroll Parish, Louisiana; Seleta Caroline Bonner born on May 4, 1823, in Lawrence County, Mississippi married John Wayles Eppes on February 9, 1837, and died on May 7, 1849 in West Carroll Louisiana; Lavinia Emeline Bonner born on November 14, 1825, married Nicholas D. Ingram on December 23, 1839, and died on July 17, 1843 in Carroll Parish, Louisiana; Cecilia Catherine Bonner born on November 14, 1825, married Benjamin C. Sample on November 10, 1841 and died on May 12, 1904; Mary Latham Bonner born on January 14, 1828, in Madison County, Mississippi and died there on September 30, 1835; Josiah Fletcher Bonner born in Madison County, Mississippi, on November 28, 1829 and died on September 20, 1852; Mary Ann Norwood Bonner born on January 2, 1833, in Madison County, Mississippi, married John M. Key on March 7, 1850, and died on March 18, 1851, in West Carroll Parish, Louisiana. After the death of Nancy Williams Hubert, Josiah Bonner married secondly Sarah K. Eppes, and thirdly Mrs. Elizabeth M. Scanland on August 24, 1848. By this third wife he had the following children: Sample Bonner born November 2, 1849, in Carroll Parish, Louisiana and died there August 4, 1852 and Josiah Bonner born on September 27, 1851, in Carroll Parish, Louisiana, and died there on January 27, 1852.

Mr. Robert Lamar Landfair, a descendant of Robert Landfair and Eliza Ann Bonner sent the Bonner Revolutionary Record, which, he reports has been established with the Daughters of the American Revolution. The father of Eliza Ann Bonner (Mrs. Robert Landfair) was Josiah Bonner. His father, Thomas Bonner, Jr., was born about 1744 in Chowan County, N. C. He married Margaret Jones there on May 6, 1767. He enlisted in Roebuck Regiment at Spartanburg, South Carolina and fought in the American Revolution. Thomas Bonner, Jr., and his wife both died in Clark County, Georgia about December, 1804.

1850 Census, Carroll Parish, Louisiana, 151, 151
John M. Key born in 1824 in Alabama
Martha Key born in 1833 in Mississippi (She was a daughter of Josiah Bonner and sister of Eliza Ann Bonner Landfair)
150, 150
Benjamin Sample born in 1815 in Louisiana
Sarah Sample born in 1826 in Mississippi
John M. Sample born in 1845 in Louisiana
William J. Sample born in 1847 in Louisiana
Lucian Sample born in 1849 in Louisiana

EMMA LANDFAIR

Born: 1848 in Louisiana
Married: Ferdinand Bullock
Children of Ferdinand and Emma (Landfair) Bullock: Ida Bullock, Lucy Bullock, Mede Bullock.
1860 CENSUS CARROLL PARISH LOUISIANA MONTICELLO 101, 92
Nancy Cole born in 1801 in E. Tennessee

Henderson J. Bullock born in 1828 in Mississippi
Ferdinand M. Bullock born in 1835 in Missississppi

1870 CENSUS WARD NO. 2 CARROLL PARISH LOUISIANA 903, 903

F. M. Bullock born in 1835 in Mississippi
Emma Bullock born in 1848 in Louisiana
Lucy Bullock born in 1863 in Louisiana
Mede Bullock born in 1867 in Louisiana (male)
Ida Bullock born in 1870 in Louisiana

HIRAM DAVID LANDFAIR

Born: December 24, 1844, in Texas

Married: 1st: Jane Lucy Coleman on August 18, 1864. She was the widow of J. S. Chandler. She was born in 1842 in Sumter County, Alabama, the daughter of James Green and Lucy (Allums) Coleman. She died May 9, 1881, in Lauderdale County, Mississippi

2nd: Marie Ludia Thrash on March 23, 1882, Lauderdale County, Mississippi. Marriage Book B1, page 312. She was born on February 13, 1848, in Alabama, the daughter of Eli and Elizabeth (Mosterd) Thrash. She died May 30, 1926 in Corinth, Mississippi

Died: December 26, 1892, in Corinth, Mississippi

Children of Hiram David and Jane Lucy (Coleman) Landfair: Lucy Eliza Landfair, Annie Lexine Landfair, Beulah Emma Landfair.

James Ingram Landfair. Born August 18, 1870 in Lauderdale County, Mississippi. Died April 3, 1947, in Memphis, Tennessee.

Octavia Prudence Landfair.

Robert Columbus Landfair. Born July 23, 1874, in Lauderdale County, Mississippi. Died August 10, 1874, in Lauderdale County.

Jesse Lamar Landfair.

Waid Hiram Landfair.

Children of Hiram David and Marie Ludia (Thrash) Landfair:

Ludia Adealion Landfair. Born March 1, 1883, in Lauderdale County, Mississippi, and died there on February 20, 1884.

George Edward Landfair.

1870 Census, Lauderdale County, Mississippi, 113, 113 Township 7
Hiram D. Landfair born in 1844 in Texas
Lucy J. Landfair born in 1842 in Alabama
Annie Landfair born in 1866 in Mississippi
Emma Landfair born in 1868 in Mississippi

1880 Census, Launderdale County, Mississippi 242, 250. Beat No. 1
H. D. Landfair born in 1842 in Texas. His father was born in Louisiana and his mother, in Mississippi

J. L. Landfair born in 1844 in Alabama where her parents were born.
Lucy Landfair born in 1867 in Arkansas
Annie Landfair born in 1869 in Mississippi
Beulah Landfair born in 1872 in Mississippi
James Landfair born in 1874 in Mississippi
Octavia Landfair born in 1875 in Mississippi
Jessie Landfair born in 1876 in Mississippi
Wade Landfair born in 1878 in Mississippi

LUCY ELIZA LANDFAIR

Born: January 20, 1866, in Arkansas

Married: 1st: Solomon L. Ethridge on December 20, 1882.

2nd: Jesse Montgomery Vinson, who was born November 26, 1861, in Louisiana and died July 23, 1918 in West Carroll Parish. He is buried in Vinson's Cemetery across from Standifer Farm, west of Forrest, Louisiana.

Died: October 4, 1905, in West Carroll Parish, Louisiana

Children of Jesse Montgomery and Lucy Eliza (Landfair) Vinson: Earl Vinson, Wade Montgomery Vinson, Hiram D. Vinson, Jessie Vinson (Married a Mr. Morgan), Beulah Vinson.

1860 CENSUS CARROLL PARISH LOUISIANA JOE'S BAYOU AND MONTICELLO 216, 208
William J. P. Vinson born in 1816 in Tennessee
Providence A. Vinson born in 1829 in Louisiana
Peter J. Vinson born in 1853 in Louisiana
Martha E. Vinson born in 1856 in Louisiana
Etta Vinson born in 1857 in Louisiana
Fanny Vinson born in 1859 in Louisiana
17 slaves

1870 CENSUS WARD NO. 5 EAST CARROLL PARISH LOUISIANA 232, 232
Wm. J. P. Vinson born in 1816 in Tennessee
Providence Vinson born in 1829 in Louisiana
Peter Vinson born in 1853 in Louisiana
Martha E. Vinson born in 1855 in Louisiana
Etta Vinson born in 1858 in Louisiana
Jesse M. Vinson born in 1862 in Louisiana

WADE MONTGOMERY VINSON

Born: April 16, 1898, in Oak Grove, Louisiana

Married: Sabra Lee May on January 8, 1925, in Forest, Louisiana. She was born on June 4, 1908, in Mendenhall, Mississippi, the daughter of Lewis Robert and Maggie (Yates) May.

Children of Wade Montgomery and Sabra Lee (May) Vinson: Doris Maxine Vinson, Wade Montgomery Vinson, Jr., Betty Jean Vinson.

DORIS MAXINE VINSON

Born: November 20, 1925 in Oak Grove, Louisiana

Married: Frederick Alfred Outlaw, Jr., on February 21, 1946. He was born on October 1, 1918.

Children of Frederick Alfred and Doris Maxine (Vinson) Outlaw:

Peggy Ann Outlaw born on December 16, 1946, in St. Joseph, Louisiana

Jerry Lee Outlaw born on February 19, 1948, in Newellton, Louisiana

Cynthia Jean Outlaw born on November 16, 1953 in Newellton, Louisiana

WADE MONTGOMERY VINSON, JR.

Born: March 24, 1928, in Oak Grove, Louisiana

Married: Sue Hall on September 22, 1949

Children of Wade Montgomery and Sue (Hall) Vinson, Junior:

Michael Wade Vinson. Born May 15, 1950 in Newellton, Louisiana

David Vinson. Born April 10, 1952, in Newellton, Louisiana

Stephen Dale Vinson. Born November 6, 1954 in Newellton, Louisiana

BETTY JEAN VINSON

Born: October 12, 1933 in Oak Grove, Louisiana

Married: J. R. Olds on November 20, 1955

Children of J. R. and Betty Jean (Vinson) Olds:

Betty Ann Olds. Born September 16, 1956 in St. Joseph, Louisiana

BEULAH VINSON

Married: William Doyle on February 10, 1910

Children of William and Beulah (Vinson) Doyle:

Clifton Doyle. Born March 12, 1916.

Lucille Doyle. Born in 1821. Married a Mr. Grigsby.

Geraldine Doyle. Born in 1927. Married a Mr. Drocher.

ANNIE LEXINE LANDFAIR

Born: September 15, 1867 in Lauderdale County, Mississippi

Married: G. A. Simmons on April 17, 1884

Died: January 18, 1893

Children of G. A. and Annie Lexine (Landfair) Simmons:

Wilson Simmons. Died February 19, 1939 in Griffin, Georgia.

BEULAH EMMA LANDFAIR

Born: December 14, 1868, in Lauderdale County, Mississippi

Married: George Edward Breno on October 8, 1884, in Lauderdale County, Mississippi. Marriage Book B2, page 22. Mr.

Breno was born November 13, 1856, in Madison, Indiana, and died in 1921 in Fort Smith, Arkansas.

Died: November 10, 1940, in Tulsa, Oklahoma

Children of George Edward and Beulah Emma (Landfair) Breno:

Catherine Terica Breno. Born October 3, 1885, in Meridian, Mississippi. Died in Tulsa, Oklahoma.

Earl Edward Breno. Born March 19, 1888, in Meridian, Mississippi

Leo George Breno. Born January 24, 1890, in Meridian, Mississippi. Died September 28, 1900.

John Joseph Breno. Born October 24, 1901. Died that day.

Charles Francis Breno. Born November 11, 1905, Memphis, Tennessee

JAMES INGRAM LANDFAIR

Born: August 18, 1870, in Mississippi

Married: Rosa Pate, daughter of William T. and Mary Ellen (Miller) Pate.

Died: April 3, 1947, in Memphis, Tennessee. Buried in Collierville, Tennessee

Children of James Ingram and Rosa (Pate) Landfair:

Clara M. Landfair. Born May 1, 1898, in Shelby County, Tennessee

Elliot G. Landfair. Born June 2, 1892, in Mobile County, Alabama. Died November 18, 1893

Mabel A. Landfair. Born August 26, 1900, in Colbert County, Alabama. Married Merriel C. Boone on June 7, 1922

Mamie L. Landfair. Born January 29, 1894, in Alcorn County, Mississippi. Married Shirley B. Cooley on June 21, 1919.

Maude C. Landfair. Born October 23, 1902, in Shelby County, Mississippi. Married Darrell H. Dacus on April 23, 1921

OCTAVIA PRUDENCE LANDFAIR

Born: July 27, 1872, in Arkansas

Married: 1st: A. A. Nelson on April 9, 1886, in Lauderdale County, Mississippi. Marriage Book B2, page 217

2nd: William Henderson Dick on December 29, 1893, in Alcorn County, Mississippi

Died: December 8, 1898, in Alcorn County, Mississippi

Children of A. A. and Octavia Prudence (Landfair) Nelson:

Hiram Nelson

Children of William Henderson and Octavia Prudence (Landfair) Dick:

Katie May Dick. Born September 21, 1894, in Alcorn County, Mississippi. Married Edgar Scott on December 15, 1910. Married secondly, John Robert Sweat.

JESSE LAMAR LANDFAIR

Born: March 11, 1876, in Lauderdale County, Mississippi

Married: Ida Louella Webb on June 10, 1903. She was born on June 23, 1877, in Chester County, Tennessee, the daughter of William Ried Finis Ewing and Cynthia Anne (Elliott) Webb. She died on September 25, 1954, in Jackson, Mississippi

Died: February 13, 1950, in Jackson, Mississippi

Children of Jesse Lamar and Ida Louella (Webb) Landfair: Herman Golden Landfair, Hiram Lamar Landfair.

HERMAN GOLDEN LANDFAIR

Born: August 14, 1907, in Harperville, Mississippi

Married: Christine Sessums on July 7, 1940

Children of Herman Golden and Christine (Sessums) Landfair:

Vivian Landfair. Born July 7, 1947, in Miami, Florida

HIRAM LAMAR LANDFAIR

Born: January 26, 1909, in Harperville, Mississippi

Married: Hazel Marie Sims, the daughter of Mark Robbins and Jennie Irene (Holloway) Sims, on June 18, 1933, in Jackson, Mississippi. She was born January 17, 1910 in Arbo, Mississippi.

Children of Hiram Lamar and Hazel Marie (Sims) Landfair:

Betty Louise Landfair.

Robert Lamar Landfair. Born March 12, 1939, in Jackson, Mississippi

BETTY LOUISE LANDFAIR

Born: April 26, 1935, in Jackson, Mississippi

Married: Jack Milton McDonald, Jr., the son of Jack Milton and Marguerita Elsie (Herring) McDonald, Sr., on December 15, 1956, in Jackson.

Children of Jack Milton and Betty Louise (Landfair) McDonald, Jr:

Susan Elizabeth McDonald. Born December 29, 1958, in Jackson

WAID HIRAM LANDFAIR

Born: December 22, 1878, in Lauderdale County, Mississippi

Married: Agnes Brady

Children of Waid Hiram and Agnes (Brady) Landfair: Marguerite Landfair, Helen Landfair, Freddie Landfair, Gladys Evelyn Landfair.

GEORGE EDWARD LANDFAIR

Born: March 6, 1885, in Lauderdale County, Mississippi

Married: Birdie Thomas on May 3, 1910

Children of George Edward and Birdie (Thomas) Landfair: George Edward Landfair, Jr., Christine Landfair, Claude Landfair, Kathleen Landfair, Ruby Landfair.

IDA LANDFAIR

Born: 1853-1855 in Louisiana

Married: John Peter Guier

Children of John P. and Ida (Landfair) Guier: Robert Clifford Guier and Samuel Peter Guier

1880 CENSUS, WARD NO. 3, WEST CARROLL PARISH, LOUISIANA
J.P. Guier born in 1845 in Louisiana
I. Guier born in 1855 in Louisiana (wife)
R. Guier born in 1873 in Louisiana (son)
S. (?   ) Guier born in 1877 in Louisiana (son)
S.E. Lanfair born in 1835 in Alabama (mother)
F. Lanfair born in 1863 in Louisiana (son)
The parents of J. P. Guier were born in Kentucky. The father of I. Guier was born in Mississippi, while her mother was born in Alabama.

1860 CENSUS, WARD NO. 6, CARROLL PARISH LOUISIANA 974, 941
Peter J. Guier born in 1807 in Kentucky
Alice M. Guier born in 1843 in Louisiana
John P. Guier born in 1845 in Louisiana
31 slaves

1860 CENSUS WARD NO. 4 CARROLL PARISH LOUISIANA 189, 185
Philip Guier born in 1798 in North Carolina
George Guier born in 1842 in North Carolina
George and Philip Guier and John Lynch of Tennessee
owned 159 slaves

1850 CENSUS WESTERN DISTRICT CARROLL PARISH LOUISIANA 86, 86
Phillip Guier born in 1798 in North Carolina
Sarah Guier born in 1808 in South Carolina
Phillip Guier born in 1840 in Louisiana
George Guier born in 1842 in Louisiana
38 slaves

87, 87
George B. Guier born in 1825 in Kentucky
Phillapina Guier born in 1823 in Tennessee
Mary Guier born in 1849 in Louisiana
Martha Guier born in 1849 in Louisiana
Margaret Guier born in 1850 in Louisiana
Estate of George Guier: 41 slaves

88, 88
John P. Guier born in 1808 in Kentucky
Mary S. Guier born in 1833 in Louisiana

Elizabeth A. Guier born in 1834 in Louisiana
Allice M. Guier born in 1843 in Louisiana
John P. Guier born in 1846 in Louisiana
Mary A. Guier born in 1781 in North Carolina
53 slaves

1840 Census, Carroll Parish, Louisiana
John P. Guier 1 male born 1780-1790, 1 female born 1780-1790, 12 slaves

Philip Guier 1 male born 1800-1810, 1 female born 1800-1810 1 female born 1830-1835, 19 slaves

George Guier. 1 male born 1800-1810, 1 male born 1830-1835, 1 female born 1810-1820, 35 slaves

1830 Census, Ouachita Parish, Louisiana (Carroll Parish was later formed out of Ouachita Parish).

Philip Guier. 1 male born 1790-1800, 1 female born 1800-1810, 6 slaves
George Guier. 1 male born 1770-1780, 1 male born 1790-1800, 1 male born 1800-1810, 1 female born 1780-1790, 1 female born 1800-1810, 13 slaves

There is a lawsuit reported in 7 Louisiana Reports, page 103, in the year 1852 between Mary Ann Guier and Phillip Guier, Administrator, over certain slaves. John P. Guier is named as the deceased husband of Mary Ann Guier. George Guier and Emanuel Guier, both deceased, are named as their sons. It is stated that Emanuel Guier left no issue. The suit was in the Parish of Carroll.

ROBERT CLIFFORD GUIER

Born: December 31, 1875
Married: Eva Roberts on March 10, 1901.
Died: October 31, 1949
Children of Robert Clifford and Eva (Roberts) Guier:

Sammie Guier. Born December 18, 1908. Married Jess Hardin on August 26, 1940. No children.

Eunice M. Guier. Born March 26, 1905. Married Don C. Shattuck, son of Frank E. Shattuck of Sand Lake, Michigan, on April 3, 1943. No children.

Robert Clifford Guier, Jr. Born February 26, 1902. Died March 4, 1902.

Robert Clifford Guier, Jr. Born November 27, 1916.

Auda Jean Guier. Born March 21, 1924. Died November 23, 1926.

Ida Mae Guier.

George Clifton Guier. Born January 27, 1907, at Pioneer, Louisiana. Married Elizabeth Drew on August 20, 1936.

1875. Mrs. S.E. Landfair bought land from Ephraim L. Kent. Book P, Page 189. East Carroll Parish, Louisiana.

IDA MAE GUIER

Born: September 2, 1903

Married: 1st: Wiley Robert Thompson on November 17, 1923.
2nd: Bernard Castleman on September 16, 1942

Children of Wiley Robert and Ida Mae (Guier) Thompson:
Eva Jean Thompson.

EVA JEAN THOMPSON

Born: July 27, 1924

Married: Mac Rae Bracken in 1943

Children of Mac Rae and Eva Jean (Thompson) Bracken:
Tommy Bracken. Born June 1, 1945

ROBERT CLIFFORD GUIER, JR.

Born: November 27, 1916

Married: Elizabeth Lonsdorf on February 20, 1943

Children of Robert Clifford and Elizabeth (Lonsdorf) Guier, Jr.:
David Michael Guier. Born May 16, 1952

SAMUEL PETER GUIER

Born: 1877

Married: Pearl Stanfill on July 8, 1909

Died: March 26, 1927

Children of Samuel Peter and Pearl (Stanfill) Guier, Sr.: Mary Guier,
Lucille Guier, Tommie Sue Guier, Samuel Peter Guier, Jr.

Mrs. Sallie Guier, Saturday, 9 August, 1851, 43 years, died Bayou
Macon Hill, Carroll Parish, Louisiana, daughter of Joel and Susan
Wilson, born in the State of South Carolina, moved to Kentucky, and
married Philip Guier, Esq., 1829. (Monticello, Carroll Parish, La.)

The above obituary is found in the New Orleans CHRISTIAN ADVO-
CATE, a publication of the Methodist Church printed in New Orleans
1851-1855. The only existing copy is in the Methodist Room, Millsaps
College, Jackson, Mississippi. It was copied into the GENEALOGICAL
REGISTER of the Louisiana Genealogical and Historical Society,
Baton Rouge, Vol. VI, No. 4, August, 1959, page 28.

MARY ANICE GUIER

Born: May 7, 1910, in Pioneer, Louisiana

Married: Lothair Arthur Newman on July 3, 1930

Children of Lothair Arthur and Mary Anice (Guier) Newman:
Lothair Arthur Newman, Jr. Born September 29, 1931
Samuel Robert Newman. Born November 25, 1937

SAMUEL PETER GUIER, JR.

Born: September 1, 1921

Married: Pattie Jane Turnage on April 4, 1942

Children of Samuel Peter and Pattie Jane (Turnage) Guier, Jr.:

Samuel Keith Guier. Born December 26, 1947

Robert Stephen Guier. Born February 7, 1951

LUCILLE NORWOOD GUIER

Born: September 5, 1914

Married: Frank Dorval Gourdon on February 12, 1933

Children of Frank Dorval and Lucille Norwood (Guier) Gourdon:

Beverly Josephine Gourdon.

Charlotte Ann Gourdon. Born November 26, 1943.

BEVERLY JOSEPHINE GOURDON

Born: May 16, 1935

Married: Andrew Morris Bruce on June 1, 1957

TOMMIE SUE GUIER

Born: July 20, 1917

Married: Leland George Megason on November 13, 1945

Children of Leland George and Tommie Sue (Guier) Megason:

Bettye Kay Megason. Born April 14, 1949

George David Megason. Born April 27, 1950

JAMES L. LANDFAIR

1860 CENSUS CARROLL PARISH LOUISIANA

James L. Landfair born in 1837 in Mississippi

James L. Landfair is described as a "merchant".

J.L. Landfair. Pvt Co. H 3rd La Inf. En May 17, 1861, New Orleans, La. Present on Roll to June 30, 1861. Roll for July and Aug 1861 absent on detached service at Springfield, Missouri. Rolls from Sept 1861 to December 1861 state Present. Apptd 4th Corpl May 15, 1862. Rolls from July 1862 to Feb 1863 state Present. Federal Rolls of Prisoners of War, Captured and Paroled at Vicksburg, Mississippi, July 4, 1863.

See Andrew B. Booth, Records of Louisiana Confederate Soldiers, Vol 3, page 636.

1870 CENSUS BRADLEY COUNTY ARKANSAS

James Landfair born in 1837 in Mississippi

Sarah Landfair born in 1844 in South Carolina

William Landfair born in 1866 in Arkansas

Conveyances, Carroll Parish, Louisiana:

Book J, pages 491 and 492. James L. Landfair to William H. Lanfair, Land. Recorded January 17, 1859

Book J, page 492. William T. Oliver exchanged land with James L. Lanfair. Recorded and dated January 12, 1859

Book K, page 456. Absolem Normon to James L. Lanfair, a lot in the Town of Oak Grove. Dated and Recorded February 13, 1860.

WILLIAM H. LANDFAIR

Born: 1833 in Mississippi

Married: Mary Jackson on February 5, 1852. See Marriage Book "A" (1832-1858) East Carroll Parish, Louisiana, page 242.

Died: November 26, 1862

1860 Census, Ward No. 5 Carroll Parish Louisiana Oak Grove 629, 606
William H. Landfair born in 1833 in Mississippi
Mary Landfair born in 1836 in Tennessee
Jno. R. Landfair born in 1854 in Louisiana
Mary E. Landfair born in 1856 in Louisiana
Salie Landfair born in 1858 in Louisiana
3 slaves

1850 Census, Carroll Parish, Louisiana 148, 148
Drury Jackson born in 1810 in Georgia
Mary Jackson born in 1813 in Georgia
Mary Jackson born in 1836 in Alabama
John Jackson born in 1838 in Alabama
Benjamin Jackson born in 1840 in Alabama
Martha Jackson born in 1842 in Alabama
Sarah Jackson born in 1844 in Alabama
James Jackson born in 1847 in Alabama

1860 Census, Carroll Parish, Louisiana
Drura Jackson born in 1812 in Georgia
Mary Jackson born in 1813 in Georgia
John R. Jackson born in 1838 in Alabama
Benjamin H. Jackson born in 1840 in Alabama
Martha Jackson born in 1842 in Alabama
Sallie F. Jackson born in 1845 in Alabama
James M. Jackson born in 1846 in Alabama
Elizabeth P. Jackson born in 1852 in Louisiana
Seburn A. Jackson born in 1854 in Louisiana
Temperance J. Jackson born in 1857 in Louisiana

Conveyances, Carroll Parish, Louisiana
Book J, pages 491 and 492. Deed of land from James L. Lanfair to William H. Lanfair. Recorded and dated January 17, 1859

Book K, page 420. Samuel C. Waugh deeded slaves to William H.

Lanfair. (Three slaves for $2,800). Dated and recorded January 19, 1860.

Book K, page 413. William H. Landfair and wife, Mary Jackson, deed to David G. Bullen. Dated January 10 and recorded January 17, 1860

JOHN R. LANDFAIR

Born: 1854 in Louisiana

Married: Mary Scott who died March 10, 1905

Died: March 19, 1920

Children of John Robert and Mary (Scott) Landfair:

Alva Dora Landfair. Born August 29, 1886. Died August 14, 1908

Emma E. Landfair. Born January 21, 1885. Died October 3, 1887.

Floyd Landfair. Born July 1, 1889

Hutchins Landfair.

Infant Landfair. Born and died February 11, 1888

James H. Landfair. Born October 21, 1901. Died August 4, 1949

Maggie M. Landfair. Born December 20, 1897. Mrs. L.E. Watkins, Lawrence, Kansas

Millie Jane Landfair. Born May 17, 1883. Died October 2, 1887.

Robert C. Landfair. Born April 13, 1893. Tulsa, Oklahoma.

Ruby Landfair. Born November 27, 1899. Died October 1904.

Virgil H. Landfair. Born February 21, 1896. Dearborn, Michigan.

William Thomas Landfair. Born December 22, 1881. Died September 23, 1888.

HUTCHINS LANDFAIR

Born: August 21, 1891

Married: Sadie Ballard

Children of Hutchins and Sadie (Ballard) Landfair:

Gerald Ivy Landfair. Born January 18, 1932 in Little Rock, Arkansas.

James Ballard Landfair. Born August 21, 1921 in Fayetteville, North Carolina

Robert Hutchins Landfair. Born February 10, 1927, in Tillar, Arkansas

Thomas Edwin Landfair. Born June 16, 1935, in Little Rock, Arkansas

Information on John Robert Landfair family is from Hutchins Landfair of Tillar, Arkansas.

DAVID LANDFAIR

Born: 1795-1802

Married: Martha Benton on August 17, 1825,, in East Feliciana Parish, Louisiana.

Died: 1842 in Carroll Parish, Louisiana.

The following deeds are from the office of the Chancery Clerk, Lexington, Holmes County, Mississippi:

Deed Book C, page 161, 17 Jan 1835. Land in Holmes County sold by Samuel Simms and Priscella, his wife, to DAVID LANDFAIR.

Deed Book A, page 514, 20 Feb 1836. David *Lanfair* and wife, Martha, of Holmes County, sell land there (Original Grant 25416, Dec 18, 1835) to Patrick Mallory. Jackson Lanfair and Robin Suggs were witnesses.

Deed Book C, pages 200-201, 4 April 1838. David Lanfair and wife, Martha, sell Holmes County land to Joel Gullidge.

Deed Book E, page 154, 27 July 1838. David Lanfair of Holmes County subscribes to 100 shares of Mississippi Union Bank Stock and pledges 400 acres as security. Acknowledged by David Lanfair and Martha, his wife, on 31 May 1839.

Deed Book F, page 427, 2 Dec 1840, to correct an irregularity in a deed dated 6 April 1840. David Lanfair and Martha, his wife, sell 480 acres in Holmes County, including 100 head of cattle, 70 sheep, 9 of oxen, all household and kitchen furniture, farming utensils, including, a gin, etc. to Robert Gray.

Deed Book G, page 702, 15 June 1844. Thomas Lockhart and Minerva T., his wife, sold Holmes County land to MARTHA LANDFAIR, MARY E. LANDFAIR, AND James E. (?   ) LANDFAIR.

Deed Book I, page 485, 15 April 1848. The widow and minor heirs of David Landfair bought land from Thomas Lockhart. James H. Dulaney, Guardian of the Minor Heirs of David Landfair, sold this land to Benjamin C. Jordan, with whom Martha Landfair had married.

1830 CENSUS, MADISON COUNTY, MISSISSIPPI
David Landfare
1 male born 1800-1810
1 male born 1810-1815
1 male born 1825-1830
1 female born 1800-1810
2 females born 1825-1830
2 slaves

1840 CENSUS, MADISON COUNTY, MISSISSIPPI
David Landfair
1 male born 1800-1810
1 male born 1810-1820
2 males born 1835-1840
1 female born 1800-1810
2 females born 1835-1840
12 slaves

Martha Landfair, wife of David Landfair, is mentioned in East Carroll Parish, Louisiana, records as selling her deceased husband's plantation. He died in 1842 in Carroll Parish.

David Landfare (Landfair) is on the tax rolls of Madison County, Mississippi, for 1828 and 1829 (one slave), 1830 (two slaves), 1834 (4 slaves), 1835 (2 slaves). Latham (probably Lorenzo Latham) and Landfair (probably David) 52 slaves in 1835. David and Jackson Landfair were on the tax rolls of Holmes County, Mississippi, in 1837 (12 slaves), David Landfair there in 1840 (9 slaves), 1841 (9 slaves). Mrs. M. Landfare is on the tax rolls of Madison County, Mississippi, for 1843 and on the tax rolls of Holmes County, Mississippi, for 1846 (11 slaves).

1840 Census, East Feliciana Parish, Louisiana
D. Landfair
1 male born 1800-1810
2 males born 1835-1840
1 female born 1800-1810
1 female born 1830-1835
1 female born 1835-1840
1 slave

1850 Census, Holmes County, Mississippi 428, 428
Benj C. Jordan born in 1820 in South Carolina
Martha Jordan born in 1819 (?   ) in South Carolina
Mery E. Lanfair born in 1834 in Mississippi
James E. Lanfair born in 1840 in Mississippi
William W. Jordan born in 1830 in Tennessee
County Court Minutes, March 1829 to April 1833
Madison County, Miss
2 March 1829 David Landfair on Jury List No. 31
17 October 1831 David Landfair on Jury List No 8
Abstracts of Lands, Book 1, p 92
Grantor No. 39 October 15, 1832 United States to David Landfair NW¼ of NW¼, Sec 11, T9, R1E
Grantor No. 50. August 19, 1833. United States to David Landfair SW¼ of NW¼, Sec. 11, T9 R1E
Deed Book I, page 246
7 September, 1833

DAVID LANDFAIR OF MADISON COUNTY, MISSISSIPPI
TO
Robert V. Davis of the State of Louisiana
Consideration: $800. Land in Madison Co., Miss.
N½ of W½ of NW¼, Sec 11 T9, R1E, 40.24 acres
S½ of W½ of NW¼, Sec 11, T9, R1E, 40.23 acres
/s/ DAVID LANDFAIR, MARTHA LANDFAIR, HIS WIFE. Ack by signers 7 September, 1833

Book X, page 143, Clerk's Office, Clinton, East Feliciana Parish Louisiana Marriage Bond for DAVID LANFAIR AND MARTHA BENTON, 17 August, 1825

EUNICE LANDFAIR

JOHN WHEELER TO UNICE LAMPHEAR 17 January 1818. Bond

STATE OF LOUISIANA

PARISH OF FELICIANA

Know all men by these presents, that we, JOHN WHEELER and ADAM PALMER are well and firmly bound unto John H. Johnson, Judge of the Parish of Feliciana and his assigns, in the full sum of Five Hundred Dollars, lawful money of the United States, which payment will and truly to be made, we bind ourselves, our heirs and adminitrators and assigns firmly by these presents. Signed and sealed and dated this 17 day of January, A.D. 1818.

Whereas, the above bounded JOHN WHEELER, has this day obtained from the judge of the Parish aforesaid, a License to celebrate a marriage between him the said JOHN WHEELER and UNICE LAMPHEAR

Now the condition of the above obligation is such, that if there exists any impediment to the celebration of said marriage, this obligation to be void and of no effect, otherwise to remain in full force and virtue.

Wit: JOHN X WHEELER

   JOHN (?   ) AUSTIN   ADAM PALMER

The above is from the marriage records of the Parish of West Feliciana at St. Francisville.

The following is from Notarial Record B, 1818-1824, pages 231-232, West Feliciana Parish, Louisiana:

STATE OF LOUISIANA

PARISH OF FELICIANA

Be it remembered that on the day of the date hereof, before me, Wm. C. Wade, Judge of the Parish aforesaid, came and appeared JOHN WHEELER of the State and Parish aforesaid, of the one part and his wife, UNICE LANDFAIR WHEELER of the same State and Parish, of the other part and the said JOHN WHEELER declared and acknowledged that he had received the sum of $200 from ADAM PALMER, CURATOR OF THE SAID UNICE LANDFAIR in part of her extradotal property or share of her father's estate, that he had laid out and apportioned the same in the purchase of a tract of land hereinafter described now with a view to replace to her the said UNICE LANDFAIR WHEELER and restore to her an indemnity and equivalent for her hereditary effects thus alienated, the said JOHN WHEELER hath bargained sold and conveyed and by these presents doth bargain sell and convey unto the said UNICE LAND-FAIR WHEELER, her heirs and assigns forever a certain tract or parcel of land lying on the west branch of Thompson's Creek, containing 120 arpants fronting on said creek and bounded on one side by lands belonging to the Estate of Hugh Coyle and on the other by land belonging to John Hamilton and the said JOHN WHEELER for himself, his heirs and assigns the before recited lands and bargained premises to the said UNICE LANDFAIR WHEELER her heirs and assigns together with all and singular the rights, titles privileges and improvements thereunto belonging or in any-wise appertaining from and against himself the said JOHN WHEELER his heirs and assigns and against the claims of all persons whomsoever shall and will warrant and by these presents ever defend and the said UNICE LANDFAIR WHEELER accepts the sale so as above made. In witness of all of which the parties aforesaid hereunto sign their names, the one granting and the other accepting in presence of me, the said Judge and in that of John Hughes and ADAM PALMER attesting witnesses this 9th day of June, A.D., 1820 and at the request of the parties I grant these presents under my signature and the parish seal the day after.

JOHN X WHEELER   UNICE LANDFAIR X WHEELER

WIT: John Hughes   Adam Palmer

Wm C. Wade, Parish Judge

Truly recorded 9th June 1820

From page 4 of the same book is the sale of the above land by William Coyle to JOHN WHEELER.

1820 Census, Feliciana Parish, Louisiana

JNO. WHEELER

1 male born 1794-1804

1 female born 1794-1804

JACKSON LANDFAIR

Born: 1813-1819 in Louisiana

Married: 1st: Susan Adaline Cade, daughter of Robert Cade and his second wife, Violet Benton, granddaughter of John Cade of Robeson County, North Carolina, and Stephen Cade of Virginia. (See William Curry Harllee's KINFOLKS, Volume II, page 1171, where she is listed as marrying "Mr. Landfair, Meridian, Mississippi". She was born about 1822 in Williamsburg, South Carolina). Mr. Harllee's book was published by Searcy and Pfaff, 931 Lafayette Street in New Orleans in 1935. This information was sent by Mr. Lamar Landfair, a descendant of Robert Landfair and also of Stephen Cade of Virginia.

2nd: Araminta Pauline Gafford, who was born on June 18 1833. She had married first on July 22, 1850, to Nathaniel Fletcher Weatherby, who died on September 8, 1862. She married Jackson Landfair on October 19,

1865. After his death she married H.M. Merrit on December 28, 1876. She died in 1907.

Died: December 26, 1868

Children of Jackson and Susan Adaline (Cade) Landfair:

Agnes, David, Erasmus, George, James, Laura, Mary, Roberta, and Sally Landfair.

Children of Jackson and Araminta (Gafford) Landfair:

Jesse Owen and Lelia Landfair.

The following deeds are from the Office of the Chancery Clerk, Lexington, Holmes County, Mississippi:

Deed Book A, pages 513-514, 3 Oct 1836. Jackson *Lanfair* sells land to Patrick Mallory. Davis Lanfair and Robin Suggs are witnesses.

Deed Book C, page 242, 21 Aug 1838. Jackson Landfair and Adaline, his wife, sell land to David Lanfair.

Jackson Landfair is likely a son of Thomas and Ann (Carter) Landfair, either listed in the Landfair Succession as Jesse or Wellington.

Deed Book F, page 427, 31 Dec 1840. Jackson Lanfair and Susannah, his wife of Holmes County sold land there to James Andrews.

Deed Book I, page 751, 16 Feb 1849. Jackson Landfair and Susannah Adaline, his wife, of Holmes County sold land there to James W. Rogers.

Deed Book S, page 189, 13 Jan 1869. Sam'l W. Weems leased land to James W. Landfair of Holmes County.

Deed Book S, page 698, 9 Dec 1869. Laura Thornton and E.H. Thornton, her husband, M.R. Thornton and J.K. Thornton, her husband, D.B. Landfair, and A.P. Landfair, Guardian of Lula (Leila) and Jesse Landfair gave a quit claim deed to A.W. McDonald.

Deed Book S, page 702, 9 Dec 1869. Arminta P. Landfair of Holmes County sold land to A.W. McDonald.

Deed Book 1, page 466, 26 Nov 1870. W.R. Baker of Holmes County sold land to Mrs. A.P. Landfair

Deed Book 3, page 290. 12 July 1875. Mrs. A.P. Landfair of Holmes County sold land to the Trustees of the Methodist Episcopal Church South and Acona Grange No. 265.

1840 CENSUS, HOLMES COUNTY, MISSISSIPPI
Jackson Landfair
1 male born 1810-1820
1 female born 1820-1825
1 female born 1835-1840
1 slave

1850 CENSUS, HOLMES COUNTY, MISSISSIPPI
Jackson Landfair born in 1813 in Louisiana
Susan A. Landfair born in 1822 in South Carolina

Laura Landfair born in 1839 in Mississippi
Erasmus Landfair born in 1841 in Mississippi
James Landfair born in 1843 in Mississippi
Roberta Landfair born in 1845 in Mississippi
David Landfair born in 1848 in Mississippi
6 slaves

1860 CENSUS, HOLMES COUNTY, MISSISSIPPI
Jackson Landfair born in 1819 in Louisiana
Adaline Landfair born in 1821 in South Carolina
James Landfair born in 1845 in Mississippi
Mary Landfair born in 1847 in Mississippi
David Landfair born in 1849 in Mississippi
George Landfair born in 1855 in Mississippi
Sally Landfair born in 1857 in Mississippi
Agnes Landfair born in 1859 in Mississippi

1860 CENSUS, HOLMES COUNTY, MISSISSIPPI 367, 367
N.F. Weatherby born in 1818 in Georgia
Araminta Weatherby born in 1838 (?   ) in Alabama
Edward Weatherby born in 1852 in Mississippi
Peyton Weatherby born in 1854 in Mississippi
Thornton Weatherby born in 1856 in Mississippi
Benjamin Weatherby born in 1858 in Mississippi
George Weatherby born in 1859 in Mississippi

JESSE OWEN LANDFAIR

Born: November 26, 1868

Married: Lela Buckley, daughter of Alonzo and Henrietta Buckley, on October 10, 1893

Died: November 7, 1922, at Maple Dale Farm, Durant, Mississippi

Children of Jesse Owen and Lela (Buckley) Landfair:

Infant Daughter. Born August 6, 1894, Durant, Mississippi. Died July 31, 1935, at Durant.

Jesse Hubert Landfair. Born October 6, 1897.

Alton Buckley Landfair. Born August 26, 1904. Married Salma Davis (nee Blankenship)

See BIBLE RECORDS. COPIED BY MISSISSIPPI DAUGHTERS OF THE AMERICAN REVOLUTION. Compiled by Edith Burton Stevens, State Chairman. West Point, Mississippi 1937-1938.

LELIA LANDFAIR

Born: September 10, 1866

Married: Doctor W.F. Gresham on September 13, 1898. See Book H, page 385, Holmes County Marriage Records, Holmes County, Mississippi

Died: ca 1950

Children of Doctor W. F. and Lelia (Landfair) Gresham: Paul Gresham, William Gresham.

See BIBLE RECORDS COPIED BY MISSISSIPPI DAUGHTERS OF THE AMERICAN REVOLUTION. Compiled by Edith Burton Stevens, State Chairman. West Point, Mississippi 1937-1938.

CONFEDERATE WAR RECORDS OF LANDFAIRS, NATIONAL ARCHIVES INDEX

J.W. LANDFAIR. Private. Company G, 4 Regiment, Mississippi Infantry. Captured as a prisoner of war in Vicksburg, Mississippi, on July 4, 1863. Received as a prisoner of war on Ship Island in 1865. He had been wounded in battle earlier that year and admitted to Way Hospital. Also filed as G.W. Landfair.

ROBERT E. LANDFAIR. Residence: Holmes County, Mississippi. Fair complexion. Light hair. Grey Eyes. Five Feet Six and one-half inches.

R.E. LANDFAIR. Company G, 4 Mississippi Infantry. Captain T.P. Nelson's Company. Enlisted Durant, Mississippi Also filed R. E. *Lanfair*

R.J. *LANFAIR* Private. Company E, 26 Arkansas Infantry. Morgan's Battalion. Enlisted Selma, Drew County, Arkansas.

J.L. LANDFAIR. Private. Company H, 3 Louisiana Infantry

JAMES C. LANDFAIR. Private. Company D, 1 Mississippi Light Infantry.

J.C. LANDFAIR. Private. Company G, 4 Mississippi Infantry. Also filed J.C. *Lamfair.*

JAMES C. LANDFAIR. Private. Company D, 1 Mississippi Light Artillery. Enlisted April 10, 1862, in Lexington, Mississippi Captured in Vicksburg, Mississippi, on July 4, 1863. Residence: Holmes County, Mississippi

SHAW

WILLIAM SHAW

Born: ca 1760

Married: Mary Anney Weekley on November 3, 178–

Died: 1840-1850

Children of William and Mary Anney (Weekley) Shaw:
Catharine Shaw; Mary Shaw; Susannah Shaw; William Shaw, Junior; Anastasia Shaw.

The old Shaw home, no longer standing, according to the recollection of Mrs. Laura Weis Whitehead, used to be near where the Old Shaw-McHugh Cemetery is. As children, they found bits of broken flowered china near there, that had been plowed up when farming.

The marriage date of William Shaw and Mary Ann Weekley is found in an old Roman Catholic Prayer Book, along with the date of birth of Mary Shaw. The old book belongs to Mrs. Elizabeth Anastasia Shaw Weis.

May Wilson McBee NATCHEZ COURT RECORDS, 1767-1805. Vol II, page 398. P. 525. Claim 514. Mississippi Territory. Jefferson County. 18 February 1804. Esther Hackler, agent and attorney for Jacob Jrokel to WILLIAM SHAW, 475 acres on the north fork of Cole's Creek actually setteled and cultivated by J. Jrokel, Sr., in 1797, being the tract that WILLIAM SHAW now lives on, for $50. Wit. John Dennis and Conrad Young.

1820 CENSUS, EAST BATON ROUGE PARISH, LOUISIANA
William Shaw
1 male born before 1775
1 male born 1794-1804
1 male born 1802-1804
2 males born 1810-1820
1 female born before 1775
1 female born 1775-1794
2 females born 1794-1804

1830 CENSUS, EAST BATON ROUGE PARISH, LOUISIANA
William Shaw
1 male born 1760-1770
1 male born 1800-1810
2 males born 1815-1820
1 male born 1815-1820
1 female born 1750-1760
1 female born 1780-1790
1 female born 1815-1820

1840 CENSUS, EAST BATON ROUGE PARISH, LOUISIANA
William Shaw
1 male born 1750-1760
2 males born 1800-1810
1 male born 1810-1820
1 male born 1820-1825
1 female born 1780-1790
1 female born 1830-1835

Thomas Martin born in the Kingdom of Ireland, the son of Hugh and Mary Martin, bequeathed a mare to William Shaw on January 20, 1802. See Spanish West Florida Records, Volume 5, page 163.

William Shaw and Mariamelia Shaw described as inhabitants of his majesty's dominions in Natchez and this district***William and Mary Shaw depose in 1809 that they have known John Savage for 18 years, that he was a native of Ireland, the County of Down, Province of Ulster, that he never married and that he had no heirs in America or Europe. Philip McHugh administered the estate. Hugh Shaw is mentioned. Spanish West Florida Records, Volume 16, page 158.

Mary A. Shaw, wife of William Shaw, died in 1837. See Probate Records, Number 580, Old Series, Number 2, East Baton Rouge Parish Louisiana.

March 24, 1804. Claim No. 161 by William Shaw, Original Claimant of 600 acres of land in St. Helena Parish under Spanish Patent issued by J. Morales July 1, 1800. The land was surveyed by C. Trudeau and was cultivated from 1800 to 1814. See American State Papers, Public Lands, Documents Legislative and Executive of the Congress of the United States, Volume 3, page 42, Published by Gales and Seaton in Washington in 1834.

William Shaw filed application number 303 on December 31, 1807, for 320 acres of land on the waters of Cole's Creek. Ibid, except Volume 2, page 248.

" I, Don Carlos Trudeau, Royal and Particular Surveyor of the Province of Louisiana, etc., certify that there was measured and bounded in favor of and in the presence of WILLIAM SHAW and with the assistance of the witnesses and the neighboring colonists a tract of land of 600 arpents plain measured by the perch of the City of Paris of 18 Royal feet of the said city and 100 perches plain to the arpent according to the Agrarian Custom in this province which tract of land situated in the District of Baton Rouge of 8 miles to the east of the River Mississippi and 12 miles to the N.N.E. of the fort is bounded on the south by land of the widow O'Connor, on the west by that of Cornelius Shaw and on the other sides by lands Royal of the Domain of his Majesty—the boundaries are parallel and forming right angles running N and S and E and W by the needle without noticing its variations this being 8 degrees and 30 minutes to the N E in which boundaries there were designated for the trees and landmarks represented on the plan which serve for landmarks natural and artificial and the survey was made in virtue of the decree of the then Governor-General Don Manuel Gayoso de Lemos to him directed, dated the 7th day of November 1798 and that all the aforesaid may appear I give the present with the figurative plan which preceded forward in conformity with the returns of survey of the 17 and 18 of May of the last year. The minutes were signed:

Mr. Ricardo Deval, Syndic, Cornelius Shaw, John Savage, Christofal Bolling, and Don Vicente Pintado, Surveyor, all of which I accredited. July 1, 1800, Carlos Trudeau. Reg. in Book B, Vol 145, under No. 1427 of the dispatch of Survey.

Carlos Trudeau

Cert. No. 4, Claim 171, Section 39, T 5, R 1 E.

In pursuance of the Act of Congress passed 3d March, 1819, entitled "An Act for Adjusting the Claims to Land and Establishing Land Offices in the District East of the Island of New Orleans" we certify that Claim No. 171 in the report of the Commissioners marked A, Claimed by William Shaw, Original Claimant, William Shaw is recognized by the said Act as valid against any claim on the part of the United States or right derived from the United States. The said claim being for 600 arpents, situated in the parish of East Baton Rouge and claimed under Spanish Patent dated (date not given)

Given under our hands this 23d day of November, 1819.

Signed:

Charles S. Cosby, Reg. and Fulwar Skipwith, Recv.

Attested:

A. Nevault, Clerk

See the Book "Spanish Land Titles" in the State Land Office Baton Rouge, Louisiana

William Shaw, Senior, and William Shaw, Junior, witnessed a deed in which Philip McHugh, Senior, sold land to Jeremiah McHugh, Mary McHugh, and Catharine McChristy. Filed September 30, 1833. See Judges Book O, page 176, East Baton Rouge Parish, Louisiana.

William Shaw, Senior, sells land to his son William Shaw, Junior. The land had been granted him by the Spanish Government. Mary Anney Shaw was named as the wife of William Shaw, Senior. William Shaw, Junior reached his majority between signing the deed on October 24, 1823, and November 20, 1824. See Judges Book L, page 255, East Baton Rouge Parish, Louisiana.

William Shaw, Senior, sells land to Mrs. Susannah McHugh. Deed filed June 11, 1831. See Judges Book I, page 421, East Baton Rouge Parish, Louisiana.

William Shaw, Senior sells land to his daughter, Mrs. Susannah

McHugh, widow. Deed filed December 10, 1823. See Judges Book L, page 311, East Baton Rouge Parish, Louisiana.

Inhabitants of the County of Feliciana to John Ballinger 1811

To Col John Ballinger

Sir: The undersigned inhabitants of the County of Feliciana in the Territory of Orleans in behalf of themselves and of a respectable number of the people inhabiting the different Parishes of the said County, authorize you as our Agent to represent to the general Government of the United States in such manner as you may find eligible and convenient, our situation and wants, our attachment to the Government of our country and the grievances which we wish and hope may be redressed consistently with the honor and Interest, as well as the Policy of that Government—We depend much on your Judgment both as to the subjects and manner of this representation and will only request that we may neither be exhibited as refractory and turbulent, or so abject as to be insensible of our rights as American citizens—The admission of the Territory of Orleans into the Union with the limits and boundaries under the late Act of Congress; Great Political Consideration may have required the division of Louisiana but the faith of Government stands too seriously pledged to admit of subdivisions without our consent;—the subjecting the land claims of the honest cultivators of the soil who settled here since the year 1803 to the same laws which have been provided for that part of Louisiana since that year; and leaving many of our citizens who made large advances of money, property and personal service to effect our emancipation from foreign oppression, without any hope of remuneration—

Relying on your prudence and perseverance in the discharge of this trust we are your fellow citizens.

Among the signatories is WILLIAM SHAW.

See Carter TERRITORIAL PAPERS OF THE UNITED STATES Volume 9, Orleans Territory, pages 970-972

SHAW-McHUGH CEMETERY IMPROVEMENTS WILL BE VIEWED BY FAMILY ON SUNDAY

The historic Shaw-McHugh cemetery near Zachary which has been undergoing a process of improvement since the beginning of this year, will be inspected this week end by the members of the families whose forefathers and relatives have been buried there for many generations.

The date and time set for the viewing of the work done on the cemetery has been set for Sunday, May 19, at 4 p.m.

A new fence has been constructed and the cemetery has been enlarged by means of a land trade made with the owners of property adjacent to it. A landscaping project is also underway, but is only partially completed.

Like many of the other family burial grounds of its type, the Shaw-McHugh cemetery has its beginning back in the late 1790's when a plot of land was granted by William Shaw for the purpose of a cemetery.

Many families, some of whose names are almost extinct in the Zachary-Baker area, have used the Shaw-McHugh cemetery as a burial place for several generations, and some of the old marble tomestones which bear the mark of the elements give mute testimony to the historical significance of the place. There are many unmarked graves, however.

The burial ground was recently incorporated under the name of the Shaw-McHugh Cemetery, Inc. It is located near the old Weis road about two miles southeast of Zachary.

The above is from the May 16, 1957, issue of THE PLAINSMAN, Zachary, Louisiana. In the paper is a picture of the cemetery and a gravestone with the following caption:

Above: The Shaw-McHugh cemetery is photographed in three separate shots by Clarence Shaw.

Right: The monument marking the graves of two McHugh men who died in the service of their country. John McHugh, son of Philip and Maria McHugh and husband of Susana Shaw, served as a private in the U.S. Army during the War of 1812. He fought in the Battle of New Orleans on January 8, 1815, and died in service a short time later. John A. McHugh, son of William B. McHugh and Helen J. Hart, was a private in World War II. He was killed on Luzon on April 18, 1945. The mounment was erected in 1946 by descendants of the first-named John McHugh.

In the May 19, 1957, Sunday edition of the Baton Rouge, Louisiana, MORNING ADVOCATE is a photograph of the SHAW-McHUGH Cemetery with the following caption:

FAMILY CEMETERY — Familes whose relatives h a v e been buried in the Shaw-McHugh Cemetery since the 1790's will gather at the cemetery shown above, at 4 p.m. today to inspect the improvements which have been made. The historic old cemetery, two miles southeast of Zachary, was recently enlarged and a landscaping project has been begun. Friends of the families who live in the Baker-Zachary area are also asked to attend.

"Cornelio Shaw" was a resident of the District of Santa Catalina of the District of Natchez under the Spanish Dominion. See Census of 1792 in the Mississippi Historical Society Publications Centenary Series Volume 1 Edited by Dunbar Rowland.

24 March 1804. Claim No. 186 by Thomas Lilly and Co. to 400 acres of land in Baton Rouge originally claimed by Cornelius Shaw. The land was surveyed on October 15, 1798 by V. Pintado. See American

State Papers, Public Lands, Documents Legislative and Executive of the Congress of the United States, Volume 3, page 43. Published by Gales and Seaton in Washington in 1834.

Catharine Shaw claimed land originally settled in 1810. Ibid, page 506. Cornelius Shaw and his wife, Catharine, bought 200 acres of land on Fairchild's Creek from John Reed. August 20, 1798. See Natchez Court Records 1767-1805. The May Wilson McBee Collection, Volume 2

Cornelius Shaw and wife, Catharine, sold the above land to Abijah Hunt on December 5, 1798. Ibid.

Cornelius Shaw joined as party plaintiff in suit of creditors against William Henderson. August 10, 1794. Ibid
Catharine Shaw donated land to Juliana McGill, the wife of John McGill. Filed June 27, 1821. See Judges Book I, page 251, East Baton Rouge Parish, Louisiana.

Land of Cornelius Shaw and land of Philip McHugh mentioned on page 163 of the Spanish West Florida Records, Volume 5.
Pedro Hernandez sued Catharine Shaw for rent. And she, in defense, proved her husband built the house and had not been paid. See Spanish West Florida Records, Volume 17.

The following persons sold land which they inherited from William Shaw, Senior: James C. Jackson and his wife, Mary Northam, Mary Shaffett of East Feliciana Parish, Daniel Shaffett and his wife, Mary Houston, Catharine Shaffett, wife of John Brashears, and William Shaffett. Conveyance Book C, page 463, East Baton Rouge Parish, Louisiana. 31 Dec. 1850.

The following persons are listed as heirs of Philip McHugh: Jeremiah McHugh, Jane McHugh, the widow Neville, Thomas McHugh, Mary McHugh, John A. McHugh, son of John McHugh, deceased, Catharine McHugh, the widow McChristy. Probate Records, number 533, Old Series, number 2, East Baton Rouge Parish, Louisiana. Filed July 18, 1836.

William Shaw, Junior, was undertutor to Mary Ann and Rachel Landfair. Sheriff's Book C, page 26, East Baton Rouge Parish, Louisiana. Oath taken November 25, 1837.

John A. McHugh mentioned in deed as son of John A. McHugh and Susannah McHugh. Notary Book O page 24, East Baton Rouge Parish, Louisiana. Filed Augst, 1840.

William Shaw, Junior, and his wife, Ellen Neville Shaw, sold to John A. McHugh land which was originally granted to William Shaw, Senior, by the King of Spain.
Conveyance Book C, page 267, East Baton Rouge Parish, Louisiana. Filed February 13, 1850.

William Shaw Junior was given land by his father William Shaw Senior in return for his promise to support his father and mother, William and Mary A. Shaw. Judges Book P, page 137, East Baton Rouge Parish, Louisiana. Filed June, 1836.

William Daniel Shaw, Mrs. Elizabeth Shaw, wife of Joseph C. Wise, and Mrs. Laura Shaw, wife of Jacob Borskey, brothers and sisters and nearest relatives of Thomas Jefferson McHugh renouce his succession in favor of the following McHughes: James, David, Thomas E., Mrs. Susannah, wife of Simeon Carmena. Conveyance Book 41, page 325, East Baton Rouge Parish, Louisiana. December 14, 1908.

ANASTASIA SHAW

Born: 1793 in Mississippi

Married: Jeremiah McHugh

Died: 1860-1870

Children of Jeremiah and Anastasia (Shaw) McHugh:

Philip McHugh; Ann McHugh; Jeremiah McHugh; Mary McHugh; Elizabeth McHugh; Joseph McHugh, died September 4, 1903, unmarried; David McHugh, died October 2, 1897, unmarried; Thomas J. McHugh, died in 1908, unmarried.

These were the children of Philip and Mary McHugh:

Jeremiah McHugh. Married Anastasia Shaw.

John McHugh. Married Susannah Shaw.

Jane McHugh. Married James Neville. Their daughter, Ellen Neville married William Shaw, Jr.

Catharine McHugh. Married a Mr. McChristy. They had a son, John.

Philip McHugh, Jr.

Mary McHugh.

Senor Don Manuel Gayoso de Lemos
Brigadier of His Majesty's Army

Governor-General and Vice Patron of the Province of Louisiana and West Florida

Inspector of the Troops and Militia of His Majesty etc.

PHILIP McHUGH, an old inhabitant of Natchez, of Irish Nationality, professing the Roman Catholic and Apostolic Church presented himself before me and said that his family which consisted of his wife and seven children desired to continue under the jurisdiction of His Most Catholic Majesty (by the Grace of God) and further:

He supplicates Your Worship to accede to him a grant of ground situated in the District of Baton Rouge that your Worship would consider sufficient to cultivate enough to produce the products of subsistence.

Don Vicente Sebastian Pintado,

Surveyor-General of West Florida for His Majesty

THIS IS TO CERTIFY: On this day the 22nd of January, 1805, was surveyed and marked for PHILIP McHUGH a piece of flat ground of 550 arpents measured by means of a Parisian perch equal to 18 feet (of Parisian measure) being 100 perches of area equal to one square arpent of area, as usual, gradetic measurement utilized in the Province; the ground being situated in the District of Baton Rouge in the place called San Juan, in the suburb commonly known as de Buhler, less than 8 miles from the east bank of the Mississippi to the western edge of this ground and to the middle of the ground 14 English miles from the Fort at Baton Rouge due north; surrounding this property is: northwest: the property of Don Santiago Roual and Don Miguel de Armes and Don Christobal, on the northeast: by the heirs of Patricio Christobal and Edward Sullivan, on the east: The property of Don Christobal and Don Miguel de Armes spoken of above, being on the west and with that of Thomas Breman completes the survey as shown preceding, in which is also shown the description of the ground and dimensions together northeast. At this time the limits of the property are marked by trees and stone bench marks.

These surveys were made by a decree dated 19th of October, 1804, by Don Vicente Folch Teran, Colonel of the Army and Governor of the Province, as ordered by his Royal Highness. The interested party is ordered to stay on the premises until all arrangements in connection with the title are finished. This survey has to be presented at the proper time to the Intendant General of this Providence after the property has been surveyed and marked so that Mr. McHugh will not have trouble in taking possession. GIVEN AT THE FORT OF BATON ROUGE.

9 January 1809.   VICENTE SEBASTIAN PINTADO

The land described above is still in the McHugh Family. Mr. and Mrs. Marshall Bond of Zachary are presently (1959) the owners. Mrs. Bond is a direct descendant of Philip McHugh through Jane (Jean) McHugh who married James Neville in Rapides Parish on March 17, 1806.

Letter from the Bishop of Natchez to Lena Carmena, dated April 1, 1946:

"From entries in Records of Baptisms of Whites, as kept by the priests of the Spanish Jurisdiction:

Page 39: May 4, 1795, Baptized Philip, son of Philip and Mary McHugh, aged one month.

Page 73: May 9, 1797 Catharine (born May 6, 1797) Daughter of Philip and Mary McHugh, both natives of Ireland, was baptized.

William and Mary Ann Shaw are said by older members of the family to have come with the McHughs and Sullivans down the Mississippi River from Pennsylvania on a flat boat. At night they would draw up along the river bank where wild geese could have been killed, had they not feared the Indians would hear the gun shots.

Camp Jackson
Six Miles Below Orleans
January 29, 1815

Most Beloved Wife:

I will inform you that I am tolerably well but have been a good part of my time very unwell, being exposed to all kinds of weather, but I hope that this scribble will find you and my little boy well and likewise all our friends. Daniel was taken sick when we first came to New Orleans and I heard he was discharged from the hospital on the 11th of this month. We have not heard from him since and do not know what has become of him if he has not gone home.

The British have retreated and there is no more to be heard of them and expect I shall see you for General Thomas says he will be discharged in a few days. It seems as if Divine Providence had interposed for our safety for on the 8th of this month the British came rushing on us when 3500 of them were killed and wounded and on our side there were 6 killed and 7 wounded. It was a shocking sight to see cut and mangled as the British were, for the ground was covered with the slain.

When I am so happy as to see you again, will tell you the particulars, so I will conclude and subscribe,

Your affectionate husband,
JOHN McHUGH

A homemade table that belonged to John and Susannah (Shaw) McHugh is still in existence. His son, John A. McHugh and his bride, Amanda Bridges, ate their wedding supper on this table. There is also in existence the arithmetic book which belonged to John McHugh.

The following is from NATCHEZ COURT RECORDS, 1767-1805 the May Wilson McBee Collection, Vol II
(page 155)

Natchez. '8 November 1797. Dennis Collins of Natchez to Philip McHugh of the same place, a tract of 248 arpents near Cole's Creek, bounded by John Fowler, Benjamin Newman, Christian Bingamin, and Alexander McIntosh as set forth in titles September 1, 1795. Witnesses: Nathaniel Tomlinson and Thomas Foster.

Daniel Fowler represents that by the death of his brother he was sole heir of his father. He asked that Gerard Brandon (father of Governor

Gerard C. Brandon of Mississippi) be appointed his guardian, as he was a minor in 1797. Philip McHugh took the Inventory of his father's estate. Among the assests was a note of James Highlands.

Jeremiah McHugh and his wife, Anastasia Shaw, with their children: Betsy, Polly, Joseph, David, Jeremiah, Jeff are buried in the Johnson Cemetery at Zachary, near the "Big McHugh" Place, so called because all these McHughs were large people. Only their son, Philip, married. Joseph, Jeff, and Dave were members of the Plains Masonic Lodge. David McHugh was a 1st Sergeant in Company F3d. Louisiana Cavalry, CSA, and T. J. McHugh was a Sergeant in the same unit.

Spanish West Florida Records:

Volume VIII, page 337

Philip McHugh and Charles Weekly witness the deed of Nehemiah Powers to John Kennard.

Volume XVIII, page 325

Cristoval de Armas, Captain of the Provincial Militia, a merchant of this post, sells to Pierre Allain 3, 150 arpents of land, bounded by the land of Gilbert Andrew, Thomas Calvit, Cornelius Shaw, Thomas Urquhart, Adam Boyd, David Bradford, Nicholas Courtois, Jacques Raoul, Philip McHugh, Patrick Sullivan and John Skinner.

Volume XVI, page 152

Philip McHugh was a witness to the Partition of the Property of Patrick Sullivan.

Volume XVI, page 153

Philip McHugh administered the Succession of John Savage, a bachelor residing in the District of Natchez.

Volume XVI, page 154

In a letter to Don Carlos Duhault de Lassus, who succeeded Don Carlos de Grand Pre as Governor, Thomas Lilley, a syndic of Springfield, writes in connection with the John Savage Estate, "I have known Mr. McHugh for some years and am confident that he will do the strictest justice to any charge that may be committeed to him." 1809.

1820 CENSUS, EAST BATON ROUGE PARISH, LOUISIANA

Romaldo Carmena

1 male born before 1775; 1 male born 1794-1804; 1 male born 1804-1810; 2 males born 1810-1820; 1 female born 1804-1810; 1 female born 1810-1820.

Philip McHugh

1 male born before 1775; 1 male born 1775-1794; 1 male born 1784-1804; 1 female born before 1775; 1 male born 1775-1794; 2 females born 1794-1804.

Jeremiah McHugh

1 male born 1775-1794; 2 males born 1810-1820; 1 female born 1775-1794; 1 female born 1810-1820.

1830 CENSUS, EAST BATON ROUGE PARISH, LOUISIANA
Philip McHugh
1 male born 1740-1750; 1 male born 1780-1790; 2 males born 1790-1810; 1 female born 1750-1760; 1 female born 1790-1800.

1840 CENSUS, EAST BATON ROUGE PARISH, LOUISIANA
Jeremiah McHugh
1 male born 1780-1790; 2 males born 1810-1820; 1 male born 1820-1825; 2 males born 1825-1830; 2 males born 1835-1840; 1 female born 1790-1800; 1 female born 1820-1825; 1 female born 1825-1830; 6 slaves.

1830 CENSUS, EAST BATON ROUGE PARISH, LOUISIANA
McHugh (The first name is not given in the census record, but this is quite obviously the family of Jeremiah McHugh.)
1 male born 1780-1790; 1 male born 1810-1815; 1 male born 1815-1820; 2 males born 1820-1825; 1 male born 1825-1830; 1 female born 1790-1800; 1 female born 1815-1820; 1 female born 1825-1830.

1850 CENSUS, EAST BATON ROUGE PARISH, LOUISIANA
Catharine McChristy born in 1800 in Mississippi
John McChristy born in 1828 in Louisiana
Mary McHugh born in 1795 in Pennsylvania
A. McHugh born in 1793 in Mississippi
Philip McHugh born in 1814 in Louisiana
Ann McHugh born in 1822 in Louisiana
Jeremiah McHugh born in 1822 in Louisiana
Mary McHugh born in 1821 in Louisiana
Elizabeth McHugh born in 1827 in Louisiana
Joseph McHugh born in 1829 in Louisiana
David McHugh born in 1832 in Louisiana
Thomas McHugh born in 1837 in Louisiana

1860 CENSUS, EAST BATON ROUGE PARISH, LOUISIANA
Anastasia McHugh born in 1793 in Mississippi
Mary McHugh born in 1825 in Louisiana
Elizabeth HcHugh born in 1830 in Louisiana
Jeremiah McHugh born in 1830 in Louisiana
Joseph McHugh born in 1829 in Louisiana
Thos. J. McHugh born in 1829 in Louisiana
3 slaves

Philip McHugh born in 1814 in Louisiana
Kezia McHugh born in 1821 in Louisiana
23 slaves

John McChristy born in 1828 in Louisiana
Catharine McChristy born in 1797 in Mississippi
15 slaves

1870 CENSUS, EAST BATON ROUGE PARISH, LOUISIANA
J. McHugh born in 1823 in Louisiana
Joseph McHugh born in 1834 in Louisiana
David McHugh born in 1836 in Louisiana
T. J. McHugh born in 1838 in Louisiana
Elizabeth McHugh born in 1830 in Louisiana
1880 CENSUS, EAST BATON ROUGE PARISH, LOUISIANA
4th Ward, 788, 820
Thomas McHugh born in 1838 in Louisiana
Dave McHugh, Brother, born in 1833 in Louisiana
Jerry McHugh, Brother, born in 1828 in Louisiana
Joe McHugh, Brother, born in 1831 in Louisiana

PHILIP McHUGH

Born: 1814 in Louisiana

Married: Kezia Ann Sullivan

Died: 1865-1867

Philip McHugh to Kezia Ann Sullivan, wife of Philip McHugh
Book MN, page 63, July 24, 1865, East Baton Rouge Parish
Book SK, page 435, October 12, 1865, East Baton Rouge Parish
Book SM, page 89, January 25, 1866, East Baton Rouge Parish
Book U, page 38, October 11, 1865, East Baton Rouge Parish
Marriage Book 8, page 249, East Baton Rouge Parish,
1867 Keziah A. McHugh and George W. Burgess

Book JP, page 256, East Baton Rouge Parish, Anastasia McHugh to
Simeon Beckham Renein, December 17, 1836 shows Anastasia was the
wife of Jeremiah McHugh.

CATHARINE SHAW

Married: William Landfair

Died: October, 1833, East Baton Rouge Parish, Louisiana

Children of William and Catharine (Shaw) Landfair: Mary Ann
Landfair, Rachel Landfair.

MARY SHAW

Born: January 15, 1784, in Louisiana

Married: John Shaffett

Died: Before 1829

Children of John and Mary (Shaw) Shaffett: Catharine Shaffett,
Mary A. Shaffett, William Shaffett, Daniel Shaffett, John C. Shaffett.

Claim No. 75 by John Shaffet, Original Claimant, on September 2,
1806, of 300 acres in Baton Rouge under patent issued by Carlos de
Grandpre. Cultivated 1796-1814.

AMERICAN STATE PAPERS, PUBLIC LANDS, Documents Legislative and Executive of the Congress of the United States, Volume 3, page 51. Published in Washington by Gales and Seaton in 1834.

John Shaffet claimed land in Baton Rouge which he cultivated in 1814. Ibid, page 505.

John Shaffet had a satisfactory settlement claim to land in East Feliciana Parish, Louisiana, which he had purchased and cultivated in 1812.

Claims to land in the Saint Helena District, No. 462, 19th Congress, 1st Session. AMERICAN STATE PAPERS, Documents of the Congress of the United States in relation to the public lands, Vol. 4, page 444. Published in Washington by Gales and Seaton in 1859.

1830 CENSUS, EAST BATON ROUGE PARISH, LOUISIANA
John Shaffet
1 male born 1770-1780; 1 male born 1800-1810; 1 male born 1810-1815; 1 male born 1820-1825; 2 females born 1810-1815.

In 1859 William and Catharine Shaffet sued James C. Jackson to recover land belonging to their mother, Mary Shaw (dead in 1829) and their father, John Shaffet (dead in 1859). The land was in East Feliciana Parish. William Shaffet was born in July, 1825, and Catharine Shaffet was born in 1817 or 1818. James C. Jackson had married a sister of the plaintiffs. See Law Report in 14 Louisiana Annual 154.

Probate No. 490. O.S. No. 2, East Baton Rouge Parish, Louisiana. Succession of John Shaffett. Daniel Shaffett mentioned as son. September 22, 1835.

1840 CENSUS, EAST FELICIANA PARISH, LOUISIANA
J. C. Jackson
1 male born 1790-1800; 1 male born 1825-1830; 1 male born 1830-1835; 1 female born 1810-1820; 14 slaves.

1850 CENSUS, EAST FELICIANA PARISH, LOUISIANA
James C. Jackson born in 1800 in Virginia; Mary A. Shaffett born in 1814 in Louisiana.

1860 CENSUS, EAST FELICIANA PARISH, LOUISIANA
J. C. Jackson born in 1800 in Virginia; M. A. Jackson born in 1824 in Kentucky (sic); Geo Jackson born in 1852 in Louisiana; J. L. Jackson born in 1853 in Louisiana (male); M. E. Jackson born in 1855 in Louisiana (female); A. Jackson born in 1856 in Louisiana; J. C. Jackson was the Recorder of East Feliciana Parish.

1870 CENSUS, EAST FELICIANA PARISH, LOUISIANA
J. C. Jackson born in 1800 in Louisiana (sic); M. A. Jackson born in 1823 in Louisiana; Geo Jackson born in 1852 in Louisiana; Jas Jackson born in 1854 in Louisiana; M. E. Jackson born in 1856 in Louisiana (female); J. D. Jackson born in 1861 in Louisiana; Emily Jack-

son born in 1864 in Louisiana; T. Lee Jackson born in 1867 in Louisiana.

CATHARINE SHAFFETT

Born: 1817-1818 in Louisiana

Married: John Brashear

Children of John and Catharine (Shaffett) Brashear: Green Brashear, Philip Brashear, Robert Brashear, Susan Brashear.

1830 CENSUS, EAST BATON ROUGE PARISH, LOUISIANA
John Brashear
1 male born 1790-1800; 1 male born 1815-1820; 1 male born 1820-1825; 1 male born 1825-1830; 1 female born 1800-1810; 2 females born 1820-1825; 1 female born 1825-1830; 1 slave.

1840 CENSUS, EAST BATON ROUGE PARISH, LOUISIANA
John Breshears
1 male born 1790-1800; 1 male born 1810-1820; 1 male born 1830-1835; 1 male born 1835-1840; 1 female born 1810-1820; 1 female born 1830-1835.

1850 CENSUS, EAST BATON ROUGE PARISH, LOUISIANA
John Brashears born in 1795 in Louisiana
Catharine Brashears born in 1816 in Louisiana
Philip Brashears born in 1833 in Louisiana
Susan Brashears born in 1841 in Louisiana
Robert Brashears born in 1844 in Louisiana
Green Brashears born in 1846 in Louisiana

1860 CENSUS, EAST BATON ROUGE PARISH, LOUISIANA
Catharine Brashears born in 1817 in Louisiana
Phillip Brashears born in 1835 in Louisiana
Susan Norwood born in 1843 in Louisiana
Robert Brashears born in 1845 in Louisiana
Green B. Brashears born in 1848 in Louisiana

1870 CENSUS, EAST BATON ROUGE PARISH, LOUISIANA
Catharine Brashears born in 1817 in Louisiana
G. W. Brashears born in 1847 in Louisiana

1880 CENSUS, EAST BATON ROUGE PARISH, LOUISIANA
Catharine Brashears born in 1820 in Louisiana
Grandchildren:
Catharine Brashears born in 1868 in Louisiana; Milton (?) Norwood born in 1870 in Louisiana; Robert Norwood born in 1873 in Louisiana; Johnie Norwood born in 1878 in Louisiana; Susan Norwood born in 1878 in Louisiana.

The parents of Catharine Brashears and all her grandchildren were born in Louisiana.

GREEN BRASHEAR

Married: Victoria Babin. See Book 13, page 497, Marriage Records, East Baton Rouge Parish, Louisiana. 1873.

Children of Green and Victoria (Babin) Brashear:

Ella Brashear; Olivia Elvena Brashear; Buffington Brashear; Walter Andrew Brashear; Gilbert Brashear.

GILBERT BRASHEAR

Born: March 1, 1891

Married: Miss L. L. Crumholdt on March 30, 1910

Died: May 30, 1956

Children of Gilbert and L. L. (Crumholdt) Brashear:

Ollie Brashear; Joseph Leon Brashear; Charles W. Brashear; Mary Elma Brashear.

JOSEPH LEON BRASHEAR

Born: January 21, 1914

Married: Nellie Lee Taylor

Children of Joseph Leon and Nellie Lee (Taylor) Brashear:

Louise Marie Brashear; Jean Ann Brashear; Bobbie Fay Brashear, born August 29, 1946.

JEAN ANN BRASHEAR

Born: December 17, 1937

Married: Ronnie O. Riley on January 21, 1957

Children of Ronnie O. and Jean Ann (Brashear) Riley: Rhonda Ann Riley. Born September 18, 1958.

LOUISE MARIE BRASHEAR

Born: October 17, 1935.

Married: Joseph Raymond Boudreaux.

Children of Joseph Raymond and Louise Marie (Brashear) Boudreaux: Karen Rae Boudreaux, born 1953; Joseph Leon Boudreaux, born January 10, 1960.

CHARLES W. BRASHEAR

Born: March 2, 1918.

Married: Loretta M. Perault.

Children of Charles W. and Loretta M. (Perault) Brashear: Ronald Wayne Brashear, born November 18, 1947.

MARY ELMA BRASHEAR

Born: October 23, 1920.

Married: Alder L. Chaney.

Children of Alder L. and Mary Elma (Brashear) Chaney: Donald

Ray Chaney, born February 3, 1944; Randy Leo Chaney, born April 13, 1956.

MARY ELLA BRASHEAR

Daughter of Green and Victoria (Babin) Brashear, granddaughter of John and Catharine (Shaffett) Brashear, great-granddaughter of John and Mary (Shaw) Shaffett, and great-great-granddaughter of William and Mary Ann (Weakley) Shaw.

Born: September 1, 1874.

Married: William Daniel Shaw, son of William and Ellen (Neville) Shaw and grandson of William and Mary Ann (Weakley) Shaw. After his wife's death, William Daniel Shaw married Mary L. McHugh, daughter of James Babin and Rachel F. (Shaffett) McHugh, granddaughter of John A. and Amanda (Bridges) McHugh, great-granddaughter of John and Susannah (Shaw) McHugh, and great-great-granddaughter of William and Mary Ann (Weakley) Shaw.

Died: May 12, 1905.

WALTER ANDREW BRASHEAR

Born: 1885.

Married: Sarah Amidee Devall in 1907.

Children of Walter Andrew and Sarah Amidee (Devall) Brashear: Alice Wilma Brashear, born 1908; Annie Lucille Brashear, born 1910; Alma Elvina Brashear, born 1914; Joseph Andrew Brashear, born 1922; Mary Annabelle Brashear, born 1915.

JOSEPH ANDREW BRASHEAR

Born: 1922.

Married: Betty Jane Wicker.

Children of Joseph Andrew and Betty Jane (Wicker) Brashear: Pamela Sue Brashear, born 1948; Gwendolyn Sherry Brashear, born 1951; Patsy Lou Brashear, born 1953; Walter Andrew Brashear, born 1956.

ALMA ELVINA BRASHEAR

Born: 1914.

Married: William Joseph Stiles.

Children of William Joseph and Alma Elvina (Brashear) Stiles: Shirley Ann Stiles, born 1936; William Joseph Stiles, Jr., born 1939; Gary Glynn Stiles, born 1942; Bradley Dale Stiles, born 1943.

SHIRLEY ANN STILES

Born: 1936.

Married: Billy Joe Haynes.

Children of Billy Joe and Shirley Ann (Stiles) Haynes: Vickie Lynn Haynes, born 1957.

ANNIE LUCILLE BRASHEAR

Born: 1910.

Married: Elisha D. Stiles.

Children of Elisha D. and Annie Lucille (Brashear) Stiles: Betty Stiles, born 1937.

BETTY STILES

Born: 1937.

Married: Sidney H. Womack.

Children of Sidney H. and Betty (Stiles) Womack: Terri Lynn Womack, born 1956; Debra Ann Womack, born 1957; Sidney H. Womack, Jr., born 1959.

MARY ANNABELLE BRASHEAR

Born: 1915.

Married: George Seguin.

Children of George and Mary Annabelle (Brashear) Seguin: George Lee Seguin; Janice Gail Seguin, born 1944; Judy Kay Seguin, born 1948; Linda Darnell Seguin, born 1954; Cyntha Ann Seguin, born 1956.

ALICE WILMER BRASHEAR

Born: 1908.

Married: Louis Ourso.

Children of Louis and Alice Wilmer (Brashear) Ourso: Louis Ourso, Jr., born 1931; Carolyn Ourso, born 1937.

LOUIS OURSO, JR.

Born: 1931.

Married: Theresa Gonzales.

Children of Louis and Theresa (Gonzales), Jr.: Joseph Lynn Ourso, born 1956; Louis J. Ourso III, born 1959.

CAROLYN OURSO

Born: 1937.

Married: Harry Lee Daigle, Sr.

Children of Harry Lee and Carolyn (Ourso) Daigle, Sr.: Harry Lee Daigle, Jr., born 1956; Drena Mae Daigle, born 1959.

OLIVIA ELVINA BRASHEAR

Married: James T. Laney.

Died: February 27, 1946.

Children of James T. and Olivia Elvena (Brashear) Laney: Mary Lillian Laney. Married Mr. Phillips. Died without issue September 30, 1956.

PHILIP BRASHEAR

Born: 1832-1835 in Louisiana.

Married: Joanna (?)

Children of Philip and Joanna (?) Brashear: Sam Brashear; Edward Brashear; Elizabeth Brashear; Annie Brashear; Catherine Brashear.

ROBERT BRASHEAR

Born: 1844-1845 in Louisiana.

Married: Estell Babin, 1867, East Baton Rouge Parish, La. Book 8, page 18.

Children of Robert and Estell (Babin) Brashear: Mary C. Brashear; Mattie Brashear; Robert Brashear.

SUSAN BRASHEAR

Born: 1843 in Louisiana.

Married: Thomas L. Norwood, 1858, East Baton Rouge Parish, La. Book 5, page 174.

Died: 1870-1880.

Children of Thomas L. and Susan (Brashear) Norwood: Chapel C. Norwood; William Norwood; Catharine Norwood; Milton Norwood; Robert Norwood; John Norwood; Susan Norwood.

Marriages East Baton Rouge Parish, Louisiana:

Catharine E. Norwood married J. E. Carpenter, 1890. Book 21, page 342.

William Norwood married Mary Frances Devall, April 9, 1888. Book 20, page 283.

John Norwood married Mary Selser, 1891. Book 22, page 15.

1880 Census, East Baton Rouge Parish, Louisiana

169, 169

Green Brashier born in 1827 in Louisiana; Victoria Brashier born in 1837 in Louisiana, Wife; Ella Brashier born in 1874 in Louisiana, Daughter; Elvena Brashier born in 1879 in Louisiana, Daughter.

171, 171

Robert Brashier born in 1844 in Louisiana; Estell Brashier born in 1850 in Louisiana, Wife; Mary Brashier born in 1870 in Louisiana, Daughter; Mattie Brashier born in 1873 in Louisiana, Daughter; Robt Brashier born in January, 1880, in Louisiana, Son.

172, 172

Philip Brashier born in 1832 in Louisiana; Joanna Brashier born in

1845 in Louisiana, Wife; Sam Brashier born in 1864 in Louisiana, Son; Edward Brashier born in 1868 in Louisiana, Son; Lizzie Brashier born in 1870 in Louisiana, Daughter; Annie Brashier born in 1872 in Louisiana, Daughter; Catherine Brashier born in 1877 in Louisiana, Daughter.

DANIEL SHAFFETT

Born: 1809 in Louisiana.

Married: Mary Houston, March 17, 1841, East Feliciana Parish, Louisiana. Book X, page 235.

Died: January 19, 1878. Succession of Daniel Webster Shaffett. Probate File No. 1361, East Baton Rouge Parish, shows date of death and heirs: John Shaffett, aged 34; Daniel Webster Shaffett, aged 26; Samuel David Shaffett, aged 19; and Benjamin Anthony Shaffett, aged 16.

Children of Daniel and Mary Houston Shaffett: John Shaffett, Sarah Shaffett; Mary Shaffett; Daniel Webster Shaffett; Samuel David Shaffett; Benjamin Anthony Shaffett. Ben Shaffett married Ernestine Wise on December 13, 1905, East Baton Rouge Parish. Book 38, page 294.

1840 Census, Ward 4, East Baton Rouge Parish, Louisiana
Daniel Shaffet
1 male born 1800-1810

1850 Census, East Baton Rouge Parish, Louisiana
Daniel Shaffet born in 1801 in Louisiana; Mary Shaffet born in 1822 in Louisiana; John Shaffet born in 1844 in Louisiana; Sarah Shaffet born in 1847 in Louisiana; Mary Shaffet born in 1850 in Louisiana; John Kelley born in 1825 in New York.

1860 Census, East Baton Rouge Parish, Louisiana
Daniel Shaffet born in 1809 in Louisiana; Mary Shaffet born in 1817 in Louisiana; John Shaffet born in 1845 in Louisiana; Sarah Shaffet born in 1847 in Louisiana; Daniel W. Shaffet born in 1852 in Louisiana; Saml. D. Shaffet born in 1859 in Louisiana.

1870 Census, East Baton Rouge Parish, Louisiana
Daniel Shaffet born in 1809 in Louisiana; Mary Shaffet born in 1820 in Louisiana; John J. Shaffet born in 1844 in Louisiana; Sarah A. Shaffet born in 1847 in Louisiana; Daniel W. Shaffet, born in 1854 in Louisiana; Samuel D. Shaffet born in 1859 in Louisiana; B. A. Shaffet born in 1861 in Louisiana.

1860 Census, East Baton Rouge Parish, Louisiana
Wm. Shaffet born in 1823 in Louisiana; Mary Gooden born in 1828 in Louisiana; Hester D. Gooden born in 1846 in Louisiana; Sarah J. Gooden born in 1849 in Louisiana; Robert Gooden born in 1856 in Louisiana; William Gooden born in 1860 in Louisiana.

1870 Census, East Baton Rouge Parish, Louisiana
William Shaffet born in 1823 in Louisiana; Mary J. Shaffet born in 1830 in Louisiana; John A. Shafet born in 1863 on Louisiana; David C. Shaffet born in 1866 in Louisiana; Samuel T. Shaffet born in 1867 in Louisiana.

1880 Census, East Baton Rouge Parish, Louisiana, 716, 733, Ward 4
Bill Shaffet born in 1832 in Louisiana; Mary Shaffet born in 1830 in Louisiana; John Shaffet born in 1863 in Louisiana; David Shaffet born in 1867 in Louisiana; Sam Shaffet born in 1870 in Louisiana.

Parents of all the above were born in Louisiana.

JOHN J. SHAFFETT

Born: October 28, 1844.

Married: Feliciana Chemin, December 21, 1887, East Baton Rouge Parish, Louisiana. Marriage Book 20, page 183. She was born on May 30, 1861, and died on June 8, 1934.

Died: March 22, 1910.

Children of John J. and Feliciana (Chemin) Shaffett: J. Wilfred Shaffett, born May 28, 1895, died July 15, 1930; Mary Louisa Shaffett.

WILLIAM SHAFFETT

Born: July, 1825, in Louisiana.

Married: Mary J. Gooden in 1861 in East Baton Rouge, Parish, Louisiana. Marriage Book 5, page 397.

Died: After 1880.

Children of William and Mary (Gooden) Shaffett: John A. Shaffett; David C. Shaffett; Samuel T. Shaffett.

East Baton Rouge Parish Marriages:

David C. Shaffett married Lizzie B. Sullivan, February 27, 1888. Book 20, page 259.

Samuel T. Shaffett married Margaret Ella Sullivan, 1891. Book 21, page 471.

John R. Shaffett married Mary E. Sullivan, 1882. Book 18, page 16.

1870 Census, East Baton Rouge Parish, Louisiana
812, 812
Robert Brashier born in 1844 in Louisiana; Estelle Brashier born in 1850 in Louisiana; Mary C. Brashier born in 1869 in Louisiana; Mary A. Babbin born in 1832 in Louisiana.

811, 811
T. L. Norwood born in 1825 in Alabama; Susan Norwood born in 1843 in Louisiana; Chapel Norwood born in 1859 in Louisiana; William Norwood born in 1864 in Louisiana; Catherine Norwood born in 1868 in Louisiana.

1860 Census, East Baton Rouge Parish, Louisiana
Thos. Norwood born in 1829 in Alabama; Chapel C. Norwood born in 1859 in Louisiana; Joana Brashears born in 1842 in Louisiana.

SUSANNA SHAW

Born: April 12, 1787.

Married: John McHugh.

Died: October 8, 1841.

Children of John and Susanna (Shaw) McHugh: John A. McHugh.
AN ACT FOR THE RELIEF OF THE LEGAL REPRESENTA-
TIVE OF JOHN McHUGH

Be it enacted etc. That there shall be, and hereby is, confirmed unto the legal representatives of John McHugh the tract of land settled upon and cultivated by John McHugh in his life time situate on White Bayou, within a survey once supposed to be the property of D. Amos, but which claim was rejected by Congress; the same lying and situate in the Parish of East Baton Rouge, in the State of Louisiana, not to exceed, in the whole, more than six hundred and forty acres and that a patent shall issue for the said tract of land in the usual form: Pro-vided, however, that the said legal representatives of the said John McHugh have not, and shall not, claim any other land in right of settlement and cultivation and that this act shall operate only as a relinquishment on the part of the United States of all the right and claim to the said lands and shall not interfere with, or affect the right or claim of other persons.

Approved June 15, 1832. 22nd Congress 1st Session

UNITED STATES STATUTES AT LARGE PRIVATE LAWS, Volume 6, page 495. Published in 1846 in Boston by Charles Little and James Brown.

"It appears from the statement of the petitioner and the accom-panying affidavits that the husband of the petitioner (John McHugh) and his family settled and made improvements on a tract of land on White's Bayou, in the Parish of East Baton Rouge, and State of Louisiana, in the month of March, 1813, and he and his family con-tinued to reside thereon till December, 1814, when he joined the army under General Jackson (as a militiaman) to aid in the defence of New Orleans, and continued in the service of the United States till his death on the 10th of March, 1815. Shortly after the death of her husband his widow, the petitioner and her family left the settlement and went to live with her parents * * *" Private Claim of Susanna McHugh to land in Louisiana No. 706, 20th Congress, 2d Session. See American State Papers, Documents of the Congress In Relation to the Public Lands, Volume 5, pages 602 and 603. Published by Gales and Seaton, Washington, 1860.

21st Congress, 1st Session, No. 804, Claim to land in Louisiana. Communicated to the House of Representatives, February 15, 1830.

Mr. Test, from the Committee on Private Land Claims to whom was referred the petition of Susanna McHugh, reported:

"The petitioner set out in her petition that she and her husband, John McHugh, settled on and improved a piece of land in East Baton Rouge, in the State of Louisiana, in the month of March 1813; that they resided thereon until December 1814; that then her husband joined the militia under General Jackson to aid in the defense of New Orleans, where died in consequence of great exposure and the severe duties he had to perform, leaving the petitioner and an infant son poor and destitute, who were thrown upon the bounty of her parents * * * the facts are uncontestably proved by William Shaw and Jeremiah McHugh who are certified by the judge taking their affidavits to be old inhabitants and residents in the parish aforesaid * * *"

Ibid, except Volume 6, page 145.

January 19, 1809. Claim No. 77 of Philip McHugh, Original Claimant of 550 acres in Baton Rouge under patent issued by Carlos Degrandpre. The land was surveyed by V. Pintado on January 22, 1802 and cultivated from 1801 to 1814.

Ibid, except Volume 3, page 51.

> Camp Morgan, February 12, 1815
> On Right Bank of the Mississippi,
> Five Miles Below New Orleans

Dear Partner of My Cares,

I can inform you that I am still alive and in tolerable health, thanks be to God for preserving me among such numbers that have died since we have been here and am in hopes that these few lines may find you and all our friends in the same state.

Tommy and myself have both been sick but have recovered. (Sickness is very great here, numbers daily die. Eight died yesterday and every day more or less.) I can yet hear no account of Daniel nor can I think what has become of him when the doctor's register says he was discharged fit for duty from the hospital on the 11th of January. James Sullivan received a few line from Jerry with some clothes which is the last I heard from you. Am a little surprised that you do not try to write to me when there is such opportunity by the post. By the post every week but I hope that we will not be many weeks here but some say we will not be discharged till the 23rd of March and others say in the course of this week. I know not for what we are detained for the British are all gone and no more to be heard of them.

I could wish if you can stay on the place and try to keep our little things together and patiently wait until I return.

If you write to me, send it out to the Plains on the day the Post comes down and direct it to me in Captain Sevens Company at the camp above mentioned. We have been transferred to another company and all the company consists of 100 men and all the supernumery officers sent home.

I have nothing more to add in particular but that you will patiently wait and pray to Him that is able to protect us till we return for He is all my hope and confidence.

In the meantime I am your affectionate and loving husband,

JOHN McHUGH

Susannah Shaw McHugh, wife of John McHugh, sent their son, John Anthony McHugh, to Baton Rouge where he stayed at the priests' house and studied under them.

JOHN ANTHONY McHUGH

Born: November 20, 1814, in Louisiana.

Married: Amanda Bridges, April 29, 1850. Marriage Book 3, page 23, East Baton Rouge Parish, Louisiana. She was born on July 5, 1826, and died January 8, 1905.

Died: April 2, 1874.

Children of John Anthony and Amanda (Bridges) McHugh: John Joseph McHugh, born August 28, 1851, died June 30, 1869; James Babin McHugh; Susannah McHugh; David Samuel McHugh; Thomas Edward McHugh; William Shaw McHugh, born June 15, 1853, died September 3, 1867.

1850 CENSUS, EAST BATON ROUGE PARISH, LOUISIANA
John McHugh born in 1814 in Louisiana; Amanda McHugh born in 1826 in Louisiana.

1860 CENSUS, EAST BATON ROUGE PARISH, LOUISIANA
John A. McHugh born in 1815 in Louisiana; Amanda J. McHugh born in 1826 in Louisiana; John J. McHugh born in 1851 in Louisiana; Wm McHugh born in 1853 in Louisiana; James B. McHugh born in 1856 in Louisiana; David McHugh born in 1858 in Louisiana; 3 slaves.

1870 CENSUS, EAST BATON ROUGE PARISH, LOUISIANA
John A. McHugh born in 1814 in Louisiana; Amanda J. McHugh born in 1826 in Louisiana; J. B. McHugh born in 1856 in Louisiana; D. S. McHugh born in 1858 in Louisiana; T. E. McHugh born in 1861 in Louisiana; S. A. McHugh born in 1866 in Louisiana; Joseph Bridges born in 1776 in Georgia; Evaline Trudeau born in 1848 in Louisiana.

1880 CENSUS, EAST BATON ROUGE PARISH, LOUISIANA
Amanda McHugh born in 1825 in Louisiana where her father and mother were also born.

Her Children, living with her in 1880: Tommie McHugh born in 1862 in Louisiana; Susan McHugh born in 1866 in Louisiana.

Amanda J. McHugh, wife of John A. McHugh, was the daughter of Joseph Bridges and was born in St. Helena Parish, Louisiana. See Fortier's *Louisiana*, Volume 3, page 274.

AMANDA JANE BRIDGES was born on June 5, 1826 and died on January 8, 1905. She attended the Greensburg Female Academy. While there in 1842, she made a sampler which is still in existence as are also her spinning wheel, parasol, four poster bed, sideboard, safe, bureau and bedside table. After her marriage to John Anthony McHugh, she was converted to Catholicism. Her sister, Lucy Jane Hunt, lived with her for many years. Her parents were Joseph Bridges and Nancy Redmond, who came from Kentucky to St. Helena Parish, Louisiana. After his wife's death, Joseph Bridges lived with his daughter, Amanda. He lived to be 104 years old and is buried in an unmarked grave in a cemetery west of Zachary, Louisiana, with his daughter, Lucy, his grandson, Thomas L. Hunt, and the first wife of his son, Guy. From Lucy Jane Hunt descend Leon and Louis Hunt of Baton Rouge and the Kirkwoods of Zachary. The descendants of Guy Bridges live at Alexandria, Louisiana. The descendants of William, another son of Joseph Bridges, are W. H. Bridges of Greenburg and J. F. Bridges of Baton Rouge. Thomas Bridges was another son.

Letter from Catharine Neville to Amanda J. Bridges

White's Bayou   August 13, 1849

Dear Friend,

Your letter received in due time and I was glad to hear of the good health of yourself and friends. I am happy to inform you that I am well and the neighborhood generally healthy. Some few are sick, but not many.

You said in your letter to Mary McHugh that you were sorry I did not like your letter to me of last fall. I can't imagine what made you think it displeased me for I assure you nothing in it that could displease anybody. The remarks you made in it about bringing *me* a beaux after saying there was no one there worthy of *yourself* I suppose must be the part you think I disliked, but when the person you meant for my beaux was a near relative of yours, of course, even that remark could not offend.

I am not able to give you any news of much importance. Nobody has been married that you know, excepting Miss Mary Sullivan to a Mr. Oswald sometime in January last. There is no prospect of any others taking place soon among the people you know. Miss Elizabeth Borskey is to be married sometime before long to a man you don't know.

I am much obliged to you for the invitation to attend the association meeting. I should like very much to be there, but I do not expect to meet with an opportunity of going. I will make known your invitation to your acquaintances and it may be that some of the young men may go, but I am not anything like certain that any of them will go. A great revivial has taken place in the Presbyterian Church in the Plains. About all the young ladies have joined and a great many of the young men. It would be almost impossible now to find enough out of the Church to make up a ball where it was so easily done two years ago.

The men in and around the Plains have organized themselves into a division of the "Sons of Temperance" and a great many have taken the pledge to drink no more: among the rest of old friends, James Sullivan. I hope they may all hold fast to their promise and that much good may come of it.

The season has been a very rainy one and the cotton crops are very much injured, the corn is good and the sugar cane is good. You must try and make it convenient to come down during the sugar making season (if not sooner) and pay them another visit.

Mr. Devall is now a candidate for the Legislature, but, as he is a Whig, and this a Democratic Parish, I suppose he will not succeed. Your old friend, the Squire, is still in very bad health, not any better than when you saw him, but rather worse. He authorized me to give you his best wishes and says he would be glad to see you.

I have nothing more, but remain your friend,

CATHARINE NEVILLE

A Poem by Catharine Neville in a Letter to Amanda J. Bridges
I need not wish thee beauty, I need not wish thee grace,
Already both are blushing in thy gentle form and face,
I will not wish thee grandeur
I will not wish thee wealth
But only a contented heart, peace, competence and health
Fond friends to love thee dearly
And honest friends to advise thee
And faithful friends to cling to thee
Whatever may betide.

May 29, 1849

UNITED STATES OF AMERICA
STATE OF LOUISIANA

Sheriff's Sales Book C page 175
East Baton Rouge Parish

I, JOHN A. McHUGH, do solemnly swear that I will support the Constitution of the United States and further, I, John A. McHugh, do solemnly swear that I will faithfuly discharge and perform all the duties incumbent on me as First Lieutenant in the 11th Regiment of the Louisiana Militia according to the best of my abilities and

understanding agreeably to the rules and regulations of the State.
SO HELP ME GOD.

/s/ JOHN A. McHUGH

Sworn and Signed before James Cooper J.P.
19 November 1840

THE DEATH OF MR. JOHN A. McHUGH

We are exceedingly pained this morning to learn that our esteemed parishoner, John A. McHugh, died suddenly this morning at about 4 o'clock. Yesterday (Wednesday) evening Mr. McHugh called at our office and after a pleasant conversation of some moments departed and to all appearances was in excellent health and frame of mind. Being late in starting for his home, he stopped at the residence of H. V. Babin, Esq. for the night, as we learn he is frequently in the habit of doing, they being warm personal friends. Mr. McHugh sat up until bedtime when he retired. At about 4 A.M. he called to Mr. Babin and stated that he felt very bad. Whereupon Mr. Babin asked what he could do for him. Mr. McHugh said he usually applied cups and used a warm mustard bath. Mr. Babin immediately sent for the doctor and prepared the bath according to request. Alas, before the arrival of the doctor the attack proved fatal and the spirit of him who had but a few hours before retired to his couch in apparent good health passed from the body to the God that gave it. Mr. McHugh was an old resident of our parish and one that was esteemed by all. For many years he had been Justice of the Peace for the 4th Ward at the Plains and had long held the position of Notary Public. In these positions he had always been a faithful servant and was well known for his good works as a man and citizen. He leaves a large family and circle of friends to mourn and regret his loss.

His remains were conveyed to his residence at the Plains and from there were conveyed to the Family Burial Ground where the body was interred by a large concourse of sorrowing relatives and sympathizing friends. Being a member of Plains Lodge, Free and Accepted Masons, the decedent was buried with Masonic Honors.
April 2, 1874.

John A. McHugh, above, was known as "Squire McHugh." He is buried with most of his family at the Old Shaw-McHugh Cemetery established by his grandfather, William Shaw, on land granted by the Royal Spanish Governor of Louisiana. His son, Thomas E. Mc-Hugh, however, is buried in Roselawn Cemetery in Baton Rouge, where he served as Clerk of Court and Deputy Sheriff.

Hall of the Plains Lodge #135
F. and A. M. East Baton Rouge Parish
April 8, 1874

WHEREAS an alarm has been given at the outer door of Our Temple by an All Wise Providence and in His Wisdom summoned from his earthly labors Brother John A. McHugh to the "narrow house appointed for all living."

RESOLVED: That in the death of our well beloved brother this Lodge has lost one of its most useful members, society a worthy citizen, but the loss to his distressed wife and bereaved family is incalculable.

RESOLVED: That his faithful adherence to the Principles of Masonry (under the surroundings of his Church and friends: Catholic) challenges the admiration of the Fraternity.

RESOLVED: That we members of Plains Lodge No. 135 deeply sympathize with his bereaved family and commend them to "Him, who tempers the wind to the shorn lamb."

RESOLVED: That in token of respect for his memory and sorrow for his death the Lodge be draped in mourning and the members wear the usual badge for thirty days.

RESOLVED: That a copy of these resolutions (with seal attached) be transmitted to the family of the deceased. Also a copy be furnished the Baton Rouge ADVOCATE for publication.

Fraternally submitted,

A. G. CARTER

(SEAL)　　　　　　　　R. T. YOUNG　　　COMMITTEE

A. Z. YOUNG

The foregoing resolutions are a true and correct copy of those passed by Plains Lodge, No. 135, F. and A. M. on the 8th day of this month.

E. L. WOODSIDE
Secretary

DAVID SAMUEL McHUGH

Born: October 8, 1858.

Married: Sarah Elizabeth Shaffett on January 28, 1877.

Died: June 12, 1926.

Children of David Samuel and Sarah Elizabeth (Shaffett) McHugh: Amanda Rachel McHugh; David Robert McHugh; Elsie McHugh, born January 25, 1891, died January 28, 1891; Guy Samuel McHugh; Ida Elizabeth McHugh; Jesse Weldon McHugh; John McHugh, born October 5, 1879, died June 18, 1922; Leona McHugh, Mary Alice McHugh, born October 19, 1889; Nettie McHugh; William Bates McHugh. Marriage Book 15, Page 327, East Baton Rouge Parish, 1876, David McHugh and Sarah E. Shaffett.

1880 CENSUS, EAST BATON ROUGE PARISH, LOUISIANA
Dave McHugh was born in 1859 in Louisiana; Sarah McHugh was born in 1855 in Louisiana.

Their children: Amanda McHugh born in 1878 in Louisiana; John McHugh born in 1879 in Louisiana.

The parents of both Dave and Sarah McHugh were born in Louisiana.

1870 Census, East Baton Rouge Parish, Louisiana 657, 657

D. R. Shaffet born in 1836 in Louisiana; Rachel Shaffet born in 1828 in Louisiana; Mary J. Shaffet born in 1855 in Louisiana; Rachel F. Shaffet born in 1852 in Louisiana; Elisa G. Shaffet born in 1859 in Louisiana; Annie P. Shaffet born in 1867 in Louisiana; Michael E. Shaffet born in 1868 in Louisiana; Sarah E. Shaffet born in 1855 in Louisiana.

1860 Census, East Baton Rouge Parish, Louisiana 1072, 1072

David R. Shaffet born in 1836 in Louisiana; Rachel Shaffet born in 1828 in Louisiana; Mary J. Shaffett born in 1855 in Louisiana; Sarah E. Shaffet born in 1855 in Louisiana; Eliza G. Shaffet born in 1859 in Louisiana; Rachel Shaffet born in 1858 in Louisiana.

AMANDA RACHAEL McHUGH

Born: July 8, 1878.

Married: Newbern Carrol Winter on January 25, 1906.

Died: August 20, 1926.

Children of Newbern Carrol and Amanda Rachel (McHugh) Winter: Leona Elizabeth Winter, born December 11, 1906, unmarried; Jesse Carrol Winter, born April 4, 1909, unmarried; Eula Gertrude Winter, born August 31, 1922, died February 25, 1942; Samuel Vernon Winter; Mary Ernestine Winter.

SAMUEL VERNON WINTER

Born: March 15, 1919.

Married: Bessie Stiles on August 13, 1948.

Children of Samuel Vernon and Bessie (Stiles) Winter: Mary Amanda Winter, born October 25, 1950; Sarah Elizabeth Winter, born September 12, 1953.

MARY ERNESTINE WINTER

Born: August 15, 1910.

Married: Philip Joseph Bertin on October 15, 1935.

Children of Philip Joseph and Mary Ernestine (Winter) Bertin: Philip Joseph Bertin, Jr., born April 1, 1937; Robert McHugh Bertin, born March 15, 1943; John Michael Bertin, born September 29, 1950.

DAVID ROBERT McHUGH

Born: February 3, 1881.

Married: Aurelie Mary Lejeune on February 18, 1917.

Died: August 4, 1953.

Children of David Robert and Aurelie Mary (Lejeune) McHugh:
David Robert McHugh, Jr.

DAVID ROBERT McHUGH, JR.

Born: November 26, 1917

Married: Barbara Miller on October 15, 1935

Children of David Robert and Barbara (Miller) McHugh: Barbara
Ann McHugh; Robert Hull McHugh; David Robert McHugh III, born
August 31, 1941; Thomas Edward McHugh, born October 3, 1943;
Jacqueline McHugh, born September 15, 1950, died September 26,
1956.

BARBARA ANN McHUGH

Born: October 11, 1936

Married: Gerald Barbin on September 26, 1956

Children of Gerald and Barbara Ann (McHugh) Barbin: Jacqueline
Ann Barbin, born July 21, 1957; Barbara Marie Barbin, born July
26, 1958.

ROBERT HULL McHUGH

Born: January 11, 1939

Married: Jo Lynette Smith on June 7, 1957

Children of Robert Hull and Jo Lynette (Smith) McHugh: Jeffry
Allen McHugh, born February 15, 1958; Jennifer Lynn McHugh, born
April 3, 1959.

GUY SAMUEL McHUGH

Born: November 26, 1893

Married: Elizabeth McMillan on December 25, 1928

Children of Guy Samuel and Elizabeth (McMillan) McHugh: Guy
Malcolm McHugh, born May 21, 1930, married Phyllis La Chapelle
on June 16, 1956; Patrick Samuel McHugh, born August 16, 1935;
Richard Anthony McHugh, born December 9, 1936.

IDA ELIZABETH McHUGH

Born: September 10, 1886

Married: Arthur Barlow Simmons on September 19, 1912. Mr. Simmons was born on December 7, 1883, and died on April 7, 1956

Children of Arthur Barlow and Ida Elizabeth (McHugh) Simmons:
Beth McHugh Simmons; Arthur Barlow Simmons, Jr.; Doctor William McHugh Simmons; David Thomas Simmons.

BETH McHUGH SIMMONS

Born: August 30, 1913

Married: 1st: Walter Herd Snider on March 19, 1931

2nd: Andrew J. Baker on December 4, 1951

Children of Walter Herd and Beth McHugh (Simmons) Snider: Lieutenant John Winfield Snider; Walter Herd Snider, Jr., born June 23, 1938.

LIEUTENANT JOHN WINFIELD SNIDER

Born: March 5, 1933

Married: Virginia Brooks on May, 1954

Children of Lieutenant John Winfield and Virginia (Brooks) Snider: Deborah Sue Snider, born November 20, 1955; John Winfield Snider, Jr., born November 8, 1957.

ARTHUR BARLOW SIMMONS, JR.

Born: February 23, 1913

Married: Sylvia Smith on April 21, 1939

Children of Arthur Barlow and Sylvia (Smith) Simmons, Jr.: Arthur Barlow Simmons III, born June 21, 1940; Susan Adele Simmons, born March 25, 1945; Timothy Simmons, born July 22, 1949; Patrick Simmons, born March 13, 1954.

DOCTOR WILLIAM McHUGH SIMMONS

Born: November 8, 1917

Married: Phoebe Bryan on June 15, 1940

Children of Doctor William McHugh and Phoebe (Bryan) Simmons: Beth Bryan Simmons, born May 22, 1941; Suzanne Simmons, born August 13, 1943; William McHugh Simmons, Jr., born April 23, 1947; Laurie Ann Simmons, born February 25, 1954.

DAVID THOMAS SIMMONS

Born: July 26, 1923

Married: Lorraine Gainey on December 24, 1945

Children of David Thomas and Lorraine (Gainey) Simmons: David Thomas Simmons, Jr., born January 21, 1948; Elizabeth Simmons, born April 25, 1949; Patricia Jean Simmons, born September 8, 1952; Michael Arthur Simmons, born June 10, 1957; Jeffrey Robert Simmons, born January 22, 1959.

JESSE WELDON McHUGH

Born: July 1, 1882

Married: Blanche Capdevielle

Died: August 2, 1960

Children of Jesse Weldon and Blanche (Capdevielle) McHugh: Weldon Capdevielle McHugh; Blanche Capdevielle McHugh.

WELDON CAPDEVIELLE McHUGH

Born: April 27, 1921

Married: Margaret Lemmon on January 24, 1948

Children of Weldon Capdevielle and Margaret (Lemmon) McHugh: Sallie Margaret McHugh, born April 11, 1950; Jess Louis McHugh, born December 7, 1954; Mary Juliette McHugh, born May 30, 1957.

BLANCHE CAPDEVIELLE McHUGH

Born: 1923

Married: R. William Collins on September 1, 1946

Children of R. William and Blanche Capdevielle (McHugh) Collins: William Collins, born 1950; Ann Collins, born 1954; Kem Collins, born 1956.

LEONA McHUGH

Born: September 4, 1896

Married: Fortune Hyacinth Maurin on June 1, 1920

Children of Fortune Hyacinth and Leona (McHugh) Maurin: Marian Elizabeth Maurin, born August 2, 1921; Elsie Desire Maurin, born September 9, 1922; Mildred Dorothea Maurin, born February 6, 1924; David McHugh Maurin, born June 4, 1926; John Harold Maurin, born March 27, 1928; Fortune Hyacinth Maurin III, born December 11, 1930; Constance Mary Maurin, born September 15, 1932; Richard Charles Maurin, born February 9, 1936; Sarah Ann Maurin, born June 16, 1938; Susan McHugh Maurin, born April 28, 1941.

MARIAN ELIZABETH MAURIN

Born: August 2, 1921

Married: Harry D. Coffee on May 13, 1947

Children of Harry D. and Marian Elizabeth (Maurin) Coffee: Harry D. Coffee, Jr., born June 4, 1948; Alfred Coffee and Grady Coffee (Twins), born April 4, 1950.

ELSIE DESIRE MAURIN

Born: September 9, 1922

Married: Leonard Lasseigne on February 9, 1943

Children of Leonard and Elsie Desire (Maurin) Lasseigne: Leonard Lasseigne, Jr., born November 8, 1946, died on March 16, 1948; David Lasseigne, born December 14, 1948; Camy Lasseigne, born September 5, 1952; Lisa Lasseigne, born July 4, 1958.

MILDRED DOROTHEA MAURIN

Born: February 6, 1924

Married: Harold Young on April 5, 1958

Children of Harold and Mildred Dorothea (Maurin) Young: Kathleen Ann Young, born prematurely on November 2, 1958.

DAVID McHUGH MAURIN

Born: June 4, 1926

Married: Peggy Lokey in June, 1952

Children of David McHugh and Peggy (Lokey) Maurin: David Mc-
Hugh Maurin, Jr., born July 14, 1953; Joseph Fortune Maurin, born
September 24, 1954; John Michael Maurin, born August 9, 1955;
Mary Elizabeth Maurin, born November 12, 1957; Mark Allen
Maurin, born December 30, 1958.

CONSTANCE MARY MAURIN

Born: September 15, 1932

Married: Doctor Verne Shaver on August 31, 1957

Children of Doctor Verne and Constance Mary (Maurin) Shaver:
Verne C. Shaver, Jr.

NETTIE McHUGH

Born: July 29, 1888

Married: Robert Watson Baird on December 17, 1937. Mr. Baird
died on March 13, 1952

WILLIAM BATES McHUGH

Born: January 26, 1884

Married: Helen Julia Hart on August 28, 1920. Miss Hart was born
on June 23, 1897

Children of William Bates and Helen Julia (Hart) McHugh: Earline
Rita McHugh; John Anthony McHugh, born January 25, 1925, killed
in the Battle of Luzon, Philippine Islands, April 18, 1945, buried at
Fort McKinley, U.S. Military Cemetery, Manila.

EARLINE RITA McHUGH

Born: April 20, 1922

Married: Raymond Smith on January 29, 1946. Mr. Smith was born
on February 23, 1924

Children of Raymond and Earline Rita (McHugh) Smith: John Mc-
Hugh Smith, born July 29, 1947; Rita Smith, born April 5, 1949;
Anthony Smith, born March 22, 1951.

JAMES BABIN McHUGH

Born: December 19, 1856

Married: Rachel F. Shaffett who was born on September 3, 1857,
and died on September 17, 1922, in 1876, marriage book 15, page
326, East Baton Rouge Parish, Louisiana

Died: May 3, 1944

Children of James Babin and Rachel F. (Schaffett) McHugh: Agnes
Barbara McHugh, born December 4, 1898, died March 13, 1905; Alice
C. McHugh, born February 21, 1883, died December 14, 1918; Annie
McHugh (Sister St. John the Baptist); Clarence Andrew McHugh,
born December 4, 1896, died April 8, 1897; Eugene S. McHugh, born

June 28, 1888, died January 5, 1916; Frederick Robert McHugh; Irene Loretto McHugh, born December 26, 1893, died July 4, 1921; James Babin McHugh, Jr., born October 11, 1886, died May 16, 1891; Joseph Laval McHugh (twin of Eugene S. McHugh); Lucy J. McHugh, born March 14, 1879; Lula G. McHugh (Sister Mary Elizabeth), born January 23, 1885, died February 6, 1941; Mary L. McHugh; Rachel Frances McHugh (Sister Mary Barbara), born August 22, 1891; Sarah Eleanor McHugh, born August 12, 1895, died August 10, 1939; Susie C. McHugh (twin of Alice C. McHugh), born February 21, 1883, died February 19, 1901; Vivian Martine Bebee McHugh, born August 7, 1900, died May 19, 1907; Zula E. McHugh (twin of Lula E. McHugh), born January 23, 1885, died September 17, 1888.

1880 CENSUS, EAST BATON ROUGE PARISH, LOUISIANA

James McHugh born in 1857 in Louisiana; Rachel McHugh born in 1858 in Louisiana.

Their children: Annie McHugh born in 1878 in Louisiana; Lucy McHugh born in 1879 in Louisiana

In Chamber's Louisiana, Volume 2, page 127, is the biography of Joseph Laval McHugh, born in 1888 in Zachary, Louisiana, the son of James Babin McHugh and Rachael (Shaffet) McHugh, who died in 1922.

ANNIE S. McHUGH
(SISTER SAINT JOHN THE BAPTIST)

Born: March 14, 1870

Died: July 7, 1960

FORMER CATHOLIC MOTHER
SUPERIOR DIES IN ORLEANS

Sister St. John the Baptist, former mother superior at the St. Joseph's convents in Baton Rouge, New Roads and Bay St. Louis, Miss., died in New Orleans at 6 a.m. today.

She was born Annie S. McHugh, eldest child of the late James Babin McHugh and the former Rachel Shaffett, Zachary.

Sr. St. John the Baptist was retired at the time of her death. Funeral services will be held tomorrow morning at St. Joseph's Provincial House, 1200 Mirabeau Avenue, New Orleans.

Baton Rouge STATE TIMES, July 7, 1960

FREDERICK R. McHUGH

Born: September 16, 1892

Married: Gertrude Priest of Gloster, Mississippi

Children of Frederick Robert and Gertude (Priest) McHugh: Frederick R. McHugh, Jr.

JOSEPH L. McHUGH

Born: June 28, 1888

Married: Ruth Johnston of Crowley, Louisiana

Children of Joseph L. and Ruth (Johnston) McHugh: Patricia Jane McHugh; Joseph McHugh, Jr.; Ann Harlan McHugh; James Samuel McHugh.

MARY L. McHUGH

Born: October 11, 1880

Married: William Daniel Shaw on September 26, 1908

Died: August 2, 1909

Children of William Daniel and Mary L. (McHugh) Shaw: Clarence Shaw, born June 20, 1909, Mr. Shaw is the great-grandson of William and Mary Ann Shaw through his father and the great-great-great grandson of William and Mary Ann Shaw through his mother. On his death the name SHAW which has been identified with the community since the closing days of the eighteenth century becomes extinct.

Marriage Records, East Baton Rouge Parish, Book 42, Page 1a September 24, 1908; William D. Shaw and Mary McHugh.

SUSANNA McHUGH

Born: March 11, 1866

Married: Simeon Fillmore Carmena on January 31, 1883. Mr. Carmena was born on February 18, 1863 and died on February 6, 1927. Marriage Book 18, Pg. 86, East Baton Rouge Parish.

Died: June 3, 1951

Children of Simeon Fillmore and Susanna (McHugh) Carmena: Helena Lee (Lena) Carmena, born December 1, 1883; Joseph William Carmena; John Allan Carmena; Martha Alma Carmena, born April 17, 1894, died December 20, 1912; Rita Angele Carmena; Robert Leo Carmena; Thomas Edward Carmena, born December 18, 1886, married Florrie Doughty, died August 13, 1949.

1840 Census, Town of Baton Rouge, Louisiana

John Carmena: 1 male born 1810-1820; 1 male born 1825-1830; 2 males born 1835-1840; 1 female born 1810-1820; 1 female born 1835-1840

1850 Census, Parish of East Baton Rouge, Louisiana

John Carmena born in 1812 in Louisiana; Mercelite Carmena born in 1822 in Louisiana; Josephine Carmena born in 1838 in Louisiana; Mary Carmena born in 1842 in Louisiana; Wm. Carmena born in 1844 in Louisiana; Louisa Carmena born in 1845 in Louisiana; Joseph

Carmena born in 1847 in Louisiana; John Carmena born in 1850 in Louisiana; Thomas Young born in 1824 in Louisiana

1860 Census, Parish of East Baton Rouge, Louisiana

John Carmena born in 1808 in Louisiana; Mar (?) Carmena born in 1830 in Louisiana; Josephine Carmena born in 1840 in Louisiana; Mary Carmena born in 1842 in Louisiana; Wm. Carmena born in 1845 in Louisiana; Louisa Carmena born in 1847 in Louisiana; Joseph Carmena born in 1848 in Louisiana; John Carmena born in 1850 in Louisiana; Manuel Carmena born in 1852 in Louisiana; Hiram Carmena born in 1856 in Louisiana; Benjamin Carmena born in 1858 in Louisiana; 8 slaves

1870 Census Parish of East Baton Rouge, Louisiana

John Carmena born in 1808 in Louisiana; Martha Carmena born in 1820 in Louisiana; Joseph Carmena born in 1840 in Louisiana; Mary Carmena born in 1846 in Louisiana; William Carmena born in 1847 in Louisiana; Louisa Carmena born in 1851 in Louisiana; Joseph Carmena born in 1849 in Louisiana; John Carmena born in 1850 in Louisiana; Manda (?) Carmena born in 1852 in Louisiana; Hiram Carmena born in 1856 in Louisiana; Benjamin Carmena born in 1858 in Louisiana; Simeon Carmena born in 1862 in Louisiana

1880 Census, Parish of East Baton Rouge, Louisiana

John Carmena born in 1808 in Louisiana, his father was born in Spain and his mother was born in Cuba; Martha Carmena born in 1820 in Louisiana where her father and mother were born.

Their children: Mary Carmena born in 1842 in Louisiana; Louisa Carmena born in 1846 in Louisiana; Simen Carmena born in 1866 in Louisiana.

JOHN ALLAN CARMENA

Born: September 30, 1897

Married: March 4, 1918 to Vera Ellen Bernard who was born on August 13, 1900

Children of John Allan and Vera Ellen (Bernard) Carmena: Frances Susanna Carmena; John Allan Carmena, Jr.; Vera Geneviene Carmena; Mary Patricia Carmena; Joycelyn Bernadette Carmena.

FRANCES SUSANNA CARMENA

Born: December 19, 1919

Married: Ed J. Hamner on February 14, 1946

Children of Ed J. and Frances Susanna (Carmena) Hamner: Sara Sue Hamner, born January 10, 1947; Richard Edward Hamner, born June 13, 1949; Margaret Ellen Hamner, born May 25, 1952.

JOHN ALLAN CARMENA, JR.

Born: October 13, 1923

Married: Glenna Kimbiel on August 24, 1948

Children of John Allan and Glenna (Kimbiel) Carmena, Jr.: Mark Allan Carmena, born November 15, 1952; John Michael Carmena, born August 30, 1954.

JOYCELYN BERNADETTE CARMENA

Born: November 17, 1933

Married: Roger Wallace on November 29, 1958. Mr. Wallace was born on January 8, 1930.

MARY PATRICIA CARMENA

Born: March 17, 1930

Married: Robert Lee Holt on April 29, 1949. Mr. Holt was born on January 20, 1925

Children of Robert Lee and Mary Patricia (Carmena) Holt: Robert Timothy Holt, born August 27, 1950; Charlotte Marie Holt, born November 8, 1952; Rebecca Anne Holt, born February 25, 1954; Grant Edward Holt, born September 5, 1956; Patricia Lee Holt, born February 18, 1958.

VERA GENEVIEVE CARMENA

Born: August 9, 1925

Married: Joseph August Bisso, Jr., on December 31, 1948. Mr. Bisso was born on December 24, 1921

Childern of Joseph August and Vera Genevieve (Carmena) Bisso, Jr.: Elizabeth Ann Bisso, born December 14, 1949; Catherine Mary Bisso, born April 22, 1952; Josephine Anne Bisso, born September 4, 1958.

JOSEPH WILLIAM CARMENA

Born: January 6, 1891

Married: Doris Ligon

Children of Joseph William and Doris (Ligon) Carmena: Joseph William Carmena, Jr., born January 5, 1929; Thomas Neil Carmena, born March 11, 1932; John Noel Carmena, born December 14, 1937.

LIEUTENANT JOHN NOEL CARMENA

Born: December 14, 1937

Married: Ethel Ursula Bogan, daughter of Mr. and Mrs. Robert Anthony Bogan, on July 23, 1960, St. Joseph's Church, Baton Rouge.

RITA CARMENA

Born: August 28, 1900, in Zachary, Louisiana

Married: William Belanger Hart on June 28, 1932. Mr. Hart was born on April 23, 1890, at Reserve, Louisiana, St. John Baptist Parish.

Children of William Belanger and Rita (Carmena) Hart: William Barry Hart, born on November 26, 1933; Thomas Edward McHugh Hart, born on August 2, 1937.

ROBERT LEO CARMENA

Born: March 6, 1909

Married: Oleta Mae McElwee, who was born on March 3, 1909

Children of Robert Leo and Oleta Mae (McElwee) Carmena: Linda Maria Carmena; Cynthia Leola Carmena.

LINDA MARIA CARMENA

Born: March 3, 1941

Married: Jesse Frank Devall, Jr., of Zachary, Louisiana, on May 7, 1960

CYNTHIA LEOLA CARMENA

Born: May 23, 1938

Married: Madison Howard Romaine on August 24, 1957

THOMAS E. McHUGH

Born: December 1, 1861

Married: Nettie Brown, daughter of Thomas B. and Sarah (Wilkins) Brown in 1889

Died: November 3, 1947

Children of Thomas E. and Nettie (Brown) McHugh: Doris McHugh; Dr. Thomas Jefferson McHugh

Nettie Brown was born on February 13, 1868, and died on August 22, 1949

THOMAS E. McHUGH, Clerk of the District Court of East Baton Rouge Parish, was born December 1, 1861, in East Baton Rouge Parish, the son of John A. and Amanda (Bridges) McHugh. His father a native of East Baton Rouge Parish died at the age of 60 and his mother who was born in St. Helena Parish passed away in her 78th year. They had six children, four now living, of whom Thomas E. is the youngest. He was educated in private schools and farming and mercantile business engaged his attention until 1900 when he became Deputy Clark and filled that position for four years. In 1904 Mr. McHugh was elected to his present office and was re-elected two successive times, the last time without opposition. Among the progressive citizens who organized the Town of Zachary none showed more energy and public spirit than Mr. McHugh who was elected the first Mayor of Zachary. In 1889 occurred his marriage to Miss

Nettie Brown, daughter of Thomas B. and Sarah (Wilkins) Brown of East Baton Rouge Parish. One son, Thomas Jefferson, and one daughter, Doris, have been born to them. The son is a graduate of Tulane University Medical Department, Class of 1914. Mr. McHugh is a Master and Royal Arch Mason, a member of the B.P.O.E. and the Woodmen of the World. Philip McHugh, great-grandfather and John McHugh, grandfather of the subject of this sketch settled in the northern part of East Baton Rouge Parish in the early days of Louisiana. Mr. McHugh is a staunch member of the Democratic Party and is always foremost in all movements affecting the public welfare.

Alcee Fortier's *Louisiana*, Volume 3, Century Historical Association 1914. Pages 274-275.

Marriage Records of East Baton Rouge Parish, Book 21, Page 116. December 14, 1889. Thomas E. McHugh and Nettie Brown.

DORIS ARWIN McHUGH

Born: October 9, 1896

Married: Arthur Taylor Prescott.

THE DOUGHERTY-PRESCOTT HOUSE. (Private) 741 North Street. The home of Colonel Arthur Taylor Prescott. It is said to have been built by a Mr. Knox in 1840. The house is of soft red brick with massive square plastered-brick columns supporting a hipped roof on all four sides. The side columns and galleries have been included in added wings; otherwise, the house retains its original form. The front gallery on the second floor has a handsome cast-iron railing. During the War Between the States, Union Cavalry rode their horses up the front steps into the house and the hoof prints are still embedded in the floors. Having ridden all over the house, the troops decided to burn it and piled firewood under the stairway, but they changed their minds when it was pointed out the house would make an excellent hospital. The house has been carefully cared for and is in today perfect repair. It has been in the hands of the same family since the year of its building. One of the rare antiques in the house is a set of china said to have been painted for a member of the family by John James Audubon. The pieces, bordered in red, are decorated with exquisitely wrought flowers.

LOUISIANA, A GUIDE TO THE STATE. Sponsored by the Louisiana Library Commission at Baton Rouge. Hastings House, New York, 1941, Page 267.

A picture of the Dougherty-Prescott House may be found in the book between pages 564 and 565.

DOCTOR THOMAS JEFFERSON McHUGH

Born: October 16, 1890, in Zachary, Louisiana

Married: Ruth Puckett, daughter of Henry L. and Addie (Kellum) Puckett, on June 8, 1920

Children of Dr. T. Jeff and Ruth (Puckett) McHugh: Ruth McHugh, born August 24, 1922

The McHugh family came from Ireland to Philadelphia, Pennsylvania, and thence to East Baton Rouge Parish in 1783. Dr. McHugh's father, Thomas E. McHugh, was also born in Zachary in 1863. He was a merchant there until 1893. For the next seven years he farmed near Baker, Louisiana. He 1900 he moved to Baton Rouge, where for 16 years the was Clerk of the District Court. In 1924 he was Deputy Sheriff of East Baton Rouge Parish. He was a Mason and served as Mayor of Zachary, Louisiana. Dr. McHugh was educated in private school in Baton Rouge. He graduated from St. Vincent's Academy, spent one year at Louisiana State University, and received his medical degree from Tulane University in 1914. He is a member of St. James Episcopal Church, Baton Rouge.

Henry E. Chambers LOUISIANA Volume II, pages 78-79.

T. Jeff McHugh, M.D., who is one of the prominent physicians and surgeons of the younger generation in the City of Baton Rouge is a representative of a sterling family whose name has been identified with the history of this part of Louisiana for nearly a century and a half. The original representative of the family in America came from Ireland and settled in Philadephia, Pennsylvania, and 142 years ago ago the family was founded in East Baton Rouge Parish, Louisiana.

Dr. McHugh was born in Zachary, East Baton Rouge Parish, Louisiana, October 16, 1890, and is the son of Thomas E. and Nettie (Brown) McHugh, both likewise natives of this parish and now residents of the City of Baton Rouge.

Thomas E. McHugh was born at Zachary, this parish, in the year 1863, was there reared and educated and there became a leading citizen and merchant. He there continued in the mercantile business until 1893 and for seven years thereafter was engaged in farm enterprise near Baker, this parish. He then in 1900 removed with his family to Baton Rouge where he and his wife have since maintained their home. Mr. McHugh served 16 years as Clerk of the District Court of East Baton Rouge Parish and at the time of this writing in the spring of 1924 he holds the office of Deputy Sheriff of the Parish. He has been active in the ranks of the Democratic Party and served for a time as Mayor of Zachary. He is affiliated with the Masonic Fraternity. Mrs. McHugh was born at Baker, this parish, in 1869. Of the two children, Dr. T. Jeff, of this review is the elder and Doris A. is the wife of Dr. Arthur Taylor Prescott, Professor of Government in the University of Louisiana and the subject of individual mention on other pages of this work. (Doris A. McHugh is the wife of Dr. Arthur Taylor Prescott, Jr., son of Professor Prescott and his wife, Nellie Daughtery, daughter of John A. and Lucy (Stewart) Daughtery. Professor Prescott was the first President of the Louisiana Industrial Institute at Ruston in 1894).

Dr. McHugh attended a private school in Baton Rouge and in 1908 he was graduated from St. Vincent Academy. Thereafter he was for one year a student at the University of Louisiana and he then entered the medical department of Tulane University. In this latter institution in New Orleans he was graduated a member of the Class of 1914 and with the degree of Doctor of Medicine. As a Collegiate the doctor is affiliated with the Kappa Alpha academic fraternity and the Kappa Psi medical fraternity.

After his graduation from the medical college Dr. McHugh further fortified himself by the experience he gained in two years of service as an interne in the Charity Hospital of New Orleans and since 1916 he has been successfully established in the general practice of his profession in the Capital City of Baton Rouge where his well appointed offices are in the New Reymond Building. He is giving effective service as Health Officer of the City. The doctor is actively identified with the East Baton Rouge Parish Medical Society, the Louisiana State Medical Society and the American Medical Society. He is a member of the Baton Rouge Chamber of Commerce. He and his wife are communicants of St. James Church, Protestant Episcopal. In the Masonic Fraternity he has received the 32nd degree of the Scottish Rite in the Consistory at Shreveport where also he is a Noble of the El Karubah Temple of the Mystic Shrine. His basic York Rite affiliation is with St. James Lodge, A.F. and A.M. in his home city where also he holds membership in the Baton Rouge Lodge No. 490 B.P.O.E.

Enduring honor shall attach to the name of Dr. McHugh by reason of the loyal and effective service of patriotism he rendered in the World War. On the 28th of March, 1917, he volunteered for service in the Medical Corps of the United States Army and at Camp Nicholls in New Orleans he received on the same date his commission as First Lieutenant in the Medical Corps. He was transferred to Camp Beauregard at Alexandria and in March, 1918, he was commissioned Captain. In the following August with the 141st Field Artillery he sailed for overseas service and he remained in France in active and valuable service until March, 1919, as Regimental Surgeon. At Camp Shelby, Mississippi, Dr. McHugh received his honorable discharge in May, 1919. He is a member of the Nicholson Post, American Legion, of Baton Rouge.

On 8th of June, 1920, was solemnized the marriage of Dr. McHugh and Miss Ruth Puckett, daughter of Henry L. and Addie

(Kellum) Puckett who reside in Baton Rouge where Mr. Puckett is
a prominent representative of the cotton brokerage business. Mrs.
McHugh was graduated from the Baton Rouge High School and thereafter continued her studies in the University of Louisiana until her
graduation with the degree of Bachelor of Arts. Dr. and Mrs. Mc-
Hugh have a winsome little daughter, Ruth, born August 24, 1922.

Henry E. Chambers HISTORY OF LOUISIANA, Volume II, pages
313-314. Published in 1925 by the American Historical Society, Chicago and New York.

RUTH McHUGH

Born: August 24, 1922

Married: G. Norman David on July 5, 1944

Children of G. Norman and Ruth (McHugh) David: Jeff McHugh
David, born November 27, 1946.

WILLIAM SHAW, JUNIOR

Born: 1803-1805 in Louisiana

Married: Ellen Neville, the Widow Hubbs. She was the daughter of
Thomas Neville and Jane McHugh, who was the daughter of
Philip and Mary McHugh and the sister of Jeremiah McHugh who
married William Shaw Jr.'s sister, Anastasia, and the sister of
John McHugh who married William Shaw Jr.'s sister, Susannah.
Ellen Neville Hubbs Shaw was the mother of Emily and Edward
Hubbs.

Died: 1870-1880

Children of William and Ellen (Neville) Shaw, Jr.: Mary Jane Shaw,
born January 11, 1846, died young; Susan Ellen Shaw, born February
9, 1848, died young; Laura Ann Shaw, born July 19, 1850, married
James Jacob Borskey; Ellen Catharine Shaw, born June 18, 1853,
died young; Elizabeth Anastasia Shaw, born December 24, 1856, married Joseph C. Weis; William Daniel Shaw, born July 9, 1858, married first Mary E. Brashears and secondly Mary McHugh, who was
the daughter of James Babin McHugh, the granddaughter of John A.
McHugh, the great-granddaughter of John McHugh and Susannah
Shaw, and the great-great granddaughter of Philip and Mary Mc-
Hugh and William and Mary Ann Weekley Shaw; John Joseph Shaw,
born April 21, 1861, died young; James Beauregard Shaw, born January 10, 1864, died young.

1850 CENSUS EAST BATON ROUGE PARISH LOUISIANA

Wm Shaw born in 1803 in Louisiana; Ellen Shaw born in 1823 in
Louisiana; Emily Hubbs born in 1841 in Louisiana; Edward Hubbs
born in 1843 in Louisiana; *Mary born in 1845 in Louisiana; *Susan
born in 1848 in Louisiana; *Lorey born in 1850 in Louisiana; Wm

Alexander born in 1815 in Louisiana; Jane Neville born in 1790 in Mississippi; Catharine Nevill born in 1830 in Louisiana

*In the original census records for 1850, no surname is given beside these first names, however, "ditto marks" follow the name "Hubbs." The 1860 and 1870 census records correctly name the children "Shaw" and not "Hubbs."

1860 CENSUS EAST BATON ROUGE PARISH LOUISIANA

Wm Shaw born in 1803 in Louisiana; Ellen Shaw born in 1824 in Louisiana; Mary J. Shaw born in 1846 in Louisiana; Laura A. Shaw born in 1850 in Louisiana; Catharine E. Shaw born in 1852 in Louisiana; Elizabeth A. Shaw born in 1855 in Louisiana; Wm. D. Shaw born in 1858 in Louisiana; Henry Chidister born in 1835 in Louisiana; Edward T. Hubbs born in 1842 in Louisiana; Wm Alexander born in 1820 in Louisiana

1870 CENSUS EAST BATON ROUGE PARISH LOUISIANA

William Shaw born in 1805 in Louisiana; Ellen Shaw born in 1822 in Louisiana; Elizabeth A. Shaw born in 1856 in Louisiana; Wm D Shaw born in 1858 in Louisiana; James B. Shaw born in 1864 in Louisiana; William Alexander born in 1815 in Louisiana; Edward Hubbs born in 1843 in Louisiana; Emily Hurst born in 1841 in Louisiana; David Hurst born in 1862 in Louisiana; Thomas Hurst born in 1867 in Louisiana

Conveyance Records, East Baton Rouge Parish: William Shaw to Leon Bonnecaze, April 24, 1860, book NJ, page 382; William Shaw to Leon Bonnecaze, June 18, 1860, book S, page 313.

See Harnett Kane's delightful PLANTATION PARADE, THE GRAND MANNER IN LOUISIANA, 1945, William Morrow and Company and particularly pages 120 through 123 for an interesting description of Leon Bonnecaze, unfortunate creditor of Charles Louis Napoleon Achille Murat, nephew of Napoleon, Crown Prince of Naples, and Master of Magnolia Mound Plantation at Baton Rouge. In 1825 Mr. Bonnecaze acted as Master of Ceremonies for the Reception of the Marquis de Lafayette, during his visit to Baton Rouge.

William Shaw to William Alexander, December 16, 1867, book W, page 318; William Shaw to John A. McHugh, March 7, 1870, book Y, page 487; William Shaw to Catharine McGuirt Bridges, March 25, 1874, book Z, page 391; William Shaw to Guy Bridges, April 29, 1878, book MI, page 373; William Shaw to Guy Bridges, April 29, 1878; book 4, page 334; Heirs of William Shaw to Joseph C. Wise, September 20, 1882, book 6, page 620; Heirs of William Shaw to the Catholic Congregation of the Church of St. John the Baptist, May 13, 1916, book 60, page 104; William Shaw to Thomas Leavey, August 23, 1854, book I, page 320; William Shaw to John A. McHugh, February

13, 1850, book C, page 267; William Shaw to Charles Whitehead, January 14, 1847, book NO, page 169; William Shaw to Charles Whitehead, October 26, 1849, book AZ, page 320; William Shaw, Senior, to William Shaw, Jr., June 29, 1836, book JP, page 137; William Shaw, Senior, to William Shaw, Jr., October 28, 1823, book JL, page 255.

1880 CENSUS EAST BATON ROUGE PARISH LOUISIANA

William Shaw born in 1858 in Louisiana; His brother, James Shaw born in 1865 in Louisiana

ELIZABETH ANASTASIA SHAW

Born: December 24, 1855

Married: Joseph C. Weis on January 12, 1879. Mr. Weis was born on September 15, 1855, and died on November 21, 1930

Childern of Joseph C. and Elizabeth Anastasia (Shaw) Weis: Laura Emily Weis, born January 11, 1880; Henry Walter Weis, born November 13, 1881; Mary Lou Ellen Weis, born March 24, 1884; Edna Alma Weis, born April 24, 1886; Margaret Lillian Weis, born January 15, 1888; Joseph David Weis, born February 9, 1890, died April 4, 1931; Alice Elizabeth Weis, born February 7, 1892; Effie Agnes Weis, born January 11, 1895, died December 5, 1900; Clarence James Weis, born October 30, 1898, died August 17, 1901.

1880 Census, 4th Ward, East Baton Rouge Parish, Louisiana 709, 842 Joe Wise born in 1856 in Louisiana, where his mother was born. His father was born in Georgia; Elizabeth Wise born in 1858 in Louisiana where her parents were born; their daughter, Laura Wise, was born in 1879 in Louisiana.

ALICE ELIZABETH WEIS

Born: February 7, 1892

Married: Charles C. Annison on July 18, 1916. Mr. Annison died on November 4, 1942

Children of Charles C. and Alice Elizabeth (Weis) Annison: Marjorie Eloise Annison, born December 15, 1917, married Ancil Branning on October 22, 1944, no children.

EDNA ALMA WEIS

Born: April 24, 1886

Married: 1st: Joseph Jay Roberts in 1904

2nd: J. B. Batson who died on December 12, 1950

Children of Joseph Jay and Edna Alma (Weis) Roberts: Ione Marie Roberts, born on September 16, 1906, married Bill Jenks on September 1, 1927. Married secondly on February 14, 1945, to Carl Wright, no children; Burnelle Melvin Roberts.

BURNELLE MELVIN ROBERTS

Born: July 27, 1911

Married: Ida Iola Bujol on August 27, 1932

Children of Burnelle Melvin and Ida Iola (Bujol) Roberts: Burnelle Melvin Roberts, Jr.; Joseph Jay Roberts II, born December 13, 1941; Marvin James Roberts, born October 24, 1943.

BURNELLE MELVIN ROBERTS, JR.

Born: June 4, 1934

Married: Mona Ray Fusilier on October 20, 1956

Children of Burnelle Melvin and Mona Ray (Fusilier) Roberts, Jr.: Christopher Michael Roberts, born September 15, 1957.

HENRY WALTER WEIS

Born: November 13, 1881

Married: Ettie Roberts

Died: 1922

Children of Henry Walter and Ettie (Roberts) Weis: Thelma Weis, deceased; Hilda Belle Weis, deceased; Mildred Weis.

JOSEPH DAVID WEIS

Born: February 9, 1890

Married: Lillie Alna Loudon on June 6, 1925

Died: April 4, 1931

Children of Joseph David and Lillie Alna (Loudon) Weis: Joseph David Weis, Jr.; Alna Mae Weis.

ALNA MAE WEIS

Born: December 2, 1930

Married: Charles Allen Abbott on December 15, 1951

Children of Charles Allen and Alna Mae (Weis) Abbott: Charles Allen Abbott, Jr., born October 9, 1952; Alna Dianne Abbott, born April 12, 1957.

JOSEPH DAVID WEIS, JR.

Born: August 13, 1928

Married: Betty Young Zimmerman on July 11, 1953

Children of Joseph David and Betty Young (Zimmerman) Weis, Jr.: Joseph David Weis III, born April 10, 1954; Dave Arthur Weis, born January 13, 1958; Karen Susan Weis, born April 6, 1959.

LAURA EMILY WEIS

Born: January 11, 1880

Married: James A. Whitehead on February 4, 1904

Children of James A. and Laura Emily (Weis) Whitehead: Nora

Ellen Whitehead, born February 28, 1905, died on December 11, 1914; Mildred Lucille Whitehead, born January 26, 1910; married Marshall Bond on November 11, 1936, no children.

LILLIAN MARGUERITE WEIS

Born: January 15, 1888

Married: Fred Odom Graves on July 8, 1926. Mr. Graves died on August 11, 1958

MARY LOU ELLEN WEIS

Born: March 24, 1884

Married: Samuel Carney Whitehead on July 9, 1903

Children of Samuel Carney and Mary Lou Ellen (Weis) Whitehead: Irma Elizabeth Whitehead; Bernice Mary Whitehead, born November 14, 1910, married St. George Lee Hines, Jr., on May 12, 1929, no children.

IRMA ELIZABETH WHITEHEAD

Born: May 3, 1904

Married: Robert Emmett Amrhein on October 18, 1925.

Children of Robert Emmett and Irma Elizabeth (Whitehead) Amrhein: Beryl Marie Amrhein; Robert Emmett Amrhein; Elizabeth Ann Amrhein.

BERYL MARIE AMRHEIN

Born: June 13, 1926

Married: Gerald Wicker on September 21, 1945

Children of Gerald and Beryl Marie (Amrhein) Wicker: Cheryl Ann Wicker, born November 21, 1946; Judith Marie Wicker, born February 6, 1953.

ELIZABETH ANN AMRHEIN

Born: December 24, 1934

Married: Joseph Gautreau on September 11, 1954

Children of Joseph and Elizabeth Ann (Amrhein) Gautreau: Theresa Marie Gautreau, born April 8, 1955; Debra Ann Gautreau, born April 9, 1956; David Joseph Gautreau, born May 17, 1959.

ROBERT EMMETT AMRHEIN, JR.

Born: July 7, 1931

Married: Ethel Mae Langley on June 3, 1951

Children of Robert Emmett and Ethel Mae (Langley) Amrhein, Jr.: Robert Michael Amrhein, born on May 7, 1955; Rodney Bryant Amrhein, born April 28, 1957; David Keith Amrhein, born August 11, 1959.

LAURA ANN SHAW

Born: July 19, 1850
Married: James Jacob Borskey on January 21, 1869
Died: November 24, 1926

Children of James Jacob and Laura Ann (Shaw) Borskey: Hannah E. Borskey; Rosalee Lilly Borskey; Nora Alberta Borskey; Bertha Mae Borskey; Benjamin A. Borskey; James William Borskey; Effie Lula Borskey

Information on the Borskeys was sent to me by Benjamin A. Borskey, 805 Blum Street, Alvin, Texas.

1870 Census, East Baton Rouge Parish, Louisiana 671, 671

James J. Borskey born in 1848 in Louisiana; Laura A. Borskey born in 1851 in Louisiana; Miss L. C. Borskey born in 1855 in Louisiana; Hannah E. Borskey born in 1870 in Louisiana; S. W. Carney born in 1849 in Louisiana.

BENJAMIN ANTHONY BORSKEY

Born: September 29, 1887
Married: Mildred Marie Stanton on August 16, 1911. She died on March 3, 1956

Children of Benjamin Anthony and Mildred Marie (Stanton) Borskey; Curtis A. Borskey; Elsie Borskey.

CURTIS A. BORSKEY

Born: August 14, 1912
Married: 1st: Gladys Trafton on July 8, 1930
2nd: Eleanor Smith in 1940
3rd: Mary Frances Leammons in 1950

Children of Curtis A. and Gladys (Trafton) Borskey: Charles Lee Borskey, born March 12, 1931

Children of Curtis A. and Eleanor (Smith) Borskey: Benjamin S. Borskey, born April 27, 1941; Curtis A. Borskey, Jr., born November 18, 1943; Leo Ray Borskey, born February 11, 1946.

ELSIE BORSKEY

Born: November 2, 1913
Married: Bert G. Phillips on July 6, 1932

Children of Bert G. and Elsie (Borskey) Phillips: Mildred Phillips; Elsie Faye Phillips, born August 14, 1942; George Wayne Phillips, born August 15, 1944; Bert G. Phillips, Jr., born October 12, 1939, married Sharon Slaughter on April 26, 1958.

MILDRED PHILLIPS

Born: July 5, 1933
Married: Arnold Wafer on April 25, 1953

Children of Arnold and Mildred (Phillips) Wafer: Lesa Wafer, born November 12, 1955; Gena Wafer, born August 16, 1957.

BERTHA BORSKEY

Born: September 12, 1886

Married: Luther Andrew Weyant

Died: December 21, 1956

Children of Luther Andrew and Bertha (Borskey) Weyant: Luther Russell Weyant; Clyde Andrew Weyant; William H. Weyant; Ralph Weyant; Mae Louise Weyant; Robert Wayne Weyant.

LUTHER RUSSELL WEYANT

Born: May 29, 1905

Married: 1st: Ruth McMullen, divorced
        2nd: Charlotte McCullough on February 13, 1958

Children of Luther Russell and Ruth (McMullen) Weyant: Phyliss Weyant.

Children of Luther Russell and Charlotte (McCullough) Weyant: Dorothy Weyant.

PHYLISS WEYANT

Born: August 7, 1925

Married: William Rose on February 5, 1944

Children of William and Phyliss (Weyant) Rose: Sandra Rose, born August 7, 1946; Catharine Rose, born July 2, 1948.

DOROTHY WEYANT

Born: August 21, 1927

Married: Steve Relinski on September 8, 1945

Children of Steve and Dorothy (Weyant) Relinski: Linda Lee Relinski, born September 26, 1946

CLYDE ANDREW WEYANT

Born: November 13, 1906

Married: Irma Ehinger on February 5, 1927

Died: October 27, 1956

Children of Clyde Andrew and Irma (Ehinger) Weyant: Patricia Weyant, born May 13, 1933; John F. Weyant.

JOHN F. WEYANT

Born: October 7, 1936

Married: Joyce David on August 27, 1937

Children of John F. and Joyce (David) Weyant: Susan L. Weyant, born December 9, 1957.

WILLIAM H. WEYANT

Born: September 8, 1908

Married: Kathleen Amy on September 15, 1928

Children of William H. and Kathleen (Amy) Weyant: William K. Weyant.

WILLIAM K. WEYANT

Born: December 5, 1934

Married: Sylvia Arrison on May 21, 1955

Children of William K. and Sylvia (Arrison) Weyant: Elizabeth Leigh Weyant, born June 12, 1957; Susan Renee Weyant, born May 5, 1959.

RALPH WEYANT

Born: May 12, 1911

Married: 1st: Peggy Fisher, divorced

2nd: Janet Cope on February 4, 1936

Children of Ralph and Peggy (Fisher) Weyant: Doris Weyant, born March 21, 1930

Children of Ralph and Janet (Cope) Weyant: James Weyant, born January 2, 1941; Judy Weyant, born February 10, 1947.

MAE LOUISE WEYANT

Born: April 24, 1913

Married: Lawrence Pope on January 2, 1932

Information on the family of Luther Andrew and Bertha (Borskey) Weyant was furnished by Mae Louise (Weyant) Pope, 7527 E. Corey Street, Downey, California.

Children of Lawrence and Mae Louse (Weyant) Pope: Ronald A. Pope, born February 10, 1933; Richard P. Pope; Charles Lawrence Pope, born February 4, 1937.

RICHARD P. POPE

Born: March 7, 1934

Married: Mariella Schmidt on September 5, 1953

Children of Richard P. and Mariella (Schmidt) Pope: James P. Pope, born July 4, 1954; Steven M. Pope, born March 23, 1958.

ROBERT WAYNE WEYANT

Born: July 23, 1925

Married: Ann Stovich on October 10, 1954

EFFIE LULA BORSKEY

Born: May 22, 1891

Married: R. W. Peebles on April 30, 1912

Children of R. W. and Effie Lula (Borskey) Peebles: Howard W. Peebles; R. R. Peebles; Marjorie Peebles.

HOWARD W. PEEBLES

Born: December, 1912

Married: Evelyn Junkins on November 24, 1936

Children of Howard W. and Evelyn (Junkins) Peebles: Tommy Peebles, born November 4, 1947.

R. R. PEEBLES

Born: January 19, 1922

Married: Addie Strantham on September 29, 1947

Children of R. R. and Addie (Strantham) Peebles: R. R. Peebles, Jr., born November 29, 1947; Bonnie Lee Peebles, born August 22, 1948; Sarah M. Peebles, born January 18, 1951; Jodie L. Peebles, born June 29, 1955.

MARJORIE PEEBLES

Born: April 4, 1918

Married: 1st: Hays Slatten in August, 1936

2nd: Dale Wyatt on September 21, 1946

Children of Hays and Marjorie (Peebles) Slatten: Robert H. Slatten, born October 19, 1943

Children of Dale and Marjorie (Peebles) Wyatt: Guy Wyatt, born March 11, 1955.

HANNAH E. BORSKEY

Born: November 24, 1869.

Married: Mr. Philbrick.

Died: May 6, 1931.

Children of Hannah E. (Borskey) Philbrick: Jack Philbrick, Maude Philbrick, Belle Philbrick.

NORA ALBERTA BORSKEY

Born: September 29, 1881.

Married: November 13, 1906, to James C. Purcell.

Died: July 28, 1955.

Children of James C. and Nora (Borskey) Purcell: Genevieve Purcell, born January 28, 1908, unmarried; Helen Purcell; Elaine Purcell, born June, 1929; Nancy Purcell, born November 13, 1941; Anna Mae Purcell; James Purcell, born September 21, 1926.

HELEN PURCELL

Born: March 8, 1909.

Married: Clyde Hering in 1927.

Children of Clyde and Helen (Purcell) Hering: Elaine Hering, born in June, 1929; Nancy Hering, born November 13, 1941.

ANNA MAE PURCELL

Born: September, 1912.

Married: Walter G. Blackburn on December 1, 1929.

Children of Walter G. and Anna Mae (Purcell) Blackburn: Walter G. Blackburn, Jr., born May 14, 1932; James Roy Blackburn, born January 28, 1934.

JAMES WILLIAM BORSKEY

Born: April 4, 1889.

Married: Lillian Crain on December 26, 1909.

Died: August 1, 1955.

Children of James William and Lillian (Crane) Borskey: James Wilbur Borskey.

JAMES WILBUR BORSKEY

Born: December 9, 1909.

Married: Mary Barrett on July 4, 1937.

Children of James Wilbur and Mary (Barrett) Borskey: Mary Ann Borskey, born April 6, 1938, married James Owens on August 30, 1958; Lawrence Borskey, born October 16, 1942; Rose Borskey, born December 27, 1949.

ROSALEE LILLY BORSKEY

Born: July 24, 1879.

Married: William M. Cummins on November 10, 1899.

Children of William M. and Rosalee Lilly (Borskey) Cummins: Frank Cummins, born July, 1900, died December, 1957; Nellie Cummins, born 1904, died young; Ernest Cummins; Jeannette Cummins, died in November, 1925.

WILLIAM DANIEL SHAW

Born: July 9, 1858.

Married: 1st: Mary Ella Brashear

2nd: Mary L. McHugh on September 26, 1908.

Died: July 3, 1938.

Children of William Daniel and Mary L. (McHugh) Shaw: Clarence Shaw, born June 20, 1909. Mr. Clarence Shaw is the great-grandson of William and Mary Ann Shaw through his father, William Daniel Shaw, and is also the great-great-great-grandson of William and Mary Ann Shaw through his mother, Mary L. McHugh. Still living in the little town where his forbears settled in the days of the Spanish

Dons, Mr. Shaw is his last descendant to bear the name of Shaw. Not far from his home in Zachary is the little cemetery established on land which since its Grant from the Spanish Crown has never been owned by anyone except the Shaw family and in it are the remains of his ancestors.

Mary E. Brashear, wife of W. D. Shaw, was born on September 1, 1874, and died on May 12, 1905.

Marriage Records of East Baton Rouge Parish, Book 35, Page 305, October 28, 1903. W. D. Shaw and Ella Brashear.

Marriage Records of East Baton Rouge Parish, Book 42, Page 1a, September 24, 1908. Mary McHugh and William D. Shaw.

Conveyance Records of East Baton Rouge Parish.

William D. Shaw to Joseph C. Wise, Book 6, Page 620, September 20, 1882.

William D. Shaw to Joseph C. Wise. Book 13, Page 157, October 4, 1890.

William D. Shaw to James B. McHugh. Book DD, Page 284, December 14, 1908.

William D. Shaw to James B. McHugh. Book 41, Page 325, December 14, 1908.

William D. Shaw to Thomas E. McHugh. Book 42, Page 556, September 15, 1909.

CARTER

COLONEL NEHEMIAH CARTER

Married: Rachel (?   )

Died: Will recorded in Natchez, Mississippi, on March 3, 1814, and probated on March 5, 1814.

Children of Colonel Nehemiah and Rachel Carter: Anna or Ann Carter; Betty Carter; Isaac Carter; Major Jesse Carter; Hannah Carter; Parsons Carter; Prudence Carter; Phebe Carter (Married Mr. Phipps); Sallie Carter (Married Mr. Hackett); Nehemiah Carter.

In the name of God Amen

I, Nehemiah Carter, late resident and inhabitant of the County of Wilkinson in the Mississippi Territory, at present confined by sickness at Second Creek in the County of Adams, and although reduced extremely low in health, yet of sound mind and memory and wishing to dispose of my goods and chattels in such manner as to prevent all future disputes and litigations among my heirs, do hereby make this my last Will and Testament in manner following, to-wit:

In the first place, I will, will and bequeath unto my beloved son Parsons Carter of the State of Louisiana a certain tract of land containing five hundred acres, lying and situate on the waters of Thompsons Creek, which land I hold by virtue of a Spanish warrant of survey, which warrant of survey has been located by Archibald Palmer, my son-in-law, who now holds the title of said land in trust for me — To have and to hold to the said Parsons Carter the above mentioned tract of land, his heirs and assigns forever

Item — I will and bequeath to my youngest son Isaac Carter of Wilkinson County in the Mississippi Territory — all that tract or parcel of land whereon I lately resided, on the Homochitto River in the said County of Wilkinson containing about ninety acres together with all the houses and buildings thereon — To have and to hold to the said Isaac his heirs and assigns the above said messuage and tenements forever.

Item — I will and bequeath unto my well beloved son Jesse Carter of Second Creek, the residue of all my goods, chattels and estates whereof I may die possessed, to be held by him, the said Jesse in trust to pay all the just dues and demands which I may owe at the time of my decease —

And should there remain any sum or sums of money in the hand of said Jesse after paying off all the debts aforesaid, then and in that case, it is my Will and request that the same be equally divided into six moieties and paid as follows, to-wit: One moietie to my daughter Hannah Palmer, one moitie to Phebe Phipps, one moietie to Anna Landfeir (this name is difficult to decipher: it could be also Landfier or Landfin), one moietie to Sally Hackett, one moietie to Prudence King and moietie to my three granddaughters, the children of my daughter Betsy Adams —

And I do hereby name constitute and appoint my well beloved son Jesse Carter to be Executor to this my last Will and Testament.

In testimony whereof I have hereunto set my Hand and Seal this Third day ofMarch A.D. Eighteen Hundred and fourteen —

(Signed)   N. CARTER   (Seal)

Signed and Sealed and declared
to be the last Will and Testament
of the said Nehemiah Carter in
presence of
Israel Smith
Wm. Walters (or Watters)

Nehemiah Carter's Will proven 5th April 1814.

State of Mississippi
County of Adams

I, Robert E. Burns, Chancery Clerk in and for said County and State do hereby certify that the above and foregoing instrument is a true and correct copy of original recorded in Will Book 1, page 107 in the Office of the Chancery Clerk, Adams County, Mississippi.

Given under my hand and official seal this the 31 day of August A.D. 1959

ROBERT E. BURNS, Chancery Clerk

By Mary Louise Curry, D. C.

AMERICAN STATE PAPERS, PUBLIC LANDS, Washington, Gales and Seaton, 1860.

Volume 4, page 444
Settlement Claim: Parsons Carter — East Feliciana — Purchase — March, 1813.

Ibid, Vol. III, page 54
Adam and A. Palmer. Original Claim of Archibald Palmer for 450 acres. Issued by Governor de Grandpre.

Adam and A. Palmer. Archibald Palmer, Original Claimant.
October 21, 1812. 590 arpents in Feliciana. V. Pintado.

(page 61)
A. and N. Palmer. Archibald Palmer Original Claimant.
October 21, 1812. 500 Arpents in Feliciana.

(Page 68)
Arch'd Palmer and Henry Bennet. 1806.

(Page 75)
H'Y Bennett and A. Palner. 1809. 1 claim by purchase.
14 claims in Feliciana.
Archibald Palmer. 1806. 1 claim by purchase. 13 claims in Feliciana.

(Page 42)
Archibald Palmer, Sen. Philip A. Grey, Original Claimant. Spanish Patent. February 15, 1802. 600 acres in Feliciana. Cultivated 1795-1814.

(page 468)
John Austin, Original Claimant. 564 acres Feliciana. Cultivated 1807-1820.

(page 472)
John Austin. Feliciana.

(page 442)
Samuel Adams. W. Knowland, Original Claimant. Spanish Patent. March 15, 1804. 291 acres. Feliciana. Issued by J. Morales. Date of Survey: December 10, 1803. Cultivated 1803-1820.

Ibid, Volume I
(page 869)
Archibald Palmer. Original Claimant. 800 acres on waters of River Homochitto. May 15, 1789.
Sarah Carter (late Kenner) Sarah Kenner, Original Claimant. 250 acres Second Creek. May 21, 1791. Spanish Patent.
Jesse Carter. Rachel Carter, Original Claimant. 500 acres Second Creek. Spanish Patent. May 16, 1791.

(page 871)
Jesse Carter. Original Claimant 800 acres River Homochitto. May 21, 1791.

(page 851)
Jesse Carter. 100 acres Second Creek British Grant. John Bolls, Original Grantee. May 26, 1777.

(page 908)
Nehemiah Carter. Jefferson County. Boyd's Creek. 640 acres.

(page 901)
Nehemiah Carter Original Claimant 90 acres on River Homochitto.

(page 614)
Nehemiah Carter. Boyd's Creek. 1200 acres. British Grant. November 21, 1798. John Gashins says "that the claimant resided in the Mississippi Territory on October 27, 1795, that he was above the age of 21 at the date of the warrant and that he has continued to be an inhabitant of the Mississippi Territory.

(Page 860)
Robert Carter. 300 acres St. Catherine's Creek. February 10, 1789. Spanish Patent.

(Page 621)
Thomas Carter. Cole's Creek. British Grant.

(page 891)
Charles Carter. 450 acres Wells Creek. Spanish Grant. January 6, 1789.

(page 893)
Vincent Carter. 640 acres Wells Creek. March 30, 1798. Occupancy.

A Petition to Governor Miro that White Cliffs, 12 miles below Natchez, one of the most picturesque spots on the Mississippi, be used for a public landing was signed on January 15, 1778, by a "few of the inhabitants of Second Creek" including NEHEMIAH CARTER AND JESSE CARTER.

MISSISSIPPI, AS A PROVINCE, TERRITORY AND STATE by John Francis Hamtramck Claiborne, Volume I, Jackson, Mississippi, Power and Barksdale, 1880, Page 129.

The following are from THE NATCHEZ COURT RECORDS, 1767-1805, by May Wilson McBee, published by Edwards Brothers, Inc., Ann Arbor, Michigan, 1953:

(Page 59) 29 Aug 1788. Thos. Irwin to Nehemiah Carter, a new negro wench, aged 20, for $475 (Mexican Dollars) payable Jan, 1790, negro mortgaged, likewise a negro of purchaser named "Bob" and two cows marked "N.C.". Jesse Carter surety for Nehemiah Carter. The undersigned having full power from Thos. Irwin, have transferred the mortgage in the foregoing to John Mapother for the amount due from N. Carter, in pursuance of an agreement between the three parties. 14 April 1792. Clark and Rees by express orders, 13 April 1792. /s/ Juan Malpother, N. Carter, Before Manual Gayoso de Lemos.

(Page 70) 3 Oct 1789. Thomas Irwin to Nehemiah Carter, two negro boys for $760, Mexican silver, payable in tobacco which has been inspected in King's Store at New Orleans, at rate of $8 per hundred pounds. Signed.

(Page 73) Clark and Rees to Nehemiah Carter, two negroes for 625 Mex. dollars on time, also mortgaged 200 acres on Second Creek bounded by John Ellis and Don Philip Trevino. Signed. One third of said plantation transferred to Ebenezer Rees for a debt of Nehemiah Carter to said Rees. 13 Apr 1792. One negro died and was replaced by Rees and one taken back.

(Page 83) Three negroes sold to Nehemiah Carter for $1,625. 20 May 1791.

(Page 85) Nehemiah Carter appointed an appraiser of a negro named "Quashee". 6 Aug 1791.

(Page 87) Nehemiah Carter one of the debtors of the Estate of Eliphalet Richards. 11 Oct 1791.

(Page 114) Post of Natchez. 7 May 1795. Rachel Carter, wife of Nehemiah Carter, of Second Creek, out of great love I bear to my three sons, Nehemiah, Parsons, and Isaac, do of my free will and accord, make them a gift of 500 arpents in this District bounded by John Bolls, Henry Phips, Samuel Phips and Osborn Sprigg, granted to me by the Governor General of this Province. 17 May 1791, with all buildings, gates and fences. /s/ Rachel Carter with the approbation of Caudel.

(Page 116) Nehemiah Carter one of the debtors of the Estate of Benjamin Monsanto, planter. 10 Oct 1794.

(Page 125) Nehemiah Carter was a witness of the Will of Pierre Surget. (Opening of the Will). 27 July 1796.

(Page 142) Nehemiah Carter was a debtor of the Estate of John Pickens. 18 Jan 1789.

(Page 144) Nehemiah Carter owed Thomas Irwin $760.

(Page 149) Nehemiah Carter owed Adam Ware money. 27 June 1792.

(Page 206) The declaration of Anthony Hutchins at the Post of Natchez on this 3rd of May 1795, before Don Carlos de Grand-Pre. At the request of Elizabeth Tomlinson, appeared Anthony Hutchins, who declared that in 1787 or 1788, talking with NEHEMIAH CARTER, concerning a tract of 100 arpents, which said Carter had bought, he told him as a friend that the buildings were out of the bounds of said land and advised the said Carter to apply for a grant to secure the said buildings but said Carter replied that he would not, observing that these people, meaning the Spaniards, would not be long here and he was glad the 100 arpents were bought in the name of his wife, for he would never hold land under a Spanish title. The deponent is near 70 years of age. /s/ Anthony Hutchins. Wit: Jean Girault, Estevan Minor, and Daniel Douglas. Before Carlos de Grand-Pre.

In his *Lower Mississippi* published by Rhinehart and Company, New York, 1959, Mr. Hodding Carter notes, "In the Natchez area lived many Britishers and Tories, who hated the Americans and who had been well treated and honored under Spain. But they still cherished the dream that the British flag would wave again over the river. Foremost among them was wiry old ANTHONY HUTCHINS, a colorful 80 year old British officer who had come years before to the Natchez country to claim a French and Indian War grant. Hutchins had remained indomitably English. He fought Spain on the river when she became the ally of the Americans, and was the principal victim of Willing's raid. Fleeing after the failure of the British coup in Natchez he ultimately returned and became the leading citizen of the conservative wealthy planters. Throughout his life he worked in behalf of England, never despairing of the return of the Cross of St. George." (page 130).

Estevan Minor succeeded Don Manuel Gayoso de Lemos as Spanish Governor at Natchez. Carlos de Grand-Pre later served as Governor of Spanish West Florida.

(Page 280) Nehemiah Carter sued Anthony Hutchins for a mare belonging to him. 3 June 1795.

(Page 282) Nehemiah Carter appointed one of the appraisers to examine work done by James Singleton on the plantation of Archibald McDuffy. 17 Nov 1792.

(Page 397) Nehemiah Carter was a witness of the lease and release of land on James Branch of Bayou Pierre (31 Aug 1777, 21 July 1779) by Francis Dolony and wife, Lucy, to William Vousdan. Mr. John Bisland was another witness. In her THIS TOO IS NATCHEZ, Nola Nance Oliver describes Somerset, plantation home of William Vousdan. In her book NATCHEZ, she describes Mount Repose, plantation home of the Bislands.

(Page 411) British land grant of 400 acres, 7 miles below White Cliffs, south of Natchez and one mile from the upper end of an island in the Mississippi River, by the Royal Governor, the Honorable Peter Chester to James Smith Yarborough, who on 21 Oct 1777 granted the land to Charles Percy. NEHEMIAH CARTER, a witness.

(Page 421) The Honorable Peter Chester, Royal British Governor, granted 1,200 acres 3 miles from Rumsey's land on Boyd's Creek, to NEHEMIAH CARTER, if it does not interfere with Harcourt's Mandamus in West Florida. 21 Nov 1778.

(Pages 532-3) Samuel Phipps, a citizen of the Mississippi Territory, County of Adams, claimed 370 acres in said county, on the waters of Second Creek, founded on a Warrent of Order of Survey granted to claimant by the Spanish Government the 24 Sept 1793, by virtue of which he took possession and continued to cultivate the same to the present time, during which time claimant has been the head of a family with wife and children. Plat shows JESSE CARTER, Colonel Hutchins and Christy Gilbert with lands adjoining. March 23, 1804. Witness: Colonel Nehemiah Carter.

(page 285) Andrew Beall sued Nehemiah Carter for the hire of negroes to saw plank in 1789.

(Page 576) Nehemiah Carter was a witness to the Claim of Elijah Pope on 31 Mar 1804 for 200 acres in Wilkinson County on the waters of Buffalo.

(Page 551) Parsons Carter, a citizen of the Mississippi Territory, Adams County, claimed 640 acres in Wilkinson County on the waters of Buffalo Creek. Parsons Carter or persons to his use did actually cultivate the tract on the day the Mississippi Territory was evacuated by Spanish Troops, Parsons Carter being then above the age of 21 years. 28 Mar 1804. Witness: Nehemiah Carter. G. Poindexter, attorney for claimant.

(Page 551) Nehemiah Carter of the Mississippi Territory claimed 640 acres on the north branch of the south fork of Buffalo Creek, Wilkinson County, by virtue of settlement by Daniel Walton prior to 1797. Daniel Walton sold the tract to Barnaby Donley and he sold it to Nehemiah Carter. The land was near Bullard's Springs. Witness: Edward Hackett.

(page 551) Edward Hackett, an inhabitant of the Mississippi Territory, claimed 200 acres on Hutchins Creek, Wilkinson County. 28 Mar 1804. Witness: Hugh Davis.

The following is copied from Mr. William B. Hamilton's "Jefferson College and Education in Mississippi, 1798-1817" published in the JOURNAL OF MISSISSIPPI HISTORY, Volume 3, page 259 (1941):

"Mrs. Edith Wyatt Moore who is on intimate terms with early Natchez documents states that to judge from the numerous papers signed with an 'X—his mark', the second generation of the upper crust in the Natchez District was allowed to grow up unlettered. At any rate the inhabitants themselves charged the despotic government of Spain with their lack of schools.

(page 262) "Another factor in the lack of good formal education was the character of some of the teachers available. Some of them were immigrants who turned to teaching in desperation with little preparation and less morals.

(page 263) "One may be permitted to hope that Joseph A. Lloyd was not typical. Lloyd came to Mississippi in the entourage of Governor Winthrop Sargent, who speedily withdrew patronage from the teacher. Lloyd remained, however, as tutor in the families of JESSE CARTER and Abner Greene and was subsequently tutor to the Surgets, the Bingamans and others. He was by 1807 a confessed drunkard, unable to govern himself, in spite of the most fearful and protracted mornings after, recorded in his diary. He was sardonically amused to discover in the same drawing room a drunken music master, a drunken dancing master, and a drunken schoolmaster."

In a letter from Carlos de Grand Pre, Natchez, March 2, 1790, to Senor Don Estevan Minor, there was enclosed a statement of the pounds of tobacco produced by the growers of Natchez in 1789, including:

ARCH PALMER: 3,700 pounds
NEHEMIAH CARTER: 5,100 pounds
JESSE CARTER: 9,500 pounds

Mississippi Genealogical Exchange, Volume 5, June, 1959, Pages 39 and 40, Edited by Katie Prince Ward Esker.

As the Carters came to Natchez in 1775, it is interesting to read about the Natchez of those days in A GENTLEMAN OF THE OLD NATCHEZ REGION: BENJAMIN L. C. WAILES, by Charles S. Sydnor, Duke University Press, Durham, North Carolina, 1938:
(page 4) In 1776, Natchez consisted of ten log cabins, two frame houses and four stores under the hill. In the whole Natchez region, *there were only 78 families, few of whom had been there more than four years.*

(page 9) From 1785 to 1800 the population increased from a little over 1,500 to about 7,500.

In 1800 there were almost 4,500 white people and 3,000 slaves. Few of the people lived more than 20 miles from the Mississippi River. By 1808 Natchez had 300 houses, mostly built of wood with balconies and piazzas.

The following shows the distribution of population in the Natchez District in 1800:

Walnut Hills	(now Vicksburg)	80 people (Warren County)
Bayou Pierre	(Claiborne County)	779 people
Cole's Creek		1493 people
Fairchild's Creek	Jefferson	352 people
Union Town	County	41 people
Ellicottsville		56 people
Pine Ridge	Adams	125 people
Natchez and St.	County	
Catherine's Creek		1696 people
Homochitto, Second		
Creek and Sandy Creek		2280 people
Buffalo River and	Wilkinson	635 people
Bayou Sara	County	

The Reverend William Winans was a pioneer Methodist minister of Mississippi and Louisiana. He founded the first Methodist Church in the City of New Orleans.

The following references are taken from Volume II of Albert Eugene Casey's AMITE COUNTY, MISSISSIPPI, 1699-1890:

(page 454) Baton Rouge. April 1, 1829. Elder Parsons Carter was appointed a Delegate to the next General Assembly of the Presbyterian Church.

(page 457) Mr. Parsons Carter from Jackson and Scott's Settlement met at Pinckneyville, Mississippi, on October 14, 1829.

(page 459) Parsons Carter from Jackson and Scott's Settlement was at the Friendship Church on October 13, 1830.

(pages 471, 475) Elder Parsons Carter from the Jackson Church attends the meeting of the Presbytery of Amite in Jackson, Louisiana, on March 15, 1837.

(page 511) The Reverend William Winans dined with Mr. Parsons Carter on Sunday, August 8, 1815, as recorded in his diary. (page 506) The Reverend William Winans mentions dining with Mr. Parsons Carter on Friday, April 14, 1815, and on Monday, April 24.

(page 592) The Reverend William Winans accompanied by Wesley rode to Brother Carter's in the Plains, 32 miles on August 29, 1842. (This must be General Carter, as his father, Parsons Carter, was dead.)

ANNA (ANN) CARTER

Married: Thomas Landfair (Lanphire, Landfare, Landfar, Landfeir, Landfier, Lamphear, Lanphier, Landphier, Lanpheir, Lamphair, Lampheir, etc.)

Died: Before April 4, 1816.

Children of Thomas and Anna or Ann (Carter) Landfair: William Landfair; Robert Landfair; Davis (or David) Landfair; Eunice (Unis) Landfair; Jesse Landfair; Wellington Landfair.

BETTY CARTER

Born: 1775-1794.

Married: 1st: Mr. Adams

2nd: Solomon Swayze who died June, 1833.

Children of Solomon and Betty (Carter) Swayze: Richard Swayze; Belinda Swayze, died at 18; William Swayze.

See DESCENDANTS OF THE JERSEY SETTLERS, KINGSTON, ADAMS COUNTY, MISSISSIPPI, page 22.

1820 CENSUS, ADAMS COUNTY, MISSISSIPPI

Solm Swayze

1 male born before 1775; 1 male born 1775-1794; 1 male born 1804-1810; 1 male born 1810-1820; 1 female born 1775-1794; 1 female born 1810-1820; 16 slaves.

A letter dated August 24, 1891, from C. F. Farrar, Kingston, Mississippi, to Isaac A. Carter of Darrington, Mississippi, says Richard Swayze of Yazoo County, Mississippi, was the son of an ADAMS, A SISTER OF ISAAC CARTER WHO LIVED AND DIED AT CARTER'S BLUFF.

BIOGRAPHICAL AND HISTORICAL MEMOIRS OF MISSISSIP-
PI, published in 1891 by the Goodspeed Company of Chicago, Volume
1, page 720, lists Dr. Caleb F. Farrar of Kingston as being "more
familiar with the early history of the Jersey Colonists than any other
man now living."

BIOGRAPHICAL AND HISTORICAL MEMOIRS OF MISSISSIPPI
(1891) Goodspeed Publishing Company, Chicago, Volume 2, page 870,
gives the biography of HENRY CLAY SWAYZE, planter of Fair-
view Plantation, a descendant of old and honored families on both
sides of the house. He was born near Kingston in 1830 and his father,
SOLOMON SWAYZE, was born in this same neighborhood on July 4,
1777 (this is an error: he was born July 4, 1776). SOLOMON
SWAYZE was the first American child born in the Settlement. He
was educated at home and although he started out for himself with
limited means, he became quite a wealthy planter. The first wife of
Solomon Swayze was ELIZABETH CARTER who was of the Colony.
Two children were born of this marriage: Richard and William. The
second wife of Solomon Swayze was Mary Custard (nee Boyd), whose
father was an extensive planter on Boyd's Lake, near Hutchins Landing. The children of this marriage were: Henry Clay, Benjamin F.
and Alexander Montgomery Swayze. Benjamin was a planter in Wilkinson County and Alexander in Adams County.

BIOGRAPHICAL AND HISTORICAL MEMOIRS OF MISSISSIPPI
(1891) Goodspeed Publishing Company, Chicago, Volume 2, pages
870-871. H. S. SWAYZE, Evans. Born in Yazoo in 1842. In 1862
Mr. Swayze enlisted in Company B, Withers Artillery. He was at the
Siege of Vicksburg, taken prisoner at Port Hudson, paroled and exchanged, captured at Mobile and imprisoned on Ship Island. In 1866
he married Jennie Handley, daughter of Sebourn and Elizabeth
(Stubblefield) Handley. Their children: Josephine, wife of James D.
McKie; Hayes, a medical student; Lizzie; Nathan; Hardy; Clayton;
and Katie. Mr. Swayze's parents, Richard and Mary E. (Sojourner)
Swayze belonged to the earliest and most prominent of Yazoo County
families.

DESCENDANTS OF THE JERSEY SETTLERS, KINGSTON,
ADAMS COUNTY, MISSISSIPPI, page 18, notes Caleb King left
New York on the first day of January, 1775, accompanied by several
families, all of whom settled on the land, EXCEPT THE FAMILY
OF NEHEMIAH CARTER. Page 22 notes the marriage of SOLO-
MON SWAYZE to BETSEY ADAMS.

The father of SOLOMON SWAYZE was Richard Swayze, Jr., who
married Hannah Budd. Besides Solomon, they were the parents of
Mary, Sarah, Lydia and Gabriel Swayze.

The grandfather of SOLOMON SWAYZE was Richard Swayze

who was born in Southold, Long Island, on August 20, 1717 and died about 1780. He was married to Sarah Horton who died in 1812 in her 99th year. Richard's brother, the Reverend Samuel Swayze's, was the first Congregational minister in New Jersey. Like most of his father's family, the Reverend Samuel Swayze was a staunch Loyalist or Tory. He bitterly opposed in public and private the aggression of the Colonies against the rule of their sovereign, King George III. The Revolution approaching, he sold his property in New Jersey and with his family, in company with his brother, Richard, moved to Western Florida, now Mississippi.

On May 13, 1767, Amos Ogden, a Captain in the English Navy, being wounded retired from service and settled in New Jersey. He received from King George III a grant of 25,000 acres of land. This was in consideration of valuable services rendered by an ancestor of the same name to King Charles I who had been secreted by Ogden in a hollow tree on his farm while being pursued by his enemies. Captain Amos Ogden met with Richard and Samuel Swayze and on April 14, 1772, sold them 19,000 acres of land, on condition that they were to survey and locate the entire claim at their own expense.

Soon after in the same year, the Swayzes sent a party including two surveyors, Caleb and Joseph King, and Captain Amos Ogden by boat from New York to Pensacola. They traveled either on pack mules through an unbroken wilderness from Pensacola to Natchez or procured small oar boats and paddled along the coast of what are now the States of Alabama and Misisippi across Lake Pontchartrain or Lake Mauripois into the Mississippi River until they came to the mouth of the Homochitto River which was the southern boundary of the "Mandamus Tract". Captain Ogden returned home after he had completed his work and died in New York City in October, 1772.

Richard and Samuel Swayze with a party consisting mostly of their married children, amounting to some 12 or 15 families, sailed from Perth Amboy, New Jersey, in the latter part of the year 1772 and after a tedious and perilous journey, landed at Pensacola. There, they discharged the boat which had been chartered for the occasion, and fitted up open boats, in which they placed their families and effects. Following the line of the coast to Pontchartrain, thence through the chaos of lakes, the Amite River to Pass Manchac to the Mississippi to the mouth of the Homochitto River until they reached the Ogden Mandamus Grant. Early in 1773, they stopped opposite what is known as CARTER'S BLUFF (named for the NEHEMIAH CARTER FAMILY).

In casting about for a suitable place to plant corn, they found a few acres not far off from which the timber had been destroyed, supposed to have been the rendezvous of Indians or hunters. Here they planted corn by making holes in the ground with sticks and cultivated it by knocking down weeds and young cane with the same implements. The season was propitious, the yield good and in the fall they went, as they said, "Into Egypt to buy corn" which name that place has ever since retained. The next year they moved and settled on a ridge near the public graveyard, about a half mile from Kingston. They built their cabins together, forming a village; nearby was a creek, which they called "Town Creek" and the location was "Jersey Settlement".

The Indians were numerous and hostile and for protection against them, these settlers built a stockade of logs. When there was an alarm of Indians, the women and children were placed in the stockade and the men stood as guards with their guns. The Swayzes remained at Jersey Settlement for several years, clearing up the ground. One of their number, Job Cory, was surprised in his field and wounded by the Indians. His was the first body placed in the graveyard.

The Indians and Spaniards becoming so troublesome about the year 1780, the colonists moved temporarily to St. Catherines Creek, near Natchez. There Samuel Swayze and his wife died and were buried on the bluffs at Natchez, below Fort Rosalie. Their remains years ago caved into the river. Soon after Richard Swayze died and his remains were carried back to the Jersey Settlement and placed in the public graveyard.

About the year 1786, the alarm of Indians having to a great extent subsided, most of the settlers returned to their Jersey Settlement.

A little later, the Spanish Governor ordered them to divide their lands and each one to settle on his portion, the object being to donate the unoccupied lands to other parties. The Swayzes sold several thousand acres, dividing 7,900 acres among the heirs of Richard Swayze and 7,900 acres among the heirs of Samuel Swayze.

The old Swayze men were highly esteemed for their moral virtues and liberal hospitality. The Reverend Samuel Swayze organized the first Protestant (Congregational) Church in Mississippi. On the Spanish Accession, only Roman Catholicism was permitted to hold public services. A search was made for Protestant Bibles and religious books. The Reverend Swayze hid the old Bible he brought from New Jersey when they came to Natchez in a cane brake on the margin of a small creek, known even today as "Sammie's Creek." Here the Protestants met to worship their God. This old Bible came into the possession of Mrs. Eliza King Farrar, a granddaughter of Richard Swayze, but was destroyed in the burning of the family home at Kingston, Mississippi, in 1866.

The Swayze records were given me by Mr. Clayton Swayze. Much of the material was furnished by Mr. J. Hereford Percy of Baton Rouge.

RICHARD SWAYZE

Born: November 15, 1810.

Married: 1st: Mary Ellen Sojourner on April 29, 1830.
2nd: Mrs. Elvira Luce Whitten Sales, a widow, on July 21, 1852.

Died: December 26, 1893.

Children of Richard and Mary Ellen (Sojourner) Swayze: Emily Swayze; Belinda Swayze; Prentiss Swayze; Missouri Swayze (Married Robert Tate) ; Hardy Sojourner Swayze; Orrin Hays Swayze.

Richard Swayze moved to Yazoo County in 1832. He homesteaded a portion of what is now Home Place. He lived in a one-room house, still standing thirty yards south of the "Big House," itself built in 1858-1859. All work was done by slaves. The head carpenter was a slave bought by Richard Swayze for $2200 for the specific purpose of building the house.

1840 CENSUS, YAZOO COUNTY, MISSISSIPPI

Richd Sweezey

1 male born 1810-1820; 1 male born 1835-1840; 1 female born 1810-1820; 1 female born 1830-1835; 1 female born 1835-1840; 16 slaves.

1860 CENSUS, YAZOO CITY, MISSISSIPPI 788, 645

Richard Swayze born in 1812 in Mississippi; Elvira Swayze born in 1820 in Mississippi; Prentice Swayze born in 1840 in Mississippi; Hardy Swayze born in 1842 in Mississippi; Orange Swayze born in 1844 in Mississippi; Missouri Swayze born in 1845 in Mississippi; 78 slaves.

1850 CENSUS, YAZOO COUNTY, MISSISSIPPI 199, 204

Richard Swayze born in 1810 in Mississippi; Emily Swayze born in 1834 in Mississippi; Belinda Swayze born in 1836 in Mississippi; Prentiss Swayze born in 1839 in Mississipp; Hardy Swayze born in 1841 in Mississippi; Missouri Swayze born in 1845 in Mississippi; Nathan H. Luce (School Teacher) born in 1824 in Mississippi; Orange Swayze born in 1843 in Mississippi; 44 slaves.

HARDY SWAYZE

Born: April 7, 1842.

Married: Jennie Handley.

Died: May 21, 1921.

Children of Hardy and Jennie (Handley) Swayze: Clark Swayze; Josephine Swayze, married 1st J. D. McKie by whom she had sons Hardy McKie and James McKie, married 2nd William H. Hoover of

Pickens; Dr. Orrin Hays Swayze, married 1st Margaret Haverkamp, married 2nd Kitty Jones, mother of Charles and Meade, Mrs. William Nichol of Memphis, married 3rd Allie Murphy, mother of Orrin Hays Swayze; Emily Swayze; Hugh Swayze; Elizabeth King Swayze, married Claud Swayze and they had these children: Claudine, Elizabeth, Josephine, Handley, Octavia, Tommy, Katie, Douglas, and Jennie; Dr. Nathan Luse Swayze, married Ann Baldwin of Canton, they had Jane Swayze (Mrs. Herbert Hogue) and Nathan Swayze; Hardy Swayze, married Mada Brown of Seasonville and they had these children: Neola, Hardy, and Sojourner; Richie; Clayton; Katie Lyle.

CLAYTON SWAYZE

Born: April 9, 1885.

Married: Visa Harris, on October 2, 1907.

Children of Clayton and Visa (Harris) Swayze: Jennie Beth Swayze, born June 20, 1908; Carl Lee Swayze (Mrs. S. P. Gaskin), born June 30, 1912; Harris Sojourner Swayze.

On June 27, 1949, Clayton Swayze married secondly to Ruth Coleman Wilburn, widow of Wyche Wilburn. Mr. Swayze was given 300 acres of land by his father, when a young man and he inherited 235 more acres. By hard work he increased his holdings to 3,600 acres. On the death of his father in 1921, he moved into the "Big House" on Home Place, built by his grandfather over a hundred year ago at the time of this writing (1960).

HARRIS SOJOURNER SWAYZE

Born: December 27, 1914.

Married: Margaret Murphy on January 12, 1938.

Children of Harris Sojourner and Margaret (Murphy) Swayze: Margaret Harris Swayze, born November 24, 1938; Clayton Swayze II, born July 19, 1941; Martha Swayze, born July 9, 1949; John Hardy Swayze, born April 25, 1952.

WILLIAM SWAYZE

Born: Ca. 1813 in Mississippi.

Married: Mary Ann Cozzens in Natchez.

1850 CENSUS, YAZOO CITY, MISSISSIPPI 198, 203

William Swayze born in 1813 in Mississippi; Mary A. Swayze born in 1816 in England; Solomon Swayze born in 1841 in Mississippi; Emma Swayze born in 1843 in Mississippi; Mary Swayze born in 1845 in Mississippi; Frances Swayze born in 1846 in Mississippi; Amanda Swayze born in 1848 in Mississippi; Virginia Swayze born in 1849 in Mississippi 25 slaves.

1860 CENSUS, YAZOO CITY, MISSISSIPPI 737, 644

Mary A. Swayze born in 1818 in England; Solomon Swayze born in

1841 in Mississippi; Emma Swayze born in 1843 in Mississippi; Mary Swayze born in 1845 in Mississippi; Frances Swayze born in 1847 in Mississippi; Amanda Swayze born in 1847 in Mississippi; Georgiana Swayze born in 1850 in Mississippi; Christiana Fallows, Teacher, born in 1840 in Mississippi; William Brown, Overseer, born in 1838 in Tennessee; 52 slaves.

HANNAH CARTER

Born: December 25, 1764.

Married: Archibald Palmer on November 14, 1782.

Died: ca. 1826 in Feliciana Parish, Louisiana.

Children of Archibald and Hannah (Carter) Palmer: Adam Palmer; Archibald Palmer, Jr.; Sarah Palmer; Nancy Palmer; Margaret Palmer; Polly Palmer; Alva Palmer; Ione Palmer; Hannah Palmer, married Samuel Turbeville; Nehemiah Palmer.

In his EAST FELICIANA, PAST AND PRESENT (1892), Mr. Henry Skipwirth describes Mr. John Palmer as "an Irish gentleman of refinement and education, an alcalde under the Spanish" and lists his three sons: Archibald, Adam and Nehemiah. Lucretia McFarland, great aunt of Dr. Henry Hobgood of Lettsworth, Louisiana (Point Coupee Parish) and a descendant of Henry and Mary Jane (Austin) Hobgood, gives Archibald Palmer's date of birth as January 3, 1758, and Hannah Carter's date of birth as December 25, 1764.

The COUNTY ARCHIVES OF MISSISSIPPI, Number 2, Adams County, Volume I, page 91 (Minutes, Court of Quarter Sessions of the Peace, 1799-1801) show a bond of Archibald Palmer and Nehemiah Carter to Governor Sargent of the Mississippi Territory in the amount of $300 for Archibald Palmer to "keep a good and orderly public house" according to license issued by the Governor. 6 August 1800.

The will of Archibald Palmer, Box 79, St. Francisville, Louisiana, is dated 1816 and proved 13 March 1817. The will was witnessed by Samuel Cresswell, John Gready, Piper Robinson, Adam Hope, Robert Collins and Lewis Davis. The heirs met on 19 January 1818 and were, Hannah Palmer, John Austin, Pearce Noland, Henry Bennett, Adam Palmer, Archibald Palmer, Jr., Margaret Gready, Alvah Palmer (minor represented by special curator, Robert McCausland), Jane, represented by special curator, Lewis Davis, Hannah Palmer represented by special curator, William Rucker and Nehemiah Palmer represented by Samuel Adams.

1820 CENSUS, FELICIANA PARISH, LOUISIANA

Hannah Palmer

1 female born before 1775; 1 female born 1794-1804; 1 male born 1794-1804; 1 male born 1804-1810; 14 slaves.

Henry Bennett:
1male born 1775-1794; 1 male born 1810-1820; 1 female born 1794-1804; 1 female born 1810-1820; 1 slave.

Saml Adams
1 male born 1775-1794; 1 female born 1775-1794; 1 female born 1804-1810; 1 female born 1810-1820; 5 slaves.

Adam Palmer
1 male born 1775-1794; 1 male born 1794-1804; 1 male born 1802-1804; 4 males born 1810-1820; 1 female born 1775-1794; 2 females born 1810-1820; 10 slaves.

1830 CENSUS, EAST FELICIANA
Adam Palmer
1male born 1750-1760; 1 male born 1780-1790; 2 males born 1810-1815; 2 males born 1815-1820; 1 male born 1825-1830; 1 female born 1800-1810; 1 female born 1815-1820; 1 female born 1820-1825; 15 slaves.

1840 CENSUS, EAST FELICIANA
A. Palmer
1 male born 1790-1800; 1 male born 1810-1820; 1 male born 1820-1825; 1 male born 1825-1830; 2 males born 1830-1835; 2 males born 1835-1840; 1 female born 1800-1810; 1 female born 1835-1840; 22 slaves.

1850 CENSUS, EAST FELICIANA 249, 249
Adam Palmer born in 1787 in Miss.; Sarah A. Palmer born in 1805 in La.; Robert Palmer born in 1833 in La.; M. W. Palmer born in 1835 in La. (M); A. M. Palmer born in 1837 in La. (M); L. E. Palmer born in 1840 in La. (F); M. L. Palmer born in 1845 in La. (M); H. O. Palmer born in 1847 in La. (F); 8 slaves.

1830 CENSUS, EAST FELICIANA
A. D. Palmer
1 male born 1790-1800; 2 males born 1800-1810; 1 male born 1815-1820; 1 female born 1780-1790; 1 female born 1790-1800; 1 female born 1810-1815; 1 female born 1815-1820; 46 slaves.

1840 CENSUS, EAST FELICIANA
A. D. Palmer
1 male born 1790-1800; 1 male born 1810-1820; 1 female born 1770-1780; 1 female born 1790-1800; 1 female born 1835-1840; 75 slaves.

1850 CENSUS, EAST FELICIANA 312, 312
A. D. Palmer born in 1790 in Miss.; Elizabeth Palmer born in 1796 S. C.; Mary Palmer born in 1836 in La.; 111 slaves.

1860 East Feliciana 338, 338

A. D. Palmer born in 1791 in Miss.; Eliz Palmer born in 1796 in S. C.; A. Palmer born in 1798 in Miss.; 166 slaves.

1830 Census, East Feliciana

William D. Carter

2 males born 1800-1810; 1 female born 1810-1815; 1 female born 1825-1830; 15 slaves.

1840 Census, East Feliciana

Wm. D. Carter

2 males born 1810-1820; 2 males born 1825-1830; 1 female born 1820-1825; 1 female born 1825-1830; 52 slaves.

1850 Census, East Feliciana

38, 38

Wm. D. Carter born in 1810 in La.; Eliz Carter born in 1812 in Ky.; Wm. P. Carter born in 1841 in La.; 100 slaves.

363,363

William A. Carter born 1819 in Miss.; Elizabeth Carter born 1830 La.; Louisiana Carter born 1841 La.; Robert Carter born 1844 La.

1840 Census, East Feliciana

Albert G. Carter

1 male born 1810-1820; 1 female born 1820-1825; 2 females born 1835-1840; 49 slaves.

1850 Census, East Feliciana

General A. G. Carter 1809 La.; Frances P. Carter 1820 La.; Howell Carter 1844 La.; William Carter 1847 La.; Charles P. Carter 1850 La.; 73 slaves.

1860 Census, East Feliciana 52, 52

General A. G. Carter 1809 La.; F. P. Carter born 1820 La.; H. Carter born 1845 La.; W. R. Carter born 1848 La.; C. P. Carter born 1849 La.; A. E. Carter born 1834 La.; H. Carter born 1839 La.; L. A. Carter born 1857 La.; E. M. Carter born 1859 La.; 95 slaves.

1830 Census, East Feliciana

Parsons Carter

1 male born 1770-1780; 2 males born 1800-1810; 1 female born 1770-1780; 1 female born 1780-1790; 1 female born 1800-1810; 1 female born 1810-1815; 1 female born 1815-1820; 1 female born 1820-1825; 2 females born 1825-1830; 15 slaves.

1840 Census, East Feliciana

N. P. Palmer

1 male born 1800-1810; 2 males born 1830-1835; 3 males born 1835-1840; 1 female born 1810-1820; 2 females born 1830-1835; 13 slaves.

261, 261

N. P. Palmer born 1803 La. (M) ; H. H. Palmer born 1811 Ky. (F) ;
L. A. Palmer born 1832 La. (M) ; C. S. Palmer born 1832 La. (M) ;
E. C. Palmer born 1834 La. (F) ; Isaac S. Palmer born 1835 La. ; N. C.
Palmer born 1837 in La. ; Adam Palmer born 1839 La. ; Arch Palmer
born 1841 La. ; C. E. Palmer born 1842 La. ; Caswell Palmer born
1844 La. ; H. S. Palmer born 1845 La. ; (female) Palmer born 1846
La. ; H. E. Palmer born 1848 La. ; 8 slaves.

1840 CENSUS, EAST FELICIANA

M. Palmer

1 female born 1810-1820; 1 female born 1835-1840; 12 slaves.
Ann H. Carter

1 female born 1800-1810; 1 female born 1820-1825; 12 slaves.

ARCHIBALD PALMER of Adams County, Mississippi Territory,
Planter, and HANNAH, his wife

Hugh Davis of same

Consideration: $1,500. Tract of land, 800 acres, French Measure on
southeast bank of Homochitto, bounded on south by lands of JESSE
CARTER, sold by him to Major John Ellis, etc., per plat annexed,
grand signed in New Orleans, 15 March 1789 by Stephen Miro, then
Governor of Louisiana Dower released by Hannah. /s/ ARCHIBALD
PALMER, HANNAH PALMER. Test. Wm. Dunbar and acknowledged by him 28 March 1801. Deed Book B, page 151, Grant and
plat on page 148, Adams County.

Harnett Kane has an interesting chapter on Sir William Dunbar who
witnessed this deed, in his NATCHEZ ON THE MISSISSIPPI. Eron
Rowland has compiled a life of Sir. William, pioneer scientist of Mississippi.

Page 465, Mrs. McBee's NATCHEZ COURT RECORDS, 1765-1805

(Book D, page 525) Claim No. 1477, Spanish Grant to Archibald
Palmer, 800 acres on South fork of the Homochitto, 17 miles south
of the Fort, adjoining Jesse Carter. New Orleans: 15 March 1789
by Miro. (p. 526) 27th March 1801. Archibald Palmer and wife, Hannah to Hugh Davis for $1,500 paid the above grant of 800 acres, etc.

The following are taken from NATCHEZ COURT RECORDS, 1767-
1805 by May Wilson McBee:

(Page 36) ARCHIBALD PALMER, N(EHEMIAH) CARTER,
JESSE CARTER, Richard Ellis, John Ellis, and John Eldergill were
witnesses to the Will of Tacitus Gaillard. 29 July 1786.

(Page 55) ARCHIBALD PALMER was a debtor of the Estate of
Richard Carpenter of Natchez, merchant. Aug. 7, 1788.

(Page 73) 800 acres of land on Homochitto belonging to Jesse Carter,

Standing, left to right — James Babin McHugh and David Samuel McHugh. Seated — Susannah McHugh (Mrs. Simeon Fillmore Carmena) and Thomas Edward McHugh

Joseph McHugh

Laura Ann Shaw (Mrs. James J. Borskey)

Julia May Briggs (Mrs. George T. Luce)

Phoebe Jane (Briggs) Parcelle

bounded by land of Richard Ellis, ARCHIBALD PALMER and lands of His Majesty. 17 Dec. 1794.

(Page 279) Robert Davis versus Barnabus Higgins. Higgins had brought suit against Davis for taking some of his hogs. Davis has proof to the contrary and wants Higgins' assertion disproved in court. Testimony to be taken before Colonel Hutchins. Witnesses: John Ellis, Abram Ellis, Stephen and Thomas Ambrose, Elijah Phipps, Elijah Ambrose, Mrs. Foley, Hugh Davis, Henry Stroud, Landon Davis, ARCHIBALD PALMER, Thos. Cummins, John Mc-Kay. Verdict rather complicated, as it was the custom for hogs to run wild "on the island" marked so they could be identified.

(Page 305) Archie Palmer versus John Farquhar, who owes him $200 by note; asks payment as petitioner is indebted to several persons. Signed. Let Farquhar be notified to pay in three days. /s/ Piernas.

(Page 314) Archibald Palmer represents that a certain John Farquhar is indebted to him for $200. 22 Dec 1783// Let John Farquhar be notified to appear at the first audience to satisfy the debt claimed. Trevino.

(Page 315) Archibald Palmer versus John Farquhar. Palmer represents that he was overseer for John Farquhar in 1782 and during that year said Farquhar went down to New Orleans to give up his property to his creditors by whom the said Farquhar and John Bisland were appointed agents; that on the said Farquhar's return with a letter of license, your petitioner inquired of him and Mr. Bisland if he should continue according to the agreement with him, the said Farquhar, and was told by them to continue. Some time afterwards a certain Cato West arrived from New England to whom the said Farquhar and Bisland sold the plantation on which your petitioner was making a crop, which he bought from your petitioner for $300 and shortly afterwards paid him $100 on the account, now said Farquhar objects to pay your petitioner the balance due him, saying that his property belongs to his creditors in general. 8 Dec 1783.

(Pages 465-6) Spanish Grant to ARCHIBALD PALMER, 800 acres on South Fork of the Homochitto, 17 miles south of the Fort, adjoining Jesse Carter. N.O. 15 Mar 1789 by Governor Miro. 27 Mar 1801. ARCHIBALD PALMER AND WIFE, HANNAH, to Hugh Davis, for $1,500 paid, the above grant of 800 acres. Both sign. Witnesses: Sir William Dunbar, Dinah Dunbar. 28 Mar 1804. Hugh Davis of Wilkinson County to Landon Davis of same for $3,500 paid, the above grant, 800 acres. Signed. Witnesses: David R. Crosby, John McCulloch. Landon Davis, Claimant, 29 Mar 1804. Wit: Mathew McCulloch, 5 Sept 1804. Certif. A-360 issued 21 June 1805. Prov. in Palmer. Landon Davis claims 800 acres by virtue of a Grant by the Spanish Government to ARCHIBALD PALMER, by him to Hugh Davis and by Hugh Davis to claimant.

(Page 466) Petition of James Nicholson, Captain of Militia in the District of Galvez Town, wishes to employ negroes I Have; asks for lands adjoining William Webb and Landon Davis, 10 Jan 1788// Spanish Government grants Order of Survey, 11 Jan 1788. Governor Miro.// Certif of Survey, 600 acres on Bayou aux Boeufs, 20 miles south of Fort adjoining John Steel, ARCH PALMER, AND JESSE CARTER

From Clerk's Office, Clinton, East Feliciana Parish, La.

Agreement as to property of each before marriage etc. Inventory of property belonging to Mrs. Charity Palmer, wife of ARCHIBALD D. PALMER, of East Feliciana Parish, State of Louisiana. One section of land 640 acres and improvements, known as the present residence of said Charity Palmer; 27 slaves, cattle, hogs, household and kitchen furniture etc. all of which property was owned by the said Charity Palmer at the time of her marriage with ARCHIBALD D. PALMER.

Inventory of separate property of ARCHIBALD D. PALMER: 870 acres of land, 802 acres of land, certain negroes, cattle, hogs, horses, etc.

Agreed to a separation of property, she to have her inventory as stated and he to have his, the same each had at marriage hereafter to be no community of property. /s/ A. D. PALMER, CHARITY X PALMER. Test: Timothy Rogers, Robert Draughan. Clinton, La. Notarial Record Book C, p 34 16 Feb 1832.

State of Louisiana, Parish of East Feliciana; Be it remembered etc., personally came and appeared the following persons who are heirs and representing heirs of Mrs. Charity Palmer, late of State and Parish aforesaid, deceased late wife of ARCHIBALD PALMER, to-wit: Lewis Watson, Senior, Michael Watson, Elizabeth Sibley, wife of William Sibley; Samuel Watson, Junior, Lewis Watson Junior; Winiford Vincent wife of James Vincent; Celia Jones, wife of Isaac Jones; Winiford Morgan, minor, Rep. by her Tutor Daniel Morgan, and her Undertutor, Robert Allison; Rachel Morgan, wife of Daniel Morgan; Elizabeth Morgan, by her husband, Thomas F. Morgan, Ephraim Smith, Junior, William W. Smith; and Putnam Powell, Edney Harrison, Lewis Watson, Elizabeth Brown absentees represented by William Dunn, Esq. All agree to previous agreement between ARCHIBALD AND CHARITY PALMER, Signed by those mentioned. Test. C. M. Smith B.M.G. Br(own) Clinton, La. Notarial Record Book D, p 328 18 Jan 1835.

FAMILY MEETING OF MARY CATHERINE PALMER, a minor child of ARCHIBALD D. PALMER and Catherine Norwood, widow. Present: Erasmus Williams, P. A. B. Williams, D. A. Palmer, Adam

Palmer, N. P. Palmer, Signed by those present. Test. R. C. Courtney, Sam'l Flemiken.

Clinton, La. Notarial Record Book G, p 70 April 28, 1838.

From: ARCHIBALD D. PALMER, SENIOR, of Parish of Feliciana, State of Louisiana, to ADAM PALMER and ARCHIBALD D. PALMER, of same. DEED OF GIFT. Natural Affection I do bear to MY BELOVED SONS. Certain tract of Land granted to me by the Spanish Government in Parish and State, aforesaid, by Certificate of Vincent Pintado as being one and a half miles South of the line of demarcation and bounded by lands of Alexander Ross and John Gready, 590 acres /s/ ARCHIBALD PALMER. Test: H. Hampton and Wm. Westberry. Ack by ARCHIBALD PALMER, SENIOR 21 October 1812.

St. Francisville, La. Notarial Book A, p. 127. 21 Oct 1812.

From: ADAM PALMER of Parish of Feliciana, State of Louisiana, to ARCHIBALD PALMER, JR., of same. In consideration of a release of claim to a certain tract of land herein described, hath given, granted, etc: All that tract of land on west branch of Thompson's Creek, between lands surveyed for Madam Watts and Major Stephen Minor — 457 arpens — granted in name of Archibald Palmer and conveyed by him to Adam Palmer, In exchange for his right or claim to interest in 590 acres in Feliciana Parish — one and a half miles South of the Line of Demarcation — bounded by lands of Alexander Ross and John Gready — conveyed this date by ARCHIBALD PALMER, FATHER OF ADAM PALMER AND ARCHIBALD PALMER by Deed of Gift, and the said Archibald Palmer, Jr. for himself, his heirs etc. /s/ ADAM PALMER, ARCHIBALD PALMER. Test: H. Hampton, Wm. Westberry. Ack by ADAM AND ARCHIBALD PALMER, JR. 21 Oct 1812. St. Francisville, La. Notarial Record Book A, p 130 21 Oct 1812.

From: ARCHIBALD PALMER, SENIOR of Parish of Feliciana, State of Louisiana to ADAM PALMER, of same. Consideration: $5. Tract of land in Feliciana Parish on west branch of Thompson's Creek between lands surveyed for Madam Watts and Major Stephen Minor — 457 arpens — per petition etc. /s/ ARCHIBALD PALMER, SENIOR. Test: H. Hampton, Wm. Westberry. St. Francisville, La. Notarial Book A. P 129 21 Oct 1812.

State of Louisiana, Parish of East Feliciana, Be it remembered etc. Came and appeared ADAM PALMER of State and Parish aforesaid, who declared etc. in consideration of the sum of $900 paid to him by James Scott, Jr., of State and Parish aforesaid: One twelve months bond given by said ADAM PALMER to DAVID LANDFAIR at the suit of said LANDFAIR vs. the said PALMER in the District Court of East Feliciana (Record No. 129, Sept 11, 1826, Minute Book 1824-

1834, p 101 simply state Court found for plaintiff), the balance on 1st January 1829, he hath granted, etc. to said James Scott, being payment for a tract of land in State and Parish aforesaid, bounded as follows: East, lands of Robert Dyer and Comite River; North, Mark Boatner and Samuel Scott; West, Samuel Scott and George Keller; South, Archibald D. Palmer, 320 acres. /s/ ADAM PALMER, JAMES SCOTT, JUNIOR. Test: Charles Carson, Randall Brown.

Clinton, La. Notarial Record Book A p 307 18 Aug 1827.

From: ARCHIBALD PALMER (SENIOR) of Feliciana Parish, State of Louisiana to ALVAH PALMER AND NEHEMIAH PALMER, of same. Deed of Gift. For natural affection which I bear to MY BELOVED SONS. A certain tract of land in Parish and State aforesaid on Mill Creek, a branch of Thompson's Creek — bounded as follows: South, by C. McMicken and Adam Palmer, North by Crisette and Regent, West by Adam Palmer and M. Watts, East by McMicken and Mulhollen agreeably to the plan drawn by Ira C. Knieland, now accompanying this deed of gift. /s/ ARCHIBALD PALMER (SENIOR) Test: H. Hampton, Wm. Westberry. St. Francisville, La. Notarial Record Book A, p 132/134 21 Oct 1812.

Book 9, Clerk's Office, St. Francisville, La. (West Feliciana Parish) Bond for marriage of Alva Palmer and Lucy Davis, May 28, 1823.

From: John Austin, Representative of Heirs of Estate of HANNAH PALMER of Feliciana Parish, La., to NEHEMIAH PALMER of same. Consideration: $105 three equal notes of $35 payable 1st January 1827, 1828, and 1829. 47½ arpens of land adjoining lands of Mrs. Mary Hale, A. P. Walsh, B. Turbeville and John Simms, /s/ John Austin and N. P. Palmer. Test: M. P. Clark, H. Ming, Joseph Barnard, N.P. St. Francisville, La. Notarial Record Book AA, p 208, 25 Feb 1826.

From John Austin, Representative of Heirs of HANNAH PALMER, deceased, of Feliciana Parish, Louisiana to ALVA PALMER of same. Consideration: $3,475. 400 arpens of land in Feliciana Parish with all improvements thereon the same whereon the deceased resided in her lifetime. Adjoining lands of Mrs. Davis, John Brown, Edmund Miles and Isam F. Woods. /s/ John Austin, ALVAH PALMER. Test: M. P. Clark, H. Meng, and Joseph Barnard, N.P. St. Francisville, La. Notarial Record Book AA, pp 211-212 25 Feb 1826.

From: John Austin Representative of Heirs of JOHN GREADY, deceased, of Feliciana Parish, State of Louisiana, to NEHEMIAH PALMER, of same. Consideration: $1,020. Four slaves: Big Lucy, Joyce, Joseph and Richard. /s/ John Austin, Nehemiah Palmer. Test: A. B. St......, W. A. Austin, St. Francisville, La. Notarial Record Book AA, p 77 29 Feb 1825.

AMITE COUNTY, MISSISSIPPI, 1699-1890 Vol III, A. E. Casey,

1957 Page 91—(Bond Book A, p 223) Wilkinson Co., Miss. Bond for marriage of Wm. Grady and Margaret Palmer. April 6, 1809.

Page 143 (License Book I, p. 106) Wilkinson Co., Miss. License for marriage of Wm. Carpenter and Margaret Posey, May 25, 1853.

ADAM PALMER

Born: ca. 1787.

Married: Sarah Williams. March 10, 1830. Book 9, Clerk's Office, St. Francisville, Louisiana.

Children of Adam and Sarah (Williams) Palmer: (As found in Inventories, 5 Jan. 1856 to 1 April 1863, #1783, pages 416-417. Estate of Adam Palmer, 9 April 1859. A suit. Inventory made previously (17 Jan 1854) confirmed by Thomas F. Dearmond and Seymour Taylor, experts)

Plaintiffs in Suit listed first: Mary E. Palmer, wife of James McCullum of Iberville Parish; Pierce A. Palmer of Bossier Parish; Jeremiah N. Palmer of Livingston Parish; Archibald Palmer of East Feliciana Parish.

Defendants listed: Sarah A. Palmer, wife of W. G. Higginbotham of East Feliciana; Lucinda Palmer, wife of Isaac B. Smith of East Feliciana; William F. Palmer of West Feliciana Parish; Robert P. Palmer of East Feliciana Parish; James E. Palmer of East Feliciana Parish; Martha W. Palmer of West Feliciana Parish; and the following minors represented by Sarah A. Palmer, Tutrix, all of East Feliciana except Louise of West Feliciana: Louisa Palmer, Adam Palmer, Michael Luther Palmer, Hannah Octavia Palmer.

LUCINDA J. PALMER

Born: ca. 1820 in Louisiana.

Married: Isaac B. Smith. March 29, 1838. Marriage Records, Clerk's Office, Clinton, La., Book A, page 90.

1850 CENSUS, EAST FELICIANA, LOUISIANA

243, 243

Isaac Smith born in 1813 in Kentucky; L. J. Smith born in 1820 in Louisiana; Sarah Smith born in 1839 in Louisiana; Drury Smith born in 1841 in Louisiana; Adam P. Smith born in 1843 in Louisiana; Eudora Smith born in 1846 in Louisiana; 3 slaves.

1860 CENSUS, EAST FELICIANA PARISH, LOUISIANA

349, 349

I. B. Smith born in 1812 in Kentucky (male); L. L. J. Smith born in 1820 in Louisiana (female); A. P. Smith born in 1844 in Louisiana (male); C. L. Smith born in 1849 in Louisiana (male); J. S. Smith born in 1852 in Louisiana (male); W. H. Smith born in 1855 in Louisiana (male); 7 slaves.

1870 CENSUS, EAST FELICIANA PARISH, LOUISIANA
4th Ward, 27, 23

I. Smith born in 1813 in Kentucky (male); Lucinda Smith born in 1813 in Louisiana; Calvin Smith born in 1851 in Louisiana; Jacob Smith born in 1853 in Louisiana; Wm. Smith born in 1855 in Louisiana.

SARAH A. PALMER

Born: 1821-1823 in Louisiana.

Married: William G. Higginbotham.

1850 CENSUS, EAST FELICIANA PARISH, LOUISIANA 260, 260

Wm. J. Higginbotham born in 1813 in Louisiana; Susan A. Higginbotham born in 1823 in Louisiana; Leonora Higginbotham born in 1842 in Louisiana; William Higginbotham born in 1843 in Louisiana; Isaac Higginbotham born in 1848 in Louisana; Jacob Sellers, School Teacher born in 1829 in Louisiana; 15 slaves.

1860 CENSUS, EAST FELICIANA PARISH, LOUISIANA 343, 343

W. G. Higginbotham born in 1819 in Louisiana (male); S. A. Higginbotham born in 1822 in Louisiana (female); J. R. Higginbotham born in 1848 in Louisiana (male); M. O. Higginbotham born in 1851 in Louisiana (female); N. C. Higginbotham born in 1852 in Louisiana (male); S. J. Higginbotham born in 1854 in Louisiana (female); A. L. Higginbotham born in 1856 in Louisiana (female); L. A. Higginbotham born in 1858 in Louisiana (male); W. Collinsworth born in 1849 in Louisiana (male); 29 slaves.

1870 CENSUS, EAST FELICIANA PARISH, LOUISIANA
3rd Ward, 178, 158

W. G. Higginbotham born in 1819 in Louisiana; S. A. Higginbotham born in 1821 in Louisiana; Riley Higginbotham born in 1848 in Louisiana; Lawson Higginbotham born in 1860 in Louisana; Boyd Higginbotham born in 1862 in Louisiana; Sarah Higginbotham born in 1854 in Louisiana; Louisa Higginbotham born in 1857 in Louisiana; Lucy Palmer born in 1864 in Louisiana; Harriet Palmer born in 1866 in Louisiana.

ARCHIBALD D. PALMER

Born: August 25, 1790.

Married: 1st: Mary Collins, widow of Robert Schofield. She was born on May 16, 1780 and died in East Feliciana Parish on March 30, 1826. She is buried in Rosehill Cemetery in Clinton. Mary Collins and Archibald D. Palmer married on March 19, 1814. Marriage Book 9, West Feliciana Parish, Louisiana.

2nd: Charity Watson, the widow Eads on June 19, 1827,

East Feliciana Parish, Louisiana, Book X, page 200. Marriages in Book X were recorded later, therefore some later marriages were recorded before earlier marriages.

3rd: Catherine E. Williams on February 15, 1835 in East Feliciana Parish, Book X, page 197. Catherine E. Williams was the widow of Abel T. Norwood. She was born March 11, 1802, the daughter of Membrance and Nancy Ann Williams.

4th: Elizabeth McCants on July 25, 1839 in East Feliciana Parish, Marriage Book X, page 196. She was the widow Chaney.

5th: Elizabeth Wall, the widow Flynn, on February 18, 1864, in East Feliciana Parish, Marriage Book X, page 194.

Died: 1865 in Caddo Parish, Louisiana.

Children of Archibald D. and Mary (Collins) Palmer: Hannah P. Palmer; David Palmer.

Children of Archibald D. and Catherine (Williams) Palmer: Mary Catherine Palmer.

ARCHIBALD D. PALMER, a deceased veteran of the War of 1812, was born in Tunica, Louisiana, August 25, 1790. His parents were natives of New Jersey and of Irish extraction. At the age of 15, our subject deserted the parental roof and came to Bayou Sara, this parish. Subsequently, he volunteered in Captain Rogers' and Captain Nessoms' Company of the 10th Louisiana Regiment commanded by Colonel Young of East Feliciana Parish and took part in the memorable Battle of New Orleans. On the restoration of peace he engaged in planting and acquired a large fortune before the Civil War began, owning many negroes and large landed property in Louisiana and Arkansas. During this struggle he was several times roughly handled by skulking and predatory soldiers, being more than once strung up to extort from him the secret of the hiding place of his money and this rough usage was really the cause of his wife's death from fright. At the age of 75 years he rode on horseback from his home to the Mississippi River, which he crossed in a skiff, holding his horse by the bridle to guide its swimming across the stream. He eventually reached Caddo Parish, where he died soon after. A contributor to the SOUTHERN WATCHMAN in speaking of the character of Mr. Palmer says, "He was born a decided character. Bold, intrepid, temperate, clean, determined, deliberate, he was born to win. Opposition was but waste paper to his onward and upward calculation. After his military term as a faithful and tried soldier in defeat and victory he returned to his beloved parish and home. The ardor of his virtuous ambition became more devoted to the true interests of his parish and state. Depending entirely upon his own personal perseverance and indefatigable genius and charity to exhibit a praiseworthy example to his friends and neighbors, to build up his much honored country, to brighten the progressive ranks of civilization in farming and agricultural purity, establishing wealth by honest industry, befriending those he could, aiding charity and schools and church, these were his leading and predominant characteristics."

DR. J. W. WORTHY, son-in-law of Mr. Palmer was a prominent and successful physician and surgeon of East Feliciana Parish and was born near Jackson November 20, 1833. He was the son of Thomas and Maria (Carney) Worthy, the former a native of Georgia who came to Louisiana when a young man and settled on the place later owned by his son, the doctor, where he died at an advanced age, a member of the Methodist Church. He had a family of four sons and three daughters, all of whom reached maturity, but of whom only Mrs. Sally Lee, wife of Zach Lee and Rhoda wife of H. Lea still survive. Of the others Thomas, William and Scott left families. Rebecca died when about grown. Dr. Worthy was the third child in order of birth. He graduated from Centenary College, studied medicine at Jackson under Dr. Thomas Jones, graduated in medicine from Tulane University in New Orleans, commenced practice in oBssier Parish in 1855 and at the close of the war returned to East Feliciana and engaged quite extensively in planting relinquishing the practice of his profession for the time being excepting as to a specialty in which he has been very successful in his immediate neighborhood and in New Orleans. While in Bossier Parish he was married to Mrs. Mary Andrews, daughter of Archibald D. Palmer. This lady was born in East Feliciana Parish May 22, 1836 and was the only child born by Mr. Palmer's third wife. Mrs. Palmer was a native of South Carolina born March 11, 1802 bore the maiden name of Catharine Williams, but, at the time of her marriage to Mr. Palmer, was the widow of Mr. Norwood. Mrs. Mary Worthy was reared in East Feliciana, but was educated at St. Michael's School in St. James Parish. She was first married to Edwin C. Andrews who was born in Hinds County, Mississippi February 18, 1830, a son of Elisha Andrews of South Carolina who early moved to Mississippi but later came to East Feliciana Parish, Louisiana where he was extensively engaged in planting. Edwin C. Andrews was a member of a family of seven children and died at Camp Moore December 22, 1861, a Lieutenant of the Nance Guard, 19th Louisville Volunteer Infantry. He left two brothers, James and Thomas A. Edwin C. Andrews was married in 1854 at Clinton, Louisiana, moved to Shreveport and followed planting in Caddo Parish. He was the father of two sons: Edward P. and Clarence, the latter of whom died in childhood. To Dr. J. D. Worthy and wife was born one child now deceased, Sallie E. Dr. Worthy died November 24, 1891 and Mrs. Mary E. Worthy August 8, 1892.

EDWARD P. ANDREWS was born in East Feliciana Parish November 10, 1855, received his literary education at Centenary College and began farming on his own account at the age of 18 and was first married to Miss Saluda Maundy, daughter of Major General G. W. Maundy. To this union were born five children: Mary who died in childhood; Worthy E., George C., Alpenia, and Saluda C. The mother died a pious member of the Methodist Episcopal Church. Mr. Andrews next married Miss Willie Haynes, daughter of Captain Frank Haynes now deceased. Mrs. Andrews was educated at Silliman Institute. She is the mother of one child, Edward, Jr. and is a consistent member of the Methodist Church. Mr. Andrews is a member of the Knights of Pythias in Clinton and in politics is a Democrat. The family is held in high esteem in the community who recognize and appreciate their many good traits of character.

BIOGRAPHICAL AND HISTORICAL MEMOIRS OF LOUISIANA. Goodspeed Publishing Company. 1892. Volume II, page 297.

Mississippi Historical Society. Dunbar Rowland. Centenary Series. Volume I. Jackson, Mississippi. 1916.

Census of Inhabitants of the District of Natchez Under the Dominion of Spain, 1792.

District of Santa Clara. ROBERTO CARTER. Page 428.

District of Homochitto. ARCHWALDO PALMER. Page 421.

District of Santa Catlina. Carlos Carter. Page 428.

Book 9, Clerk's Office, St. Francisville, La. (West Feliciana Parish). Bond for Marriage of Archibald D. Palmer and Mary Schofield March 19, 1814. Consent by Hannah Palmer. Also signing: Henry Bennett and Adam Palmer.

October 4, 1815, Petition of ARCHIBALD PALMER, JUNIOR and WIFE, MARY, request to be appointed Curator and Curatria of Robert Schofield, late of Parish, aforesaid, deceased, former husband of Mary, died in the year 1812, leaving three minor children, to-wit: Nancy, Betsy, and Robert. /s/ARCHIBALD PALMER, JUN'R AND MARY PALMER.

November 18, 1815. William Collins of Mississippi Territory files Petition as Tutor for minor children under the age of 12 years, St. Francisville, La. Succession of Robert Schofield, Probate File 103.

Received of Parish of Feliciana, State of Louisiana and of ARCHIBALD PALMER, $247.96½ in full of what may be due my wife, Emily Scofield, daughter of Robert Scofield, deceased, whose wife by second marriage was Mary Collins now wife of the aforesaid ARCHIBALD PALMER, and who has children Nancy, Elizabeth and Robert

Scofield. /s/ Fenton Cook. Test: A. G. Scott, A. H. McDermott, Wm. C. Wade, Parish Judge. St. Francisville, La. Notarial Record Book B, page 191 9 Mar 1820.

Emancipation of DAVID ADAM PALMER. Be it remembered etc. came ARCHIBALD D. PALMER, of East Feliciana Parish, State of Louisiana, Father and Natural Tutor of his minor son, DAVID ADAM PALMER, over 18 years of age, etc., is fully competent, etc. so he emancipates his son, etc. /s/ A. D. PALMER, Test: Lee Hardesty, John Morgan. Clinton, La. Notarial Record Book D, p 310 29 Dec. 1834.

License Book F, p 35, Wilkinson County, Mississippi, License for Marriage of DAVID A. PALMER and Martha A. Hester, Dec. 3, 1834. AMITE COUNTY, MISSISSIPPI, 1699-1890. A. E. Casey, 1957.

U.S.A., State of Mississippi, County of Wilkinson: Be it known on the 9th July 1833, personaly came and appeared HANNAH TURBE-VILLE, WIFE OF SAMUEL TURBEVILLE, FORMERLY, HAN-NAH PALMER, who releases all right and claim in a tract of 640 acres. Signed by them. Test: R. N. Schofield. Clinton, La. Notarial Record Book C, p 41. July 1833.

DAVID ADAM PALMER

Born: December 26, 1816

Married: Martha Ann Hester in Wilkinson County, Mississippi. Marriage Book F, page 35. She was born in Wilkinson County, the daughter of Charles Hester of Granville County, North Carolina and Mary Eliza Dickson who was born in Greene County, Georgia. She was a niece of Michael Dickson who married Hannah P. Palmer. She married secondly Leonard K. Barber of Woodville, Miss., where she died December 24, 1899 and is buried in the Evergreen Cemetery.

Died: February 18, 1835. Buried in Rosehill Cemetery, Clinton, Louisiana near his son and mother.

Children of David Adam and Martha Ann (Hester) Palmer: Archibald D. Palmer, born October 1, 1835, died August 7, 1838, buried Rosehill Cemetery, Clinton, La.; Mary Eliza Palmer, born December 29, 1835, married 1st William Noland Tigner in Wilkinson Co., Miss., marriage book K, page 17. May 22, 1856, married 2nd J. D. Carr March 24, 1879, Warren County, Miss., marriage book H, page 728.

MARY ELIZA PALMER

Born: December 29, 1835

Married: 1st: William Noland Tigner on May 22, 1856. Mr. Tigner was born in Wilkinson County, Mississippi, on Oc-

tober 30, 1833, the son of William Tigner and his
second wife, Lydia Ellen Noland of Georgia.

2nd: John (Jonathan) Dalton Carr, the son of William
Carr of North Carolina and Susan Smith of Patrick
County, Virginia. Mr. Carr was born in Tennessee
in 1817. Later, the family moved to Morehouse Parish, Louisiana where Mr. Carr died September 6,
1890. He is buried in the cemetery of the Episcopal
Church of Oak Ridge, Louisiana.

Died: April 25, 1915.

Children of William Noland and Mary Eliza (Palmer) Tigner: Mary
Lydia Tigner, born March 28, 1857, in Wilkinson County, Missississi;
Noland Barber Tigner, born August 2, 1858, in Wilkinson County,
Mississippi, unmarried, died October 1, 1905; Caroline Hester Tigner,
born June 4, 1860, in Wilkinson County, Mississippi, died March 24,
1895, unmarried; Martha Lavinia Tigner, born January 17, 1863, in
Morehouse (now Richland) Parish, Louisiana, died August 17, 1864;
William Noland Tigner was shot and killed from ambush on April 30,
1863, in what is now Richland Parish, Louisiana. He is buried in
New Salem Cemetery in Richland Parish, not far from Rayville,
Louisiana, together with his wife and all his children except Martha
Lavinia Tigner who died in Lafayette County, Arkansas, where the
family stayed as Civil War refugees.

MARY LYDIA TIGNER

Born: March 28, 1857, in Wilkinson County, Mississippi.

Married: Williamson Argyle Moore on March 30, 1879. Marriage
Book C, page 32, Richland Parish, Louisiana. Mr. Moore was
born August 5, 1852 at Crew Lake, now Richland Parish, Louisiana, the son of Dr. Madison Tyler Moore of Patrick County, Virginia, and Mary Emily Webb of Stokes County, North Carolina.
His parents first settled in Madison County, Mississippi, then
moved to Panola County, Mississippi, and to North Louisiana ca
1850. Mr. Moore died at Oak Ridge on April 3, 1915.

Died: February 18, 1930, at the home of her daughter, Mrs. Windsor
Pipes in Morehouse Parish, Louisiana. She is bured at New Salem
Cemetery, Richland Parish, Louisiana, in the same plot with her
husband and parents.

Children of Williamson Argyle and Mary Lydia (Tigner) Moore:
Dalton Tazette Moore.

DALTON TAZETTE MOORE

Born: March 1, 1880

Married: Windsor Pipes on December 19, 1899. Mr. Pipes was born in East Feliciana Parish, Louisiana, and was the second son of David Washington and Ella Victoria (Norwood) Pipes. Windsor Pipes came to Morehouse Parish, Louisiana, in 1896. He died January 8, 1958, in Bastrop, Louisiana, and is buried there in Christ Church Cemetery.

Children of Windsor and Dalton Tazette (Moore) Pipes: Henry Alexander Pipes, born July 11, 1901, married Zelma Bradley Snyder on June 18, 1930, died March 16, 1956; Windsor Tigner Pipes, born January 22, 1905, drowned in ferry accident on December 22, 1927; Ella Norwood Pipes, born October 17, 1906, married October 11, 1931, to Clark Griffith Dumas; David Washington Pipes, born October 24, 1910, married Flora Kate McDuff on February 2, 1934; Williamson Moore Pipes, born September 20, 1913, married Thelma Nanette Keebler; Lady Dalton Pipes, born October 20, 1916, married Joel Mendel Rich on June 24, 1939; Duncan Norwood Pipes, born April 26, 1918, died June 15, 1918; Mary E. Pipes, born August 27, 1919, married Tenneille Benjamin McEnery on July 5, 1945; Paullette Clifton Pipes, born February 11, 1921, married Elizabeth Ann Walcott on August 23, 1942.

HANNAH P. PALMER

Born: 1815

Married: Michael Dickson on March 27, 1832, in East Feliciana Parish, Louisiana, Book X, page 57.

Died: 1882

Children of Michael and Hannah P. (Palmer) Dickson: Mary A. Dickson, born July 27, 1833, died September 21, 1834, buried Rosehill Cemetery, Clinton, Louisiana; William L. Dickson, born May 26, 1836, died May 1, 1837, buried Rosehill Cemetery, Clinton, Louisiana; Archibald P. Dickson, born January 28, 1840, twin of Augustus Hester Dickson, died July 23, 1841, buried Rosehill Cemetery, Clinton, Louisiana; Augustus Hester Dickson, born January 28, 1840, died April 23, 1846 (?), buried Rosehill Cemetery, Clinton, Louisiana; David P. Dickson, born April 1, 1848, died August 10, 1848, buried Rosehill Cemetery, Clinton, Louisiana; Victoria Dickson, born ca 1837, married Milton Thomas on April 26, 1855, in East Feliciana Parish, Louisiana; Elizabeth Dickson, born ca 1832, unmarried; Mary Eliza Dickson, born cs 1843; Emily C. Dickson, born 1845; Palmer Dickson, unmarried; Hugh Dickson, unmarried; Michael A. Dickson

1850 CENSUS, EAST FELICIANA PARISH, LOUISIANA 575, 575

Michael Dickson born in 1800 in South Carolina; Hannah Dickson born in 1814 in Louisiana; M. A. Dickson born in 1835 in Louisiana (male); Hannah V. Dickson born in 1838 in Louisiana; Elizabeth

Dickson born in 1842 in Louisiana; Mary E. Dickson born in 1843 in Louisiana; Emily C. Dickson born in 1845 in Louisiana; 66 slaves

1860 CENSUS, BOSSIER PARISH, LOUISIANA, BENTON 564, 564

Dr. J. D. Worthy born in 1834 in Louisiana; 3 slaves

566, 566

J. W. Dickson born in 1837 in Louisiana; N. H. Dickson born in 1842 in Louisiana; E. G. Cook, Overseer born in 1821 in South Carolina; J. W. Dickson, 27 slaves; N. H. Dickson, 24 slaves

568, 568

M. Dickson born in 1800 in Georgia (male) ; Mrs. M. P. Dickson born in 1814 in Louisiana; E. A. Dickson born in 1841 in Louisiana (female) ; M. E. Dickson born in 1844 in Louisiana (female) ; M. C. Dickson born in 1846 in Louisiana (female) ; Palmer Dickson born in 1852 in Louisiana; Hugh M. Dickson born in 1855 in Louisiana; 122 slaves

The following is from *Biographical and Historical Memoirs of Northwest Louisiana,* published in 1890 by the Southern Publishing Company of Nashville and Chicago, page 61

W. L. Dickson, M.D., is one of the leading physicians of Caddo Parish and is especially well known at Rush Point and that vicinity. He is a prominent representative of one of the oldest families of Louisiana, his grandfather Michael Dickson, having been born near Macon, Georgia, but moved to East Feliciana Parish at a very early day and in 1855 came to Bossier Parish. He had some money left him and by using it judiciously he became one of the wealthiest men in the state, owning 10,000 acres of some of the most valuable and fertile land in Louisiana, being also the owner of real estate in Arkansas. At his death in 1865, he was 69 years of age. His wife whose maiden name was Hannah Palmer a native of South Carolina (this is wrong. She was born in Louisiana. See census records above,) was brought by her father, Adam D. Palmer, to Louisiana when a child when she met and married Mr. Dickson. (This is an error. Her father was Archibald D. Palmer, the son of Archibald Palmer and Hannah Carter and the grandson of Mr. John Palmer who came from South Carolina). See also under date of April 16, 1869, Acts of Partition, Heirs of Archibald D. Palmer, in East Feliciana Parish, Louisiana, "Before Henry Hawford, N.P., at the Residence of Dr. J. Worthy came and appeared MADAM HANNAH P. PALMER, RELICT OF MICHAEL DICKSON, DECEASED, Madam Mary Catharine Palmer, wife of Dr. John Worthy, and Madam Mary E. Palmer, relict of Wm. N. Tigner, deceased, ALL MAJORS AND HEIRS OF ARCHIBALD D. PALMER, DECEASED) Her father was also very wealthy and she and her husband were members of the Methodist Episcopal Church, South. Nine of the children born to them grew to maturity and Michael A., the father of the subject of this sketch was educated in the Centenary College of Jackson, Louisiana, graduating from the same. In 1862 he joined the Confederate Army. He controlled and managed the property belonging to his father for some years prior to the latter's death. He was married in 1853 to Miss Mattie Lipscomb of East Feliciana Parish, she being still alive and a resident of Shreveport. (Mr. Casey's AMITE COUNTY RECORDS, Volume 3, show the date of marriage as March 6, 1856). Mr. Dickson was a Democrat, a Royal Arch Mason and his wife is an earnest member of the Methodist Episcopal Church, South. To them were born five children, four living: Dr. W. L. Michael A., a planter of Lafayette County, Arkansas, S.A., a graduate in medicine of the University of Louisiana at New Orleans, but gave up this calling to enter a drug store in Shreveport, and J. O. (Error: should be J(ohn) C(arter)) who is a partner in the firm of Dickson and Dickson at Rush Point. A daughter named Annie died when an infant. The father of these children passed from life in 1870, when just in the prime of life, being 41 or 42. Dr. W. L. Dickson attended Centenary College of Jackson, Louisiana, until he was in his senior year, then left school to represent his mother in the settling up of his grandfather's estate. In 1877 he commenced the study of medicine under Dr. T. G. Ford at Charity Hospital, Shreveport, Louisiana, and from 1879 until the spring of 1881 he attended Bellevue Hospital Medical College of New York City graduating from the same in the spring of the latter year after which he located on Rush Point, his plantation and brothers land amounting to 1,500 acres. His practice is large and the success which has attended his efforts is fully deserved for he is deeply enamored of his profession and gives every case that comes under his care the utmost attention and study. He is a Democrat, his first presidential vote being cast for Hancock and English and socially he is a member of the K.P., Dixie Lodge No. 32.

MICHAEL A. DICKSON

Born: 1835

Married: Mattie Lipscomb on March 6, 1856, in East Feliciana Parish, Louisiana

Died: December 16, 1870

Children of Michael A. and Mattie (Lipscomb) Dickson: William Lipscomb Dickson, born December 4, 1858, married Claudia L. Sentell on February 24, 1897, in New Orleans, Louisiana, died June 18, 1912; Michael Alexander Dickson; Samuel Augustus Dickson; John Carter Dickson; Anna Elizabeth Dickson, born December 2, 1856, died November 12, 1857.

MICHAEL ALEXANDER DICKSON

Born: June 22, 1860

Married: Lizzie J. Cryer on April 25, 1882

Died: February 3, 1924

Children of Michael Alexander and Lizzie J. (Cryer) Dickson: Michael Hugh Dickson, born February 3, 1883, died without issue; Wilhelmina Dickson, born December 30, 1884, died without issue; William B. Dickson, born December 15, 1886, married Cora V. Minor on May 3, 1922, divorced July 2, 1932.

SAMUEL AUGUSTUS DICKSON

Born: March 18, 1862

Married: 1st: Mildred Sentell on February 5, 1885, in New Orleans, La.

2nd: Bula Dillingham on July 10, 1911

Died: June 2, 1916

Children of Samuel Augustus and Mildred (Sentell) Dickson: Martha A. Dickson, born May 22, 1886, died in infancy; George Sentell Dickson, twin of Martha A. Dickson; Mildred Dickson; Carter Bickham Dickson, born April 10, 1889. His son, Carter Bickham Dickson II married Caroline Haywood on August 15, 1943, and they have three sons: Michael Augustus Dickson born November 6, 1946; Carter Bickham Dickson III born July 6, 1949, and James Scott Dickson born March 13, 1960.

Samuel Allen Dickson, born April 6, 1890, married Emily Hunt on January 2, 1918, no issue; Claudius Markham Dickson; Susie Vaughn Dickson.

Children of Samuel Augustus and Bula (Dillingham) Dickson: Brice Dillingham Dickson.

GEORGE SENTELL DICKSON

Born: May 28, 1886

Married: Martha S. Holmes on June 28, 1911

Died: April 11, 1917

Children of George Sentell and Martha (Holmes) Dickson: George Sentell Dickson II; Mildred Edna Dickson, born October 29, 1912; married J. Sam McConathy II on September 8, 1934. They have one son, J. Sam McConathy III born January 15, 1937.

GEORGE S. DICKSON II

Born: Janaury 10, 1917

Married: Ruth Eggleston on July 14, 1932

Children of George S. and Ruth (Eggleston) Dickson II: George S. Dickson III, born August 11, 1934.

MILDRED DICKSON

Born: June 22, 1887

Married: Mahlon H. Levy on November 6, 1912

Children of Mahlon H. and Mildred (Dickson) Levy: Mahlon Howell Levy, Jr., born January 11, 1916.

MAHLON HOWELL LEVY, JR.

Born: January 11, 1916

Married: Utha Spinks on January 19, 1943

Children of Mahlon Howell and Utha (Spinks) Levy, Jr.: Howell Dickson Levy, born October 17, 1952.

CLAUDIUS MARKHAM DICKSON

Born: October 8, 1892

Married: Marjorie Ross Fields on September 28, 1920

Children of Claudius Markham and Marjorie Ross (Fields) Dickson: Claudia Ross Dickson, married William F. Standke; Markham Allen Dickson, married Margaret Shaffer.

SUSIE VAUGHN DICKSON

Born: November 25, 1894

Married: T. Russell Welsh

Children of T. Russell and Susie Vaughn (Dickson) Welsh: Mildred Russell Welsh.

MILDRED RUSSELL WELSH

Born: October 5, 1920

Married: Moulton A. Storey on March 12, 1942

Died: August 14, 1958

Children of Moulton A. and Mildred Russell (Welsh) Storey: Susan Storey, born April 23, 1945; Moulton Russell Storey, born November 25, 1947.

JOHN CARTER DICKSON

Born: October 25, 1863

Married: Julia Payne Ogden on July 17, 1901

Died: July 26, 1927, Shreveport, Louisiana

Children of John Carter and Julia Payne (Ogden) Dickson: Martha Louisa Dickson; Carter Ogden Dickson, born January 25, 1904, Dixie, Louisiana, married Martha Rice Fulton on September 5, 1943; Julia Payne Dickson, born September 8, 1906, Dixie, Louisiana; William Lipscomb Dickson, born December 13, 1909, Shreveport, Louisiana, married Nell Haile Maroney on May 10, 1952.

Sue S. Briggs
(Mrs. Jason Uriah Johnson)

Catherine Lee Owen
(Mrs. Frederick Wespy)

Laura Sue Schroeder
(Mrs. Frank Stone Owen)

Col. William Frazer Owen

MARTHA LOUISA DICKSON

Born: July 20, 1902, in Shreveport, Louisiana

Married: Selden Senter on October 20, 1927

Children of Selden and Martha Louisa (Dickson) Senter: Martha Louisa Senter; Mary Lester Senter, born March 10, 1942.

MARTHA LOUISA SENTER

Born: July 4, 1931, in Shreveport, Louisiana

Married: Thomas Zopher Green on September 4, 1954

Children of Thomas Zopher and Martha Louisa (Senter) Green: Thomas Zopher Green, born July 12, 1955, Lafayette, Louisiana; Mary Shannon Green, born September 30, 1957, Lafayette, Louisiana; Martha Louisa Green, born December 12, 1959, Lafayette, Louisiana.

MARY CATHERINE PALMER

Born: May 22, 1836, in East Feliciana Parish, Louisiana

Married: 1st: Edwin C. Andrews in 1854.

       2nd: Doctor John D. Worthy.

Died: August 8, 1892

Children of Edwin C. and Mary Catherine (Palmer) Andrews: Edwin P. Andrews; Clarence Andrews, died in childhood.
Children of Dr. John D. and Mary Catherine (Palmer) Worthy: Sallie E. Worthy.

1850 CENSUS, EAST FELICIANA PARISH, LOUISIANA 221, 221

Thomas Worthy born in 1801 in Georgia; Maria Worthy born in 1807 in Louisiana; Thomas Worthy born in 1831 in Louisiana; John Worthy born in 1833 in Louisiana; Barbara Worthy born in 1836 in Louisiana; William Worthy born in 1837 in Louisiana; Sara Worthy born in 1840 in Louisiana; James Worthy born in 1842 in Louisiana; Henrietta Worthy born in 1844 in Louisiana; Rhoda Worthy born in 1847 in Louisiana; 30 slaves.

1860 CENSUS, EAST FELICIANA PARISH, LOUISIANA 265, 265

T. Worthy born in 1800 in Georgia (male); M. Worthy born in 1808 in Louisiana (female); T. A. Worthy born in 1832 in Louisiana (male); W. G. Worthy born in 1837 in Louisiana (male); S. J. Worthy born in 1842 in Louisiana (male); S. E. Worthy born in 1841 in Louisiana (female); R. J. Worthy born in 1847 in Louisiana (female); 43 slaves.

1870 CENSUS, EAST FELICIANA PARISH, LOUISIANA, 3RD WARD 575, 520

J. D. Worthy born in 1834 in Louisiana (male); M. C. Worthy born in 1836 in Louisiana (female); P. E. A. (must be Edward P. Andrews) born in 1856 in Louisiana; Sally Worthy born in 1864 in Louisiana.

EDWARD P. ANDREWS

Born: November 10, 1855, in East Feliciana Parish, Louisiana

Married: 1st: Saluda Maundy, daughter of Major General G. W. Maundy

2nd: Willie Haynes, daughter of Captain Frank Haynes

Children of Edward P. and Saluda (Maundy) Andrews: Mary Andrews (died in childhood); Worthy E. Andrews; George C. Andrews; Alpenia Andrews; Saluda C. Andrews.

Children of Edward P. and Willie (Haynes) Andrews: Edward P. Andrews, Jr.

1860 CENSUS, EAST FELICIANA PARISH, LOUISIANA 461, 461

G. W. Munday born in 1817 in Mississippi; S. E. Munday born in 1828 in Louisiana (female); L. L. Munday born in 1845 in Louisiana (female); M. Munday born in 1849 in Louisiana (female); G. W. Munday born in 1851 in Louisiana (male); L. L. Munday born in 1855 in Louisiana (female); S. Munday born in 1857 in Louisiana (female); 41 slaves.

1870 CENSUS, EAST FELICIANA PARISH, LOUISIANA, TOWN OF CLINTON 117, 117

G. W. Munday born in 1817 in Mississippi; S. E. Munday born in 1840 in New York; George Munday born in 1851 in Louisiana; Mary Munday born in 1850 in Louisiana; Laura Munday born in 1856 in Louisiana; Seluda Munday born in 1858 in Louisiana.

Major General G. W. Munday was born in Pass Christian, Mississippi, in 1817, the son of Robert and Susan Ann Kyler Munday. Robert Munday was a native of Virginia, reared at Munday's Landing, Kentucky, now in Mercer County, while his wife was a native of Lancaster, Pennsylvania. The parents were married in Pennsylvania and moved from Kentucky to New Orleans in 1815.

In 1837 General Munday bought an interest in THE LOUISIANA, a paper in Clinton, Louisiana. He served as Deputy Sheriff and was Clinton agent for the Clinton and Port Hudson Railroad. General Munday married Laura Ann Felps, daughter of Joseph Felps, a native of Georgia, in 1841. They were parents of Mary Munday, wife of Sheriff William E. Woodward, Laura L. Munday, wife of John M. Beauchamp, George W. Munday living in Mississippi, Loulie Munday who died at 16, and SALUDA MUNDAY, WIFE OF PALMER ANDREWS, DECEASED WITH FOUR CHILDREN SURVIVING AND LIVING IN THE PARISH.

General Munday married secondly Sallie Daniels and they were the parents of Daniel Eaton Munday, Bessie E. Munday, Effie Munday who died at age 11, and Willie Munday who died in infancy.

General Munday was a Major General of the Militia before the Civil War. He served in the House and Senate before and after the War. He was a member of the Constitutional Convention which sent delegates to nominate Buchanan and Douglas. He was a delegate to the Southern Convention in Montgomery in 1858. While in the Legislature, General Munday introduced bills for widow's dower, the homestead law, and the local option law. General Munday has one of the finest libraries in Louisiana.

BIOGRAPHICAL AND HISTORICAL MEMOIRS OF LOUISIANA. Goodspeed. Chicago. Volume II. Pages 266-268.

MARGARET PALMER

Born: ca. 1790 in Wilkinson County, Mississippi

Married: 1st: William Gready, April 6, 1809, Wilkinson County, Mississippi Book A, page 223

2nd: John Posey, May 9, 1818, West Feliciana Parish, Louisiana, Book 10

Died: September 20, 1862, West Feliciana Parish, Louisiana, buried Bethesda Church

Children of John and Margaret (Palmer) Gready: Mary P. Gready. Children of John and Margaret (Palmer) Posey: Hezekiah A. Posey; Margaret L. Posey, married William Carpenter in Wilkinson County, Mississippi, May 25, 1853, Book I, page 106; Isabella J. Posey, married Stephen Jones on January 4, 1856, West Feliciana Parish; Martha A. Posey, married Samuel Goodrich, 15 Feb. 1839, West Feliciana Parish; Hannah (Anna) Posey, perhaps married first a Mr. Dear, then, H. P. Wright.

1850 CENSUS, WEST FELICIANA PARISH, LOUISIANA 300, 305

Margaret Posey born in 1790 in Mississippi; H. A. Posey born in 1829 in Louisiana (male); M. L. Posey born in 1832 in Louisiana (female); Isabella J. Posey born in 1834 in Louisiana; 11 slaves. Box 78, West Feliciana La for Succession of Margaret Palmer Gready Posey; West Feliciana Marriage Records; Death Notice of Mary Hudson in West Feliciana.

MARY P. GREADY

Born: June 14, 1815 in West Feliciana Parish, La.

Married: Henry Hudson on January 12, 1832

Died: July 2, 1893 in West Feliciana Parish, La.

Children of Henry and Mary P. (Gready) Hudson: Margaret Hudson, born ca. 1834, married Mr. Moore; Henrietta Marion Hudson; Martha

A. Hudson, born ca. 1839; Robert Hudson, Born ca. 1844; Erastus A. Hudson, born ca. 1845.

HENRIETTA MARION HUDSON

Born: August 1, 1837

Married: Charles Bushnell Austin on August 15, 1856

Died: January 7, 1915

Children of Charles Bushnell and Henrietta Marion (Hudson) Austin: James Newson Hines Austin; Gertrude Z. Austin.

For record of these children, see listings for James Newsom Hines Austin and Charles Bushnell Austin.

NANCY PALMER

Born: ca. 1790 in Mississippi

Married: Pierce (or Pearce) Noland in 1809

1820 CENSUS, FELICIANA PARISH, LOUISIANA

Pierce Noland

1 male born 1775-1794; 1 male born 1794-1804; 1 male born 1804-1810; 2 males born 1810-1820; 1 female born 1775-1794; 4 females born 1790-1800; 5 slaves.

1830 CENSUS, EAST FELICIANA PARISH, LOUISIANA

Pierce Noland

1 male born 1790-1800; 1 male born 1800-1810; 2 males born 1810-1815; 1 male born 1815-1820; 1 male born 1825-1830; 1 female born 1780-1790; 1 female born 1810-1815; 1 female born 1815-1820; 3 females born 1820-1825; 9 slaves.

1840 CENSUS, EAST FELICIANA PARISH, LOUISIANA

Pierce Noland

1 male born 1780-1790; 1 male born 1825-1830; 1 female born 1750-1760; 1 female born 1780-1790; 1 female born 1810-1820; 1 female born 1820-1825; 1 female born 1825-1830; 1 female born 1830-1835; 15 slaves.

1850 CENSUS, EAST FELICIANA PARISH, LOUISIANA

259, 259

Nancy Nolan born in 1790 in Miss.; Jenny Nolan born in 1829 in La.; Jane Nolan born in 1816 in La.; Hannah Nolan born in 1826 in La.; James Bennett born in 1824 in La.

State of Louisiana, Parish of East Feliciana: Be it remembered, etc., on the 30 July 1833, came and appeared: PEARCE NOLAND AND HIS WIFE, NANCY PALMER, ADAM PALMER AND SARAH WILLIAMS, HIS WIFE, who state that they release all rights, claims, etc. in the 640 acres formerly owned by A. PALMER. /s/ by them. Test: R. N. Schofield, J. N. Palmer. J. C. White, N.P. Clinton, Louisiana, Notarial Record Book D, page 5. 30 July 1833.

His Will. 1816. Proved: 30 March 1817. Property Community, joint labor of myself and my wife, HANNAH. Have already given children in manner I designated. My will is that all property I die possessed with to my dearly beloved WIFE, HANNAH PALMER. Wife, HANNAH, sole executrix of this my last will. Wife HANNAH appointed guardian of all my minor children. /s/ ARCHIBALD D. PALMER. Witnesses: Samuel Creswell, John Gready, Jesse Roberson, Adam Hope, Robert R. Collins, Lewis Davis. Proved by Gready Roberson, Hope and Davis. A paper in the file, dated 19 Jan 1818 indicates Hannah was living then.

St. Francisville, Louisiana. SUCCESSION OF ARCHIBALD D. PALMER. SENIOR, DECEASED. Probate File No. 79.

Same Probate File, No. 79. SUCCESSION OF HANNAH PALMER. Partition of her estate. 27 February 1829. Present: John Austin, husband of Sarah Palmer, Archibald D. Palmer, Jr., Margaret Gready, Nehemiah A. Palmer, Adam Palmer, Alva Palmer, Hannah P. Turbeville by Attorney Bradford, Mary Bennett and Nancy Nolan by Robert Haile, Jane Palmer, by Lewis Davis, Curator.

St. Francisville, Louisiana. Conveyance File, Book E, page 116. 8 July, 1833. Relinquishment of the Heirs of HANNAH PALMER, Deceased, Personally came and appeared, to-wit: HENRY BENNETT AND MARY PALMER, HIS WIFE: JOHN POSEY AND MARGARET PALMER, HIS WIFE, ALVAH PALMER AND NEHEMIAH PALMER, all residents of this Parish who certify that they have no claims etc as heirs of A. Palmer, deceased in a certain tract of land of 640 acres confirmed by Certificate No. 189 to Palmer and Bennett, to the said tract of land, it having been conveyed away by the Representatives of HANNAH PALMER, DECEASED. Signed by all those mentioned therein.

State of Louisiana. Parish of East Feliciana: Be it remembered, etc., personally appeared, PHILLIP NOLAND, of the State of Mississippi, Wilkinson County, who declared for and in consideration of one tract of land in West Feliciana Parish, Louisiana, 400 arpens, bounded: East by lands of Mrs. Bennett, and West prong of Thompson's Creek, North by lands of Isam Wood; South, by lands of Edward McGehee and East by lands of John Brown; Sold by Adam Palmer of State and Parish aforesaid. . . Swap for 600 acres in State and Parish aforesaid bounded as follows: West, by lands of Heirs of Sarah Palmer, East by land of Heirs of Robert Scott, South by lands of Jeremiah Noland, North by land of Pierce Noland and Jeremiah Noland, etc. /s/ PHILLIP NOLAND, ADAM PALMER. Test: Samuel Wattman,

Henry Skipwith. Clinton, Louisiana, Notarial Record Book D, page 303. 13 Dec. 1834.

From: ARCHIBALD PALMER, SENIOR, of the Parish of Feliciana, State of Louisiana, to HENRY BENNETT and MARY BENNETT, his wife of same. DEED OF GIFT. In consideration of Natural Love and Affection I bear towards my daughter, the said MARY BENNETT and $5. The one sixth part of a tract of 600 arpens of land in Feliciana Parish, fronting on Thompson's Creek, granted to Phillip A. Gray by the Spanish Government, containing 100 square arpens to be laid off in such manner that the buildings and improvements already made thereon by the said HENRY BENNETT AND MARY, HIS WIFE, will be in the center of the said 100 arpens. /s/ ARCHIBALD PALMER, MARY BENNETT, HENRY BENNETT. Test: John Sneed, John H. Mills, William Rucker, and John H. Johnson, Parish Judge.

St. Francisville, Louisiana. Notarial Book A, page 421. 15 February 1817.

From: John Austin of Feliciana Parish, Louisiana, Representative of Heirs of Hannah Palmer, deceased, to Henry Bennett, of same. Consideration: $1,040, in three equal installments, payable 1st of January, 1827, 1828, and 1829. 10% interest. Certain slaves: Sarah, Cato, and Ceasar. /s/ JOHN AUSTIN, HENRY BENNETT. Test: M. P. Clark and John Brown. St. Francisville, Louisiana, Notarial Book AA, page 211. 25 February 1826.

FAMILY MEETING. 31 March 1834. MINOR CHILDREN OF HENRY BENNETT: ADAM, JAMES, MARGARET, SARAH JANE and HENRIETTA BLOUNT. Widow: MARY. Inventory of his Estate, 12 December 1833. St. Francisville, Louisiana, Succession of HENRY BENNETT. File No. 16.

FAMILY MEETING. 23 September 1835. Present: Alvah Palmer, Tutor, N. D. Palmer, M. P. Clark, John Posey, Isaac Draughan, Calvin Smith and Wm. A. Austin. MINOR HEIRS: ADAM J. BENNETT, JAMES C. BENNETT, SARAH JANE BENNETT. Married Daughter: MARGARET, WIFE OF GEORGE H. PATTILLO. St. Francisville, Louisiana. SUCCESSION OF MARY BENNETT. FILE No. 8.

RENUNCIATION OF RIGHTS BY HEIRS OF PEARCE NOLAND: William A. Noland, Archibald P. Noland for himself and as Undertutor for Hannah, Martha, Jeremiah and Amanda Noland, minors, Jane F. Noland and Sarah Ann Phares, represented by Charles Richardson, by a Power of Attorney from said Sarah Ann and her husband, Samuel Phares. 27 June, 1844. Book J, pages 208-210, East Feliciana Parish, Louisiana. Index to Conveyances, Vendor, Vendee.

Noland Marriages, East Feliciana Parish, Louisiana

Book A, page 206 Hannah E. Noland and Calvin S. Smith January 21, 1852

Book A, page 162 Martha N. Noland and Sterling L. Jeter November 16, 1848

Book B, page 80 Amanda Noland and J. E. Ware December 14, 1865

Book 2, page 23 Nancy E. Noland and John Tannett October 30, 1873

Noland Marriages from Wilkinson County, Mississippi, as sent by Mrs. J. V. Parker, 2017 Van Street, Alexandria, Louisiana (Stella W. Parker) : Pierce Noland to Nancy Palmer 4/5/1809; Jeremiah Noland to Jane Ogden 6/24/1811; Phillip Noland to Mary Mayes 3/30/1809; Sarah Ann Noland to Samuel Phares 2/5/1840; Jeremiah D. Noland to Helen Ann Downs 5/9/1837; Jane Noland to Mason E. Saunders 5/12/1836; Lydia Noland to Wm. Tignor 11/6/1820; George W. Noland to Julia D. Norwood 11/18/1852; Thomas V. Noland to Lydia J. Tignor 1/18/1859.

WILLIAM NOLAND

Born: 1810 in Louisiana

Married: Anne Phares, daughter of William Phares of East Feliciana
    Parish, Louisiana, on January 1, 1838, in West Feliciana Parish.
Children of William and Anne (Phares) Noland: Pierce A. Noland, married Fannie McClain (McLean) ; Elizabeth Noland, married John Tannett 30 Oct 1873, married secondly Joseph Gore; Amanda Noland, born 4 March 1846, East Feliciana Parish, Louisiana, married Julian Eugene Ware 14 December 1865, (grandparents of Mrs. J. V. Parker, 2017 Van Street, Alexandria, Louisiana) ; Martha Noland; Jeremiah N. Noland, married Mary Ann Stafford 4 Sept 1873; Hannah Noland, born 1851; Mary Noland, married Samuel A. Stanley 5 Dec 1878; Sallie Noland, married Samuel A. Stanley 21 June 1885.

1850 CENSUS, EAST FELICIANA PARISH, LOUISIANA

241, 241

William Nolan born in 1810 in Louisiana; Anne Nolan born in 1821 in Louisiana; Pierce Nolan born in 1842 in Louisiana; Elizabeth Nolan born in 1844 in Louisiana; Amande Nolan born in 1846 in Louisiana; Martha Nolan born in 1847 in Louisiana; Jeremiah Nolan born in 1849 in Louisiana; Susannah Arnold born in 1769 in Virginia; 4 slaves.

1860 CENSUS, EAST FELICIANA PARISH, LOUISIANA

350, 350

W. Noland born in 1810 in Louisiana (male) ; A. Noland born in 1821 in Louisiana (female) ; P. A. Noland born in 1842 in Louisiana (male) ; E. Noland born in 1844 in Louisiana (female) ; A. Noland born in 1846 in Louisiana (female) ; J. Noland born in 1849 in Louisiana (male) ; H. Noland born in 1851 in Louisiana (female) ; M. Noland born in 1853 in Louisiana (female) ; S. Noland born in 1855 in Louisiana (female) ; E. Noland born in 1858 in Louisiana (male) ; E. Noland born in 1859 in Louisiana (male) ; 9 slaves.

1870 CENSUS, EAST FELICIANA PARISH, LOUISIANA

35, 30 Ward 4

Wm. Nolan born in Louisiana; Ann Nolan born in Louisiana; Eliz Nolan born in Louisiana; Mary Nolan born in Louisiana; Jenny Nolan born in Louisiana; Sally Nolan born in Louisiana.

1880 CENSUS, EAST FELICIANA PARISH, LOUISIANA

Ward 4, 35, 35

Ann Nolan born in 1822 in Louisiana, her parents were born in North Carolina; Sally Nolan born in 1855 in Louisiana where her parents were born, Daughter; Elizabeth Tannett born in 1846 in Louisiana where her parents were born Daughter.

Grandchildren whose father was born in Wales and their mother in Louisiana: Annie Tannett born in 1874 in Louisiana; Charles A. Tannett born in 1875 in Louisiana; Avery M. Tannett born in 1877 in Louisiana; J. Amanda Tannett born in 1879 in Louisiana.

AMANDA JANE NOLAND

Born: March 4, 1846

Married: Julian Eugene Ware, son of James Ware of West Baton Rouge Parish, on December 14, 1865.

Children of Julian Eugene and Amanda Jane (Noland) Ware: William Parish Ware, born 1866, married 1st Sallie Sanders on August 24, 1896, 2nd Elma Earl Austin on December 4, 1907, and 3rd Emma Dubois; Charles Noland Ware, born March 8, 1868, died April 8, 1956, never married; Edward Lesley Ware; Lydia Eugenia Ware, born 1871, died 1951, married T. J. Henderson of Wilkinson County, Mississippi, on February 4, 1892; Harvy Ware, born 1873, died young; Annie Ware, born 1875, died 1895; Sallie Ware, born 1878, died young; Jerry Ware, born 1880, died young; Stella Margaret Ware, born May 28, 1882, married William O. Smith on October 13, 1903, married 2nd Louis Hall in 1938; Julian Eugene Ware, Jr., born March 16, 1884, married Barbara Sanders on February 15, 1919, died April 26, 1936.

EDWARD LESLEY WARE

Born: September 22, 1869

Married: Stella Eliza Hagewood, daughter of James Duncan Hagewood and Sarah Jane Stapleton, on December 19, 1901. She died on October 28, 1921

Died: January 7, 1954

Children of Edward Lesley and Stella Eliza (Hagewood) Ware: Josie Amanda Ware, born July 10, 1903, married on May 7, 1919 to J. N. Oksenholt. Their children: J. N. Oksenholt, Jr., born October 18, 1924; Karl Edward Oksenholt, born October 10, 1926; Stella Jensine Oksenholt, born January 4, 1931; Dagma Virginia Oksenholt, born December 2, 1932.

Edward Hagewood Ware, born November 22, 1905, married Laura Ruth Kennidy on May 23, 1934. Their children: Melba Ann Ware born December 6, 1934; Dolores Jean Ware born October 5, 1936; Edward Newton Ware born December 24, 1938; Larry Joseph Ware born August 31, 1940; and twins William Ray Ware and Gerald Lynn Ware born September 13, 1941.

Lillian Louise Ware, born July 17, 1907, married William L. Luttrell on August 7, 1926. Their children: Diane Ware Luttrell born June 22, 1931 and Barbara Rue Luttrell born November 8, 1932 and died October, 1956. Married secondly Louis S. Drewett. Their children: Judith Louise Drewett born October 29, 1943.

Stella Mae Ware, born November 22, 1909. Married Joseph V. Parker January 20, 1938. Their children: James Lesley Parker born April 1, 1940 and Rodney Allen Parker born October 29, 1945.

Julian Eugene Ware (female), born January 31, 1911. Married Clarence D. Long on August 13, 1937. Their children: Wayne Edward Long born September 11, 1938.

Irene Wood Ware, born July 7, 1913. Married Edward B. Swafford on December 23, 1933. Their children: Patricia Hope Swafford born May 7, 1939; Jennifer Marie Swafford born May 18, 1946; Angela Elizabeth Swafford born October 31, 1947; Marianne Swafford born September 13, 1951.

Ernest Lesley Ware, born January 24, 1915, never married.

James Francis Ware, born March 31, 1918, married Edythe Grace Painter on September 29, 1945. Their children: Linda Susanne Ware born July 14, 1946, and Edward Lesley Ware born June 29, 1950.

Sterling Neilson Ware, born October 15, 1921, married Emmie Muhleder on May 6, 1951. Their children: James Neilson Ware born March 19, 1951, and Nancy Lee Ware born September 10, 1953.

POLLY (MARY) PALMER

Married: Henry Bennett

Died: Before September 23, 1835

Children of Henry and Polly (Mary) Palmer: Adam J. Bennett, Henrietta Blount Bennett; James C. Bennett; Margaret Bennett (married George H. Pattillo) ; Sarah Jane Bennett.

ADAM J. BENNETT

Born: 1814-1815 in Louisiana

Married: Mary J. E. Harvey in East Feliciana Parish, Louisiana

Children of Adam J. and Mary J. E. (Harvey) Bennett: Henry Bennett; Mary Ann Bennett; Burtis Bennett; Sarah Jane Bennett; William H. Bennett; Adam J. Bennett; Robert E. Bennett; Margaret Bennett; Major A. Bennett; Archie B. Bennett; Alva Bennett.

1850 CENSUS, SABINE COUNTY, TEXAS 146, 146

Adam J. Bennett born in 1815 in Louisiana; Mary J. E. Bennett born in 1826 in Louisiana; Mary Ann Bennett born in 1841 in Louisiana; Henry L. Bennett born in 1842 in Louisiana; Burtus C. Bennett born in 1844 in Texas; Sarah Jane Bennett born in 1846 in Texas; William H. Bennett born in 1850 in Texas.

1860 CENSUS, SABINE COUNTY, TEXAS 225, 225

A. J. Bennett born in 1814 in Louisiana: Mary J. Bennett born in 1823 in Louisiana; Mary A. Bennett born in 1840 in Louisiana; Henry Bennett born in 1842 in Louisiana; Bertes C. Bennett born in 1845 in Texas; Sarah J. Bennett born in 1848 in Texas; William Bennett born in 1850 in Texas; A. J. Bennett born in 1853 in Texas; Robert Bennett born in 1855 in Texas; Major A. Bennett born in 1859 in Texas.

H. S. BENNETT, a well-to-do planter and a native of West Feliciana Parish, Louisiana, was born on the 26th of July, 1842, a son of Adam J. and Mary J. E. (Harvey) Bennett, the former of whom was a planter. In 1843 he moved with his family to Sabine County, Texas. Besides H. S. Bennett, they were: Mary A., B. C., Sarah J., W. H., A. J., R. E., Margaret, Major A., Archie B., and Alva.

In 1873, H. S. Bennett married Sallie B. Cotton. They were the parents of the following children: C. S., H. S., Jr., Archie E., Elizabeth F., Sallie B., George S.

Mr. Bennett owns several plantations: "Hardesty," "Tosner," "Ditto," "East and West Cypress Grove" and the homestead, 'Mound."

BIOGRAPHICAL AND HISTORICAL MEMOIRS OF LOUISIANA. Goodspeed. Chicago. Volume 1, pages 283-284.

1870 CENSUS, SABINE COUNTY, TEXAS, BEAT NO. 5, 286, 286

A. J. Bennett born in 1815 in Louisiana; Mary Jane Bennett born in 1822 in Louisiana; Sarah Jane Bennett born in 1847 in Texas; William H. Bennett born in 1850 in Texas; Adam J. Bennett born in 1853 in Texas; Robert E. Bennett born in 1855 in Texas; Margaret A. Bennett born in 1859 in Texas; Major A. Bennett born in 1857 in Texas; Jessee A. Bennett born in 1864 in Texas; Alan Bennett born in 1869 in Texas.

1880 CENSUS, SABINE COUNTY, TEXAS

5th Precinct, 244, 244

Burtis Bennett born in 1850 in Texas. His father was born in La. Mary Bennett wife born in 1850 in Georgia where her parents were born.

Children: Lee Bennett born in 1869 in Texas; Henry Bennett born in 1871 in Texas; Willie Bennett born in 1873 in Texas; Mary J. Bennett born in 1877 in Texas.

245- 245

Major Bennett born in 1859 in Texas. His father was born in La. and his mother was born in S. C.

Louisa Bennett wife born in 1857 in Georgia where her parents were born.

240, 240

Adam J. Bennett born in 1815 in La. where his mother was born. His father was born in Geo (?)

Mary J. Bennett wife born in 1822 in S. C. where her parents were born.

Children: Arch Bennett born in 1864 in Texas; Alva Bennett born in 1869 in Texas.

SARAH PALMER

Born: January 29, 1786

Married: John Jones Austin on September 20, 1804, by Father Brady in Wilkinson County, Mississippi, or West Feliciana Parish, Louisiana. John Jones Austin was married first ca 1794, possibly in New Jersey, to Jane Meeker born in 1777. They had children, David Austin born ca 1795-6 in New Jersey, wed Charlotte Cooke, daughter of Appolo Cooke, and died after 1880 in Mississippi living with his daughter Abigail who had married a Mr. Chisholm and Sarah Jane Austin born 1797, died 1878, married in Chatham, Connecticut to Asahel Goodrich. They are both buried in Braceville, Ohio, and left issue. Records in West Feliciana Parish, La., Braceville, Ohio, Waterville, Oneida County, New York and THE GOODRICH FAMILY IN AMERICA by L. W. Case.

Died: June 4, 1861. She and her husband are burnied in the Family Cemetery on the Charles Hamilton Place.

Children of John Jones and Sarah (Palmer) Austin: (All born in West Feliciana Parish, Louisiana) William A. Austin, married Elizabeth Draughan on January 29, 1829; Lewis Stirling Austin; Aurelia Austin, married Martin P. Clark on December 29, 1826, married secondly William Noble on February 9, 1842; Robert McCausland Austin, married Louisa Bogan before 1841; Sarah Ann Austin, married Calvin S. Smith on December 20, 1832; Mary Jane Austin; Hannah Louisa Austin; John Quincy Adams Austin, married Milly Ann Turberville on October 26, 1848; Susan Jones Austin, married Samuel K. Smart on January 9, 1840; Meranda Elizabeth Austin, born June 10, 1826, died September 5, 1835; Charles Bushnell Austin.

1830 CENSUS, WEST FELICIANA PARISH, LOUISIANA
John Austin
1 male born 1770-1780; 1 male born 1810-1815; 1 male born 1820-1825; 1 male born 1825-1830; 1 female born 1780-1790; 1 female born 1815-1820; 2 females born 1820-1825; 2 females born 1825-1830; 12 slaves.

1840 CENSUS, WEST FELICIANA PARISH, LOUISIANA
Sarah Austin
2 males born 1820-1825; 1 female born 1780-1790; 12 slaves.

1850 CENSUS, WEST FELICIANA PARISH, LOUISIANA
347, 352
Sarah Austin born in 1786 in Mississippi; Chs B. Austin born in 1828 in Louisiana; Margaret Austin born in 1829 in Louisiana; Sarah Austin born in 1849 in Louisiana; Mary Austin born in 1850 in Louisiana.

1860 CENSUS, WEST FELICIANA PARISH, LOUISIANA
325, 328
S. Austin born in 1787 in Louisiana (female); J. K. Austin born in 1856 in Louisiana (female); W. W. Miller, Overseer, born in 1839 in Mississippi (male); S. H. Austin born in 1850 in Louisiana (female); M. J. Austin born in 1850 in Louisiana (female); 15 slaves.
The will of John Austin is in Box 1, St. Francisville, Louisiana. It names his wife Executrix, and is witnessed by E. D. McCarstle, William Draughan and N. N. McCarstle. Among interesting personal effects are these books: *Scott's Family Bible, Jeffersons Correspondence, Methodist Magazine, One large Bible, Martins's Large Digest, Louisiana Civil Code, Louisiana Code of Practice, Dodd's Common Place Book.* 10 June 1833.
Will of Sarah (Palmer) Austin in Box 1, St. Francisville, Louisiana. May 27, 1861. Witnessed by L. S. Austen, Margret (sic) Posey, Mary Jane Hobgood. Her children and grandchildren accepting distribution of the estate: L. S. Austen, A. A. Zug, H. L. Eddins, Joel Eddins, Mary J. Hobgood, H. Hobgood, Wm. A. Austen, Susan J. Smart, S. K. Smart, A. M. Palmer, A. J. (?) Hawsey, (?) Conner, Robert J. Elliott, Chas. B. Austin, and J. Q. Austen, Administrator. 13 March 1862.
License Book A, p 134, Wilkinson County, Mississippi, License for Marriage of Dr. Adam Palmer and Sarah Noland, August 3, 1809.

(Bond dated July 29, 1809). Page 99, AMITE COUNTY, MISSIS-SIPPI, 1699-1890, Vol III, By A. E. Casey, 1957.

Partition of Community Property between the children and Heirs of Mrs. Sarah A. Palmer, deceased, and her surviving husband, ADAM PALMER, made this 30 November 1842, by L. Saunders, Parish Judge, etc. Recipients: ADAM PALMER, ARCHIBALD D. PALM-ER, Under Tutor of minor children of Sarah A. Palmer, deceased, Mary P. McCollum wife of James McCollum, Jeremiah N. Palmer, Philip N. Palmer, Pierce A. Palmer, Archibald Palmer, Sarah A. Hig-ginbotham, wife of William G. Higginbotham, Lucinda L. S. Smith, wife of Isaac B. Smith. Signed by all. Test: Robt. Dyer, John Jeter. Clinton, La. Notarial Record Book I, p 482. 10 Dec 1842.

State of Louisiana, Parish of East Feliciana; FAMILY MEETING of relations of minor heirs of Sarah Palmer, deceased, late of State and Parish aforesaid: Present: Jeremiah Palmer, brother; Pearce Noland and Phillip Noland, Maternal Uncles; Nehemiah Palmer, Paternal Uncle; Mrs. Margaret Posey and Mrs. Nancy Noland, Paternal Aunts; John Posey, Uncle by marriage. Mention of ADAM PALMER, father of the minors (who are not named). Signed by the relations.
Test: Lewis Austin, William Noland.
Clinton, La. Notarial Record Book D, p 303. 13 Dec 1834.

State of Louisiana, Parish of East Feliciana. FAMILY MEETING for minor heirs of Sarah Palmer, deceased late of State and Parish, aforesaid, etc. relations present: J. N. Palmer, Pearce Noland, A. P. Palmer, Nancy X Noland, Margaret Posey, and John Posey, Acting on Petition of Adam Palmer, father of said minors (who are not named).
Clinton, La. Notarial Record Book D, p 303 13 Dec 1834.

Clerk's Office, Clinton, East Feliciana Parish, Louisiana:
Phillip N. Carter married Martha E. M. Chaney. Oct 8, 1851 Book A, p 200.

Jeremiah N. Palmer married Martha J. Ambrose, 8 Jan 1835 Book X, p 202.

AMITE COUNTY, MISSISSIPPI, 1699-1890 Vol III A. E. Casey 1957 Page 136—(License Book G, p 137) Wilkinson County, Miss., License for marriage of JEREMIAH N. PALMER and Minerva Blount. Dec 24, 1841.

CHARLES BUSHNELL AUSTIN

Born: July 14, 1828, in West Feliciana Parish, Louisiana.

Married: 1st: Margaret Louretta Ferguson, daughter of Robert and Bridget (Higgins) Ferguson, who was born January 5, 1828, and died August 5, 1855. Marriage October 12, 1848

2nd: Henrietta Marion Hudson on August 15, 1856 in Wes Feliciana Parish. She was a daughter of Henry Hudson and Mary P. Gready (married as Mary Posey), the daughter of William Gready and Margaret Palmer. She had a sister Margaret Hudson born about 1834 and married to a Mr. Moore a sister, Martha A. Hudson born ca 1839 and brothers, Robert and Erastus A. Hudson born ca 1844 and 1845 respectively.

3rd: Louise Jane Posey on July 27, 1869

Died: January 18, 1909, in West Feliciana Parish. Buried at the Concord Church Cemetery, Rogillioville, Louisiana

Children of Charles Bushnell and Margaret Louretta (Ferguson) Austin: Sarah Helen Austin, born August 20, 1849, in West Feliciana Parish, married James Z. Richardson on December 23, 1869; Mary Jane Austin, born August 19, 1850 in West Feliciana Parish, married Stephen Garner Smith, Jr., on February 26, 1873; Margaret Louretta Austin, born August 3, 1855 in West Feliciana, also a twin brother buried with his mother.

Children of Charles Bushnell and Henrietta Marion (Hudson) Austin: James Newsom Hines Austin, named for the Reverend Hines, a Methodist minister; Gertrude Z. Austin, born July 15, 1859 in West Feliciana, married Alonzo R. Rogillio on December 23, 1883; a foster son, William E. Early, the son of Thomas William and Martha Ann (Posey) Early, born November 27, 1868.

1870 CENSUS, WEST FELICIANA PARISH, LOUISIANA, 12TH WARD 62, 63

Chas. B. Austin born in 1830 in Louisiana; Henrietta Austin born in 1838 in Louisiana; M. J. Austin born in 1850 in Louisiana; Margaret Austin born in 1855 in Louisiana; J. N. H. Austin born in 1857 in Louisiana; Gertrude Austin born in 1859 in Louisiana.

JAMES NEWSOM HINES AUSTIN

Born: August 20, 1857, in West Feliciana Parish, Louisiana

Married: Mary Penelope Smith on November 18, 1880, in West Feliciana Parish

Died: March 31, 1943, in Jackson, Louisiana

Children of James Newson Hines and Mary Penelope (Smith) Austin Hugh Carlyle Austin; Clara Irene Austin, born November 9, 1883 in West Feliciana Parish, married Augustus William De Lee on January 18, 1905; Grover Cleveland Austin, born February 3, 1885, in West Feliciana Parish, married Dora (Bonnette) Simpson in January, 1916; Edith Ella Austin, born August 8, 1886, in West Feliciana Parish, married Robert F. Rogillio on November 10, 1909; Ruby Ethel Austin, born November 29, 1888, in West Feliciana Parish, unmar-

ried; Sidney Eustis Austin, born September 27, 1890, in West Feliciana Parish, died September 21, 1930; Nellie Gertude Austin, born
February 5, 1893, in West Feliciana Parish, married Alexander Stott
on November 15, 1931; Clarence Ernest Austin, born June 3, 1895
in West Feliciana Parish, married Early Hotard on August 31, 1925;
Marion Hines Austin, born February 23, 1897 in West Feliciana
Parish, married Oneida Englade; Carl Lionel Austin, born November
1, 1898, in West Feliciana Parish, married Carrie Eudora Austin on
August 24, 1935; Son, born May 1, 1901, died same day; daughter born
December 11, 1887, died December 12, 1887; James Newsom Hines
Austin and Mary Penelope Smith are buried in the Town Cemetery,
Jackson, Louisiana, all the above information furnished by Mamie
Austin Rouzan, Rt. 1, Box 57, Jackson, Louisiana, Miss Ethel Austin
and Mrs. Hugh C. Austin of Jackson.

HUGH CARLYLE AUSTIN

Born: December 22, 1881 in West Feliciana Parish, Louisiana

Married: Emma Jeannette Lucas on January 28, 1909, in East Feliciana Parish, Louisiana

Children of Hugh Carlyle and Emma Jeannette (Lucas) Austin:
Mamie Penelope Austin, born April 20, 1914, in East Feliciana Parish, married Carniel Matthew Rouzan on October 10, 1936; Hugh
Carleton Austin, born April 19, 1926 in East Feliciana Parish, married Anna Rachal in January, 1950; Jeannette Austin, born July 24,
1928 in East Feliciana Parish, married Marvin Galloway Calhoun,
two daughters, Sallie Jeannette Calhoun and Jeanne Calhoun, both
born in Knoxville, Tennessee; Ruby Eva Austin, born March 11, 1911
in East Feliciana Parish, married Leo Lafayette Gerald on January
2, 1935, two children, James Ogden Gerald born January 6, 1947,
Washington, D. C. and Leo Meffre Gerald born in 1950 in Washington; Thelma Eugenie Austin, born November 25, 1918 in Pointe
Coupee Parish, Louisiana, married Harvey Lorraine McClinton;
three children, Miriam Lorraine McClinton born August 21, 1941,
at Baptist Hospital in New Orleans; Harvey Austin McClinton, born
January 28, 1943 in Jackson, Alabama and Sandra Juarine McClinton, born October 4, 1945 in Jackson, Alabama.

HANNAH LOUISA AUSTIN

Born: June 16, 1820, Laurel Hill, West Feliciana Parish, Louisiana

Married: William Joel Eddins in August, 1839

Died: August 20, 1892, Cottonwood, Callahan County, Texas

Children of William Joel and Hannah Louisa (Austin) Eddins: Lewis
Sterling Eddins, born June 14, 1840, married Sue Hays, died October
27, 1918; Allen Eddins, born 1842 in Louisiana, died 1858; Josephine
Eddins, born 1844 in Louisiana, married George Selman; Laura

Eddins, born 1848 in Texas, married Jim Powell; Dora Eddins, (twin of Laura Eddins), born 1848 in Texas, married 1st Jim Montgomery, married 2nd Ira Holden; John Eddins, born 1850; Alonzo Austin Augustus Eddins.

ALONZO AUSTIN AUGUSTUS EDDINS

Born: February 14, 1861, in East Carroll, Red River Parish, Louisiana

Married: Mary Eugenia Morton, daughter of Doctor William and Jane Elizabeth (Moose) Morton, in 1888

Dide: June 18, 1935, in Pecos, Reeves County, Texas

Children of Alonzo Austin Augustus and Mary Eugenia (Morton) Eddins: Ina Claire Eddins; Carol Morton Eddins, born December 30, 1890, in Paradise, Wise County, Texas, married 1st Leta Heard, daughter of Lee F. and Frank Heard, They were the parents of Carl Lee Eddins, born September 4, 1924, in Pecos, Texas and married Barbara Gingras on June 21, 1947; Elizabeth Eddins; Sue Vern Eddins, born December 10, 1893, in Paradise, Wise County, Texas, died December 13, 1953, in Pecos Texas, married Sully Ikard, they were the parents of Betty Ikard who married Bob Jenkins; Louis Addison Eddins; Lester Eddins, born March 4, 1897, in Paradise, Wise County, Texas, married and had a child, Peggie Ann Eddins; Lillian Claude Eddins; Lynn Bates Eddins.

INA CLAIRE EDDINS

Born: September 28, 1889, in Paradise, Wise County, Texas

Married: Harry Tweedle, son of John Walter and Elsie (Kenans) Tweedle on September 2, 1907, in Pecos, Texas.

Children of Harry and Ira Claire (Eddins) Tweedle: Audley Tweedle, born August 27, 1910, Sterling, Texas, died at birth; Thelma Eugene Tweedle, born October 28, 1911, Sterling, Texas, died August 27, 1912; Harry Tweedle, Jr., born September 20, 1913, in Sterling, Texas, married Mary Elizabeth Johnston, they had a son James Edward Tweedle, born July 23, 1939, in San Angelo, Tom Green County, Texas; Dorothy Aileen Tweedle, born July 26, 1916, married 1st Clayton Precure, they had a son, Eugene Precure born July 23, 1935, married second the Reverend Roy V. Hibbard; Jane Evelyn Tweedle, born January 9, 1920, married 1st Harold Piffer in Oklahoma City, Oklahoma, married 2nd Fred Nibling, son of Dr. George B. Nibling, in San Angelo, Texas, they had a son Kenneth Nibling, born June 28, 1939, in Greenville, Texas; Maxine Imogene Tweedle, born August 21, 1921, married Warren Charles Albert on August 28, 1943, they had: Thomas Warren Albert, born August 10, 1944, in Greenville, Texas; Carol Ann Albert, born July 5, 1947, in San Angelo, Texas; John Albert, born December 6, 1953 in San Angelo, Texas; John

Alonzo Tweedle, born December 6, 1928, died January 29, 1929; Jack Keith Tweedle, born November 18, 1929, married 1st Joan King, married 2nd Billie McClain.

ELIZABETH EDDINS

Born: August 21, 1892, in Paradise, Wise County, Texas
Married: Tom Crum
Children of Tom and Elizabeth (Eddins) Crum: J. Y. Crum, born in Pecos, Texas, Texas, died 1950, married 1st Martha Wade, they had two children: Jay Crum and Tom Crum, Jr., married 2nd Katherine Lipscomb of Fort Worth, Texas, no issue; Myrtle Verne Crum, born Pecos Texas, married Ralph Homes of Pecos, Texas, they had two children, Mary Bess Homes and Freddy Jean Homes; Mable Crum, married Henry Dingee, Jr., they had: Henry Dingee III; Barbara Dingee; Diana Dingee, and Jane Dingee; Tom Crum; Lillian Crum, married Billy Wilson, they were the parents of Billy Crum Wilson; Bess Jean Crum, married 1st Frank Bourland, they were the parents of Frank Bourland, Jr., and Judy Bourland, married 2nd Edward Malovly; Fred Addison Crum, married Jean Farrar Omer and they were the parents of Marcia Crum.

LYNN BATES EDDINS

Born: March 22, 1901 in Palo Pinto, Texas
Married: Frances Inez Armstrong, daughter of J. B. and Cynthia
    Hadley Armstrong, on May 21, 1931
Children of Lynn Bates and Frances Inez (Armstrong) Eddins; Mary Frances Eddins, born October 2, 1935 in Pecos, Texas; Addison Morton Eddins, born December 24, 1940 Wink, Texas.

LOUIS ADDISON EDDINS

Born: March 4, 1897, in Paradise, Wise County, Texas
Married: Alice Alverson, on January 23, 1928
Died: January 23, 1942
Children of Louis Addison and Alice (Alverson) Eddins: Fred Lester Eddins, born November 3, 1929, married Dorothy Prichard, daughter of Floyd Vance and Verna (Drennan) Prichard, they had Eric Lester Eddins, born May 3, 1953; Helen Eddins, born June 9, 1932 in Lubbock, Texas, married 1st Worth Trammel and they had Alvin Ray Trammel, married 2nd Clyde Freeman, son of John Clarence and Hattie Sturdivant Freeman, on March 10, 1951; Sue Alice Eddins, born November 13, 1933 in Lubbock, Texas, married William Noland Barbee, son of Edward Perry and Mable Blanche (Phillips) Barbee, on April 30, 1951 and they were the parents of Billie Sue Barbee, born on March 7, 1952 in Lubbock, Texas.

LILLIAN CLAUDE EDDINS

Born: September 3, 1899, in Gordon, Palo Pinto County, Texas

Married: Arthur White Taylor on June 12, 1920

Children of Arthur White and Lillian Claude (Eddins) Taylor: John Eddins Taylor, born September 14, 1925, in St. Louis, Mo.; Anne Eddins Taylor, born August 10, 1927 in St. Louis, Mo., married William Squire Holmes on January 11, 1952.

MARY JANE AUSTIN

Born: August 19, 1850, at Laurel Hill, West Feliciana Parish, Louisiana

Married: Steven Garner Greene Smith on February 26, 1873. Mr. Smith, the son of Steven Garner and Mary Virginia Elizabeth (Jones) Smith was born on March 5, 1852, at Beech Grove Plantation, West Feliciana Parish, Louisiana, and died on June 10, 1910

Died: May 23, 1925

Children of Steven Garner Greene and Mary Jane (Austin) Smith: L. Marion Smith, born April 12, 1874, at Beech Grove Plantation, West Feliciana Parish, Louisiana, died February 26, 1942, married December 21, 1893, to L. W. Doherty, they were parents of: Leon Alba Doherty; Nattalee Ruth Doherty; Phillip Sample Doherty; Garner Smith Doherty; Lil White Doherty; Charles A. B. Doherty; Kemp Smith Doherty; Mary Helen Doherty; Lucie Louise Doherty; and Marion Eunice Doherty; Steven Garner Smith, born January 21, 1876, at Beech Grove Plantation West Feliciana Parish, Louisiana, died June 8, 1943, married Lena M. Dawson on December 21, 1904, they were parents of: Garner Leland Smith (died as a baby); Albert Kenneth Smith; Mary Jane Smith; F. L. Smith; Joseph Elliot Smith; and twins: Garner and Gladys Smith; Sophie Jones Smith, born September 8, 1878, at Beech Grove Plantation West Feliciana Parish, Louisiana, married John Brandon Campbell, son of John Brandon and Margaret Campbell, in 1896, they were parents of: Walter Lynn Campbell, born December 18, 1896, in West Feliciana Parish, married September 30, 1917, to Effie Banks and they were the parents of Lelya Lynette Campbell, born December 11, 1921, in Woodworth, Louisiana and married on June 27, 1944 to Raymond T. O'Neil and the mother of Barbara Gail O'Neil and Johnnie May Campbell, born July 13, 1929, in Maryville, Louisiana, and married to Edward Charles Palmer on August 7, 1954; Stella Mary Campbell, born September 9, 1898, in West Feliciana Parish, Louisiana, married Milton Thomas Sessions on April 10, 1920; Nettie Jeanette Campbell, born October 23, 1900, in West Feliciana Parish, Louisiana, married Charles V. Romer on November 16, 1926; Albert Smith Campbell, born July 17, 1904 in West Feliciana Parish, Louisiana, married September 19, 1926, to Vida Baker and they were the parents of Vida E. Campbell, born May 4, 1927 and married Paul Gaudin; John Albert Campbell, born March 1, 1929 and married Mrs. Evelyn David; Elizabeth Christine Campbell, born June 13, 1931 and married Riley J. Jeansonne; William Lynn Campbell, born June 13, 1931; and Meryal Ann Campbell, born November 31, 1942; Mary Christine Campbell, born August 12, 1902 in West Feliciana Parish, Louisiana, married Ralph Bloom of Rochester, New York, on May 31, 1936 and they were the parents of Rachel Margaret Bloom born January 20, 1938, in Rayville, Louisiana; Albert B. Smith, born November 25, 1880, Beech Grove Plantation, West Feliciana Parish, Louisiana, died August 20, 1881; Mable Smith, born April 22, 1883, on Beech Grove Plantation, West Feliciana Parish, Louisiana, married March 1, 1905, to Howard W. Toms and they were the parents of: Lucille Inez Toms; Louis Oliver Toms; Mary Katherine Toms; Lydia Wickliff Toms; Johnnie B. Toms; Ruby Dean Toms; Grady Alington Toms; and Annie Mable Toms; Lillie Helen Smith, born November 15, 1886, on Beech Grove Plantation, West Feliciana Parish, Louisiana, married James J. Griffin on March 18, 1909 and they were the parents of: Arthur Don Griffin; Mary Ruth Griffin; Robert Wickliff Griffin; Ida Mary Griffin; Clyde S. Griffin; Walter C. Griffin; Sophie Griffin; Sarah Griffin; Lillie Helen Griffin; Emma Gertude Griffin; Beatrice Griffin; Greene Griffin; Hazel Pauline Griffin; and James Joseph Griffin; Margaret Ferguson Smith, born March 6, 1892 on Beech Grove Plantation, West Feliciana Parish, Louisiana, married Lawrence B. Smith on July 30, 1913, they were the parents of Ladie Ruth Smith, born July 10, 1913, in Orange, Texas.

LEWIS AUSTIN

Married: 1st: Nancy Sanders Liles on December 27, 1827

2nd: Sarah A. Reames on November 28, 1938, East Feliciana Parish, Louisiana

1840 CENSUS, EAST FELICIANA PARISH, LOUISIANA

Lewis Austin; 1 male born 1800-1810; 1 male born 1820-1825; 1 male born 1835-1840; 1 female born 1810-1820; 7 slaves

1850 CENSUS, EAST FELICIANA, LOUISIANA 219, 219

Lewis Austin born in 1806 in Louisiana; Sarah Austin born in 1820 in Louisiana; Lewis Austin born in 1836 in Louisiana; Alonzo Austin born in 1841 in Louisiana; John Austin born in 1843 in Louisiana; Robert Austin born in 1846 in Louisiana; William Austin born in 1849 in Louisiana; 19 slaves

1860 CENSUS, EAST FELICIANA PARISH, LOUISIANA 261, 261

L. S. Austin born in 1807 in Louisiana (male); S. A. Austin born in 1820 in Louisiana (female); J. G. Austin born in 1843 in Louisiana (male) ; K. L. Austin born in 1846 in Louisiana (male) ; W. McR Austin born in 1849 in Louisiana (male) ; H. B. Austin born in 1851 in Louisiana (male) ; J. E. Austin born in 1853 (male) in Louisiana; J. Austin born in 1859 in Louisiana (male) ; M. J. Austin born in 1855 in Louisiana (female) ; L. L. Austin born in 1845 in Louisiana (male) ; S. A. A. Smith born in 1847 in Louisiana (female) ; H. P. Smith born in 1849 in Louisiana (female) ; C. P. Russell born in 1812 in Pennsylvania (male, teacher) ; L. S. Austin 38 slaves; L. S. Austin, Jr., 1 slave

1880 CENSUS, EAST FELICIANA PARISH, LOUISIANA, 3RD. WARD

220, 227

Lewis Austin born in 1845 in Louisiana where his parents were born; Lewis Austin, Jr., born in 1868 in Louisiana where his parents were born.

221, 228

John Austin born in 1843 in Louisiana; Mary Austin born in 1850 in Louisiana; Alonzo Austin born in 1868 in Louisiana; John Austin, Jr., born in 1872 in Louisiana; Robert Austin born in 1877 in Louisiana; Eugene Austin born in 1879 in Louisiana; parents of all above were born in Louisiana, except those of Mary Austin who were born in South Carolina.

225, 232

William Austin born in 1849 in Louisiana; Mary Austin born in 1852 in Alabama; Sallie Austin born in 1876 in Louisiana; Holcombe Austin born in 1877 in Louisiana; the father of Mary Austin was born in Georgia and her mother was born in Maryland.

226, 233

Robt Austin born in 1846 in Louisiana where his parents were born; Anna Austin born in 1848 in Alabama, her father was born in Georgia and her mother was born in Maryland.

228, 235

Lewis S. Austin born in 1807 in Louisiana. HIS FATHER WAS BORN IN NEW JERSEY; HIS MOTHER WAS BORN IN MISSISSIPPI. Harriet Austin born in 1827 in Mississippi. Her father was born in South Carolina and her mother was born in Georgia; Mary Jane Austin born in 1855 in Louisiana where her parents were born.

1870 CENSUS, EAST FELICIANA PARISH, LOUISIANA, 3RD WARD

L. S. Austin born in 1806 in Louisiana; S. A. Austin born in 1820 in Louisiana; W. W. Austin born in 1849 in Louisiana; M. J. Austin born in 1855 in Louisiana

222, 197

E. K. Austin born in 1863 in Louisiana; J. G. Austin born in 1865 in Louisiana; L. C. Austin born in 1850 in Louisiana

144, 133

W. A. Austin born in 1810 in Louisiana, Druggist in Jackson; Eliz Austin born in 1825 in Louisiana.

MARY JANE AUSTIN

Born: March 22, 1819, Tunica, Louisiana

Married: On June 18, 1837 John Henry Hobgood, who was born September 14, 1810, on Prospect Plantation, Tunica, Louisiana, and died on December 1, 1867.

Died: October 13, 1867, Tunica, Louisiana

Children of John Henry and Mary Jane (Austin) Hobgood: Nehemiah Palmer Hobgood; Lucretia Hobgood; John Henry Hobgood; Married Jenny O'Toole of Virginia.

NEHEMIAH PALMER HOBGOOD

Born: June 5, 1852, in Tunica, Louisiana.

Married: Mary Conville White on November 20, 1873. Mary Conville White, born June 18, 1853, in West Feliciana Parish, Louisiana, and died January 1, 1902, in Tunica, was descended from the Bingaman and Surget families, who are prominently mentioned in Harnett Kane's *Natchez On The Mississippi*, particularly in the chapters "The Golden Surgets" and "Always Invite the Right People."

Died: October 9, 1920, in St. Francisville, Louisiana

Children of Nehemiah Palmer and Mary Conville (White) Hobgood: Catharine White Hobgood. Never married; Annie Heath Hobgood; Doctor John Henry Hobgood; William Conville Hobgood; Agnes Lucretia Hobgood, marreid Ovide Lejeune, no children; Mary Eliza Hobgood; Louis Hobgood, died young; Alice Hobgood, died young.

ANNIE HEATH HOBGOOD

Married: Jacob Lewis Row

Children of Jacob Lewis and Annie Heath (Hobgood) Row: Lewis Row who married Bernice Cotton of Baton Rouge, Louisiana; Palmer Row who married Sarah Thompson of Baton Rouge; Mary Conville Row who married Howard Staples of Alexandria, Louisiana, and had a son, Louis Staples.

DOCTOR JOHN HENRY HOBGOOD

Married: Vera Lee Coyle

Children of Doctor John Henry and Vera Lee (Coyle) Hobgood: John Henry Hobgood, Jr. who married Margie Frances Terrell on

February 26, 1943, in Crowley, Louisiana, and had Elizageth Terrell Hobgood born April 15, 1946, and Mary Lee Hobgood born May 5, 1949; Vera Lee Hobgood who married Blyn Olds of Baton Rouge, Louisiana, and had Glyn Hobgood Olds, John Russell Olds, and Vera Lee Olds; Walter Palmer Hobgood who married Velma Davis and had Lyndahl Irene Hobgood, Walter Palmer Hobgood, Jr., Mary Catharine Hobgood, and Leslie Ann Hobgood; and Emmett Hobgood who married Mary Jane Steed of Alexandria, Louisiana, and had Henry Herbert Hobgood.

WILLIAM CONVILLE HOBGOOD

Married: Willia Leake

Children of William Conville and Willia (Leake) Hobgood: Conville Hobgood who married Charlotte Sturdevant and had William Keith Hobgood; Margaret Leake Hobgood who married Rodney Lemoine and had Edine Lemoine, Rodney A. Lemoine, Jr., Conville Hobgood Lemoine, Willia Leake Lemoine, and Walter Emmett Lemoine; and Katheryn Hobgood who married Paul Courrege of Baton Rouge, Louisiana, and had Paul Robert Courrege, Jr., William Hobgood Courrege, Renee Courrege, and Frank Wall Courrege.

MARY ELIZA HOBGOOD

Born: June 5, 1887, in Tunica, Louisiana

Married: Rodolph George Osterberger the son of Charles Henry Osterberger and Mary Stingle. Charles Henry Osterberger was born in Haspelschiedb, Germany, the son of Charles Osterberger of Paris, France, and of Mary Stingle, herself the daughter of Henry Stingle and Clara von Phul.

Children of Rodolph George and Mary Eliza (Hobgood) Osterberger: Marjorie Heath Osterberger; Mary Beverly Osterberger; and Rolly George Osterberger.

MARJORIE HEATH OSTERBERGER

Born: October 9, 1912, in White Castle, Louisiana.

Married. Lieutenant Colonel John Greaves Bennett on June 25, 1938, in Rayne Memorial Church in New Orleans, Louisiana. Colonel Bennett was born on May 1, 1905, in Madison, Mississippi. He is a chemical engineer with Kerr-McGee Oil Industries in Oklahoma City, Oklahoma.

Children of Lieutenant Colonel John Greaves and Marjorie Heath (Osterberger) Bennett: John Overton Bennett. Born May 28, 1939, in Beaumont, Texas; George Dewees Bennett born June 27, 1942 in Canton, Mississippi; and Beverly Carter Bennett born on February 8, 1949.

MARY BEVERLY OSTERBERGER

Born: August 23, 1914, in New Orleans, Louisiana.

Married: Robert Charles Gunness on June 18, 1936, in New Orleans. Mr. Gunness has served as a director of the Standard Oil Company of Indiana since 1953 and as an Executive Vice President since 1956. He served as Vice Chairman of the Research and Development Board of the Department of Defense, 1951, and is a Trustee of the University of Chicago. See *WHO'S WHO IN AMERICA* (1960-1).

Children of Robert Charles and Mary Beverly (Osterberger) Gunness: Beverly Ann Gunness born February 20, 1945, in Chicago; Robert Charles Gunness born February 24, 1939 in Chicago and married Barbara Jane Wolfe of Tulsa, Oklahoma, on June 8, 1960 and had Pamela Lynn Gunness born March 31, 1961; and Donald Austin Gunness born August 18, 1941.

ROLLY GEORGE OSTERBERGER

Born: October 5, 1921, in New Orleans, Louisiana

Married: John Eldred Swearingen, Jr., on September 19, 1942. Since 1958, Mr. Swearingen has served as President of the Standard Oil Company of Indiana. He has served as a director of the company since 1952 and Executive Vice President, 1956-8. He is a director of the Chase Manhattan Bank, the First National Bank of Chicago, and the American Petroleum Institute and is a trustee of the Carnegie Institute of Technology. See *WHO'S WHO IN AMERICA*.

Children of John Eldred and Rolly George (Osterberger) Swearingen, Jr.: Marcia Lynn Swearingen born September 18, 1945, in Chicago; Sarah Cathryn Swearingen born June 16, 1949, in Tulsa, Oklahoma; and Linda Sue Swearingen born October 29, 1953, in Chicago.

LUCRETIA HOBGOOD

Born: May 24, 1844

Married: Doctor Lewis Row of Birmingham, Alabama

Died: January 21, 1932

Children of Doctor Lewis and Lucretia (Hobgood) Row: Laura Row

LAURA ROW

Born: July 25, 1871

Married: Watson Bradford

Died: January 1, 1940, in Birmingham, Alabama

Children of Watson and Laura° (Row) Bradford: Lewis Bradford; Born June 7, 1892; James Bradford, Born October 3, 1894, Tunica, Louisiana—Died, 1935 Birmingham, Alabama; Lyndahl Bradford

LYNDAHL BRADFORD

Born: October 25, 1896

Married: Bert Kent Smith

Children of Bert Kent and Lyndahl (Bradford) Smith: Bert Kent Smith, Jr. Born August 25, 1921; James Watson Smith. Born in 1923

ISAAC CARTER

Married: 1st: Elizabeth Lambert. January 25, 1808. Marriage License Book 1, pages 54-55, Adams County, Mississippi

2nd: Jane Floyd. March 1, 1817. Marriage License Book 1, page 342, Adams County, Mississippi

Children of Isaac and Elizabeth (Lambert) Carter: David L. Carter. Children of Isaac and Jane (Floyd) Carter: Lydia Floyd Carter, Alvah Carter; Jesse Abraham Carter; Nehemiah Carter.

Isaac Carter and Edward Hackett signed a Memorial to Congress on November 25, 1803. C. E. Carter's *Territorial Papers of the United States, Territory of Mississippi*, Vol. 5, page 286.

Note: Some of my records list Nehemiah Carter as the son of Isaac by his first wife, but Mrs. Paul H. Laroussini of Baton Rouge, who knows more of the Isaac Carter genealogy than anyone else says his mother was Jane Floyd. For that reason I have listed him as the son of Jane Floyd.

DAVID L. CARTER

Born: 1808-1810 in Mississippi

Married: 1st: Ann Nancy Netterville on February 23, 1836, Richard C. Clampitt, Bondsman. Marriage License Book F, page 105, Wilkinson County, Mississippi

2nd: Ophelia Ford, daughter of Thomas Ford, on September 14, 1841, William B. Netterville, Bondsman. Marriage License Book G, page 114, Wilkinson County, Mississippi

Wilkinson County, Mississippi, marriages of the Isaac Carter *descendants* can be found in Volume 3 of Albert Eugene Casey's *Amite County, Mississippi*

Mrs. Paul Henri Laroussini (Winona Netterville) of Baton Rouge made available to me several bulletins of the Jeremiah Netterville Family Association, of which she is genealogist. In them is given the record of Ann Nancy Netterville born about 1818-1820. After she and David Lambert Carter were married, it is stated that they lived in the "Plains" just north of Baton Rouge. They had a child born about 1837, who was dead when the estate of Jeremiah Netterville was settled on February 13, 1844. Jeremiah Netterville, father of

Ann Nancy Netterville was born on November 23, 1777, and died in May, 1824, in Wilkinson County, Mississippi, where he had come from Charleston, South Carolina, between 1810 and 1820. Jeremiah's home, "Magnolia Dale," was on Ford's Creek.

1820 CENSUS, WILKINSON COUNTY, MISSISSIPPI
David Carter: 1 male born before 1775; 1 male born 1810-1820; 1 female born 1775-1794; 59 slaves

1840 CENSUS, WILKINSON COUNTY, MISSISSIPPI
David Carter: 1 male born 1800-1810; 1 female born 1835-1840; 7 slaves

1850 CENSUS, WILKINSON COUNTY, MISSISSIPPI 162, 165
Nehemiah Carter born in 1811 in Mississippi; David L. Carter born in 1808 in Mississippi; 27 slaves

1860 CENSUS, WILKINSON COUNTY, MISSISSIPPI 190, 190
D. L. Carter born in 1810 in Misissippi; 26 slaves

LYDIA FLOYD CARTER

Married: Richard Clampitt. March 31, 1832, Wm. E. Green, Bondsman. Marriage License Book E, page 241, Wilkinson County, Mississippi.

Children of Richard and Lydia Floyd (Carter) Clampitt: John Clampitt; Richard Clampitt, Jr.

1830 CENSUS, WILKINSON COUNTY, MISSISSIPPI

Richd Clampett: 1 male born 1800-1810; 1 female born 1780-1790; 1 female born 1810-1815; 2 females born 1815-1820

1840 CENSUS, WILKINSON COUNTY, MISSISSIPPI

Richd Clempitt: 1 male born 1800-1810; 1 male born 1810-1820; 2 males born 1835-1840; 1 female born 1770-1780; 5 slaves

1860 CENSUS, WILKINSON COUNTY, MISSISSPPI 271, 271

Richd Clampitt born in 1804 in South Carolina; Emeline Clampitt born in 1823 in Mississippi; James Clampitt born in 1844 in Louisiana; William Clampitt born in 1845 in Louisiana; Nehemiah Clampitt born in 1847 in Mississippi; Samuel Clampitt born in 1849 in Mississippi; Mary J. Clampitt born in 1850 in Mississippi; Henry Clampitt born in 1852 in Mississippi; Caroline Clampitt born in 1854 in Mississippi

ALVA(H) CARTER

Born: ca 1821 in Mississippi

Married: 1st: Mary A. Leek. February 7, 1852. Marriage Book I, page 141, Wilkinson County, Mississippi

2nd: Sarah Ann Duval. January 19, 1854. Marriage Book I, page 234, Wilkinson County, Mississippi

Children of Alva(h) and Sarah Ann (Duval) Carter: Jesse Monroe Carter, had 14 children; Nehemiah Carter, married Susan Leek, February 1, 1877, David L. Smith, Bondsman, marriage book L, page 361, Wilkinson County, Mississippi, has descendants; Margaret Carter, died before maturity; Isaac Carter, married, left family; Mary Carter, married a Mr. Leake, had family, married Will Hayes, had family, lived in Woodville, Mississippi; Louis Carter, married Mary Holmes, moved to Fort Worth, Texas, has family; Henry Carter, died in youth; Will Carter, married first, Elizabeth Rabb, they had Bessie Carter and Printiss Carter, married second, E. J. Curtain on October 6, 1898, marriage book N, page 236, Wilkinson County, Mississippi, they had a daughter, Doris Carter.

1860 Census, Wilkinson County, Mississippi 314, 314

Alva Carter born in 1821 in Mississippi; Sarah A. Carter born in 1827 in Mississippi; Jesse C. Carter born in 1855 in Mississippi; Nehemia Carter born in 1846 in Mississippi; Margaret J. Carter born in 1848 in Mississippi; Henry J. Carter born in 1860 in Mississippi; 1 slave; Estate of Jesse Carter, 20 slaves
1870 Census, Dist 4, Wilkinson County, Mississippi

Alvey F. Carter born in 1821 in Mississippi; Sarah Ann Carter born in 1827 in Mississippi; Jesse C. Carter born in 1855 in Mississippi; Nehemiah Carter born in 1858 in Mississippi; Henry J. Carter born in 1860 in Mississippi; Mary E. Carter born in 1862 in Mississippi; Isaac L. Carter born in 1864 in Mississippi; William J. Carter born in 1866 in Mississippi; Lewis C. Carter born in 1868 in Mississippi; Amand C. Carter born in May, 1870 in Mississippi
Dist 1, 1870 Census, Wilkinson County, Mississippi
Nehemiah Carter, Sr. born in 1810 in Mississippi

1880 Census, Beat No. 4, Wilkinson County, Mississippi 18, 22

S. A. Carter born in 1832 in Mississippi (female); children: M. E. Carter born in 1863 in Mississippi; Isaac D. Carter born in 1864 in Mississippi; William J. Carter born in 1866 in Mississippi; Lewis E. Carter born in 1867 in Mississippi

JESSE MONROE CARTER

Born: cs 1855 in Mississippi

Married: Sarah A. Leake. February 17, 1879 Marriage Book L, page 438, Wilkinson County, Mississippi

1880 Census, Beat No. 4, Wilkinson County, Mississippi 18, 23

Jesse Carter born in 1855 in Mississippi; Sarah A. Carter born in 1861 in Mississippi, wife Mary Carter born in 1870 in Mississippi, daughter

JESSE ABRAHAM CARTER

Born: February 15, 1818, Cold Springs, Wilkinson County, Mississippi

Married: 1st: Elizabeth Lanehart, daughter of Abraham and Cynthia Ann (Enlow) Lanehart, August 6, 1840, Nehemiah Carter, Bondsman. Marriage License Book G, page 50, Wilkinson County, Mississippi.

2nd: Cynthia Ann Lanehart, daughter of Abraham and Cynthia Ann (Enlow) Lanehart.

Died: November 26, 1858, Frogmore Plantation, Wilkinson County, Mississippi

Children of Jesse Abraham and Elizabeth (Lanehart) Carter: Isaac Abraham Carter; Katherine T. Carter; Nehemiah L. Carter; David Carter; Lydia Rebecca Carter.

Children of Jesse Abraham and Cynthia Ann (Lanehart) Carter: Sarah Elizabeth Carter (died young) and Addie Ellen Carter.

1850 CENSUS, WILKINSON COUNTY, MISSISSIPPI 537, 541

Jesse Carter born in 1818 in Mississippi; Eliz Carter born in 1820 in Mississippi; Isaac Carter born in 1842 in Mississippi; Catharine Carter born in 1845 in Mississippi; Nehemiah Carter born in 1847 in Mississippi; David Carter born in 1850 in Mississippi; Cynthia Lanhart born in 1839 in Mississippi; Alvia Carter born in 1791 in Mississippi; 12 slaves

1860 CENSUS, WILKINSON COUNTY, MISSISSIPPI 315, 316

Cynthia A. Carter born in 1839 in Mississippi; Jane Enlow born in 1791 in Mississippi; Isaac Carter born in 1843 in Mississippi; David Carter born in 1849 in Mississippi; Lydia R. Carter born in 1853 in Mississippi; Ellen A. Carter born in 1859 in Mississippi; Francis Truax born in 1839 in Mississippi; Wm. J. Truax born in 1856 in Mississippi; Mary L. Truax born in 1858 in Mississippi; 3 slaves.

ISAAC ABRAHAM CARTER

Born: March 15, 1842, Cold Springs, Wilkinson County, Mississippi

Married: 1st: Eula Ann Phipps, the daughter of John and Ellen (Enlow) Phipps. July 12, 1866. Her first husband was a Mr. Ikards. She was born on November 7, 1844, Piney, Wilkinson County, Mississippi and died there on April 28, 1877. Marriage Book K, page 408 Wilkinson County, Mississippi

2nd: Mrs. Martha J. (Phipps) Netterville, the daughter of of John and Ellen Phipps. May 26, 1878. Marriage Book L, page 408. Wilkinson County, Mississippi

Died: October 10, 1909, Piney, Wilkinson County, Mississippi

Children of Isaac Abraham and Eula Ann (Phipps) Carter: Charles Gregory Carter, born October 10, 1867, Piney, Wilkinson County, Mississippi, died December 7, 1870; Jesse Alvin Carter; Lillian P. Carter; John Edwin Carter;Rose D. Carter, born February 6, 1874, Piney, Wilkinson County, Mississippi, died December 26, 1943; Isaac William Carter; Eula Phipps Carter, born April 13, 1877, Piney, Wilkinson County, Mississippi, died October 29, 1877.

Children of Isaac Abraham and Martha J. (Phipps) Carter: Catherine Maude Carter; Richard Thomas Carter, twin of Catherine Maude Carter, born February 12, 1879, Piney, Wilkinson County, Mississippi, dead; Elizabeth Jane Carter; Phipps Carter; Benjamin Carter; Lydia Georgia Carter; Walter Carter, born June 6, 1887, Piney, Wilkinson County, Miss., married Elizabeth Whitehead; Wallace Carter, twin of Walter Carter, born June 6, 1887, Piney, Wilkinson County, Mississippi, married a Miss Yolande.

1870 CENSUS, WILKINSON COUNTY, MISSISSIPPI

Isaac A. Carter born in 1842 in Mississippi; Julia A. Carter born in 1844 in Mississippi; Charles G. Carter born in 1868 in Mississippi; Jesse A. Carter born in 1869 in Mississippi; N. L. Carter born in 1842 in Mississippi (male); David Carter born in 1850 in Mississippi; Lydia R. Carter born in 1860 in Mississippi; E. A. Carter born in 1858 in Mississippi.

1880 CENSUS, BEAT NO. 4, WILKINSON COUNTY, MISSISSIPPI 63, 69

Isaac A. Carter born in 1842 in Mississippi; Martha J. Carter born in 1848 in Mississippi (Wife).

Children: Jesse A. Carter born in 1870 in Mississippi; Lillie R. Carter born in 1871 in Mississippi; John E. Carter born in 1873 in Mississippi; Rosa D. Carter born in 1874 in Mississippi; Isaac W. Carter born in 1876 in Mississippi; K. M. Carter born in 1879 in Mississippi (female); R. T. Carter born in 1879 in Mississippi (male).

Stepchildren: L. E. Netterville born in 1869 in Mississippi; Mary E. Netterville born in 1871 in Mississippi; Jessey Netterville born in 1872 in Mississippi; Mattie R. Netterville born in 1873 in Mississippi; Eveline Netterville born in 1874 in Mississippi.

JESSE ALVIN CARTER

Born: August 22, 1861, Piney, Wilkinson County, Mississippi

Married: Eva Ruth Smith, daughter of John Wesley and Mary E. (Dawson) Smith, on April 13, 1902, Marriage Book N, page 383, Wilkinson County, Mississippi

Died: May 22, 1910, Woodville, Mississippi

Children of Jesse Alvin and Eva Ruth (Smith) Carter: Howard Lee Carter.

HOWARD LEE CARTER

Born: March 22, 1904, Woodville, Mississippi

Married: Jane Arden Wells, in Liberty, Amite County, Mississippi, on January 5, 1939.

Children of Howard Lee and Jane Arden (Wells) Carter: Annie Ruth Carter, born July 19, 1940, Woodville, Mississippi; Howard Lee Carter, Jr., born August 9, 1941, Woodville, Mississippi; Martha Jane Carter, born November 29, 1943, Woodville, Mississippi; Jesse Alvin Carter, born March 25, 1947, Woodville, Mississippi; Bythella Arden Carter, born July 17, 1950, Woodville, Mississippi.

LILLIAN P. CARTER

Born: January 25, 1871, Piney, Wilkinson County, Mississippi

Married: John Gower Netterville, son of Jesse Mathis and Nancy (Gower) Netterville on January 24, 1897, at Piney. Marriage Book N, page 139, Wilkinson County, Mississippi

Died: January 19, 1940

Children of John Gower and Lillian P. (Carter) Netterville: Nancy Eula Netterville, born November 15, 1897, died on January 4, 1904; Clarinda Eleanor Netterville; Isaac David Netterville; Jesse Mathis Netterville, born August 5, 1902, died June 7, 1903; John Gower Netterville, Jr., born December 3, 1904; Evelyne Catherine Netterville; Lafayette Netterville; Addie Juanita Netterville; Lillian Augustine Netterville, born August 9, 1913.

CLARINDA ELEANOR NETTERVILLE

Born: January 13, 1899, Wilkinson, Wilkinson County, Mississippi

Married: Grover Curtain, son of William James and Elizabeth (Geter) Curtain, on September 18, 1926

Children of Grover and Clarinda Eleanor (Netterville) Curtain: Annie Ruth Curtain; Margie Estelle Curtain; Lillian Ruby Curtain, born September 14, 1936, Wilkinson, Mississippi, married Jesse Wayne Reagan, son of Albert and Myrtis (Bullock) Reagan.

ANNIE RUTH CURTAIN

Born: July 22, 1927, Wilkinson, Mississippi.

Married: Fred F. Perry, son of Harper and Lydia E. (Ashley) Perry, August 30, 1946, Natchez, Mississippi

Children of Fred F. and Annie Ruth (Curtain) Perry: Frances Ann Perry, born October 22, 1947, Natchez, Mississippi; Fred Wright Perry, born April 5, 1949, Natchez, Mississippi.

MARGIE ESTELLE CURTAIN

Born: January 24, 1931, Wilkinson, Mississippi

Married: Marvin Billy McKinney, son of Benjamin and Myrtle (Hall) McKinney, on May 1, 1950.

Children of Marvin Billy and Margie Estelle (Curtain) McKinney: Alma Patricia McKinney, born February 15, 1951, Natchez, Mississippi.

ISAAC DAVID NETTERVILLE

Born: July 11, 1900

Married: Mable C. Leake, daughter of George and Maggie (McNealy) Leake, on January 17, 1924

Children of Isaac David and Mable C. (Leake) Netterville: Delsa Mae Netterville; Isaac David Netterville, Jr., born September 11, 1926, Wilkinson, Mississippi, married Lela Irby, daughter of Rodney N. and Sadie (Hardy) Irby, on September 1, 1945, Vidalia, Louisiana; Glyn Douglas Netterville, born July 2, 1932, Wilkinson, Mississippi; Hilton Lynn Netterville, born July 12, 1934, Wilkinson, Mississippi.

DELSA MAE NETTERVILLE

Born: November 10, 1924, Wilkinson, Mississippi

Married: Broomfield McCurley, son of John P. and Julia (Day) McCurley, on June 12, 1943.

Children of Broomfield and Delsa Mae (Netterville) McCurley; Linda Fay McCurley, born April 20, 1947, Wilkinson, Mississippi; Gary Dean McCurley, born June 17, 1949, Wilkinson, Mississippi.

EVELYNE CATHERINE NETTERVILLE

Born: May 28, 1906, Wilkinson, Mississippi

Married: Leon Cavin, son of Henry Lee and Ollie (Leake) Cavin, on October 27, 1925

Children of Leon and Evelyne Catharine (Netterville) Cavin: Leon Chancy Cavin; Noland Clyde Cavin; John Lee Cavin, born January 5, 1931, Wilkinson, Mississippi; Wallace Neal Cavin, born December 21, 1932, Wilkinson, Mississippi; Ollie P. Cavin, born November 8, 1949, Wilkinson, Mississippi.

LEON CHANCY CAVIN

Born: August 13, 1926, Wilkinson, Mississippi

Married: Dorothy Sturdivant, daughter of William and Nina (Hazlip) Sturdivant, on July 15, 1946

Died: May 16, 1952

Children of Leon Chancy and Dorothy (Sturdivant) Cavin: Kenneth Wayne Cavin, born June 19, 1948, Natchez, Mississippi; Donald Lane Cavin, born November 14, 1949, Wilkinson, Mississippi; Nina Kathryn Cavin, born March 27, 1952, Wilkinson, Mississippi.

NOLAND CLYDE CAVIN

Born: January 16, 1928, Wilkinson, Mississippi

Married: Barbara Mae Frost, daughter of Edward Louis and Lottie Mae (Black) Frost, on August 1, 1950

Children of Noland Clyde and Barbara Mae (Frost) Cavin: Lynn Ruth Cavin, born July 31, 1952, Natchez, Mississippi.

LAFAYETTE NETTERVILLE

Born: May 28, 1908, Wilkinson, Mississippi

Married: Mattie Phipps, daughter of Joseph A. and Mattie (Caffery) Phipps, on November 10, 1932

Children of Lafayette and Mattie (Phipps) Netterville: Ernest Melvin Netterville, born July 15, 1933, Wilkinson, Miss.; Lafayette Netterville, Jr., born May 10, 1935, Wilkinson, Mississippi; Jean Netterville, born May 11, 1939.

ADDIE JUANITA NETTERVILLE

Born: November 17, 1910, Wilkinson, Mississippi

Married: John Ashley, son of Weathersby and Lula (Howard) Ashley, on March 5, 1924

Children of John and Addie Juanita (Netterville) Ashley: John Dudley Ashley, born December 27, 1929, Wilkinson, Mississippi, married Bobbie Jean Carter, daughter of David and Myrtle Jane Carter, on August 19, 1949; William Joe Ashley, born August 30, 1935.

JOHN EDWIN CARTER

Born: January 4, 1873, Piney, Wilkinson County, Mississippi

Married: Stella Cassels.

Died: November 23, 1953

Children of John Edwin and Stella (Cassels) Carter: Edwina Carter, born November 30, 1903, Wilkinson, Mississippi, married David M. Owens on June 7, 1937; Richard Clifton Carter; Eula Ann Carter.

RICHARD CLIFTON CARTER

Born: July 21, 1906, Wilkinson, Mississippi

Married: Margaret Leake, daughter of George Douglas and Margaret (McNealy) Leake, on July 2, 1944

Children of Richard Clifton and Margaret (Leake) Carter: Margaret Ann Carter, born February 16, 1936, Wilkinson, Miss.; Richard Clifton Carter, Jr., born December 30, 1939, Woodville, Mississippi.

MARGARET ANN CARTER

Born: February 16, 1936, Wilkinson, Mississippi

Married: Dr. Joseph Mattox on April 5, 1955

Children of Dr. Joseph and Margaret Ann (Carter) Mattox: Mark Carter Mattox, born August 6, 1959.

EULA ANN CARTER

Born: December 13, 1908, Wilkinson, Mississippi

Married: Jefferson E. Whitley on October 26, 1935

Children of Jefferson E. and Eula Ann (Carter) Whitley: S. Frances Whitley, born August 30, 1936, Wilkinson, Mississippi; Sarah Evelyn Whitley, born July 19, 1938, Wilkinson, Mississippi; Jo Ann Whitley, born July 2, 1940, Woodville, Mississippi.

ISAAC WILLIAM CARTER

Born: December 20, 1875, Piney, Wilkinson County, Mississippi

Married: Mary Carter, daughter of Jesse and Minnie (Leake) Carter, on February 8, 1900. Marriage Book N, page 291, Wilkinson County, Mississippi

Died: January 2, 1954

Children of Isaac William and Mary (Carter) Carter: Dave Carter; Vernon Carter; Ray Carter, born March 3, 1909, Wilkinson County, Mississippi, married Hazel Pritchard; Ardis Carter, born July 4, 1912, Wilkinson County, Mississippi, died July 5, 1914; Middie Lee Carter, born November 17, 1917, Wilkinson County, Mississippi, married Eddie Davis; Isaac Abraham Carter.

DAVE CARTER

Born: December 29, 1900, Wilkinson, Mississippi

Married: Myrtle Jane Floyd on January 20, 1921. Marriage Book O, page 457, Wilkinson County, Mississippi

Children of Dave and Myrtle Jane (Floyd) Carter: Ardis Carter; Bobby Carter, married John Ashley on August 19, 1949.

ARDIS CARTER

Born: June 27, 1925, Wilkinson, Mississippi

Married: 1st: Hiram Clayton Freeman
2nd: Leo A. Geter, son of Leo and Emily (Leake) Geter, on January 11, 1947

Children of Hiram Clayton and Ardis (Carter) Freeman: Billy Wayne Freeman, born July 21, 1945, Woodville, Mississippi.

Children of Leo A. and Ardis (Carter) Geter: Jerry Leo Geter, born October 19, 1948, Centerville, Mississippi; Marie Ann Geter, born April 11, 1950, Woodville, Mississippi.

VERNON CARTER

Born: September 16, 1903, Wilkinson County, Mississippi

Married: Doris Carter, daughter of Will and Bessie Geter (Curtain) Carter.

Children of Vernon and Doris (Carter) Carter: William Vernon Carter; Elizabeth Carter, married H. Geter.

ISAAC ABRAHAM CARTER

Born: April 2, 1919, Wilkinson County, Mississippi

Married: Mary Elizabeth Leake, daughter of Alex Boyd and Clara (Cavin) Leake, on December 26, 1945

Children of Isaac Abraham and Mary Elizabeth (Leake) Carter: Kay Frances Carter, born 1947, Wilkinson County, Mississippi; Isaac Abraham Carter, Jr., born 1948, Wilkinson County, Mississippi; Alex Boyd Carter, born 1950, Wilkinson County, Mississippi; William Thomas Carter, born 1952, Wilkinson County, Mississippi.

CATHERINE MAUDE CARTER

Born: February 12, 1879, Piney, Wilkinson County, Mississippi

Married: Frederick Paddock Leake, son of Alex Boyd and Mary Catherine (Netterville) Leake

Died: October 7, 1929

Children of Frederick Paddock and Catherine Maude (Carter) Leake: Mary A. Leake, born January 2, 1902, Wilkinson, Mississippi, died July 20, 1909; R. T. Leake; Mattie Elbertine Leake, born January 25, 1905, Wilkinson, Mississippi, married Emmett Howard Morris, son of John D. and Marcella (Bryant) Morris on October 7, 1934; Frederick Paddock Leake II; Carter Leake, born November 28, 1909, Wilkinson, Mississippi, died February 12, 1910; Theodore Leake, born February 20, 1911, Woodville, Mississippi, married Miss J. V. Geter, daughter of Henry Parham and Eunice (McGraw) Geter; Katherine Leake, born December 28, 1912, Woodville, Mississippi, died January 30, 1913.

R. T. LEAKE

Born: August 13, 1903, Wilkinson, Mississippi

Married: Ernest Isaiah Watson, son of the Reverend Isaiah and Loula (Towns) Watson

Children of Ernest Isaiah and R. T. (Leake) Watson: Richard Thomas Watson, born May 31, 1924, Alexandria, Louisiana, married Margaret Glenn Brabston, U.S. District Attorney, 962 Witworth Street, Jackson, Mississippi; George Ernest Watson, born December 12, 1927, Monroe, Louisiana, married Janice Dean Savage on September 9, 1950; Patricia Juanita Watson.

PATRICIA JUANITA WATSON

Born: January 27, 1930, Centerville, Mississippi

Married: Benjamin Arthur Talbert on May 29, 1947

Children of Benjamin Arthur and Patricia Juanita (Watson) Talbert: Patricia Morris Talbert, born February 2, 1948, Woodville, Mississippi; Elias Leake Talbert, born August 30, 1951, Centerville, Mississippi; Benjamin Arthur Talbert, Jr., born April 11, 1954, Centerville, Mississippi.

FREDERICK PADDOCK LEAKE, JR.

Born: August 27, 1906, Wilkinson, Mississippi

Married: Mary Ruth Boatner, daughter of David Phares and Fannie Ruth Caufield Boatner, on May 20, 1937

Children of Frederick Paddock and Mary Ruth (Boatner) Leake, Jr.: Frederick Paddock Leake III, born May 15, 1938, Centerville, Mississippi.

ELIZABETH JANE CARTER

Born: February 12, 1881, Piney, Wilkinson County, Mississippi

Married: John Cassels

Children of John and Elizabeth Jane (Carter) Cassels: John Paul Cassels, born December 20, 1908, Wilkinson County, Mississippi, married Dodie L. Cooke on September 18, 1948; Claude Carter Cassels; Alvin Maxion Cassels; Thelma I. Cassels, born February 28, 1920, Woodville, Mississippi, married Horace Preston Jones December 15, 1945.

CLAUDE CARTER CASSELS

Born: August 23, 1910, Piney, Wilkinson County, Mississippi

Married: Mrs. Celeste Patterson Walker on September 28, 1941, she was daughter of George and Fannie (Brown) Patterson

Children of Claude Carter and Celeste (Patterson) Cassels: Susan Carter Cassels, born April 15, 1948, Hattiesburg, Mississippi.

ALVIN MAXION CASSELS

Born: April 2, 1918, Woodville, Mississippi

Married: Vernel Hughes, daughter of Melton Henry and Lelan (McCurley) Hughes, on September 4, 1947

Children of Alvin Maxion and Vernel (Hughes) Cassels: Bessie Ann Cassels, born August 3, 1948, Centerville, Mississippi; Jimmie Oliver Cassels, born January 21, 1950, Centerville, Mississippi

PHIPPS CARTER

Born: May 11, 1882, Piney, Wilkinson County, Mississippi

Married: Sallie Cassels on September 20, 1905. Marriage Book N, page 514, Wilkinson County, Mississippi

Died: July 14, 1947

BENJAMIN CARTER

Born: November 29, 1883, Piney, Wilkinson County, Mississippi

Married: Mary Ethel Enlow, daughter of Tom and Susan (Felter) Enlow.

Children of Benjamin and Mary Ethel (Enlow) Carter; Lloyd Alvin Carter, born November 13, 1910, Piney, Wilkinson County, Mississippi; Olivia Georgia Carter; Beatrice Susan Carter; Juanita Sarah Carter, born June 24, 1918, Natchez, Mississippi, died September 3, 1937; Martha Lee Carter, born July 28, 1921, Piney, Wilkinson County, Mississippi, married Floyd Lusk on October 28, 1945; Thomas Bernard Carter, born July 7, 1923, Natchez, Mississippi, married Madaline Booker on June 29, 1949; Lillie Mae Carter; Nina Merle Carter.

OLIVIA GEORGIA CARTER

Born: February 18, 1912, Piney, Wilkinson County, Mississippi

Married: Henry Roberts, son of John and Frances (Smith) Roberts, on June 23, 1930

Children of Henry and Olivia Georgia (Carter) Roberts: Charles Eldridge Roberts, born January 1, 1931, Natchez, Mississippi; Fannie May Roberts, born December 21, 1933, Natchez, Mississippi, married William Taylor, son of Henry Wesley and Annie Rebecca (Melton) Taylor, on August 9, 1952; Donald Jewel Roberts, born July 16, 1936, Natchez, Mississippi; Julia Erline Roberts, born July 16, 1936, Natchez, Mississippi, twin of Donald Jewel Roberts, married Freddie Geter March 29, 1952; Henry Alva Roberts, born April 2, 1940, Natchez, died April 2, 1940; Ethel Juanita Roberts, born April 4, 1941, Natchez; Alvis Cecil Roberts, born June 29, 1943, Natchez, died Nov. 9, 1943; Patricia Ann Roberts, born September 24, 1945, Natchez, Mississippi; Betty Sue Roberts, born November 28, 1948, Natchez, Mississippi.

BEATRICE SUSAN CARTER

Born: May 3, 1916, Natchez, Mississippi

Married: Jesse Forest Leake, son of William Netterville and Hannah Janet (Rabb) Leake, on May 5, 1934

Children of Jesse Forest and Beatrice Susan (Carter) Leake: Wallace Leake, born March 1, 1935, Natchez, Mississippi; Myrtle Pauline Leake, born January 30, 1936, Natchez, Mississippi; Jerry Wayne Leake, born November 8, 1940, Oak Grove, Louisiana.

LILLIE MAE CARTER

Born: January 4, 1926, Natchez, Mississippi

Married: Benford Moak on February 20, 1946

Children of Benford and Lillie Mae (Carter) Moak: Linda D. Moak, born January 2, 1947, Natchez, Mississippi; Thomas M. Moak, born September 27, 1948, Natchez, Mississippi.

NINA MERLE CARTER

Born: August 14, 1930, Natchez, Mississippi

Married: Rayford Wilson, son of Kirby and Mildred (Byrd) Wilson, on October 23, 1948

Children of Rayford and Nina Merle (Carter) Wilson: Stanley Lloyd Wilson, born December 22, 1950, Natchez, Mississippi.

LYDIA GEORGIA CARTER

Born: May 19, 1885, Piney, Wilkinson County, Mississippi

Married: Lee Thompson, Jr., in 1912.

Children of Lee and Lydia Georgia (Carter) Thompson, Jr.: Leroy Thompson.

LEROY THOMPSON

Born: September 22, 1915, Woodville, Mississippi

Married: Opal May McElwee, daughter of Henry Dwight and Katie Lee (Shaw) McElwee, on February 29, 1930

Children of Leroy and Opal May (McElwee) Thompson: Thomas Leroy Thompson, born January 29, 1937, Woodville, Miss.; Carol Joan Thompson, born June 4, 1938, Woodville, Mississippi.

KATHERINE T. CARTER

Born: August 23, 1844, Cold Springs, Wilkinson County, Mississippi.

Married: Alonzo Tyler Rabb, the son of Nicholas and Katherine (Tyler) Rabb, on January 18, 1866. Mr. Rabb was born in Darrington, Wilkinson County, 1844, and died on November 19, 1920.

Died: January 11, 1912.

Children of Alonzo Tyler and Katherine T. (Carter) Rabb: James Bunyon Rabb; Elizabeth Emma Rabb; David Carter Rabb; Isaac Franklin Rabb, born October 22, 1871, Piney, Wilkinson County, died August 24, 1873; Lydia Lou Rabb, born March 27, 1874, Piney, Wilkinson County, married Will E. McGraw on February 8, 1910, died October 12, 1950; Kirk Rabb; Irene Rabb, born September 22, 1877, Piney, Wilkinson County, married L. L. Laneheart on September 23, 1901, died September 10, 1909, had issue; Hanna J. Rabb; Adaline Rabb, born October 30, 1881, Piney, Wilkinson County, died May 4, 1890; Bertha Rabb, born February 27, 1884, Piney, Wilkinson County, died July 28, 1885; Belle Rabb, born April 25, 1886, Piney, Wilkinson County, died May 8, 1886; Jesse V. Rabb, twin of Belle Rabb, born April 25, 1886, Piney, Wilkinson County, married Lottie Brown on December 23, 1909, left issue.

1880 Census, Beat No. 4, Wilkinson County, Mississippi 47, 53
Alonzo Rabb born 1844 in Mississippi; Kate Rabb born in 1847 in
Mississippi; J. B. Rabb born in 1867 in Mississippi (male); Elizabeth
Rabb born in 1869 in Mississippi; David Rabb born in 1870 in Missis-
sippi; Lydia Rabb born in 1874 in Mississippi; Kirk Rabb born in
1876 in Mississippi; Irene Rabb born in 1878 in Mississippi; Hanner
(Hannah) Rabb born in 1880 in Mississippi.

JAMES BUNYON RABB

Born: October 24, 1866, Piney, Wilkinson County, Mississippi

Married: Jessie Emma Cavin, daughter of Carroll B. and Clarinda
Catharine (Netterville) Cavin, in 1887

Died: July 15, 1952

Children of James Bunyon and Jessie Emma (Cavin) Rabb: Carroll
A. Rabb; Bertha Rabb; Wiley Rabb, born May 19, 1894, Wilkinson
County, Mississippi, died December 20, 1908; Elizabeth Rabb, born
May 18, 1896, Wilkinson County, Mississippi, died November 19,
1897; Alonzo James Rabb; Franklin Rabb, born November 25, 1900,
Wilkinson County, Miss., died November 25, 1900; Edgar Rabb; Etta
Rabb, born July 26, 1904, Wilkinson County, Mississippi; Lela Rabb,
born October 17, 1906, Wilkinson County, Mississippi, died February
17, 1907; Conley Rabb; Gladys Edith Rabb.

CARROLL A. RABB

Born: December 8, 1889, Wilkinson County, Mississippi

Married: Claudia King, daughter of John T. and L. Ann (Stubbs)
King, on September 1, 1923

Children of Carroll A. and Claudia (King) Rabb: Johnnie Beatrice
Rabb.

JOHNNIE BEATRICE RABB

Born: November 25, 1930, Baker, Louisiana

Married: Otto Morgan Keating, son of Martin R., and Ida Lucille
(Galloway) Keating, on November 25, 1950

Children of Otto Morgan and Johnnie Beatrice (Rabb) Keating:
Lawanna Rae Keating, born February 25, 1952, Baton Rouge, Louisiana.

BERTHA RABB

Born: May 23, 1892, Wilkinson County, Mississippi

Married: Morris Sibley on June 20, 1923. He was the son of Charles
C. and Mary Melvina (Hodge) Sibley.

Children of Morris and Bertha (Rabb) Sibley: Elma Sibley, born
March 22, 1924, Jackson, Louisiana, married Frank H. Griffin; Dor-

othy Alma Sibley, born December 22, 1926, Baton Rouge, Louisiana, died July 4, 1930; Robert Morris Sibley, born November 6, 1928, Baton Rouge, Louisiana; Mary Louise Sibley; Milton Sibley, born December 28, 1932, Baton Rouge, Louisiana, died June 28, 1947; Leona Sibley.

MARY LOUISE SIBLEY

Born: March 4, 1930, Baton Rouge, Louisiana

Married: Wesley E. Smith, son of Grover Cleveland and Ella Jane (Elliot) Smith, on February 3, 1948

Children of Wesley E. and Mary Louise (Sibley) Smith: Gordon Milton Smith, born November 24, 1948; Grover Morris Smith, born February 11, 1951, Vicksburg, Mississippi.

LEONA SIBLEY

Born: January 11, 1934, Baton Rouge, Louisiana

Married: Adrian J. Noland, son of A. T. and Ida Noland, on May 30, 1951

Children of Adrian J. and Leona (Sibley) Noland: Robert Randolph Noland, born March 30, 1952, Oceanside, California.

ALONZO JAMES RABB

Born: September 15, 1898, Wilkinson County, Mississippi

Married: Eva King, daughter of John T. and L. Ann (Stubbs) King, on August 30, 1924

Children of Alonzo James and Eva (King) Rabb: Mildred Rabb; Betty Jo Rabb; Barbara Jean Rabb, born January 13, 1933, Baton Rouge, Louisiana, married Jewel McLain Wilson, son of Duncan and Katie Ellen (Taylor) Wilson, on July 5, 1952.

MILDRED RABB

Born: October 25, 1926, Baton Rouge, Louisiana

Married: Thomas J. Loudon on December 8, 1941. Mr. Loudon is the son of William and Ollie (Roberts) Loudon.

Children of Thomas J. and Mildred (Rabb) Loudon: Michael James Loudon, born July 8, 1951, Baton Rouge, Louisiana.

BETTY JO RABB

Born: January 29, 1931, Baton Rouge, Louisiana

Married: Earl Andrew Kling on May 29, 1954

Children of Earl Andrew and Betty Jo (Rabb) Kling: Shela Ann Kling, born June 9, 1956, Baton Rouge, Louisiana.

EDGAR RABB

Born: January 18, 1902, Wilkinson County, Mississippi

Married: Mattie Keowen on November 3, 1928

Died: February 26, 1938

Children of Edgar and Mattie (Keowen) Rabb: Lois June Rabb.

LOIS JUNE RABB

Born: December 19, 1929, Baker, Louisiana.

Married: William Robert Large on December 19, 1948.

Children of William Robert and Lois June (Rabb) Large: Karen Lynn Large, born October 28, 1949, Baton Rouge, Louisiana.

CONLEY RABB

Born: February 21, 1910, Wilkinson, Mississippi

Married: Ernie Day, daughter of Luther L. and Sarah Eugenia (Flowers) Day, on November 5, 1932

Children of Conley and Ernie (Day) Rabb: Carlos David Rabb, born May 18, 1934, Rosetta, Wilkinson County; Marvin Alonzo Rabb, born May 4, 1943, Baton Rouge, Louisiana.

GLADYS EDITH RABB

Born: November 25, 1913, Wilkinson County, Mississippi

Married: Sam Tubberville, son of Bowan A. and Elizabeth (Howard) Tubberville, on April 2, 1938

Children of Sam and Gladys Edith (Rabb) Tubberville: Jessie Elizabeth Tubberville.

JESSIE ELIZABETH TUBBERVILLE

Born: April 21, 1939, Denham Springs, Louisiana

Married: Rodney C. Ballard, son of Herbert and Irene (Hull) Ballard, on December 16, 1956

Children of Rodney C. and Jessie Elizabeth (Tubberville) Ballard: Patricia Ann Ballard, born July 3, 1952.

ELIZABETH EMMA RABB

Born: January 7, 1868, Piney, Wilkinson County, Mississippi

Married: Will Carter

Died: June 11, 1896

Children of Will and Elizabeth Emma (Rabb) Carter: Bessie Carter, lives near Sicily Island, Louisiana; Printiss Carter, lives near Sicily Island, Louisiana, married.

DAVID CARTER RABB

Born: November 16, 1869, Piney, Wilkinson County, Mississippi

Married: Mary Ellen Netterville, daughter of William A. and Martha P. (Phipps) Netterville, on April 10, 1892

Died: September 14, 1900

Children of David Carter and Mary Ellen (Netterville) Rabb: Richard Baxter Rabb, born June 8, 1894, Piney, Wilkinson County, Mississippi, died October 6, 1900; Isaac Alonzo Rabb.

ISAAC ALONZO RABB

Born: August 22, 1898, Piney, Wilkinson County, Mississippi

Married: Catherine V. Smith, daughter of William and Mary K. (Patrick) Smith, on September 3, 1930

Children of Isaac Alonzo and Catherine V. (Smith) Rabb: Isaac Alonzo Rabb, Jr., born July 12, 1931, New Orleans, Louisiana; Verity Anne Rabb, born October 9, 1933, New Orleans, Louisiana; Derrye Adrienne Rabb, born December 14, 1937, New Orleans, Louisiana.

KIRK RABB

Born: December 11, 1875, Piney, Wilkinson County, Mississippi

Married: Mattie Netterville, daughter of William A. and Martha J. (Phipps) Netterville, on December 19, 1898

Died: November 11, 1945

Children of Kirk and Mattie (Netterville) Rabb: Alonzo K. Rabb, Mattie Evelyn Rabb, Regina Rabb, Natalie Rabb, Audry Rabb.

ALONZO K. RABB

Born: March 30, 1901, Piney, Wilkinson County, Mississippi

Married: Sallie Kate Cavin, daughter of Thomas Walter and Elizabeth Jenny (Knight) Cavin, on April 25, 1922

Died: January 2, 1949

Children of Alonzo K. and Sallie Kate (Cavin) Rabb: Alonzo K. Rabb, Jr., born August 10, 1923, Woodville, Mississippi; Mattie Elizabeth Rabb.

MATTIE ELIZABETH RABB

Born: October 25, 1925, Woodville, Mississippi

Married: Claude Melson II, son of Claude and Lois (Newton) Melson, on May 30, 1946

Children of Claude and Mattie Elizabeth (Rabb) Melson II: Claude Everett Melson III, born October 23, 1947, Centerville, Mississippi.

MATTIE EVELYN RABB

Born: September 20, 1903, Piney, Wilkinson County, Mississippi

Married: 1st: William S. Lee, son of David S. and Grace (Hooper) Lee, on June 2, 1925

2nd: Phillip Buckman Williams, son of Henry Davis and Emma ((Holliday) Williams, on September 13, 1939

Children of William S. and Mattie Evelyn (Rabb) Lee: William S. Lee, Jr., born December 19, 1926, married Geraldine Kirby on December 15, 1950; Robert Douglas Lee, born March 5, 1930, Cleveland, Mississippi.

Children of Phillip Buckman and Mattie Evelyn (Rabb) Williams: Phillip Buckman Williams, Jr., born June 27, 1945, Woodville, Mississippi.

REGINA RABB

Born: May 16, 1906, Piney, Wilkinson County, Mississippi

Married: William T. Cakes, Jr., son of William T. and Martha (Herrod) Cakes, on February 15, 1935

Children of William T. and Regina (Rabb) Cakes, Jr.: Betty Jo Cakes, born September 13, 1937, Centerville, Mississippi.

NATALIE RABB

Born: July 2, 1908, Piney, Wilkinson County, Mississippi

Married: Walter P. Jensen, son of Herbert and Lelah Ellen (Leake) Jensen, born May 30, 1933

Children of Walter P. and Natalie (Rabb) Jensen: Walter P. Jensen, Jr., born May 9, 1927, married Stella Louise Smith on June 9, 1951; William R. Jensen, born June 12, 1929, Woodville, Mississippi; Natalie Imogene Jensen, born July 18, 1939, Woodville, Mississippi.

AUDRY RABB

Born: January 23, 1913, Piney, Wilkinson County, Mississippi

Married: Eugene Brock Hill, son of A. S. and Leola (Brock) Hill, on May 24, 1933

Children of Eugene Brock and Audry (Rabb) Hill: Eugene Brock Hill, Jr., born August 12, 1938, Cleveland, Mississippi; Kirk Rabb Hill, born May 19, 1945, Cleveland, Mississippi.

HANNAH J. RABB

Born: December 6, 1897, Piney, Wilkinson County, Mississippi

Married: William Netterville Leake, son of Alex Boyd and Mary A. (Netterville) Leake, on June 16, 1901

Children of William Netterville and Hannah J. (Rabb) Leake: Mable Leake; Chancy L. Leake, born September 17, 1903, Wilkinson County, Miss.; Jesse Forest Leake; William Alexander Leake; Irene Leake; Estelle Ann Leake, born January 18, 1910, Piney, Wilkinson County, Mississippi, married Michael Laughlin McElligott in 1932, died November 19, 1935; Irving B. Leake, born February 10, 1913, Piney, Wilkinson County, Mississippi, married Ida Mae Ashley, daughter of William and Gertrude Ashley, on December 13, 1945; Lydia Catherine Leake; Woodrow Wilson Leake, born April 18, 1916, Piney, Wilkinson County, Mississippi, died August 8, 1916; Mary Bell Leake; Elizabeth Leake; Alonzo Rabb Leake.

MABLE LEAKE

Born: May 2, 1902, Wilkinson County, Mississippi

Married: Wilber Henry Brehm, son of John Henry and Nancy Brehm, on November 26, 1926

Children of Wilber Henry and Mable (Leake) Brehm: Rebecca Leake Brehm; Wilma Ann Brehm, born February 26, 1930, Natchez, Mississippi, died June 24, 1946; Wilber Henry Brehm, Jr., born June 13, 1932, Natchez, Mississippi, died September 12, 1947; Nancy Janet Brehm, born July 17, 1936, Natchez, Mississippi.

REBECCA LEAKE BREHM

Born: June 2, 1928, Natchez, Mississippi

Married: Billie T. Gaddis, son of James Truman and Ida (Tillman) Gaddis, on December 23, 1950

Children of Billie T. and Rebecca (Leake) Gaddis: Gene Henry Gaddis, born December 27, 1951, Fort Benning, Georgia.

JESSE FOREST LEAKE

Born: April 17, 1904, Wilkinson County, Mississippi

Married: Beatrice Carter, daughter of Benjamin and Mary Ethel (Enlow) Carter

Children of Jesse Forest and Beatrice (Carter) Leake: Wallace Leake, born March 1, 1935, Natchez, Mississippi; Myrtle Pauline Leake, born June 30, 1936, Natchez, Mississippi; Jerry Wayne Leake, born November 8, 1940, Oak Grove, Louisiana.

WILLIAM ALEXANDER LEAKE

Born: September 1, 1906, Piney, Wilkinson County, Mississippi

Married: Esta Orgeron on February 2, 1938

Children of William Alexander and Esta (Orgeron) Leake: L. Ann Leake, born October 5, 1938, New Orleans, Louisiana; Elaine Rita Leake, born June 1, 1942, New Orleans, Louisiana; William Alexander Leake, Jr., born December 6, 1944, New Orleans, Louisiana; Hannah Janett Leake, born December 19, 1946, New Orleans, La.; Alvin Charles Leake, born August 6, 1948, Harvey, Jefferson Parish, Louisiana.

IRENE LEAKE

Born: September 15, 1908, Piney, Wilkinson County, Mississippi

Married: Alvin Cecil Reed, on November 9, 1903

Children of Alvin Cecil and Irene (Leake) Reed: William Cecil Reed, born October 31, 1940, Clifton, Texas; Catherine Irene Reed, born July 3, 1942, Dallas, Texas; Irving Leon Reed, born February 9, 1944, Baton Rouge, La.; Walter Ray Reed, born September 26, 1948, Lake Charles, La.

MARY BELL LEAKE

Born: May 30, 1919, Piney, Wilkinson County, Mississippi

Married: Lawrence Hockman on August 25, 1950

Children of Lawrence and Mary Bell (Leake) Hockman: Barbara Jean Hockman, born April 8, 1951, Grand Rapids, Michigan; Joan E. Hockman, born March 18, 1954.

LYDIA CATHERINE LEAKE

Born: October 21, 1914, Piney, Wilkinson County, Mississippi

Married: Louis Hoffman

Children of Louis and Lydia Catherine (Leake) Hoffman: Lydia Estelle Hoffman, born October 19, 1942, Natchez, Mississippi

ELIZABETH LEAKE

Born: January 21, 1921, Piney, Wilkinson County, Mississippi

Married: Michael L. McElligott on November 13, 1937

Children of Michael L. and Elizabeth (Leake) McElligott: Michael Laughlin McElligott, born Cleveland, Mississippi; Rose Lucille McElligott, born December 15, 1942, Los Angeles, California; James Patrick McElligott, born June 16, 1945, Charleston, South Carolina; William Henry McElligott, born November 23, 1947, Paoli, Indiana; Mary Margaret McElligott, born June 18, 1949, Paoli, Indiana; Katherine Ann McElligott, born November 23, 1951, Paoli, Indiana.

ALONZO RABB LEAKE

Born: September 30, 1923, Piney, Wilkinson County, Mississippi

Married: Margarette Michael on September 16, 1947

Children of Alonzo Rabb and Margarette (Michael) Leake: Linda Kay Leake, born July 4, 1952.

NEHEMIAH L. CARTER

Born: 1846 in Wilkinson County, Mississippi

Married: Emma Netterville, daughter of John Thomas and T. (Lanehart) Netterville

Died: September 3, 1883

Children of Nehemiah L. and Emma (Netterville) Carter: Emma Eula Carter, born July 13, 1877, Wilkinson County, Miss., died September 4, 1881; Elizabeth Eveline Carter, born November 29, 1878, Wilkinson County, died September 4, 1881; Warren J. Carter, born March 4, 1880, Wilkinson County, died December 19, 1882; John Jesse Carter, born January 21, 1882, Wilkinson County, died November 6, 1885; Nehemiah Carter, born August 17, 1883, Wilkinson County, died June 22, 1885.

DAVID CARTER

Born: October 3, 1849, Wilkinson County, Mississippi

Married: Lizzie Havard, daughter of John and Adaline (Coon) Havard, February 13, 1879. Marriage Book L, page 433, Wilkinson County, Mississippi.

Died: January 22, 1928.

Children of David and Lizzie (Havard) Carter: Charles Sessions Carter; Katie Amanda Carter; Dudley Edward Carter; Dannie H. Carter; David Carter, born April 11, 1888, Wilkinson County, Mississippi, died May 26, 1888; Seymore Carter, born July 19, 1889, Wilkinson County, Mississippi, died January 6, 1892; Mattie Annette Carter, born July 31, 1893, Wilkinson County, Mississippi, married Archie Carter on March 3, 1912, has family; James Sessions Carter. 1880 CENSUS, BEAT NO. 4, WILKINSON COUNTY, MISSISSIPPI 6, 6

David Carter born in 1850 in Mississippi; Elizabeth W. Carter born in 1855 in Mississippi, wife; Charles S. Carter born in 1879 in Mississippi, son; Betsey Middleton born in 1801 in Mississippi, grandmother.

CHARLES SESSIONS CARTER

Born: November 14, 1879, Wilkinson County, Mississippi

Married: Lillie Charlotte Lanehart, daughter of Abraham Donley and Charlotte (Montgomery) Lanehart, on December 26, 1905. Marriage Book N, page 524, Wilkinson County, Mississippi

Children of Charles Sessions and Lillie Charlotte (Lanehart) Carter: Katie Amanda Carter, born October 27, 1906, Wilkinson County, Mississippi; Lizzie A. Carter.

LIZZIE A. CARTER

Born: February 10, (?), Wilkinson County, Mississippi

Married: Judson Holloway, son of Algy and Percy (Ashley) Holloway, on January 1, 1945.

Children of Judson and Lizzie (Carter) Holloway: Dolores Holloway, born August 13, 1946, Rosetta, Wilkinson County, Mississippi; Henry O. Holloway, born December 2, 1947, Rosetta, Wilkinson County, Mississippi; William Thomas Holloway, born June 12, 1949, Rosetta, Wilkinson County, Mississippi.

KATIE AMANDA CARTER

Born: September 24, 1881, Wilkinson County, Mississippi

Married: Henry Geter on June 29, 1901

Died: October 25, 1902

Children of Henry and Katie Amanda (Carter) Geter: Leve Magruder Geter, married Bernie Leake, died 1960, has descendants.

DUDLEY EDWARD CARTER

Born: December, 1883, Wilkinson County, Mississippi

Married: Sally F. McGregory on February 27, 1908. She was the daughter of Frank and Alice (Brown) McGregory.

Children of Dudley Edward and Sally F. (McGregory) Carter: David Elliot Carter, born November, 1908, Wilkinson County, married 1935 to Elene Parker, has issue; Dannie Wilson Carter, born June 20, 1910, Wilkinson County, died 1915; Albert Elwyn Carter, born February 23, 1912, Wilkinson County, married June 3, 1941, Mary Estelle Flowers, died September 23, 1954, has issue; Mary Kathleene Carter; Henrietta Carter, born October 2, 1915, Wilkinson County, married William Hammock on December 24, 1939, has issue; Dudley Sessions Carter, born July 26, 1917, Wilkinson County, married 1935 to Ruth Flowers, has issue; Ralph Davis Carter; Stella Bernice Carter; Alvin Franklin Carter, born March 27, 1923, Wilkinson County, married a Miss Smith on December 24, 1949, has issue; Seymore R. Carter, born December 18, 1926, Wilkinson County, married 1948 Mary Jane Roberts, has issue; Sally Irene Carter, born October 1, 1933, Wilkinson County, married Leroy Smith on October 17, 1951, has issue.

MARY K. CARTER

Born: December 18, 1913, Wilkinson County, Mississippi

Married: Myrle C. Flowers, son of John Earl and Vera (Leake) Flowers, on June 14, 1936

Children of Myrle C. and Mary K. (Carter) Flowers: Mary Louise Flowers, born June 27, 1939, Wilkinson County, Mississippi, married Bailey Elwood Howell on July 12, 1959; Theresa J. Flowers, born June 4, 1943, Wilkinson County, Mississippi.

RALPH DAVIS CARTER

Born: December 4, 1919, Wilkinson, Mississippi

Married: Clara L. Leake, daughter of Alex Boyd and Clara C. (Cavin) Leake, on June 22, 1946

Children of Ralph Davis and Clara L. (Leake) Carter: Ralph Davis Carter, Jr., born April, 1948, Natchez, Mississippi.

STELLA B. CARTER

Born: November 16, 1921

Married: Alex Boyd Geter, son of Leo Arglass and Emily (Leake) Geter, on June 5, 1942

Children of Alex Boyd and Stella B. (Carter) Geter: Alex Boyd Geter, Jr., born March 29, 1944, Wilkinson County, Miss.; Robert Gregory Geter, born October 14, 1948, Baton Rouge, La.

DANNIE H. CARTER

Born: April 5, 1886, Wilkinson County, Mississippi.

Married: Emma Cavin, daughter of Thomas Walter and Elizabeth

(Knight) Cavin on June 9, 1915. Marriage Book O, page 243, Wilkinson County, Mississippi

Died: 1960

Children of Dannie H. and Emma (Cavin) Carter: Annette Carter; Lezena Carter, born on September 21, 1919, in Laneheart, Wilkinson County, Mississippi, maried Harold Smith, son of Peter and Ruth (Day) Smith, on May 3, 1941, died March 9, 1945; Edna Mae Carter; Dannie H. Carter, Jr.

ANNETTE CARTER

Born: May 21, 1916, in Lanehart, Wilkinson County, Mississippi

Married: Robert Hensley, son of Wiley Russell and Mary Frances
(Jordan) Hensley, on August 30, 1936. He was born on August 21, 1906, in Oakland, Benton County, Mississippi

Children of Robert and Annette (Carter) Hensley: Barbara Ann Hensley, born July 15, 1938, Woodville, Mississippi; Bonnie Lea Hensley, born September 3, 1939, Woodville, Mississippi; Robert Gene Hensley, born February 15, 1941, Woodville, Miss.

DANNIE H. CARTER

Born: September 23, 1926, Lanehart, Wilkinson County, Missisippi.

Married: June Smith, daughter of Edward L. and Willie (Cage)
Smith on May 25, 1949.

Children of Dannie H. and June (Smith) Carter: Pamela L. Carter, born June 23, 1952, Natchez, Mississippi.

EDNA MAE CARTER

Born: October 20, 1922, Lanehart, Wilkinson County, Mississippi

Married: Clemens Fife on May 3, 1941

Children of Clemens and Edna Mae (Carter) Fife: Melvin L. Fife, born February 11, 1951, Baton Rouge, Louisiana; James Carter Fife, born November 3, 1953, Baton Rouge, Louisiana.

JAMES SESSIONS CARTER

Born: March 29, 1895, Wilkinson County, Mississippi

Married: Orilla Leake, daughter of Alex Boyd and Mary A. (Netter-
ville) Leake, on February 28, 1917. Marriage Book O, page 283, Wilkinson County, Mississippi

Died: October 30, 1946

Children of James Sessions and Orilla (Leake) Carter: Alex Dave Carter; Mary Elizabeth Carter, born February 13, 1924, Wilkinson County, Mississippi, married George Matthews on July 19, 1955; Mattie Clara Carter; James Sessions Carter, Jr., born November 3, 1928, Wilkinson County, married Pauline Virginia Hughes; Elbertine Leake Carter; Orilla Lee Carter, born November 24, 1933, Wilkinson

County, married Glen Powell Butler on December 31, 1955; Arilla Bea Carter, twin of Orilla Lee Carter, born November 24, 1933, Wilkinson County; Lydia L. Carter, born August 10, 1938, Wilkinson County, died January 29, 1941; Charles D. Carter, born November 3, 1939, Wilkinson County; Melva Lena Carter, born March 5, 1942, in Centerville, Mississippi.

ALEX DAVE CARTER

Born: December 5, 1921, Wilkinson County, Mississippi

Married: Doris Hazlip, daughter of John Rayford and Bertie (Sturdivant) Hazlip, on August 17, 1947.

Children of Alex Dave and Doris (Hazlip) Carter: Alex Dave Carter, Jr., born July 2, 1951, Baton Rouge, Louisiana.

MATTIE CLARA CARTER

Born: May 23, 1926, Wilkinson County, Mississippi

Married: Homer C. Reed, Jr. on May 31, 1947

Children of Homer C. and Mattie Clara (Carter) Reed, Jr.: Dorothy C. Reed, born June 12, 1948, Hattiesburg, Mississippi; James Sessions Reed, born August 7, 1950, Natchez, Mississippi.

ELBERTINE LEAKE CARTER

Born: August 15, 1931, Wilkinson County, Mississippi

Married: Milton Davis Westberry, son of Ernest and Lona (Jester) Westberry, on June 7, 1947

Children of Milton Davis and Elbertine Leake (Carter) Westberry: Milton Davis Westberry, Jr., born April 15, 1948, Centerville, Mississippi; Ernest Gregory Westberry, born June 17, 1950, Centerville, Mississippi.

LYDIA REBECCA CARTER

Born: August 17, 1853, Cold Springs, Wilkinson County, Mississippi.

Married: Frederick A. Leak, Feb. 22, 1872, Wilkinson County, Miss.

Died: April 11, 1904.

Children of Frederick A. and Lydia Rebecca (Carter) Leak: Walter Leak, born 1882, Cold Springs, died in infancy; Lelah Ellen Leak; Mary Leak; Harrison Carter Leak; Thomas Anthony Leak, born 1890, Wilkinson County, died 1911; Dave Leak; Pearle Leak, born February 24, 1894, Wilkinson County, died August 2, 1902; Addie Elizabeth Leak, born January 31, 1897, Wilkinson County.

LELAH ELLEN LEAK

Born: 1884, Cold Springs, Wilkinson County, Mississippi

Married: Herbert Jensen.

Children of Herbert and Lelah Ellen (Leake) Jensen: Nelson Jensen, born 1902, Doloroso, Wilkinson County, Mississippi, married Bettie Davis, has issue; Anthony Carter Jensen, born May 23, 1904, Doloroso, Mississippi, died August 16, 1906; Walter P. Jensen; Frederick Kimbel Jensen, born January 28, 1908, Doloroso, Mississippi, died April 25, 1910; Lydia Jensen, born 1911 Doloroso, Mississippi, married Francis B. Holliday, has issue; Sarah Jensen, born 1913, Doloroso, Mississippi; Mary Elizabeth Jensen, born 1916, died 1941.

WALTER P. JENSEN

Born: 1906, Doloroso, Mississippi

Married: Natalie Rabb, daughter of Kirk and Mattie (Netterville) Rabb, on May 20, 1933

Children of Walter P. and Natalie (Rabb) Jensen: Walter P. Jensen, Jr., born May 9, 1927, Woodville.

MARY LEAK

Born: 1886 Cold Springs, Wilkinson County, Mississippi

Married: 1st: Mr. A. Smith
         2nd: Carrol Hackett

Died: 1915

Children of A. and Mary (Leake) Smith: Elmo Smith, born April, 1900, Wilkinson County, married and has issue; Freddie Smith, born 1902, Wilkinson County, Mississippi.

HARRISON CARTER LEAK, JR.

Born: August 14, 1885, Wilkinson County, Mississippi

Married: Maude Caulfield on September 4, 1918

Died: September 1, 1959

Children of Harrison Carter and Maude (Caulfield) Leak: Anna Douglas Leak, married Thomas L. Robertson, lives in Anderson, Indiana; Harrison Carter Leak, Jr.; James Caulfield Leak, deceased, married Mildred E. Breland.

Address of Mrs. Harrison Carter Leak, Sr.: P.O. Box 3, Woodville, Mississippi.

HARRISON CARTER LEAKE, JR.

Born: February 16, 1922, Woodville, Mississippi

Married: Mary Collins Hewes, daughter of Cecil and Elizabeth (Collins) Hewes

Children of Harrison Carter and Mary (Hewes) Leak, Jr.: Harrison Carter Leak III, born August 14, 1948, Baton Rouge, Louisiana; James C. Leak, born March 1952, Baton Rouge, Louisiana

Address: 9566 Donna Drive
         Baton Rouge, Louisiana

DAVE LEAK

Born: 1892 in Wilkinson County, Mississippi

Married: Blanche Sturgen

Died: 1959

Children of Dave and Blanche (Sturgen) Leak: Fred Leak, married Doris Birdwell, has issue; Mary Leak, married Raymond J. Parkins, has issue.

ADDIE ELLEN CARTER

Born: March 26, 1859, in Wilkinson County, Mississippi

Married: Charles Thomas Netterville, the son of Jesse Mathis and Rebecca Catharine (Lanehart) Netterville, on January 8, 1878

Died: February 12, 1947

Children of Charles Thomas and Addie Ellen (Carter) Netterville: Ethel Addie Netterville; Mary Eveline Netterville; Katherine Rebecca Netterville, born November 6, 1882, Wilkinson County, Mississippi, died May 17, 1928; Lydia Ann Netterville; Jessie Netterville; Charles Thomas Netterville, Jr.; William Magruder Netterville; Annie Sessions Netterville, born October 2, 1895, Wilkinson County, Mississippi, died August, 1896; Winona Ellen Netterville, born July 27, 1898, Wilkinson County; Mississippi, married Paul Henri Laroussini, the son of Pierre Hypolite and Pauline (Bechet) Laroussini, of New Orleans, on March 15, 1938.

ETHEL ADDIE NETTERVILLE

Born: December 30, 1878, Wilkinson County, Mississippi

Married: Thomas Walter Cavin, son of Moses and Sallie (Shropshire) Cavin, on January 16, 1910.

Died: December 26, 1954

Children of Thomas Walter and Ethel Addie (Netterville) Cavin: Rita Rebecca Cavin.

RITA REBECCA CAVIN

Born: June 16, 1911, Wilkinson, Mississippi

Married: Horace Elbert Smith on August 22, 1930

Children of Horace Elbert and Rita Rebecca (Cavin) Smith: Imogene Smith, born February 29, 1932, Baton Rouge, Louisiana, died March 3, 1932; Thomas James Smith, born January 29, 1940, Natchez, Mississippi; Robert Alvin Smith, born October 30, 1946, Natchez, Mississippi.

MARY E. NETTERVILLE

Born: September 17, 1880, Wilkinson County, Mississippi

Married: Clarence Clifton Cassels on January 29, 1907

Children of Clarence Clifton and Mary E. (Netterville) Cassels: Cleo

Clifton Cassels, born August 23, 1908, Wilkinson County, Mississippi, married Mary Kate Skinner on June 4, 1933.

LYDIA ANN NETTERVILLE

Born: September 16, 1885, Wilkinson County, Mississippi

Married: Fernand Vaughan Gasquet, son of Francis James and Louise Gasquet, on December 23, 1916.

Died: December 12, 1946

Children of Fernand Vaughan and Lydia Ann (Netterville) Gasquet: Francis James Gasquet.

FRANCIS JAMES GASQUET

Born: January 10, 1919, Memphis, Tennessee

Married: Mary Rainwater on February 6, 1944

Children of Francis James and Mary (Rainwater) Gasquet: Mary Gasquet, born August 1, 1945, Charleston, South Carolina; Dorothy Ann Gasquet, born July 28, 1948, Natchez, Mississippi; Francis James Gasquet, Jr., born June 28, 1951, Natchez, Mississippi; Norma Elizabeth Gasquet, born January 18, 1959, Natchez, Mississippi.

JESSIE NETTERVILLE

Born: December 17, 1887, Wilkinson County, Mississippi

Married: Thomas Wesley Flowers, Jr., son of Thomas Wesley and Mary (Jacobs) Flowers on October 25, 1905.

Children of Thomas Wesley and Jessie (Netterville) Flowers, Jr.: Fay Flowers; Lavada Flowers; Thomas Wesley Flowers III; Charles Lesley Flowers, twin of Thomas Wesley Flowers III, born January 28, 1912, New Orleans, Louisiana, married Mnomi McCraine, daughter of David and Mae (Miller) McCraine, on June 6, 1937; Commander Elton Ernest Flowers, U.S.N.; Mary Ellen Flowers; Lydia Katherine Flowers; Annie Mae Flowers; Winona Ethel Flowers; W. Eugenia Flowers; Rubin P. Flowers.

FAY FLOWERS

Born: August 8, 1906, Wilkinson County, Mississippi

Married: George T. Head on December 25, 1928

Children of George T. and Fay (Flowers) Head: George Wesley Head.

GEORGE WESLEY HEAD

Born: March 5, 1931, Nashville, Tennessee

Married: Etta Maxine Finch, daughter of Henry Carl and Annabelle (Douglas) Finch, on March 21, 1955

Children of George Wesley and Etta Maxine (Finch) Head: Harriet Fay Head, born May 17, 1957, Nashville, Tennessee.

LAVADA FLOWERS

Born: July 21, 1908, Wilkinson County, Mississippi

Married: January 4, 1925 to Robert West McGraw, son of Harry William and Louise (Floyd) West McGraw

Children of Robert and Lavada (Flowers) West McGraw: Robert E. McGraw, born April 2, 1926, Baton Rouge, Louisiana; Roger Yates McGraw; Roy West McGraw.

ROGER YATES McGRAW

Born: April 20, 1928, Woodville, Mississippi

Married: Betty Jo Bass in 1948

Children of Roger Yates and Betty Jo (Bass) McGraw: Diane McGraw, born May 29, 1949, Centerville, Mississippi; Roger Yates McGraw, Jr., born August 24, 1957, in Marksville, Louisiana; Susan A. McGraw, born June 25, 1957, Centerville, Mississippi.

ROY WEST McGRAW

Born: April 19, 1930, Woodville, Mississippi

Married: Joyce Olivia Maher, daughter of Joseph Alfred and Barbara Olivia (Whitehead) Maher, on November 27, 1951

Children of Roy West and Joyce Olivia (Maher) McGraw: Roy West McGraw, Jr., born November 7, 1952, Baton Rouge, Louisiana; Gena McGraw, born March 1, 1955, Baton Rouge, Louisiana; David Wayne McGraw, born June 23, 1956, Baton Rouge, Louisiana.

THOMAS WESLEY FLOWERS III

Born: January 28, 1912, New Orleans, Louisiana

Married: Mary Pauline Colly, daughter of Newell Gaston and Mary Ellen (Johns) Colly

Children of Thomas Wesley and Mary Pauline (Colly) Flowers III: Thomas Wesley Flowers IV, born July 8, 1936, Manchester, Coffee County, Tennessee, married Peggy Ruth Reinecke on April 13, 1960; Charles Lesley Flowers, born November 24, 1938, La Grange, Troup County, Georgia; Dale Colly Flowers, born January 2, 1940, Clarksville, Tennessee; William Paul Flowers, born October 30, 1942, Unionville, Tennessee; James Neil Flowers, born September 30, 1945, Shelbyville, Tennessee; Mary Paulette Flowers, born December 31, 1951, Columbia, Tennessee.

COMMANDER ELTON ERNEST FLOWERS, U.S.N.

Born: September 26, 1915, Wilkinson County, Mississippi

Married: Dorothy Lillian Lutjens on April 8, 1936

Children of Commander Elton Ernest and Dorothy Lillian (Lutjens) Flowers; Dorothy Jean Flowers; Alton Paul Flowers, born February 20, 1948, Brooklyn, New York.

DOROTHY JEAN FLOWERS

Born: August 15, 1938, Brooklyn, New York

Married: Edward Eugene Morgan on June 19, 1932

Children of Edward Eugene and Dorothy Jean (Flowers) Morgan: Nancy Jean Morgan, born January 3, 1960, Olney, Illinois.

ANNIE MAE FLOWERS

Born: March 3, 1922, Natchez, Mississippi

Married: Andrew Thompson on August 2, 1942

Children of Andrew and Annie Mae (Flowers) Thompson: Jessica Ann Thompson, born August 24, 1949, Baton Rouge, Louisiana.

MARY ELLEN FLOWERS

Born: September 14, 1917, Natchez, Mississippi

Married: Ernest Scott Baragona on December 10, 1938

Children of Ernest Scott and Mary Ellen (Flowers) Baragona; Joy M. Baragona; Ernest Scott Baragona, Jr., born November 5, 1946, Natchez, Mississippi; Thomas Charles Baragona, born January 23, 1948, Natchez, Mississippi.

JOY M. BARAGONA

Born: January 24, 1940, Natchez, Mississippi

Married: Alfred Carson III on March 7, 1958

Children of Alfred and Joy M. (Baragona) Carson III: Alfred Carson IV, born February, 1960, Baton Rouge, Louisiana.

LYDIA KATHERINE FLOWERS

Born: November 18, 1919, Natchez, Mississippi

Married: William M. Marsh, son of David Garfield and Ann H. Marsh, on February 26, 1944

Died: September 9, 1953

Children of William M. and Lydia Katherine (Flowers) Marsh: William Francis Marsh, born November 26, 1944, San Mateo, California; Robert Wesley Marsh, born August 6, 1947, San Mateo, California.

WINONA ETHEL FLOWERS

Born: December 29, 1923, Natchez, Mississippi

Married: Robert Stanley Fant on June 5, 1946

Children of Robert Stanley and Winona Ethel (Flowers) Fant: Suzane Winona Fant, born March 29, 1947, Glasgow, Kentucky; David Robert Fant, born January 3, 1949, Glasgow, Kentucky; Dennis Robert Fant, born November 12, 1950, Glasgow, Kentucky.

W. EUGENIA FLOWERS

Born: April 19, 1926, Natchez, Mississippi

Married: Julius Wesley Andrews, son of Julius Wesley and Mary Edna (Blanchard) Andrews, on May 1, 1948

Children of Julius Wesley and W. Eugenia (Flowers) Andrews: Judy Marie Andrews, born February 17, 1949, Baton Rouge, La.; Joan Flowers Andrews, born June 25, 1950, Shreveport, La.; Jane Edna Andrews, born November 18, 1953, Shreveport, La.

RUBIN P. FLOWERS

Born: November 6, 1927, Natchez, Mississippi

Married: Flora Mae Enlow, daughter of Dudley and Donna (Ashley) Enlow, on August 31, 1946

Children of Rubin P. and Flora Mae (Enlow) Flowers: Jerry Wayne Flowers, born August 16, 1948, Natchez, Mississippi; Donna Fay Flowers, born September 3, 1952, Charleston, South Carolina.

CHARLES THOMAS NETTERVILLE, JR.

Born: March 24, 1890, in Wilkinson County, Mississippi

Married: Jennie McCraine, daughter of Walter and Ella McCraine, on September 22, 1912

Children of Charles Thomas and Jennie (McCraine) Netterville, Jr.: Lieutenant Colonel Rush Edwards Netterville; Charles Thomas Netterville III, born August 4, 1916, in Wilkinson County, Mississippi, died August 22, 1918; Robert Lavelle Netterville; Katherine Lydia Netterville; Richard James Netterville; William Noland Netterville, born October 12, 1928, in Wilkinson County, Mississippi, married Marie Joyce Thompson, daughter of James Franklin and Etta Mae (Williams) Thompson, on December 15, 1956; Frederick Harold Netterville; Mary Louise Netterville.

LIEUTENANT COLONEL (DOCTOR) RUSH EDWARDS NETTERVILLE

Born: August 8, 1913, in Wilkinson County, Mississippi

Married: Lieutenant Frances McAllister of Concord, North Carolina, on April 12, 1945, in France.

Children of Lieutenant Colonel Rush Edwards and Frances (McAllister) Netterville: Rush Edwards Netterville, Jr., born March 7, 1946, in Winston, North Carolina; Cynthia Dianne Netterville, born August 11, 1947, in Baltimore, Maryland; Elizabeth Ann Netterville, born July 31, 1953, in Jackson, Mississippi.

ROBERT LAVELLE NETTERVILLE

Born: April 24, 1918, Wilkinson County, Mississippi

Married: Anna Clarice Peggy Sharp Junk, daughter of Merritt and Ann Clarice (Sharp) Junk, on July 31, 1948

Children of Robert Lavelle and Anna Clarice Peggy Sharp (Junk)

Netterville: Constance Netterville, born February 19, 1950, Natchez, Mississippi; Richard Burnell Sharp Netterville, born April 21, 1953, Natchez, Mississippi.

KATHERINE LYDIA NETTERVILLE

Born: December 6, 1921, Wilkinson County, Mississippi

Married: Alonzo DeWitt Welch, son of Samuel L. and Lucy Emily (Garner) Welch, on June 21, 1942

Children of Alonzo DeWitt and Katherine Lydia (Netterville) Welch: Rosaland Ann Welch, born June 8, 1943, Oakland, California; Katherine Netterville Welch, born February 26, 1948, Oxford, Mississippi; Mary Louise Welch, born October 18, 1949, Oxford, Mississippi.

RICHARD JAMES NETTERVILLE

Born: December 25, 1926, Wilkinson County, Mississippi

Married: Annie Lee Rabb, daughter of Edward and Amanda (Stewart) Rabb, on June 22, 1946

Children of Richard James and Annie Lee (Rabb) Netterville: Winona Netterville, born August 8, 1950, Centerville, Mississippi; Yvonne Netterville, born November 8, 1953, Centerville, Mississippi; Brenda Lee Netterville, born December 15, 1956, Centerville, Mississippi.

FREDERICK HAROLD NETTERVILLE

Born: October 25, 1930, Wilkinson County, Mississippi

Married: Tommie Jo Olive, daughter of Ray Seacy and Claudie Mae (Holt) Olive, on October 25, 1957

Children of Frederick Harold and Tommie Jo (Olive) Netterville: Charles Thomas Netterville IV, born December 13, 1958, Natchez, Mississippi; Claudia Rae Netterville, born February 26, 1960, Natchez, Mississippi.

MARY LOUISE NETTERVILLE

Born: December 2, 1932, Wilkinson County, Mississippi

Married: Leroy Hunter Howell, son of Virgil Marion and Eula (Sullivan) Howell on December 23, 1950

Children of Leroy Hunter and Mary Louise (Netterville) Howell; Leroy Hunter Howell, Jr., born December 20, 1952, Natchez, Mississippi; Charles Virgil Howell, born February 4, 1955, Natchez, Mississippi; Marilyn Eloise Howell, born October 5, 1956, Natchez, Mississippi; Rachel Malinda Howell, born February 25, 1960, Natchez, Mississippi.

WILLIAM MAGRUDER NETTERVILLE

Born: August 2, 1892, in Wilkinson County, Mississippi

Married: Lottie Mae Keele, daughter of John Alexander and Della Bee (Feltus) Keele, on December 25, 1916

Children of William Magruder and Lottie Mae (Keele) Netterville: Dorothy Mae Netterville, born September 20, 1917, in Nashville, Tennessee, died January 2, 1935; Tula Marie Netterville; Lottie Neva Netterville; William Magruder Netterville, Jr.; John Thomas Netterville; Benjamin Netterville, born January 2, 1934, in Nashville, Tennessee, died January 4, 1934; Catharine Juanita Netterville.

TULA MARIE NETTERVILLE

Born: March 1, 1919, in Wilkinson County, Mississippi

Married: George Burkehalter, the son of Nicholas A. and Nannie (Campbell) Burkehalter on February 19, 1936

Children of George and Tula Marie (Netterville) Burkehalter: Dorothy Joyce Burkehalter, born November 29, 1937, in Nashville, Tennessee, married Bobby Kenneth Barnes of DeKalb County, Tennessee, on October 10, 1956; Barbara Clarie Burkehalter, born October 4, 1942, in Nashville, Tennessee; William Nicholas Burkehalter, born April 20, 1950, in Nashville, Tennessee.

LOTTIE NEVA NETTERVILLE

Born: May 8, 1921, in Baton Rouge, Louisiana

Married: James Franklin Fowler, the son of Thomas G. and Jessie Florence (Mullins) Fowler, on August 17, 1942

Children of James Franklin and Lottie Neva (Netterville) Fowler; James Franklin Fowler, Jr., born June 23, 1943, Temple, Texas; Lois E. Fowler, born September 6, 1945, Temple, Texas; Judy Caroline Fowler, born October 10, 1948, College Station, Texas; Dorothy Anne Fowler, born May 2, 1951, College Station, Texas.

WILLIAM MAGRUDER NETTERVILLE, JR.

Born: April 20, 1923, in Nashville, Tennessee

Married: Jennie Prococcini on February 8, 1947

Children of William Magruder and Jennie (Prococcini) Netterville: William Magruder Netterville III, born April 10, 1959 in New Providence, New Jersey.

CATHERINE JUANITA NETTERVILLE

Born: March 30, 1928, in Nashville, Tennessee

Married: Harold Wayne Hammontree on July 17, 1948

Children of Harold Wayne and Catharine Juanita (Netterville) Hammontree: Harold Wayne Hammontree, Jr., born September 25, 1949, Nashville, Tennessee; Leslie Ruth Hammontree, born January 2, 1952, in Nashville, Tennessee; William James Hammontree, born July 13, 1954, in Nashville, Tennessee.

JOHN THOMAS NETTERVILLE

Born: October 26, 1930, Nashville, Tennessee

Married: Annie Ruth Johnson, daughter of James L. and Martha
Jane (Grantham) Johnson, on December 15, 1951

Children of John Thomas and Annie Ruth (Johnson) Netterville:
John Thomas Netterville, Jr., born September 17, 1952, Nashville,
Tennessee; James Lee Netterville, born March 13, 1954, Nashville,
Tennessee; Joseph David Netterville, born February 9, 1959, Nash-
ville, Tennessee.

MAJOR JESSE CARTER

Died: Before April 21, 1818

Children of Major Jesse Carter: Eliza (Betsy) Carter, married
Colonel Israel Elliot Trask; Lydia Carter, married Governor George
Poindexter, divorced, married Lewis Williams of Brimfield, Massachusetts. The following is from Clarence Edwin Carter's *Territorial
Papers of the United States, Territory of Mississippi*, excerpt from
letter of Governor Williams of Mississippi to the Secretaries of State
and Treasury of the United States, November 3, 1807:

(Pages 576-7) "Claiborne has used his influence since his dismissal
to induce the officers, particularly of the Militia, to resign, but in
this he has had little success, only two, one of which is Major Carter,
Poindexter's father-in-law, having resigned; Major Trask and Major
Bowman having accepted the Command of the Regiment, in lieu of
Claiborne and Carter and both of them of their own families; the
former, son-in-law to Carter and the latter brother-in-law to Claiborne, have cast a damp on his further attempts as these are Gentlemen of the First Standing and Respectability in Society, admired for
their moderation in private and public life and of considerable military knowledge and experience and have been witnesses to Claiborne's
conduct."

(Pages 570-1) Petition to Thomas Jefferson, President of the United
States, Signed by Jesse Carter, later Major, the First Regiment,
Militia of Adams County, Mississippi. October 25, 1807.

(Pages 569-70)

Town of Washington
October 17, 1807

HIS EX, GOVERNOR WILLIAMS,

Having discharged the duties lately assigned me by yourself as
Commander-in-Chief of the Forces of this Territory, I make use of
the present as a favorable opportunity to resign my Commission as
Major in the First Regiment, Mississippi Militia.

JESSE CARTER

Monies received by John Henderson, Receiver of Public Monies, at the Town of Washington, on account of Land purchased by them on 1st day of January, 1807.

No. 96. NEHEMIAH CARTER. $45.00 for 90 acres.

Deed Book "D", page 281, Wilkinson County, Mississippi. 31st August 1815. Sheriff's Sale. From H. Cornell, Sheriff, Wilkinson County.

To: JESSE CARTER.

Consideration: $27.90

Tract of Land in Wilkinson County, 90 acres, "D" No. 156, Section 11, Township 4, Range 2 West, land formerly the property of NEHEMIAH CARTER.

Test: (Signed) H. Cornell
Wm. Vaughan   Sheriff
A. Reid   Wilkinson County

Deed Book "D", page 281, Wilkinson County, Mississippi

21 April 1818.

From: ISRAEL E. TRASK, ELIZABETH, his wife; and LYDIA
      CARTER of Adams County, Mississippi, Executors of the last
      Will and Testament of JESSE CARTER of said County, Deceased

To: ISAAC CARTER of Adams County

Consideration $5.00 and Love and Affection we bear the said ISAAC CARTER, have assigned, etc., etc. and by power and authority in us vested, etc., etc. by Last Will and Testament the foregoing Indenture, together with the said tract of land therein described. To have and to hold, etc., forever.

Test: (Signed) I. E. TRASK
Rich'd Pearce   ELIZA TRASK
Dana H. Pearce   LYDIA CARTER

Acknowledged by the witnesses: July 27, 1824. Filed same day.

Minutes of Probate Court, Wilkinson County, Mississippi. Book 3, page 202, 26th March 1827. "The Last Will of WILLIAM P. TRASK (the Will not recorded in Will Book) was brought into Court and proved by the Oath of Dick H. Eggles, et al. Letters to JAMES L. TRASK, Executor and HARRIETT TRASK, Executrix, therein named, etc.

Will Book 1, page 147, Adams County, Mississippi. The Will of Jesse Carter of the County of Adams in the Mississippi Territory.

Dated: 3rd of February, 1816.

Proved: No date shown, though another document indicates it was
        shortly before the 21st April 1818.

Legatees: Samuel Postlethwait, Esquire, of the County of Adams
         250 acres on Second Creek, conveyed to me by George Poindexter,
         Esquire, by indenture dated the second April last passed, also,

fourteen negro slaves, etc., also one half of the residue of my estate after payment of my just debts, etc., etc.

My daughter Lydia be permitted to occupy and enjoy three fourth parts of said premises during her natural life, etc., etc. she to have custody, care and superintendence of education of my grandson, George Poindexter, Junior, during his minority, etc.

Rest and residue to my daughter, Eliza Trask, wife of Israel E. Trask, Equire, her heirs, etc.

Emancipates certain slaves.

Executors: Esteemed Son-in-law, Israel E. Trask, Esquire, and my beloved Daughters, Eliza and Lydia, etc.

(Signed)   JESSE CARTER

Test: Lyman Harding
      Wm. Walters
      Isaac Carter

See also: MISSISSIPPI COURT RECORDS, 1799-1835, J. Estelle Stewart King, 133 N. Wetherly Drive, Beverly Hills, California, page 25.

Book of Deeds "E", pages 358-359. Date: 3rd March 1828. "An Agreement." A. G. (Albert George) Poindexter, son of Lydia and George Poindexter: Whereas, an article of separation between George Poindexter and Lydia Poindexter, his then wife, was entered into between Jesse Carter, farther of said Lydia on the one part and behalf of the said Lydia and the offspring of the marriage which has existed between said George and Lydia, of whom I am one mentioned in said article and the said George Poindexter on the other part, which said article was decreed in all its parts by the Superior Court of Law and Equity for Adams County, State of Mississippi, etc., etc., An Agreement by Jesse Carter to educate the subscriber, etc., etc.

(Signed) A. G. POINDEXTER

Test. A. M. Scott
Recorded 4 March 1828

See MISSISSIPPI COUNTY COURT RECORDS
The May Wilson McBee Papers, Page 3

The Samuel Postlethwait named in the will of Major Jesse Carter, above, was the builder of the beautiful ante-bellum home, Clifton, in Natchez. Clifton, later sold to the Frank Surgets, is engagingly described in Stark Young's SO RED THE ROSE, Charles Scribner's Sons, New York, 1935, and the story told of its destruction by the Federals during the occupation of Natchez. See particularly pages 231-233 and 288, 295-296. The family of Samuel's brother, Henry Postlethwait, bought King's Tavern, the oldest building in Old Natchez. Pictures and description of this old building may be found in

Nola Nance Oliver's *OLD NATCHEZ, SYMBOL OF THE OLD SOUTH*, Hastings House, New York, 1940, and in Harnett Kane's *NATCHEZ ON THE MISSISSIPPI*, William Morrow and Company, New York, 1947, pages 73-78.

Lyman Harding who witnessed Major Carter's will built Auburn in 1812. The old home was later sold to Stephen Duncan, whose mother was a Postlethwait. Later, the old home and grounds were given to the City of Natchez and are now maintained as a park. See Mr. Kane's book, pages 204-219.

Among the protestors against the Code of Laws drawn by Winthrop Sargent, first Territorial Governor of Mississippi were the "most active, intelligent and influential men in the community." JESSE CARTER was one of them according to *A HISTORY OF MISSISSIPPI* by Robert Lowry and William H. McCardle, Jackson, Mississippi, Henry and Company, 1891, page 171. For the story of Governor Sargent and a picture of Gloucester, his plantation home, one of the loveliest in Natchez, see Mr. Kane's book, pages 112-124.

Will of William Shunk
May 7, 1802

Legatees: Three sisters: Nancy, Polly and Sally, friend, Jesse Carter, who is a partner in a cotton gin.

Executors: Jesse Carter, Nehemiah Carter, Jr.

Witnesses: William Nicholls, Thomas Pollard, Israel Smith

MISSISSIPPI COURT RECORDS, 1799-1835, J. Estelle Stewart King, 133 N. Wetherly Drive, Beverly Hills, California, Page 15.

The following entries are from Mrs. McBee's NATCHEZ COURT RECORDS, 1765-1805:

Page 461 (Book D, page 463) Land Claim No. 1390, etc. British Grant to John Bolls, 100 acres on Second Creek. Pensacola, 26 May, 1777 and by him sold to Robert Collingwood. Claimed by JESSE CARTER, 28 March 1804. Certificate No. A-355 issued to claimant JESSE CARTER who was an actual settler in Mississippi Territory, 27 October 1795, claims 600 acres in Adams County, by virtue of two grants, (1) for 100 acres granted by the British Government to John Bolls and by him conveyed to Robert Collingwood and by him to Nehemiah Carter, 27 November 1777, being part of the land hereby claimed and the other (2) was granted by the Spanish Government to RACHEL CARTER on 16 May, 1791, both of which tracts are joined and were conveyed by the said NEHEMIAH CARTER and RACHEL, his wife to the claimant, 26 March, 1804. Robert Collingwood to NEHEMIAH CARTER lease and release $300, 100 acres granted to John Bolls as above. 20 December 1777. Deed 26 March 1804 NEHEMIAH CARTER and wife RACHEL to JESSE CARTER, $350 paid; the above tract about 7 miles south of Natchez, adjoining HENRY

PHIPPS, Samuel Phipps, John Ellis, Osborn Sprigg on Second Creek. /s/ N. CARTER, RACHEL CARTER

Page 42. Book A, p. 388. 3 August 1787. Alexander Moore, merchant, sells to JESSE CARTER of the District, two slaves.

Page 61 (Book B, p 209) 10 January 1789. Thomas Irwin to JESSE CARTER and SARAH CARTER, his lawful wife, 4 negro boys and 2 negro wenches for $2,760, Mexican silver, etc. Mortgaged plantations, etc. /s/ JESSE CARTER, SARAH CARTER, Thos. Irwin.

Page 461. (Book D, p 477) Land Claims. Claim No. 1391. Spanish Grant to Mrs. SARAH KENNER, 250 acres on Second Creek, 9 miles southeast of Fort. New Orleans, 21 May 1791 by Miro. Claimant SARAH CARTER, 28 November 1804. Certificate A-354, issued 21 June 1805 SARAH CARTER, LATE KENNER, WIFE OF JESSE CARTER, claims 250 arpents on Second Creek by virtue of a complete Spanish Patent as above. This claim signed: Washington, Mississippi 19 March 1804 by JESSE CARTER FOR SARAH CARTER. The original Spanish Grant is made out to MADAM SARAH KENNER, as was plat.

Page 462. (Book D, p 479) Claim No. 1392. Spanish Grant to MADAM SARAH CARTER, 500 acres 7 miles South of Fort, bounded by the Grantee, Osborn Sprigg, Samuel and HENRY PHIPPS. New Orleans 16 May 1791 by Miro.

Page 73. Book B, page 380. Clark and Rees sell to JESSE CARTER an african negro, for $525, Mexican silver, on terms, mortgages also another negro and 800 arpents of land on Homochitto bounded by Richard Ellis, ARCHIBALD PALMER and lands of his Majesty. Signed. 17 Dec 1794. Negro taken back and sale null and void. /s/ Ebenezer Rees. Mercer House built in 1816 in Natchez for Jane Ellis Rapalje, daughter of Richard Ellis, is pictured and described in Nola Nance Oliver's *This Too Is Natchez.*

(Page 88) Jesse Carter was a debtor of the Estate of Eliphalet Richards. 11 Oct 1791.

(Page 110) 800 arpents of land at Buffalo Creek owned by Richard Ellis, bounded by JESSE CARTER and Mrs. Farar.

(Page 116) JESSE CARTER was a debtor of the Estate of Benjamin Monsanto, planter. 10 Oct 1794.

(Page 294) JESSE CARTER versus John Smith. There is a balance due to JESSE CARTER by John Smith which we do order to be paid in three months with the costs. /s/ Thomas Green, John (X) Perry. Cole's Creek. Jan 27, 1782.

(Pages 343-4) JESSE CARTER versus Thomas Irwin. JESSE CARTER in 1789 purchased from Mr. Irwin six negroes and gave his bond for the same and on 12 Feb 1790. He delivered to the said Irwin 9 hogshead and 400 carrots of tobacco on his account and in March of the same year he delivered him a flat valued at $100, one half of which was to be passed to the credit of your petitioner; since then Mr. Irwin has negotiated the said bond without giving the necessary credits thereon agreeable to contract, which will more fully appear to Your Excellency by the different vouchers hereunto annexed. Signed. Natchez. 28 April 1797.

(Page 428) Book C, page 457. Spanish Grant to JESSE CARTER, 800 acres near the Homochitto, 18 miles south of Fort bounded by vacant lands. N.O. 21 May 1791. Don Estevan Miro, Governor. JESSE CARTER, of the Township of Second Creek, County of Adams, Mississippi Territory, and WIFE, SARAH, to John Ellis, Major of Militia of said Township, for $1,200 paid the above 800 acres. Signed by both. Wit: Patrick Foley, J. W. A. Lloyd. Prov. by Lloyd, 10 Sept 1800 before Sir William Dunbar, J.P. 24 May 1800.

(Page 431) Spanish Land Grant to Wm. Cocke Ellis, 800 acres on waters of Buffalo Creek, 25 miles southeast of the Fort, bounded by JESSE CARTER and John Ellis, Sr. N.O. 16 Feb 1789.

(Page 586) Heirs of Joseph Miller claim 350 arpents of land in Adams County on Buffalo River by virtue of a Spanish Order of Survey dated about 1794. Justis Andrews, James Nicholson, JESSE CARTER, and William Cocke Ellis have adjoining lands.

(Page 332) Don Carlos de Grand-Pre appointed Jesse Greenfield and JESSE CARTER to visit the plantation of Mrs. Charles White to examine the work of Calvin Smith in making a crop. 21 May 1795.

Nola Nance Oliver in her book Natchez, Symbol of the Old South, describes Cherokee, the home built by Jesse Greenfield about 1794.

(Page 267) Israel Smith versus Arthur Cobb.

Testimony of Sarah Carter (Certificate to the same, signed Sarah Williams) : This is to certify that when Mrs. Smith lay on her death bed she bequeathed her riding horse to her husband and desired that he would keep it.

Deposition of JESSE CARTER that Arthur Cobb attacked Smith (Israel) on the road and Philander Smith came between them and Cobb used much abusive language. Sept. 2, 1793.

/s/ JESSE CARTER.

Deeds Recorded in Chancery Clerk's Office, Natchez, Adams County, Mississippi:

JESSE CARTER of Township of Second Creek, Adams County, Mississippi Territory, Planter, and his wife, Sarah, to: John Ellis, Major of Militia in Buffalo Township, County and Territory, aforesaid, Planter. Consideration: $1,200. 800 French acres, Southeast bank of River Homochitto, beginning at a Tupelo Gum on the southeast bank of said river, measurement being such as was customary under the

Spanish Government, per Patent from the Spanish Government to JESSE CARTER, dated 25th May, 1791 etc. Signed: JESSE AND SARAH CARTER. Deed Book B, page 73. 24 May, 1800.

JESSE CARTER and SARAH CARTER, his wife, of Adams County, Mississippi Territory.

To: ISRAEL E. TRASK and ELIZABETH, his wife, of same. Consideration: $1. Tract of 600 acres, on which said Carters now live; situate on Second Creek in County aforesaid, the same tract of land granted RACHEL CARTER in the year 1791 by Don Stephen Miro, Governor General of Louisiana and including the tract of 100 acres purchased in the year 1777 by NEHEMIAH CARTER of Robert Collingwood under a British Survey, bounded on north by land of George Rapalge, etc. Signed: JESSE CARTER, SARAH CARTER.

Test. Israel Smith.

Deed Book D, page 276. 19 September 1806.

Received of GEORGE POINDEXTER the sum of $1129, full satisfaction for the balance due from him for twelve African slaves delivered to him as his portion of slaves purchased by ISRAEL E. TRASK in Charleston, South Carolina, in 1805, for the use of said Trask, Poindexter, and myself, etc. Signed: JESSE CARTER.

Test. L. Brooks, John Hutchins.

Deed Book G, page 281. 12 September 1811

Orphan's Court, Minute Book 2, 1815-1820, page 82, January Term, 1817. The last will of JESSE CARTER, deceased, late of this county, was proven by oaths of Lyman Harding and William Walters. Letters to Executors therein named. Bond $30,000. Philander Smith, William Baker, and Francis Surget, Appraisers. Philander Smith and Jonathan Thompson, Securities.

Mr. Harding was the first Attorney General of Mississippi. For an interesting account of the Surget family see Harnett Kane's NATCHEZ ON THE MISSISSIPPI. Mr. Thompson bought "Twin Oaks" built in 1806 by Lewis Evans, first Territorial Sheriff and still standing in Natchez.

Orphans Court, Adams County, Mississippi, Minute Book 1, 1803-1815, page 22, October Term, October 8, 1803; On application of PARSONS CARTER, Letters of Administration were granted him on the Estate of Nehemiah Carter, Junior, deceased, he having taken the usual oath and entered into bond in the sum of $2,000 with Philander Smith and JESSE CARTER, Sureties. Abner Green, Israel Smith and John H. White appointed appraisers.

Mr. Green belonged to the family which owned "Springfield," the plantation home, still standing, where President Andrew Jackson, then a merchant on Bayou Pierre, married his beloved Rachel.

The following are from Mrs. McBee's NATCHEZ COURT RECORDS, 1765-1805:

Page 552. Unrecorded Land Claims, No. 1394. Claimant: JESSE CARTER, 28 March 1804. Witnesses: NEHEMIAH CARTER. Rejected, 12 May, 1807. Mississippi Territory. JESSE CARTER, PARSONS CARTER, AND ISAAC CARTER, Legal Representatives of NEHEMIAH CARTER (Junior), deceased, claim 640 acres in Wilkinson County on Buffalo Creek. The above mentioned tract was actually inhabited and cultivated by the said NEHEMIAH CARTER, prior to and on the day the Mississippi Territory was finally evacuated by the Spanish Troops, he being at that time above the age of 21 years.

Page 114. (Book C, p 273)
Post of Natchez
7 May 1795

RACHEL CARTER, wife of NEHEMIAH CARTER, of Second Creek, out of great love I bear to my three sons, NEHEMIAH, PARSONS, and ISAAC, do of my free will and accord make them a gift of 500 arpents in this District, bounded by John Bolls, Henry Phipps, Samuel Phipps, and Osborn Sprigg, granted to me by the Governor Generall of this Province, 16 May 1791 with all buildings, gates and fences. /s/ RACHEL CARTER with approbation of (FRANCISCO) CAUDELL.

Page 36 (Book A, pp 305-308)
29 July 1786.
The Will of Tacitus Gaillard.
Witnesses: JESSE CARTER N(ehemiah) CARTER ARCHIBALD PALMER

Page 551. Unrecorded Land Claims. No. 1387.
EDWARD HACKETT, 28 March 1804.
Certificate N. D-156 issued 16 December 1806. Edward Hackett as inhabitant of the Mississippi Territory claims 200 acres on Hutchins Creek, Wilkinson County, by virtue of a settlement made by James Knowles, previous to 1795 for which he, the said James Knowles had a certificate from the Surveyor General of the Province. Signed: EDWARD HACKETT

ELIZA (BETSY) CARTER

Married: Colonel Israel Elliot Trask
1820 CENSUS, WILKINSON COUNTY, MISSISSIPPI
James L. Trask
1 male born 1810-1820; 1 male born 1804-1810; 3 males born 1775-1794; 1 female born 1810-1820; 1 female born 1804-1810; 1 female born 1794-1804; 143 slaves.

1830 CENSUS, WILKINSON COUNTY, MISSISSIPPI

James L. Trask

1 male born 1790-1800; 1 male born 1800-1810; 1 male born 1810-1815; 1 female born 1790-1800; 185 slaves.

1840 CENSUS, WILKINSON COUNTY, MISSISSIPPI

J. L. Trask

1 male born 1780-1790; 1 male born 1790-1800; 4 males born 1800-1810; 1 male born 1810-1820; 1 male born 1830-1835; 1 male born 1835-1840; 4 females born 1810-1820; 1 female born 1830-1835; 1 female born 1835-1840; 234 slaves.

1850 CENSUS, WILKINSON COUNTY, MISSISSIPPI

James L. Trask

245 slaves.

I. E. Trask appointed Brigade Major and Inspector of Artillery in Natchez by Governor Claiborne in 1802.

MISSISSIPPI, AS A PROVINCE, TERRITORY AND STATE by John Francis Hamtramck Claiborne Volume I, Jackson Mississippi Power and Barksdale 1880 Page 225.

Isaac E. Trask was one of the first members of the Mississippi Society for the Acquirement and Dissemination of Useful Knowledge. NATCHEZ, ITS EARLY HISTORY by Joseph Dunbar Shields Edited by his granddaughter, Mrs. Elizabeth Dunbar Murray. John P. Morton and Company. Louisville, Kentucky. 1930. Pages 56-7.

In speaking of Governor Williams, George Poindexter says in a letter to the Secretary of War in 1808, in reference to his brother-in-law, "He has appointed Israel E. Trach, formerly a Captain in the Provisional Army, raised under the Administration of President Adams and a decided and warm Federalist, Colonel of Adams County.

TERRITORIAL PAPERS OF THE UNITED STATES, TERRITORY OF MISSISSIPPI, Volume V, page 607. By Clarence Edwin Carter.

James L. Trask signed Petition to Congress in 1808. Ibid, page 662.

J. E. Trask, as a member of the Territorial Bar, signed a Petition to Congress. Ibid, page 180.

Trask licensed to practice law. Ibid, page 255.

Israel Elliot Trask and other Citizens of Natchez write to Governor Winthrop Sargent on the Eve of his Departure. March 28, 1801. Ibid, page 123.

From INDEX OF DEATHS IN MASSACHUSETTS CENTINEL AND *COLUMBIAN CENTINEL*, 1784-1840, Library of Congress.

Colonel Israel E. Trask of Springfield, Mass., died near Woodville, Mississippi. December 26, 1835. C.C.

Augustus Trask died in Woodville, Mississippi, aged 30. C.C. January 16, 1819.

William C. Trask, only son of Colonel Israel C. Trask of Brimfield died in Boston Sunday aged 11. C.C. June 14, 1815.

Brimfield, Massachusetts, Vital Records, Published by the New England Historic Genealogical Society of Boston in 1931:

(Pages 139-140)

Births of the children of Colonel Israel E. and Elizabeth (Bety) Trask:

Eliza born June 7, 1805, in Natchez; Eliza born on August 2, 1809 in Natchez; Eliza born on July 18, 1810, in Natchez; Elizabeth Lawrence born on February 25, 1813, in Brimfield; Frederick Augustus born July 1808 in Natchez; Israel Carter born October 17, 1815 in Brimfield; Sarah born on October 21, 1816 "on the Ohio River near Indian Creek, 18 miles above Cincinnati."; William Carter born December 17, 1803 in Natchez; William Elliot born December 5, 1820.

(Page 331)

Deaths

William Carter son of Colonel Israel E. and Elizabeth Trask died June 11, 1815, in Boston; Augustus, son of Dr. Israel and Sarah Trask died on October 26, 1818 in Woodville, Mississippi; Eliza, daughter of Colonel Israel E. and Elizabeth Trask died January 17, 1813 in Brimfield aged 2 years and 10 months; Dr. Israel Trask died October 1, 1801, in Greenwich, aged 63; Sarah Lawrence Trask widow of Dr. Israel Trask died August 3, 1827, aged 71.

(Page 248)

William P. Trask of Natchez married Harriet Morgan on July 14, 1818.

The James L. Trask mentioned above was a brother of Colonel Israel Elliot Trask, who married Eliza Carter. Their sister, Sarah Trask married Judge Stephen Pynchon of Hampden County, Massachusetts. Judge Pynchon, a graduate of Yale in 1789, was descended from Colonel William Pynchon, who came to America in 1630, was a Charter Member, first Treasurer and Assistant Governor of the Massachusetts Bay Colony, as well as the author of several theological works and the founder of Springfield, Massachusetts, which he named after his home in England. Among his other ancestors were the Reverend William Hubbard, the early historian of New England, and George Wyllys, Colonial Governor of Connecticut and owner of the celebrated Charter Oak.

In 1848 Charlotte Davis Pynchon, daughter of Judge Stephen Pynchon and Sarah Trask, married James Alexander Ventress, who had spent nine years in Europe in various universities including the

University of Edinburgh, the Academy in Paris, and the University of Berlin. Mr. Ventress was a friend of Sir Walter Scott, John Wilson (Christopher North), author of *Lights and Shadows of Scottish Life*, Jeremy Bentham, the philosopher and John Baptiste Say, the political economist. He was a frequent visitor at La Grange, home of the Marquis de Lafayette. He authored several plays, was a contributor to several French and English scientific and literary magazines and had several of his papers read before the Institute of France.

Mr. Ventress received his License to practice law in 1841 from William L. Sharkey, then Chief Justice of the Supreme Court of Mississippi. He served as Speaker of the House of Representatives and State Senator. The first story of his plantation home, La Grange, had been built by Major James Lawrence Trask, who willed his Mount Pleasant Plantation to his niece, Charlotte Davis (Pynchon) Ventress. (See the will of J. L. Trask, Will Book 2, page 107, Wilkinson County, August Term of Court, 1855, in which also Major Trask left a cash bequest to his niece, Sarah Anderdonk). Another story and observatory were added before the Civil War, to the Trask home. This home, since burned, was on the Woodville to Fort Adams Road and was described in *Mississippi, A Guide to the Magnolia State*, (Federal Writers Project of the Works Progress Administration, Hastings House, New York) as a "handsome place similar in appearance to the Hermitage near Nashville, Tennessee" (home of President Andrew Jackson).

Mr. Ventress served as a member of the Board of Trustees of the University of Mississippi from its creation in 1844 until his death and is known as the "father of the University."

This material on the Ventress and Trask families was found in *Biographical and Historical Memoirs of Mississippi* (1891), Volume II, pages 952-956, Goodspeed Company, Chicago. Also noted in the article is the parentage of the Trask children, their father being Dr. Israel Trask of Brimfield, Massachusetts, a Revolutionary Veteran and member of the Massachusetts Constitutional Convention and their mother being Sarah Lawrence, the daughter of Dr. James Lawrence, a descendant of Sir Robert Lawrence of Ashton Hall, Lancashire, England, who accompanied Richard Coeur de Lion to the Holy Land and at the Siege of Acre was the first to plant the Banner of the Cross on the battlement for which he was knighted. In reference to Charlotte Davis (Pynchon) Ventress, the article contains the following: "After completing her education at Springfield, Mrs. Ventress, a beautiful and accomplished young lady came to Mississippi with a cousin to make her home with her uncle, Major James L. Trask who was a bachelor and remained with him until his death. Major Trask settled in Mississippi in 1805. He was a veteran of the War of 1812 and served under General Jackson at the Battle of New Orleans. A man of remarkable energy and business tact, he amassed a large fortune, most of which he bequeathed to his niece. His brothers, Augustus and Dr. William P. Trask also lived in Wilkinson County and are buried in the family burying ground, as is also his eldest brother, Colonel Israel E. Trask. Colonel Trask was a man of considerable ability. Harvard University conferred on him the honorary degree of A.M. He represented his county in the legislature and Constitutional Convention of Massachusetts and was one of the Incorporators of Amherst College."

From Dunbar Rowland's Mississippi Territorial Archives, 1798-1803, Volume I:

(Page 175) 28 Sept 1799 Governor Winthrop Sargent appointed Jesse Carter, Ensign in the Militia of Adams County.

(page 400) Governor William C. C. Claiborne appointed J. E. Trask Brigade Major and Inspector of the Artillery in Natchez.

ELIZA LAWRENCE TRASK

Born: February 25, 1813

Married: John Gallison Tappan on May 8, 1839. Mr. Tappan was born in Boston on February 5, 1808. He died in Brookline on August 29, 1883. Mr. Tappan attended the Phillips Academy, Andover, and Harvard College. He was President of the Boston Belting Company.

Died: November 1, 1894

Children of John Gallison and Eliza Lawrence (Trask) Tappan: John Eliot Tappan; Elizabeth Wild Tappan, born August 17, 1845, died November, 1909; Mary Swift Tappan, born August 20, 1848; Frederick Herbert Tappan; Walter Tappan, born September 15, 1854, died July 18, 1887; Herbert Tappan, born May 6, 1857, died April 30, 1902; In 1915 Miss Mary Swift Tappan resided at 29 Edgehill Road, Boston, Massachusetts, in Brookline.

ANCESTORS AND DESCENDANTS OF ABRAHAM TOPPAN OF NEWBURY, MASSACHUSETTS, 1606-1672. By Daniel Langdon Tappan. Printed in Arlington, Massachusetts, pages 31 and 32.

FREDERICK HERBERT TAPPAN

Born: January 31, 1850

Married: Elizabeth Loring Meredith of Baltimore, Maryland

Died: December 7, 1900

Children of Frederick Herbert and Elizabeth Loring (Meredith) Tappan: Frederick Tappan, born August 7, 1876, lived in British Columbia in 1913; Mary Farnsworth Tappan, born August 10, 1879, married in October, 1904, to George P. Hamlin; Robert Meredith Tappan, born July 9, 1885, married on October 9, 1912, to Catharine

Foster (Residence: Clay Brook, Charles River Village, Massachusetts).

JOHN ELLIOT TAPPAN

Born: August 31, 1840

Married: Margaret P. Wilson on February 20, 1865

Died: November 2, 1907

Children of John Eliot and Margaret P. (Wilson) Tappan: John Tappan, born September 12, 1866; David Henry Scott Tappan, born December 20, 1867; Margaret Tappan, born June 8, 1869; Mary Elizabeth Tappan, born August 20, 1870, died December 28, 1898.

SARAH TRASK

Born: October 21, 1816, "on the Ohio River near Indian Creek, 18 miles above Cincinnati"

Married: John Remsen Onderdonk on January 5, 1839. Mr. Onderdonk was born November 6, 1815 and died April 15, 1857.

Children of John and Sarah (Trask) Onderdonk: John Remsen Onderdonk II; Elizabeth Carter Onderdonk; Maria Holmes Onderdonk, born in New York in 1843, died 1844; Sarah Trask Onderdonk, born in New York on May 14, 1845, died in New York on October 9, 1891; Andrew Onderdonk; William Holmes Onderdonk; James Lawrence Onderdonk, born in New Jersey on May 24, 1854, died in Alaska in 1900.

ONDERDONK FAMILY IN AMERICA. By Elmer Onderdonk of Philadelphia and Andrew Onderdonk of New York. 1910. Pages 164-165, 213-215.

ANDREW ONDERDONK

Born: August 30, 1848, in New York

Married: Sarah D. Hillman in March 1871

Died: 1906 in Oscawan, New York

Andrew Onderdonk was a Civil Engineer and Contractor. He built the sea wall in San Francisco, the Canadian Pacific Railway and the subway in New York City.

Children of Andrew and Sarah D. (Hillman) Onderdonk: Sherby Onderdonk, born December 11, 1871 in Bergen, New Jersey; Eva Onderdonk, born May 5, 1873 in Plainfield, New Jersey; Percy Onderdonk, born May 26, 1876 in San Francisco; Arthur Onderdonk, born January 29, 1881, at Yale, British Columbia; Gladys Onderdonk, born December 23, 1888 in Chicago, married October 10, 1908 to Bradfor Gage Weekes, son of Arthur D. Weekes.

ELIZABETH CARTER ONDERDONK

Born: September 26, 1841

Married: Henry Bell Laidlaw in Jersey City. Mr. Laidlaw was a Vestryman of Trinity Parish. He was born in New York on December 25, 1838 and died there in 1902.

Children of Henry Bell and Elizabeth Carter (Onderdonk) Laidlaw: Louise Laidlaw, born in 1865 in New Jersey, married William Herbert Judson; James L. Laidlaw, born in New Jersey in 1868, married Harriet Burton; Edith Elizabeth Laidlaw, born in New Jersey in 1871; Alice Laidlaw, born in New Jersey in 1873, married Jesse Lynch Williams; Jesse Laidlaw, born in New Jersey in 1875, married Edward Roesler; Agnes Laidlaw, born in New York in 1876, married August Roesler; Robert Remsen Laidlaw, born in New York in 1881, married Isabella Wood; Elliot Carter Laidlaw.

Henry Bell Laiwlaw, husband of Elizabeth Carter Onderdonk, was the son of Robert Laidlaw and his wife, Huldah Bell. Robert Laidlaw was born in Scotland in 1798. He was Professor of English Literature at Edinburgh University. He died in Jersey City in 1862.

Henry Bell Laidlaw was born in 1839. He joined Laidlaw and Company (Stockbrokers established in 1842) in 1854 and became its President in 1873. He died in 1902.

AMERICAN BIOGRAPHIES, Editorial Press Bureau, Inc., Washington, D. C., Volume III, page 163.

JAMES LEES LAIDLAW

Born: December 10, 1868

Married: Harriet Wright Burton on October 25, 1905, in New York City.

Died: May 9, 1932, Sands Point, Long Island, New York

Children of James Lees and Harriet Wright (Burton) Laidlaw: Louise Burton Laidlaw; James Lees Laidlaw was a founder and director of Standard and Poors Corporation (Business and Financial Counselors) and served as President of Laidlaw and Company.

AMERICAN BIOGRAPHIES, Editorial Press Bureau, Inc., Washington, D. C. Volume III, page 163.

LOUISE BURTON LAIDLAW

Married: Dana Converse Backus on September 16, 1933

Children of Dana Converse and Louise Burton (Laidlaw) Backus: Mary Backus, wife of Douglas Rankin; Janet Backus; Elizabeth Backus; Harriet Meredith Backus; Anne Converse Backus.

See listing of Dana Converse Backus in *WHO'S WHO IN AMERICA*, 1958-1959.

JOHN REMSEN ONDERDONK II

Born: March 31, 1840, in New York

Married: Rosina Jacobs in 1867

Died: November 22, 1888, in Chicago

John Remsen Onderdonk II was an Architect and Civil Engineer. He assisted his brother, Andrew Onderdonk, on the Canadian Pacific Railroad and in introducing water to Chicago, when he died.

Children of John Remsen and Rosina (Jacobs) Onderdonk II: John Remsen Onderdonk III, born October 14, 1869, graduated in 1889 from the Stevens Institute.

WILLIAM HOLMES ONDERDONK

Born: March 19, 1852 in New Jersey

Married: Matilda Hendrickson in 1875

Died: 1903 in Chicago

Children of William Holmes and Matilda (Hendrickson) Onderdonk: William Holmes Onderdonk, Jr., born October 13, 1877 in Jersey City; Dudley Onderdonk, born April 11, 1879 in Jersey City; Forman Hendrickson Onderdonk, born February 18, 1881 in Jersey City, lives in Chicago; James Lawrence Onderdonk, born October 21, 1888 in New York.

LYDIA CARTER

Born: 1788-1789

Married: 1st: George Poindexter, later Governor of Mississippi, in 1804. Divorced in 1815.

2nd: Lewis Williams on June 20, 1820, in Brimfield, Massachusetts.

Died: August 28, 1824, in Brimfield, Masachusetts.

Children of Governor George and Lydia (Carter) Poindexter: Albert Poindexter and George Littleton Carter Poindexter.

GEORGE POINDEXTER. (1779-September 5, 1853). Delegate, Representative, Senator from Mississippi, was born in Louisa County, Virginia, the seventh child of Thomas and Lucy (Jones) Poindexter. His own restless nature and the thinness of the family pocketbook made his schooling sporadic and he read law in several offices before he was admitted to the practice of law which he began at Milton, Virginia. In 1802 he moved to Natchez, Mississippi, taking little with him beyond his own great ability and deep loyalty to Jeffersonian Democracy. Shortly after he reached his destination William Charles Cole Claiborne, the newly chosen Governor of the Mississippi Territory, appointed him Attorney General and in this capacity he took part in the efforts to bring Aaron Burr to trial. In 1805 he became a member of the Territorial Assembly which soon sent him to Congress as a Delegate. Possibly the most important event of his three terms from March 4, 1807, to March 3, 1813, was his spirited opposition to the celebrated disunion speech of Josiah Quincy of Massachusetts (Annals of Congress, 11 Cong., 3 Sess., Col 525). In 1813 he became a District Judge for the Territory and though he was bitterly assailed by Andrew Marschalk, an able newspaper editor of the Territory, the bar considered him an able and upright judge. In 1815 he published TO THE PUBLIC, a pamphlet designed to meet the charges against him. He was a very influential member of the Convention that framed the First Constitution of Mississippi in 1817 and he founded the document on the philosophy of the Virginia School of Democracy. Reentering Congress as the first Representative of the State of Mississippi he served from December 10, 1817, to March 3, 1819. He defended Andrew Jackson's conduct in the Seminole Campaign "and the national verdict then was that his arguments were unanswerable" (Claiborne, page 391). He was Governor of Mississippi from 1820 to 1821 and at the request of the Legislature, while he was Governor, he codified the laws of the State and in 1822 was able to present his work to the legislature, the consideration of which was the principal object of the Session of 1822. This REVISED CODE OF THE LAWS OF MISSISSIPPI (1824) was the first real code in Mississippi and it met with instant and sustained approval. He was defeated for Congress in 1822.

This and other troubles sent him into gloomy retirement. His health was poor and at times he was unable to walk. The enemies he made were bitter and unrelenting in exposing the seamy side of his life, particularly by accusing him of unfairness in a duel in which he killed Abijah Hunt. His family life was also embittered for with public charges he had divorced Lydia (Carter) Poindexter and his second wife, Agatha (Chinn) Poindexter and their only son died. Though one of the ablest men in Mississippi in his day he was constantly involved in personal quarrels and newspaper altercations, for he was moody and variable in temper. Because of poor health he refused the Commission of Chancellor offered him by Governor Brandon in 1828 and this was also the probable cause of his defeat for the Senate in the following year.

His condition improving, he was appointed to the Senate to fill the unexpired term of Robert H. Adams, and later he was elected with negligible opposition to this office. He served from October 15, 1830, to March 3, 1835. In the Senate he underwent a change that was important in his own career and in national affairs. Beginning with a dispute over the distribution of patronage in Mississippi he became an unrelenting enemy of Andrew Jackson. The Democratic Party in Mississippi detested his course and hints were dropped that financial transactions with the Bank of the United States explained the change yet it seems true that he sensed the essential difference between Jacksonian and Jeffersonian Democracy and he believed his course was more consistent with that of the Democratic Party. This Party nominated Robert J. Walker to succeed him; thereupon, he campaigned on the Whig ticket in 1835, but was defeated. He did not again serve his State in public office. Broken in body by dissipation and by a severe fall, he removed to Lexington, Kentucky, but later returned to Jackson, Mississippi, where he practiced law until his death.

DICTIONARY OF AMERICAN BIOGRAPHY. Volume XV, pages 29 and 30. Edited by Dumas Malone. New York. 1935 Charles Scribner's Sons.

1830 CENSUS, WILKINSON COUNTY, MISSISSIPPI

George Poindexter

1 male born 1770-1780; 1 male born 1800-1810; 1 male born 1820-1825; 111 slaves.

The original will of Lydia Carter Williams of Brimfield, Hampden County, Massachusetts is in Hampden County. A certified copy is in Natchez, Will Book 1, page 327.

Dated: 12 March 1824

Proven: January Term, 1825

Legatees: Beloved Husband, Lewis Williams in Trust, etc., Also Executor and Guardian of George Littleton Poindexter, a minor.

Son: George Littleton Poindexter, real and personal property at age 21.

Son: Albert Poindexter, a gold watch.

Mention of real estate in Mississippi and Louisiana.

/s/ LYDIA C. WILLIAMS

Test. Jno. B. Cooley
    Eben Knight
    Chester A. Keyes

GEORGE POINDEXTER of Adams County, Mississippi Territory
To
JESSE CARTER of same

Consideration: $5,000. Tract of land situated on waters of Second Creek, in said County, now in occupancy of said GEORGE POINDEXTER, 250 acres originally granted by the Spanish Government to SARAH KENNARD and conveyed by JESSE CARTER and his wife to GEORGE POINDEXTER the 12th of September, 1811. /s/ GEO. POINDEXTER. Test. John Steel and Theodore Stark.

Deed Book H, page 434, Adams County, Miss. 2 April 1815.

Colonel Steel was Secretary of the Mississippi Territory under Governor Winthrop Sargent and Acting Governor in 1801.

GEORGE POINDEXTER and LYDIA, his wife of the County of Adams, Mississippi Territory
To
Archibald Terrill of Same.

Consideration: $1,000. Tract of land in County and Territory afore-said, 400 arpents, beginning corner dogwood, then north 39 degrees, East 166 poles, etc.

/s/ G. POINDEXTER and L. POINDEXTER. Acknowledged by them 28 September 1812. Josiah Simpkins, Judge.

Deed Book H, page 260, Adams County, 14 September, 1811.

1820 CENSUS, ADAMS COUNTY, MISSISSIPPI

Lydia Carter

1 male born 1775-1794; 42 slaves.

On the left 124.2 miles from Vicksburg to the Louisiana line, which is 128.2 miles from Vicksburg is Ashwood (open by appointment) the former plantation of George Poindexter (1779-1855), Author of the first Mississippi Code and Second Governor of the State. Pages 345-6, MISSISSIPPI, A guide to the Magnolia State, Federal Writers Project, Works Progress Administration, Viking Press, New York, 1938. VITAL RECORDS OF BRIMFIELD, MASSACHUSETTS TO THE YEAR 1850. Published by the New England Historic Genealogical Society, 1931

(page 37)

George Littleton Carter son of Lydia of Natches baptized on November 28, 1820

(pages 175 and 257)

Lydia Carter of Natches, Miss. and Lewis Williams married on June 20, 1820.

(page 334)

Lydia Carter wife Lewis Williams died on August 28, 1824 in Brim-field (Lydia Carter Williams August aged 35 gravestone record Brim-field Center Cemetery; Aug 27 aged 36, a private record of deaths and burials in Brimfield kept 1808-50 by the Chairman of the Cemetery Commission.

The J. F. H. Claiborne Papers are housed in the Department of Archives. The Poindexter Papers are part of the Claiborne Papers. Contents are listed in the Publications of the Mississippi Historical Society, Volume 5.

The following is from MISSISSIPPI AS A PROVINCE, TERRI-TORY AND STATE by John Francis Hamtramck Claiborne, Volume I, Jackson, Mississippi, Power and Barksdale, 1880:

(pages 363-4)

"In 1804 he (George Poindexter) married Lydia, the daughter of Major Jesse Carter, a wealthy planter of Adams County. His friend Mr. Trist (H. B. Trist, Collector of Customs) wrote to him: 'You have drawn a valuable prize in the matrimonial lottery. Her great beauty is, as far as I can judge, her least recommendation, for she blends grace and intelligence with every amiable trait that adorns her sex.' "

(page 371)

"1808. He had already separated from his beautiful wife, who had borne him two sons, and he had publicly accused her of criminal relations with one who had been a favorite with both — I have critically examined the evidence in his own papers against this lady and though she may have been indiscreet and the more so from resentment of her husband's suspicions, I am sure she was never criminal — that she was a pure and true wife. She subsequently married Mr. Williams, a clergyman of Brimfield, Massachusetts and maintained an unexcelled reputation.

Excerpts from EARLY LIFE OF GEORGE POINDEXTER. By Mack Swearingen. Published by Tulane University Press, 1934.

(Page 66)

"For example in 1804 he married Lydia* beautiful daughter of Major Jesse Carter, a rich and prominent planter.* No other details of the match are known. The next year, however, Poindexter appeared for the first time on the tax rolls and was listed as possessing 400 hundred acres of land on Sandy Creek, valued at $800.00. This was very likely Lydia's dowry, but there can be no certainty on that point."

*"Her gallant contemporaries said she was beautiful; beautiful she must have been. There is, at any rate, no evidence to the contrary. Claiborne, p. 363, is the only authority for the date."

*"In the tax rolls for 1805 Major Carter is put down for 850 acres of land, 40 slaves and other property, the whole valued at $23,620.00. This was a considerable fortune."

(Page 133-)

"*** Poindexter was vitally interested in another case. This was his suit for divorce. There is not much of a problem here. As early as May, 1814, Poindexter had begun to quarrel with his father-in-law over a loan. Major Carter was apparently refusing to pay interest on this and naturally Poindexter's incredibly sensitive nature caused him to construe this as an effort to impose on him. This was the way in which all his domestic relations became sooner or later embroiled. Poindexter had positive hallucinations on supposed violations of his rights. In this way arose his divorce suit. Some time early in 1815 (perhaps even sooner) he got it into his head that his wife was having illicit relations with Thomas G. Percy, an unmarried planter who lived near the Poindexters and was a favorite with both of them. On Janu-

— 466 —

ary 11, Percy advertised his property together with that of his brother-in-law, Dr. Samuel Brown for sale. This might have been the cause or the result of Poindexter's suspicions. At any rate it was on January 15 that Poindexter filed his bill and in a very little while Percy and Brown were residents of Kentucky rather than the Mississippi Territory.

"The exact date of the trial at which Poindexter was granted his divorce is not known, but it was during this term *** His divorce decree left two sons, Albert and George in the care of their mother, but stipulated that Poindexter should provide for their education. Albert, the elder, was sent to school in Philadelphia, but George, being too young remained with his mother.

"Mrs. Poindexter's guilt need not be determined. Claiborne claims that he investigated all the papers left by Poindexter and that from these it appeared she must have been innocent. But the Poindexter papers were preserved by Claiborne and were available to the author and unless some of them have been destroyed, there is not a scrap of evidence one way or another on Mrs. Poindexter's guilt. Claiborne was nothing if not gallant. Sparks (W. H. Sparks THE MEMORIES OF FIFTY YEARS. Philadelphia. 1870 Pages 341-2) in his account intimates a strong suspicion of her guilt. Who could blame her? Any person who had to put up with the vile disposition of Poindexter could be, even must be, forgiven for seeking a little comfort and consolation wherever it was to be found. If Percy was even the least sympathetic, there was every chance that the distressed Lydia would confess to him that she was abused or perhaps "misunderhood". What was there then for neighbor Percy to do? The whole point, however, is that it really mattered little whether she was guilty — she probably was not. But if Poindexter suspected her, she might just as well have been. His insane jealousy knew no bounds and having once got the idea that she was unfaithful, all the other developments were only natural, even his denial of the paternity of his sons."

"Such was the extremities of Poindexter's jealousy he professed to doubt the paternity of these boys and throughout his whole life refused to claim them as his own; 36 years later in his will, after he had married the third time, the old rancor was still so strong that he denied having any male descendants and thus cut off the two sons of George Poindexter from a share in his fabulous wealth. Poindexter's will is recorded and proved in the Clerk's Office at Raymond, Mississippi. The property he disposed of in it was so extensive the author would almost sacrifice his claim on the credulity of readers if he listed it. Among other things were 20 sections of land on the Rio Grande, to half of which he had a clear title. He likewise had large quantities of land in Kentucky, Louisiana, and six counties in Mississippi, property which today certainly would be worth many millions. Albert and George both died before their father, the former in poverty and disgrace after a career of crime. The latter had two sons, one of whom had descendants who are still living and with whom the author had some correspondence."

An interesting description of Thomas G. Percy may be found on pages 271 and 272 of *LANTERNS ON THE LEVEE*, the incredibly beautiful autobiography of the late William Alexander Percy of Greenville, Mississippi, great-grandson of Thomas G. Percy and son of the renowned United States Senator from Mississippi, Leroy Percy. The father of Thomas G. Percy and the first of the family in this country was Charles Percy who settled on a Spanish Land Grant in Wilkinson County, Mississippi. His plantation was called Northumberland Place and he was known by the Spaniards as Don Carlos.

PARSONS CARTER

Born: March 6, 1776

Married: Ann Hays Dortch on August 1, 1805. Ann Hays Dortch was born on April 17, 1786, and died on November 24, 1854. She was the daughter of David Dortch, known as John and also as Daniel. David Dortch's ancestors had spelled their name "Deutsch", until Nathan Deutsch went from Holland to England with William of Orange and from England to Virginia and changed the spelling to Dortch. From him all of the name in America are descended. This branch of the Dortch family eventually settled in the Florida Parishes of Louisiana, particularly in East Feliciana and East Baton Rouge Parishes, in that part of these two parishes known as Sts. John Plains; now called Buhler Plains, about five miles east of Port Hudson, lying along each side of the Baton Rouge-Bayou Sara Highway, extending from about ten miles north of Baton Rouge to the old Clinton and Port Hudson Railroad, which intersected the highway and ran through the A. G. Carter plantation. The home of Parsons Carter and his wife, Ann Hays Dortch, was on the highway, some two miles south of the railroad.

Died: February 29, 1839

"PARSONS CARTER * * * a scion of the Carters of Shirley Hall of Old Virginia, migrated from Natchez, certainly before the country passed from under the Spanish jurisdiction and founded a home on the Baton Rouge and St. Francisville Road, just where it emerges from Buhler's Plains * * * WILLIAM D. CARTER AND GENERAL ALBERT G. CARTER lived near the old family seat, useful, public-spirited citizens, warmly honored and loved by their neighbors. Many of the descendants of General A. G. Carter still uphold the social prestige of the family, in close vicinity to their ancestral seat."

EAST FELICIANA, LOUISIANA, PAST AND PRESENT by Henry Skipwith, Page 7. Published in New Orleans by the Hopkins Printing Office, 1892. Mr. Howell Morgan, 162 Albany Avenue, Shreveport, Louisiana, who compiled the Carter genealogy knew Mr. Skipwith, who was at one time Clerk of Court of East Feliciana Parish. His son, John, also held the same office. His other sons were Henry, Jr., and Wyndham Skipwith. The "Florida Parishes" comprised East Feliciana, West Feliciana, East Baton Rouge, St. Tammany, Washington, St. Helena, Livingston and Tangipahoa Parishes. It was called West Florida and at one time the County of Feliciana. It was not included in the Louisiana Purchase in 1803. Spain claimed it from 1763 to 1810. The land grants were Spanish. That to "Linwood" was validated Nov. 17, 1873 and signed by the President, U. S. Grant, By S. D. Williamson, Secretary, etc.

Children of Parsons and Ann Hays (Dortch) Carter: William Dortch Carter; General Albert Gallatin Carter; Elizabeth Penny Carter; Mary Dortch Carter; Mary Ann Rebecca Littleton Carter, born June 5, 1806, died September 11, 1815; Lydia Carter, born June 3, 1817, died August 23, 1832; John Dortch Carter, born October 15, 1819, died July 24, 1820.

The home of Parsons Carter and his wife, Ann Hays Dortch, in Sts. John Plains, now called Buhler Plains, was only two miles from "Linwood" on the Baton Rouge and Bayou Sara (St. Francisville) Road. St. Francisville was named Fort Sainte Heine by the French and Bayou Sara was also known by that name during French rule. Port Hudson was called "Les Ecores au de Lait" or Milk White Cliffs.

General Albert Gallatin Carter was born at "Distant View," the home of his father, Parsons Carter, and so were his children, except the youngest, Charles Parsons Carter, who was born at "Linwood," which he built while living at "Distant View." Also born at "Linwood" were his grandchildren, Albert Carter, Thos. Gibbes III, and Howell Morgan; and Daisy and Lydia Purnell; all of the children of Howell (Polk) Carter except Ethel Lillian who was born in Detroit, Michigan. George W. Purnell, Jr., was born in Jefferson, Texas. Also born at "Linwood" were his great-grandchildren, Thomas Gibbes IV, and Howell Morgan, Jr. Besides "Linwood," the home, General Carter built one of the largest brick sugar houses in the State of Louisiana on Linwood Plantation. His slaves made all the bricks and did all common labor in the construction. This sugarhouse was used by the Federal soldiers as a hospital, during the Siege of Port Hudson and afterwards. Port Hudson surrendered July 9, 1863.

From: David Dortch of East Feliciana Parish, La., to PARSONS CARTER of same. Consideration: $200., recording transfer of a negro Fanny, aged six years in 1817, this written conveyance dated

2 April 1833. /s/ David Dortch, PARSONS CARTER. Test: L. Hardesty, W. Waddell.

Clinton, La., Notarial Record Book C, p 332. 1 March 1817
Power of Attorney. PARSONS CARTER of East Feliciana Parish, La. to WILLIAM D. CARTER of same. PARSONS CARTER expects to leave the State for some months and appoints WM. D. CARTER his lawful attorney, etc. /s/ PARSONS CARTER, WM. D. CARTER. Test: Thos. L. Andrews, Franklin.

Clinton, La. Notarial Record Book B, p 72, 21 April 1829
From: James Henderson of West Feliciana Parish, La., to PARSONS CARTER of East Feliciana Parish, Louisiana. Consideration: $360 cash and notes payable to WILLIAM D. CARTER and indorsed by him etc. 10% interest. Lot of land in East Feliciana Parish, No. 15 at Port Hudson, Square 2, etc. /s/ James Henderson PARSONS CARTER. Test: Daniel McRay, John C. White.

Clinton, La. Notarial Record Book C, p 133. 20 July 1830.
From: David Dortch of East Feliciana Parish, La. to PARSONS CARTER OF SAME. Consideration: $350. One plantation in East Feliciana Parish, La. on White's Bayou near Robert W. Newport's also two negroes, the present residence of David Dortch etc. /s/ D'd Dortch, PARSONS CARTER. Test: Reub. N. Short, W. Waddell
Clinton, La. Notarial Record Book C p 373. 30 April 1833
Power of Attorney. From Mrs. Ann H. Carter of East Feliciana Parish, La. wife of PARSONS CARTER to PARSONS CARTER, her husband. Power of Attorney for all purposes. /s/ Ann H. Carter PARSONS CARTER. Test: David Dortch, John W. Barnhill

Clinton, La. Notarial Record Book D, p 141 13 February 1834
Acknowledgment: Came and appeared Ann H. Dortch, WIFE OF PARSONS CARTER and Robert W. Newport, all of said Parish of East Feliciana, State of Louisiana. Said Ann H. Dortch and her husband, said PARSON CARTER, declared etc. that a sale made by CARTER to Newport some time in the year 1823, 55 acres etc. bounded by lands of said CARTER on South and East by lands formerly owned by Nath'l Harlon, on west by lands of Newport on North by land formerly owned by David Dortch, was made with the concurrence etc. of said Ann Dortch, wife as aforesaid but that she was not made a party thereto. Now she ratifies etc. /s/ Ann H. Carter, PARSONS CARTER, R. Newport. Test: Alex Spears, James C. Jackson.
Clinton, La. Notarial Record Book E, p 174 31 August 1835

From: PARSONS CARTER AND HIS WIFE, ANN H. CARTER of East Feliciana Parish, La. to ALBERT G. CARTER of same. Consideration: $10, 395 cash and notes. Tract of land on which said PAR-

SONS CARTER now resides /s/ PARSONS CARTER, ANN H. CARTER Test: John C. Walker, S. Fletcher.

FAMILY MEETING: Present — Robert H. Lewis, Nehemiah P. Palmer, Adam Palmer, John C. Walker, Albert Baily, Sworn, etc. Touching the interest of Mary Carter, minor child of PARSONS CARTER, deceased, after having read the petition of Ann H. Carter, Tutrix of said minor, filed in court Feb 5, 1840, etc. do advise that the land and negroes belonging to said deceased Parsons Carter, be sold etc. Signed by those present and by William D. Clark, Under-tutor. Test: R. Bonner, Hy. Henford.

Clinton, La. Notarial Record Book H, p 247, 6 Mar 1840

Before me Andrew Atchison, Notary Public etc. came and appeared Mrs. Ann Carter, widow in community, William D. Carter, Albert G. Carter, Eliza P. Carter, wife of John C. Walker, Mary D. Carter, wife of Wallace Badger, heirs at law of PARSONS CARTER deceased, all of East Feliciana Parish, Louisiana, who renounce any further claim on Estate of PARSONS CARTER, THEIR DECEASED FATHER. All sign, including Walker and Badger.

Clinton, La. Notarial Record Book I, p 248 1 March 1841

From: Lee Hardesty of East Feliciana Parish, La. to William Dortch Carter and his wife, Sarah Ellen Carter of same. Consideration: $1,930.25 cash and notes. Deed and mortgage 439½ acres, same land sold to Benjamin Anthony Williams and Frederick Williams by James L. Williams on 13 January 1823, also certain negroes, etc. /s/ L. Hardesty, WILLIAM D. CARTER, Sarah E. Carter, Test: Robert Penny, Lafayette Saunders, Thomas M. Scott, Parish Judge.

Clinton, La. Notarial Record Book B, p 231   5 April 1830

FAMILY MEETING, on order of Parish Judge. Present: Thomas W. Scott, Albert G. Perry, Malachi Weston, Geo. M. Catlett, Sanford Perry, relations connections and friends of the minor, FRANCES P. HOWELL, WIFE OF ALBERT G. CARTER, of East Feliciana Parish, La., to advise in matter of selling certain real estate. Signed by all. Test: Bartlett F. Cook, J. P. Davis.

Clinton, La. Notarial Record Book E, p 403, 30 June 1836

Came Elizabeth Howell, wife of Malachi Weston, of full age; FRANCES HOWELL, WIFE OF ALBERT G. CARTER, and de-clared that whereas in the partition of Estate of William Kirkland, Senior, and William Kirkland, Junor, among the children of William Kirkland, Senior and the collaterals of said William Kirkland, Jr. a tract of land, 1600 arpens, known as Redwood Plantation in East Feliciana Parish, La., bounded by Redwood on the west, on the north by Nancy Kirkland, on the south by Brashears, and on the east by Public Land fell to the two appearers and their two half brothers, William Llewellyn, and Samuel C. Llewellyn, conjointly, they being the children of a deceased child of said William Kirkland, Senior and sister to said William Kirkland, Junior; that subsequently to that partition among the said children, a partition of the property that fell to them, to-wit, the said Elizabeth, Frances, William and Samuel C. was made and this tract of land was then laid off

GENERAL ALBERT GALLATIN CARTER

Born: October 31, 1809

Married: 1st: Rebecca McManus on November 20, 1830. She was born on February 28, 1814, and died on September 1, 1834

2nd: Frances Priscilla Howell on January 14, 1836. She was born on May 9, 1819, and died on April 26, 1884. She was a granddaughter of Richard Howell, Governor of New Jersey, 1792-1801, and a first cousin of Mrs. Jefferson Davis, wife of the President of the Confederacy and of Daniel Agnew, Chief Justice of Pennsylvania.

Died: July 25, 1876

Children of General Albert Gallatin and Rebecca (McManus) Carter: Albert Eugene Carter.

Children of General Albert Gallatin and Frances Priscilla (Howell) Carter: Lydia Annie Carter; Mary Elizabeth Carter, born January 11, 1839, died February 29, 1848; Frances Rebecca Carter, born November 9, 1841, died September 18, 1847; Howell Polk Carter; William Ruffin Carter, born March 28, 1847, died September, 1895; Charles Parsons Carter.

From LOUISIANA, A Guide to the State, Sponsored by the Louisiana Library Commission at Baton Rouge, Hastings House, New York, 1941

Natchez-St. Francisville, Baton Rouge, New Orleans Mississippi Line to Baton Rouge, US 61-65 Highway

(Page 515)

At 27,8 miles. Junction with unmarked, unimproved road built on abandoned roadbed of the Old Clinton and Port Hudson Railroad.

Right here one mile to LINWOOD (private), the home of Mr. and Mrs. Malcolm Dougherty. The house was built by General Albert G. Carter in 1838-1840 and remained in possession of the Carter Family until 1910. After the defeat of the Confederates, the plantation was overrun by Union soldiers who burned the outhouse, sacked the big house, and partially destroyed the sugarhouse. The house is a white frame building with four heavy plaster-covered brick columns of the Doric order across front and galleries upstairs and down.

US 61-5 enters the plateau area of East Baton Rouge Parish at 29.5 miles. This section has been various known as White Plains, Buhler's Plains, and the Plains of St. John. In the days of the West Florida Rebellion delegates from the surrounding districts met in this neighborhood and marched on the Spanish Fort at Baton Rouge.

Plains. 30.7 miles. A hamlet centered around the Plains Presbyterian Church (Right), a white frame building with green shutters. The land for the church property was bequeathed by the widow of John Buhler in 1829.

See the interesting book PLANTATION LIFE IN THE FLORIDA PARISHES OF LOUISIANA 1836-1846 AS REFLECTED IN THE DIARY OF BENNET HILLIARD BARROW by Edwin Adams Davis. Printed by the Columbia University Press in New York in 1943. Mr. Barrow belonged to the family in West Feliciana Parish that built several beautiful plantation homes. Among them were Highland, Greenwood, and Afton Villa. Mr. Barrow in his diary mentions the visit of General Carter and voting for the General in 1842 for Senator. See particularly pages 162, 163 and 264. The book is highly recommended for those wishing to know what life was like in the ante-bellum years for a member of the plantation gentry.

GENERAL ALBERT G. CARTER, a prominent planter and native of East Feliciana Parish, Louisiana, was born in 1809. He was the son of PARSON CARTER, a native of Georgia who came to Louisiana sometime about 1790 and settled in this place near where the son of our subject now lives. He entered land from the Spanish Government which he improved until it became the fine plantation it now is and where he lived until his death which occurred in 1842. He was a leader in the Presbyterian Church of which he was an elder for a number of years. He was quite successful as a planter and accumulated quite a property and owned a great many slaves. His wife was Miss Ann Dortch of German descent who survived him until 1864, aged 63 years. To this union were born five children: Mrs. Mary Badger who lives in Austin, Texas, William D., the eldest son who died in 1858 leaving a family in the parish, Albert G. was the next in order of birth, Mrs. Eliza Walker who died in 1851 leaving a family and the other child died when young. Albert G. Carter was reared on the home place and was educated at Jackson, Louisiana, at what is now known as Centenary College, then the Louisiana College. He settled in this parish where he following planting until the breaking out of the war, when, in 1863, he went to Georgia and remained until 1866. He then returned to this parish and resumed planting which he continued until his death in 1876. He was commissioned General of the State Militia soon after the Mexican War and took a very active part in politics. He was a Democrat and represented this parish in the Legislature in 1846. He did not aspire to office, preferring to remain free of any of the incumbrances of official duties, but accepted office only at the earnest solicitation of his friends. During the latter part of his life, he took a very active interest in the affairs of his church, the Presbyterian. His first wife was Miss Rebecca McManus, a native of this state and parish. She was the daughter of Samuel McManus, one of the earliest settlers of this parish. She died in 1834, comparatively young, leaving one son, Eugene Carter, who was born in 1833. He was reared by his grandmother, Mrs. Sarah McManus until he was eight years of age when he returned to his father's home. His father had married a second time, his wife being Miss Frances P. Howell of this parish. She died April 13, 1884, leaving three sons and three daughters of whom three sons and a daughter are still living: Howell Carter who lives in Baton Rouge, Mrs. Lydia Purnell, wife of G. W. Purnell of this parish; William R. Carter lives in Bolivar County, Mississippi; Charles P. Carter lives in Longview, Texas. The mother of these children died a consistent member of the Presbyterian Church. The subject lived with his parents until maturity, attending school at Oakland, Mississippi, then at Columbian College in the District of Columbia where he graduated in a class of five in 1855. He then returned to this parish and engaged in planting. He has since resided on the old home place. He served in the late war about three years in the 1st Louisiana Cavalry for one year and then in the Ogden Battalion until the close of the war. He was in the siege of Port Hudson where he was taken prisioner. After the war he resumed planting and is now the owner of a fine plantation of well cultivated land. He was married to Miss Helen Moore of Abbeville Parish who was the daughter of Edmund Moore, a native of Tennessee and who came to Louisiana where Mrs. Carter was born in 1828. He settled in Ascension Parish and later in Abbeville Parish where he is yet living, being now at the advanced age of 85 years — hale and hearty for one that age. He reared a family of four children, two of whom are now living, B. Frank Moore who lives at Harrisburg, Kentucky, and Helen M., the widow of Mr. Carter. She was reared in Abbeville Parish and educated at the Convent of the Sacred Heart and at Patapsco Institute near Baltimore, Maryland. To this union have been born nine children, three of whom are now dead, Helen wife of J. W. Anderson, Edna Carter, Millie, the wife of Walter McLaurin, Alberta living at home, Minnie H. also at home, Lillie A. was the wife of James H. McManus and died leaving a family of five children, one of whom is now deceased, Florence died in 1863, Albert Edgar at the age of nine years. Mrs. Carter is a member of the Presbyterian Church of which her children are also attendants. Politically Mr. Carter is a Democrat and takes much interest in the advancement of his party.

Biographical and Historical Memoirs of Louisiana. Goodspeed Publishing Company. Chicago. 1892. Volume 1, pages 340-341.

1820 CENSUS, FELICIANA PARISH, LOUISIANA

Parson Carter: 1 male born before 1775; 1 male born 1775-1794; 1 male born 1794-1804; 1 male born 1802-1804; 2 males born 1804-1810; 1 female born 1775-1794; 1 female born 1794-1804; 2 females born 1810-1820; 16 slaves

ALBERT EUGENE CARTER

Born: December 3, 1833

Married: Helen A. Moore on June 19, 1856

Children of Albert Eugene and Helen A. (Moore) Carter: Lillie Almedia Carter; E. Moore Carter, married Margaret Smiley; Florence Carter, died in infancy; Helen Adele Carter; Edna Earl Carter; Willie Carter; Alberta Carter, married Dr. Will D. Anderson; Albert Eugene Carter, Jr., died in early youth; Minnie Hynson Carter, married Dr. Harry Johnston, no issue.

HELEN ADELE CARTER

Born: April 13, 1865

Married: John Way Anderson

Children of John Way and Helen Adele (Carter) Anderson: John Way Anderson, married Margaret Graves on September 16, 1908, their daughter, Helen Louise Anderson born January 1, 1910 married Julius Pratt on June 16, 1936; Maggie Helen Anderson, born March 28, 1886, married V. T. McCleland; Lillie Belle Anderson, born December 12, 1887, married Halley Earl Townsend, their son Halley E. Townsend Jr. married Frances Maricelli on April 15, 1939; Charles Lafayette Anderson, born February 23, 1890, married Portia Christian; Eugene Carter Anderson, born May 23, 1892, married Ramona Weigle; Edward Moore Anderson, born June 23, 1894, married secondly to Myrtle Hughes, their daughter was Myrtle Helen Anderson; Eugenia Anderson, born September 15, 1896, married R. G. Jones; Katie Adele Anderson, born December 1898, married R. V. Wilson, they were the parents of Robert V. Wilson, Jr., born 1922; Katherene Adele Wilson, born 1925 and died 1936; Margaret Helen Wilson, born 1928; James Anderson Wilson, born in 1932; and William Hudnahl Wilson, born 1935.

LILLIE ALMEDIA CARTER

Born: May 24, 1857

Married: James Hoard McManus at "Linwood" on December 24, 1874. Mr. McManus was born on December 10, 1849 and died on October 1, 1905

Died: May 11, 1882

Children of James Hoard and Lillie Almedia (Carter) McManus: Annie Evelyn McManus; Albert Hugh McManus; Helen Adele McManus.

ANNIE EVELYN McMANUS

Born: December 18, 1875

Married: William Edward Miller in St. James Episcopal Church in Baton Rouge on June 1, 1903. Mr. Miller was born January 14, 1864 and died on August 11, 1923

Children of William Edward and Annie Evelyn (McManus) Miller: Evelyn Ann Miller, born September 18, 1909, married Horace Wesley Russell on November 30, 1929 in St. James Episcopal Church in Baton Rouge, Mr. Miller was born July 24, 1906.

ALBERT HUGH McMANUS

Born: August 13, 1877

Married: Emma Schleicher

Died: November 23, 1924

Children of Albert Hugh and Emma (Schleischer); McManus: Infant son, died October, 1910, Albert McManus, Jr.

HELEN ADELE McMANUS

Born: March 15, 1880

Married: John Perry Dickinson on August 4, 1904, at the Presbyterian Church in Norwood

Children of John Perry and Helen Adele (McManus); Dickinson: John Willie Dickinson, born October 31, 1905, married Rose A. Vincent in the Catholic Church in Lake Charles; Albert Russell Dickinson, born November 19, 1906; Ida Lillie Dickinson, born May 17, 1908, married Charles A. Carver on April 20, 1939 at the Presbyterian Church in Lake Charles; Perry Adolphus Dickinson, born August 16, 1910, married Emma Lyonne Jones at the Christian Church in Lake Charles on March 23, 1936; Helen Adele Dickinson, born October 19, 1911; Doris Dickinson, born January 28, 1913; Henry Allen Dickinson, born March 2, 1918.

WILLIE CARTER

Married: Walter McLaurin

Died: January 15, 1919

Children of Walter and Willie (Carter) McLaurin: Walter McLaurin born August 21, 1889, married Annie Wall Whitaker, their son James Walter McLaurin born on July 1, 1910, married Lady Katherine Kretschmar on September 28, 1935; John Purvis McLaurin, born 1891, married Emma Loyse Steidly, their son John Purvis McLaurin, Jr. was at Old Miss College in 1940.

ALBERTA CARTER

Married: Dr. William D. Anderson, brother of John W. Anderson, who married Helen Adele Carter

Children of Dr. William D. and Alberta (Carter) Anderson: William D. Anderson of Centerville, Mississippi, Mr. Anderson has three sons, Harry, William Towne, and Scott Anderson and one daughter, Carolyne Anderson; Lillie Lee Anderson; Bertie Anderson, married J. W. McCulloch of Charleston, Mississippi, their daughter Pauline married James Edward Davis and has a son, James Edward Davis, Jr.

HOWELL POLK CARTER

Born: September 14, 1844

Married: 1st: Adele Purnell, no issue

        2nd: Minnie Hynson, no issue

        3rd: Dora L. Johnston

Died: April 30, 1918

Children of Howell Polk and Dora L. (Johnston) Carter: Dora Maud Carter, born October 23, 1882; Howell Carter, Jr., married Florence Otis. They had two children, Marjorie Carter born August 22, 1923, and Howell Carter III born February 9, 1929; Ethel Lillian Carter, married Sidney Calongne, they had Dorothy Calongne, born March 25, 1910, who married Paul Geddes Borron and were the parents of Barbara Ann Borron, born July 22, 1935 and Paul Geddes Borron Jr., born June 14, 1938; Ethel Calongne, born October 9, 1911 and married James Hunter Dorman and were the parents of James H. Dorman, Jr., born September 26, 1936 and Carol Carter Dorman, born December 30, 1939. Sydney E. Calongne, born November 7, 1914; Mabel Anna Carter, born June 21, 1888 and married H. Watterson Reily. They had Gladys Beryl Reily who married Carlton C. Kemp and had Carlton Christie Kemp, Jr., Beverly Carter Reily who married Dr. Thomas B. White and had Beverly Stuart White, born August 27, 1937; Lillie Mary Carter. Married Wood H. Thompson. They had Lillie Carter Thompson, born November 8, 1915 and married James D. Sparks and had James Dilling Sparks, Jr. and Wood Thompson Sparks.

LYDIA ANNIE CARTER

Born: December 16, 1836

Married: 1st: Thomas Gibbes Morgan who was born on March 21, 1835 and died January 21, 1864, a prison of war on Johnson's Island in Lake Erie, when his youngest son, Howell, was 7 months and 20 days old. He was Captain of Company C, 7th Louisiana Infantry. He was born in Baton Rouge where the Old Capitol was built afterwards. That square of ground belonged to his father, Judge Thomas Gibbes Morgan and there his two older sisters and two brothers were born. Magnolia trees were planted to commemorate the birth of each and are still there in all their pristine glory, having changed their name from "Laurier" to "Magnolia." The Morgans who spoke French in their home, as do many in Louisiana, called the tree "Laurier-Amande" (Almond-Laurel) because of an imaginary similarity of its shape of flower to the almond.

2nd: George William Purnell on March 27, 1870

Died: December 31, 1915, in Dallas, Texas

Children of Thomas Gibbes and Lydia Annie (Carter) Morgan: Albert Carter Morgan, died in infancy; Thomas Gibbes Morgan III; died at age of twelve; Howell Morgan.

Captain Thomas Gibbes Morgan, who married Lydia, one of General Carter's daughters, was the son of Judge Thomas Gibbes Morgan of Baton Rouge and a member of an interesting and highly talented family.

David Morgan, first ancestor to come to America, went to Philadelphia in 1717, but returned to Wales, leaving his son, Evan Morgan, as a permanent settler. Evan was a partner in the Mount Holly, New Jersey, Iron Works. His son, George Morgan, married Mary Baynton and was a partner in the Philadelphia firm of Baynton, Wharton and Morgan. He served as Deputy Commissary General of Washington's Army at Valley Forge. One of his daughters, Anne Morgan, married Thomas S. Gibbes of South Carolina and was the grandmother of Charlotte Augusta Gibbes of Charleston, later the wife of John Jacob Astor. His son, John Morgan, married Margaret Bunyan and was the father of Judge Thomas Gibbes Morgan of Baton Rouge.

By his first wife, Eliza McKennan, Judge Morgan had a son, Philip Hickey Morgan, related through his mother to Thomas McKean, Signer of the Declaration of Independence, Chief Justice and Governor of Pennsylvania. Philip Hickey Morgan, born November 9, 1825, was educated in the public schools in Baton Rouge and in Paris, France. He served as a First Lieutenant in the Louisiana Volunteer Company in the Mexican War. He helped his father annotate the Louisiana Civil Code. On May 22, 1852 he married Beatrice Leslie Ford, daughter of Judge James Ford of Baton Rouge. He went to New Orleans where he was elected Judge of the Second District Court. During the War Between the States, he remained loyal to the Union. After the War he served as United States District Attorney in Louisiana, as a Justice of the Louisiana Supreme Court, a Judge of the International Court in Egypt, and Envoy Extraordinary and Minister Plenipotentiary to Mexico. He died August 12, 1900, and is buried in Allegheny Cemetery, Pittsburg, Pennsylvania. Two of the better known descendants of Philip Hickey Morgan are his granddaughters, Gloria Morgan (Mrs. Reginald Vanderbilt) and Thelma Morgan (Lady Furness), who have written the story of their lives in *Double Exposure*, published in 1958 by David McKay Company of New York. Their father, Harry Hays Morgan, who had been born at Aurora Plantation at Baton Rouge, was in the diplomatic service.

By his second wife, Judge Thomas Gibbes Morgan, had a daughter, Sarah Morgan, who was born in New Orleans on February 28, 1842. During the War Between the States, Sarah Morgan stayed with General Carter at his home "Linwood." Her diary, illustrated with pictures of her family and their home in Baton Rouge, as well as a picture of "Linwood" was first published in 1913 by Houghton Mifflin Company (*A Confederate Girl's Diary*). In 1960 the diary was republished in annotated form by the Indiana University Press. Sarah Morgan was married to Francis Warrington Dawson, a young Englishman who came South to fight for the Confederacy. Mr. Dawson was born in London on May 17, 1840, and was educated at the famous Crookall Academy in London and by private tutors. He served as Chief Ordnance Officer in General FitzHugh Lee's Cavalry Division. After the War he was editor of the Charleston, South Carolina, *News and Courier* and authored several books. He was a Knight of the Order of St. Gregory the Great.

Lavinia Morgan, another daughter of Judge Morgan, married Colonel Richard Coulter Drum, a native of Westmoreland County, Pennsylvania. In the foreword to Sarah Morgan Dawson's diary, Warrington Dawson, her son, says "Colonel Drum was largely instrumental in checking the Seccession movement in California, which would probably have assured the success of the South." During President Cleveland's first administration Colonel Drum, then a Brigadier, was Adjutant General of the United States Army.

George Mather Morgan, a Captain in the First Louisiana, served with Jackson in Virginia and was killed in service, the second of Judge Morgan's sons to die in the Confederate Army.

Eliza Morgan. Married Count Charles de la Noue.

James Morris Morgan, another son of Judge Morgan, was born in New Orleans on March 10, 1845. He entered the United States Naval Academy in 1860 and served as a Midshipman in the Confederate Navy. Since his sister-in-law, Lydia Carter, was a cousin of Mrs. Jefferson Davis, he was detailed to accompany her on her flight from Richmond. In October, 1865, he married Helen, daughter of George Trenholm of Charleston, Secretary of the Treasury of the

Confederacy. She died leaving a daughter. Mr. Morgan then went to Egypt to train Egyptian troops. In 1873 he married Gabriella Burroughs, granddaughter of Chancellor de Saussure of South Carolina. They had a daughter. Mr. Morgan served as Consul General of the United States to Australasia. He collaborated with John P. Marquand on *Prince and Boatswain: Sea Tales from the Recollections of Rear Admiral Charles E. Clark.*

The autobiography of James Morris Morgan was published by Houghton Mifflin in 1917 as *Recollections of a Rebel Reefer.* On page 11, Mr. Morgan comments, "I used to delight in going to beautiful Lynwood, the plantation of General Carter in the Parish of East Feliciana and some twenty miles from Baton Rouge. Howell Carter, one of the General's sons was near my own age and we were great friends. Howell had a beautiful sister whom I adored: the fact that she was a young lady in society made no difference to me. She acknowledged that I was her sweetheart and it was heaven for me to stand by the piano while she sang for me and besides my favorite brother, Gibbes, some ten years my senior, approved of my choice and complimented my good taste. One day Gibbes and Lydia Carter got married and it took me a long time to recover from the effects of their treachery. Gibbes was the last man I would have suspected of being my rival." On page 45 Mr. Morgan remarks, "A cavalry regiment appeared on the scene and among the privates I saw my old playmate and dear friend, Howell Carter, mounted on a fine big horse with a sabre as long as himself tied to him. Howell was only about a year older than I but he was big for his age."

Children of George William and Lydia Annie (Carter) Purnell: George William Purnell, Jr., born June 21, 1871 in Jefferson, Texas, married Pearl Brownlee in Dallas where they live. They had a son Dana Purnell who married a Miss Turquette and had a daughter, Barbara; Daisy Purnell, married Judge Cecil L. Simpson of Dallas County, Texas; Lydia Adele Purnell, born June 9, 1876, married Dr. William Frederick Hagaman, their daughter Ruth Hagaman married Will H. Benners and had a son Will H. Benners III and a son Frederick Hagaman Benners. Their son Frederick Purnell Hagaman married Hilda Bienvenue and they had a son John Frederick Hagaman, born May 1, 1939, their son Elmer Cook Hagaman died in infancy. Their daughter, Nettie Hagaman, born in March 1901 married Frank L. Norwood and had Nettie Adele Norwood and Frank L. Norwood, Jr., their son, George Hagaman married Beth Gilbert and had Carolyn and Mary Lou Hagaman. Their daughter Lydia Isabel Hagaman married Noel Fillastre and adopted a daughter, Sue.

HOWELL MORGAN

Born: June 1, 1863
Married: Thisba Ann Hutson of the H. Rider Haggard and the

famous Drs. Haggard family and of the Odell family of Odell, Bedfordshire, England on July 3, 1895

Children of Howell and Thisba Ann (Hutson) Morgan: Cecil Morgan; Mildred Morgan; Thomas Gibbes Morgan IV, born at "Linwood" on March 11, 1907, cadet, freshman year L.S.U. 1923-4. Member of Lambda Chi Alpha and Demolay, died in Alexandria, Egypt on August 16, 1924; Howell Morgan, Jr.; Howell Morgan is the compiler of the Carter Genealogy, a copy of which was lent to me by Mrs. C. M. Rouzan, Route 1, Box 57, Jackson, Louisiana; Mr. Morgan was a member of Sons of the Revolution, District of Columbia, May 6, 1903, and of the Louisiana Society, Sons of the American Revolution, 1919; Mr. Morgan spent ten years in the United States Indian Service in South Dakota, Oklahoma Territory, Nebraska, and Minnesota in the several successive capacities of Clerk, Agency Clerk, Chief Clerk, and Acting Indian Agent. For two years he farmed at "Linwood." He was a farmer and banker from 1904 to 1912. Assistant Supervisor of Public Accounts in Louisiana 1912-1919. Treasurer of the State of Louisiana, 1920-1924. State Bank Examiner, 1924-1928. Democrat, Mason, Episcopalian.

JUDGE CECIL MORGAN

Born: August 20, 1898

Married: Margaret Harriet Geddes on April 20, 1932

Children of Judge Cecil and Margaret Harriet (Geddes) Morgan: Cecil Morgan; Margaret Morgan

Judge Morgan received his Bachelor of Laws Degree at Louisiana State University in 1919. He served as Deputy Clerk of Court of East Baton Rouge Parish, 1919-1920, and was admitted to the Louisiana Bar in 1920. From 1920 to 1941 he practiced law in Shreveport, Louisiana, part of that time with the Esso Standard Oil Company. He was United States Commissioner for the Western District of Louisiana, 1922-1925. He served in the Louisiana Legislature from 1928 to 1932 and in the Louisiana Senate from 1932 to 1934. He was a Judge of the First Judicial District of Caddo Parish from 1934 to 1936. From 1943-1945 he was Associate General Counsel of the Esso Standard Oil Company, Vice President in Charge of Manufacturing Operations, Louisiana Division, 1949 to 1952. Since 1952 he has been a member of the Board of Directors of the Company and Executive Assistant to the Chairman of the Board since 1955. Since 1952 he has served as Counsellor to the Standard Oil Company of New Jersey and Vice President of the Esso Standard Oil Company. Judge Morgan is a member of the International House and Boston Club in New Orleans and of the Metropolitan Club in New York. Office: 30 Rockefeller Plaza. *Who's Who in America.*

HOWELL MORGAN, JR.

Born: April 8, 1910, at "Linwood."

Married: Doris Mildred Dupuy on June 16, 1939. She was born on August 28, 1916. Doris Dupuy is a lineal descendant of Light Horse Harry (General Henry) Lee, who put down the Pennsylvania Whiskey Insurrection in 1794. Howell Morgan's ancestor, Major Richard Howell, Governor of New Jersey, led his New Jersey troops in support of General Lee.

Children of Howell and Doris Mildred (Dupuy) Morgan, Jr.: David Lee Morgan, born March 11, 1940; Howell Morgan, Jr., is a graduate of the Baton Rouge High School, attended Centenary College and L.S.U., member of Kappa Alpha Fraternity.

CHARLES PARSONS CARTER

Born: April 3, 1850

Married: Lou Lum, a niece of George Kelly, a noted foundryman and manufacturer of Kelly plows.

Children of Charles Parsons and Lou (Lum) Carter: William Howell Carter, married Nellie Cline; their daughter, Lou Jane Carter married Chris Reisor and had a child, Nancy Nell Reisor; George Kelly Carter; Roy Carter, died in infancy.

ELIZABETH PENNY CARTER

Born: 1816

Married: Captain John Caffery Walker on March 22, 1836, in Feliciana Parish, Louisiana. Captain Walker was born March 18, 1796 and died in 1861. He was a great-nephew of Rachel Donelson, wife of President Andrew Jackson, through his mother, Rachel Caffery (wife of George Walker) and his grandmother, Mary Donelson (sister of Mrs. Andrew Jackson and wife of John Caffery)

Died: November, 1853

Children of Captain John Caffery and Elizabeth Penny (Carter) Walker: Annie Eliza Walker; Wilhelmina Walker, born 1839, died July 15, 1871, married a Mr. McNair; Parsons Carter Walker, born 1848, married Emma Woolford, died 1904; Fanny Walker, born 1846, married Harry Hendy, has descendants in Cincinnati, Ohio

Vera Morel of New Orleans sent information on this branch. She is compiling *The Descendants of George Walker of Virginia*, from whom Captain John Caffery Walker descends.

ANNIE ELIZA WALKER

Born: June 22, 1837

Married: John Barrett Sydnor (1835-1877)

Died: December 21, 1904

Children of John Barrett and Annie Eliza (Walker) Sydnor: Mary Badger Sydnor, born October 22, 1859, married Octave J. Morel, died March 7, 1924; Annie Baylor Sydnor, born November 26, 1871, married October 16 1895, to William E. Hamilton of Houston, Texas, their children: Annie Hamilton, born September 26, 1896; Brooke Hamilton, born August 7, 1899 and married August 1934 to Jewel Kendall; Eleanor Hamilton, born March 5, 1902 and married Dr. Carl B. Young on February 1, 1922, Annie B. Sydnor died Jan. 30, 1952; Sarah Sydnor, born July 22, 1863, married Charles C. Oden on October 8, 1888, they have a son Sydnor Oden born May 25, 1902, he married Olga Poe, they live in Houston and have one son, Sarah Sydnor died June 19, 1944; Kate Sydnor, born November 20, 1865, married Frank Sawyer on June 27, 1888, they had a daughter, Nadine Bettina Sawyer, born August 17, 1889, married 1st Albert Thomas Kung on June 6, 1914 and 2nd Pat Robinson, Kate Sydnor died Jan. 6, 1934; Barrett G. Sydnor, born Jan. 12, 1873, married Fannie Thomas on February 6, 1896, their son, Edward Sydnor was born Jan. 23, 1897, married Nora Delaney Wallace on Feb. 22, 1947 and have a son, Edward Sydnor, Barrett G. Sydnor died Jan. 20, 1942; Edward Garland Sydnor, born October 14, 1861, died Jan. 25, 1892; John Walker Sydnor, born February 15, 1857, died April 14, 1902.

MARY SYDNOR

Married: Octave Morel

Children of Octave and Mary (Sydnor) Morel: May Morel; Vera Morel, 1472 Arabella St., New Orleans; Octa Morel, Holly Bluff, near Covington, Louisiana, married James Lyman Crump; Anita Morel, married a Mr. Tipping, 1472 Arabella St., New Orleans; Louise Morel, married a Mr. Townsend, lives in New Orleans; Ruth Morel, lives in New Jersey.

MARY ANN DORTCH CARTER

Born: 1814 in St. Francisville, West Feliciana Parish, Louisiana
Married: 1st: David Smith
        2nd: Wallace Badger

Children of David and Mary Ann Dortch (Carter) Smith: A. D. Smith; William Smith; Ida Lillie Smith; Mary E. Smith, born 1839, died 1924, married Joseph H. Barnett, they had children: Mary Ida Barnett, born 1858, died at seven years old, and Thomas L. Barnett, born 1860, died 1931, married Emily Louise Shaffett

Children of Thomas L. and Emily Louise (Shaffett) Barnett: Eula Barnett; Lucy Barnett; Louise Barnett; Bessie Barnett; Mary L. Barnett; Claude Barnett; Thomas Barnett.

Children of Wallace and Mary Dortch (Carter) Badger: Francis Edmond Badger, married Mary Ann Dortch, daughter of David Dortch and Mary A. Young, the sister of R. T. Young; they were the parents of Edward E. Badger, born in 1854 and died in 1878, of Emma Badger, of Nonie Badger who died aged 6; of Mollie Badger who died aged 2; of Frances Badger who married a Mr. Black; Anna Mary Badger, married Joseph H. Stewart, they had the following children: Claude, Wallace, Odell, and Joseph H. Stewart, Jr.; Wallace Badger.

WILLIAM DORTCH CARTER

Born: January 30, 1808
Married: 1st: Sarah Cammack
        2nd: Mrs. Elizabeth Dortch, nee Worley, widow of his cousin, Washington Dortch
Died: July 25, 1859
Children of William Dortch and Sarah (Cammack) Carter: Esther Ann Carter
Children of William Dortch and Elizabeth (Worley) Carter: William Parsons Carter.

ESTHER ANN CARTER

Married: 1st: Caleb Worley
        2nd: Major E. C. Wharton
Children of Caleb and Esther Ann (Carter) Worley: George Worley.

GEORGE WORLEY

Married: 1st: Prim Woolford
        2nd: Leona Tilford
Children of George Worley: Eunice Worley; George C. Worley (married Anita Barber); Thisba Morgan Worley; Leona Worley (married Ray Miller); Frances Day Worley (died aged 14); Amelia Cecile Worley.

EUNICE WORLEY

Married: Walter P. Spencer
Children of Walter P. and Eunice (Worley) Spencer: Priscilla Spencer, married Noel van Riel; Eunice Worley Spencer, married Wilbur T. Hoffman.

PRUDENCE CARTER

Born: 1780-1790
Moved with her husband George King, nephew of Caleb King, to Clermont County, Ohio in 1814. Letter of C. F. Farrar, Kingston, Mississippi, to Isaac A. Carter, Darrington, Miss. Aug. 24, 1891

1820 CENSUS, GOSHEN TOWNSHIP, CLERMONT COUNTY, OHIO
George King: 1 male born 1775-1794; 1 male born 1810-1820; 1 female born 1775-1794

1830 CENSUS, GOSHEN, CLERMONT COUNTY, OHIO

George King: 1 male born 1780-1790; 1 male born 1815-1820; 1 female born 1780-1790; 1 female born 1810-1815; I female born 1820-1825

1840 CENSUS, GOSHEN, CLERMONT COUNTY, OHIO

Village of Goshen, George King: 1 male born 1780-1790; 1 male born 1820-1825; 1 male born 1830-1835; 1 female born 1790-1800; 1 female born 1820-1825; 1 female born 1825-1830

Thomas King: 1 male born 1810-1820; 1 female born 1810-1820

From HENRY PHIPPS of Mississippi Territory to Isaac Gaillard of same. Consideration $400. Tract of land bounded on south by Buffalo River on west by *torn*, other sides by vacant land at time of Grant; 500 acres etc. (s) HENRY X PHIPPS. Test: Adam Ellis and William Conner. Dower released by PHOEBE PHIPPS, WIFE OF THE WITHIN MENTIONED HENRY PHIPPS. /s/ PHOEBE X PHIPPS 16 January 1801. Deed Book B, page 334. Adams County, Mississippi. Page 470 Mrs. McBee's NATCHEZ COURT RECORDS, 1765-1805. (Book E, p 68) Claim No. 1077 Spanish Grant to HENRY PHIPPS, 500 acres on Buffalo Creek, 20 miles south of Natchez, adjoining Joseph Dove, New Orleans, 30 August 1793 by Carondolet. (Book E, p 71) 16 January 1801. HENRY PHIPPS for $400 to him paid conveyed the above to Isaac Gaillard. /s/ HENRY X PHIPPS, PHOEBE X. PHIPPS who renounced dower.

Deed Book O. p 157, Adams County, Mississippi 26 August 1822. An agreement. Whereas: the late JESSE CARTER of Adams County, Mississippi, deceased, did by his last will and testament convey unto Samuel Postlethwaite, Esq. of Natchez all that tract of land on Second Creek in said County, containing 250 acres, the same tract originally granted to SARAH KENNARD, also slaves mentioned in will, etc. together with one-half the residue of said JESSE'S Estate (after payment of just debts) in trust to Samuel Postlethwaite for the use of LYDIA, daughter of said JESSE and GEORGE POINDEXTER, JR., grandson of said JESSE, etc. Now the undersigned Executor and Execturix deeming it both necessary and expedient that whole estate, real and personal, as conveyed by the said JESSE afsd. be sold by the said Trustee agreeably to the provisions of the last will and testament of the said JESSE and we so hereby authorize and direct the same. /s/ I. E. TRASK, ELIZA TRASK, LYDIA C. WILLIAMS, LEWIS WILLIAMS. Test. Stephen Pynchon and J. L. Trask for Israel *L*. TRASK and ELIZA'S signing. Stephen Pynchon and Nehemiah Willis for LEWIS AND LYDIA C. WILLIAMS, signing. Proof: Commonwealth of Massachusetts, Hampden County: August 29, 1822, personally appeared I. E. TRASK, Esq., and ELIZA TRASK, his wife above named and August 26, 1822 personally appeared

LEWIS WILLIAMS AND LYDIA C. WILLIAMS, HIS WIFE, and severally acknowledged the above instrument to be their free act and deed. Before me, Stephen Pynchon, Chief Justice of the Court of Sessions and Justice of the Peace for Hampden County. Deed Book O, p 158 sold the slaves and Deed Book O p 220 sold the 250 acres of land.

Executors Bonds 1811-1814 p 135, Adams County, Miss. Bond of JESSE CARTER, Executor of Estate of NEHEMIAH CARTER (Senior) April 5, 1814. $1,500. Israel Smith, Security.

WRIGHT

No WRIGHTS in the 1792 Spanish Census of the Old Natchez District.

Claiborne County, Mississippi, formed in 1802 from Pickering (later Jefferson) County, which itself had formed part of the Old Natchez District.

Claiborne County Records exist from the following dates:

Deeds (1802)

Marriage (1816)

Orphan's Court Minutes (1803) ; Not indexed.

Probate (1831)

Tax Rolls (1802)

Wills (1803)

Claiborne County Tax Rolls:

1802: NO WRIGHTS

1803: NO WRIGHTS

1805: JAMES WRIGHT

1807: JOHN WRIGHT (1) white poll and 2 slaves.

1810: Two WILLIAM WRIGHTS

Warren County, Mississippi, formed in 1809 from Claiborne County.

Warren County Records exist from the following dates:

Deeds (1810)

Marriage (1811)

Probate (1818)

Wills (1810)

Tax Rolls (1818)

Warren County Tax Roll:

1818: Jesse Wright; Abel Write; Thomas Write; James Oliver.

Joint 1810 Census of Claiborne and Warren Counties, Mississippi

Abel Wright

Elizabeth Wright

Hezekiah Wright
Jane (maybe James) Wright
Thomas Wright
William Wright
William Wright
Mary Right 1 male born after 1789; 1 female born before 1789
John Right 1 male born before 1789; 1 female born before 1789; 1 female born after 1789
James Oliver 1 male born before 1789; 1 male born after 1789; 1 female born before 1789; 1 female born after 1789
1816 Census, Warren County, Mississippi
James Oliver
Jame Wright

ABEL WRIGHT

1820 CENSUS, WARREN COUNTY, MISSISSIPPI

Abel Wright

1 male born 1775-1794; 2 males born 1810-1820; 1 female born 1794-1804; 2 females born 1810-1820.

1830 CENSUS, WARREN COUNTY, MISSISSIPPI

Abel Wright

1 male born 1780-1790; 1 male born 1810-1815; 1 male born 1820-1825; 1 female born 1790-1800; 1 female born 1810-1815; 1 female born 1820-1825; 1 slave.

Abel Wright to Jesse Wright. Sale of negro man and a black mare. Test: Thomas H. Dearwood. 5 Oct. 1811. Deed Book A, page 23, Warren County, Mississippi.

Wm. H. and Mary Wright sold land adjoining that of Abel Wright. 6 April 1854. Deed Book Y, page 483, Warren County.

JESSIE WRIGHT, JUNIOR

Absolem Stampley sold land to Jesse Wright, Junior, which land was first granted by the Spanish Government to Hugh Matheese and by him transferred to John Stampley, Sen'r, deceased, joining land granted to Jacob Stampley, now owned by James Hyland. 24 July 1829. Witnessed by Hugh Russell and Abel Wright. Deed Book E, page 200, Warren County, Miss.

Tract Book page 8, Entry No. 122, Warren County, Miss. U.S.A. to Jesse Wright, Junior. Dec. 8, 1826. The E½ of NE¼, Sec. 9, T13, R3E.

Probate File No. 983. Estate of Jesse Wright, Junior. Warren County, Mississippi. Bond 25th Nov. 1839, Mary Wright, Admx, Benjamin Wright and Isaac Hamilton. Appraised same date by James E.

Sharkey, Hugh Russell, Alexander Russell, Wm. Blackburn, and Reuben Gibson.

1840 CENSUS, WARREN COUNTY MISSISSIPPI

Mary Wright

1 male born 1820-1825; 1 male born 1830-1835; 1 female born 1790-1800; 1 female born 1820-1825.

1850 CENSUS, WARREN COUNTY, MISSISSIPPI

748, 772

Mary Wright born in 1791 in South Carolina; James B. Wright born in 1831 in Mississippi; 2 slaves.

Deed of Gift. From James Russell, his wife, Laura Russell; John Russell, his wife, Rebecca Russell; and Eli W. Russell TO: Mary Ann Maples, the wife of John W. Maples. . . Consideration, Love and Affection. . . All our interest in the property of the Estate of Jesse Wright, deceased, descending to us through our deceased half brother, William Bradford, the real estate being from NE¼ of Sec. 9, T13, R3E (land Jesse Wright, Jr., bought from Absolem Stampley in 1829). 5 March 1866. Deed Book DD, page 283, Warren County, Mississippi.

Marriages, Warren County, Mississippi:

John W. Wright married Mary Ann Russell. Oct 22, 1854, A. S. Allen, Surety. Book G, page 287.

William Bradford married Jane Owens. Dec. 13, 1849. Claiborne Steele, Surety. Book G, page 56.

Alexander Russell Married on March 10, 1819, but bride's name is not shown. Jacob Hyland, Surety. Book C, page 29.

Eli W. Russell married Laura D. Fortner. Jan 8, 1867, Martin Fortner, Surety. Book H, page 73.

John Russell married Rebecca E. Mathis. Oct. 31, 1847. John Blackman, Surety. Book A, page 97.

James Russell married Laura Ford. Mar 4, 1858. J. C. Chappell, Surety. Book G, page 448.

Real Estate belonging to Heirs of late Jesse Wright equally divided between Mary Ann Maples and James B. Wright P. H. Webb and James Russell, witnesses. Deed Book EE, page 146. 4 Oct 1866.

1850 CENSUS, WARREN COUNTY, MISSISSIPPI, 749, 773

William Bradford born in 1817 in Mississippi; Jane Bradford born in 1815 in Mississippi; John Owen born in 1827 in South Carolina; Robt Dixen born in 1826 in Mississippi.

1850 CENSUS, WARREN COUNTY, MISSISSIPPI, 751, 775

John Russell born in 1821 in Mississippi; Rebecca Russell born in 1828 in Mississippi; Mary E. Russell born in 1849 in Mississippi; Martha W. Russell born in 1850 in Mississippi.

1860 CENSUS, WARREN COUNTY, MISSISSIPPI 1332, 1310

P. Knowland born in 1816 in Mississippi; W. Bradford born in 1816 in Mississippi.

1860 CENSUS, WARREN COUNTY, MISSISSIPPI, 1324, 1302

Jas. Russell born in 1820 in Mississippi; Laura Russell born in 1840 in Mississippi; Charles Russell born in 1860 in Mississippi.

1860 CENSUS, WARRENTON, WARREN COUNTY, MISSISSIPPI 1440, 1407

J. Maples born in 1820 in Virginia; Mary Maples born in 1837 in Mississippi; Martha Maples born in 1855 in Mississippi; Charles Maples born in 1852 in Mississippi; William Maples born in 1849 in Mississippi; George Maples born in 1858 in Mississippi.

1870 CENSUS, RED BONE, WARREN COUNTY, MISSISSIPPI 280, 270

James Russel born in 1827 in Mississippi; Looren (?) Russel born in 1840 in Mississippi; Sally Russel born in 1851 in Mississippi; Samuel Russel born in 1867 in Mississippi; Thomas Russel born in 1869 in Mississippi.

1870 CENSUS, RED BONE, WARREN COUNTY, MISSISSIPPI 281, 271

M. A. Maples born in 1839 in Mississippi; Mattie Maples born in 1856 in Mississippi; George Maples born in 1851 in Mississippi.

1870 CENSUS, RED BONE, WARREN COUNTY, MISSISSIPPI 293, 283

E. W. Russel born in 1841 in Mississippi (male); L. Dee Russel born in 1848 in Mississippi (female); H. A. Russel born in 1868 in Mississippi (male); E. A. Russel born in 1870 in Mississippi (male).

JAMES B. WRIGHT

Born: ca 1831 in Mississippi

Married: 1st: Arrabella Bean. Aug 2, 1855. James D. Oliver, Surety. Book G, page 330. Warren County, Miss.

2nd: Julia Casey. May 6, 1872. J. H. Chappell, Surety Book H, page 358, Warren County, Miss.

James B. Wright and Juliet (sometimes Julia), his wife of Warren County, Miss. sold land conveyed by Absolem Stampley to Jesse Wright, Jr., in 1829 to Adaline Cowan. J. E. Arnold, Witness. 25 Feb 1878. Acknowledged 11 June 1878.

Deed Book 92, page 220, Warren County, Miss. 26 Sept. 1899. From George H. Jewell of Morehouse Parish, Louisiana To Mary Wright. Consideration. . . Love and Affection which I bear toward my sister-in-law, Mary Wright. . . all my interest in NW¼ of NE¼ and part of NE¼ of Sec 9, T13, R3E, it being all my interest as heir at law of Betty Wright, daughter of James Wright.

Deed Book 93, Warren County, Miss. 16 April 1900. George W. Hirsch, Julia Girod and Mary Wright sold to E. H. Russell interest in lands owned by late James B. Wright, deceased, in Warren County described as N½ of NE¼, Sec 9, T13, R3E, except part sold to Adaline Cowan.

Ed Girod married Mrs. Julia (widow of James B. Wright). June 16, 1890. Theo G. Birchett, Surety. Book I, page 390, Warren County, Miss.

JAMES D. OLIVER

Born: June 9, 1784

Married: Polly Wright on April 16, 1812. James Estell on the bond.

Marriages, Book B, page 23, Warren County, Mississippi. J. E. S. King's MISSISSIPPI COURT RECORDS, 1799-1835.

Died: June 18, 1829

In a letter written to Owen Johnson from Eudora, Arkansas, on March 28, 1942, A. A. Wright, son of Robert Wright and grandson of Dorrell Wright, says that Dorrell Wright's mother, after Dorrell Wright's father (John Wright) died, married a Mr. Oliver and had a son, Bill Oliver who died in the War between the States. All these Wrights and Olivers, he says, are buried in Cedars, Mississippi, south of Vicksburg. Further he writes that Dorrell Wright and his second wife, Mary Ann Landfair, are buried at Bayou Mason Church, five miles west from Old Floyd, Louisiana. William Landfair, father of Mary Ann Landfair, is buried in a graveyard two miles south of Forest, Louisiana.

Gravestones in the Beard Cemetery, Yokena, Mississippi:

JAMES D. OLIVER	MARY
Born: June 9, 1784	WIFE OF JAMES D. OLIVER
Died: June 18, 1829	Born: December 30, 1787
Aged	Died: January 9, 1868
45 years, 9 days	

1820 Census, Warren County, Mississippi, JAMES OLIVER, 1 male born 1775-1794; 2 males born 1810-1820; 2 females born 1810-1820; 1 female born 1775-1794; 1 slave.

Deed Book Z, page 11, Warren County, Mississippi.
24 October 1854. Mary A. Fortner of Warren County to Wm. L. Sharkey of same.

Sale of my undivided interest being one sixth part of Lot 4, Sec 25, Township 14, Range 3 East in Warren County ON WHICH MRS. MARY OLIVER NOW LIVES, WHICH TRACT OF LAND WAS ENTERED BY MY FATHER, JAMES D. OLIVER and descended to me jointly with four other children, as one of his heirs at law; 85 acres. /s/ Mary A. Fortner. Test: D. and F. Maynadier.

Probate File 425. THE ESTATE OF JAMES D. OLIVER, DE-CEASED. July Court, 1829.

Application of MARY OLIVER as Administratrix, approved and bond of $1,500 with Peter G. Miller and JESSE WRIGHT as Sureties.

1830 CENSUS, WARREN COUNTY, MISSISSIPPI
Mary Oliver
1 male born 1790-1800; 1 male born 1810-1815; 1 male born 1815-1820; 1 male born 1820-1825; 1 female born 1780-1790; 2 females born 1815-1820; 1 female born 1825-1830; 1 slave.

1840 CENSUS, WARREN COUNTY, MISSISSIPPI
Mary Oliver
1 male born 1820-1825; 1 male born 1825-1830; 1 female born 1790-1800; 2 females born 1825-1830; 3 slaves.

1850 CENSUS, WARREN COUNTY, MISSISSIPPI
786, 810
Mary Oliver born in 1787 in South Carolina; John Oliver born in 1824 in Mississippi; 2 slaves.

1860 CENSUS, WARREN COUNTY, MISSISSIPPI 986, 977
Jno Oliver born in 1823 in Mississippi; Mary Oliver born in 1800 in South Carolina; 2 slaves.

1870 CENSUS, RED BONE PRECINCT, WARREN COUNTY, MISSISSIPPI 297, 287
John Olliver born in 1823 in Mississippi.

1880 CENSUS, KLEIN'S STORE AND RED BONE, WARREN COUNTY, MISS. 611, 621
John Oliver born in 1822 in Mississippi where his parents were born. Tract Book, page 123, Warren County, Miss. ca 1831-1834. U.S.A. to J. D. Oliver, Lot No. 4, Sec 25, T14, R3E.

Deed Book NN, page 767, Warren County, Miss. From Benjamin F. Oliver of Warren County to John Oliver of the same: 1/12th part of Lot 2, Sec. 25, T14, R3E, also 1/12th part of Lot 4, Sec. 25, T14, R3E, known as the Oliver Tract. It being my entire interest as heir at law to said tract of land. 18 April 1871.

Deed Book NN, page 768, Warren County, Miss. From Martha Jane Bolls and J. W. Bolls, her husband of Hinds County, Miss., to John Oliver of Warren County, 1/12 part of Lot 5, Sec. 25, T14, R3E and also 1/12th part of Lot 4, Sec. 25, T14, R3E, the Oliver Tract. 25 Jan. 1872.

Deed Book 77, page 3, Warren County, Miss. From Nancy Ann Beard and J. Warren Beard of Warren County, Miss. to John Bolls their part of Lot 4, Sec. 25, T14, R3E. 15 June 1892.

Deed Book 204, page 501, Warren County, Miss. From John Oliver of Warren County to the Heirs of Caroline and William Readen of the same one half interest in Lot 5, T14, R3E. Heirs of Caroline and William Readen: George, Marry, John, and Annie. (Marry was married to Mr. Thompson and Annie was married to Mr. Beard). 3 Nov 1883.

1850 CENSUS, WARREN COUNTY, MISSISSPPI, 788, 812

William Reden born in 1814 in Louisiana; Caroline Reden born in 1815 in Mississippi; James Reden born in 1838 in Mississippi; William Reden born in 1840 in Mississippi; George Reden born in 1845 in Mississippi; Mary Reden born in 1848 in Mississippi.

1860 CENSUS, WARREN COUNTY, MISSISSIPPI, 985, 976

Wm Redding born in 1820 in Mississippi; Caroline Redding born in 1820 in Mississippi; Wm Redding born in 1840 in Mississippi; Mary Redding born in 1850 in Mississippi; George Redding born in 1851 in Mississippi; John Redding born in 1854 in Mississippi; Lucy Redding born in 1856 in Mississippi; Laura Redding born in 1857 in Mississippi; Agnes Redding born in 1858 in Mississippi.

1850 CENSUS, WARREN COUNTY, MISSISSIPPI, 759, 783

Hiram Fortner born in 1814 in Mississippi; Mary A. Fortner born in 1818 in Mississippi; Mary J. Fortner born in 1838 in Mississippi; Elizabeth M. Fortner born in 1840 in Mississippi; John W. Fortner born in 1843 in Mississippi; Martin Fortner born in 1845 in Mississippi; Laura Fortner born in 1848 in Mississippi.

1860 CENSUS, WARREN COUNTY, MISSISSIPPI, 1323, 1301

Mary Fortner born in 1810 in Mississippi; Wm Fortner born in 1848 in Mississippi; Martin Fortner born in 1850 in Mississippi; Laura Fortner born in 1846 in Mississippi; Anna Fortner born in 1852 in Mississippi.

1870 CENSUS, RED BONE PRECINCT, WARREN COUNTY, MISSISSIPPI 279, 279

Martin Fortner born in 1845 in Mississippi; Eliza Boden born in 1841 in Mississippi; Preston Boden born in 1859 in Mississippi; Charlie Maples born in 1851 in Mississippi.

1880 CENSUS, KLEIN'S STORE AND RED BONE PRECINCT, WARREN COUNTY, MISS. 525, 535

Martin L. Fortner born in 1846 in Mississippi; Anna E. Fortner born in 1844 in Mississippi; Ewing Fortner born in 1876 in Mississippi.

1880 CENSUS, KLEIN'S STORE AND RED BONE PRECINCT, WARREN COUNTY, MISSISSIPPI 609, 619

Warren Beard born in 1844 in Mississippi; Anna Beard, wife, born in 1853 in Mississippi.

Children: James Beard born in 1874 in Mississippi; Lucien Beard born in 1876 in Mississippi; Samuel Beard born in 1878 in Mississppi; Carrie Beard born in December, 1879, in Mississippi.

WILLIAM H. OLIVER

Born: June 29, 1820, in Mississippi

Married: 1st: Frances (Fanny) Wright. September 2, 1847. Tobias Stephens on the bond. Marriages, Book A, page 114, Warren County, Mississippi.

2nd: Mrs. Laura A. Powers on May 4, 1854.

Died: February 15, 1865.

Children of William H. and Frances (Wright) Oliver: Benjamin Oliver, John William Oliver, Martha Jane Oliver, Henry Clay Oliver. Guardian Bonds and Letters, March 1859, to April 1871, page 63: Wm. H. Oliver, Guardian of the minor heirs of Frances Oliver: Benjamin Oliver, John William Oliver, Martha Jane Oliver, and Henry C. Oliver. Wm. H. Oliver, John J. Higdon, and Thomas Tompkins gave bond on November 28, 1853.

1850 CENSUS, WARREN COUNTY, MISSISSIPPI 763, 787

William Oliver born in 1823 in Mississippi; Francis Oliver born in 1831 in Mississippi; Benjamin F. Oliver born in 1848 in Mississippi; Martha J. Oliver born in 1849 or 1850 in Mississippi; Mary M. Wright born in 1808 in Mississippi; John Wright born in 1833 in Mississippi; Elizabeth Wright born in 1837 in Mississippi; Henry C. Wright born in 1843 in Mississippi; Elizabeth Clark born in 1828 in North Carolina; John Clark born in 1830 in North Carolina; 30 slaves.

1860 CENSUS, HINDS COUNTY, MISSISSIPPI 1325, 1343

W. H. Oliver born in 1820 in Mississippi; L. Oliver born in 1829 in Mississippi; W. Powers born in 1848 in Mississippi; B. Oliver born in 1848 in Mississippi; C. Powers born in 1848 in Mississippi; M. Oliver born in 1849 in Mississippi; J. Oliver born in 1851 in Mississippi; W. E. Watson born in 1839 in Mississippi; 40 slaves.

In Chapel Hill Cemetery, nine miles east of Utica, Mississippi, and seven miles south of Learned, Mississippi, is the grave of William H. Oliver born June 29, 1820, and died February 15, 1865, and the grave of John Oliver, born February 15, 1851, and died August 28, 1866. See Marriage and Cemetery Records of Hinds County, Mississippi by Mary J. Berry (1951), pages 430 and 434.

Among the graves in the Wright Family Plot in the Presbyterian Churchyard in Yokena, Mississippi, is that of Fanny M. Oliver born February 24, 1831, and died September 1, 1853. She is named on her tomb as the wife of William H. Oliver.

Marriage License, Book 6, page 328, Claiborne County, Miss. W. H. Oliver and Mrs. Laura A. Powers; License 2 May 1854; Ceremony 4 May, 1854. Bondsman: John R. Powers.

From: Chancery Clerk's Office, Raymond, Hinds County, Miss.:

Deed Book 23, page 434, 4 Oct 1854. From: WILLIAM H. OLIVER OF CLAIBORNE COUNTY, MISS. To: Reuben Collins of Hinds County, Miss. Trustee Amos R. Johnson and John Shelton of Hinds County, Miss. Oliver indebted to Collins for $6,400, two notes and as security pledges lands in Hinds County, the NE¼ and E½ of NW¼, Sec 21, T5, R4W; the N½ of Sec 21 and W½ of NW¼, Sec 21, T5, R4W, 640 acres. /s/ W. H. Oliver, R. Collins, A. R. Johnson, John Shelton. Ack. by Oliver 18 Dec 1854.

Deed Book 25, page 104. 7 Feb 1857. From: WILLIAM H. OLIVER AND LAURA A., HIS WIFE OF HINDS COUNTY, MISS. To: John D. Cobb of Vicksburg, Miss. Trustees William R. Miles and Dan'l Adams and Douglas West of New Orleans, La. Whereas: 3 Feb 1857 Oliver drew two bills of exchange, one for $5,000 payable ten months after date and one for $6,000. . . . and as security Oliver has pledged certain lands in Hinds County, the NE¼ and E½ of NW¼, Sec 21, T5, R4W, etc. 640 acres. /s/ W. H. OLIVER, L. A. OLIVER, John D. Cobb. Ack by W. H. OLIVER AND L. A. OLIVER ON 7 Jan 1860.

Probate File 1949. ESTATE OF WILLIAM H. OLIVER OF HINDS COUNTY, MISS. He died 15 Feb 1865. Widow Laura A. Oliver applied for Administration on the Estate 6 Nov 1865, mentioning children, hers and also stepchildren, none named. Later 4 Dec 1865, S. B. Thomas was Administrator. Estate finally adjudged insolvent: List of some of creditors and amount they received: J. B. Wright: $2.65 on a claim of $100; B. F. Oliver, minor, J. B. Wright, Guardian, $145.10 on a claim of $5,568.64; Martha J. Bolls (Mattie J. Oliver married J. W. Bolls in 1865) $48.30 on a claim of $1,856.21 and many others. J. B. Wright put in a claim as Guardian of B. G. and J. W. Oliver, minor heirs of Frances M. Oliver, for $11,137.28 for hire of slaves from Oct 11, 1853 to Feb 15, 1865, claim dated 6 Aug 1866. On 14 Jan 1867 a memo states that J. W. Oliver is now deceased.

BENJAMIN F. OLIVER

B. F. Oliver married Jessie Stauer. April 11, 1887. Tobias Stevens on the bond. Marriages, Book I, page 258, Warren County, Mississippi.

1880 Census, Warren County, Mississippi, Klines Store, 50, 54
Ben F. Oliver born in 1849 in Mississippi.

MARTHA J. OLIVER

Book 5, page 392, Hinds County, Miss. (Back of p 31)
J. W. Bolls and MATTIE J. OLIVER. Bond Date 23 May 1865. Bondsman: W. L. Tucker.

Deed Book 31, page 254, Chancery Clerk's Office, Raymond, Hinds County, Mississippi. 17 March 1868. From: Sarah A. Ellison of Hinds County, Mississippi. To: MARTHA J. BOLLS, WIFE OF J. WESLEY BOLLS OF SAME. Consideration: $720 for land in Hinds County, Miss., the S½ of SW¼ and S½ of W½ of SW¼, all Sec. 7, T5, R1W, 180 acres. /s/ Sarah A. Ellison and ack. 17 March, 1868.

1870 Census, Township 5, R 3, Hinds County, Mississippi

P.O. Edwards, 240, 240

John W. Bolls born in 1834 in Mississippi; Martha Bolls born in 1849 in Mississippi; Fanny Bolls born in 1866 in Mississippi; Anna Bolls born in 1868 in Mississippi; S. A. Ellerson born in 1815 in Tennessee (female).

1880 Census, 4th District, Raymond Precinct, Hinds County, Mississippi, 616, 616

J. W. Bolls born in 1835 in Mississippi; Mat (?) Bolls born in 1842 in Mississippi, wife.

Children: Fannie Bolls born in 1865 in Mississippi; Annie Bolls born i n1868 in Mississippi; Lizzie Bolls born in 1870 in Mississippi; Mary Bolls born in 1874 in Mississippi; Nannie Bolls born in 1875 in Mississippi; Dudley Bolls born in 1877 in Mississippi; Olive Bolls born in January, 1880, in Mississippi.

DORRELL WRIGHT

Born: 1809-1810 in Mississippi.

Married: 1st: Nessa Saunders on April 25, 1831, in Warren County, Mississippi.

2nd: Mary Ann Landfair on February 24, 1848, in East Carroll Parish, Louisiana.

Died: 1870-1880.

Children of Dorrell and Nessa (Saunders) Wright: Christopher Columbus Wright; Dorrell Wright; Gibeon or Gideon Wright; Keightly Wright; Lafayette Wright; Mary Jane Wright; Robert Wright; William Wright.

Children of Dorrell and Mary Ann (Landfair) Wright: Anna Wright; Mattie Wright; Sarah Elizabeth Wright; Susan Wright; Thomas Wright.

1850 CENSUS, CARROLL PARISH, LOUISIANA

Dorrell Wright born in 1810 in Mississippi; Mary A. Wright born in 1830 in Louisiana; Lafayette Wright born in 1832 in Mississippi; Robert Wright born in 1833 in Mississippi; Kultz (?) Wright born in 1834 in Mississippi; Gibeon Wright born in 1836 in Mississippi; Dorrell Wright born in 1838 in Mississippi; William Wright born in 1839 in Arkansas; Mary Wright born in 1846 in Louisiana.

1860 CENSUS, CARROLL PARISH, LOUISIANA

Dorrell Wright born in 1810 in Mississippi; Mary A. Wright born in 1827 in Louisiana; Dorrell Wright Jr. born in 1838 in Mississippi; Mary J. Wright born in 1846 in Louisiana; Sarah E. Wright born in 1851 in Louisiana; Susan Wright born in 1854 in Louisiana; 30 slaves.

1870 CENSUS, EAST CARROLL PARISH, LOUISIANA

Dorrell Wright Sr. born in 1809 in Mississippi; Mary Wright born in 1830 in Louisiana; Lizzie Wright born in 1852 in Louisiana; Susie Wright born in 1856 in Louisiana; Mattie Wright born in 1860 in Louisiana; Anna Wright born in 1866 in Louisiana; Thomas Wright born in 1867 in Louisiana.

Dorrell Wright Jr. and Nessa Saunders married on April 25, 1831, in Warren County, Mississippi.

Dorrell Wright and Nessa (Saunders) Wright, who died March 7, 1846, had the following children aged as follows in 1846: Lafayette 15, Robert 14, Keightly 12, Gibeon (or Gideon) 10, Dorrell 8, William 6, Christopher Columbus 4; and Mary Jane, infant. See Succession of Nessa Wright, Drawer No. 73, East Carroll Parish, Louisiana.

Dorrell Wright married Mary Ann Landfair on February 24, 1848. See Marriage Book A (1832-1858) page 134, East Carroll Parish, Louisiana.

ANNA WRIGHT

Married: John Troup who was born August 21, 1867 and died in July, 1941.

Died: January 18, 1896

Children of John and Anna (Wright) Troup: Frank Troup, born November 8, 1892, died March 28, 1896; Sooner Troup, born May 15, 1894, died at birth; Ida May Troup, born January 4 and died January 18, 1896; Mattie Troup.

MATTIE TROUP

Born: March 2, 1891

Married: William Austin Hays on December 20, 1915

Children of William Austin and Mattie (Troup) Hays: Katherine Hays, born November 9, 1916, in Oak Grove, Louisiana. Address: Rural Route, Briggs Community, Oak Grove, Louisiana; James Morgan Hays, born November 10, 1918; Jeanette Hays; Mary Lee Hays, married first, Pershing J. Vizina on February 24, 1942, divorced, married second, George Maslin in March, 1954; Joseph Austin Hays, born July 15, 1925; William Scott Hays, born November 29, 1933, married Florence Abigail Rouse on October 8, 1955.

JEANETTE HAYS

Born: May 7, 1921

Married: Audis W. Hatten on February 24, 1941.

Children of Audis W. and Jeanette (Hays) Hatten: Sandra Jean Hatten, born July 4, 1942.

DORRELL WRIGHT

Born: 1838 in Mississippi

Married: Nancy E. McIntyre

Died: 1870-1871

Children of Dorrell and Nancy E. (McIntyre) Wright: Mary E. Wright.

1870 CENSUS, CARROLL PARISH, LOUISIANA

Dorrell Wright born in 1838 in Mississippi; Nancy E. Wright born in 1848 in Louisiana; Mary E. Wright born in 1869 in Louisiana; (No Name) Wright born in March 1870 in Louisiana (female).

Nancy E. McIntyre was the wife of Dorrell Wright Jr. and the sister of Reuben L. A. McIntyre. The Wrights had a minor child, Mary E. Wright, to whom Dorrell Wright Sr. was appointed guardian in 1871. See Succession of Dorrell Wright Jr. in Drawer 73, East Carroll Parish, Louisiana.

See record of Robert Wright. The Wright brothers, Robert and Dorrell, married the McIntyre sisters, Margaret and Nancy, respectively.

MATTIE WRIGHT

Born: 1860-1861 in Louisiana

Married: Robert Oldham

1880 Census Ward 3 West Carroll Parish Louisiana 114, 120

Robt W. Oldham born in 1857 in Alabama; Mattie Oldham born in 1861 in Louisiana.

The parents of Robt Oldham were born in North Carolina.

The father of Mattie Oldham was born in Mississippi and her mother was born in Louisiana.

ROBERT WRIGHT

Born: 1833-1834 in Mississippi

Married: Margaret McIntyre

Children of Robert and Margaret (McIntyre) Wright: Archy Wright; John D. Wright; Robert S. Wright; William D. Wright.

1860 CENSUS, CARROLL PARISH, LOUISIANA 254, 244

Robert Wright born in 1834 in Mississippi; Margaret Wright born in 1834 in Mississippi; John D. Wright born in 1860 in Louisiana.

1870 CENSUS, CARROLL PARISH, LOUISIANA

Robert Wright born in 1833 in Mississippi; Margaret Wright born in

1833 in Mississippi; John D. Wright born in 1859 in Louisiana; Robert S. Wright born in 1862 in Louisiana; William D. Wright born in 1866 in Louisiana; Archy Wright born in 1870 in Louisiana.

1850 CENSUS, CARROLL PARISH, LOUISIANA 213, 213

A. M. McIntyre born in 1788 in North Carolina; Elizabeth McIntyre born in 1808 in Mississippi; John H. McIntyre born in 1825 in Mississippi; Mary J. McIntyre born in 1827 in Mississippi; Reuben A. McIntyre born in 1829 in Mississippi; Margaret A. McIntyre born in 1832 in Mississippi; Hugh L. McIntyre born in 1837 in Mississippi; Flora McIntyre born in 1840 in Mississippi; Nancy McIntyre born in 1846 in Louisiana.

1860 CENSUS, WARD NO. 4, CARROLL PARISH, LOUISIANA 255, 245

John H. McIntyre born in 1830 in Mississippi; Reuben L. A. McIntyre born in 1831 in Mississippi; Elizabeth McIntyre born in 1809 in Mississippi; Mary J. McIntyre born in 1835 in Mississippi; Flora S. McIntyre born in 1842 in Mississippi; Daniel C. McIntyre born in 1846 in Louisiana; Nancy E. McIntyre born in 1848 in Louisiana; John H. McIntyre owned $50,000 Real Estate and $11,600 Personal Estate. Elizabeth McIntyre owned $6,400 and Reuben McIntyre owned $6,000 Real Estate.

1870 CENSUS, WARD NO. 6, CARROLL PARISH, LOUISIANA, FLOYD 35, 35

Reuben McIntyre born in 1825 in Mississippi

220, 220

John H. McIntyre born in 1824 in Mississippi; Margaret McIntyre born in 1847 in North Carolina; Mary E. McIntyre born in 1869 in Louisiana; Daniel C. McIntyre born in 1847 in Mississippi; Mary Oldham born in 1815 in North Carolina; Thomas Oldham born in 1848 in North Carolina; Malcolm Oldham born in 1855 in North Carolina; George Oldham born in 1857 in Alabama; Robert Oldham born in 1859 in Alabama; Mary Oldham born in 1852 in North Carolina.

SARAH ELIZABETH WRIGHT

Born: May 11, 1851, in East Carroll Parish, Louisiana

Married: Henry Delos Briggs on January 19, 1871, in East Carroll Parish, Louisiana

Died: January 10, 1918, in Oak Grove, Louisiana

Children of Henry Delos and Sarah Elizabeth (Wright) Briggs: Delia Elizabeth Briggs; Dorrell D. Briggs; Eri Briggs; Henry Delos Briggs; John Cheatham Briggs; Mary Briggs; Ollie Briggs; Orrin Briggs; Sue Saphronia Briggs.

SUSAN WRIGHT

Born: 1854-1856 in Louisiana

Married: Young J. Settoon

1880 CENSUS, WARD NO. 1, WEST CARROLL PARISH, LOUISIANA

Y. J. Settoon born in 1853 in Louisiana; Susan Settoon born in 1856 in Louisiana; Cuba Settoon born in 1879 in Louisiana (female); Infant Son born in 1880 in Louisiana.

1860 CENSUS, WARD 5, CARROLL PARISH, LOUISIANA 771, 745

Saml G. Settoon born in 1823 in Louisiana; Eliza E. Settoon born in 1827 in Louisiana; Livingston Settoon born in 1846 in Louisana; California Settoon born in 1848 in Louisiana; Cuba Settoon born in 1850 in Mississippi; Young Settoon born in 1852 in Louisiana; Hamden Settoon born in 1854 in Arkansas; Nancy Settoon born in 1857 in Louisiana; 6 slaves.

THOMAS McCUE WRIGHT

Born: September 21, 1868

Married: 1st: Annie Tharpe

2nd: Lily Warrington on June 12, 1910, in Lambert, Mississippi. She was born on August 12, 1881, in Yazoo County, Mississippi.

Died: November 13, 1931

Children of Thomas McCue and Annie (Tharpe) Wright: William Thomas Wright.

Children of Thomas McCue and Lily (Warrington) Wright: Warrington Arvil Wright.

Lily Warrington Wright is living in Oak Grove, Louisiana (1959).

WILLIAM THOMAS WRIGHT

Born: February 14, 1906, in Epps, Louisiana

Married: Jo Gardner on June 27, 1929, in Crossett, Arkansas. She was born on March 9, 1907, in Hamburg, Arkansas, Ashley County.

Children of William Thomas and Jo (Gardner) Wright: William Gardner Wright, born August 24, 1930, in Hamburg, Arkansas; Max Allen Wright, born August 17, 1932, in Hamburg, Arkansas.

WARRINGTON ARVIL WRIGHT

Born: September 16, 1911

Married: Isola Elizabeth Butler on November 19, 1941, in Jackson, Mississippi

Children of Warrington Arvil and Isola Elizabeth (Butler) Wright: Mary Elizabeth Wright, born March 3, 1943, in Delhi, Louisiana; Rebecca Ann Wright, born September 4, 1944, in Delhi, Louisiana.

ELIZABETH WRIGHT

Deed Book A, page 10, Chancery Clerk's Office, Warren County, Mississippi. From ELIZABETH WRIGHT of Warren County, Mississippi Territory. To: BENJAMIN WRIGHT, SARAH WRIGHT, AND FRANCES WRIGHT, MY THREE CHILDREN, certain slaves and other property. /s/ ELIZABETH WRIGHT. Test: JOHN J. WRIGHT AND MARY WRIGHT. "26 March 1810

There is a land entry numbered 129 in Warren County, no date, for B. WRIGHT, the NW¼, Section 18, Township 14, Range #3 East. Then there is another entry numbered 122, also in Warren County for BENJ. WRIGHT, JR., Dec 8, 1826, for W½ of NE¼, Section 9, Township 13, Range #3 East. The first item was sold by Mary Matilda (Wright) Steed, Administratrix of the Estate of Benjamin Wright, deceased, as was a small item of 11.51 acres which proves that the item for B. Wright, NW¼ Section 18, was in reality for Benjamin Wright. See Warren County Deed Book S, page 731, July 31, 1837, and Deed Book X, page 356, July 12, 1851.

Mary Matilda Jones mentioned above married first Benjamin Wright and after his death she married Moses H. Steed, who in the 1850 Census is listed as Overseer for James Glass, a relative of Mary Matilda Jones through the Hyland family.

1860 Census, Warren County, Mississippi 1070, 1058

H. M. Steed born in 1820 in Tennessee
Mary Steed born in 1810 in Mississippi.

Book C, page 243, Marriage Licenses of Warren County, Mississippi: Levi Gibson Owen and Frances Wright. 15 Dec 1825. Abel Wright, Surety.

Book C, page 134. Samuel L. Blanchard and Sarah Wright. 16 Sept 1822 Robt McClure, Surety.

BENJAMIN WRIGHT

Born: February 6, 1801

Married: Mary Matilda Jones on September 17, 1829. On October 2, 1850, she married Moses H. Steed, William H. Sparke, Surety, in Warren County, Mississippi

Died: March 2, 1844

Children of Benjamin and Mary Matilda (Jones) Wright: Frances M. Wright; John Benjamin Wright; Henry Clay Wright, born February 4, 1842, died March 14, 1858; Sarah Elizabeth Wright, died August 24, 1853, aged 16 years, 8 months and 16 days; Martha Jane Wright, died August, 1847.

The following are from the Chancery Clerk's Office, Warren County, Mississippi:

Probate File No. 1054 THE ESTATE OF BENJAMIN WRIGHT, DECEASED. March Term of Court. MATILDA WRIGHT appointed

Administratrix. Fourth Monday, November Court, 1847. Division of the Estate: Mrs. Matilda Wright, widow of Benjamin Wright, one part; Wm. H. Oliver and Frances, his wife, in her right, lately Frances Wright, one of the children and heirs, one part; Mrs. Matilda Wright, as Guardian for John B. Wright, Elizabeth Wright, and Henry C. Wright, three parts;

September Term of Court, 1848. The Administratrix asks for additional time to make a final report, due to yellow fever in Vicksburg.

Petition of Wm. H. Oliver and Frances his wife lately Frances Wright, is one of the children, etc. of Benjamin Wright, who departed this life on 1st of March, 1844. That decedent died intestate, leaving a widow, Matilda M. Wright and five children, his legal heirs, etc.; to wit: Your petitioner Frances and three others, John Wright, Elizabeth Wright, Henry C. Wright, now living, and Martha Jane Wright, who departed this life last of August, 1847. October Term, 1847.

Probate File No. 1147. The Estate of HENRY CLAY WRIGHT, minor heir of BENJAMIN WRIGHT, deceased. Died 14th March, 1858, intestate. His heirs are: JOHN B. WRIGHT, A BROTHER: BENJAMIN OLIVER, JOHN OLIVER AND MARTHA OLIVER, MINOR HEIRS OF HIS SISTER, FRANCES OLIVER OF WHOM WM. H. OLIVER IS GUARDIAN: AND MARY M. STEED, HIS MOTHER AND GUARDIAN.

Deed Book S, page 731. Date 31st July 1837. Deed Samuel D. McCray of Warren County, Mississippi. To BENJAMIN WRIGHT, of same. Consideration $10 per acre for 11.51 acres of Section 18 Township 14, Range 3 East of Warren County.

Deed Book X, page 356. Date: 12 July, 1851. From MARY MATILDA STEED, GUARDIAN OF MINOR HEIRS OF BENJAMIN WRIGHT, DECEASED, LATE OF THE COUNTY OF WARREN. To: Joseph S. Acuff of same. Consideration: $651. Court of April Term, 1851, ordered sold the NW¼ of Sec 18, T 14, Range 3 East 147.87 acres, also 11.51 acres in same Section. /s/ MARY MATILDA STEED and M. H. STEED.

1830 Census, Warren County, Mississippi
Benjamin Wright
1 male born 1800-1810; 1 female born 1800-1810; 8 slaves.

1840 Census, Warren County, Mississippi
Ben Wright
1 male born 1800-1810; 1 male born 1830-1835; 1 female born 1810-1820; 2 females born 1830-1835; 2 females born 1835-1840; 16 slaves.

These Wrights are buried in the Presbyterian Churchyard at Yokena, Warren County, Mississippi.

Marriage Licenses from Circuit Clerk's Office, Warren County, Mississippi:

Book D, page 169. Benjamin Wright and Matilda Jones, 17 Sept 1829, Thomas D. Downs, Surety.

Book G, page 85. Moses H. Steed and Mary (Matilda) Wright, 2 October, 1850. Wm. H. Sparke, Surety.

The mother of Mary Matilda Jones was Elizabeth Hyland, born about 1785 and died May 15, 1854. Elizabeth Hyland was the daughter of James and Eve Hyland, Senior. James Hyland, Senior, (Jaime Hilands) is listed in the Spanish Census of 1792. James and Eve Hyland had these children: Sarah Hyland who married Henry Maynadier. 29 March 1816, Andrew Glass, Surety. Book B, page 73, Circuit Clerk's Office, Warren County, Mississippi, Marriage Licenses. It was this Henry Maynadier who as Justice of the Peace married Dorrell Wright, Jr., and Nessa Saunders on 25 April 1831, Gideon Blackman, Surety. Book D, page 234, Marriage Licenses, Warren County, Mississippi. This Henry Maynadier is listed in the Spanish Census of 1792 as Enrique Manadue, el joven. John Hyland who married Sarah Edwards. April 12, 1821, John Blanchard, Surety. Book C, page 85, Marriage Licenses, Warren County, Mississippi. Lavinia Hyland who married Edmond Reeves. November 5, 1818, Andrew Glass, Surety. Book C, page 12, Marriage Licenses, Warren County, Mississippi. Martha Hyland who married Edmond Reeves (after the death of Lavinia Hyland Reeves). 27 February 1820, John M. Henderson, Surety. Book C, page 59, Marriage Licenses, Warren County, Mississippi. Christopher Hyland whose estate was administered by his brother, James Hyland with another brother, Jacob Hyland, Surety. 5 August 1824. Probate File No. 163, Warren County, Mississippi. Jacob Hyland who married Matilda Steele on October 20, 1809. James Hyland, Junior, who married 1. Betsy McCord. 29 January 1811, Marmadue Simms, Surety. Book B, page 11, Marriage Licenses, Warren County. 2. Sarah Phillips, 2 January 1817. Andrew Glass, Surety. Book B, page 85, Marriage Licenses, Warren County. 3. Frances Knowland. 6 March 1827. Robert Boardman, Surety. Book D, page 59, Marriage Licenses, Warren County. Frances Hyland. Married a Glass. Her sole heir was Eliza Glass who married Claiborne Steele (Book D, page 176). As guardian of Leigh Richmond and Eliza Steele, he deeded land inherited from James Hyland, Senior, to William L. Sharkey. Deed Book M, pages 161-2. James Glass and Mary Kirkwood (Mary Glass married Robert Kirkwood. Book B, page 253) deeded land inherited from James Hyland, Senior to Claiborne Steele. Deed Book F, page 30. The Will of Anthony Glass (Book A, page 44) mentions wife, Helen, brother-in-law, George Rapalge, uncle, Andrew Glass, sister, Elizabeth Whittington, brother, James Glass, and children of sister Mary Kirkwood. Elizabeth Hyland who married a Jones and was the mother of Mary Matilda Jones who married first Benjamin Wright and then

Moses H. Steed. See Probate File No. 1494. Estate of Elizabeth Jones, deceased. Mary M. Steed, Administratrix, Moses H. Steed and Joseph S. Acuff, Sureties. Elizabeth Jones died May 15, 1854, leaving Mary Matilda Steed, her sole heir. William Hyland who married Nancy Wright. 16 April 1816, James Oliver, Surety. Book B, page 80, Marriage Licenses, Warren County.

Of the above Hylands, William Hyland and Nancy Wright left children who are named under the listing for Nancy Wright. The children of Elizabeth and Frances Hyland were given above. John Hyland and Sarah Hyland left no children. See Probate File No. 119, Warren County, Estate of John Hyland, Sarah Hyland, Administratrix. Elizabeth Hyland Jones was guardian of Christopher and Jane Reeves, minor children of Edmond Reeves. (Deed Book G, page 689, Warren County). Christopher Hyland died unmarried. Jacob Hyland had a son, William S. Hyland, for whom William L. Sharkey was guardian. Probate File No. 359, Warren County. Mr. Sharkey served as Chief Justice of the Supreme Court of Mississippi and as Provisional Governor of the State. For "love and affection" Mr. Sharkey conveyed two acres, including the old graveyard on his plantation on Boguesha in Warren County to William S. Hyland on November 3, 1865. Deed Book DD, page 270, Warren County. James Hyland, Jr., had a son, James N. Hyland for whom his wife, Frances Hyland was guardian, Jesse Wright and Peter G. Miller, Sureties. Probate File No. 363, Warren County. He also had a son, John Hyland for whom William L. Sharkey was guardian. Probate File 364, Warren County.

The will of Eve Hyland, wife of James Hyland, Senior, (Will Book A, page 17, Warren County) was signed 15 September 1828 and proved 27 June 1831. Legatees of the estate were the children of Henry and Sarah Maynadier, daughter, Elizabeth Jones, Granddaughter, Matilda Jones, grandson, John Jones, granddaughter Eliza Glass, granddaughter, Jane Reeves, son Jacob Hyland, granddaughter, Martha Hyland who married William Knowland on April 2, 1829, John M. Henderson, Surety. Book D, page 151, Marriage License, Warren County. Jacob Hyland who had been appointed Executor predeceased his mother and Elizabeth Jones served as Executrix.

Several sizeable Spanish Land Grants were made to the Hylands. McBee's *Natchez Court Records 1767-1805* shows the following: Page 381. Grant of 300 acres from Don Manuel Gayoso de Lemos to James Hyland, on Big Black River. Page 363. Don Manuel Gayoso de Lemos grants 800 acres seven miles northwest of the Big Black River, adjoining land of Donna Catalina Lintot. Natchez, Feb 4, 1797. James Hyland is described as "A resident of this district before the Spanish accession". Donna Catalina Lintot described as the "Yellow Duchess" by Mr. Harnett Kane in his NATCHEZ ON THE MISSISSIPPI later presided over Concord, built by Governor Manuel Gayoso de Lemos and later acquired by her husband, Don Esteban Minor, last of the Spanish Governors. Page 363. Don Manuel Gayoso de Lemos granted 700 acres of land adjoining that granted to James Hyland to Jacob Hyland. Feb 4, 1797. From AMERICAN STATE PAPERS, PUBLIC LANDS: Vol. 2, p 747, Glass and Hyland original claimants of 768 acres in Louisiana. Vol 2 p 813 Andrew Glass and Jas. Hyland claimed 640 acres in Concordia Parish, Louisiana. May 7, 1811. Vol. 1 p 894 James Hyland, Senior, claimed 640 acres on Big Black River. Vol. 1 p 903 James Templeton and James Hyland granted 300 acres on Big Black River. Dec 22, 1806. Vol 1, 904 Jacob Hyland granted 300 acres on the Mississippi River. Dec 29, 1806. Vol 1 p 904 James Hyland, Jr., granted 200 acres on the Big Black River.

JOHN B. WRIGHT

Born: April 11, 1833
Married: Cynthia Eunice Wells
Died: January 1, 1922
Children of John B. and Cynthia Eunice (Wells) Wright: Allen Wright; Edward Wright; Hardy Wright; Henry Clay Wright; Hyland Wright; Mary Wright; Minna Em Wright; Percy Wright; Thomas Wright; John W. Wright; Nannie Wright.

1860 CENSUS, HINDS COUNTY, MISSISSIPPI, 1338, 1357
J. B. Wright born in 1834 in Mississippi; C. E. Wright born in 1838 in Mississippi; J. W. Wright born in 1857 in Mississippi; 18 slaves.

1870 CENSUS, RED BONE PRECINCT, WARREN COUNTY, MISSISSIPPI 397, 387
J. B. Wright born in 1833 in Mississippi; Cynthia Wright born in 1839 in Mississippi; John Wright born in 1858 in Mississippi; Hyland Wright born in 1862 in Mississippi; Thomas Wright born in 1864 in Mississippi; Hardy Wright born in 1866 in Mississippi; Mary Wright born in 1869 in Mississippi; M. M. Steele born in 1810 in Mississippi; B. F. Oliver born in 1849 in Mississippi.

1880 CENSUS, KLINE'S STORE AND RED BONE PRECINCT, WARREN COUNTY, MISSISSIPPI 478, 488
John B. Wright born in 1833 in Mississippi; Cynthia Wright born in 1837 in Mississippi; Hyland Wright born in 1862 in Mississippi; Hardy Wright born in 1867 in Mississippi; Mary Wright born in 1869 in Mississippi; Thomas Wright born in 1871 in Mississippi; Percy Wright born in 1873 in Mississippi; Allen Wright born in 1875 in Mississippi; Edward Wright born in 1878 in Mississippi. The parents of all the above were born in Mississippi.

In the Bethesda Presbyterian Churchyard, eight miles southeast of Utica, Mississippi, are the graves of John B. Wright born April 11,

1833, and died January 1, 1922, of Cynthia Eunice Wells, wife of John B. Wright, born March 30, 1838, and died May 22, 1904, of Minna Em daughter of J. B. and C. E. Wright born January 8, 1863, and died August 1, 1868, and their Infant Son. See Marriage and Cemetery Records of Hinds County Mississippi by Mary J. Berry (1951), pages 447, 449, 450. On page 443 is listed grave of their son Henry Clay Wright born April 10, 1850 and died May 21, 1860.

1850 CENSUS, HINDS COUNTY, MISSISSIPPI 620, 620

William Wells born in 1808 in Mississippi; Nancy Wells born in 1811 in Mississippi; Nathaniel Wells born in 1830 in Mississippi; Cynthia Wells born in 1838 in Mississippi; Mary A. E. Wells born in 1840 in Mississippi; Martha Wells born in 1842 in Mississippi; Narcissa A. Wells born in 1848 in Mississippi; 17 slaves.

1860 CENSUS, HINDS COUNTY, MISSISSIPPI 924, 935

Wm. M. Wells born in 1809 in Mississippi; Nancy Wells born in 1811 in Georgia; M. A. E. Wells born in 1840 in Mississippi (female); M. E. Wells born in 1842 in Mississippi (female); N. A. Wells born in 1849 in Mississippi (female); 28 slaves.

From: The Chancery Clerk's Office, Raymond, Hinds County, Miss. Deed Book 26, page 179 1 Aug 1858 From: Benjamin F. Osborn of Hinds County, Miss. To: JOHN B. WRIGHT of same. Consideration: $5,174 for lands in Hinds County, the NW¼ of Sec 10; the E½ of NE¼ and E½ of SE¼, Sec 9; the E½ of SW¼ and W½ of SE¼, Sec 9; all T3, R3W, 476 acres, less 4 acres. /s/ B. F. Osborn Ack 21 Aug 1858.

Deed Book 27, page 404 6 Jan 1860 From: W. H. OLIVER AND LAURA A. OLIVER OF HINDS COUNTY, MISS. To: JOHN B. WRIGHT OF SAME, Consideration: $1,437.50 for lands in Hinds County, Miss., 115 acres in the E½ of SW¼ and W½ of SE¼, lying south of the south prong of Tallahala, Sec 3, T3, R3W etc. /s/ W. H. OLIVER AND L. A. OLIVER. Ack by signers on 7 Jan 1860.

Deed Book 28, page 747 4 Dec 1865 From: JOHN B. WRIGHT AND C. E. WRIGHT, HIS WIFE OF HINDS COUNTY, MISS. To: W.H.B. Carlisle of same. Consideration: $700 for lands in Hinds County Miss., the E½ of SE¼ and E½ of W½ of SE¼, Sec 9, T3, R3W, 120 acres. /s/ J. B. WRIGHT AND C. E. WRIGHT and ack by signers on 13 Dec 1865

Deed Book 30, page 202 10 Jan 1867. From: J. B. WRIGHT OF HINDS COUNTY, MISS. AND CYNTHIA, HIS WIFE, To: J. W. and D. E. Slater of same. Consideration: $1,000 for land in Hinds County, Miss., the E½ of NW¼, Sec 10, the W½ of W½ of SE¼, Sec 9; also 115 acres on south side of Little Tallahala, Sec 3, T3, R3W in E½ of SE¼ and W½ of SE¼, total, 315 acres. /s/ J. B. WRIGHT AND C. E. WRIGHT and ack by them 14 Jan 1867.

Book 3, page 309, Hinds County, Miss. Jno. B. Wright and Miss C(ynthia) E. Wells; Marriage License 24 Nov 1856; Ceremony 26 Nov 1856. Bondsman: W. H. OLIVER

Deed Book 2, page 705. 25 March 1840. From: Samuel L. Blanchard and Carolina, his wife of Warren County, Miss. To: BENJAMIN WRIGHT OF SAME. Consideration: $1,200 for land in Hinds County, Miss., the SW¼ of W½ of SE¼ and W½ of NE¼ Sec 24; S½ of NE½ and N½ of SE¼, Sec. 23; E½ of NE¼ and N½ of SW¼, Sec 25, all T5, R4W, 640 acres. /s/ S. L. Blanchard and Carolina M. Blanchard and ack by them 26 March 1840.

Book D, page 344, Warren County, Miss. S. L. Blanchard and Carolina Marshall; Marriage License 7 Aug 1833; Ceremony 8 Aug 1833; Bondsman J. M. Henderson.

JOHN WILLIAMS WRIGHT

Born: 1857-1858 in Mississippi

Married: Hattie Anna Johnson, daughter of William Warren Johnson and Lucinda Jane Lawhorn of Morton, Mississippi in 1884. Hattie Johnson Wright died in February, 1913

Died: December 29, 1931

Children of John Williams and Hattie Anna (Johnson) Wright: William Cummings Wright, born August 11, 1885; Anna Tresillian Wright; Lenora Beatrice Wright, born March 27, 1888; Benjamin F. Wright, born February 14, 1891; Lula Cynthia Wright, born January 24, 1893; Annie Aline Wright, born February 19, 1895; Albert Sidney Wright, born February 1, 1897; Mrs. Emmett Reed, R.F.D. 3, Box 8, Vicksburg, Mississippi, lists the death of Cynthia Eunice Wells Wright as May, 1903; Mrs. Alma Wright Beard, Route 2, Box 181, Vicksburg, Mississippi, says her grandfather, John Benjamin Wright was born and partly reared in Hinds County, near Edwards, Mississippi, and that he owned some 3,000 acres of land and a number of slaves.

ALBERT SIDNEY WRIGHT

Born: February 1, 1897

Married: Mary Drusella Wilson on December 24, 1924

Children of Albert Sidney and Mary Drusella (Wilson) Wright: Albert Sidney Wright, Jr., born February 27, 1928; Mary L. Wright, born September 20, 1925; Everett James Wright, born February, 1937; William Wright, born December 10, 1938, married Brenda Jones; Emma Louise Wright, born May 30, 1940; Lillie B. Wright, born February 26, 1946; Beverly Ann Wright, born December 12, 1948; Ann Helen Wright, born January 8, 1935, married Harver Luckett, their children: Debbie Luckett, born 1956; Jerry Dean

Luckett, born 1953; John William Wright, born December 30, 1933, married May Kliemnon, their children: Timothy Wright, born 1958; John William Wright, Jr., born 1957; Margie Marie Wright, born November 8, 1926, married Claude Wright in 1955, their children: Claudie Marie Wright; Lorrie L. Wright; Claude Wright, Jr.

ALMA TRESSILLIAN WRIGHT

Born: December 24, 1886

Married: 1st: James Fletcher, who died on September 2, 1913

2nd: Walter Douglas Beard who died on October 10, 1947

Children of James and Alma Tressillian (Wright) Fletcher: Joseph Warren Fletcher, born on August 21, 1905; Mamie Mae Fletcher; Edward Lee Fletcher, born on December 29, 1909; Josie Lee Fletcher. Children of Walter Douglas and Alma Tressillian (Wright) Beard: Helen M. Beard; John Douglas Beard

MAMIE MAE FLETCHER

Born: September 2, 1907

Married: 1st: Ben Bolt Beard on September 22, 1923. Mr. Beard died on October 11, 1946

2nd: Emmett F. Reed on April 21, 1949

Children of Ben Bolt and Mamie Mae (Fletcher) Beard: Josie Louise Beard; Linnie Mae Beard, born on April 9, 1927; Alma Elizabeth Beard, born on June 24, 1929; Benjamin Edward Beard, born on August 18, 1931; Anna Marie Beard, born on May 13, 1934

JOSIE LEE FLETCHER

Born: September 25, 1913

Married: James Riley Morris on December 19, 1936

Children of James Riley and Josie Lee (Fletcher) Morris: James Riley Morris, Jr., born May 1, 1939; Alma Frances Morris, born June 29, 1946

HELEN M. BEARD

Born: September 5, 1918

Married: Robert D. Peden

Children of Robert D. and Helen M. (Beard) Peden: Walter Howard Peden, born March 27, 1953; Ella Loraine Peden, born June 1, 1956

JOHN DOUGLAS BEARD

Born: August 4, 1921

Married: Frances Louise Jones

Children of John Douglas and Frances Louise (Jones) Beard: John Douglas Beard, Junior

HARDY WRIGHT

Married: Lula Rollison

Children of Hardy and Lula (Rollison) Wright: Edward Wright.

MARY WRIGHT

Married: 1st: Mr. Sadler

        2nd: Charles Wright

        3rd: Mr. Rollison

Children of the Sadlers: Sam Sadler; Mattie Sadler

Children of Charles and Mary (Wright) Wright: Edward Wright; Charles Lee Wright.

Children of the Rollisons: Taft Rollison; Edna Rollison.

PERCY WELLS WRIGHT

Born: June 21, 1873

Married: Gertrude Emma Letting who was born March 28, 1876 and died March 2, 1949

Died: April 30, 1932

Children of Percy Wells and Gertrude Emma (Letting) Wright: Thelma Annie Wright, born November 8, 1911, died December 31, 1913.

THOMAS WRIGHT

Married: Ida Rollison, sister of Lula Rollison who married Hardy Wright, brother of Thomas Wright

Children of Thomas and Ida (Rollison) Wright: Nannie Lane Wright; Irene Wright; Addie Wright; Alice Wright; Cynthia Wright; Lula Wright.

NANNIE WRIGHT

Married: Henry Marsh

Children of Henry and Nannie (Wright) Marsh: Eunice Marsh (married Fred Templeton); John Marsh; Nannie May Marsh.

FRANCES (FANNY) WRIGHT

Born: February 24,1831

Married: William H. Oliver. September 2, 1847. Tobias Stephens on the bond. Marriages, Book A, page 114, Warren County, Mississippi.

Died: September 1, 1853

Children of William H. and Frances (Wright) Oliver: Benjamin Oliver; John William Oliver; Martha Jane Oliver; Henry Clay Oliver.

Frances (Wright) Oliver is buried in the Yokena Cemetery, Yokena, Mississippi, with her son, Henry Clay Oliver, her father, Benjamin

Wright, her mother, Mary Matilda Jones, her brother, Henry Clay Wright, and her sisters, Sarah Elizabeth Wright and Martha Jane Wright. Her mother, Mary Matilda Jones was born December 6, 1808, and died September 5, 1871. After the death of Benjamin Wright, she married Moses H. Steed who died January 24, 1866, aged 47 years. Also buried here is John G. Jones, born October 26, 1810, and died June 23, 1837. (See will of Eve Hyland mentioning her grandchildren, Matilda and John Jones).

SARAH WRIGHT

Nimrod Selser and William Hyland were named guardians of Sarah Wright on June 3, 1822. She was over age 14. Courthouse records, Warren County, Mississippi

JESSE WRIGHT

1820 Census, Warren County, Mississippi
Jesse Wright: 1 male born 1775-1794; 1 female born 1794-1804; 2 females born 1810-1820

1830 Census, Warren County, Mississippi
Jesse Wright: 1 male born 1790-1800; 1 male born 1810-1815; 2 males born 1820-1825; 1 female born 1800-1810; 1 female born 1815-1820; 1 female born 1825-1830; 3 slaves
Probate File No. 821, Warren County, Mississippi. Estate of Jesse Wright. July 19, 1938, Lucretia Wright, widow of Jesse Wright relinquished claim to administration in favor of Elias Woodburn. Granted. Bond $15,000. /s/ Elias Woodburn, E. W. Hankinson, E. D. Downs, July 23, 1838. Petition of Elias Woodburn, Adm, for permission to sell Lot 2, Sec 25, T14, R3E, mentions children: Nancy of full age and minors, George S., William H. and Eliza Wright, George Clark, Guardian. In 1842 Woodburn resigned the administration and James Rawls petitioned the court for the same, stating Nancy Rawls, his wife, was an heir of Jesse Wright and naming his four children: George, William, Eliza (deceased on March 28, 1842), and Nancy Rawls. George S. Wright was Guardian of his brother, William H. Wright, 1847 to final settlement of the Estate, April 23, 1849.
Tract Book, page 47, October 30, 1831. U.S.A. to Jesse Wright, Entry No. 130, Lot No. 2, Sec. 25, T14, R3E, Warren County, Miss.

NANCY WRIGHT

James Rawls married Nancy Wright. December 20, 1838. John Gibson on the bond. Marriages, Book #E, page 331, Warren County, Mississippi.
Will Book A, page 52, Warren County, Mississippi; Will of Claudius Rawls. Mentions wife, Elizabeth; daughter, Nancy Middleton; three youngest children, Mary, Claudius, and Elizabeth; and three sons,

Isaac, James and William Rawls. Witnesses: Elias Woodburn, Henry Monkhouse, and Henry Hyland. 29 March 1835.

Will Book A, page 241, Warren County, Mississippi. Will of Elizabeth Rawls. Son Claudius Rawls appointed Executor. Witnesses: Benj. F. Owen, W. Reden, and D. A. Cameron. 6 May 1856.

WILLIAM H. WRIGHT

Wm. H. Wright married Mary Urie. Dec 4, 1851. George Barnes, Surety. Book G, page 134, Warren County.

Deed Book Y, page 483, Warren County. From Wm. H. and Mary Wright of Claiborne County, Miss. to Louis M. Savoy, 400 acres in Warren County know nas "the Spanish Grant," bounded on the north by land of W. S. Hyland and A. Russell; on the south by lands of Wm. Fortner and Abel Wright; on the east by lands of D. E. Martin; on the west by Bogue de Sha; also land entered by Robert Urie and land from Sharkey to Robert Urie. 6 Apr 1854.

GEORGE S. WRIGHT

Deed Book W, page 151, Warren County, Miss. 19 June 1849. George S. Wright and wife, Susan, of Claiborne County, Miss., sell land in Warren County to William H. Wright. This land was bounded on the north by the Valentine Tract; on the east by land belonging to the Widow and Heirs of Thomas Wright; on the south by lands belonging to Mary Oliver and William L. Sharkey, and on the west by lands of Sharkey.

JOHN J. WRIGHT

Deed Book C, page 35, Claiborne County, Mississippi. 31 October 1808. Deed of JOHN J. WRIGHT AND JANE WRIGHT, HIS WIFE OF CLAIBORNE COUNTY, MISSISSIPPI TERRITORY. To: John Patterson, Consideration: $1,400 for two lots in Town of Port Gibson, Mississippi on South Fork of Bayou Pierre, numbered lots 2 and 5 of plat of Square 7. /s/ JOHN J. WRIGHT, JANE X WRIGHT. Wm. C. Cessna, Tho. Hanes, and Oliver W. Fuller, witnesses.

JAMES J. WRIGHT

J. J. Wright married Caroline M. Stoker. October 8, 1846. James W. Jones, Surety. Book A, page 32, Warren County, Miss.

J. J. Wright married Ellen N. Stoker. February 26, 1857. Thomas Wright, Surety. Book G, page 404, Warren County, Miss.

Deed Book GG, page 99. James J. Wright and Ellen N. Wright, his wife, of Warrenton, Warren County, Miss., sell lots 68, 69, 82, and 83 in the Town of Warrenton to Mrs. Sallie Monett. 31 Dec 1866.

JAMES C. WRIGHT

James C. Wright married Harriett B. Cook. Sept. 28, 1832, Nathaniel Bonner, Surety. Book D, page 310, Warren County, Miss.

Deed Book H, page 9. From James C. Wright and Harriett B. Wright of Warren County, Miss. to Stephen Jackson, land in Warren County entered by Edwin Cook and allotted to Harriett B. Cook by the Commissioner of the Probate Court. 5 Jan 1836.

Deed Book H, page 140, Warren County, Miss. 20 Feb 1836. Mary McCawley gave a Quit Claim deed to James C. Wright in Warren County land sold by Samuel McCauley to Simon T. Lane.

Tract Book, page 42, Warren County, Miss. U.S.A. to James C. Wright. Land in Section 31, Township 16, Range 5E.

Deed Book K, page 163, Warren County, Miss. 5 Aug 1837. Alfred Graham and wife, Martha, of Warren County, sell land to J. C. Wright.

Deed Book GG, page 304, Warren County. 25 Aug 1869. Charles E. Wright of Issaquena County, Miss., Adm'r of James C. Wright, Dec'd, sells lands in Warren County to Thomas J. Wright, 636 acres.

1840 CENSUS, WARREN COUNTY, MISSISSIPP

Jas. C. Wright: 1 male born 1800-1810; 1 male born 1810-1820; 2 males born 1835-1840; 1 female born 1810-1820; 1 female born 1830-1835; 18 slaves

1850 CENSUS, WARREN COUNTY, MISSISSIPPI 960, 990

James C. Wright born in 1812 in Mississippi; Rebecca L. Wright born in 1825 in Mississippi; Martha M. Wright born in 1834 in Mississsppi; Thomas J. Wright born in 1836 in Mississippi; James W. Wright born in 1838 in Mississippi; Charles Wright born in 1841 in Misissippi; John F. Wright born in 1844 in Mississippi; Jane B. Wright born in 1837 in Mississippi; Emma S. Wright born in 1850 in Mississippi; Mary J. Barnett born in 1834 in Louisiana; Elizabeth Biddle born in 1811 in North Carolina; Elizabeth D. Biddle born in 1835 in Virginia; 45 slaves

1860 CENSUS, WARREN COUNTY, MISSISSIPPI 1207, 1186

Jas. Wright born in 1811 in Mississippi; Rebecca Wright born in 1827 in Mississippi; Emma Wright born in 1850 in Mississippi.

THOMAS J. WRIGHT

T. J. Wright married Minerva Wright. April 14, 1870. C. C. Fryer, Surety. Book H, page 52, Warren County, Miss.

T. J. Wright married Mary Middleton. 19 Dec 1875. Moses Jones, Surety. Book H, page 581, Warren County, Miss.

Deed Book GG, page 144. 15 June 1869. Quit Claim Deed from Richard S. Buck of Warren County, Miss., to Mary B. Wright of same, land in Townships 15 and 16, Warren County.

Deed Book 54, page 338. 14 Dec 1882. Deed of Trust from Mary

B. Wright and Thomas J. Wright, her husband, of Warren County to Albert S. Caldwell of Vicksburg. 14 Dec 1882.

Probate File No. 3864, Warren County, Miss. Estate of Mrs. Mary B. Wright, widow of Thomas J. Wright, son of James C. Wright. She died January, 1895. Delia Nelson, Executrix. Mentioned in will: Mrs. Delia A. Nelson, Anna G. Wright, and James C. Wright. Statement of Delia Nelson listing heirs of Mrs. Mary B. Wright: Mrs. A. G. Pollard of Warren County; Mrs. Elizabeth Green of Warren County; Walter Fletcher of Warren County; Dick Thompson, of Warren County, all of 21 years; and minors, Nettie G. Wright and James C. Wright, the former a resident of Memphis, Tennessee, and the latter of Nashville. See also Deed Book 87, pages 255-8. 1 March 1898

THOMAS WRIGHT

Thomas Wright married Nancy Evans. May 24, 1817. James Knowland on the bond. Marriages, Book B, page 89, Warren County, Mississippi.

Will Book B, page 25, Warren County, Mississippi. WILL OF NANCY J. WRIGHT. Dated April 13, 1870. Filed January 4, 1873. Witnesses: Thomas K. Knowland, John B. Gibson, William Redden, and C. Rawls. Mentions daughter, Rebecca Alston, son Lycurgus Wright, and grandchildren of deceased son, Thomas M. Wright.

Probate File No. 816, Warren County, Mississippi. Estate of Thomas Wright, deceased. 24 July 1837. Nancy Wright, widow and relict of Thomas Wright, deceased surrenders right of administration on the Estate of "my friend" Benjamin Wright. Bond for $6,000 signed by Benjamin Wright, Adm., Jesse Wright and Jos. Templeton. Benjamin Wright died in 1844.

Tract Book page 47. Entry No. 130, Sept. 14, 1831. Lot No. 1, Sec 25, T14, R3E, Warren County, Miss. U.S.A. to Thomas Wright. Deed Book T, page 601, 2 Oct 1843. Tax Collector of Warren County sold certain property of Mrs. Thomas Wright to Ann F. Walker.

Deed Book W, page 464, Warren County. 16 Oct 1848. Anna F. Walker sold property to Mary Wright. Corrected to read Nancy Wright.

1820 CENSUS, WARREN COUNTY, MISSISSIPPI

Thomas Wright: 1 male born 1794-1804; 1 male born 1810-1820; 1 female born 1794-1804

1830 CENSUS, WARREN COUNTY, MISSISSIPPI

1 male born 1790-1800; 1 male born 1815-1820; 1 male born 1820-1825; 1 male born 1825-1830; 1 female born 1790-1800; 2 females born 1820-1825; 1 female born 1825-1830; 2 slaves

1840 CENSUS, WARREN COUNTY, MISSISSIPPI

Nancy Wright: 2 males born 1810-1820; 1 male born 1820-1825; 1 male born 1825-1830; 1 female born 1790-1800; 1 female born 1810-1820; 1 female born 1820-1825; 1 female born 1825-1830; 1 female born 1835-1840; 2 slaves

1850 CENSUS, WARREN COUNTY, MISSISSIPPI 783, 807

Nancy Wright born in 1796 in South Carolina; Eveline Wright born in 1820 in Mississippi; Thomas Wright born in 1825 in Mississippi; Rebecca Wright born in 1827 in Mississippi; 5 slaves

1860 CENSUS, WARREN COUNTY, MISSISSIPPI 984, 975

Nancy Wright born in 1795 in North Carolina Blind; Eveline Wright born in 1822 in North Carolina; Wm Rawls born in 1816 in Mississippi; Elizabeth Rawls born in 1830 in Mississippi; Lawson Rawls born in 1842 in Mississippi; Ann Rawls born in 1846 in Mississippi; Burck Rawls born in 1848 in Mississippi; Jennie Rawls born in 1851 in Mississippi; Wm Rawls born in 1854 in Mississippi; James Rawls born in 1857 in Mississippi; Jane Rawls born in 1858 in Mississippi; 8 slaves

LYCURGUS WRIGHT

1880 CENSUS, KLEIN'S STORE AND RED BONE PRECINCTS, WARREN COUNTY, MISSISSIPPI 607, 617

Lycurgus Wright born in 1818 in Mississippi. His parents were born in South Carolina; Nancy Wright, his wife, born in 1823 in Mississippi where her parents were born; Caroline Wright born in 1863 in Mississippi, Daughter; Moses Jones born in 1857 in Mississippi where his parents were born. Son-in-law; Maggie Jones born in 1853 in Mississippi. Daughter; Charles Jones born in 1877 in Mississippi. Grandson; Jim Jones born in 1878 in Mississippi. Grandson.

1860 CENSUS, WARREN COUNTY, MISSISSIPPI 983, 974

L. Wright born in 1818 in Mississippi; Nancy Wright born in 1822 in Mississippi; Wm Wright born in 1844 in Mississippi; Macy Wright born in 1847 in Mississippi (feminine); Sophia Wright born in 1850 in Mississippi; Chas Wright born in 1851 in Mississippi; Margaret Wright born in 1855 in Mississippi; Minerva Wright born in 1853 in Mississippi; Nancy Wright born in 1858 in Mississippi; 1 slave

1850 CENSUS, WARREN COUNTY, MISSISSIPPI 784, 808

Lycurgus Wrght born in 1817 in Mississippi; Nancy Wright born in 1823 in Mississippi; William W. Wright born in 1843 in Mississippi; Nancy M. Wright born in 1848 in Mississippi; Sophia D. Wright born in 1850 in Mississippi

Lycurgus Wright married Nancy Johnson. February 22, 1838. John

F. Miller on the bond. Marriages, Book E, page 208. Waren County, Mississippi.

Elias Woodburn, Adm. of the Estate of Jesse Wright, deceased, of Warren County, Mississippi, sold land to Lycurgus Wright. This property was later repossessed and sold by the heirs of Jesse Wright. 26 Feb 1839. Deed Book N, page 435, Warren County.

THOMAS M. WRIGHT

Thomas M. Wright married Nancy J. Barefield. October 17, 1858. Wm. A. Royall on the bond. W. W. Bolls, Minister. Marriages, Book G, page 468, Warren County, Mississippi.

NANCY WRIGHT

Wm. Hyland married Nancy Wright. License 16 April 1816. Jas. Oliver, Surety. Book B, p 80, Circuit Clerk's Office, Warren County, Mississippi. Marriage Licenses.

Probate File No. 204, Warren County, Mississippi. Estate of William Hyland, deceased. Nancy Hyland Administratrix. Bond $3000 27 Feb 1826. James Hyland and Jesse Wright Sureties. Mentions minor heirs but does not name them.

One fifth part of estate set aside for Boswell Burbridge, one of the heirs by reason of his marriage with the widow of William Hyland. March 15, 1834.

Deed Book K, p 349, Warren County, Mississippi. 2 Jan 1838. From Jesse Wright, Guardian of Andrew Hyland and Maria Hyland, minors under 21 years, children of William Hyland deceased of Warren County. To Wm L. Sharkey of same. Consideration $30 an acre. Have obtained permission of the Orphans' Court to sell real estate of said wards, an undivided interest in Sec 20, 23, and 24, T14 R3E, in Warren County on Bogue desha. /s/ JESSE WRIGHT.

Boswell Burbridge married Nancy Hyland. 3 Sept 1829. John Miller, Surety. Book D, p 166 Circuit Clerk's Office, Warren County, Mississippi. Marriage Licenses.

1830 CENSUS, WARREN COUNTY, MISSISSIPPI

Boswell Burbridge

1 male born 1800-1810; 1 male born 1810-1815; 1 male born 1815-1820; 1 male born 1820-1825; 1 female born 1790-1800; 1 female born 1800-1810; 1 female born 1815-1820; 1 female born 1825-1830; 6 slaves.

1840 CENSUS, WARREN COUNTY, MISSISSIPPI

B. Burbridge

1 male born 1790-1800; 1 male born 1810-1820; 1 male born 1820-1825; 1 male born 1830-1835; 16 slaves.

1820 CENSUS, WARREN COUNTY, MISSISSIPPI

William Hyland

1 male born 1775-1794; 1 male born 1804-1810; 1 male born 1810-1820; 1 female born 1794-1804; 1 female born 1810-1820.

Probate File No. 1093, Warren County, Mississippi. Estate of Boswell Burbridge. Bond $10,000. /s/ Joel Hullum, Adm'r and Susan Evans, Adm'x, B. L. Hullum, Thomas W. Tompkins, bondsmen, 28 April 1845. Only heir, William R. Burbridge, a minor.

1850 Census, Warren County, Mississippi, 735, 759

Benj. Johnson born in 1828 in South Carolina, Overseer
William R. Burbridge born in 1830 in Mississippi, Planter

THE END

INDEX

The spelling of names in this book varies from place to place quite often, as the names are given in each instance as written in the original source record. In the Index, the spelling is the one generally found. Names are often found more than once on a page.

In the Addendum following the Index there are some early baptismal records of especial interest to the Landfair and Carter families. The records were discovered too late for entry in the appropriate section of the book.

— 519 —

— 539 —

The following baptismal records pertaining to the Landfair and Carter families were found by Mamie Austin (Mrs. C. M. Rouzan) of Jackson, Louisiana, after the book had already been printed and are consequently printed here rather than under the record of those families. These records are from the ancient Parish Church of St. Francis, but are now kept in St. Mary's Church in New Roads, Louisiana. The following baptisms all appear in Book Number 3 (1786-1814) and all took place on the same day. There follows first the baptism of Guillaume (William) Lamphier (Landfair), as written in French and then an English translation. For the other children, I have given the names of the godparents, who were different.

Page 141
"L'an mil huit cent deux

Le quatorze de Septembre je cure de Saint Francois a la Pointe Coupee ai batise avec les ceremonies ordinaires Guillaume fils legitime de Thomas Lamphier et Anne Carter habitans de Nlle. Feliciana age de quatre ans, les ayeux (aieux) paternels Jean Lamphier et Anne Howard, les maternels Nehemias Carter et Rachel Minthorn, son parrain David White, la marraine Marie Raoul. En foi de quoi j'ai Signe.   De Saint Pierre."

"1802.
On September 14, I curate of St. Francis, baptized with the customary ceremonies William, legitimate son of Thomas Landfair and Anne Carter, inhabitants of Feliciana, aged four years, the paternal ancestors, John Landfair and Anne Howard, the maternal ancestors Nehemiah Carter and Rachel Minthorn, godfather, David White and godmother, Marie Raoul. In testimony of which I sign, De Saint Pierre."

Other baptisms of the children of Thomas Landfair and Anne Carter: (Page 141) David Landfair, aged six months, godfather William Hawthorn and godmother, Marie Jeanne Bourg.

(Page 142) Julie Landfair, aged two years, godfather Zachaus Barshers (?) and godmother, Julie Lilly.

Baptisms of two children of Rachel Carter, a daughter of Nehemiah and Rachel (Minthorn) Carter, and her husband, William Cunningham, the son of H. Cunningham:

(Page 142) Sarah Cunningham, aged two years, godfather Jacques Higgins and godmother, Sarah Horry.

(Page 142) Nehemia Cunningham, aged six years, godfather Daniel Walkman and godmother Catherine Walkman.